The Medieval Peasant House in Midland England

by

Nat Alcock and Dan Miles

with contributions by
John Chenevix Trench†, Christopher Currie, Chris Dyer,
Bob Laxton† and Cliff Litton

Oxbow Books

Oxford and Philadelphia

Published in the United Kingdom by
OXBOW BOOKS
10 Hythe Bridge Street, Oxford OX1 2EW

and in the United States by
OXBOW BOOKS
908 Darby Road, Havertown, PA 19083

Paperback Edition: ISBN 978-1-78297-714-8
Digital Edition: ISBN 978-1-78297-117-7

A CIP record for this book is available from the British Library

The Library of Congress has cataloged the hardcover edition as follows:

Alcock, N. W. (Nathaniel Warren)
    The medieval peasant house in Midland England / by Nat Alcock and Dan Miles ; with contributions by John Chenevix
Trench ... [et al.]. -- 1st ed.
        p. cm.
    Includes bibliographical references and index.
    ISBN 978-1-84217-506-4
    1. Architecture, Medieval--England--Midlands. 2. Architecture, Domestic--England--Midlands. 3. Dwellings--England--
Midlands. 4. Crucks--England--Midlands. 5. Archaeological dating--England--Midlands. I. Miles, D. W. H. II. Title.
    NA963.A445 2013
    728.09424'0902--dc23
                            2012041704

Printed in the United Kingdom by Berforts Information Press

For a complete list of Oxbow titles, please contact:

UNITED KINGDOM
Oxbow Books
Telephone (01865) 241249, Fax (01865) 794449
Email: oxbow@oxbowbooks.com
www.oxbowbooks.com

UNITED STATES OF AMERICA
Oxbow Books
Telephone (800) 791-9354, Fax (610) 853-9146
Email: queries@casemateacademic.com
www.casemateacademic.com/oxbow

Oxbow Books is part of the Casemate Group

Front cover right: Phoenix Cottage, 1 Birmingham Road, Stoneleigh, Warwickshire (STO-F, p. 248); top left: Mill Farm, Mapledurham, Oxfordshire (MDM-A, p. 200); bottom left: Abel's Cottage, 43 High Street, Long Crendon, Buckinghamshire (LON-A). Back cover top: Reconstructed elevation for Phoenix Cottage (p. 249); bottom: Re-creation of the home of Robert Dene of Stoneleigh, Warwickshire (p. 158).

To J. T. Smith
who compiled the first detailed cruck distribution map,
laying the foundation for all our later work

Contents

Appendices

CD-ROM

Reports on individual buildings [pdf files]

Preface

This volume presents the results of a study of almost 120 medieval houses in the four Midland counties of Buckinghamshire, Leicestershire, Oxfordshire and Warwickshire (with a few in Gloucestershire and Nottinghamshire), using a combination of tree-ring dating (dendrochronology) and architectural survey, together with the documentary background to another twenty houses. Most of these buildings are of cruck construction – to the extent that the summary title 'The Cruck-Dating Project' has often been applied to the project as a whole.

The survey was initiated by Bob Laxton in collaboration with Nat Alcock, in succession to the successful Kent tree-ring dating project carried out by the Nottingham University Tree-ring Dating Laboratory (NUTRDL) from 1986–9. The primary evidence was obtained between 1988 and 1991 by a team consisting of Robert Howard of NUTRDL (dendrochronology) and Dan Miles (architectural survey) under the direction of Nat (N. W.) Alcock (co-ordinating the architectural and documentary study), Bob (R. R.) Laxton and Cliff (C. D.) Litton (tree-ring dating). Most of the plans and sections were measured by Dan Miles during the main phase of the project, but some have come from external sources or from later work and the conventions employed sometimes vary, for example in the inclusion or omission of roof materials. We are extremely grateful to Bob Meeson for redrawing the more than one hundred sections to a uniform scale and style.

Although frustrating for the contributors, the delay in completing this book has had its advantages, through the opportunity both to include additional buildings, and to undertake further research on those already studied. Work after the formal end of the project has included the recording and tree-ring dating by Dan Miles of other medieval houses allowing us to include a dozen extra houses, the updating of sapwood estimates and more detailed documentary research. Very recently, also, it has been possible to apply high-precision radiocarbon dating to some buildings. As a particular example of the positive aspects of this extended period of research, fieldwork by Eric Sewell in Long Crendon, the village already notable for having more cruck buildings than anywhere else in England, has, astonishingly, identified three more cruck-built houses there. Similarly, documentary research on the social background to the medieval houses in Steventon has been transformed by the discovery of extensive hitherto unknown documentary sources.

Apart from sections for which individual authors are named, Nat Alcock has been primarily responsible for chapters 3 and 4 on Planning and Structure, and Dan Miles for chapter 5 on Carpentry. We have worked jointly on the other chapters. We thank the various contributors for their unstinting efforts, and for their patience in waiting for this publication to appear. We are especially grateful to Dr Christopher Currie for making available his research, both published and unpublished, on houses in the Vale of the White Horse, and in discussing the buildings there with us.

The project was funded by the Leverhulme Trust, without whose support it could not have been undertaken. The radiocarbon dating was funded by the Society of Antiquaries (one site), the Vernacular Architecture Group (four sites) and the Oxfordshire Building Record (one site). Generous grants in support of the publication have been made by the Aurelius Charitable Trust. Sadly, during the long period that it has taken for this book to be completed, Bob Laxton, one of the original project directors, has died, as has John Chenevix-Trench, who undertook the initial documentary research on Long Crendon. We hope that they would have approved of the final results.

We thank everyone who has assisted the project, and in particular those who have allowed us free access to record and date their houses. Without their co-operation, the study would have been impossible. Several people provided substantial help with the surveying, notably Catherine Murray (Buckinghamshire), Nick Hill (Leicestershire and Rutland), and members of the Oxfordshire Buildings Record (Oxfordshire, led by David Clark). The archivists at the many repositories where documents have been consulted have been unfailingly helpful.

Despite the long wait between our original survey work and the final appearance of this volume, we hope that everyone interested in the subject of medieval houses will consider the results worth waiting for.

Nat Alcock
Dan Miles

List of Figures and Tables

Tables

Part II

Figures

Picture Credits:

We thank the following organisations and individuals for permission to reproduce figures. Copyright remains with the original owners. Centre for Buckinghamshire Studies (6.3; 8.4.4, 8.5.10); The Master, Fellows and Scholars of Christ's College, Cambridge (6.15); English Heritage (8.1.1); J.J. Eyston (8.6.11); Neil Finn (8.8.1; 8.8.4); Nick Hill (5.11); The National Archives (8.87); Eric Sewell (8.4.1, 8.5.1); Shakespeare Centre Library and Archive (6.12, 8.11.5); Steventon Parish Council (8.10c.1); John Walker (8.5.4). Acknowledgements for images reproduced in the reports are included in the individual figure captions.

Coastline and boundaries on maps are based on data provided through EDINA UKBORDERS with the support of the ESRC and JISC and uses boundary material which is copyright of the Crown and the ED-LINE Consortium. Acknowledgements for images reproduced in the reports are included in the individual figure captions.

PART I

Analysis of the Medieval Peasant House

CONVENTIONS

Labelling of features

In descriptions and reports and on plans, bays are labelled as I, II, etc, and trusses as T1, T2, etc.

Dates

Dates cited in the text are given in forms that are intended to indicate their source, their precision and their reliability. A suffix 'd' indicating a tree-ring date is occasionally used when this is not self-evident. In the original reports and the dates as published in *Vernacular Architecture*, central felling dates within the date ranges were given but, following current practice, only the felling date ranges are used.

The following conventions are used:

1408 *or* Spring 1408	Timber felled in 1408 (incomplete growth for that year), possibly with the season identified
1407/8	Timber felled in the winter of 1407–8 (complete growth for 1407)
1405/8	Several timbers with precise felling dates, covering this range of years
c. 1408	Felling with a year or two of this date (usually with slight uncertainty about the completeness of the sapwood)
1406–10	(short felling date range) Used when an individual timber or a group of timbers are believed to have had virtually complete sapwood, but where a small amount (estimated here at 4 rings) were lost in coring or could not be measured or counted.
1398–1428	Felling date range (incomplete sapwood or only heartwood/sapwood boundary present
1297–1308	Italics indicate that the felling date range has been refined by the use of the OxCal computer program. The unrefined felling date range is given in the individual report.
1405	Earliest likely felling date for timber without sapwood (last ring plus 10 or13 years). This is the *terminus post quem* (*tpq*) date.
early 15th cent	Date estimated from typology or other evidence (see individual report for details) (subdivided as early; mid; late)
1408doc	Date from documentary evidence
1620i	Date from building inscription

Sapwood estimates

Felling date ranges have been revised from those originally presented, using the best currently available sapwood estimates. Most of the ranges have also been refined using OxCal (see p. 268). Both the original and revised estimates are given in the individual reports. The following 95% probability estimates are used

Leicestershire, Nottinghamshire, West Midlands	12–45 rings; mode 21 rings
Buckinghamshire, Gloucestershire, Oxfordshire, Warwickshire	9–41 rings; mode 17 rings

The modal dates are used for plotting and statistical analysis but are not cited in the text, since they do not provide precise dates for buildings. When no sapwood survives and only a *terminus post quem* (*tpq*) date is known, the modal date is taken to be 25 years after the *tpq* date.

Dendrochronology Abbreviations

FMR = first measured ring	LMR = last measured (complete) ring	Dat Cat = Dating Category (see p. 266)
LHR = last heartwood ring	NM = not measured	

Sapwood: B = complete to bark on sample
C = complete to waney edge on sample
c = complete on timber but not on sample
¼C/ ½C = complete sapwood with some spring/spring and summer growth (ring not measured)

Units and conversion factors

Dimensions are given in Imperial measure throughout, since these are the units that the carpenters would have used originally. Thus, any standard dimensions or other regularities will be most obvious when expressed in these units. For reasons of space and readability, the metric equivalents of individual dimensions are not included in the text, but can be calculated using the following factors:

Linear dimensions	*Land (area) measure*
1 yard = 3 feet = 0.914 metres	1 acre = 4 rods = 0.405 hectare
1 foot = 12 inches = 0.305 metres	1 rod = 40 perches = 0.101 hectare
1 inch = 2.54 centimetres	1 perch = 25.3 square metres

The *yardland* (virgate in Latin) was a conventional measure of the size of an open-field holding, which varied from place to place (and to some extent from holding to holding). At Long Crendon, Buckinghamshire, a yardland contained 30 customary acres, corresponding to 25 statute acres; at Steventon, Oxfordshire, it contained 24 acres; at Stoneleigh, Warwickshire (1597), the yardland was calculated to contain 28 acres on average, and at Diseworth, Leicestershire (1797) each contained 24 acres, although conventionally they were reputed to be of 18 acres.

1

Introduction

T[homas?] Hopkyns is required to build a house of five pairs of forks (*edificare super unum toftum unam domum de v per' forkes*) within two years [at Long Itchington, Warwickshire] (1346–7, Bodleian Library, Ms Trinity 84, p. 65).

When our project on the *Medieval Peasant House* began, the long-held view of historians and archaeologists was that houses such as that to be built by Thomas Hopkyns at Long Itchington would have lasted for no more than a generation.[1] However, the investigation of documentary sources was undermining these views,[2] as was evidence that most of the several hundred cruck houses in the Midlands were of medieval date and, simply from their numbers, they could not all be of superior social status. Writing in 2011, the position is reversed. The new orthodoxy is that peasant houses were substantial, and built to last – and that 'later medieval houses survive in their thousands'.[3] However, less attention has been paid to the details of these houses, or to their social status, which may not be as uniform as the label *peasant* might suggest. Some types of medieval houses, such as the Wealden buildings of Kent, are linked to an emerging group of prosperous yeomen.[4] In contrast, many of smaller medieval houses in the Midlands, in particular those of cruck construction, can be associated with people of much more modest status. Both these groups, however, fall within the overall definition of *peasant* within late medieval English society, as the mass of village householders.[5] They merge at one end into the landless labourers who might occupy their own houses or sometimes live with the masters they served, and at the other into the substantial villagers who had perhaps amassed several originally separate holdings and were farming on a considerable scale. They would normally hold their house and land by customary or copyhold tenure, although a few were free tenants. However, this tenurial distinction was of less importance than the nature and extent of the agricultural and other resources available to them.

Our aim is to provide an in-depth study of the many medieval peasant houses still standing in Midland villages, and of their historical context. In particular, the combination of tree-ring and radiocarbon dating, detailed architectural study and documentary research illuminates both their nature and their status. Within the volume, this introduction examines the strands of evidence used and sets out the detailed strategy adopted in the project, with the study of cruck-built houses at its heart. The four central chapters present the primary results. Chapter 2 examines the dating results in relation to their geographical and chronological range. Chapters 3, 4 and 5 present an examination of the buildings surveyed, correlated with the dating evidence, looking at the developments in planning, structure and carpentry from the thirteenth to the sixteenth centuries. Chapter 6 examines the documentary evidence for medieval peasant houses, both in general terms and in case studies of villages for which exceptionally good documentary and architectural evidence survives. A short additional section examines the social background to the base-cruck houses included in the survey. In Chapter 7, the results are brought together, demonstrating how our work has provided a new and detailed view of the medieval peasant house, resolving the contradiction between the archaeological and architectural evidence. We hope here to show how its social organisation developed in the period before we have extensive documentary evidence for the use of space within the house.

Technical details of the dating methodology are given in Appendix 1, and Appendix 2 provides a complete tabulation of the buildings studied with the codes assigned to each (which are used for reference in the main text). It also includes a list of the buildings rejected on preliminary examination. The dates obtained are listed in Chapter 2.

The heart of an architectural study lies in the individual buildings examined, even more than in the generalisations derived from them. The main text is extensively illustrated with sections and plans of the houses studied; their interpretation, however, requires a close analysis of the buildings, especially in relation to the reconstruction of missing portions or the evidence for such features as smoke louvres. Descriptions of each of the 117 buildings surveyed, accompanied by plans, drawings and photographs, are included on the accompanying CD-ROM. In addition, reports for a further 21 buildings have been compiled, which focus on their documentary history and give only brief details of the buildings (generally based on earlier work). A small selection of these reports are printed in Part II. These include both typical peasant houses and also the most remarkable buildings discovered: LON-G, an aisled hall built in 1205; AST-A, a box-framed chamber block of 1282–6; MDM-A, a virtually complete three-bay cruck house of 1335.

The Evidence for Peasant Houses

Three strands of evidence contribute to our knowledge of medieval peasant housing. Each provides specific insights and each also has its specific weaknesses.

Documents

Documentary sources give good evidence of the dates at which some houses were being constructed. They are concerned to specify the structural character and size, indicating clearly that they were regarded as valuable assets. However, we cannot generally demonstrate that the particular houses referred to might have survived to the present day. The extensive sources, such as probate inventories and surveys, that illuminate post-medieval houses,[6] are generally non-existent or very sparse until after the Middle Ages. A few exceptions have been discovered, including Stoneleigh, Warwickshire, for which inventories survive from as early as 1537 and regularly include room names; the earliest of these inventories can be seen as describing medieval houses still furnished in medieval style; such other early inventories as have been studied only rarely name the rooms.

Caution is needed in relating the documentary evidence directly to surviving buildings, because it seems clear that by the fifteenth century rural society in some areas was undergoing differentiation, with the emergence below the manorial level of wealthier sub-classes within village society. These groups are identifiable, for example, as the builders of the elegant Wealden houses in Kent.[7] This trend seems to be associated more with pastoral than arable farming regions and might therefore be relatively unimportant in the Midland counties. Significant late medieval changes have been identified in the sizes of village holdings, but the distribution of land remained generally even (but see the discussion of Oxfordshire in Chapter 6).

The direct identification of the original status for individual standing medieval village houses is exceptionally difficult, because evidence linking post-medieval village holdings with their medieval counterparts is very sparse. However, when the pattern of land-holdings within the village was uniform, it is not necessary to relate a particular house to a particular medieval holding, to demonstrate that it must have belonged to, say, a yardland (30 acre) farm. The documentary case studies focus on places where we can either make links of this type or can find information about the status of individual houses.

Excavation

Excavation can be expected to date house sites reasonably closely and to provide good evidence for their size and room layout, and for the overall pattern of buildings within the croft, but it is unable to identify their associated land-holding. The inevitable hiatus caused by later destruction mean that a complete picture is disappointingly rare. More important in relation to the permanence or impermanence of peasant building, is the difficulty of identifying the character of the standing structure from the below-ground evidence. This is exemplified by the reinterpretation of the excavations at Wharram Percy, from single-generation insubstantial structures to long-lived cruck houses, identical in form to those still standing in neighbouring villages.[8] Thus, archaeological results are of only moderate value in establishing the detailed nature of peasant houses. Rather, the evidence of standing buildings informs the interpretation of excavation results. Partly for this reason and partly because a major review of excavated medieval houses is close to publication,[9] the evidence of excavation finds only a limited place in the present volume.

Standing Buildings

The third strand of evidence for medieval peasant houses, that of standing buildings, has often only contributed to the discussion in rather general terms. To identify an actual medieval peasant house, three questions must be answered. Is it medieval in date and, if possible, precisely when was it built? Secondly, what was its original form? Thirdly, was it of peasant status? The answers to these three questions for our surveyed houses are given in Chapters 2, 3–5 and 6 respectively.

Research in vernacular architecture has gradually led to the recognition of surviving small medieval houses, by working back from the well-established structural and plan features of sixteenth or seventeenth century houses.[10] The latter can easily be recognised, since from around 1575, many carry inscribed dates.[11] In particular, the literary evidence for improvement from the later sixteenth century onwards has been confirmed.[12] The upper floors and chimneys reported as new features in this period are amply exemplified in standing buildings.

Houses that are more primitive than these sixteenth or seventeenth century examples must, by elimination, be medieval. They share in particular the touchstone of the medieval house, the open hall: the main living room originally without an upper floor or a chimney, recognisable by the soot from its central hearth encrusting the roof timbers. Such houses have now been identified in very considerable numbers over the whole of southern England.[13] In some areas, notably Kent, Sussex and much of East Anglia, the medieval houses have sufficient distinctive details (in such features as their roof structure, crown posts, beam mouldings and bracing patterns), that a reasonably precise typology can be established, linked to buildings of known date. As noted above, the quality of many of the houses in these regions suggests that their builders belonged to a relatively wealthy sub-class within the village

community. Smaller and simpler medieval houses have been recorded there, but they are too rare to provide a detailed picture of the houses of more modest peasants.[14]

In the Midlands, the medieval houses generally lack such detailing. They are dominated by one structural form, the *cruck*, in which the roof and walls are supported by paired timbers (cruck blades), reaching from ground to apex in a single sweep. A typical cruck house has three bays (structural units), with four cruck trusses (Fig. 1.1). Most often, the central bay was the open hall, with the roof timbers sooted by the smoke rising from a hearth on the floor; one end bay had an original upper floor, providing sleeping rooms, and the other end was used as service space.

In Fig. 1.2A, the components of a cruck truss are drawn and labelled. Some Midlands *box-frame* houses (Fig. 1.2B) have also been identified as late medieval as, for example, Cuttle Pool Farm, Knowle, Warwickshire, dated to 1478/9.[15] This structural form becomes dominant in the region after crucks passed out of use, but the present survey and other recent studies have shown that box-framing formed a more significant component of the medieval carpenter's repertoire than expected, appearing as early as the late thirteenth century in chamber blocks (see Chapters 3 to 5). Surprisingly, perhaps, the earliest surviving houses in the region are not cruck-built, but are *aisled* (Fig. 1.2C), with free-standing posts set within the walls, or use the more substantial *base crucks*. These have large curved cruck-like blades that rise only to the tiebeam. They often

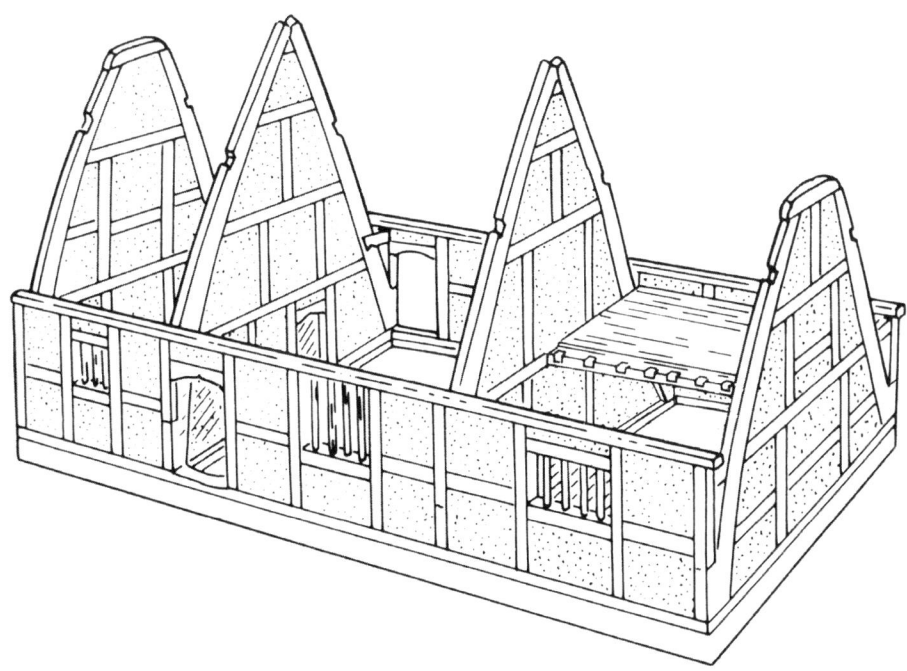

Fig. 1.1. A typical Midlands cruck house. Redrawn from Alcock, Meeson *et al.* (1996) Recording timber-framed buildings: an illustrated glossary.

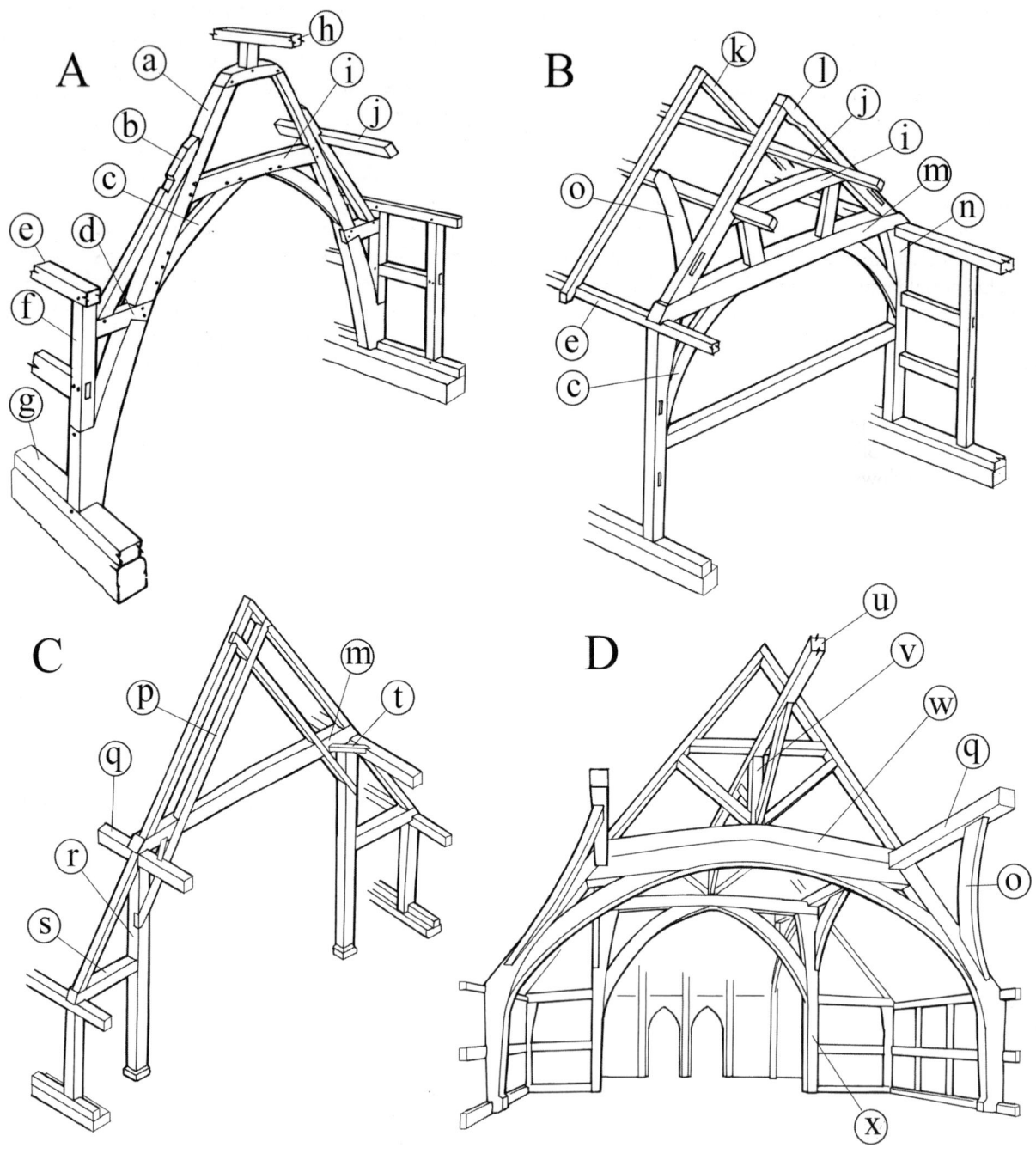

Key to components (* for more than one label):

a	cruck blade	h	ridge piece	n	wall post	u	collar plate (or purlin)
b	packing piece	i	collar	o*	windbrace	v	crown post
c*	arch brace	j*	purlin (trenched in A;	p	passing brace	w	double tie
d	cruck spur		clasped in B)	q*	arcade plate	x	spere truss.
e*	wall plate	k	common rafter	r	arcade post		
f	cruck stud	l	principal rafter	s	aisle tie		
g	sill beam	m*	tiebeam	t	dragon tie		

Fig. 1.2. Typical timber-framed trusses: (A) a cruck truss; (B) a box-framed truss with clasped purlin roof; (C) an aisled truss; (D) a base-cruck truss with crown-post upper roof and, beyond it a spere truss of aisled form. Drawings by Bob Meeson, based on Alcock, Meeson *et al.* (1996) *Recording Timber-Framed Buildings.*

have *aisled* end or spere (screen) trusses and use square-set arcade plates rather than the diagonally-set purlins found with crucks (Fig. 1.2D).

Despite these alternative forms, the dominance of cruck construction in the southern half of Britain is amply demonstrated by the distribution map of cruck houses (Fig. 1.3), and by the absence in the Midlands of similar numbers of box-framed houses. In midland and southern England, the great majority of the crucks are undoubtedly medieval, demonstrated both by their tree-ring dates and their architectural features. Furthermore, the sheer number of cruck houses confirms that they must be peasant houses, rather than being of manorial status or restricted to the wealthiest of villagers. When a village has ten or even twenty such houses, it is a safe deduction that they were the homes of ordinary people including, as our study indicates, the whole hierarchy of rural society, from substantial and middling peasants down to a few smallholders (though not equally likely to survive for all these groups). The status is less obvious for the aisled and the substantial base-cruck houses, for which the evidence is considered in Chapter 6. This map also shows how the cruck distribution has a sharply defined eastern boundary, with crucks being completely absent from the eastern third of England; the cause of this boundary has been an enigma since it was first recognised, but its further examination lies beyond the scope of the present study.[16]

Understanding the original form of these houses requires detailed structural analysis, working back from the existing building, mentally stripping away later modernisation and interpreting minute details to re-create the form of the medieval house. This is undertaken, house-by-house, in the individual reports, and an overview of their characteristics is given in chapters 3–5, and summarised in chapter 7.

A particularly significant aspect of the dominance of cruck construction in the region relates to the interpretation of the documentary evidence. Almost invariably, when they give information about the structure itself, they are described as composed of *furcae*, either individually or in pairs, a term which has long been translated as *cruck*.[17] Although this meaning has recently been challenged, the suggested alternatives are not convincing. In particular, if this standard term, used in the region where crucks are dominant (and not generally elsewhere), had a different significance, we are left without a plausible word for cruck.[18] Thus, we can use the documentary evidence to support that obtained from standing buildings for the dating and use of cruck construction

Project Strategy

The objective of this project has been to study a considerable sample of what were expected to be medieval peasant houses, applying structural recording and analysis, dendrochronology, and documentary research.[19] Within this overall aim, strategic choices inevitably had to be made. The first was to concentrate on cruck houses. This decision was primarily based on the belief that they dominated the surviving early buildings in the region, and that most such houses from the Midlands southwards were of medieval date. Furthermore, the continuing interest in this form of construction had led to the compilation of a comprehensive list of cruck buildings, providing a ready-made database of examples for study.[20] Although some small medieval box-framed buildings (Fig. 1.2B) survive within the region dominated by cruck construction (especially as wings associated with cruck halls), they had not previously been the subject of detailed analysis. However, a number of examples have been included in the study and it has been possible to re-evaluate their significance as components of the regional medieval building tradition.

The project area

The second choice was of the areas to be examined. The distribution map of crucks (Fig. 1.3) shows notable concentrations in north-east and west Yorkshire, along the Severn (Herefordshire, Worcestershire and Shropshire), in south-east and central Wales, and in south Oxfordshire. For the study of medieval peasant houses, the northern areas were rejected because it appeared that almost all the standing buildings were post-medieval, although some evidence suggested that crucks might have been reused from earlier houses.[21] In the Severn-side counties and Wales, the cruck houses are believed to be medieval, but many of them are very elegant, with strikingly decorative carpentry. It was unclear whether they were the houses of typical medieval peasants or belonged to an elite group of villagers.[22]

In the Midlands, the cruck houses in Warwickshire and Leicestershire seemed to be the most 'ordinary', often lacking any distinction in their construction. Here, surely, might be found the homes of typical medieval peasants. Detailed study of buildings immediately to the south, in the limestone regions of Oxfordshire and Northamptonshire, seemed less likely to be rewarding. Few crucks had been recorded in this area and these appeared generally to be fragmentary survivals after an extensive sixteenth and seventeenth century rebuilding. However, many cruck houses were known in the southern half of Oxfordshire and the adjoining county of Buckinghamshire, and the area included several 'cruck villages' (those containing half-a-dozen or more crucks).[23] Notably early dates had been suggested for some of the Oxfordshire examples, for which confirmation by dendrochronology would be particularly valuable.[24] Thus, our survey has concentrated on these four counties (including also that part of West Midlands formerly in Warwickshire) (Fig. 1.4).[25] The northern two counties are representative of the grouping of crucks from the Cotswolds northwards, the southern ones of the cruck

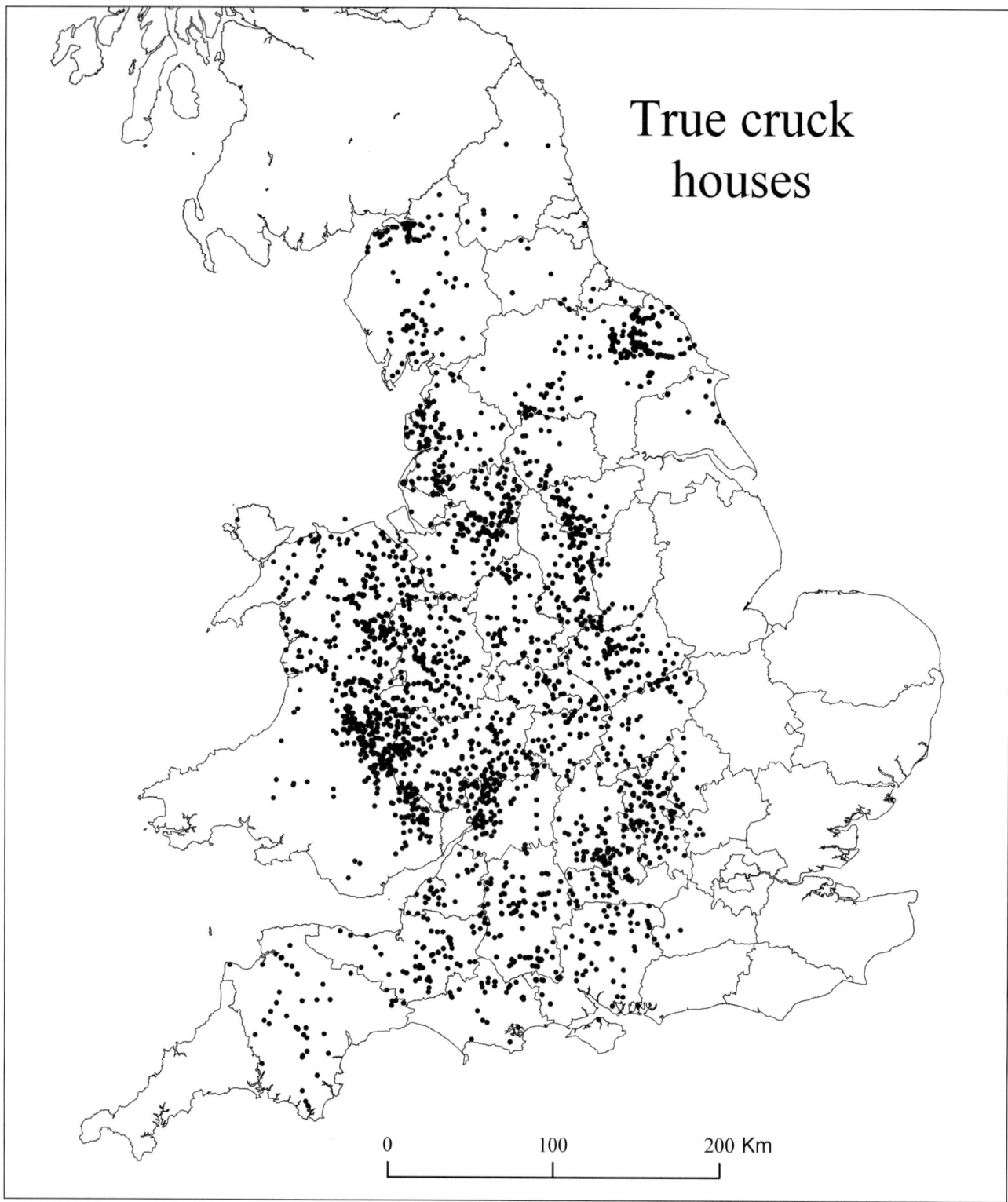

Fig. 1.3. Distribution of cruck houses in England and Wales. A total of 3086 examples are plotted. (Updated from the map published in Alcock, 'Distribution of crucks', to include newly identified examples.)

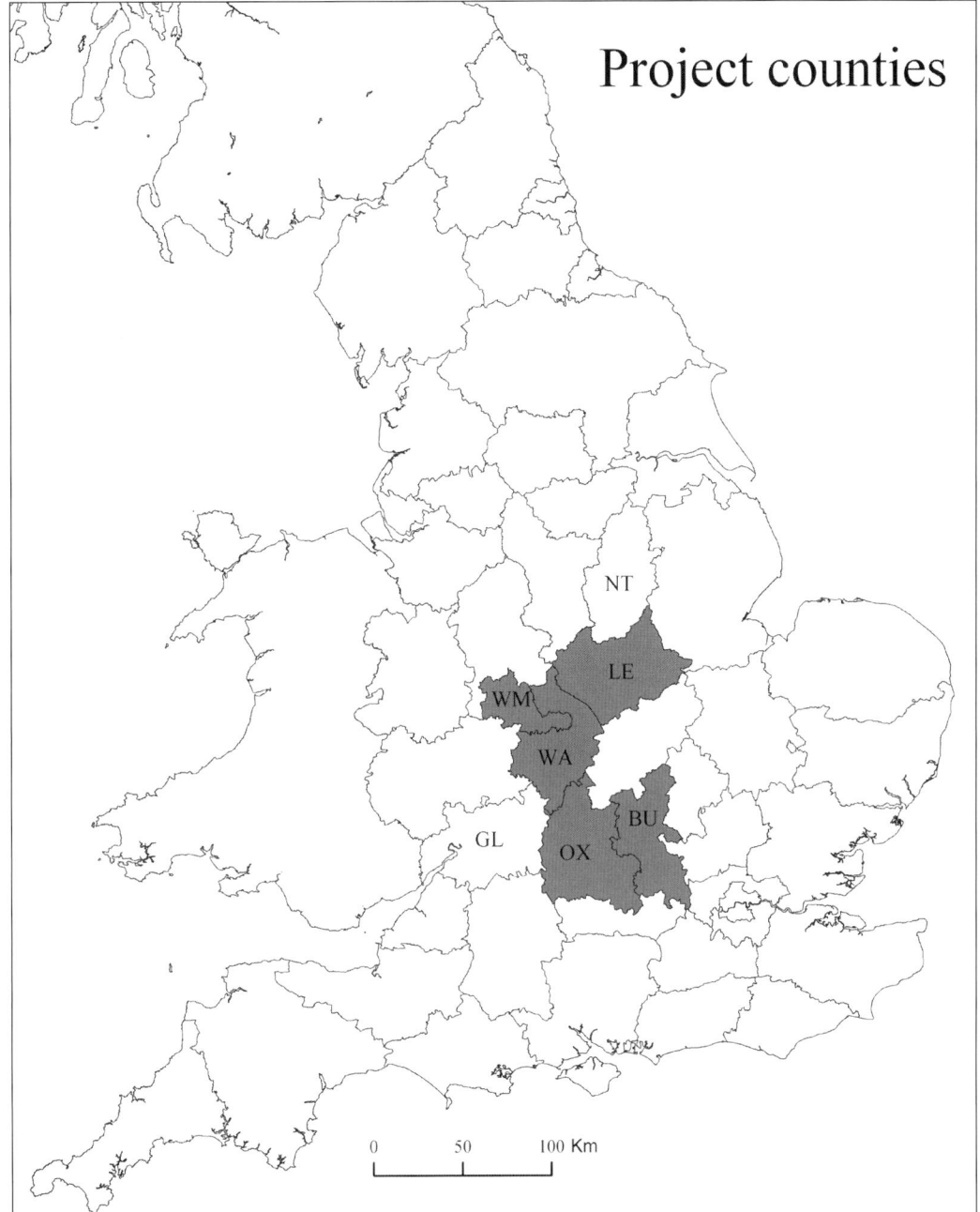

Fig. 1.4. The project counties. Two houses in Gloucestershire, three in Nottinghamshire and one in Rutland were also examined. Those parts of West Midlands formerly in Staffordshire and Worcestershire were not included in the project; neither, apart from one house, was Rutland, administratively part of Leicestershire from 1974 to 1997.

concentration in the Chilterns and the Vale of White Horse.[26] The survey might have been extended to the south, into the rest of Berkshire (from which that part of the study area in south Oxfordshire had been removed in 1974), Wiltshire and Hampshire, but this seemed likely to spread out the buildings that could be recorded too thinly, while proportionately fewer crucks are known there than in the chosen counties.[27]

We also examined one village in Gloucestershire, Frampton-on-Severn, where eight cruck houses had been recorded and an architectural survey had been carried out.[28] Disappointingly, this extension to the project area was not very successful in that only two houses were deemed worthy of detailed study and only one of these provided a tree-ring date. One of the very few surviving cruck houses in Nottinghamshire was also included, since independently-funded dating had already been carried out there.

The choice of individual buildings to sample started from the county lists of cruck houses and decisions about the best villages to study. In general, the most complete houses have been selected, because they should provide the best evidence for structure and function. However, this strategy introduces a real danger of sampling bias, because of potential correlation between age and state of preservation. We believe, though, that this problem has been reduced by another aspect of the project strategy. Rather than sample randomly in the survey area, we concentrated on the major groups of houses in the 'cruck villages', Long Crendon (Buckinghamshire), East Hendred, Harwell and Steventon (Oxfordshire), Rothley (Leicestershire) and Stoneleigh (Warwickshire). As far as possible every cruck house was examined within these villages, whether well or badly preserved, though some then had to be rejected as unlikely to date. It should be noted, too, that fragmentary structures have proved difficult to date, in part because they may include only two or three suitable timbers. We have included in the lists and plots of dated buildings any other cruck houses within the survey area for which tree-ring dates have been obtained.[29]

It was not usually possible to arrange a preliminary visit, and the survey team was virtually committed to surveying and sampling on the day, and would only reject houses if they were clearly going to be unsatisfactory. Many of the houses were selected on a 'cold calling' approach where house owners were written to without prior contact and, happily, most of these owners turned out to be very co-operative and enthusiastic. Very few householders refused permission, although one leading member of the Society for the Preservation of Ancient Buildings objected on the philosophical grounds that the physical intervention involved in the removal of even a cubic centimetre of historic fabric was not worth the information gained,[30] and another lady was concerned that the coring would reactivate long-dormant insects.

Fieldwork was intensive, with houses pre-arranged and both the sampling and building recording taking place at the same time, to lessen the inconvenience for the householders. In retrospect, this was less than ideal, in that often it would take a day just to record a section through the house, and the drawings were therefore not made on site, but drawn out later from measured sketches. This time pressure also limited the details that could be noted, particularly about secondary phases. A few buildings were examined while they were in a state of repair or conversion, and these opportunities were seized on as they allowed better access to more timbers. Fate sometimes took a hand, for instance when the survey team turned up at Manor Cottage, Sutton Courtenay (SUC-A), to discover that it had caught fire the night before. Fortunately, we were able to revisit the property the following year during its reconstruction and obtain some excellent samples with bark edge which had escaped the flames – indeed these samples probably would not have been accessible before the fire!

In one respect, the project was extended beyond its original objectives, by including a number of base-cruck buildings, two of them in Nottinghamshire and one in Rutland. This construction allows a greater width than is normally achievable with true crucks and thus, as larger buildings, they are generally believed to be of higher status than the ordinary cruck houses. They have been identified as manor houses, well-endowed rectories, and urban gentry houses.[31] They were expected to contain good quality timber, from which we hoped to obtain long tree-ring sequences that would be of value for dating other buildings. We were indeed able to obtain some long sequences, but the buildings were found to date to the fourteenth century and earlier, and the sequences did not overlap extensively with those for most of the other buildings. Serendipitously, close examination of the status of these base-cruck houses has shown that several of them were probably built by superior peasants rather than the manorial lords that previous work had indicated, and they are therefore more directly relevant to the project than had been supposed (see p. 151).[32]

2

Sampling and Dating of the Surveyed Houses

Nat Alcock, Dan Miles, Bob Laxton† and Cliff Litton

Project Results

In the first part of this chapter, the survey results and the statistical validity of the survey sample are examined, through a comparison of the number of buildings surveyed for the project with the totality of cruck houses recorded in the project region. The results, for buildings either successfully dated or failing to date, and their distributions are then considered.

Surveyed buildings

The numerical data for the project are summarised in the first and second parts of Table 2.1. Within the four principal counties, 477 cruck houses have been recognised (and also 48 barns), but of these 63 have been demolished or contain only reused timbers.[1] At the start of the project, we estimated that the available resources would allow about 100 buildings to be surveyed, about a 25% sample of the total number of cruck houses in the surveyed counties.

In all, 155 houses have been examined, 147 of them in the core project counties, including eight non-cruck houses (mainly base crucks). From these, 38 buildings were eliminated on preliminary visits as unlikely to give useful results, either because they seemed unlikely to give successful tree-ring dating, for reasons such as the use of elm or of timbers with very wide rings, or because their structural evidence was concealed or was very fragmentary. The remaining 117 buildings have been surveyed, generally during the course of the project, though occasionally earlier

or later work has been incorporated. In the main survey counties, 102 cruck houses have been surveyed (almost 25% of those standing). Although a relatively higher proportion of the Warwickshire crucks have been examined than elsewhere, this resulted from a wish to equalise the numbers of buildings surveyed in the four counties; the smaller numbers surviving there probably result from the destruction inflicted by nineteenth and twentieth century urban development. The lists in Appendix 2 cover both the surveyed and rejected buildings.

Fig. 2.1 shows the distributions of the project cruck houses, whether dated, undated or rejected, and of other cruck houses within the four counties. The map shows a generally good match between the overall distribution of cruck houses and that of the surveyed houses with no obvious sampling bias, apart from a lack of surveyed buildings in central Oxfordshire and north Buckinghamshire; this is the result of the strategic concentration on individual villages in the south of both counties, particularly Harwell in Oxfordshire and Long Crendon in Buckinghamshire. The map also highlights the sparsity of identified cruck houses in a strip cutting across the centre of the project region between south Warwickshire and central Oxfordshire; this corresponds to the stone-building region of the Cotswolds where cruck buildings are either concealed by later stone walls and so are difficult to recognise, or have been replaced. This strip where cruck houses are uncommon is also apparent on Fig. 1.3.

Table 2.1. Cruck and base cruck buildings within the project counties and adjacent areas, and numbers of project buildings surveyed, rejected, dated and undated. Source for cruck and base-cruck buildings: http://archaeologydataservice.ac.uk/archives/view/vag_cruck/ (accessed 1 Dec 2010).

		Project Counties						Other Counties				
County (and abbreviation)		Buckinghamshire (BU)	Leicestershire (LE)	Oxfordshire (OX)	Warwickshire (WA)	West Midlands (Warw) (WM)	Totals	Gloucestershire	Nottinghamshire	Rutland	West Midlands (Worcs /Staffs)	Totals
Recorded cruck buildings	Standing houses	131	94	117	63	9	414	81	6	6	2	
	Standing barns	7	7	18	5	2	39	29	1		0	
	Demolished / reused cruck houses	6	27	9	12	9	63	12		7	4	
	Demolished / reused cruck barns	2	2	3	1	1	9	10	1	2	0	
	Total cruck buildings	146	130	147	81	21	525	132	15	8	6	
	Base-cruck houses	10	6	12	8	0	36	18	2	3	2	
Project buildings	Surveyed	27	22	29	29	4	111	2	3	1		117
	Rejected	7	10	14	5		36	2				38
	Total	34	32	43	33	4	147	4	3	1		155
	Base-cruck houses:	(2)			(2)		(4)		(2)	(1)		(7)
	non-cruck houses:	(1)		(2)	(2)		(5)					(5)
	% of standing cruck houses	18	23	23	38	44	25					
	(Documentary study)	(9)		(9)	(3)		(21)					
Dating of surveyed buildings	Dated (primary structure)	18	15	25	24	2	83	1	3	1		88
	Undated (primary structure)	9	7	4	5	2	28	1				29
	% dated	67	68	86	83	50	75					75

Dated buildings

Both the general and the more technical aspects of tree-ring and radiocarbon dating are described in Appendix 1. For interpreting the dates themselves, it is important to emphasise that what is provided by dendrochronology is either a precise *felling date* or an *estimated felling-date range*, identifying when the tree or trees were felled. Radiocarbon dating invariably gives a *felling date range*. It is unfortunately the case that tree-ring dating is not always successful, if the ring-width sequences cannot be matched satisfactorily with master sequences of known date. However, radiocarbon dating almost always gives a reasonably precise date.[2]

Felling dates and ranges

All the timbers dated in this study were of oak, apart from one elm cruck (MDM-A) and two elm timbers for which radiocarbon dates were obtained (WOA-A and LON-

G). Oak shows an important characteristic: a distinction between the inner heartwood and the outer sapwood annual rings, separated by the heartwood/sapwood boundary. This allows for three possible types of tree-ring dates:

(a) A timber complete to the outermost ring, to which the bark was attached, can be given a *felling date* precise to the year – or sometimes to the season, if the final ring was only part-grown.

(b) If the sapwood is incomplete, then an *estimated felling date range* is obtained. This includes a statistical estimate of the number of sapwood rings the timber might have had. Much research has been undertaken to improve the precision of these estimates. Felling date ranges presented in italics have been refined using the dating program OxCal (see Appendix 1).[3]

(c) If no sapwood at all survives, it is only possible to give a *terminus post quem* ('after which') date. This corresponds to the final ring date plus the minimum number of

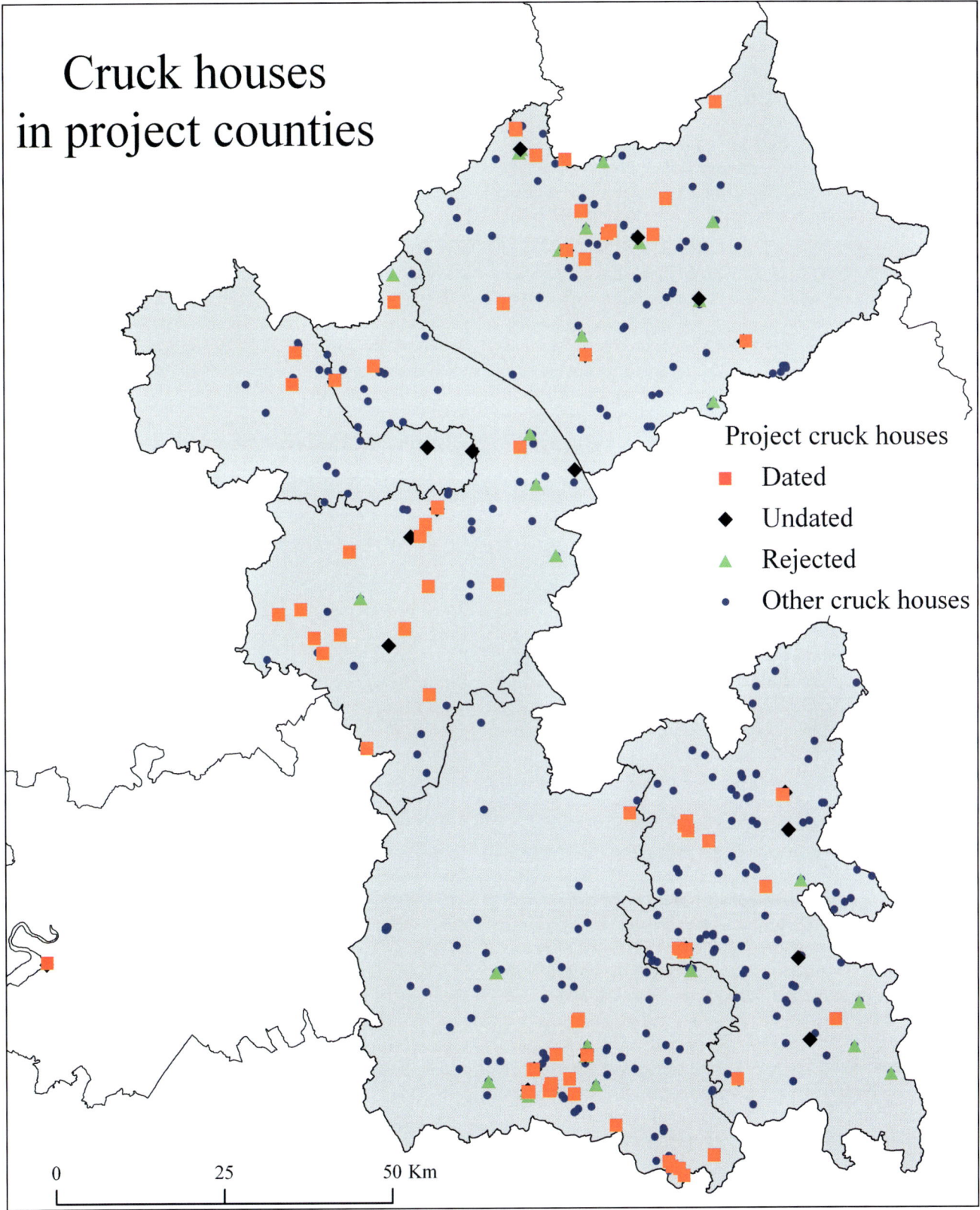

Cruck houses in project counties

Project cruck houses
- ■ Dated
- ◆ Undated
- ▲ Rejected
- • Other cruck houses

Fig. 2.1. Cruck houses recorded in the project counties identifying those dated, undated and rejected. Non-project cruck houses recorded in Gloucestershire and Nottinghamshire are not mapped. Note the outlying examples at Frampton-on-Severn, Gloucestershire (one dated to 1496/7, one undated and two rejected), which are not included on later maps.

sapwood rings appropriate for the location, with no allowance for lost heartwood rings. It is thus the earliest possible felling date. Because trees were generally chosen to be of the smallest size necessary for their particular function,[4] it is reasonable to presume that only a moderate number of heartwood rings have been lost, and that felling probably took place within 25 to 50 years of this *terminus*. Fortunately, this only had to be applied to one building studied (SOF-A), and it was possible to suggest from architectural evidence that construction took place comparatively soon after the *terminus post quem* date.

Radiocarbon dates have an intrinsic range, larger or smaller depending on their position on the calibration curve or on the fit to the curve of multiple ('wiggle-matched') dates (Appendix 1). If necessary, this also has to be convoluted with the appropriate sapwood allowance to obtain the *calibrated felling date range*. These dates are described as 'calibrated', because of the need to apply the calibration correction, and they are presented in italics (e.g. *cal AD 1423–1446*). One date (STE-E) has been obtained by the joint application of radiocarbon and tree-ring dating.

Felling and construction

It is always an assumption that a building was constructed at or very soon after the felling date of its timbers (e.g. in the summer following winter felling). In general, this assumption is confirmed by medieval building accounts, which include in one year both the payments for felling timber, and those for the conversion into building timber. It is also not uncommon to discover mortices that were clearly cut square in green timber, but have distorted as the wood seasoned. This demonstrates that construction took place within a few years of felling. The inferred equivalence of felling and building dates is strengthened when several timbers give the same precise felling date (e.g. STC-A), or some were felled in the winter and others in the following spring. However, it is more common for felling dates to span a few years, when we can presume that construction followed soon after the latest date. The felling dates rarely differ by more than a year or two although an unusually broad spread was found in AST-A, with felling dates between 1282 and 1286. Sometimes, however, one timber has a felling date ten or twenty years earlier than the remainder (e.g. STE-E); it is then presumed to have come from a dead tree, or perhaps from a stockpiled timber. The danger is evident that, if one timber only in a building is dated, its felling date may precede construction by rather more than the few years just suggested. Fortunately a knowledge of construction dates to the precise year has not been of great importance in the present study.

The dates

The results of the tree-ring and radiocarbon dating are summarised in the third part of Table 2.1, and a full list of the project dates is in Table 2.2a; other dated buildings in the project counties are listed in Table 2.2c. They include all the dated cruck, box-frame, base-cruck and aisled houses within the study area, that were not part of the project itself, and they are included on the relevant maps.

Primary building phases were dated for 83 of the 117 buildings surveyed (the great majority cruck-built), the rate of success ranging from almost 86% in Oxfordshire, to a disappointing 67% in Buckinghamshire, despite having already rejected significant numbers of houses there as unlikely to give dates.[5] In 13 houses, second or third construction phases and in 12 houses, minor work or repairs were also dated (included in Table 2.2, but not in the statistics in Table 2.1); these include three chimneys with inscribed dates.

The first criterion for identifying the buildings surveyed as medieval peasant houses, their dating, has been emphatically satisfied. Primary construction dates start in 1205 for an aisled hall, 1265–88 (range) for a cruck, and run through to the 1550s (with a handful of later dates). For the cruck houses, our ability to locate them within this 350 year period allows us to identify trends in features that would otherwise appear as arbitrarily chosen alternatives.

We can use this information to suggest typological dates for those houses which failed to date, by identifying similar structural features. Virtually all these undated buildings appear to be of the later fifteenth to sixteenth centuries, indicating an above-average dating failure rate for this period. This may arise from the greater use of fast-grown timber or of elm rather than oak (even though most buildings that used elm extensively were rejected prior to surveying and attempted dating).

Distribution of dated houses

Table 2.3 and Figures 2.2–2.4 show the distribution of the dated buildings over the project counties. In examining the correlation between geographical location and date, striking differences are immediately obvious, both for cruck houses and for buildings of other types.[6]

Cruck Houses: From both the mapping of crucks and the tabulation, the contrast between Oxfordshire at one extreme and Buckinghamshire at the other is very marked. Oxfordshire has the only crucks dating from before 1350, and no less than eleven built by 1400, compared to only five in Warwickshire and one in Leicestershire (all of the 1380s–90s), while in Buckinghamshire the earliest dated cruck houses are of the 1430s–40s. At the other end of the timescale, the latest identified cruck houses in Warwickshire are of *1496–1515* and 1508/9 (apart from one anomalous house of *1655–87*), while in the other three counties, crucks continued in use until almost 1600.

Although it is easy to identify these distinctions, to understand and perhaps explain them is only possible

Table 2.2. Summary of buildings and dates.

(a) Surveyed buildings

The first date always relates to the primary phase of the building; if only a second date is given, the primary phase is undated. Dates in italics indicate felling date ranges refined using OxCal (Miles, 2006); for the unrefined estimates, see the individual reports. Dates in the form *cal AD 1301–28* are calibrated radiocarbon dates (95.4% probability ranges). For the date conventions, see p. 2. Note that most previously published felling date ranges have been amended.

Drw identifies the 1:100 scale cross-section drawing(s) for the building (A–ZZ, pp. 52–78); *rep*, see Report.

For a listing in county order including the grid references, see Appendix 2, Table A2.1a

Code	Cou	Drw	Address	Date 1	Type 1	Date 2	Type 2
ALC-A	WA	E	Alcester, 19 Henley Street	*1398–1407*	Cruck		
ANS-A	LE	I	Anstey, Green Farm, Bradgate Road	1449/50	Cruck		
ASH-A	WA	J W	Ashow, Trinity Cottage	*1464–75*	Cruck & box-frame	1385+	Reused timber
AST-A	OX	V	Aston Tirrold, The Cottage, Aston Street*	1282/6	Box-framed chamber block	1517/19	Hall; chamber block re-roofing
BAT-A	NT	Y	Bathley, The Hollies	1294/6	Base cruck		
BIF-A	OX	I	Shiplake, Barn Grounds, Binfield Heath	1453–5	Crucks reused		
BIL-A	LE	R	Billesdon, The Gables, 6 Church Street		Cruck		
BIN-A	WA	K	Binton, Kineton Cottage	1474/5	Cruck	1473/4	Cruck
BIT-A	WA	D X	Bishops Tachbrook, The Leopard	1413/14	Cruck		
BOT-A	BU	M	Botolph Claydon, Rosamond Cottage*	1507–9	Cruck	1366–98	Windbrace
BRN-H	RU	Z	Braunston, Quaintree House	*1306–9*	Base cruck		
CAD-A	LE	K	Cadeby, Church Cottage	1472/3	Cruck		
CAS-A	LE	N	Castle Donington, 1 Apiary Gate	*1512–35*	Cruck		
CAS-B	LE	O	Castle Donington, 31 Bondgate	1553/4	Cruck		
CLI-B	NT	ZZ	Clifton, TIL House, 56 Village Road	1319/20	Base cruck	1466	Box-framed wing
COS-A	LE	R	Cosby, 9 The Nook		Cruck		
COS-B	LE	P	Cosby, Coates Barn, Main Street	*1566–77*	Cruck	1734–61	Extension
COU-A	WM	U	Coundon, Alveston Cottage		Cruck		
CUB-A	WA	Z	Cubbington, Old Manor House	*1313–41*	Base cruck		
DID-A	OX	N S	Didcot, 26 Manor Road		Cruck	*1517–28*	Cruck wing
DID-B	OX	O	East Hagbourne, Kingsholm	*1549–60*	Cruck		
DIS-A	LE	R	Diseworth, Plough Inn, 33 Hall Gate		Cruck		
EAH-A	OX	O	East Hendred, Old Forge, Church Street	1553/6	Cruck		
EAH-B	OX	T	East Hendred, Inglenook/Penny Green, Catte Street		Cruck		
EAH-C	OX	E W	East Hendred, Godfrey's Farm, 2 St Marys Road	1418/20	Cruck & box-frame		
ERD-A	WM	D W	Erdington, Lad in the Lane, Bromford Lane	1400	Cruck	1461	Box-framed wing
FOS-A	GL	L	Frampton-on-Severn, Old House (Advowson Farm)	1496/7	Cruck		
FOS-B	GL	R	Frampton-on-Severn, Wildgoose Cottage		Cruck		
FRI-A	OX	O	Fringford, Fringford Mill	*1550–65*	Cruck		
HAL-A	LE	K	Hallaton, 29 High Street	*1465–83*	Cruck		

Code	Cou	Drw	Address	Date 1	Type 1	Date 2	Type 2
HAL-B	LE	S	Hallaton, 34, 36 Churchgate		Cruck		
HAR-A	OX	T	Harwell, Dell Cottage, Church Lane		Cruck	1517–49	Inserted beam
HAR-B	OX	E	Harwell, Church Farm, Church Lane	1420/1	Cruck	1513–40	Repair?
HAR-C	OX	D V	Harwell, Abbey Timbers, Broadway Hill	1399/1400	Cruck & box-framed wing		
HAR-D	OX	B	Harwell, Pomander House, Townsend	*cal AD 1305–57*	Cruck		
HAR-E	OX	A	Harwell, Tibberton Cottage, Wellshead Lane	*1294–1324*	Cruck		
HAR-F	OX	M	Harwell, Holywell Cottage, Wellshead Lane	1504/5	Cruck		
HBY-C	LE	C	Harby, Home Farm	1380	Cruck	1657	Ceiling
HIW-A	WA	K	Leek Wootton, Old Thatched Cottage, Hill Wootton	*1470–8*	Cruck		
HOB-A	LE	G	Hoby, Roof Tree Cottage	1440/1	Cruck		
HUG-A	BU	Q	Hughenden, Grange Farm, Widmer End		Cruck		
IVI-A	BU	Y	Ivinghoe, Pendyce House, 12–14 Station Road	*1250–77*	Aisled hall	*1288–1323*	Base cruck
LEW-A	WA	T	Leek Wootton, Old Forge Cottage		Cruck		
LNG-M	WA	ZZ	Long Marston, Hopkins, Wyre Lane	1339/40	Base cruck		
LON-A	BU	M	Long Crendon, Abel's Cottage, 43 High Street	*1506–36*	Cruck		
LON-B	BU	Q	Long Crendon, Woodpeckers, 25 High Street		Cruck		
LON-C	BU	J	Long Crendon, Church Green Cottage, 102–104 High Street	*1466–97*	Cruck		
LON-D	BU	L	Long Crendon, 96-98 High Street (96)	*1494–1506*	Cruck	1731	Cupboard
LON-E	BU	H	Long Crendon, Cordwainers, 2 Bicester Road	1447	Cruck		
LON-F	BU	O	Long Crendon, Dragon Fm, 121 Bicester Road	*1551–9*	Cruck		
LON-G	BU	Y	Long Crendon, Sycamore Farm, 9 Bicester Road	1205	Aisled hall	*cal AD 1301–28*	Crown post
LON-H	BU	G	Long Crendon, Old Bakehouse, 61 Bicester Road	*1441–51*	Cruck		
LON I	BU	Q X	Long Crendon, Warwick Farm, 31 Bicester Road		Cruck		
LON-J	BU	Q	Long Crendon, Wapping, 66 High Street		Cruck		
LON-K	BU	F	Long Crendon, 96–98 High Street (98)	*1430–58*	Cruck		
LON-L	BU	Q	Long Crendon, 82 High Street		Cruck		
LOW-A	OX	B T	Long Wittenham, Terret Close, High Street	*1352–62*	Cruck		
LOW-B	OX	T	Long Wittenham, Cruck Cottage (Cruckfield)		Cruck		
LOW-C	OX	B	Long Wittenham, 33 High Street	*1323–49*	Cruck		
LOX-A	WA	U	Loxley, Loxley Farm		Cruck		
LWH-A	LE	P	Long Whatton, 4 Main Street (The Boot)	*1558–62*	Cruck		

Code	Cou	Drw	Address	Date 1	Type 1	Date 2	Type 2
MDM-A	OX	A V	Mapledurham, Mill Farm	1335	Cruck & box-frame		
MDM-B	OX	J	Mapledurham, Pithouse, Trench Green	1454/5	Cruck		
MDM-C	OX	J	Mapledurham, Three Chimneys, Jackson's Lane	1458	Cruck		
MOU-A	OX	P	Moulsford, Pye Corner	1559	Cruck		
NEB-A	WA	U	Newton-and-Biggin, Stag & Pheasant		Cruck		
NEW-A	LE	S	Newtown Linford, Vine Cottage, 9 Main Street		Cruck		
NEW-B	LE	F	Newtown Linford, Rose Cottage, 11–13 Main Street	1437/8	Cruck		
NOS-C	NT	I	Normanton-on-Soar, Old Post Office*	*1447–54*	Cruck	*1475–92*	Added box-framed bay
NWH-A	WA	rep	Nether Whitacre, Church End Farm	*cal AD 1423–46*	Crucks reused		
NWL-A	BU	N	Newton Longville, Jasmine Cottage, 52 Westbrook End	*1536–8*	Cruck		
NWL-B	BU	I	Newton Longville, Ivy Lodge, 46 Westbrook End	1454/5	Cruck		
NWL-C	BU	Q	Newton Longville, Paradise Cottage, Paradise Lane		Cruck		
NWL-D	BU	M	Newton Longville, Beverley Cottage, 34 Westbrook End	1492	Cruck		
OXH-A	WA	I	Oxhill, Old Post Office	*1450–6*	Cruck		
POL-A	WA	M	Polesworth, 64 High Street	1508/9	Cruck		
RAD-A	OX	N	Radley, Thatched Cott, 46–8 Lower Radley	1522/3	Cruck		
RAD-B	OX	A N	Radley, Bakers Close, 104 Lower Radley	1513/14	Cruck	1256–88	Cruck
ROT-A	LE	S	Rothley, Old House, 89 Town Green Street		Cruck		
ROT-B	LE	G	Rothley, April Cottage, 12 Church Street	1444–8	Cruck		
ROT-C	LE	P	Rothley, 13 Fowke Street	*1290–1319*	Box-frame	*1576–1610*	Cruck
ROT-D	LE	L	Rothley, 91 Town Green Street	*1492–9*	Cruck		
ROW-A	WA	C	Rowington, Holywell Farm	*1383–1408*	Cruck		
SKI-A	BU	H X	Hambledon, Old Crown House & Isabel Cottage, Skirmett	*1444–74*	Cruck	1618	Inserted fireplace
SOF-A	WA	E	Stretton-on-Fosse, Manor Farm	1415+	Cruck	1589i	Inserted fireplace
SOU-A	WA	E	Southam, 26 Warwick Road	1418/19	Cruck & box-framed wing		
STC-A	BU	H	Steeple Claydon, Willow Vale Farm, West End	1448	Cruck		
STC-B	BU	F	Steeple Claydon, Rhenold's Close, 28 North End	*1431–6*	Cruck		
STC-C	BU	G	Steeple Claydon, Well Cottage, 40–44 Queen Catherine Road	1444/5	Cruck		
STE-A	OX	T	Steventon, Folly Ho, 53 The Causeway		Cruck	*1555–70*	Box-framed wing
STE-B	OX	B V X	Steventon, Tudor House, 67 The Causeway*	1355/6	Cruck	1299	Box-framed wing
STE-C	OX	C	Steventon, 83 The Causeway	1365/6	Cruck	*1317–46*	Reused cruck

Code	Cou	Drw	Address	Date 1	Type 1	Date 2	Type 2
STE-D	OX	W	Steventon, 71 The Causeway	1463/7	Box frame	Framed	
STE-E	OX	B V	Steventon, 39 The Causeway*	*1350/1*	Cruck	1356/65	Box-framed wing
STK-A	BU	ZZ	Stokenchurch, Kensham Farm		Base cruck		
STO-A	WA	*rep*	Stoneleigh, 10 Vicarage Road		Crucks reused		
STO-B	WA	H	Stoneleigh, Skep Cottage, 3 Birmingham Road	*1444–57*	Cruck		
STO-C	WA	U	Stoneleigh, High Beams, 8–9 Vicarage Road		Cruck		
STO-D	WA	L	Stoneleigh, 23–5 Birmingham Road	*1496–1515*	Cruck		
STO-E	WA	W	Stoneleigh, Motslow Cottages	1537	Box frame		
STO-F	WA	K	Stoneleigh, Phoenix Cott, 1 Birmingham Road	1480–2	Cruck		
STO-G	WA	W	Stoneleigh, Pypes Mill	1490doc	Box frame		
STR-A	WA	J	Stratford-upon-Avon, Anne Hathaway's Cottage, Shottery	1462/3	Cruck	1697i	Chimney
STW-A	BU	R	Stewkley, 28 High Street North		Cruck		
SUC-A	OX	A V	Sutton Courtenay, Manor Cottage	1317/18	Cruck		
SUF-A	WA	L	Stretton-under-Fosse, Old Forge	*1480–92*	Cruck		
SUT-A	WM	G	Sutton Coldfield, Smithy, 78 Birmingham Road	1442–4	Cruck		
SYS-A	LE	S	Syston, 72 High Street		Cruck		
WAL-A	WA	C	Haselor, Cruck Cottage, Walcote	1384/5	Cruck		
WEE-A	BU	G	Weedon, Eastgate House, East End	1446–50	Cruck		
WEL-A	WA	F	Wellesbourne, 2 School Road	1430	Cruck		
WEN-A	BU	R	Wendover, 6–8 Pound Street		Cruck		
WOA-A	WA	P	Weston-on-Avon, Low Thatch	*cal AD 1655–87*	Cruck		
WOE-A	LE	F	Woodhouse, Golden Cottage, 280 Forest Road	1426–30	Cruck & box-framed wing		
WOE-B	LE	J	Woodhouse, Old Post Office, 244 Forest Road	1455/6	Cruck		
WOR-A	WA	D	Water Orton, The Chestnuts, Church Lane*	1398/9	Cruck	*cal AD 1415–53*	Box-framed wing
WOS-A	WM	U	Walsgrave-on-Sowe, Cruck House, 14–16 Hinckley Road		Cruck		

* Third dates: AST-A, 1508, replaced sill. BOT-A: 1643i, chimney. NOS-C: 1546–1576, beam of inserted ceiling. STE-B: 1448/9, reconstruction of crosswing. STE-E: 1518/19, kitchen range. WOR-A: 1579/80, replacement of lower end.

(b) Documentary histories (italic codes).

Code	Cou	Address
LON-M	BU	Long Crendon, Lower End House, 72 Bicester Road,
LON-N	BU	Long Crendon, Harfield Cottage, 7 Bicester Road
LON-O	BU	Long Crendon, Manor House, Frogmore Lane [*Drawing Y*]
LON-P	BU	Long Crendon, 'Manor Garage' (at Manor House)
LON-Q	BU	Long Crendon, 2 The Square
LON-R	BU	Long Crendon, 27–29 High Street
LON-S	BU	Long Crendon, Eight Bells, 51 High Street
LON-T	BU	Long Crendon, 58–60 High Street
LON-U	BU	Long Crendon, Northend Farm
STE-F	OX	Steventon, Priory Cottages, 127 The Causeway & The Priory, 123–5 The Causeway

Code	Cou	Address
STE-G	OX	Steventon, 99 The Causeway [Botleys]
STE-H	OX	Steventon, 87 The Causeway
STE-I	OX	Steventon, 79 & 81 The Causeway
STE-J	OX	Steventon, 35–7 The Causeway
STE-K	OX	Steventon, 12 Milton Lane
STE-L	OX	Steventon, Home Fm, 14–16 Milton Lane
STE-M	OX	Steventon, Green Fm (I), 1 Milton Lane
STE-N	OX	Steventon, Old Farm, 5 Kennel Lane
STO-H	WA	Stoneleigh, 2 Church Lane
STO-I	WA	Stoneleigh, Bridge Cottage
STO-J	WA	Stoneleigh, Croom Cottage, Birmingham Road

(c) Non-project buildings (principally dated), with codes assigned for reference purposes.
For a listing in county order with grid references and sources, see Appendix 2, Table A2.1b.

Code	Cou	Location and reference	Date	Type
X-BEA	BU	New Beaconsfield, Baylins Farm	1453–77	Box-framed hall and wing
X-BUR	WA	Burmington, Burmington Manor	1159+	Aisled hall
X-CHA	OX	Chalgrove, Chalgrove Manor,	1447–68 1488	Box-framed wing Box-framed hall
X-CLI	WA	Clifford Chambers, Old Rectory	1433/4	Post-and-rafter hall; two box-framed wings
X-CR1	OX	Crowmarsh Gifford, Queens Head	1341	Base cruck
X-CR2	OX	Crowmarsh Gifford, 17–19 The Street	1435/8	Box-framed, six in-line bays
X-EAH	OX	East Hendred, Wisteria House & The Stores	1472/3	Box-framed hall with two wings
X-FRI	LE	Frisby-on-the-Wreake, 7 Main Street	1417	Box-framed, four in-line bays
X-HA1	OX	Harwell, Lime Tree House, High Street [*Drawing Y*]	1243–7 1294–1306	Aisled hall base cruck
X-HA2	OX	Harwell, Middle Farm, south range hall and north range	1323 1367–71	Box-framed wing Base cruck
X-HAM	BU	Hambledon, Burrow Farm, chamber block	1494/5	Box-framed wing (hall replaced)
X-HIA	WA	Henley-in-Arden, Heritage Centre, 150 High St	1345 1451	Box-framed wing Box-framed hall
X-KNO	WM	Knowle, Cuttle Pool Farm, Cuttle Pool Lane	1479	Box-framed hall and in-line floored chamber
X-LOU	LE	Loughborough, Warners Lane/Churchgate	1343–53	Base cruck derivative
X-MAX	WA	Maxstoke, Castle	1345doc	Base cruck
X-MD4	OX	Mapledurham, Whittles Farm, cross wing hall	1412/13 1471/2	Box-framed wing Cruck hall
X-MED	LE	Medbourne, Manor House (original roof) (reconstructed)	1238 1287	Aisled hall Short-principal roof
X-MEL	LE	Melton Mowbray, 5 King Street	1330	Base cruck
X-MIL	OX	Milton, 42–42A High Street [*Drawing ZZ*]	undated	Base-cruck hall and box-framed wing
X-NEV	LE	Nevill Holt, Nevill Holt Hall, great hall	1275–99	Base cruck
X-OAK	RU	Oakham, Flores House, hall range cross wing	1378 1407–10	Stone-walled base cruck Box-framed over stone ground floor
X-QUE	LE	Queniborough, 86-8 Main Street	1427/8	Integral cruck hall and box-framed wing
X-SAW	WA	Sawbridge, Hall House	1449	Post-and-rafter hall; box-framed wing
X-STM	BU	Stoke Mandeville, Old Moat Farmhouse, Marsh Lane	1498/9	Box-framed wing (hall replaced)
X-TAN	WA	Tanworth-in-Arden, Old Bell Cottages	1449	Box-framed (Wealden house)
X-TEM	WA	Temple Balsall, Old Hall	1176–1221	Aisled hall

Code	Cou	Location and reference	Date	Type
X-UFT	WA	Ufton, 1–2 Ufton Fields	1407	Cruck house
X-WAN	OX	Wantage, 57 Grove Street	1449	Cruck house
X-WHA	OX	West Hagbourne, York Farm	1284/5	Base cruck hall and box-framed wing
X-WIL	WA	Wilmcote, Glebe Farm	1514	Box-framed hall and wing

Table 2.3. Ranges and numbers of dates.

(a) Cruck houses. The four dated cruck houses in the supplementary table (X-MDM4; X-QUE; X-UFT; X-WAN) are included, but for the undated houses only those surveyed are counted.

Dates	Buckinghamshire	Leicestershire	Oxfordshire	Warwickshire & West Midlands	Gloucestershire	Nottinghamshire
Earliest	1431–77; 1444/5	1380	1256-88	1384/5	1496/7	1447–54
Latest	1551–74	1576–1601	1554–76; 1559	1508–9; cal AD 1655–87		
13th century	-	-	2	-	-	-
14th century	-	1	9	5	-	-
15th century	12	10	7	16	1	1
16th century	4	5	8	1	-	-
17th century	-	-	-	1	-	-
Undated	8	7	6	7	1	-

(b) Dated box-framed cross-wings and chamber blocks, including those in the supplementary table but excluding wings of box-framed hall ranges (in (c)).

Dates	Buckinghamshire	Leicestershire & Rutland	Oxfordshire	Warwickshire & West Midlands	Nottinghamshire
13th century		1	3		
14th century			2		
15th century	2	3	1	3	1
16th century			1		

(c) Box-framed (including post-and-rafter) hall ranges. Dated houses only, including those in the supplementary table.

Dates	Buckinghamshire	Leicestershire & Rutland	Oxfordshire	Warwickshire & West Midlands	Nottinghamshire
15th century	1	1	3	6	1
16th century				2	

(d) Aisled halls.

As well as the surveyed houses and those listed in Table 2.2 (c), the undated Buckinghamshire aisled halls at Denham Court, The Savoy, Denham, and The Manor, Long Crendon (*LON-O*) are included.

Dates	Buckinghamshire	Leicestershire & Rutland	Oxfordshire	Warwickshire
12–13th century	2		1	2
Undated	3			

(e) Base-cruck houses.

All base cruck houses in the survey counties are included.

Dates	Buckinghamshire	Leicestershire & Rutland	Oxfordshire	Warwickshire	Nottinghamshire
13th century	1	1	1		1
14th century		3	4	2	1
Undated	8	3	2	6	

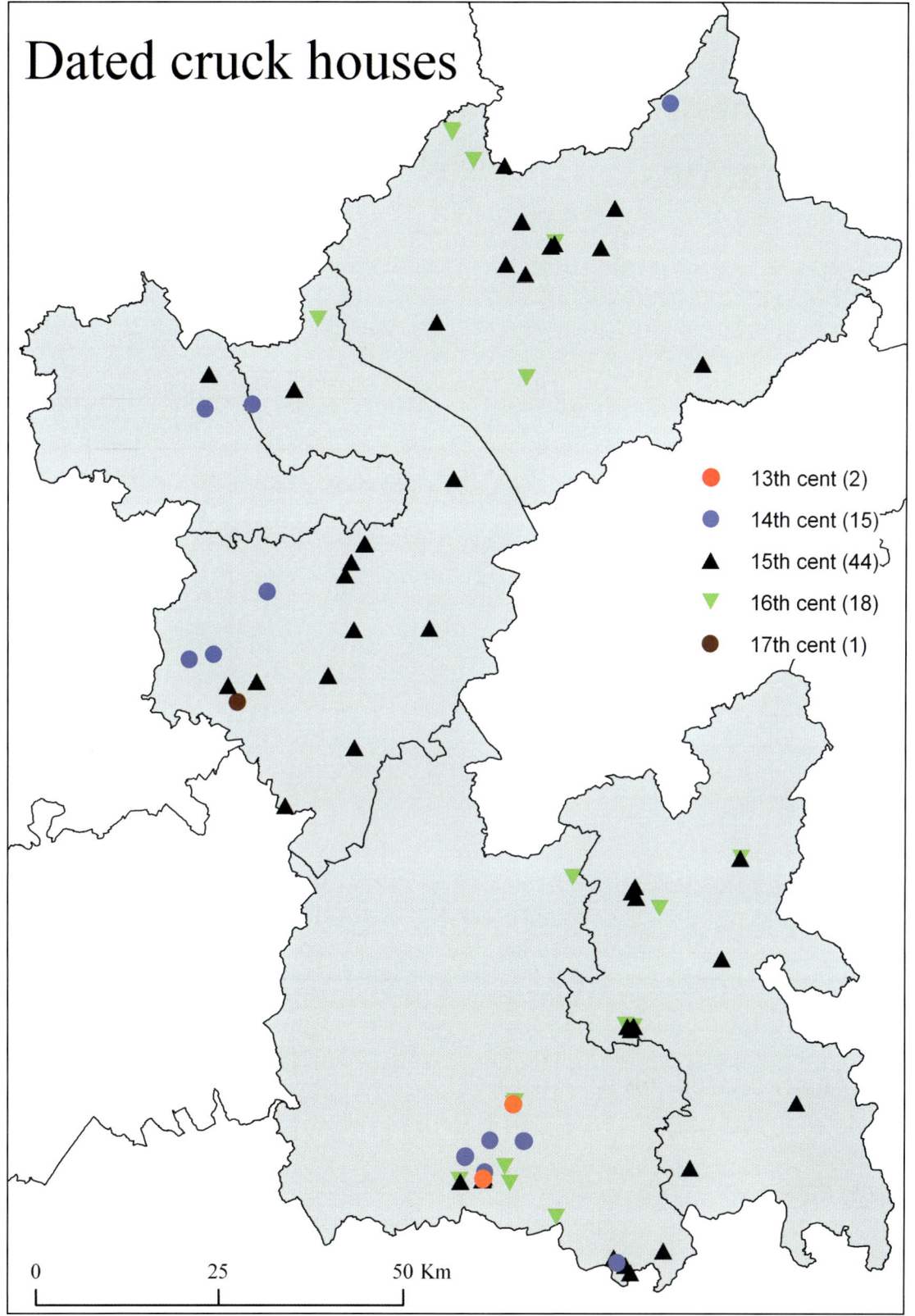

Fig. 2.2. Dated cruck houses in the project counties.

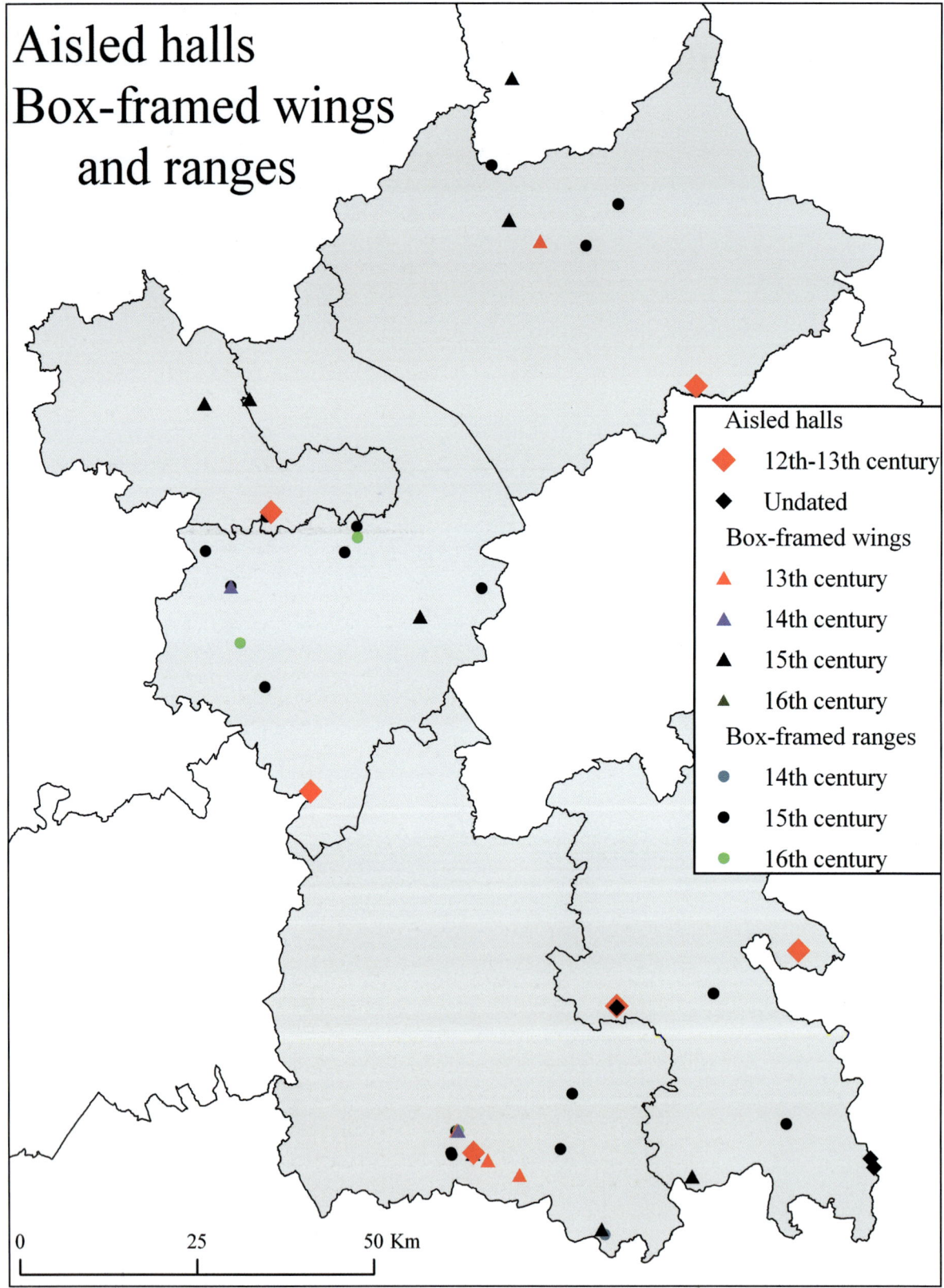

Aisled halls
Box-framed wings
and ranges

Aisled halls
◆ 12th-13th century
◆ Undated
Box-framed wings
▲ 13th century
▲ 14th century
▲ 15th century
▲ 16th century
Box-framed ranges
● 14th century
● 15th century
● 16th century

0   25   50 Km

Fig. 2.3. Dated and undated aisled halls and dated box-framed free-standing ranges and attached wings in the project counties.

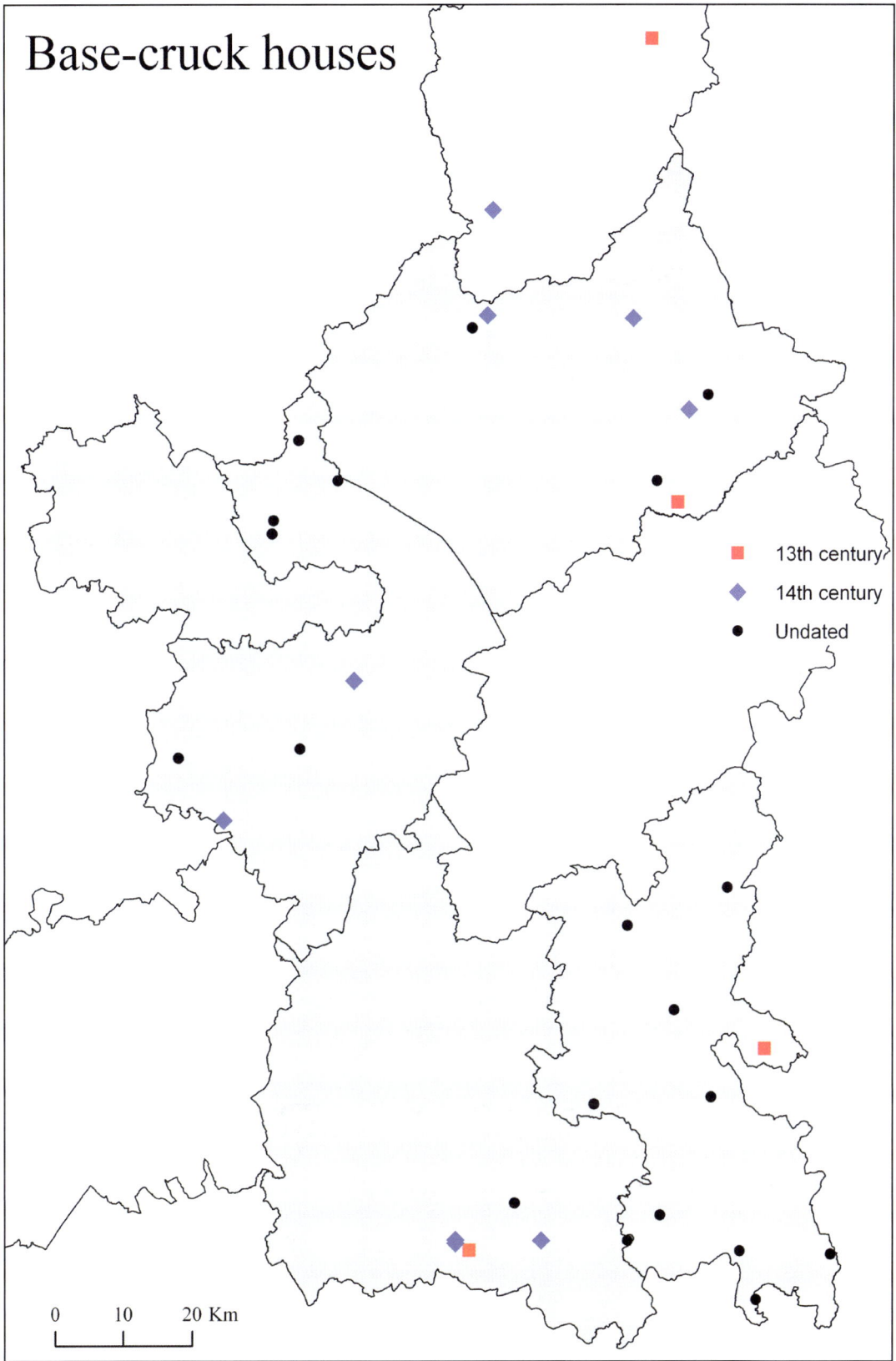

Fig. 2.4. Dated and undated base-cruck houses in the project counties (including Nottinghamshire and Rutland). The map includes all base crucks whether surveyed as part of the project or not.

after exploring the planning, structure and carpentry of the houses, and their documentary background (following chapters).

Box-framed buildings: For box-framed construction (Fig. 2.3 and Table 2.3b–c), our knowledge is more limited than for crucks, since no systematic research on medieval Midlands box-framed buildings has been undertaken. Box-framing appears in the later thirteenth century, for storeyed chamber blocks or crosswings attached to open halls (presumably of cruck form); it is assumed that the fragment at 13 Fowke Street, Rothley, Leicestershire (ROT-C, *1290–1319*) is of this type, although only one side wall survives and the inferred hall has completely disappeared.

The earliest complete box-frame building is the free-standing chamber block at The Cottage, Aston Tirrold, Oxfordshire (AST-A), dated to 1282/6. The attached crosswing at York Farm, West Hagbourne (X-WHA, 1284/5) is of virtually the same date. Apart from the Rothley building, all the thirteenth and all but one of the fourteenth-century box-framed ranges are in Oxfordshire. In Leicestershire and Rutland, early box-framed crosswings are found with cruck halls at Woodhouse (WOE-A, 1426–30) and Queniborough (X-QUE, 1427/8) and with the base-cruck hall at Braunston (BRN-H, *1306–9*).

The earliest box-framed truss in a mostly cruck-built house is at Mill Farm, Mapledurham (MDM-A), of 1335, and a couple of later houses use the same unusual combination, Godfrey's Farm, East Hendred (EAH-C) in 1418/20 and Trinity Cottage, Ashow (ASH-A) in *1464–75*.

Fully box-framed single-range houses only appear among the dated buildings in the fifteenth century. Unlike the early crosswings, these buildings are relatively uniformly distributed across the project counties. A house at Frisby-on-the-Wreake, Leicestershire, has been dated to 1417 (X-FRI), and in Oxfordshire the first complete box-framed house (including a hall with an open arch-braced truss) was built in 1435–8 (17–19 The Street, Crowmarsh Gifford, X-CR2). In Warwickshire, the Old Rectory, Clifford Chambers (X-CLI) is of 1433–4. In considering these buildings, the caveat already noted about our lack of knowledge is important, and other early box-frame buildings surely exist in the project counties.

It also seems very likely that box-framing was already fully established by the fourteenth century in the larger towns, Coventry, Leicester and Oxford, which show only minimal indications of a cruck tradition; dated buildings in these towns have not been included on the map. Furthermore, three of the fully box-framed houses dated to before 1450 (7 Main Street, Frisby-on-the-Wreake, Leicestershire (X-FRI, 1417), the Old Rectory, Clifford Chambers (X-CLI, 1443/5) and Red Roofs Farmhouse, Sawbridge, Warwickshire (X-SAW, 1449)) do not appear to be straightforward peasant houses; they are identified respectively as a sub-manor house, a substantial rectory, and the home of an upwardly-mobile gentry family.[7] Another, Old Bell Cottages, Tanworth-in-Arden (X-TAN, 1449), is of Wealden form and should probably regarded as a an urban stray, since, outside south-east England, this house-type is overwhelmingly found in towns.[8]

Base Crucks: Base crucks have been of particular interest in tree-ring dating studies, because they include many of the earliest houses yet identified. Almost 50 examples from England and Wales have so far been tree-ring dated, mostly to the earlier and mid-fourteenth century, with rather fewer of the later thirteenth century and after 1350.[9] Both the seven base-cruck houses that were surveyed (all but one dated), and the other examples in the project counties are mapped on Fig 2.4 (see Table 2.3d–e). Although some are substantial manor houses, several of those studied can be shown to have been the homes of superior peasants (Chapter 6.5). They are evenly distributed across the survey region, apart from the central stone belt, where it appears that short principal trusses were used rather than base crucks.[10]

Their dating is relatively uniform, all falling between the later thirteenth and mid-fourteenth centuries, and from their typology, the undated houses are broadly of the same period. The earliest and latest dated examples are both from Oxfordshire, of 1285 and 1369 respectively.[11]. This pattern contrasts with the results from other parts of England and Wales, where base crucks continued in use into the later fifteenth century, and sometimes developed as a preferred type for yeoman houses.[12]

Aisled halls. Aisled halls (Fig. 2.3) are reasonably well recorded nationally, with a published gazetteer listing 170 buildings.[13] They are rare within the Midlands compared to East Anglia or Yorkshire, but the few examples include the earliest timber-framed halls found in the project counties, with all the known dates falling in the twelfth or thirteenth centuries. Their distribution is widespread, but they can only be seen as a minor component of the surviving buildings in the region.

The Planning and Organisation of the Surveyed Houses

INTRODUCTION

The structural choices made in a medieval house are intimately related to its plan form. Thus, a two-bay hall requires an open central truss, while the provision of a floored chamber imposes constraints on the height (and therefore the width) of the building. The direct evidence for plan and layout is discussed here followed, in the next chapter, by an examination of the structural variations. More specific aspects of carpentry and wood technology are considered in chapter 5.

PLAN AND FUNCTION

Identifying patterns in layout and room use in these medieval houses is often difficult, because alteration and replacement has a greater effect on the plan than on the shape of the individual trusses. The relatively few houses that have survived essentially unaltered are particularly valuable, but for a number of others either the full plan can be extrapolated, or information about one or two rooms can be obtained. Table 3.1 summarises the plan evidence grouped by county. for cruck and box-framed houses. Houses comprising a single range are examined first (both cruck and box-framed), followed by those with crosswings, and then by base-cruck and aisled buildings.

Three of the houses have good evidence that an additional lean-to bay formed part of the original structure (FOS-B, LON-A and MDM-A); in each, the purlins stop at the end cruck, but this truss is unweathered or shows other evidence that it did not originally form the end of the house.[1] Although none of these lean-tos survive, similar structures have been recorded in Hampshire and Bedfordshire.[2] Such lean-to sections and the likelihood of detached service buildings having once existed need to be borne in mind in considering the plans.

House and hall size: Single-range houses

Houses with all their rooms in a single range are the most numerous. Figure 3.1 presents block diagrams for all those dating from before 1438, and Figures 3.2–3 give

Table 3.1. Numbers of hall and house bays in complete cruck and box-framed houses. Source: Entries in Table A2.3, where the size is known or inferred (Y or Y? in the table). '+1', '+2' identify houses with passage bays or probable lean-tos (not included in the numbers of bays).

House bays	One-bay halls				One-bay totals	Two-bay halls				Two-bay halls with wings			Two-bay totals
	2	*3*	*4*	*5*		*2*	*3*	*4*	*5*	*3W*	*4W*	*5W*	
Buckinghamshire	2+2	2+1			7	1	6	3					10
Gloucestershire						0+1			1				2
Leicestershire	2	9			11		1	1			0+1		3
Nottinghamshire		1			1								
Oxfordshire	1	1	1	1	4		7+2	3		1*	0+1*	2+1	17
Warwickshire & West Midlands	4	6	2		12		1	5				3	9
Totals	11	20	3	1	35	2	17	12	1	1	2	6	41

* DID-A: two-bay hall and one-bay wing, after the addition of bay III. STE-E: one-bay hall with passage and three-bay wing. Overall totals: two-bay houses: 13; three-bay houses: 38; four-bay houses: 17; five-bay houses: 8.

representative examples of similar diagrams for later houses, arranged by size. The most straightforward indicator of the scale of these houses is the number of bays, which can be estimated for 73 cruck and 3 box-frame houses (Table 3.1; tabulated for the individual houses in Appendix 2). Half of them (37) have three bays, while twelve and thirteen respectively have two or four in-line bays. It is noticeable that the earliest houses (Fig. 3.1) are relatively large, the majority with four bays (or three and a lean-to, as at MDM-A). Two-bay houses survive only from the mid-fifteenth century onwards. For five-bay houses in a single range, one firm and one probable example survive (FOS-A, 1496/7 and DID-B, *1549–60*), although the majority of the houses with crosswings are of this size. This dominance by three-bay houses matches the pattern of documentary references to medieval crucks (see Chapter 6, e.g. p. 131).

Slightly more houses have two-bay rather than one-bay halls, but this summary conceals a marked regional variation. Almost all the Oxfordshire houses have two-bay halls, Buckinghamshire has almost equal numbers of each, while in Leicestershire and Warwickshire the two-bay hall is in a minority. Thus, the characteristic three-bay house in the south of the region has a two-bay hall with one bay for a chamber, but the more northerly houses have single bay halls flanked by service and chamber bays. In Warwickshire, the latest of the houses with two-bay halls (all with arch-braced open trusses) dates from 1451. Elsewhere, both plain and arch-braced trusses are found in the centre of two-bay halls and these continued to be built until the very end of the cruck period (NWL-B of 1542 in Buckinghamshire; CAS-A of 1521 in Leicestershire), although the latest arch-braced truss is of 1492 (NWL-A). Even one of the two late houses where the hall was fully floored from the outset (LON-F) still has a two-bay ground floor hall, though with two chambers over.[3]

Upper floors

The identification of originally floored bays is sometimes straightforward, typically through the survival of heavy lodged joists (most often running axially). However, these floors leave little or no trace if removed and it is not always clear if a later floor was inserted into an originally open bay or replaced an earlier floor. Despite this complication, the evidence for flooring is clear and would not be greatly altered if some originally floored bays have not been recognised. Before 1400, none of the main house ranges appear to have been floored, although crosswings were invariably of two storeys.[4] The earliest floored rooms in dated houses are found in the first half of the fifteenth century: EAH-C (1418/20, probable floor replaced); HOB-A (1440/1); ROT-B (1447); SKI-A (*1444–74*); WEL-A (1430).[5] They become more common as the century progressed and all the sixteenth-century houses for which we have satisfactory evidence had original floors in at least one bay. Indeed, two

of the latest houses, CAS-B (1553/4) and LON-F (*1551–9*) have both their bays floored.[6] At this point, the fading cruck tradition impinges on the new lifestyles developing in the later sixteenth century. Apart from these houses, the original floored bays are believed to have been used as chambers with solars over, or sometimes as service rooms with chambers over.

Box-framed houses

Apart from the crosswings and chamber blocks considered next, only five wholly or partly box-framed houses were included in the project (Fig. 3.3), and it is significant that two of the earliest houses each includes a cruck truss, in the centre of the open hall at EAH-C (1418/20) but in a subsidiary room at ASH-A (*1464–75*). One house (STO-G, 1490doc) is of two bays with an open hall and floored chamber, indistinguishable in form from most of the two-bay cruck houses. The others all have four bays, two (EAH-C, STO-E) with the relatively standard layout of a two-bay hall flanked by service and chamber bays, although STO-E is very wide (almost 22 ft), but has very short bays. ASH-A has a fairly standard plan among Warwickshire houses, with chamber/service, hall and kitchen, but has an extra bay beyond the kitchen, which might possibly have been a barn or other agricultural space. Unusually, here, we have evidence that the inner room was divided (used apparently in 1639 for a buttery and dairy).

STE-D (1463/7) (Fig. 3.4) is exceptional in having a two-bay floored chamber, but its location and history indicate that it was not a standard house. It stands touching Tudor House, Steventon (STE-B), with which it was in common ownership from when it was built until 1897, and they formerly had communicating doors on both the ground and first floors. It has an open hall and service bay, as well as the chamber bays, so it most probably had a dual function, depending on the family requirements. It could either have served as an ordinary house, perhaps sub-let, or it could have accommodated an overflow of family members or farm servants from the main house, when this was more convenient.

Houses with chamber blocks or crosswings

Figures 3.4–5 show block plans for all of the dozen houses known or believed to have halls associated with either detached chamber blocks or attached crosswings. Most of the relatively few examples are among the earliest buildings identified in our survey, with half of them constructed partly or completely before the mid-fourteenth century. It is also notable that in only one of these early houses is the hall and wing of the same date (SUC-A, 1317–18). Two halls (HAR-D and HAR-E) are believed to have been associated with vanished chamber blocks, while three chamber blocks predate their surviving medieval halls. Tudor House,

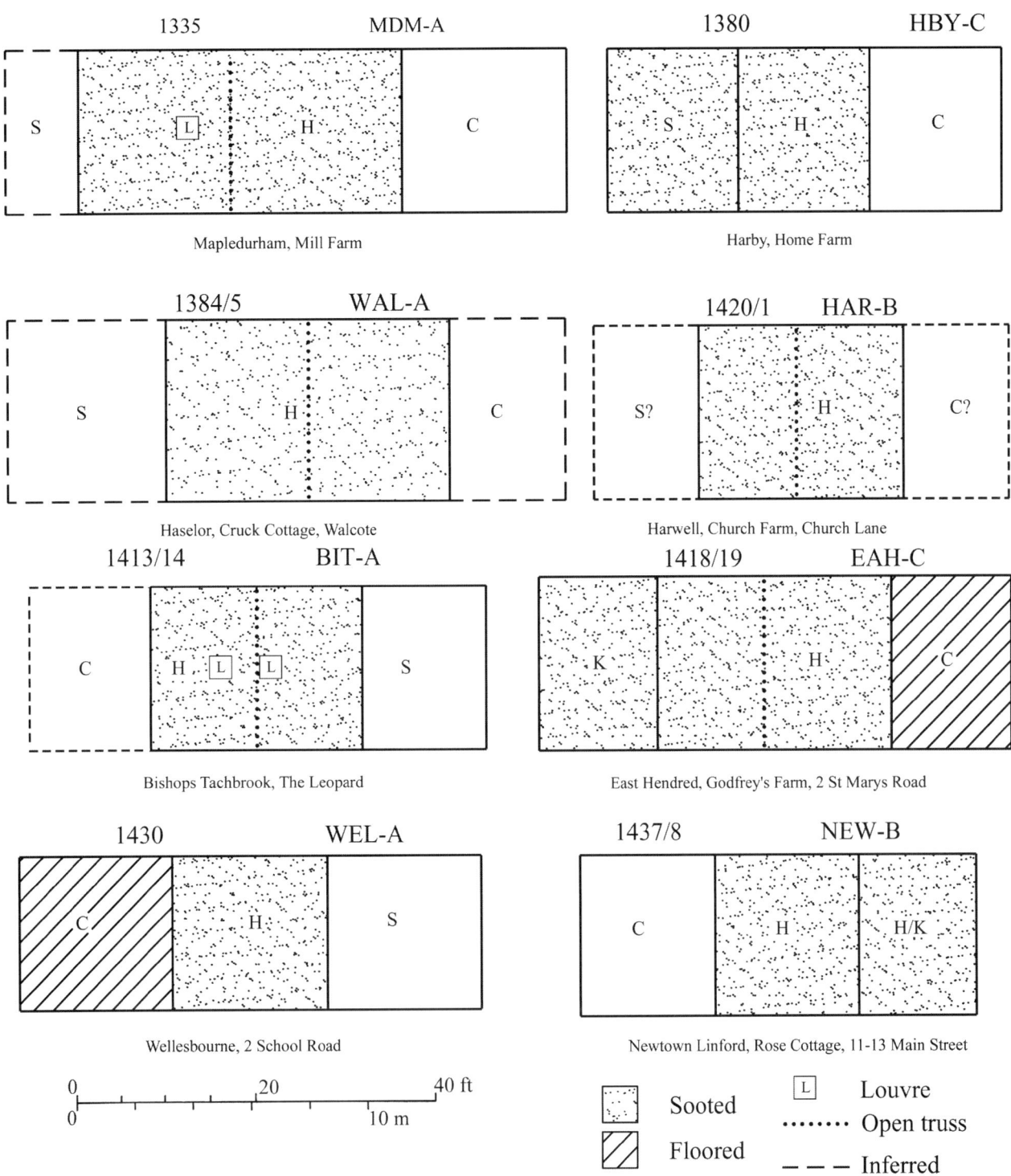

Fig. 3.1. Block plans to scale of early houses with in-line plans:. The drawing includes all houses dating from before 1440 whose plans can be recovered, (see also STC-B, 1431-47, on Fig. 3.2). Room letters: H Hall, C Chamber, S Service, K Kitchen.

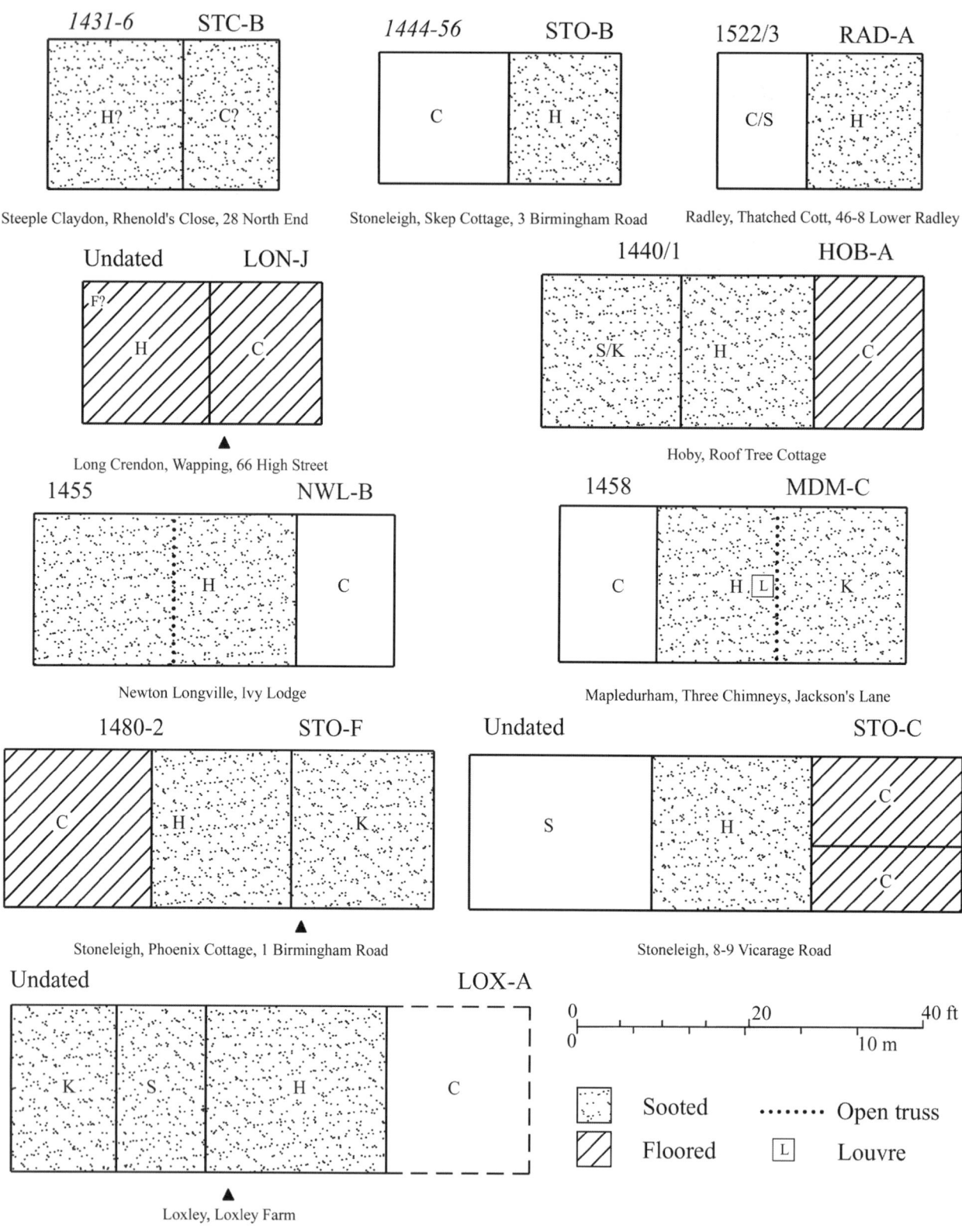

Fig. 3.2. Block plans to scale of selected houses with two- or three-bay in-line plans, 1431 to 1523, arranged by number of bays. Room letters: as Fig. 3.1.

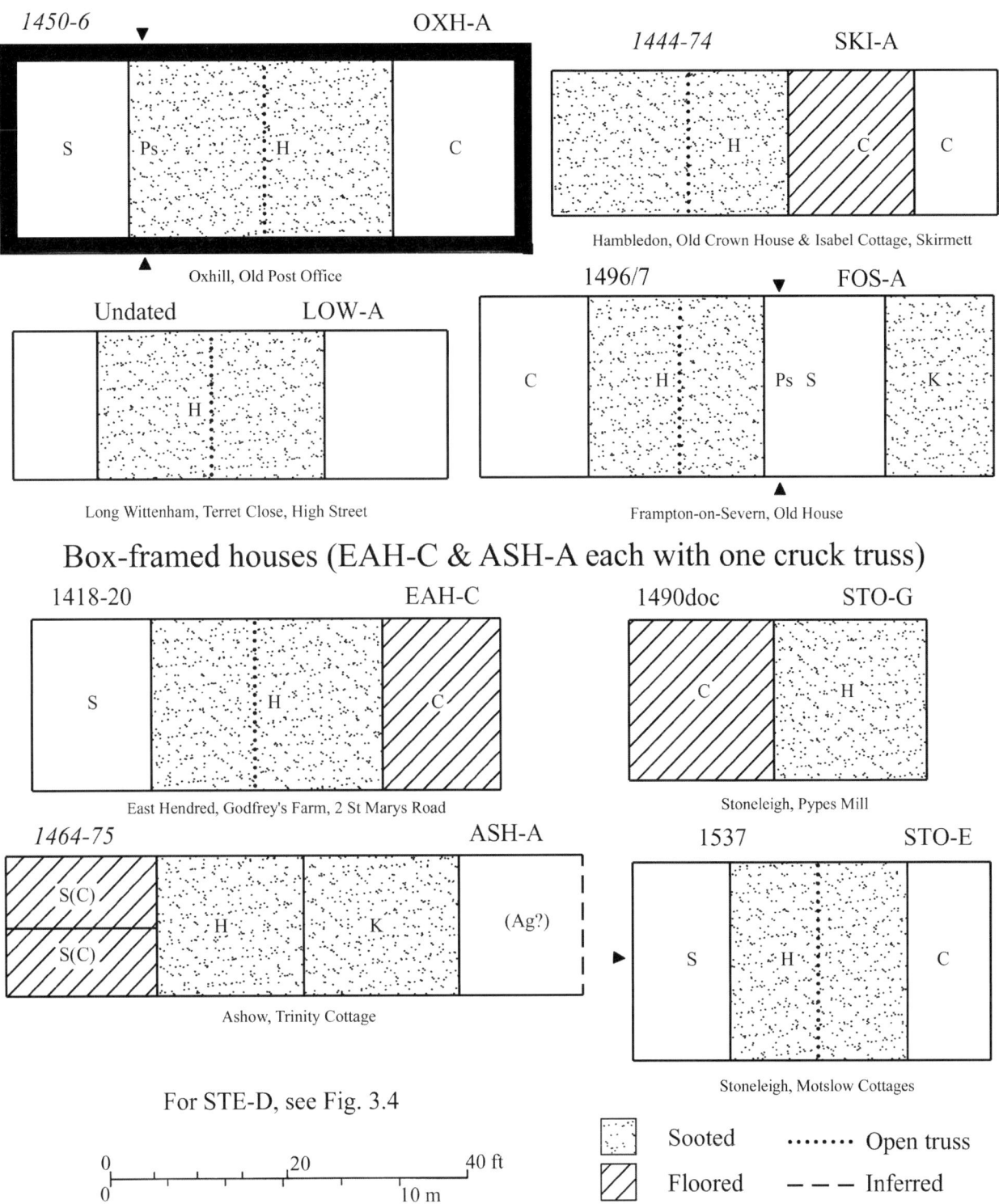

Box-framed houses (EAH-C & ASH-A each with one cruck truss)

For STE-D, see Fig. 3.4

Fig. 3.3. Block plans to scale of selected houses with four- or five-bay in-line plans, 1450 to 1496, and of box-framed houses. Room letters: as Fig. 3.1, with Ps Passage. OXH-A is the only house with stone external walls.

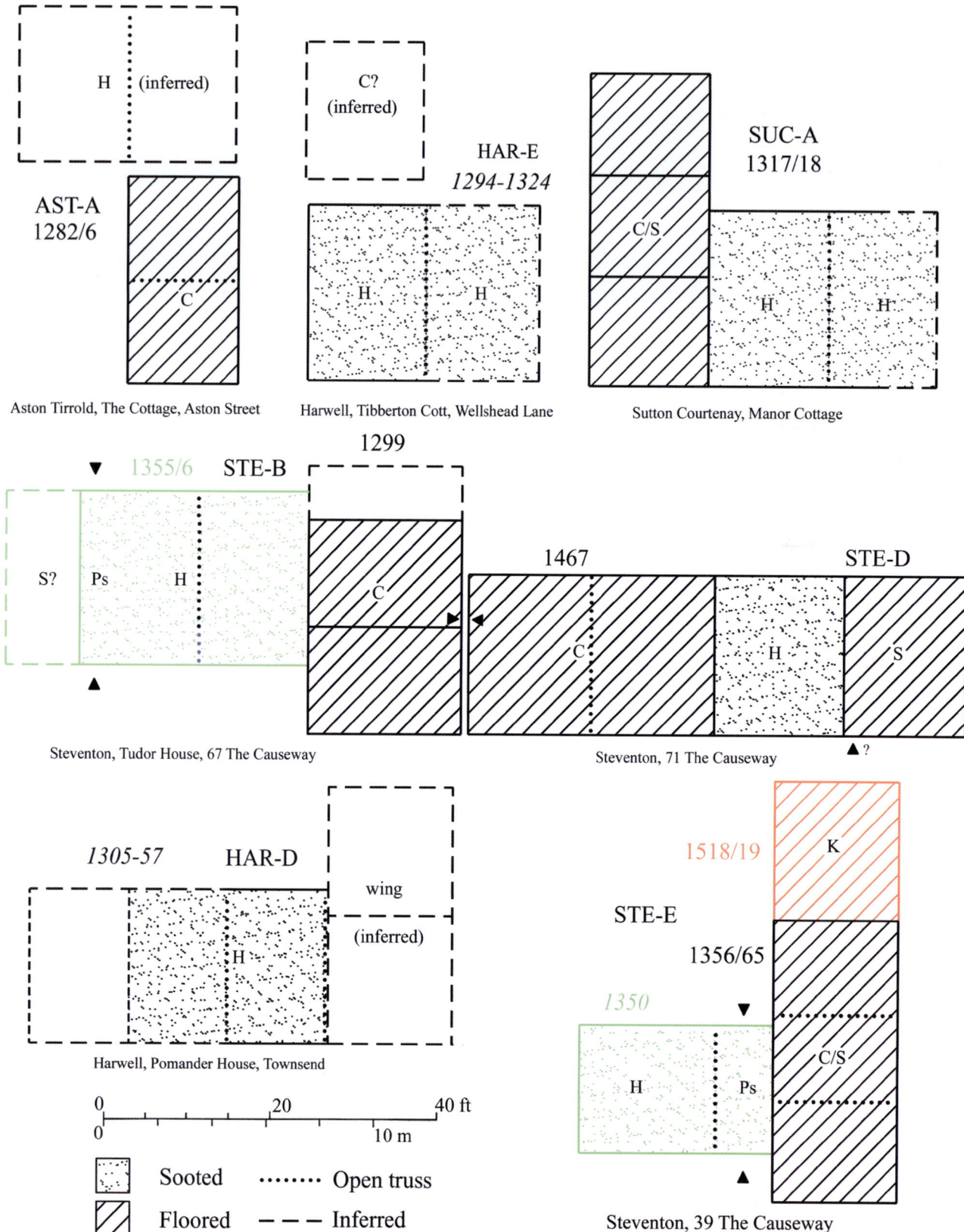

AST-A
1282/6

H (inferred)

C

Aston Tirrold, The Cottage, Aston Street

HAR-E
1294-1324

C?
(inferred)

H   H

Harwell, Tibberton Cott, Wellshead Lane

SUC-A
1317/18

C/S

H   H

Sutton Courtenay, Manor Cottage

1355/6   STE-B

S?   Ps   H

Steventon, Tudor House, 67 The Causeway

1299

C

1467

C

STE-D

H   S

Steventon, 71 The Causeway

1305-57   HAR-D

wing
(inferred)

H

Harwell, Pomander House, Townsend

1518/19   K

STE-E

1356/65

1350   C/S

H   Ps

Steventon, 39 The Causeway

0 ————————— 20 ————————— 40 ft
0 ——— 10 m

· · · Sooted   ········ Open truss
/// Floored   – – – Inferred

Fig. 3.4. Block plans to scale of houses with halls and chamber blocks or crosswings, 1286–1365. Room letters: as Fig. 3.1. The plan of STE-D, associated with STE-B is also included.

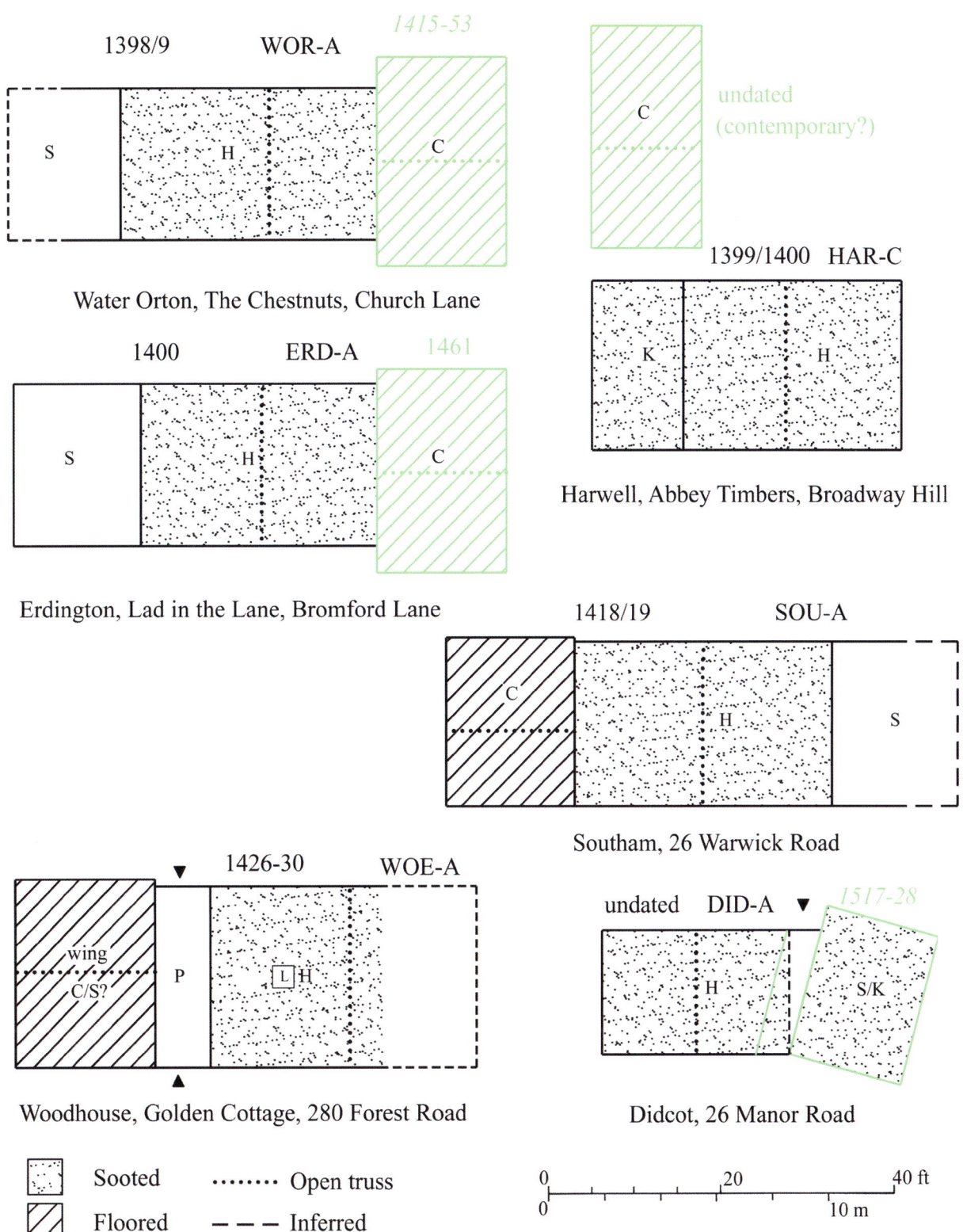

Fig. 3.5. Block plans to scale of houses with crosswings, late fourteenth to sixteenth centuries. Room letters: as Fig. 3.1.

Steventon (STE-B; see p. 222) is particularly notable, with its chamber block dated to 1299, now attached to a splendid hall of 1355/6, but perhaps originally adjacent rather than attached to its hall. Here, as elsewhere, we must conclude that the original hall (possibly even earlier than the surviving chamber block) was found too modest for the aspirations of the house's owners. The earliest box-frame building identified, the chamber block at The Cottage, Aston Tirrold, Oxfordshire (AST-A, 1282–6) was free-standing suggesting, with the other examples, that this plan form preceded the attached layout.[7] It is reminiscent of the plans of houses known only from excavation in which each domestic function occupied a separate building.[8]

This pattern of extension and rebuilding persists after 1400, although the sequence is reversed, with crosswings added to earlier halls. Two substantial cruck halls (WOR-

A and ERD-A) have crosswings built some 30–60 years after the hall. In each, the structure makes it more likely that the new wings replaced another wing, rather than an in-line chamber bay. In any case, they clearly represent an improvement in the quality of the private rooms. Three houses from 1400 onwards have hall and wing ranges of the same date: Abbey Timbers, Harwell (HAR-C, 1399–1400) (probable), 26 Warwick Road, Southam (SOU-A, 1418/19), and Golden Cottage, Woodhouse (WOE-A, 1426–30), and it is noticeable that the wings in the last two houses are hardly longer than the width of the main ranges.[9] Perhaps the suggested earlier wings at WOR-A and ERD-A were also of this type.

The most unusual crosswing is the cruck-built single bay at 26 Manor Road, Didcot (DID-A, 1509–41), for a kitchen or heated service room. The hall is earlier (though

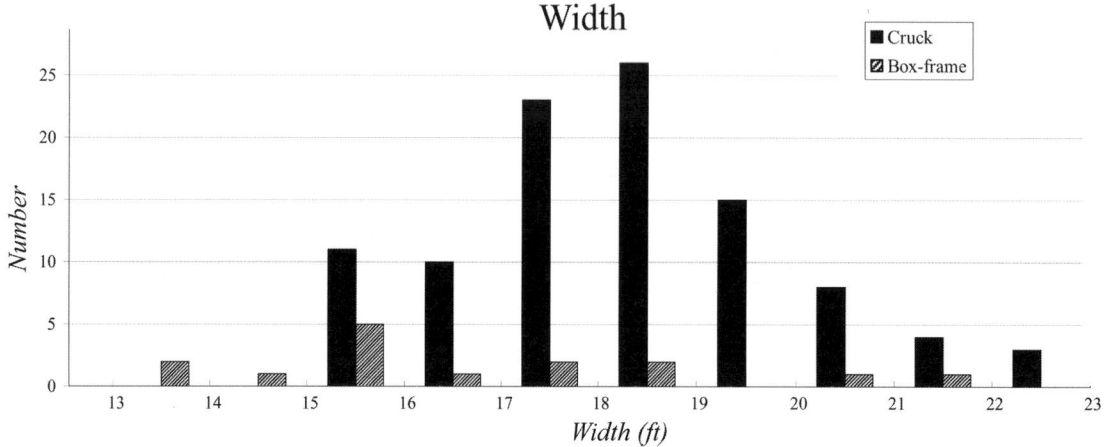

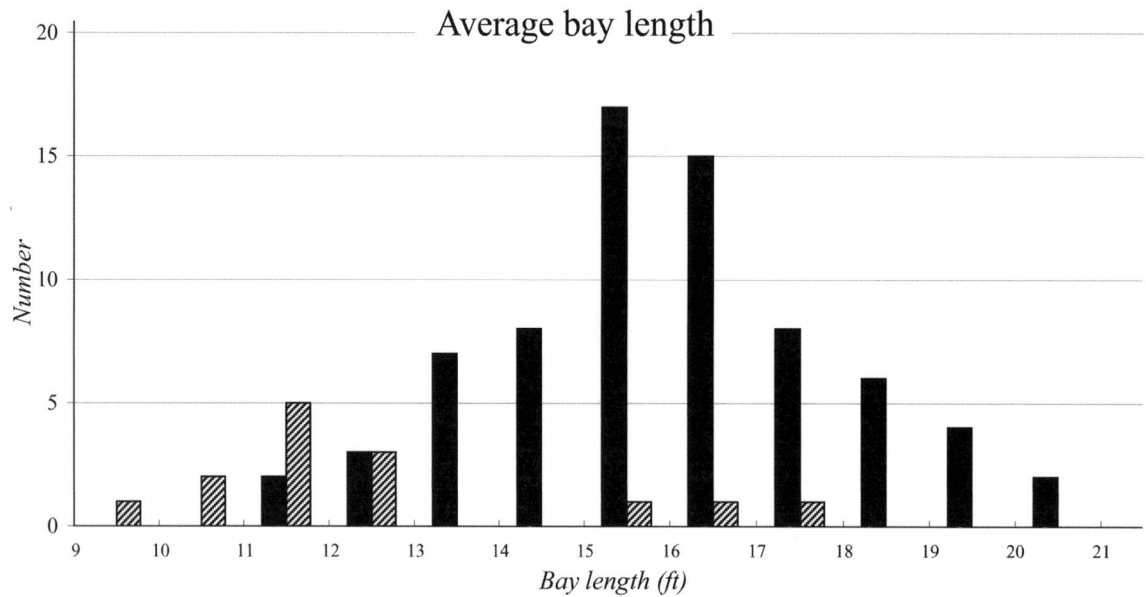

Fig. 3.6. Width (upper) and average bay length (lower) for cruck and box-frame houses.

undated) and the wing must have been a convenient way to extend the original house, similar to the in-line extensions to other houses.[10] Since the two primary bays comprise only an open hall, this wing presumably replaced a chamber bay and, when it was built, the end hall bay was presumably cut off for a chamber, possibly floored.

Dimensions[11]

Evidence on the size of the houses is limited because only about 40 houses are complete as constructed. For a similar number, one bay has been lost or replaced, and the assumption can be made that this bay was the same size as the adjacent one.[12] This is reasonable, since very few of the complete houses have more than one chamber or service bay, and the inferred dimensions do not differ appreciably from those for complete houses. However, if the end of the hall itself is missing, we cannot be certain of the total size since, in the complete houses, almost equal numbers of halls stand at the end of the house or are flanked by an additional bay. For the remaining, incomplete, houses the width is known, and usually the length of one or two bays, but not the full number of bays or the length.

The range of width and length is shown in Figure 3.6. In width, the 100 cruck houses range from 15 to 22ft, with half falling between 17 and 19ft. The ten box-framed buildings (houses and wings) are generally narrower, with one main range and one crosswing no more than 13ft 6in wide (HAR-C and AST-A). The average bay length for the cruck houses is 15ft, while the box-framed ranges have shorter and narrower bays, averaging only 12ft long, with the bays in one house (SOU-A) only 9.5ft long, giving a two-bay crosswing hardly longer than the width of the main house (see Fig. 3.5). As this example perhaps suggests, no correlation is seen between bay length and width.

The floor area naturally depends to a large extent on the number of bays, as shown in Fig. 3.7, and summarised in Table 3.2. The average ground area increases from 540 to 1205 square feet for two to five bays, with an area of

Table 3.2. Floor areas (square feet). The three box-framed houses (Table A2.3c) are included. Cross passages and probable lean-tos are counted as half bays.

Bays	*2–2.5*	*3–3.5*	*4–4.5*	*5–5.5*	*All*
Number of houses	13	38	17	8	76
Average ground floor area	540	863	1027	1205	881
Min ground floor area	446	547	722	994	446
Max ground floor area	715	1268	1396	1619	1619
No with upper floor	2	16	6	8	32
Average total area, houses with upper floors	915	1206	1347	1601	1313
Max area, houses with upper floors	936	1497	1523	2377	2377

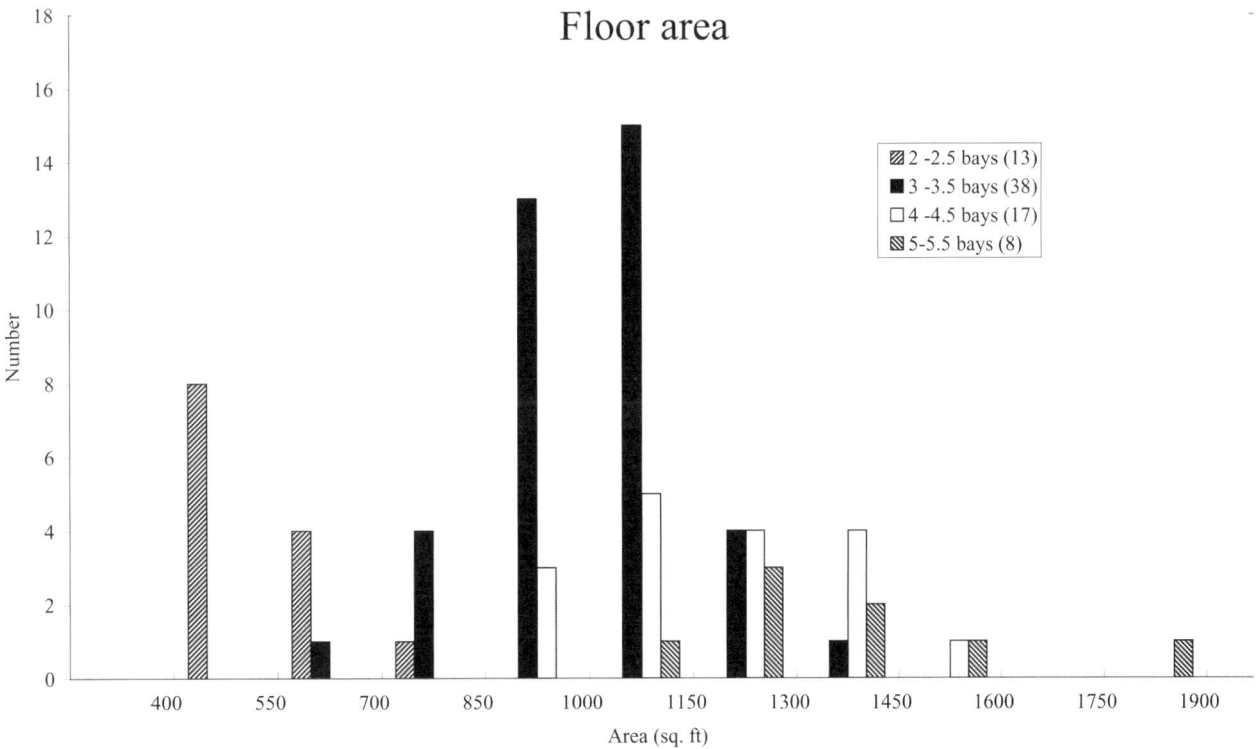

Fig. 3.7. Ground floor areas of cruck and box-frame houses, arranged by number of bays.

about 850 square feet typical for a three-bay cruck house, although these range between 547 and 1268 square feet – remarkably, both probably in fourteenth century houses (LOW-B, undated and MDM-A, 1335).[13]

A complication in working out the size of houses is the extent of upper flooring, since the existence of original upper floors in cruck ranges is often uncertain, although all the surviving box-framed wings were floored. Including these wings, 32 houses have evidence for upper floors, which contributed between 200 and an exceptional 760 square feet to the house (respectively for HAL-A and STE-B), adding on average about a third extra to the ground floor area. From the average dimensions identified here, a characteristic three-bay house would be about 18ft wide and 45 ft long, with a floor area of 850 square feet (1100 square feet if it had an upper floor in one bay).

Rooms and their use

Two-bay and one-bay halls

Halls of two bays slightly outnumber those of one bay.[14] They are identified by their central open trusses, often arch-braced, with confirmation from the presence of smoke-blackening in the roof on both sides of this truss. Generally, the only direct evidence for the use of these comparatively large spaces is the sooting from the open hearth. If this can be localised, it seems to be thickest beside the open truss, but not always in the central bay. A few houses retain traces of smoke louvres and these are more often in the end bay (LON-I, MDM-A, MDM-B) than the centre (EAH-B). Remarkably, two houses (BIT-A, MDM-C) had louvres in *both* hall bays. Both these examples and the other louvre positions indicate a differentiation in the use of the two hall bays. We can envisage the central bay as the living area, heated by a small fire, and the end bay as the kitchen, with the main cooking hearth located under the louvre.

Further evidence for differentiation of the hall space comes from the open trusses themselves. A surprising number had tiebeams as well as collars.[15] One house (STW-A) includes also a chamfered central post spanning between collar and tiebeam, an example of a type that has a wide but sparse national distribution, dating from the late fourteenth to the early fifteenth centuries.[16] Close examination of the small visible length of the tiebeam here shows the presence of stave holes, indicating the presence of a spere partition at least at one end of the beam. In general, these low beams also imply differentiation of the hall space. Previously it has been suggested that that they might carry curtains or hangings, subdividing the hall. This remains their most plausible function. If the end bay was in full use for cooking, the hanging would probably have been pulled back, creating a large working area. When the household gathered around the hearth in the living bay,

drawing a curtain across the open truss would certainly have made them more comfortable.

In other houses, the smoke-blackening is sparser in the end than the central hall bay. Here, the functional division was probably into one bay for living and cooking, with the other bay for storage, food preparation, dairying and similar activities not needing heat.

Chambers

After the hall, the next requirement was for separate sleeping space. No specific features identify a room used as a chamber, but documentary sources which give room names (see Chapter 6) invariably mention chambers as well as halls in village houses. Thus it is inferred that one end bay in houses with one-bay halls and the third bay in houses with two-bay halls provided a chamber. The chamber bay was at first single-storey and had a solar above it in the later houses. The floored crosswings in the more sophisticated houses seem to have served principally as chambers, although the low-ceilinged ground floors of some wings suggest that they had service space at this level (e.g AST-A; STE-E). Of course, not every member of the household would necessarily have slept in the chamber, although the earliest peasant probate inventories rarely list beds or mattresses in the hall.[17]

The most modest houses had only two bays altogether. One bay was always a hall with open hearth and it is inferred that the second bay was the chamber. In two houses (STC-B, *1433–6*; FOS-B, undated) both bays are smoke-blackened, apparently indicating that each had a hall only. However, both open trusses had tiebeams as well as collars and it seems likely that the two bays were separated by a low partition, possibly of light-weight wattle and daub, with one of them used as a chamber with its upper part still open to the hall bay. FOS-B also has evidence for a lean-to at one end, presumably used as a service room.

The two-bay houses with upper floors (LON-J and NWL-C) show no evidence (e.g. from low ceilings) that one ground floor was used for service with the principal chamber above, so the hall presumably combined both living and service space, with a ground floor chamber and two upper chambers.

High and low ends

A few houses suggest a differentiation in status of the ends of the hall, usually by the position of the door or the hall window, which are expected to be placed respectively at the low and the high end of the hall. Their positions confirm that the chamber was at the high end of the hall.[18] At MDM-A, although no direct evidence identifies the higher end of the hall, the louvre is placed in what is interpreted as the lower bay of the hall, and beyond it was the lean-to bay (since removed), presumably for service.

Service Rooms

Separate service bays presumably had the same functions as the end bays in two-bay halls. The axial division expected in grander houses into buttery and pantry is not seen in these houses.[19] The service rooms occasionally show evidence for their own open hearths, and two of the clearest examples are in Warwickshire (LOX-A; STO-F), perhaps reflecting the trend there towards single bay halls.[20] The former existence of detached kitchens also cannot be discounted, since their occurrence elsewhere in England identifies them as a frequent element of peasant housing.[21] Indeed, one surviving fragmentary building (*LON-P*) can be interpreted as a cruck-built kitchen or brewhouse. Similarly, in East Hendred, Oxfordshire, detached kitchens, apparently of two different types, perhaps normal kitchens and back kitchens/brewhouses, are recorded in a survey of 1607 (see p. 131).

Only four houses in all have additional in-line bays beyond the standard complement of chamber, one- or two-bay hall and service. One Warwickshire and one Gloucestershire house (LOX-A; FOS-A) probably had kitchens in their fourth or fifth bay, and the very late Oxfordshire house (DID-B, *1549–60*) may have been similar. The final Warwickshire example (ASH-A) is more enigmatic because of the lack of structural evidence. However, the two long end bays divided by the only cruck truss in the structure seem to have been of lower status than the hall and inner room. Use as a barn, stable or byre (or a combination of these) seems a possibility. The extra space created by the insertion of upper floors in modernisation after 1500 certainly led to originally domestic sections of some houses being turned over to agricultural use (e.g. STO-F and WEE-A).

Floored Bays

Floored chamber bays only appear in the fifteenth century, and their upper rooms are of modest quality with low eaves and lacking roof decoration. Thus, they provided lower rather than higher status accommodation. Sixteenth-century probate inventories show that they were used as subsidiary chambers though they also provided the most secure storage for valuables in chests and coffers (that must surely have been firmly padlocked).[22] Surprisingly, these subsidiary chambers were called *solars* (sometimes spelt *celer*); it would seem that this term was semantically associated with any upper floor sleeping room, not exclusively the best chambers.

In two houses (NOS-C and STO-C (Fig. 3.2)), the floored inner bay was subdivided on the ground floor. This would suggest that the principal chamber was on the upper floor with paired service rooms below. However, a probate inventory of 1610 for the Stoneleigh house identifies the divided rooms as the little chamber 'next the street' and 'next

the yard', thus the division seems to have been intended to provide an extra chamber rather than service rooms.[23]

Entries and Cross Passages

In post-medieval houses, the position and form of the entrance is generally used to classify plan forms, the most prominent distinction being between lobby-entry and cross passage plans. In the cruck houses, evidence for the original entry is sparse. Of two Stoneleigh houses with known door positions, one was entered into the lower end bay, the kitchen (STO-F), and the other apparently into the chamber end (*STO-H*). Typically, these houses developed in the post-medieval period into lobby-entry plan forms. At least in some cases, the inserted stack seems to occupy the position of the original hearth, so it is possible that the medieval plan form also included a door adjacent to the hearth. This is consistent with the occasional evidence for entries at the low end of the hall. Original cross passages are rare, generally only in houses with early wings (e.g. WOE-A and STO-E), whose plans should probably be related to those of higher status houses with a cross passage separating hall and service end.

Crosswings

Some of the early crosswings (Fig. 3.4) are strikingly sophisticated, although their rarity identifies them as a very minor component of peasant building. The earliest surviving wings seem to have provided service rooms on the ground floor with chambers above, since the halls had no additional service bays.[24] The upper floors often have decorative crown post roofs and must be seen as 'great chambers', while the ground floors often have low ceilings.[25] These chamber blocks must surely be the timber-framed counterparts of the thirteenth-century stone solar wings found, for example at Old Soar, Plaxtol, Kent and Charney Bassett, Oxfordshire.[26]

The apparent similarity between these early two-storeyed chamber blocks or wings and those of later date seems to conceal different functions. The halls being built from the mid-fourteenth century onwards (Fig. 3.5) incorporated service bays, so their wings could then contain ground-floor parlours with additional chambers above. This was certainly the function of most of the wings built with or added to houses from 1400 onwards, as it is of the floored chamber bays found in houses without wings.

The possibility exists that a few of the three-bay cruck houses comprised a two-bay hall with a service bay rather than a chamber, and that their chambers were in box-framed blocks which have since disappeared, as indeed seems to be the case for the houses whose chamber blocks are later than their halls. Although this interpretation is difficult to disprove in individual cases, particularly when one of the house bays has been replaced, it seems implausible as a general explanation of the three-bay houses. In particular, the survival pattern in Steventon and elsewhere in Oxfordshire is for the chamber block to survive when the halls have been replaced, rather than the reverse. The successors to single-storey three-bay houses typically had one end floored, and these surely must have been used as chambers with solars over, as is indicated in the documents.

Aisled Halls and Base Crucks

Because of the close structural links between the houses using aisled trusses and those with base crucks, they are considered together. The use of base crucks in the central truss of an open hall is generally seen as a device for eliminating free-standing aisle posts from the hall, though these were retained in closed trusses and spere trusses. The base crucks also allowed a wider span than was normally achieved with true crucks. The base-cruck halls show many features in common with aisled construction: not only their aisled end trusses, but also square-set arcade plates rather than diagonally-set purlins and the use of common-rafter upper roofs. Indeed, in three houses it has been established that base crucks were inserted into mid-thirteenth century

aisled halls (IVI-A, LON-O, X-HA1). Base cruck houses have been recognised as of relatively high status, for example manor houses, well-endowed rectories, or urban gentry houses, although later houses often appear to be of rather lower standing.[27] However, the present study has shown that even the early base-cruck houses had a wider social range than expected; the documentary evidence for their status is discussed in Chapter 6 (p. 151).

Dimensions and planning of aisled and base-cruck halls

This section examines the planning of four aisled halls, the three later converted into base crucks, and the exceptionally early aisled house, Sycamore Farm, Long Crendon (Figs. 3.8–9). Eight houses originally constructed with base crucks are considered with them (listed in Table 3.3, with their dimensions).[28] The four aisled halls are closely similar in span, with external widths of 24–26ft, and the modest status and early date of Sycamore Farm is only reflected in its 10ft bay length, and the small scantling of its timbers. Unfortunately, this structure is the least complete of the four, with only one full hall bay surviving, which apparently extended further at both ends. All the other houses have

Table 3.3. Dimensions of aisled and base-cruck halls. Passage bays (P) are not included in the hall areas. Heights are measured from the floor to the top of the rafters, the top of the arcade plate and the top of the wallplate. Dimensions in feet, bracketed values estimated.

Code	Location	Type	Date	Bays		Width		Length	Area (ft²)	Height		
				Hall	Other	External	Between plates	Hall	Hall	Ridge	Arcade	Wall
LON-G	Long Crendon, Sycamore Farm, 9 Bicester Rd	Aisled hall	1205	3(?)		(24)	14.2	32.7	(785)	21.4	11.9	
X-HA1	Harwell, Lime Tree House, High Street	Aisled hall Base cruck	1243–7 1294–1306	3(?)	1 +W?	23.5	13.4	(33.0)	775	25.7	15.7	9.2
IVI-A	Ivinghoe, Pendyce House, 6 Station Road	Aisled hall Base cruck	*1250–77 1288–1323*	1 + 2*½	2?	26.6	14.0	27.8	740	25.0	13.8	
LON-O	Long Crendon, Manor House, Frogmore Lane	Aisled hall Base cruck	13th cent c. 1300	2	1+	22.3	11.1	28.2	628	20.3	12.6	7.4
BAT-A	Bathley, The Hollies	Base cruck	1295/6	2	1	26.0	16.0	28.6	744	28.7	14.9	
BRN-H	Braunston, Quaintree House	Base cruck	1306-9	2	P + W?	24.6	14.9	32.1	791	32.5	21.4	
CLI-B	Clifton, TIL House, 56 Village Rd	Base cruck	1319/20	1½	1 + W?	20.3	13.1	20.9	424	22.0	11.9	8.7
CUB-A	Cubbington, Old Manor House	Base cruck	*1313–41*	1½	P + 1?	22.5	12.0	21.7	488	25.7	16.5	
LNG-M	Long Marston, Hopkins, Wyre Lane	Base cruck	1339	2	1	26.0	13.7	32.0	832	24.4	13.6	
X-MIL	Milton, 42–42A High Street	Base cruck	early 14th century	2	1+2(W)	17.1	10.0	22.8	391	20.2	12.9	9.0
STK-A	Stokenchurch, Kensham Farm	Base cruck	end 14th century	2	1+	(21)	11.1	30.0	(630)	23.5	15.5	
X-WHA	West Hagbourne, York Farm	Base cruck	1284/5	2	1+2(W)	24.5	12.2	22.8	561	24.5	14.8	8.1

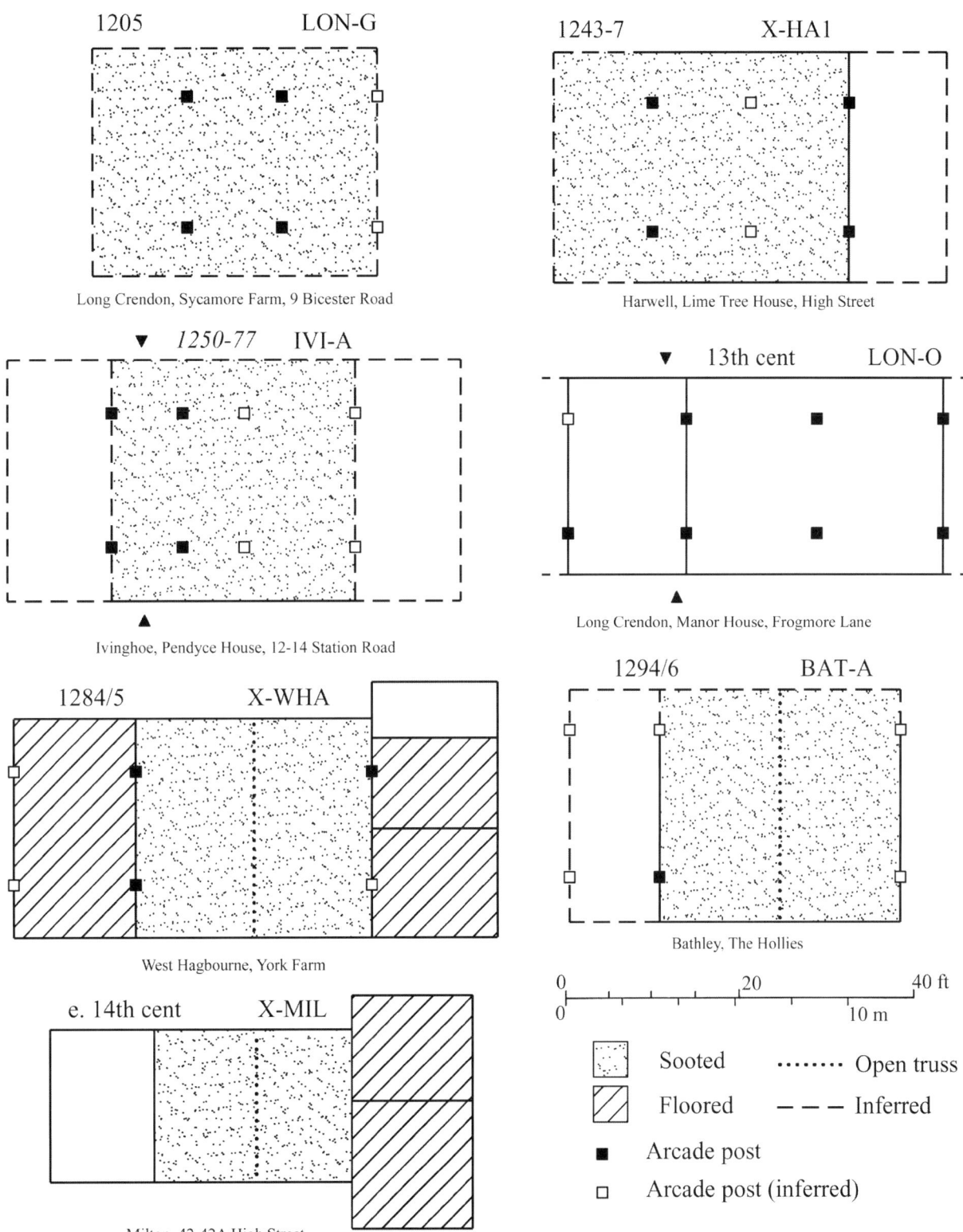

Fig. 3.8. Block plans to scale of houses with aisled halls and the earliest houses with base-cruck halls. The missing aisles of LON-G, IVI-A and BAT-A are drawn in their approximate original positions.

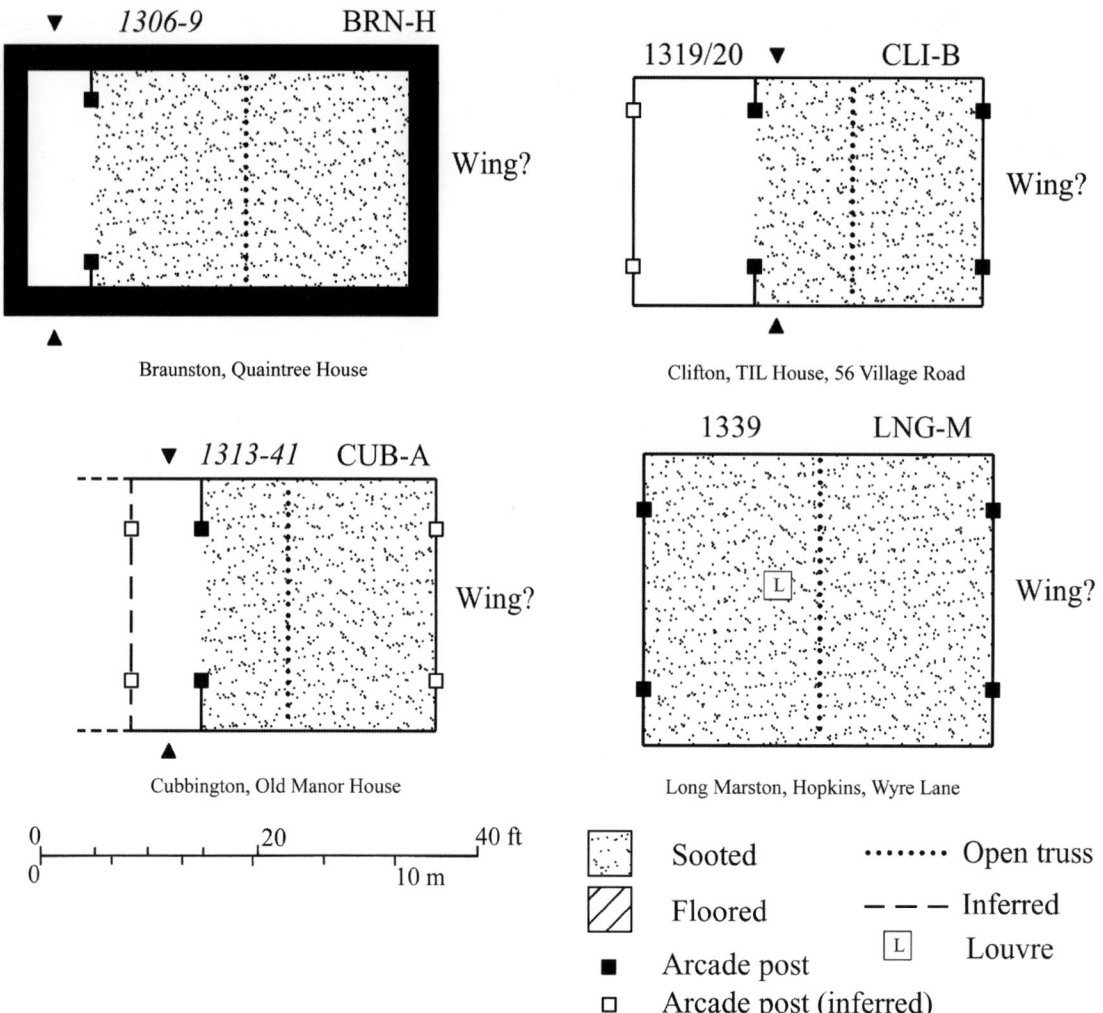

Fig. 3.9. Block plans to scale of later houses with base-cruck halls. STK-A is omitted as the plan is too incomplete for reconstruction.

two-bay halls with at least one service bay as well. Only for Lime Tree House, Harwell (X-HA1) is the original plan reasonably clear. At one end of its hall, the wall plates are cantilevered out for half a bay. An aisled (outshot) end is inferred beyond this, which was replaced by a fourteenth century crosswing; the length of this end bay was apparently similar to the main bays. Another cantilevered bay is inferred at the other end, which was partitioned from the hall with wattle and daub; thus use of this end as the chamber is suggested.[29]

At Pendyce House, Ivinghoe (IVI-A) the two hall bays also survive but one bay is bisected by what appears to be a spere truss with the half-bay beyond it containing a wide passage. Beyond the other end, the (later) collar purlin extends for a further 1–2ft, but no further truss has been identified. Thus, it is possible that this end was cantilevered and aisled as at Lime Tree House. At the other end, the

house extended beyond the hall end truss but no further structure is visible. Long Crendon Manor has two hall bays and a low-end bay including a cross passage, but nothing is known of its high-end accommodation.

Most of the base-cruck halls are rather similar in size, with spans of 24 to 26ft and hall floor areas of 600–700 ft^2. They are considerably more generously proportioned than even the largest cruck houses. However, Clifton, Kensham, Cubbington and especially Milton are notably smaller than the remainder. With an overall width of no more than 17ft, Milton lies well within the size range of ordinary crucks (as discussed above), while the other two are at its upper end. In these buildings, the choice of a more sophisticated constructional technique must have been made for reasons of prestige rather than to achieve extra space.

In the houses in which base crucks replaced aisled open trusses, the plans remained unchanged, and it appears that these improvements affected only the appearance and convenience of the hall. The majority of the houses originally built with base crucks have not survived complete, but they include two-bay halls with an additional in-line bay. In some houses this bay was certainly at the lower end, so presumably was for service. At Long Marston, the house ended at the closed truss of the hall, so any service bay must have been detached. The absence of parlours or chambers in most of these houses strongly suggests that they all originally had upper-end wings. This likelihood is confirmed by the two houses which survive intact, West Hagbourne (X-WHA) and Milton (X-MIL). Both include just such a wing which, in contrast to the other houses, is structurally integrated with the main range.

4

The Structure of the Surveyed Houses

Introduction

This chapter gives a structural overview of Midland peasant houses and of their variation with place, time and status. It starts with true cruck houses, followed by those with box-framing, the intermediate and hybrid trusses found in a few houses, and finally the aisled halls and base crucks. The more technical aspects of timber conversion, jointing, wall-framing and related topics (including decoration) are considered in chapter 5. Cross-sections at uniform 1:100 scale are presented in Figures A-U for cruck trusses, V-ZZ for other types of structure; Table 2.2 identifies which page includes a particular building. Some characteristic examples are reproduced below at a larger scale.

As discussed above, the great majority of the houses studied use true crucks, and complete box-framed houses do not appear until the later fifteenth century, although box-framed cross wings are among the earliest structures identified. Virtually all the houses had timber-framed outer walls, the only definite exception being the stone walls of OXH-A, and most probably BRN-H. The two houses at Hallaton, Leicestershire (HAL-A and HAL-B) are in an area where early mud walls have been recorded, and this material has been suggested for both; however, each of their cruck trusses have or had spurs which would be expected to link to framed walling.

Cruck Houses

The development of cruck-trussed houses before 1350

Only a handful of cruck buildings dating from before the Black Death have been found during our survey, all of them from Oxfordshire. In view of the small number, their lack of common features is perhaps not surprising. As will be seen from the dimensional analysis (below), these houses have relatively broad and low profiles. The only undoubted thirteenth-century cruck identified is at Baker's Close, Lower Radley (RAD-B, 1256–88), but of this structure only one blade survives, in a house reconstructed in 1514 (Fig. A).[1] The blade is very neatly formed, with a sharply cranked elbow, but provides no other structural evidence.

The earliest complete cruck truss is that at Tibberton Cottage, Harwell (HAR-E, *1294–1324*, Fig. A), probably dating from close to 1300. This is the half-hipped truss at the end of an open hall. Again it has elbowed blades, with a double collar, probably with straight braces to the lower one; it is unusual to find such braces in a closed truss. The collars and braces are tenoned, although the tiebeam is halved, projecting past the blades to support the (replaced) wall plate.[2] A fragment of the central truss of the open hall is also visible, comprising part of the arch-braced collar that capped the blades, supporting upper principals.

In Manor Cottage, Sutton Courtenay (SUC-A, 1317/8) (Fig. 4.1), the central hall truss survives but one end truss has been replaced while at the other end the hall is fully integrated with the contemporary box-framed wing, without a separate truss. The central truss is again strongly elbowed, with an arch-braced collar (removed). A fragment of a small house of similar date, 33 High Street, Long Wittenham (LOW-C, *1323–49*) (Fig. B) also has angled blades.

Mill Farm, Mapledurham (MDM-A) is an exceptional survival of an almost complete early fourteenth-century house, whose timbers were felled in winter 1334/5 and spring 1335. It has three cruck trusses with a tiebeam truss at one end, which show a fully developed range of structural techniques (Figs. 4.1, A, V; p. 200). The elbowed crucks of the elegant open truss (T2) carry a tenoned collar and arch-braces, with halved spurs to support the wall plate. In the closed truss (T3), the collar and tiebeams are halved. Both internal trusses are capped by saddles, though T2 carries an additional short post supporting the ridge; the end truss (T1) carries a half-hip and the rafters originally extended down over a short lean-to bay (since removed). The northern end is fully hipped, with the end truss (T4, Fig. V) of box-frame form. This truss is unusual in having reversed assembly, i.e. the wall plates are on top of the tiebeam, which was probably adopted because it gave the plates similar support to that provided by the cruck spurs. As well as some surviving original wall-framing and traces of a louvre (Chapter 5), the original roof of Mill Farm is mostly intact, with one pair of purlins supporting the small-section common rafters (typically 3 by 2in). The missing

original truss at the other end was almost certainly of the same form, since the house had a lean-to half bay at this point. It would thus have been completely symmetrical, fully hipped at both ends.

Mid- and late fourteenth-century crucks

Felling dates for a dozen cruck buildings fall in the mid- to later fourteenth century, including the first houses outside Oxfordshire (Figs. B–D). The majority have steep-pitched and elegant arch-braced open trusses, exemplified by a magnificent example, Tudor House, Steventon (STE-B, 1355/6) (Fig. 4.2), which dwarfs most of the other cruck houses. Its open truss has heavy arch-braces to the high collar, which carries short cusped principals.[3] Similar but plainer open trusses are found in several other houses,

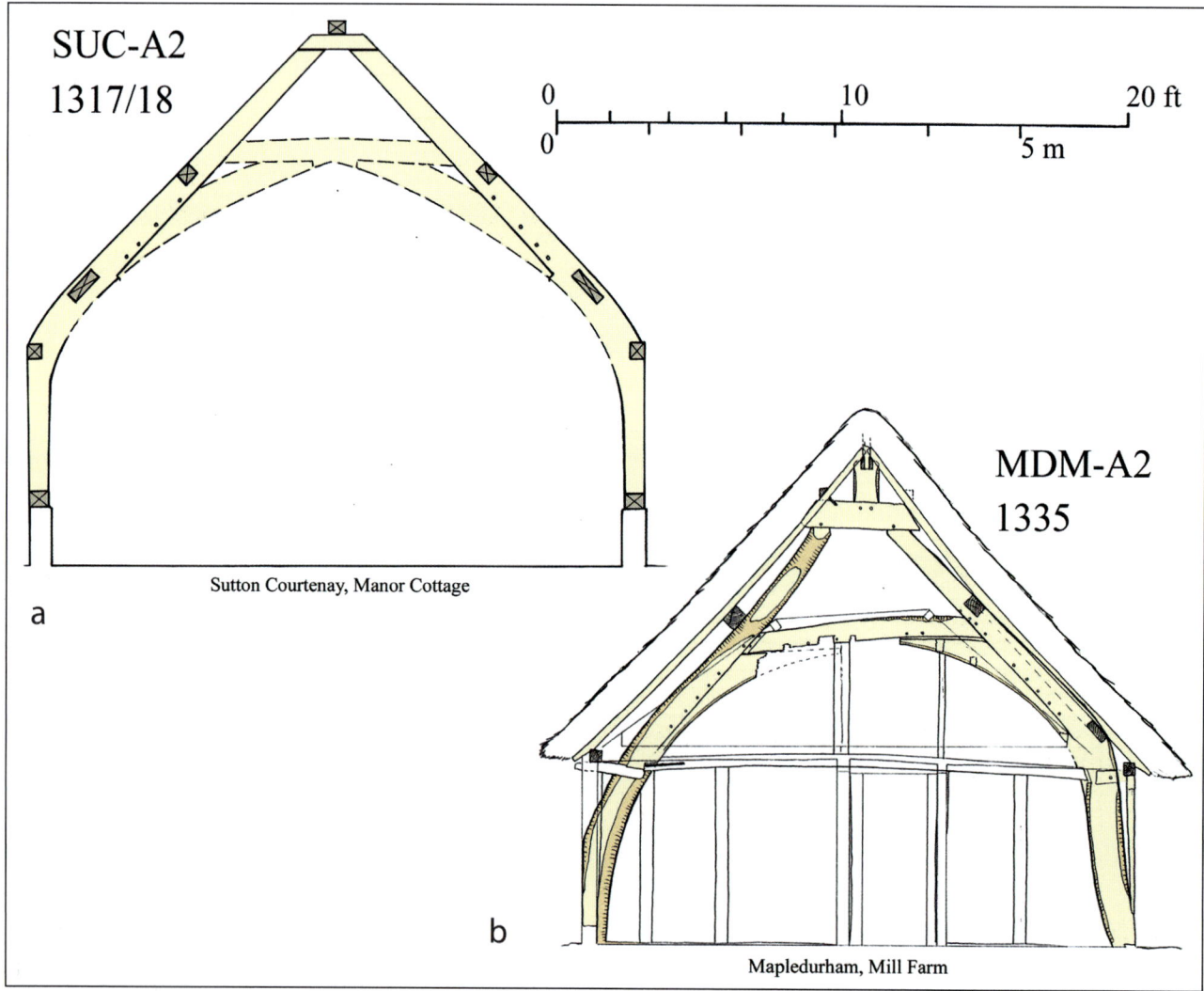

SUC-A2
1317/18

0   10   20 ft
0   5 m

Sutton Courtenay, Manor Cottage

a

MDM-A2
1335

Mapledurham, Mill Farm

b

Fig. 4.1. Cruck trusses before 1350: (a) Manor Cottage, Sutton Courtenay, Oxon (SUC-A), truss T2: 1317/18, based on Currie (1992). (b) Mill Farm Cottage, Mapledurham, Oxon (MDM-A), truss T2: 1335.

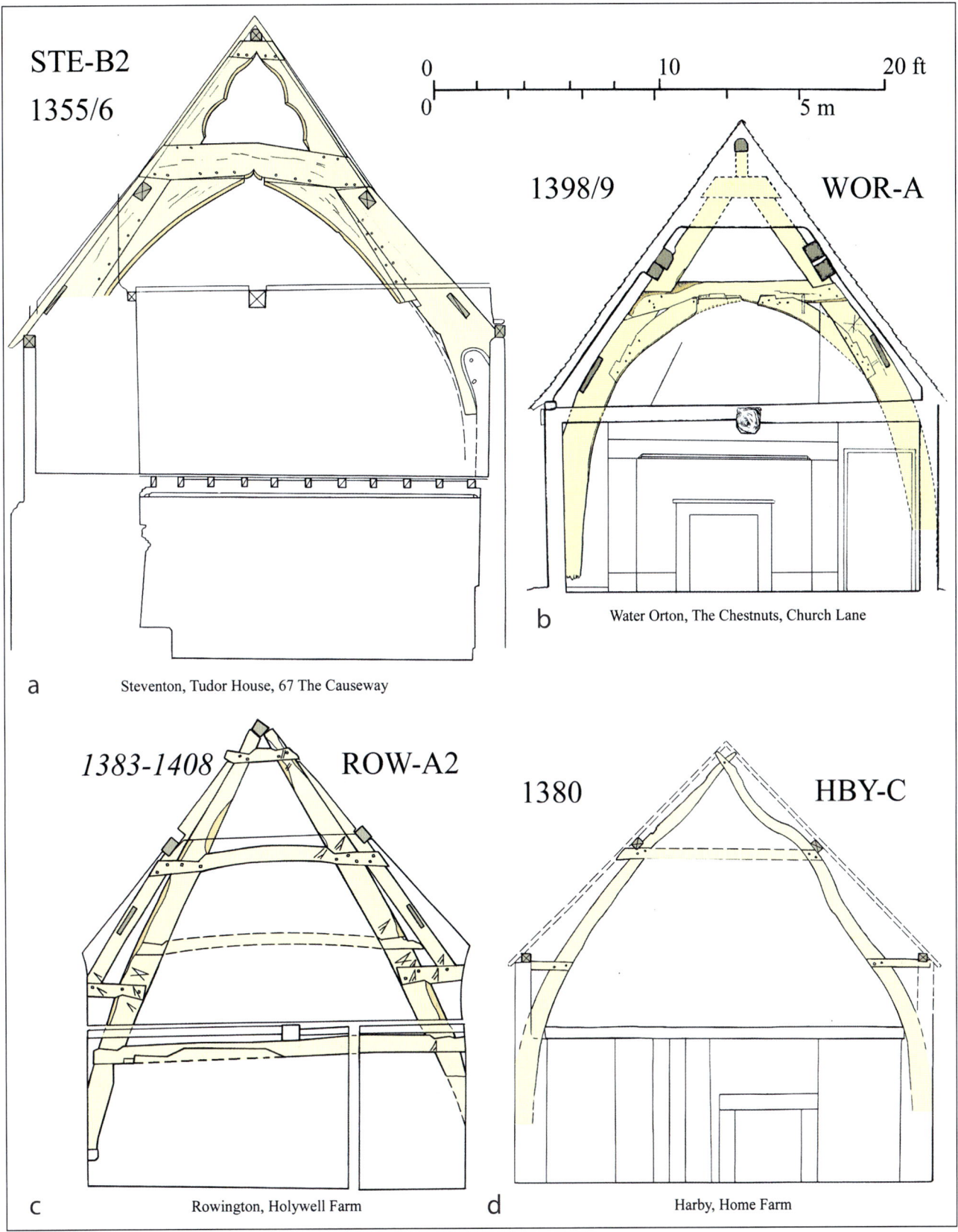

Fig. 4.2. Cruck trusses from 1356 to 1399. (a) Tudor House, Steventon, Oxon (STE-B), truss T2: 1355/6. (b) The Chestnuts, Water Orton, Warws (WOR-A): 1398/9 (The upper roof can be seen but is not accessible for measurement.). (c) Holywell Farm, Rowington, Warws (ROW-A), truss T2: *1383–1408*. (d) Home Farm, Harby, Leics (HBY-C): 1380.

including 83 The Causeway, Steventon (STE-C) dated to 1365/6 (Fig. C), and Pomander House, Harwell (HAR-D, *1304–57*, Fig. B). The former originally included spandrel struts (between the blades and the arch-braces), the only examples noted during the survey. Both these houses also have trusses whose blades are truncated above the collars, either closed or standing against a crosswing wall.

At 83 The Causeway (STE-C, 1365/6), the house appears to have been reconstructed in the fifteenth century, but with the trusses retained intact, although the original open truss became the end of the hall.[4] A more striking case of reconstruction, amounting in effect to reuse, is found at Terret Close, Long Wittenham (LOW-A, *1352–62*; Fig. B). The central truss of this four-bay cruck house has mortices for long arch-braces which do not fit the existing collar and tiebeam or match the other trusses. The open truss in a somewhat later house, Abbey Timbers, Harwell (HAR-C, 1399/1400, Fig. D) probably gives a good impression of how this truss might have looked originally.

This period also includes the earliest surviving cruck houses in both Leicestershire and Warwickshire, demonstrating clearly the differentiation between crucks of higher and lower quality that is hinted at in comparing MDM-A and LOW-C with STE-B (Figs. 4.1, B and 4.2). Four of the Warwickshire houses dating from 1400 or before have two-bay halls with arch-braced open trusses, all including individual features that did not become part of the later carpentry repertoire of the area. In the open cruck truss at The Chestnuts, Water Orton (WOR-A, 1398/9, Fig. 4.2), the arch-braces have 'joggled halvings', distinctive joints found otherwise only in a house at Ufton, Warwickshire (X-UFT).[5] In the earliest Warwickshire cruck house, Cruck Cottage, Walcote, Hazelor (WAL-A, 1384/5. Fig. C), the blades are carried in V-cuts in the cruck studs rather than reaching the sill; these joints are reinforced only by pairs of heavy face pegs.

The open truss at the Lad in the Lane, Erdington (ERD-A, 1400, Fig. D), has a beam spanning the open truss just above head height, with a chamfered post rising from it to the collar, as does the undated open truss at 28 High Street, Stewkley, Buckinghamshire (STW-A, Fig. R), and the later Three Chimneys, Mapledurham (MDM-C, 1458, Fig. J) (without a post). The open trusses at both Holywell Farm, Rowington (ROW-A3, 1384–1415, Fig. C) and the earlier Pomander Cottage Harwell (*1305–57*, HAR-D, Fig. B) were apparently also spanned by low beams, though without central posts. The significance of these unusual beams in relation to the plans of these houses has been discussed above (p. 34).

The closed trusses in these houses are well-shaped, though that at ROW-A has a proliferation of transverse members: a yoke and two collars as well as spurs and a tiebeam (Fig. 4.2). In contrast, the earliest Leicestershire cruck, Home Farm, Harby (HBY-C, 1380, Fig. 4.2) is remarkably crude, with irregular spindly blades using exclusively halved joints. Similarly, the cruck truss at 19 Henley Street, Alcester (ALC-A, *1398–1407*, Fig. E) is very plain, with halved tiebeam and collar. As it is the single surviving truss in this house, we do not know how it related to the structure, and it could have been an end truss.

Early fifteenth-century crucks

The differentiation in decoration and carpentry that becomes apparent in the later fourteenth-century is even more marked after 1400. All but one of the houses dated before about 1430 have arch-braced central trusses, and for the only exception (HAR-B) the character of the central truss is unknown (Figs. D, E, F).[6] By contrast, of the examples from the mid-century, only a couple have arch-braced trusses (Figs. F, G, H, I). The apparent suddenness of this change must be an accident of survival as a few later fifteenth-century crucks have arch braces, but the difference in quality between the two groups is very striking. This contrast also has a geographical aspect, since only one Leicestershire cruck is arch-braced (WOE-A, Fig. F), compared to three in Buckinghamshire, ten in Warwickshire/West Midlands and no less than fourteen in Oxfordshire. Three of the well-carpentered early fifteenth-century crucks are from Warwickshire, continuing and improving on the late fourteenth-century group already noted. The open truss at The Leopard, Bishops Tachbrook (BIT-A, 1413/14, Fig. 4.3) was particularly impressive, with a chamfered beam spanning the hall and ogee scissor-braces above it (inferred from the surviving mortices). The rest of the structure at BIT-A is also remarkable although it seems more to reflect innovative carpentry than established traditions. One closed truss has massive short blades extended by thinner rafters, while the other can only be described as a very distant relative of an aisled truss, with an arch-braced post apparently engaging the principal rafter (Figs. D, X).

Manor Farm, Stretton-on-Fosse (SOF-A, 1409+, Fig. E)[7] is as sophisticated as BIT-A, but with more typical carpentry; it has shapely symmetrical timbers decorated with double chamfers, with all joints tenoned. The set of three studs filling the space between the two collars has no parallels in the survey. We can also infer the status of the house from its location within the village of Stretton-on-Fosse, as it backs onto the late seventeenth-century manor house. With the name Manor Farm, it seems very likely to have been the original manorial site. The house was improved in 1589 (dated on the inserted hall chimney), and again in the seventeenth century (with the addition of the parlour wing); it must have been superseded soon after this.

Two other Warwickshire houses from this period, 26 Warwick Road, Southam (SOU-A, 1418/9) and The Old Smithy, Sutton Coldfield (SUT-A, 1442–4), and one in

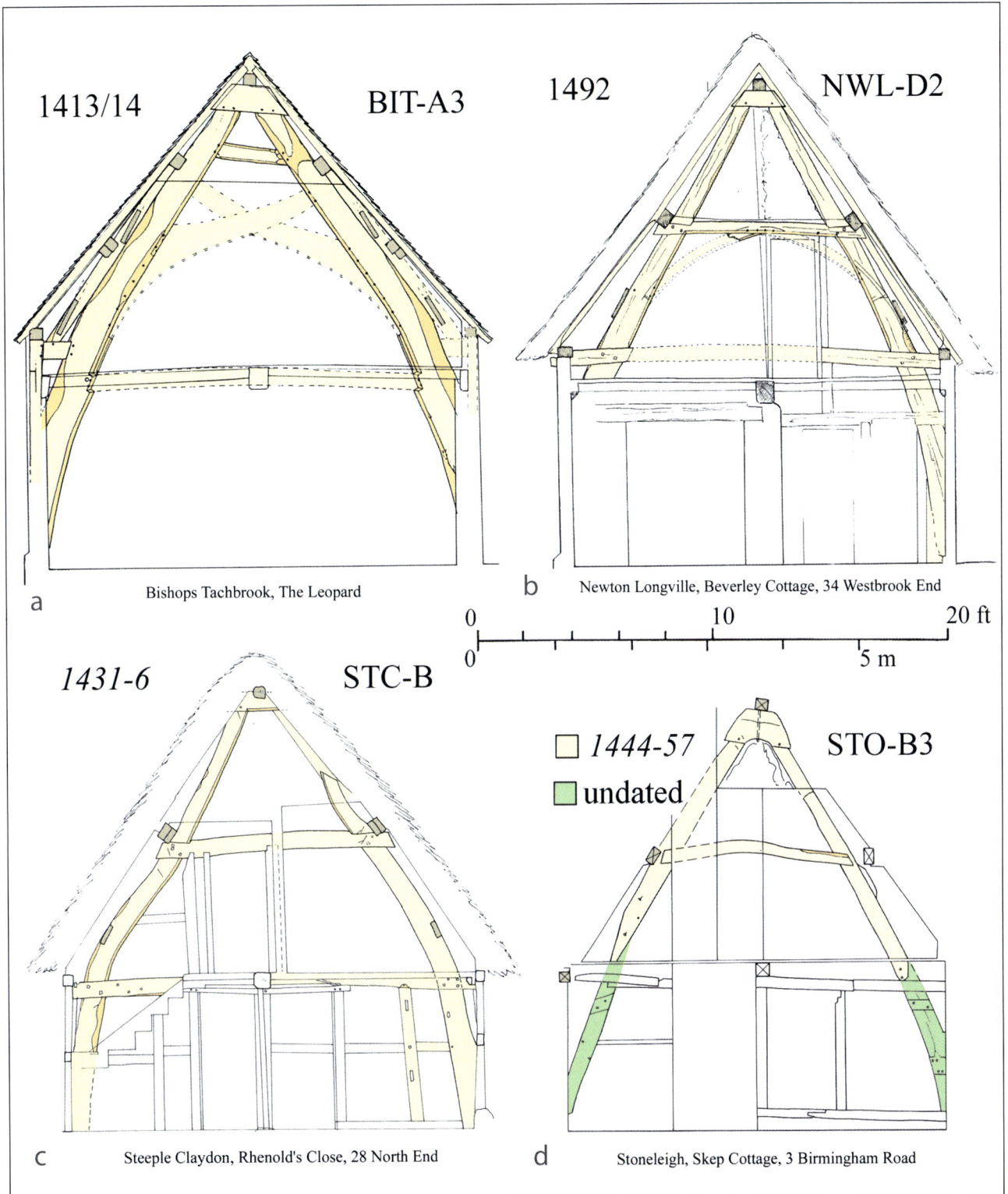

Fig. 4.3. Arch-braced and plain fifteenth-century crucks. (a) The Leopard, Bishop's Tachbrook, Warws (BIT-A), truss T3: 1413/4. (b) Beverley Cottage, Newton Longville, Bucks (NWL-D), truss T2: 1492. (c) Rhenold's Close, Steeple Claydon, Bucks (STC-B): *1431–6*. (d) Skep Cottage, 3 Birmingham Road, Stoneleigh, Warws (STO-B), truss T3: *1444–57*. Both blades of this truss are in two sections, partly oak and partly elm, presumably reused from earlier buildings. The date (from both blades of truss T2 and the purlin between T2 and T3) clearly relates to the present form.

Leicestershire, Golden Cottage, Woodhouse Eaves (WOE-A, 1426–30) have arch-braced open trusses (Figs. E, F, G); unexpectedly for an open truss, SUT-A seems to have had original infill above the collar. The open arch-braced truss at Godfrey's Farm, East Hendred, Oxon (EAH-C, 1418/20, Fig. E) is exceptionally high, with the crown of the collar a full 5ft higher than at Woodhouse Eaves. This height undoubtedly correlates with the use of box-framing for all the remaining trusses. It demonstrates that an arch-braced cruck was still valued in a large open hall, though it might no longer be the main structural type used in a house of this quality.

Only a handful of arch-braced crucks were constructed after the 1450s. The most notable is the Old Post Office, Oxhill, Warws (OXH-A, *1450–6*, Fig. I). As well as its well-finished braces, it has curved struts above the collar, braces to the ridge and even small decorative blocks pegged to the each side of the collar. It also shares with BIT-A and SOF-A the unusual use of doubled purlins and windbraces. The remaining houses with arch-braced trusses include the only examples from Buckinghamshire: Eastgate House, Weedon (WEE-A, 1446–50, Fig. G), Beverley Cottage, Newton Longville (NWL-D, 1492, Fig. 4.3) and the undated 28 High Street North, Stewkley (STW-A, Fig. R), and one Gloucestershire house, Advowson Farm, Frampton-on-Severn (FOS-A, 1496/7) (the arch-braced central truss is not drawn); the reused cruck fragments at Binfield Heath (BIF-A, 1453–5. Fig, I) also came from an arch-braced truss.[8] Buckinghamshire (perhaps with Gloucestershire where the dating evidence is very limited) seems to have lagged behind the other counties in its building styles, for example having no cruck houses surviving from before 1430. Even so, the arch-braced cruck at Newton Longville (NWL-D, Fig. 4.3) must by 1492 have been an old-fashioned response to the desire for something better than one's neighbour; it could only have impressed on a very local stage at a time when more serious status-seekers had turned away from crucks altogether.

Plain crucks of the mid-fifteenth century onwards

Apart from the handful of arch-braced trusses just discussed, all the Buckinghamshire crucks are plain. The earliest complete dated cruck there, Rhenold's Close, Steeple Claydon (STC-B, *1431–6*, Fig. 4.3), is apparently an open truss with soot blackening on both sides. However, the two 'hall' bays make up the entire house, with half-hipped crucks at each end. The truss lacks any of the decorative features, apart from a simple chamfer on one blade and the saddle, while all the joints (except the apex) are halved.

This simplicity is typical of most crucks from this date onward. Their overall character is very uniform, with only a few regional variations, notably in the cruck apexes (discussed in detail in Chapter 5, p. 83f). Saddle apexes (C-type) remained in use in Leicestershire and

Warwickshire, with only occasional variations. However, in Buckinghamshire and Oxfordshire, crucks with truncated blades (W-apexes) became very popular. Their rationale must lie in the opportunity they provided for the building to be taller without the blades needing to be excessively long. A similar height to that available with box-framed construction could thus be achieved, while retaining the simplicity and undoubted cheapness of a plain cruck truss. Most of these houses had original upper floors (p. 97f) but whether this was the case for any individual house is not very significant, since the extra height also made it easier to insert a floor. It thus contributed to the ability of these houses to survive.

In Leicestershire, although crucks continued in use even longer than in the south, extra height was less often sought. When wanted, it was usually achieved by setting a king-post on top of the cruck saddle (apex F1), a device also adopted in Warwickshire. A popular alternative in the later fifteenth century was an exceptionally thick saddle, sometimes built up from two or three chunks of wood; the underside might be hollowed out to give a curving cap to the cruck blades (e.g. STO-B, Fig. 4.3). Several saddles with a total depth of 15–18in have been recorded (contrasted to the normal 7–9in). The largest of all is no less than 22in thick (BIL-A, undated, Fig. R).

Upper floors

Original upper floors in cruck ranges are very simply supported on plain square-section joists, which can easily be removed or replaced, so the lack of recognisable early joists is not definitive evidence for an originally unfloored bay; indeed, in a few houses the position of the mid-rail or the presence of high windows has led us to suggest that an early floor has been replaced (e.g. at Godfrey's Farm, East Hendred, EAH-C). In a house which has not survived completely, it is also possible that a demolished bay had an original floor, even though the existing structure does not. Thus, although early floors can be identified, their absence does not always indicate unfloored bays. Of the plain undated houses, a fair number have original floors, adding weight to the structural indications that they are predominantly of the later fifteenth century. None of the more decorative undated houses have original floors, again confirming that they are generally earlier than the plainer ones.

Dimensions

The dimensions of the cruck frames provide a quantitative parallel to the changes in structure just examined. Two measurements are used: the width (between the outer faces of the wall plates, precise or estimated) and the height (from the floor to the upper face of the ridge); additionally, the wall height (to the top of the wall plate) is tabulated when it is known, as a further guide to the proportions of

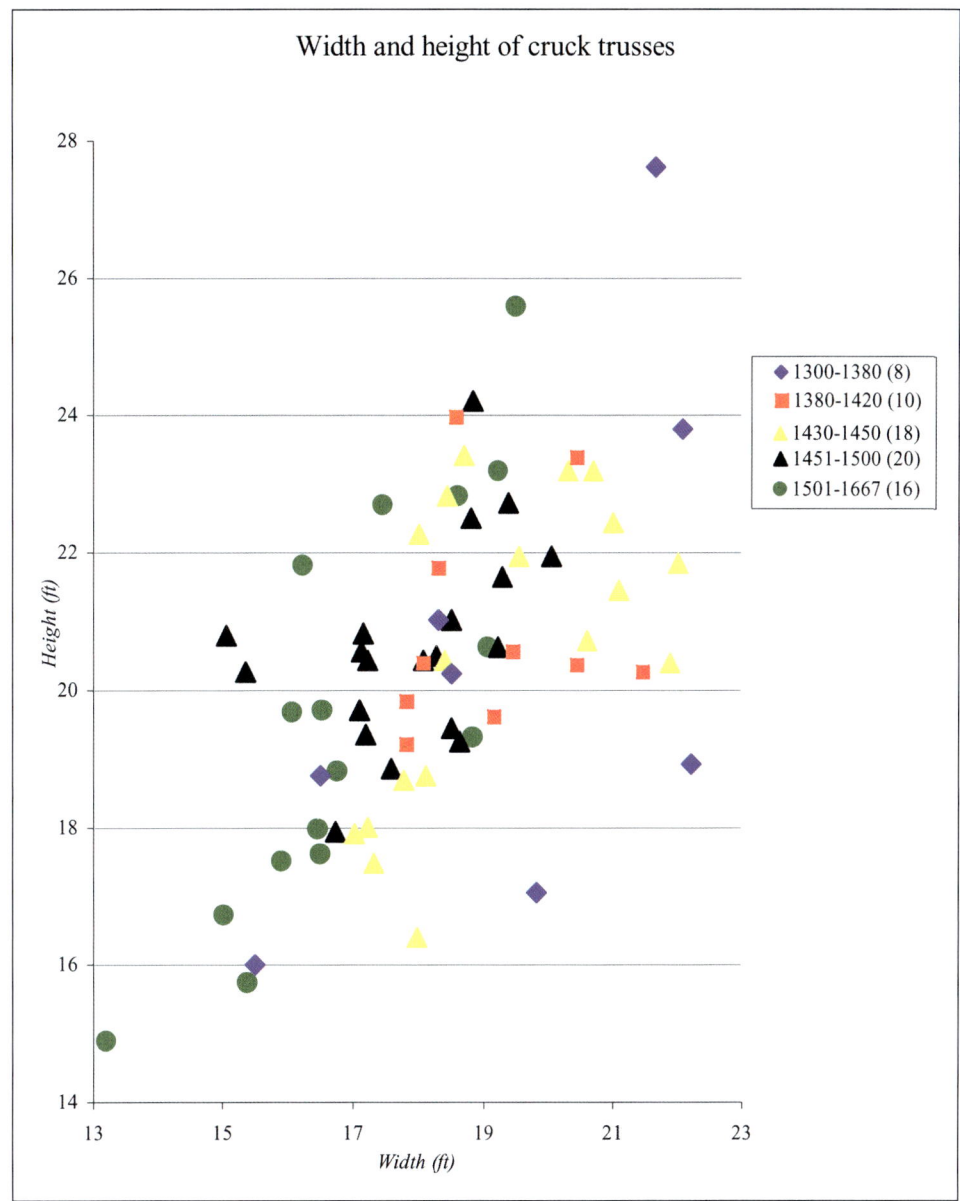

Fig. 4.4. Width and height of cruck trusses, with symbols corresponding to their date (data in Table A2.3).

the structure. These dimensions are listed in Appendix 2, Table A2.3.

The correlation of width, and height with date is shown in Fig. 4.4. In their overall proportions, most cruck trusses have a span (13 to 22ft) somewhat less than their height (15–28ft). When compared by date, clear differences appear. The earliest houses (from before 1380) are distinctive. They are generally wide and low, including two houses which are considerably wider than they are high (SUC-A and MDM-A, Fig. 4.1). This group also includes two houses that are exceptionally wide and high, the fragmentary HAR-E (Fig. A) and STE-B (Fig. 4.2). The survival of these earliest houses may well be directly correlated with their generous

size. If they had the same proportions but were two or three feet narrower, the corresponding reduction in height would have made it almost impossible to insert upper floors, and they would probably have been replaced rather than modernised. Only one early house, LOW-C (*1323–49*, Fig. B), has the dimensions (width 15.5ft, height 16.0ft) that might be expected for the most modest early houses, although STE-E (*1350*, width 16.5ft, height 18.7ft, Fig. B) is only slightly wider.

The shapely arch-braced crucks dating from the late fourteenth to the mid-fifteenth century are also relatively wide (average 19.2ft), but are often 2ft higher than most of the early houses, clustering together towards the top right of the plot. However, the second half of this period contains two distinct populations, one corresponding to the earlier houses, mostly 20ft or more wide, but the other considerably smaller, with widths in the 16–18ft range.

The plain examples of the later fifteenth century form a central block in the plot, sharing the same general proportions as their more decorated counterparts, but on average are about a foot narrower. They are also rather more homogeneous, with none exceeding 20ft in width, and only one more than 22ft high. The sixteenth century saw a further reduction in size, with houses on average a foot narrower and a foot lower than the previous group. However, several are notably high in proportion to their width, confirming the pressure to provide space for upper storeys already suggested by the preceding analysis. Exceptionally, Pye Corner, Moulsford (MOU-A, 1559, Fig. P), measuring no less than 25ft to the ridge, is an example of the carry-over of cruck construction beyond the medieval period. It achieved sufficient height for full upper floors by setting a tall king post onto the collar of the truncated crucks. The undated crucks (not plotted) generally correspond in their dimensions to those dated to 1450–1500, supporting the later fifteenth to early sixteenth-century dates suggested for most of them.

The dozen crucks less than 16ft wide merit closer examination. Most have the relatively tall proportions typical of the later houses, with heights of 16 to 19ft, which would provide some headroom for an upper storey; their dates fall between *1464–75* and *1566–77* (with three undated). In complete contrast, the tiny cruck in the service wing at 26 Manor Road, Didcot (DID-A, *1517–28*, Fig. N) is only 13ft wide and 15ft high, and must surely have been single-storeyed originally (as it remains). The latest cruck identified in our survey, Low Thatch, Weston-on-Avon, Warwickshire (WOA-A, Fig. P), radiocarbon-dated to *1655–87*, is not only very narrow (15.4ft) but also very low, 15.7ft to the ridge (and with walls only 7ft high). Although an upper room has been inserted, access through the cruck truss was only achieved by completely cutting out the collar. It is by no means clear that this house belongs in the same category as the other narrow buildings, and the possibility has been suggested that it originated as a small barn attached to a house into which it was later incorporated.

Box-framed wings and houses (Figs. V, W)

In structure, the box-framed trusses are broadly similar to each other, differing most obviously in scale, from the massive wing at Tudor House, Steventon (STE-B, 1299), 20ft wide by 30ft high to the modest Abbey Timbers, Harwell (HAR-C, probably 1400), only 13ft by 22ft. All are two-storeyed at least in part, except for the fully-hipped end truss at Mill Farm, Mapledurham (MDM-A, discussed above). At STE-D (1463/7), ASH-A (*1464–75*), STO-G

(1490doc) and STO-E (1537), the framed ranges included both open halls and floored chambers, as indeed has been found in other houses in the region.

Several of the wings and chamber blocks show primitive structural features (discussed in Chapter 5), indicating that standard framing techniques were not fully developed by the early fourteenth century. The Aston Tirrold house (AST-A, 1282/6, Fig. V) is notable as the earliest complete small box-framed building yet discovered, with most of its thirteenth-century wall framing surviving. The precise original form of the roof is uncertain; it apparently had principal rafters and the street-facing end of the roof was fully hipped (see p. 166). The roof was replaced in about 1500, and the section drawing shows its later form (a reconstruction, as it was destroyed by fire in the 1960s).

Almost all the fourteenth-century crosswings have crown-post and common-rafter roofs, as does the earlier wing at York Farm, West Hagbourne (X-WHA, 1284/5). Notably, though, that at 39 The Causeway, Steventon (STE-E, 1356/65, Fig. V) has a clasped-purlin roof, although the gable truss includes a crown strut, suggesting misleadingly that the roof behind it included crown posts. This is the earliest example in a box-framed range of what was to become the standard later design. The fifteenth century crosswings in Leicestershire and Warwickshire, where crown-posts are rare, also have clasped purlins.[9]

Intermediate and hybrid trusses (Fig. X)

One unexpected discovery during our survey has been of a small group of unusual trusses, neither of standard cruck nor box-frame form. Two resemble the intermediate trusses that occasionally provide additional roof support in the centre of long hall bays in substantial houses. They comprise arch-braced principal rafters and collars, resting on the wall plates, but without tiebeams or substantial wall posts. The truss at Warwick Farm, Long Crendon (LON-I3, undated) spans a two-bay hall (slightly off-centre) and was perhaps used to avoid the cost of a full cruck truss. That at Tudor House, Steventon (STE-B3, 1355/6; Chapter 8.10) stands at the end of the hall, against the earlier crosswing. Since it can have provided no transverse restraint for the wall plates, these were presumably attached to the crosswing wall plate, and the truss only supported the purlins and ridge.[10]

The truss at the other end of the Tudor House hall (STE-B1) has a unique form. It uses a dropped tiebeam carried on solid jowls cut on the wall posts, with the plates supported on the tops of the posts, and with doubled principal rafters. The house undoubtedly had a service bay (probably a lean-to) beyond this truss and a possible explanation for the form of the truss is that the wall plates in this bay were lower, being supported by the dropped tiebeam. This construction can then be seen as an *ad-hoc* adaptation to an unusual situation.

Two cruck halls incorporate aisled components. At Old Crown House, Skirmett (SKI-A, *1442–74*), the central open truss has a standard aisled form including aisle ties tenoned into the wall plates. This must have been viewed as a partial partition truss dividing the hall into functional units. A closely similar truss has more recently been identified at 2–6 Old School Lane, Wilmcote, Warwickshire (SP 164 579), although this house has not been dated nor recorded in detail. Truss T4 at The Leopard, Bishop's Tachbrook (BIT-A, 1413/4), was similar, but less efficiently designed, apparently with the posts joined to the principal rafters rather than to the tiebeam/collar.

Aisled Halls and Base Crucks

In base-cruck construction, the open hall trusses have large curved cruck-like blades that rise only to the tiebeam. The structures show many features derived from aisled construction, usually having aisled end trusses and square-set arcade plates rather than diagonally-set purlins; it is generally accepted that one of the main reasons for using base crucks was to avoid the presence of aisle posts in the open hall. Close structural examination and the precision of dendrochronology has led to the firm identification and dating of houses in which base crucks were actually inserted into pre-existing aisled halls; these include Lime Tree House, Harwell (X-HA1) and Pendyce House, Ivinghoe (IVI-A), where the aisled halls have been dated to 1243–7 and *1250–77* respectively, and the base crucks to 1294–1306 and *1288–1323* (Fig. Y). The same alteration also took place at Long Crendon Manor (LON-O, undated), which seems from the form of the aisled truss to be somewhat later.[11]

The earliest base-cruck hall so far dated by dendrochronology is in Staffordshire, the Manor House, West Bromwich of 1270–88, and only a handful of other examples were definitely built before 1300, with the great majority dating from the first half of the fourteenth century.[12] It is clear from these dates and from the evidence for reconstruction of aisled halls, that we are seeing the actual beginning of the base-cruck structural tradition in the Midlands. The concept of the base cruck had been developed by the 1240s, and was being adopted for houses of middling status towards the end of the thirteenth century, when it became an option for a prosperous yeoman freeholder or copyholder (see Chapter 6.5).

Aisled Halls

The four aisled halls that predate the emergence of the base cruck are remarkably uniform in character. They each use passing braces, with their varying status reflected only in modest differences in size and structure (Fig. Y). The nave spans are the same to within a few inches, as are the overall widths, as far as these can be determined from the surviving structures (Table 3.4).[13] They differ most in their height, which is controlled almost entirely by the length of the aisle posts. These range from 12ft (to the top of the arcade plates) at Sycamore Farm (LON-G) and Long Crendon Manor (LON-O) to 14ft at Pendyce House (IVI-A) and 15ft at Lime Tree House (X-HA1).[14] Although the timbers at Sycamore Farm are considerably less substantial than at Long Crendon Manor, their cross-sectional envelopes are virtually superimposable. One enigmatic features of Sycamore Farm deserve special comment, that its arcade plates have been re-used from an even earlier building (Fig. 8.5.4). These timbers could not be dated, but they must belong to a rather similar structure to the present one, and we can suggest that it was not very much earlier, but quickly required rebuilding, perhaps through structural failure.

Base Crucks

In their structure, the base crucks recorded during the project (Figs. Y–ZZ) find their place within the established framework for the development of the type.[15] They all retain aisled construction at the ends of the hall (BRN-H and CUB-A, Fig. Z; CLI-B, Fig. ZZ) although, at Milton the modest width allowed a simple tiebeam truss at the end of the hall and the residual aisled structure consists of no more than queen posts standing on the tiebeam (X-MIL2, Fig. ZZ). The earliest examples have passing braces, either retained from the pre-existing aisled halls (X-HA1; IVI-A; LON-O), or used in new construction (BAT-A, Fig. Y). These were being gradually superseded by crown posts with collar plates from the later thirteenth century onwards. A similar development is seen in the use of doubled tiebeams. These seem originally to have been adopted as a practical solution to the insertion of a base-cruck component in what was otherwise an aisled structure, as seen at Lime Tree House (X-HA1), where the arcade plate is trapped between the two tiebeams. Doubled tiebeams were retained at Old Manor House, Cubbington, The Hollies, Bathley and Quaintree House, Braunston (CUB-A; BAT-A; BRN-H, Figs. Y–Z), even though none of these were originally aisled, with a residual form at Long Marston in which the upper tiebeam was reduced to a clasping piece (Fig. ZZ).

Kensham Farm, Stokenchurch (STK-A, Fig. ZZ), although undated, belongs typologically to the end of the fourteenth century, making it the latest of the group. The roof above the tiebeam is constructed with principals rather than common rafters, typical of the late base crucks found for example in Herefordshire.[16] The upper roof had unusual inner braces starting just within the rafters, which must either have risen to a lost collar, or have been of scissor form, reaching the opposite rafters (perhaps like BIT-A, Fig. D).

CROSS-SECTION DRAWINGS
OF CRUCK, BASE-CRUCK, AISLED
AND BOX-FRAME TRUSSES
SCALE: 1:100

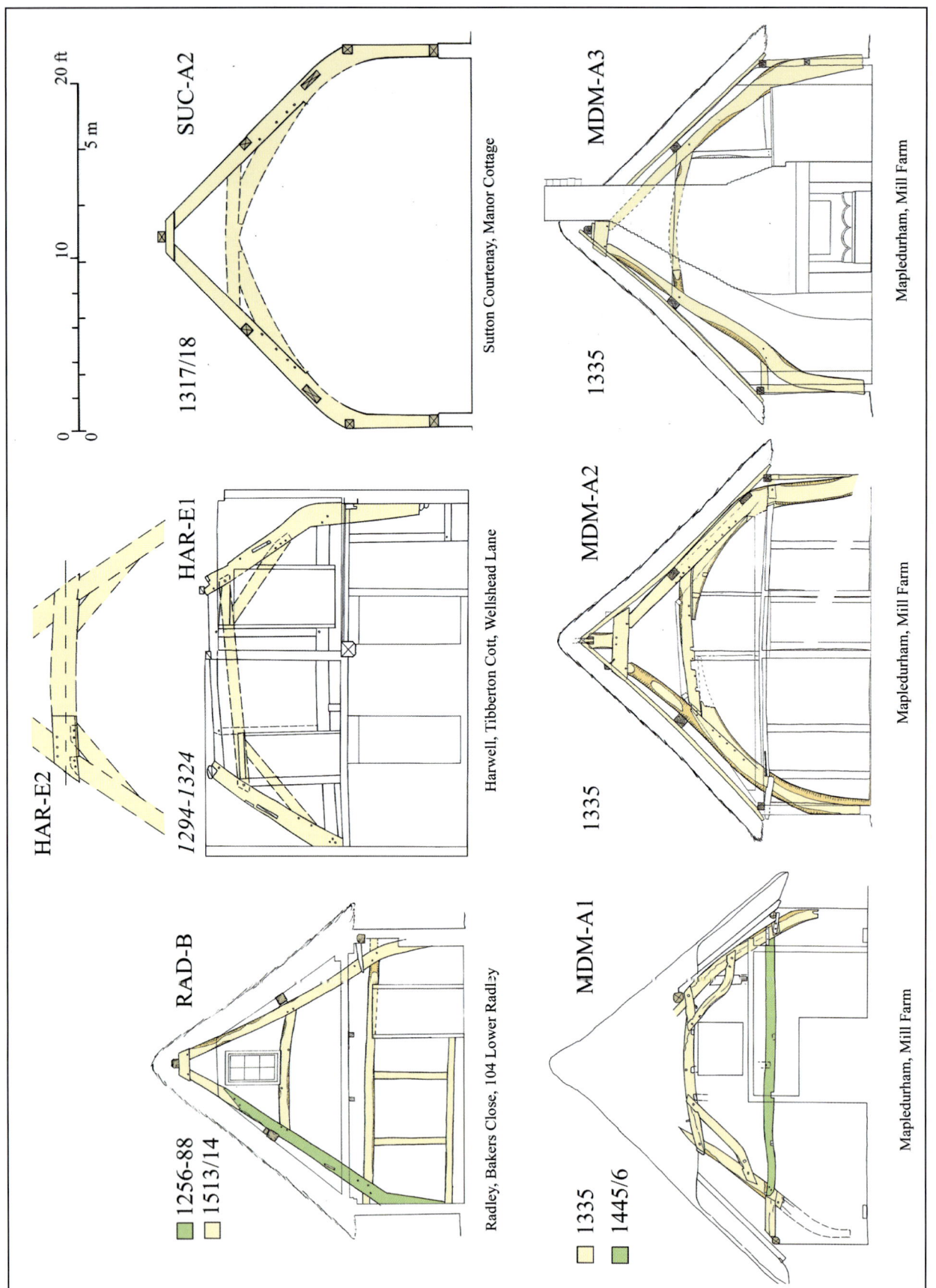

20 ft

5 m

SUC-A2

1317/18

Sutton Courtenay, Manor Cottage

HAR-E2

HAR-E1

1294-1324

Harwell, Tibberton Cott, Wellshead Lane

RAD-B

1256-88
1513/14

Radley, Bakers Close, 104 Lower Radley

MDM-A3

1335

Mapledurham, Mill Farm

MDM-A2

1335

Mapledurham, Mill Farm

MDM-A1

1335
1445/6

Mapledurham, Mill Farm

Fig. A. Crucks. Late thirteenth to early fourteenth century.

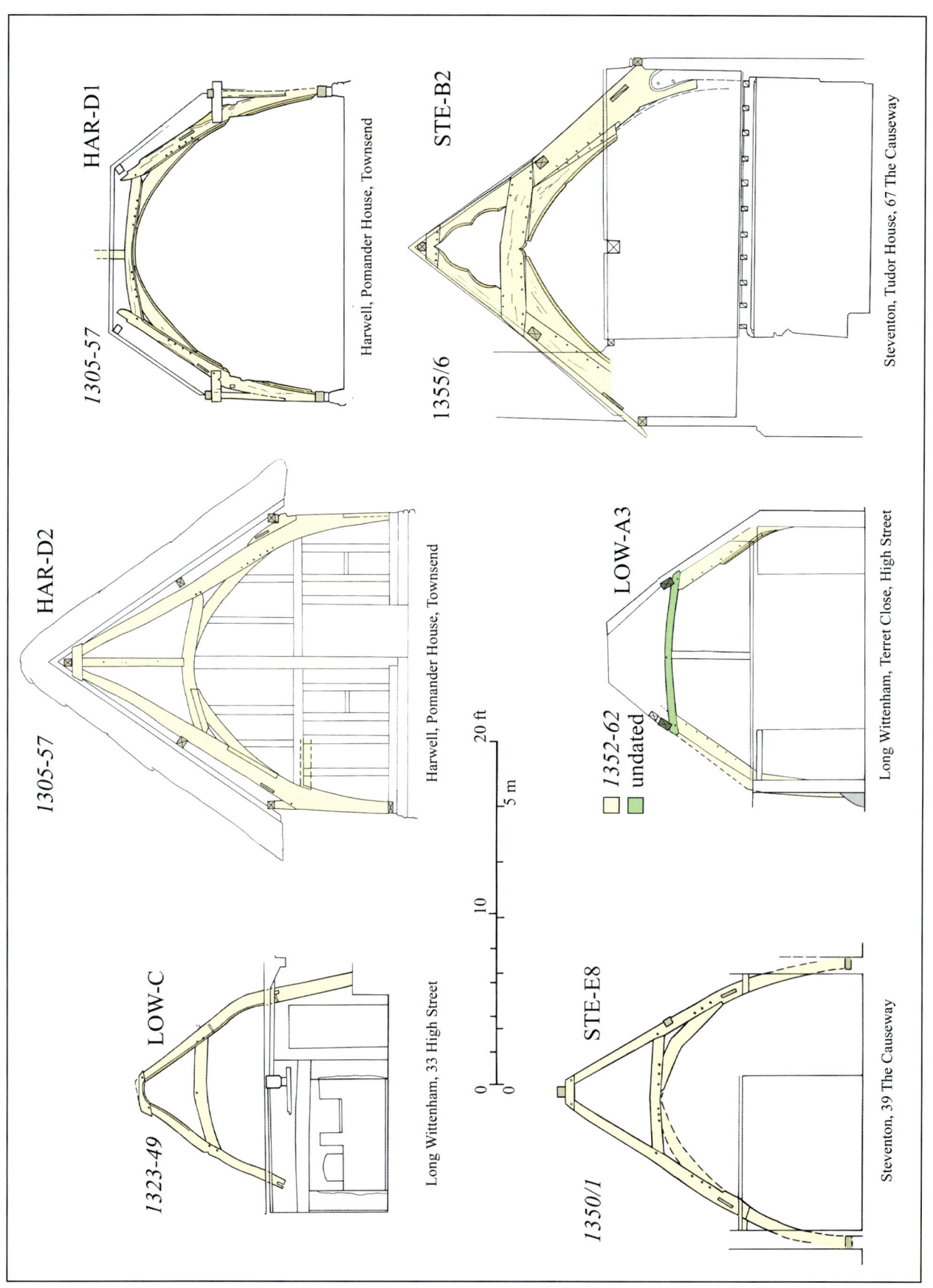

HAR-D1 *1305-57* Harwell, Pomander House, Townsend

STE-B2 *1355/6* Steventon, Tudor House, 67 The Causeway

HAR-D2 *1305-57* Harwell, Pomander House, Townsend

LOW-A3 *1352-62* undated Long Wittenham, Terret Close, High Street

LOW-C *1323-49* Long Wittenham, 33 High Street

STE-E8 *1350/1* Steventon, 39 The Causeway

20 ft

5 m

10

Fig. B. Crucks. Early to mid-fourteenth century.

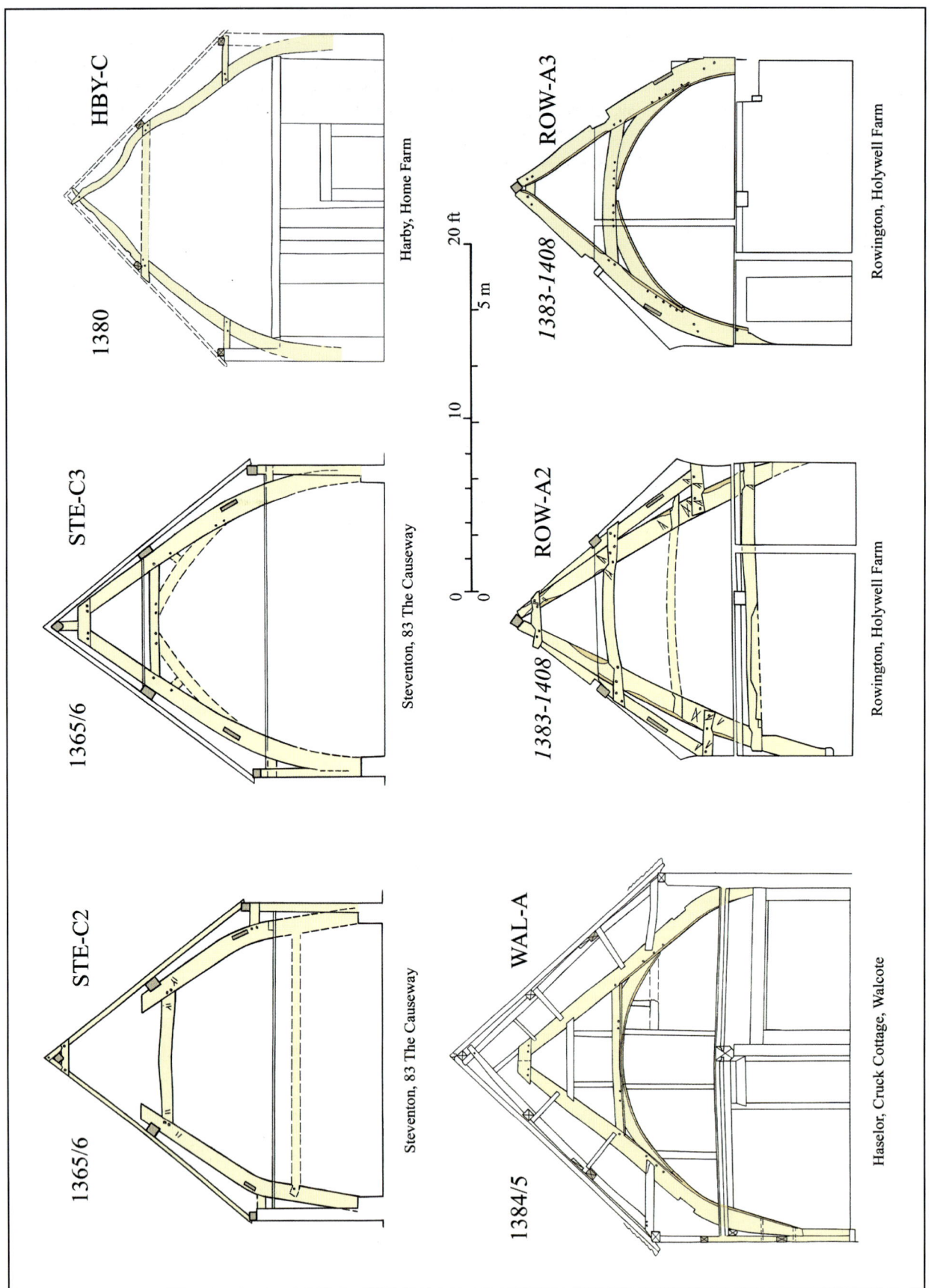

HBY-C

1380

Harby, Home Farm

STE-C3

1365/6

Steventon, 83 The Causeway

STE-C2

1365/6

Steventon, 83 The Causeway

ROW-A3

1383–1408

Rowington, Holywell Farm

ROW-A2

1383–1408

Rowington, Holywell Farm

WAL-A

1384/5

Haselor, Cruck Cottage, Walcote

20 ft

10

0

5 m

0

Fig. C. Crucks 1365/6 to 1383–1408.

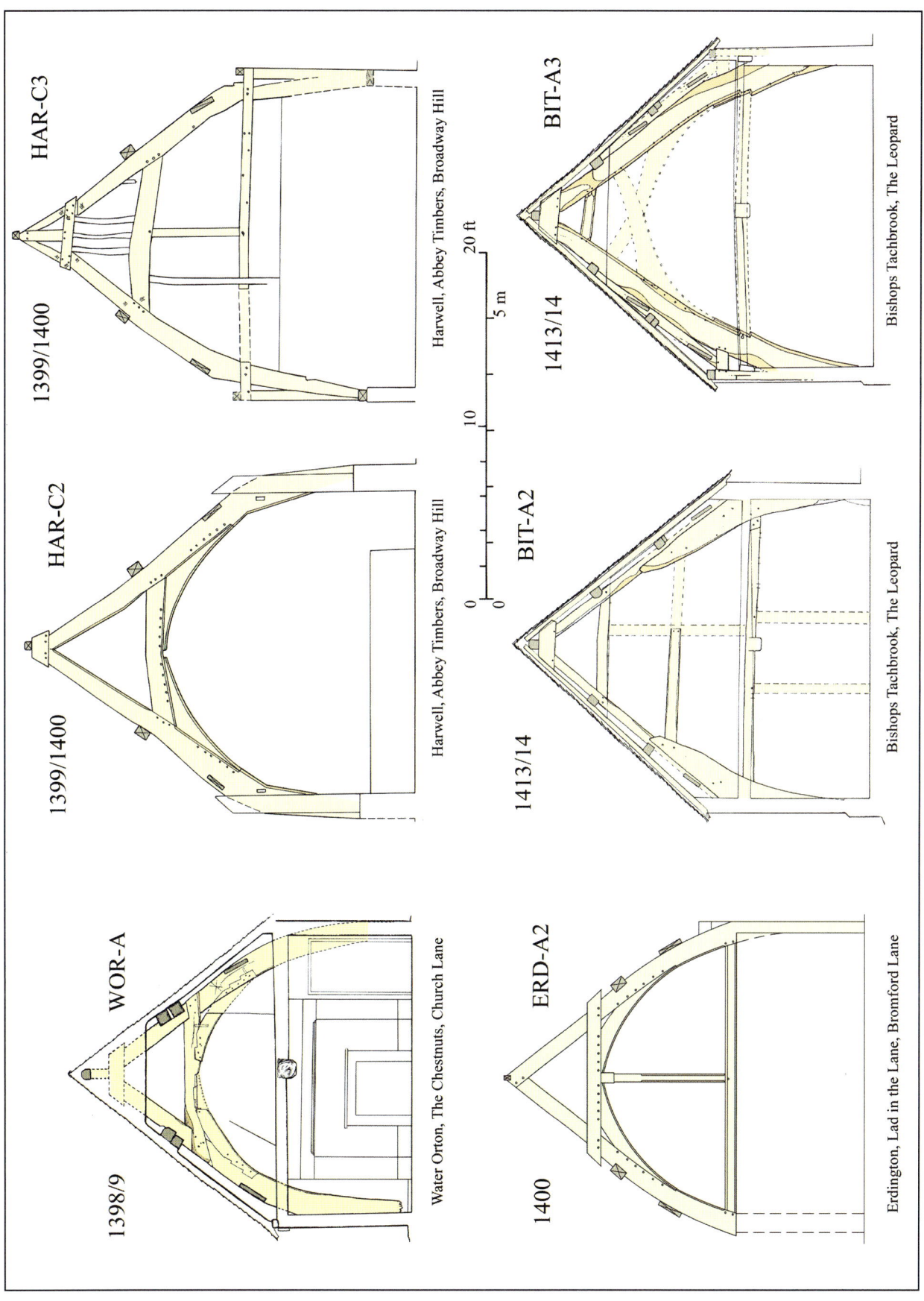

HAR-C3

1399/1400

Harwell, Abbey Timbers, Broadway Hill

HAR-C2

1399/1400

Harwell, Abbey Timbers, Broadway Hill

WOR-A

1398/9

Water Orton, The Chestnuts, Church Lane

BIT-A3

1413/14

Bishops Tachbrook, The Leopard

BIT-A2

1413/14

Bishops Tachbrook, The Leopard

ERD-A2

1400

Erdington, Lad in the Lane, Bromford Lane

20 ft

10

5 m

0

0

Fig. D. Crucks. 1398/9 to 1413/14.

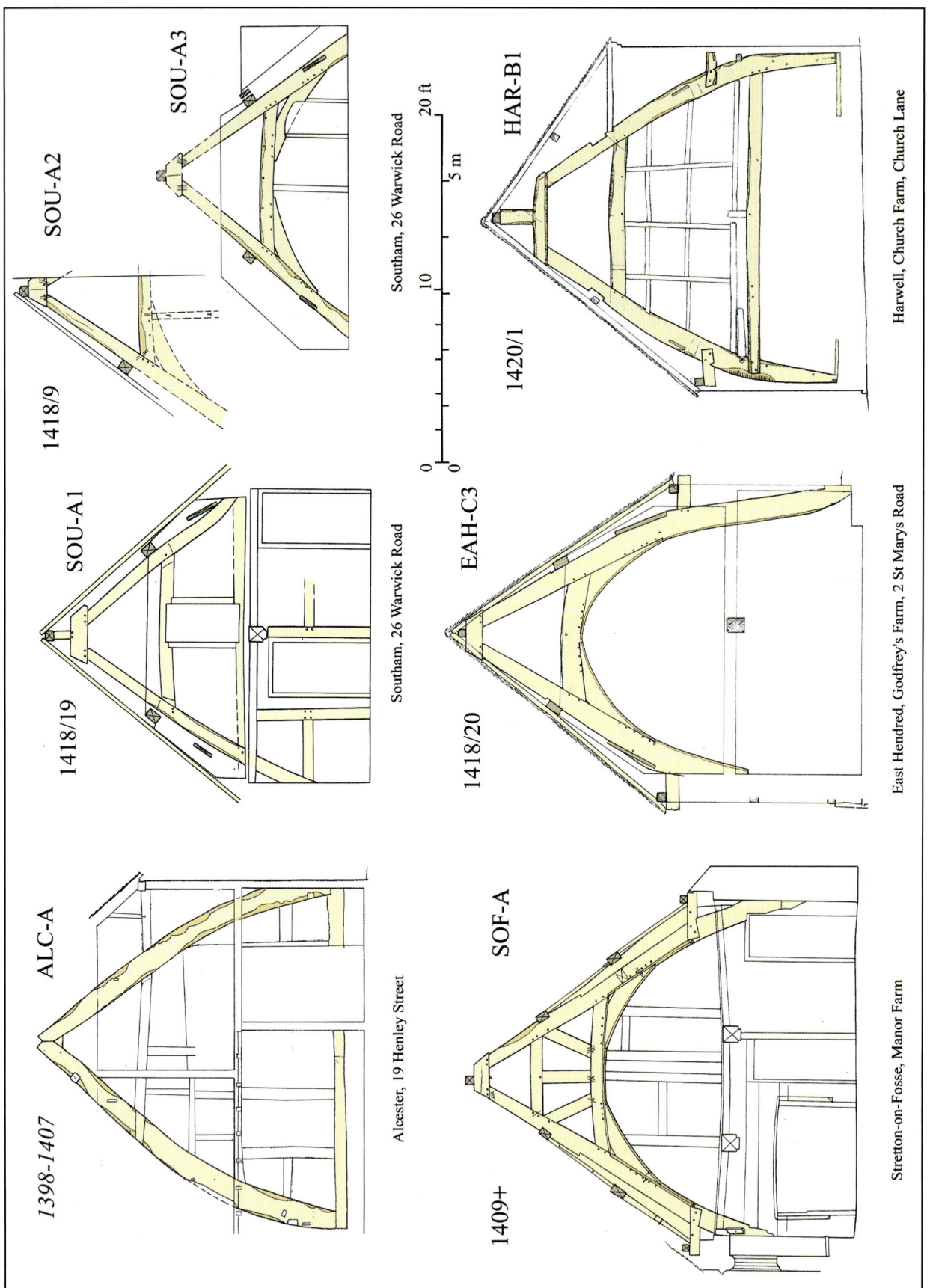

SOU-A3

SOU-A2

1418/9

Southam, 26 Warwick Road

HAR-B1

1420/1

Harwell, Church Farm, Church Lane

SOU-A1

1418/19

Southam, 26 Warwick Road

EAH-C3

1418/20

East Hendred, Godfrey's Farm, 2 St Marys Road

ALC-A

1398–1407

Alcester, 19 Henley Street

SOF-A

1409+

Stretton-on-Fosse, Manor Farm

20 ft

5 m

10

0

0

Fig. E. Crucks. 1398–1407 to 1420/1. For HAR-B3 (very similar to HAR-B1) see the report.

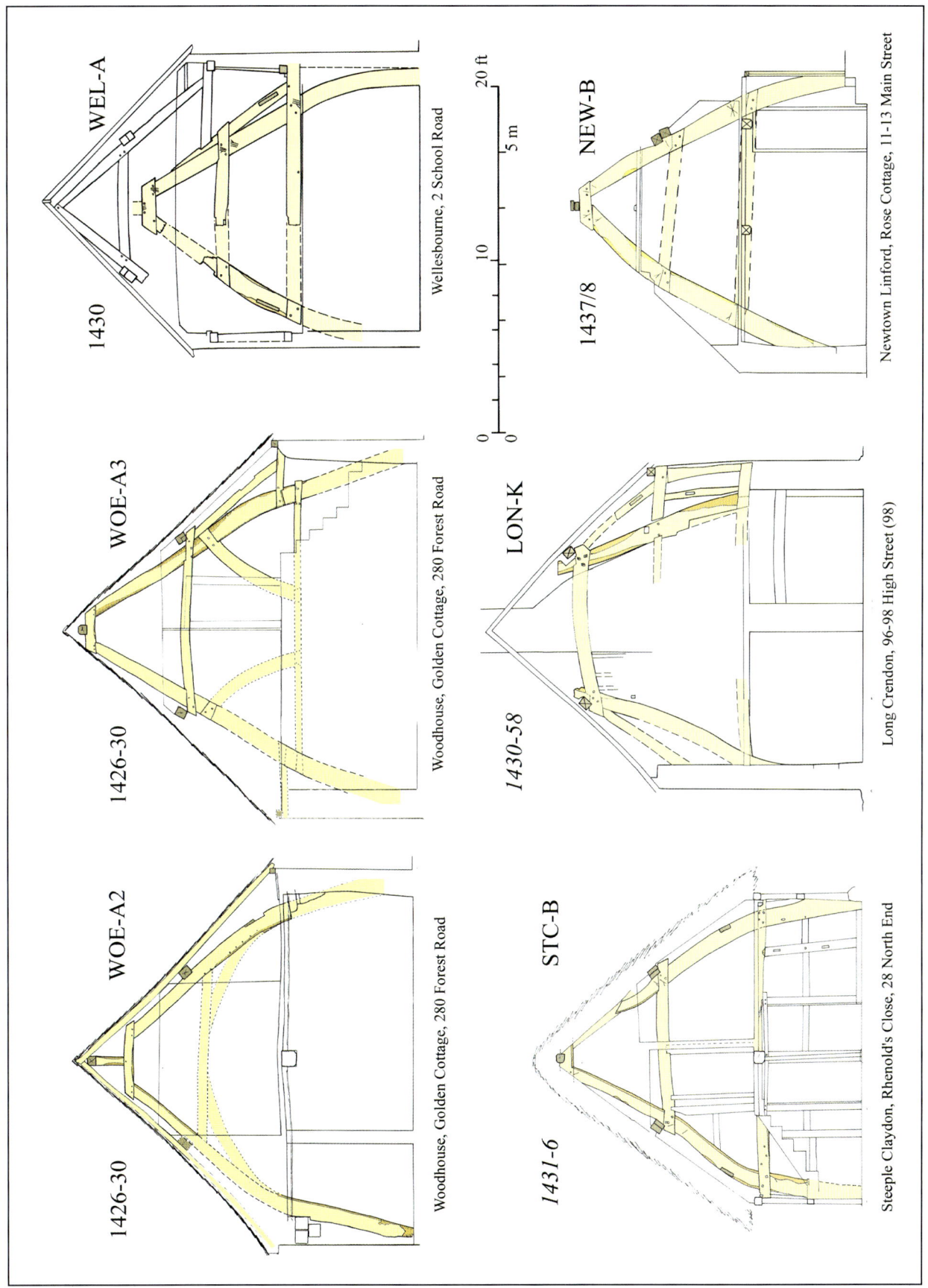

WEL-A

1430

Wellesbourne, 2 School Road

20 ft

5 m

10

0

0

NEW-B

1437/8

Newtown Linford, Rose Cottage, 11-13 Main Street

WOE-A3

1426-30

Woodhouse, Golden Cottage, 280 Forest Road

LON-K

1430-58

Long Crendon, 96-98 High Street (98)

WOE-A2

1426-30

Woodhouse, Golden Cottage, 280 Forest Road

STC-B

1431-6

Steeple Claydon, Rhenold's Close, 28 North End

Fig. F. Crucks. 1426–30 to 1437/8.

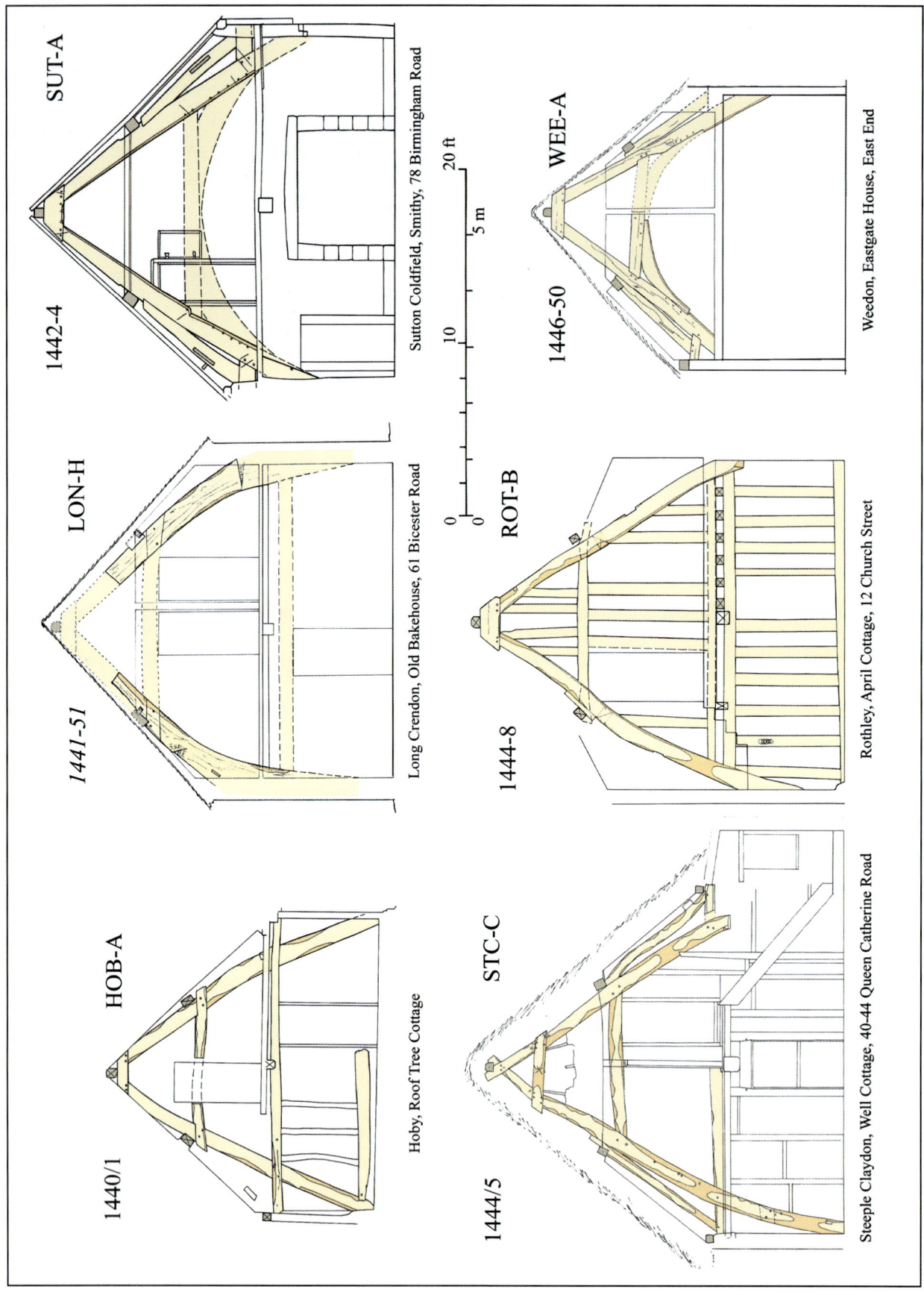

SUT-A 1442-4 Sutton Coldfield, Smithy, 78 Birmingham Road

LON-H 1441-51 Long Crendon, Old Bakehouse, 61 Bicester Road

HOB-A 1440/1 Hoby, Roof Tree Cottage

WEE-A 1446-50 Weedon, Eastgate House, East End

ROT-B 1444-8 Rothley, April Cottage, 12 Church Street

STC-C 1444/5 Steeple Claydon, Well Cottage, 40-44 Queen Catherine Road

20 ft

5 m

10

0

0

Fig. G. Crucks. 1440/1 to 1446–50.

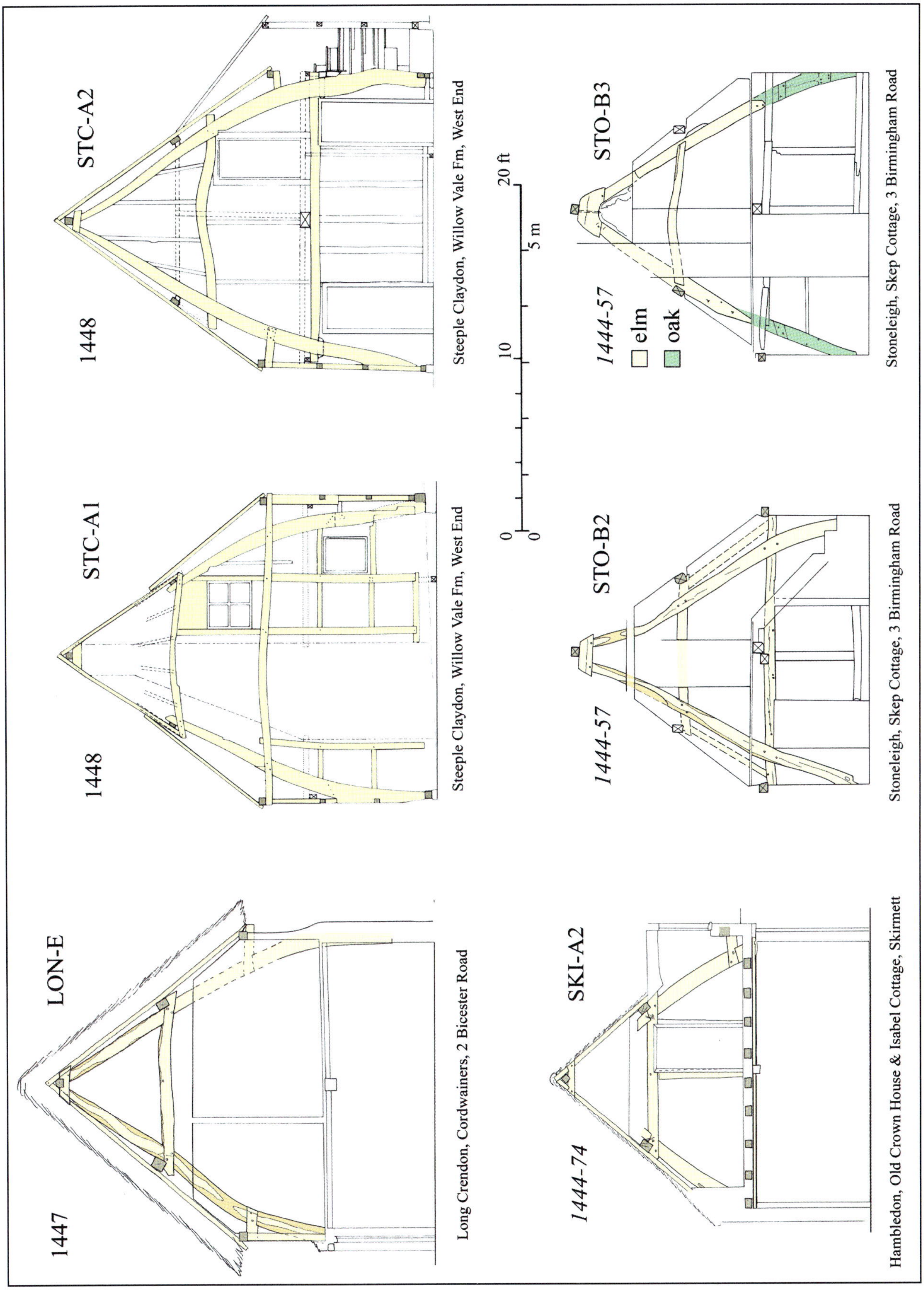
1447
LON-E
Long Crendon, Cordwainers, 2 Bicester Road
1448
STC-A1
Steeple Claydon, Willow Vale Fm, West End
1448
STC-A2
Steeple Claydon, Willow Vale Fm, West End
1444-74
SKI-A2
Hambledon, Old Crown House & Isabel Cottage, Skirmett
1444-57
STO-B2
Stoneleigh, Skep Cottage, 3 Birmingham Road
1444-57
STO-B3
Stoneleigh, Skep Cottage, 3 Birmingham Road
elm
oak
0
10
20 ft
0
5 m

Fig. H. Crucks. 1447 to 1444–57.

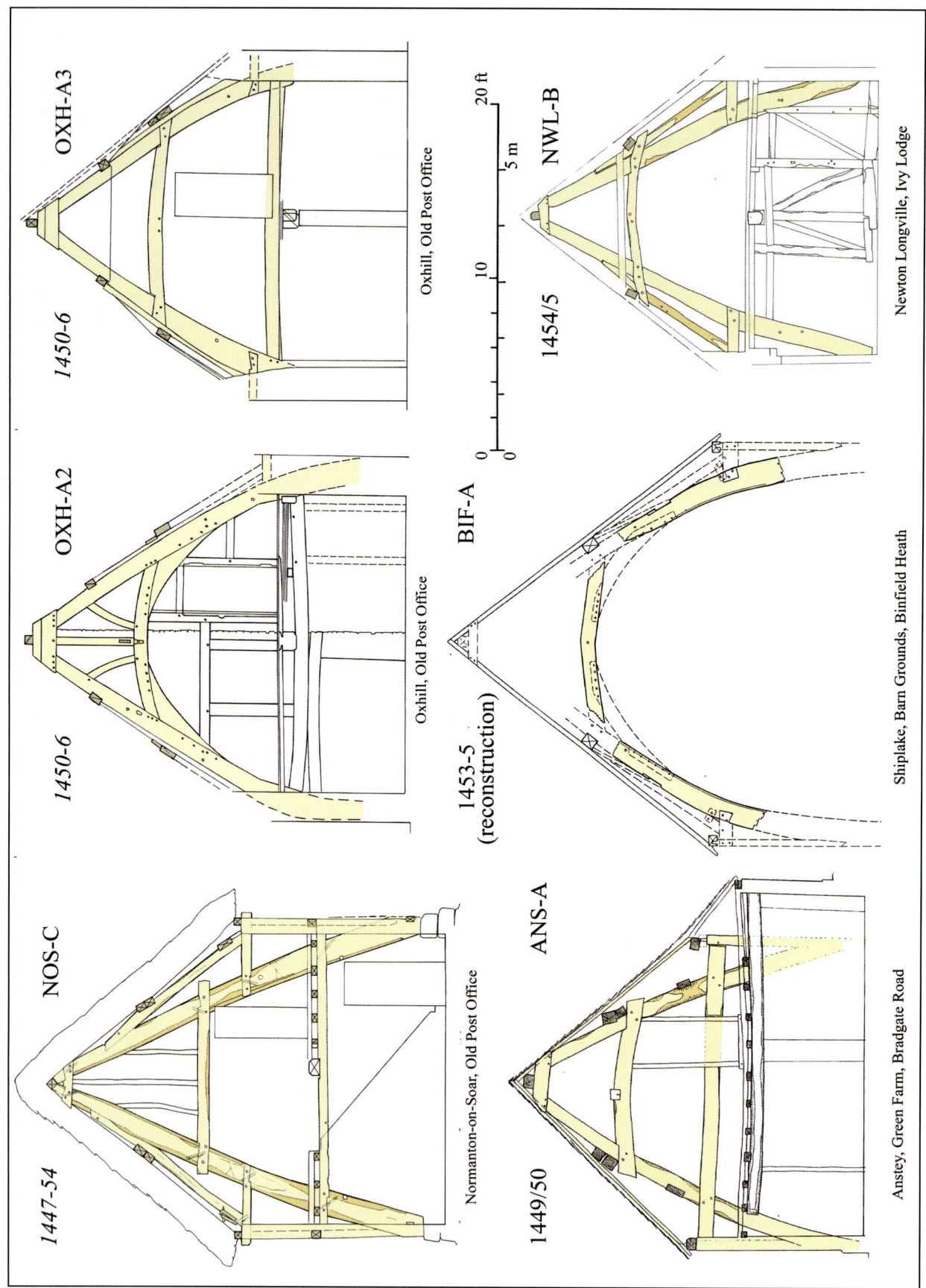

OXH-A3

1450-6

Oxhill, Old Post Office

OXH-A2

1450-6

Oxhill, Old Post Office

NOS-C

1447-54

Normanton-on-Soar, Old Post Office

NWL-B

1454/5

Newton Longville, Ivy Lodge

BIF-A

1453-5 (reconstruction)

Shiplake, Barn Grounds, Binfield Heath

ANS-A

1449/50

Anstey, Green Farm, Bradgate Road

20 ft

5 m

10

0

0

Fig. I. Crucks. 1447–54 to 1454/5.

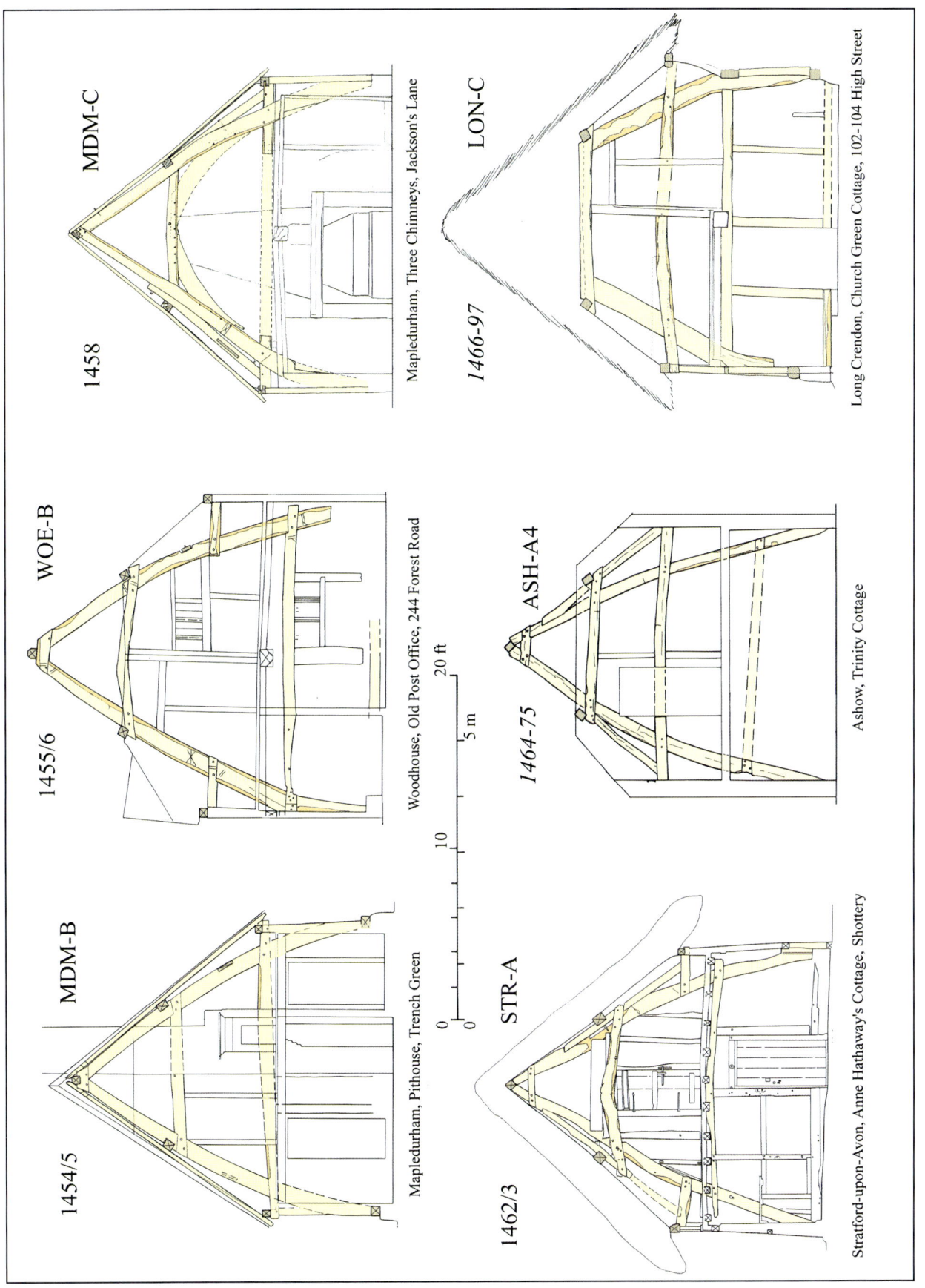

MDM-C

1458

Mapledurham, Three Chimneys, Jackson's Lane

LON-C

1466-97

Long Crendon, Church Green Cottage, 102-104 High Street

WOE-B

1455/6

Woodhouse, Old Post Office, 244 Forest Road

ASH-A4

1464-75

Ashow, Trinity Cottage

MDM-B

1454/5

Mapledurham, Pithouse, Trench Green

STR-A

1462/3

Stratford-upon-Avon, Anne Hathaway's Cottage, Shottery

20 ft

5 m

10

0

0

Fig. J. Crucks. 1454/5 to 1466–97.

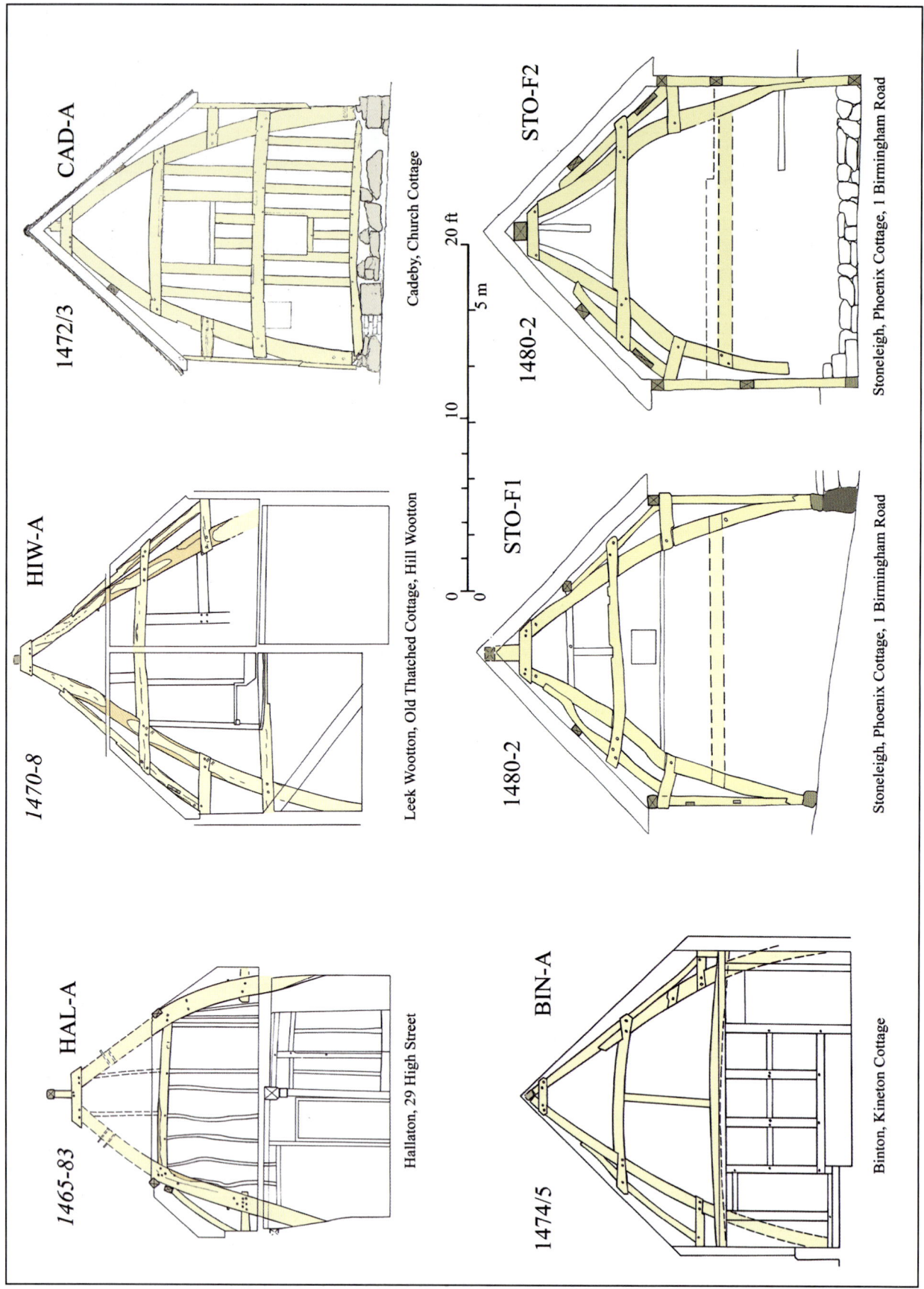

CAD-A
1472/3
Cadeby, Church Cottage

HIW-A
1470-8
Leek Wootton, Old Thatched Cottage, Hill Wootton

HAL-A
1465-83
Hallaton, 29 High Street

STO-F2
1480-2
Stoneleigh, Phoenix Cottage, 1 Birmingham Road

STO-F1
1480-2
Stoneleigh, Phoenix Cottage, 1 Birmingham Road

BIN-A
1474/5
Binton, Kineton Cottage

20 ft
5 m
10
0
0

Fig. K. Crucks. 1465–83 to 1480–2.

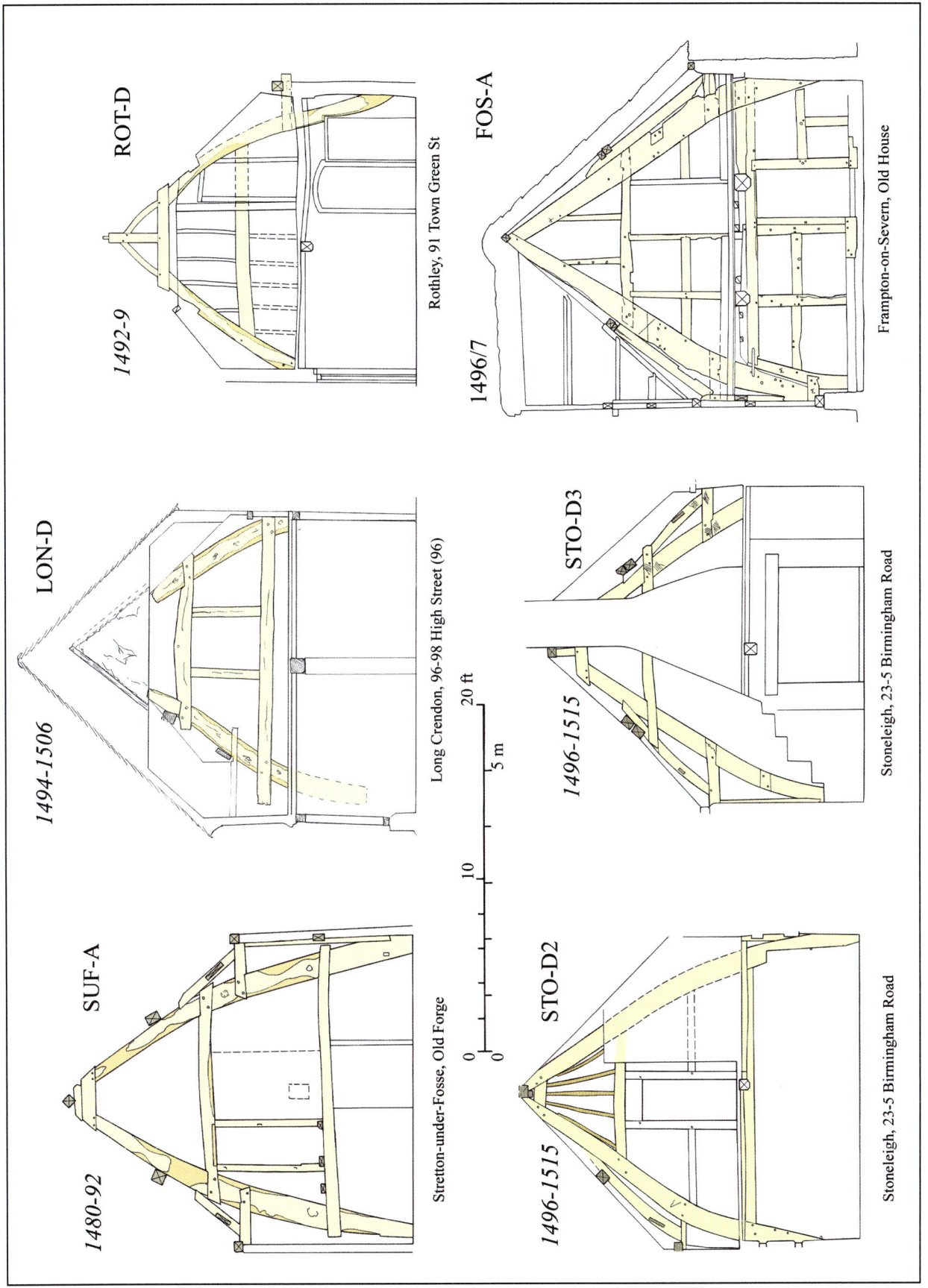

ROT-D

1492-9

Rothley, 91 Town Green St

FOS-A

1496/7

Frampton-on-Severn, Old House

LON-D

1494-1506

Long Crendon, 96-98 High Street (96)

STO-D3

1496-1515

Stoneleigh, 23-5 Birmingham Road

SUF-A

1480-92

Stretton-under-Fosse, Old Forge

STO-D2

1496-1515

Stoneleigh, 23-5 Birmingham Road

20 ft

5 m

10

0

0

Fig. L. Crucks. 1480-92 to 1496/7.

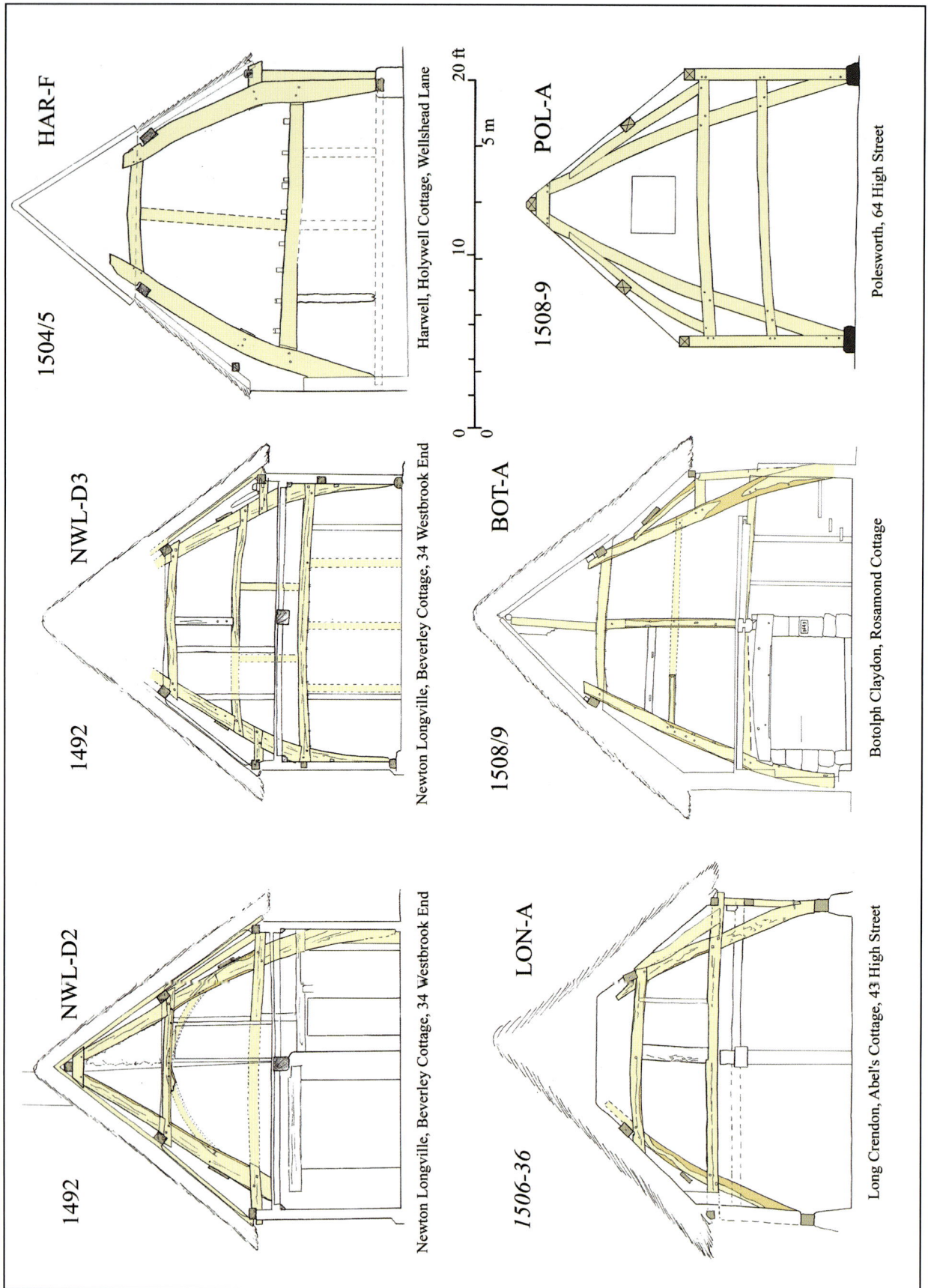

HAR-F 1504/5 — Harwell, Holywell Cottage, Wellshead Lane

POL-A 1508-9 — Polesworth, 64 High Street

NWL-D3 1492 — Newton Longville, Beverley Cottage, 34 Westbrook End

BOT-A 1508/9 — Botolph Claydon, Rosamond Cottage

NWL-D2 1492 — Newton Longville, Beverley Cottage, 34 Westbrook End

LON-A 1506-36 — Long Crendon, Abel's Cottage, 43 High Street

20 ft
5 m
10
0
0

Fig. M. Crucks. 1492 to 1508–9.

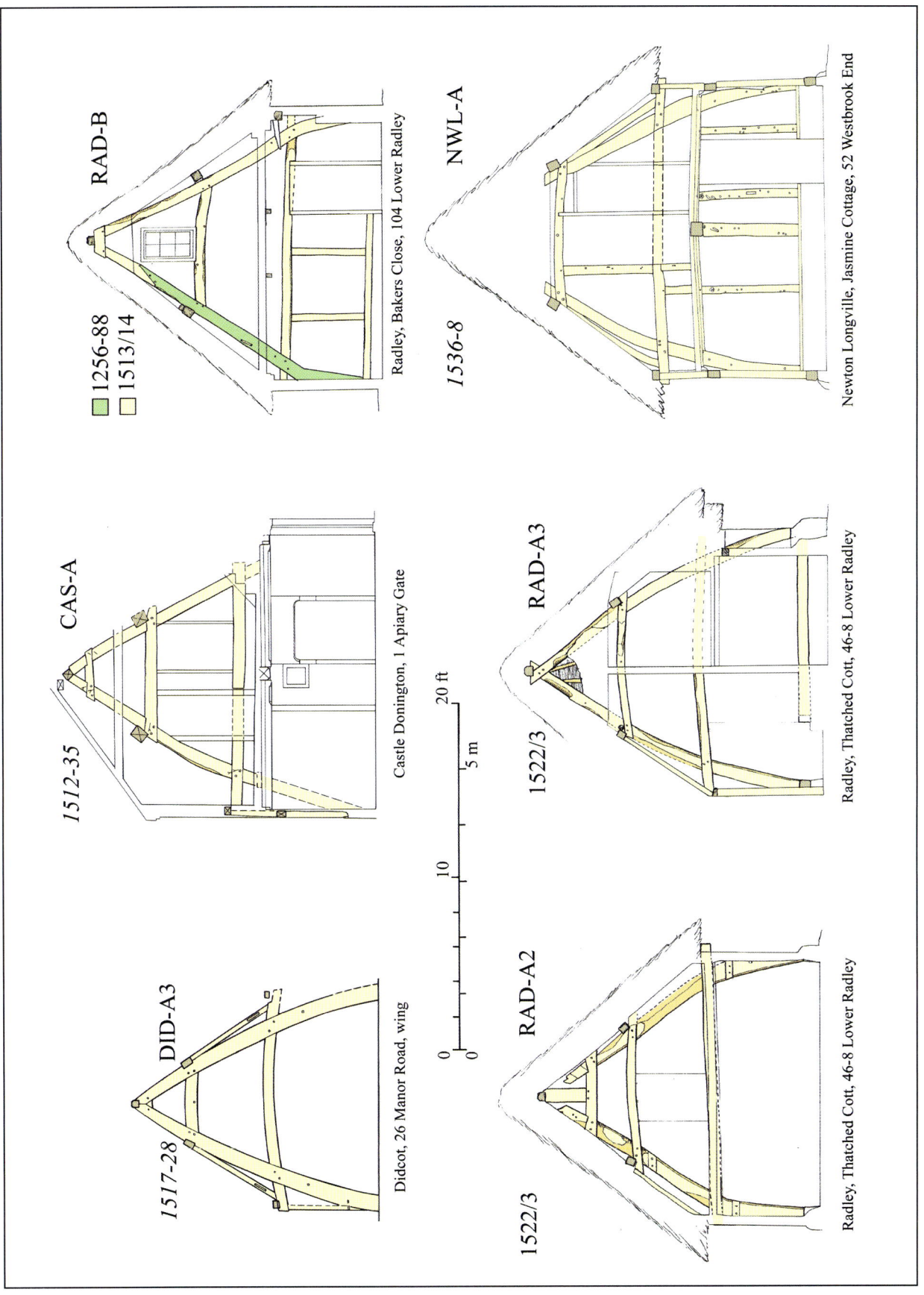

RAD-B

1256-88
1513/14

1513/14

Radley, Bakers Close, 104 Lower Radley

NWL-A

1536-8

Newton Longville, Jasmine Cottage, 52 Westbrook End

CAS-A

1512-35

Castle Donington, 1 Apiary Gate

RAD-A3

1522/3

Radley, Thatched Cott, 46-8 Lower Radley

DID-A3

1517-28

Didcot, 26 Manor Road, wing

RAD-A2

1522/3

Radley, Thatched Cott, 46-8 Lower Radley

20 ft

5 m

10

0
0

Fig. N. Crucks. 1509–41 to 1535–60.

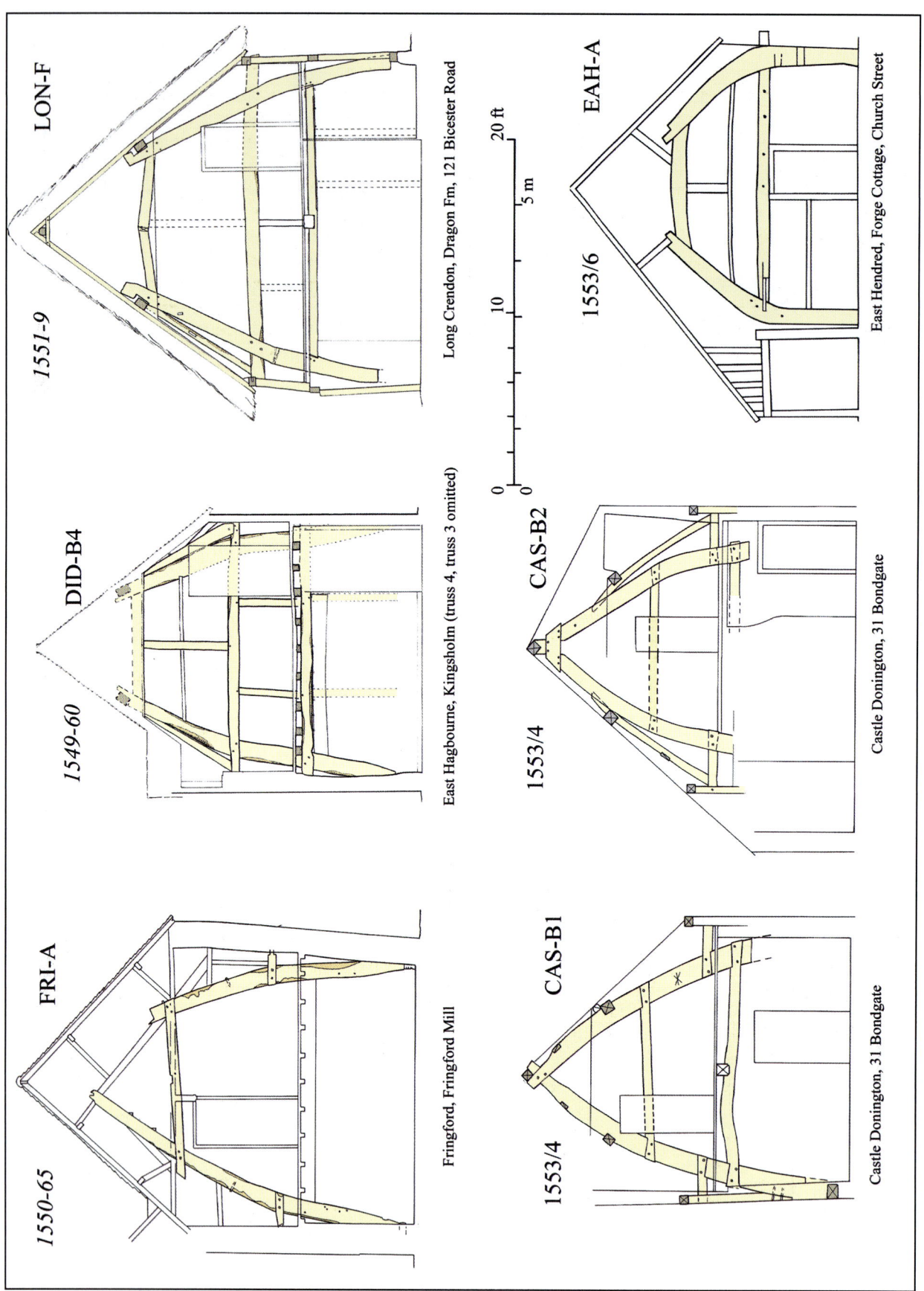

LON-F

1551-9

Long Crendon, Dragon Fm, 121 Bicester Road

EAH-A

1553/6

East Hendred, Forge Cottage, Church Street

DID-B4

1549-60

East Hagbourne, Kingsholm (truss 4, truss 3 omitted)

CAS-B2

1553/4

Castle Donington, 31 Bondgate

FRI-A

1550-65

Fringford, Fringford Mill

CAS-B1

1553/4

Castle Donington, 31 Bondgate

20 ft

5 m

10

0

0

Fig. O. Crucks. 1544–76 to 1556.

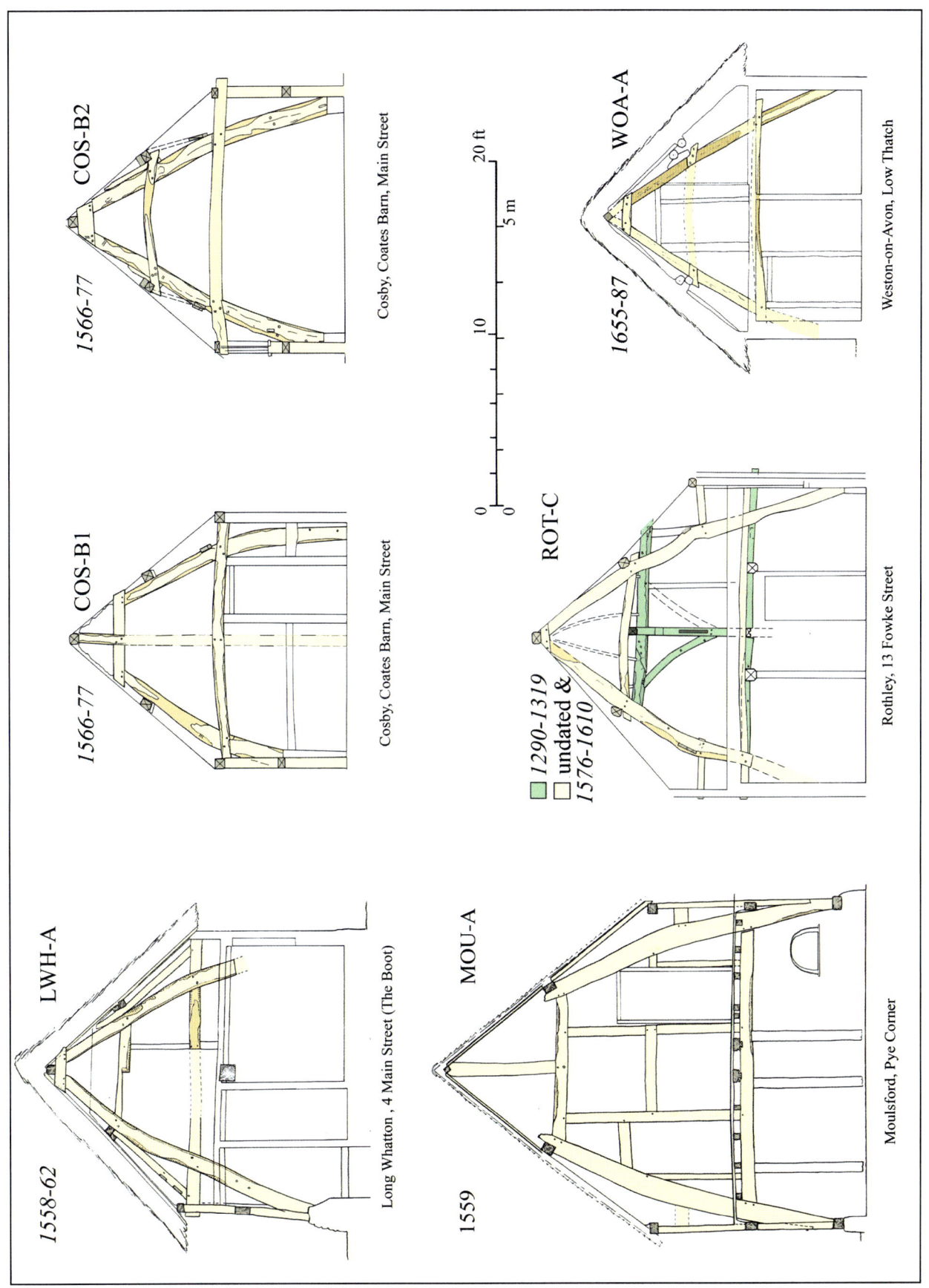

COS-B2
1566-77
Cosby, Coates Barn, Main Street

WOA-A
1655-87
Weston-on-Avon, Low Thatch

COS-B1
1566-77
Cosby, Coates Barn, Main Street

ROT-C
1290-1319
undated &
1576-1610
Rothley, 13 Fowke Street

LWH-A
1558-62
Long Whatton , 4 Main Street (The Boot)

MOU-A
1559
Moulsford, Pye Corner

20 ft
5 m
0   10

Fig. P. Crucks. 1558-83 to 1655-87.

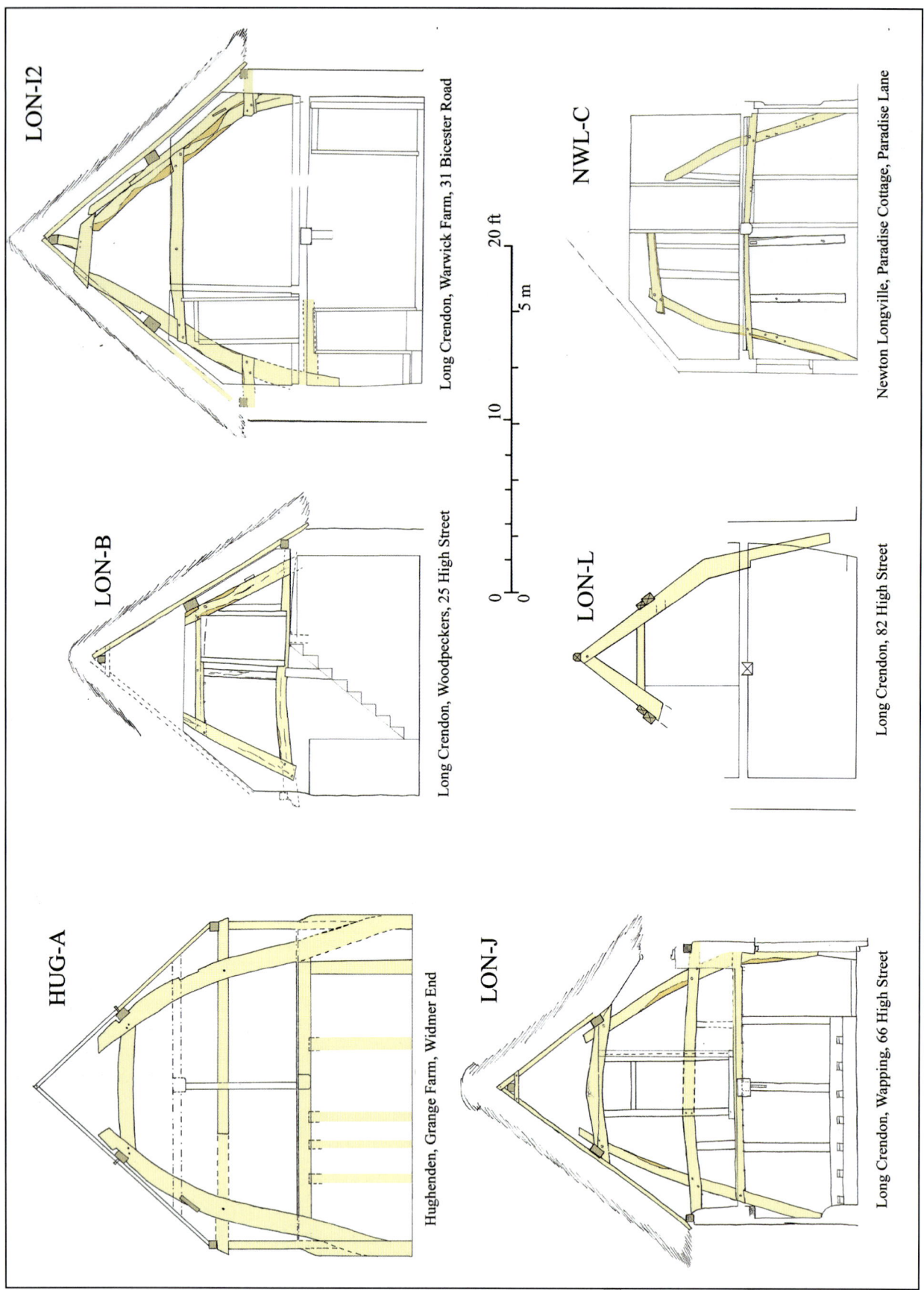

LON-I2

Long Crendon, Warwick Farm, 31 Bicester Road

LON-B

Long Crendon, Woodpeckers, 25 High Street

HUG-A

Hughenden, Grange Farm, Widmer End

NWL-C

Newton Longville, Paradise Cottage, Paradise Lane

LON-L

Long Crendon, 82 High Street

LON-J

Long Crendon, Wapping, 66 High Street

20 ft

5 m

10

0

0

Fig. Q. Undated crucks: Buckinghamshire, HUG-A to NWL-C.

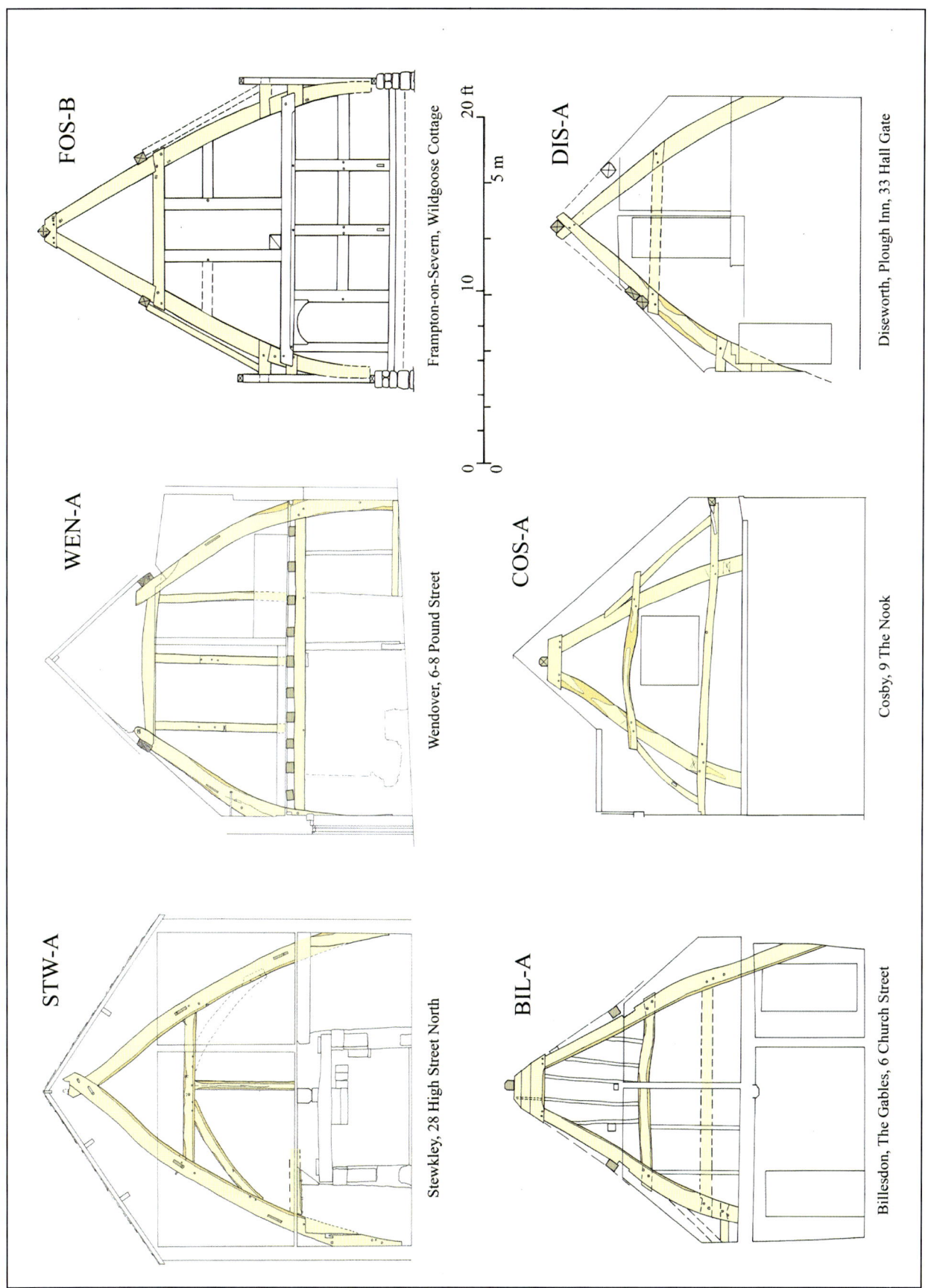

FOS-B
Frampton-on-Severn, Wildgoose Cottage

DIS-A
Diseworth, Plough Inn, 33 Hall Gate

WEN-A
Wendover, 6-8 Pound Street

COS-A
Cosby, 9 The Nook

STW-A
Stewkley, 28 High Street North

BIL-A
Billesdon, The Gables, 6 Church Street

20 ft
5 m
10
0
0

Fig. R. Undated crucks: Buckinghamshire, STW-A to WEN-A; Gloucestershire, FOS-B; Leicestershire, BIL-A to DIS-A.

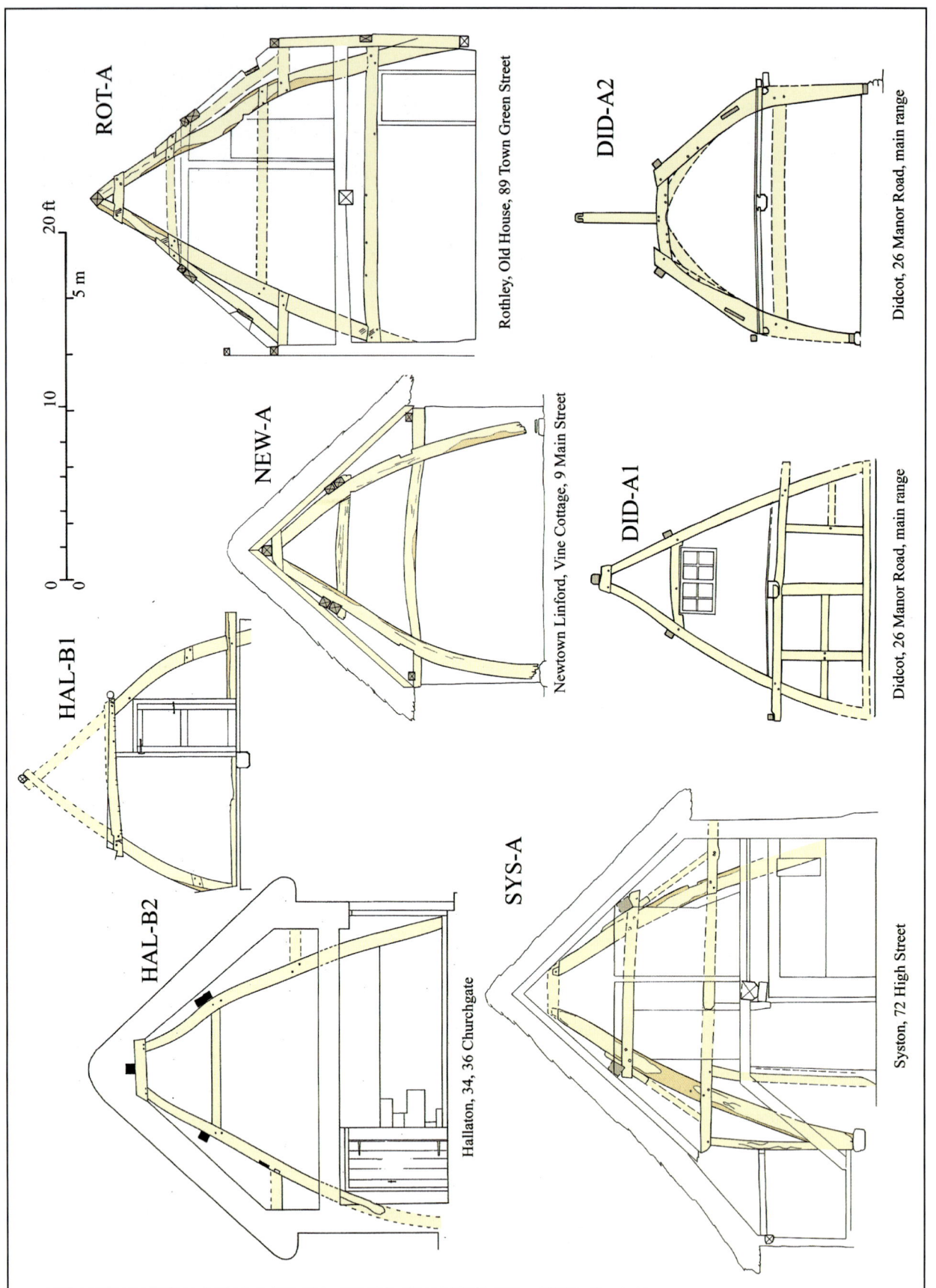

ROT-A

Rothley, Old House, 89 Town Green Street

DID-A2

Didcot, 26 Manor Road, main range

NEW-A

Newtown Linford, Vine Cottage, 9 Main Street

DID-A1

Didcot, 26 Manor Road, main range

HAL-B1

HAL-B2

Hallaton, 34, 36 Churchgate

SYS-A

Syston, 72 High Street

20 ft
5 m
10
0
0

Fig. S. Undated crucks: Leicestershire, HAL-B to SYS-A; Oxfordshire, DID-A.

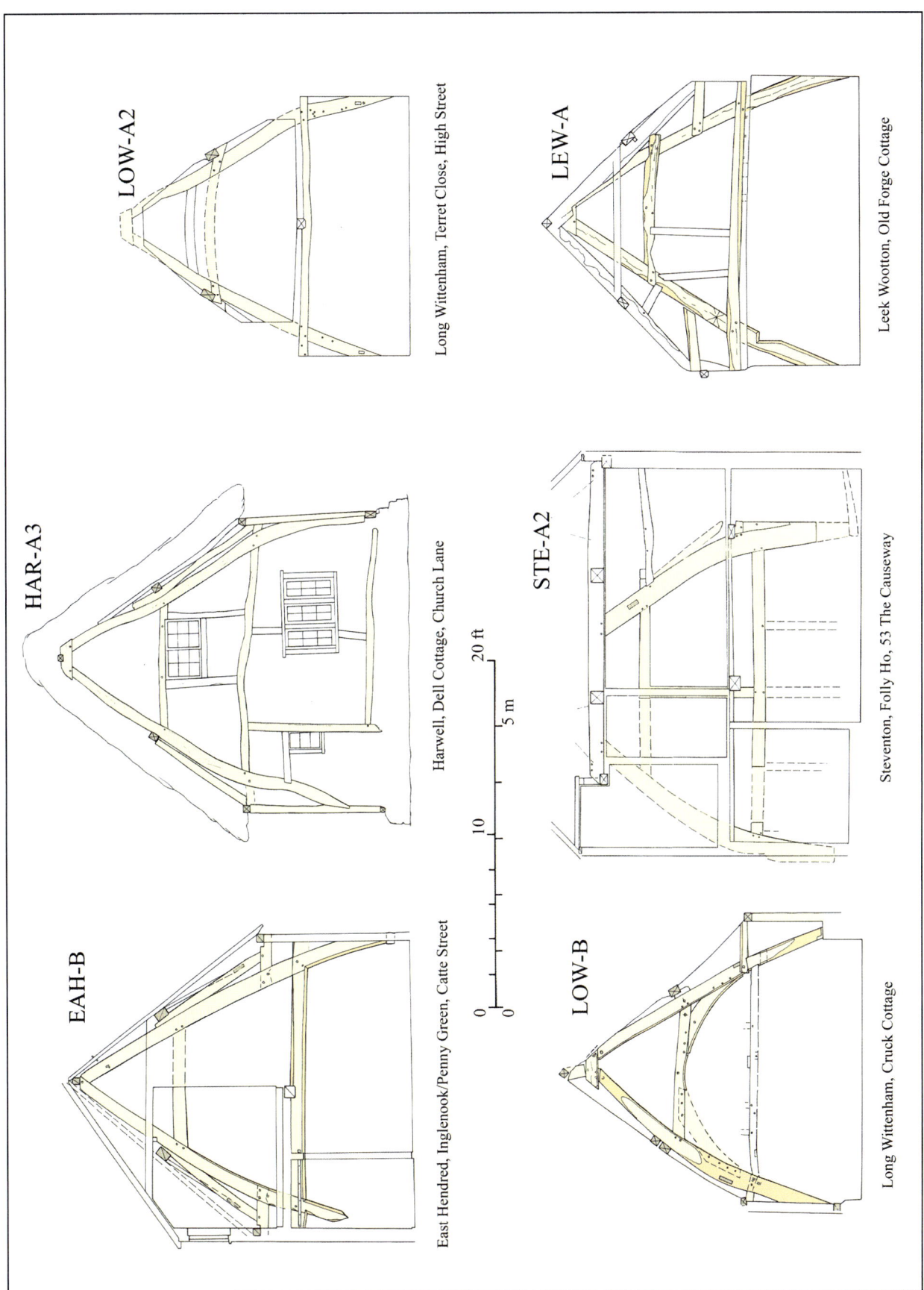

LOW-A2

Long Wittenham, Terret Close, High Street

LEW-A

Leek Wootton, Old Forge Cottage

HAR-A3

Harwell, Dell Cottage, Church Lane

STE-A2

Steventon, Folly Ho, 53 The Causeway

EAH-B

East Hendred, Inglenook/Penny Green, Catte Street

LOW-B

Long Wittenham, Cruck Cottage

20 ft

10

0

5 m

0

Fig. T. Undated crucks: Oxfordshire, EAH-B to STE-A; Warwickshire, LEW-A. For HAR-A1, see the report.

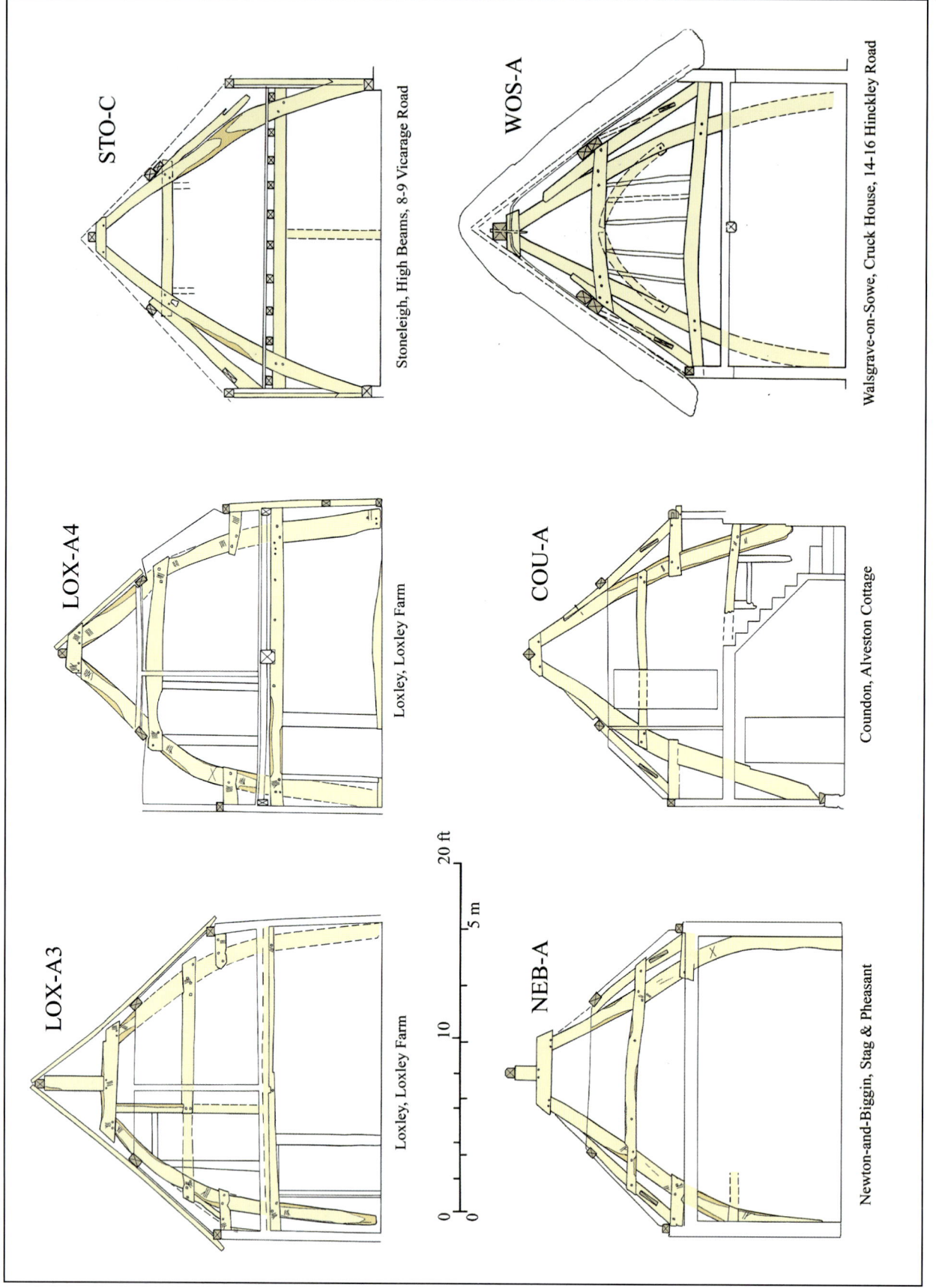

STO-C

Stoneleigh, High Beams, 8-9 Vicarage Road

WOS-A

Walsgrave-on-Sowe, Cruck House, 14-16 Hinckley Road

LOX-A4

Loxley, Loxley Farm

COU-A

Coundon, Alveston Cottage

LOX-A3

Loxley, Loxley Farm

NEB-A

Newton-and-Biggin, Stag & Pheasant

20 ft

5 m

10

0

0

Fig. U. Undated crucks: Warwickshire, LOX-A to STO-C; West Midlands, COU-A and WOS-A.

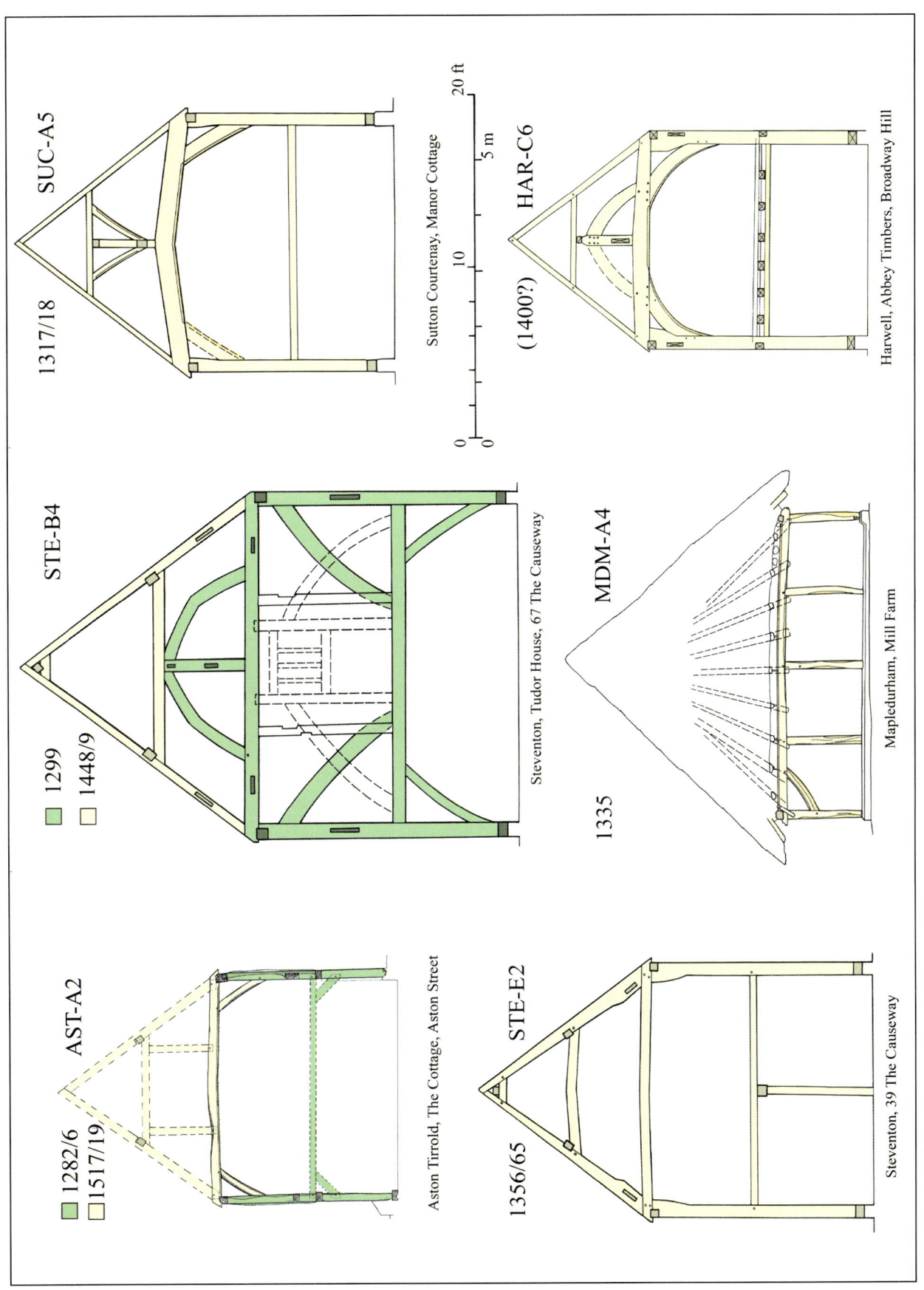

Fig. V. Box-frame trusses (1). For ROT-C, see Fig. P.

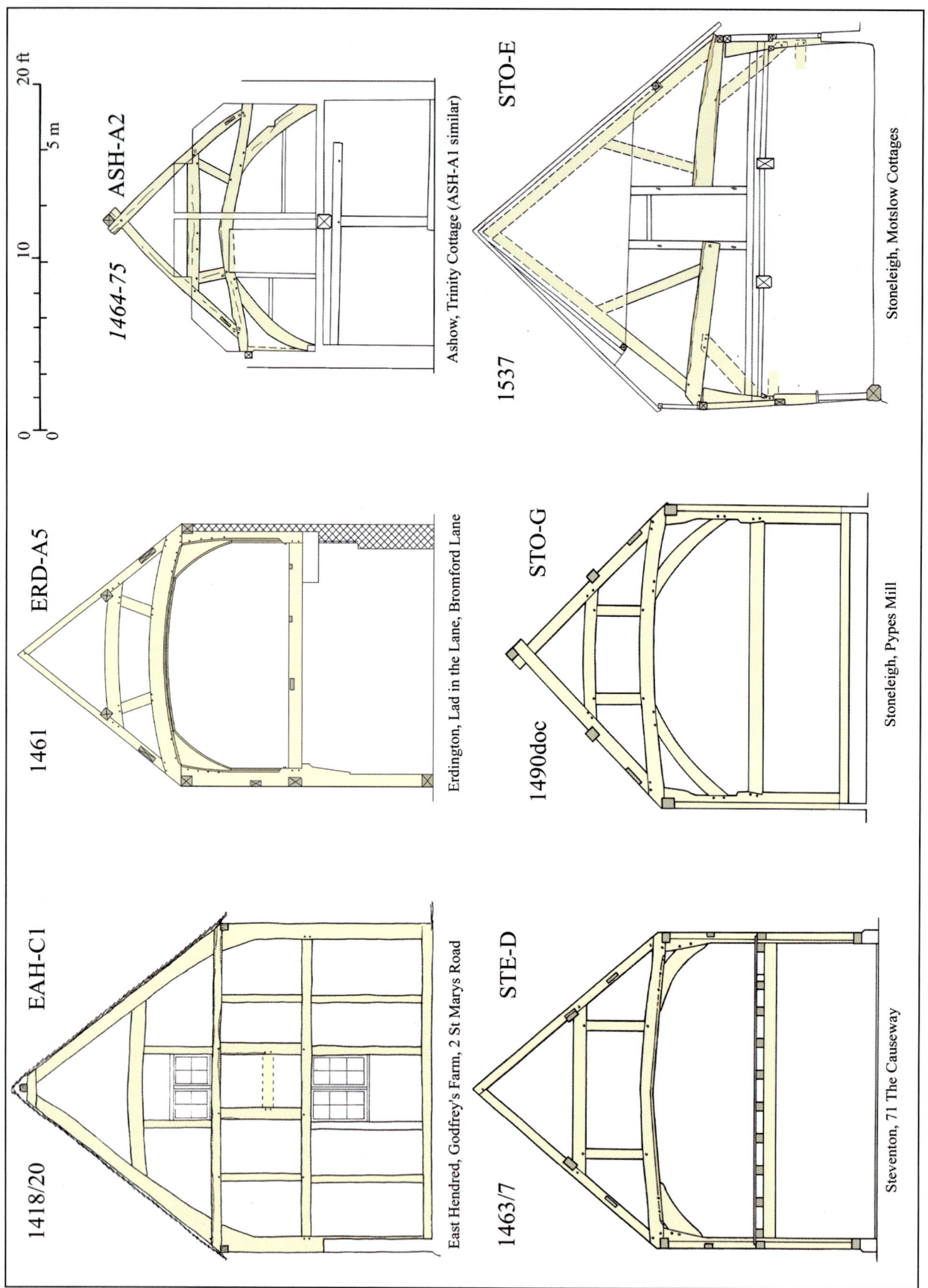

20 ft

5 m

10

0

0

ASH-A2

1464-75

Ashow, Trinity Cottage (ASH-A1 similar)

STO-E

1537

Stoneleigh, Motslow Cottages

ERD-A5

1461

Erdington, Lad in the Lane, Bromford Lane

STO-G

1490doc

Stoneleigh, Pypes Mill

EAH-C1

1418/20

East Hendred, Godfrey's Farm, 2 St Marys Road

STE-D

1463/7

Steventon, 71 The Causeway

Fig. W. Box-frame trusses (2).

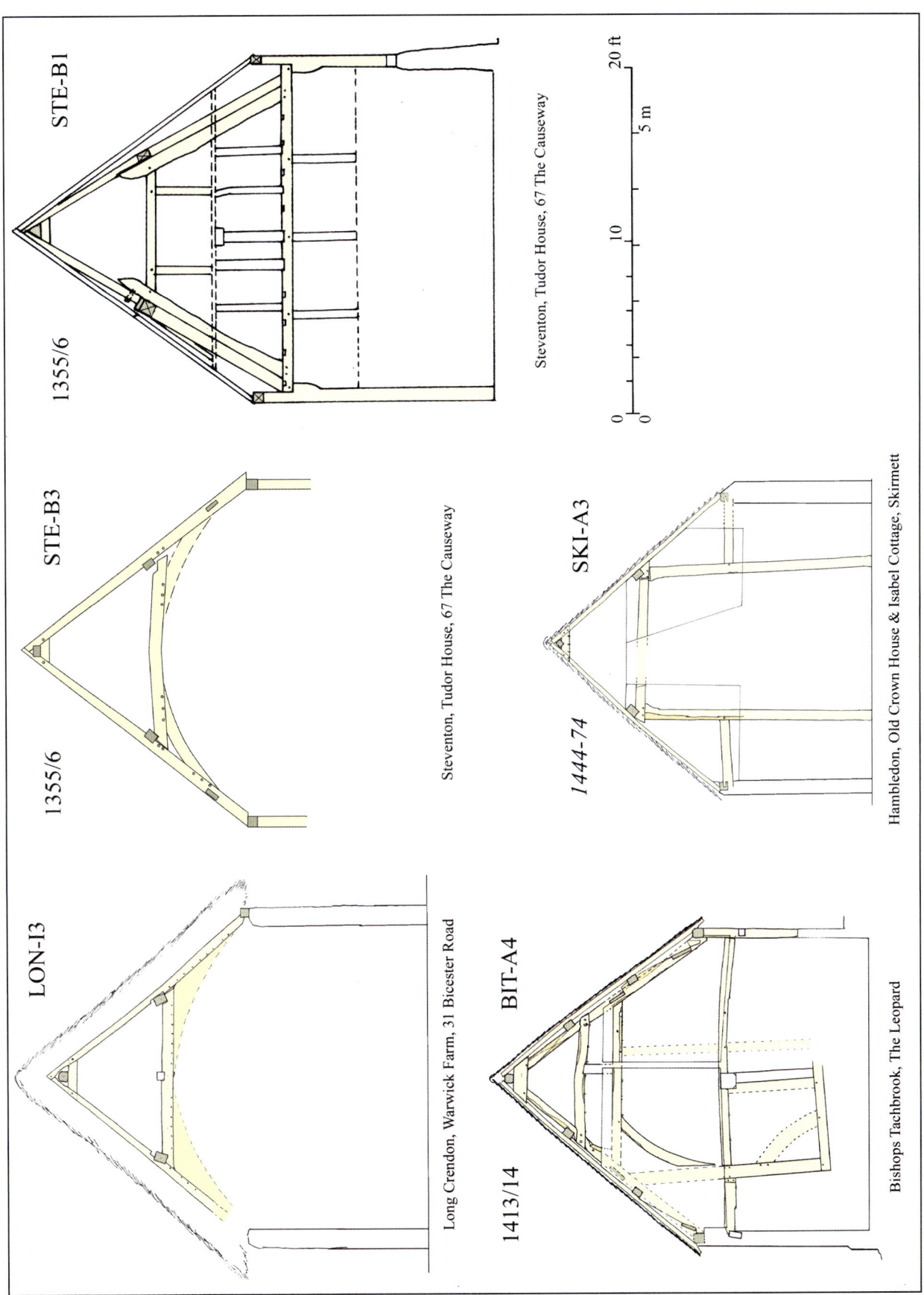

STE-B1

1355/6

Steventon, Tudor House, 67 The Causeway

STE-B3

1355/6

Steventon, Tudor House, 67 The Causeway

SKI-A3

1444-74

Hambledon, Old Crown House & Isabel Cottage, Skirmett

LON-I3

Long Crendon, Warwick Farm, 31 Bicester Road

BIT-A4

1413/14

Bishops Tachbrook, The Leopard

20 ft

5 m

10

Fig. X. Intermediate and unusual trusses.

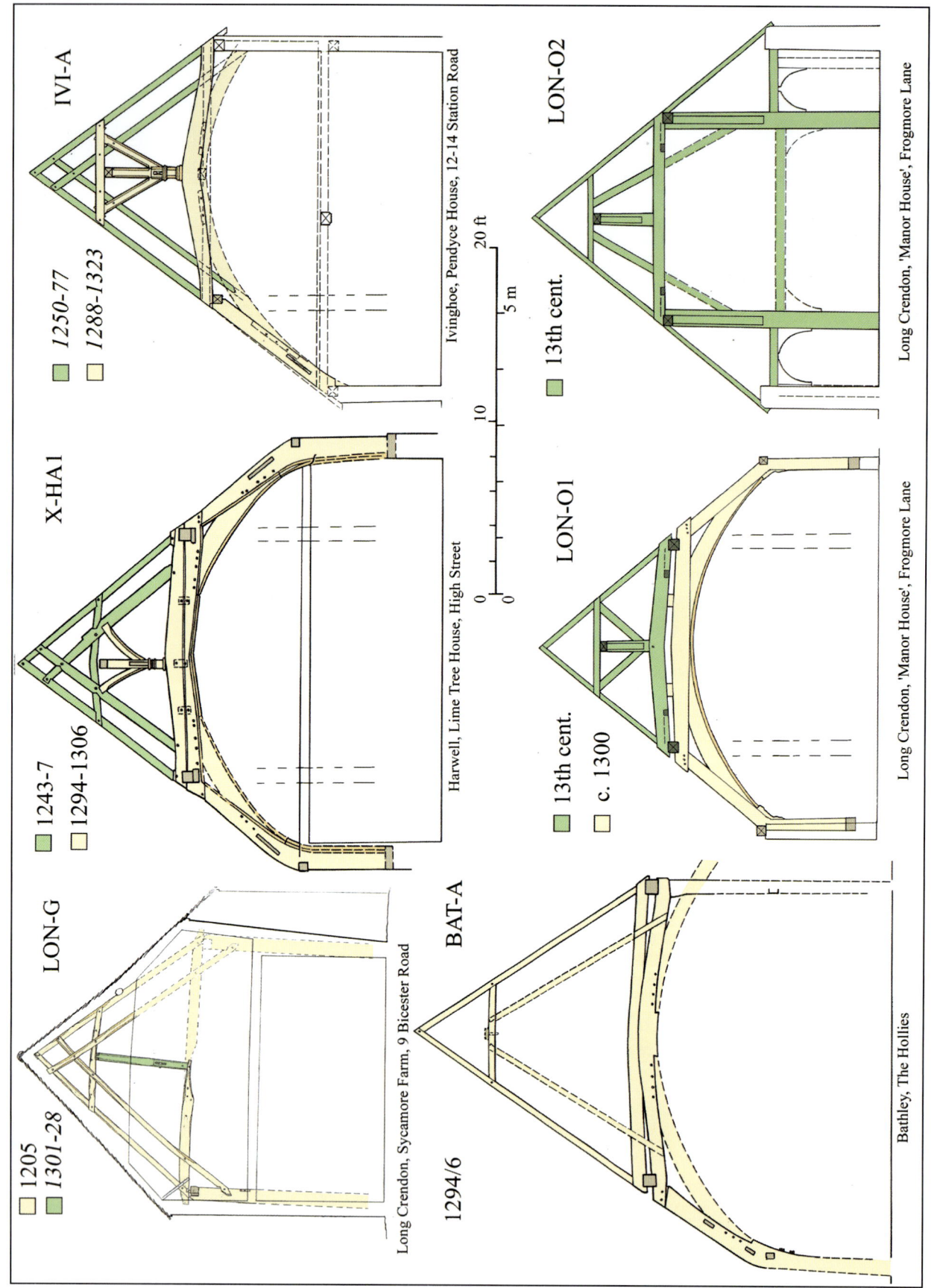

IVI-A

■ *1250-77*
□ *1288-1323*

Ivinghoe, Pendyce House, 12-14 Station Road

X-HA1

■ 1243-7
□ 1294-1306

Harwell, Lime Tree House, High Street

LON-G

□ 1205
■ 1301-28

Long Crendon, Sycamore Farm, 9 Bicester Road

LON-O2

■ 13th cent.

Long Crendon, 'Manor House', Frogmore Lane

LON-O1

■ 13th cent.
□ c. 1300

Long Crendon, 'Manor House', Frogmore Lane

BAT-A

1294/6

Bathley, The Hollies

20 ft

5 m

10

0

0

Fig. Y. Aisled trusses and base-cruck trusses (1). Notes: Dashed lines show the positions of the removed aisle posts in X-HA1, IVI-A and LON-O. LON-O has not been fully surveyed.

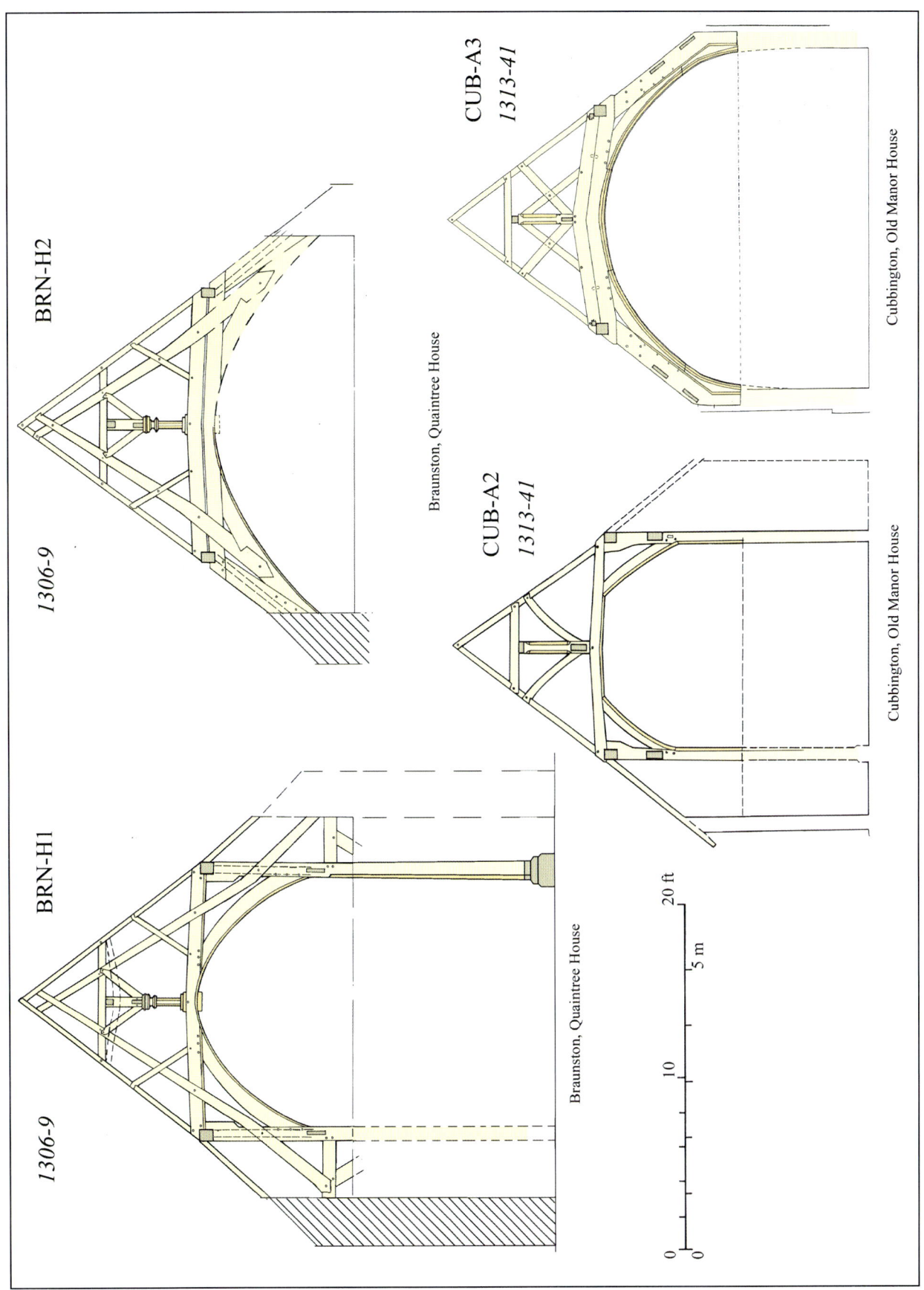

BRN-H2

1306-9

Braunston, Quaintree House

CUB-A3
1313-41

Cubbington, Old Manor House

CUB-A2
1313-41

Cubbington, Old Manor House

BRN-H1

1306-9

Braunston, Quaintree House

20 ft

5 m

10

0

0

Fig. Z. Base-cruck trusses (2).

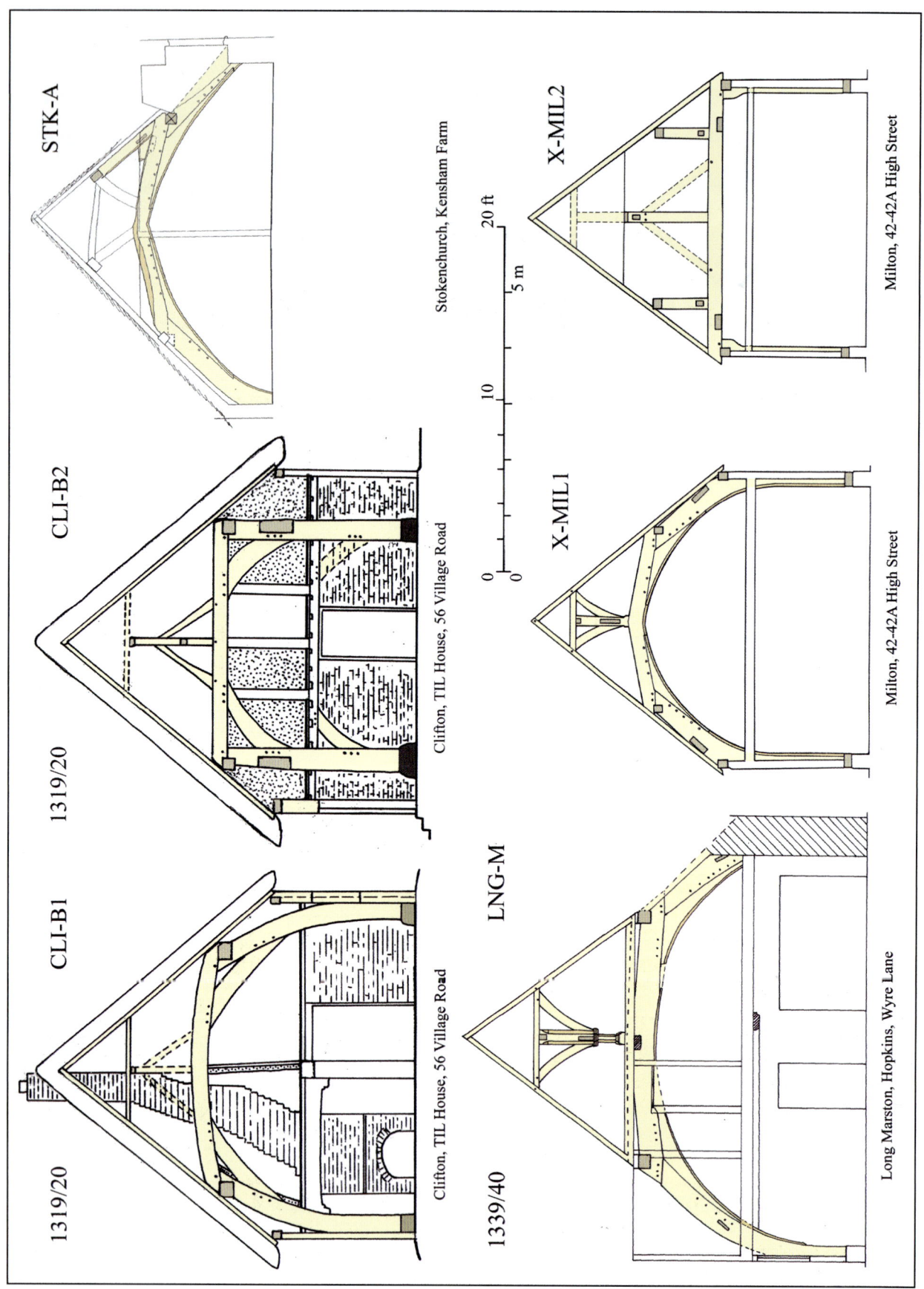

STK-A

Stokenchurch, Kensham Farm

CLI-B2

1319/20

Clifton, TIL House, 56 Village Road

CLI-B1

1319/20

Clifton, TIL House, 56 Village Road

LNG-M

1339/40

Long Marston, Hopkins, Wyre Lane

X-MIL2

Milton, 42-42A High Street

X-MIL1

Milton, 42-42A High Street

20 ft

5 m

10

0

0

Fig. ZZ. Base-cruck trusses (3).

5

The Carpentry
of the Medieval House

Introduction

The principal concern of this chapter is the examination of carpentry details in the cruck-built medieval houses that make up the great majority of the buildings investigated. It also considers parallels, drawn mainly from the cruck-building zone. The chapter begins with the carpentry of the cruck trusses themselves, followed by the longitudinal timbers connecting them; the wall-framing, windows and doors; roof timbers and smoke louvres. The occasional decorative details are then considered. Taken together, these features illuminate the character of these houses, demonstrating that they are more sophisticated in their carpentry and detailing than the term 'peasant' might suggest. Carpentry features specific to aisled, base-cruck and box-framed buildings are examined at the end of the chapter, but those shared with cruck buildings are included in the main sections.

Timber conversion and carpentry techniques

The conversion of whole trees to useable timbers took place in a number of ways. For cruck blades, the simplest procedure involved roughly squaring whole trees, producing what is known as 'boxed-heart' timber, while the principal alternative was to saw the tree in two, creating 'halved' or 'heart-sawn' timber. The two blades produced by halving are identical and of equal width, but half as thick as they are wide, and it is perhaps surprising that this technique was not used universally. The overriding criterion must have been that the tree needed to be large enough and flat enough in one dimension to be sawn in two; if it curved in both directions, it could only be used as a whole tree. Tiebeams, collars, arch-braces, and purlins also often used halved timbers. Smaller components were occasionally 'quarter-sawn', producing four members from each tree, or were made from timber sawn into several planks. However, most frequently, the smallest possible timber for a particular position was used whole. Thus, rafters might be made from whole small poles, rather than cut from larger trees.[1]

Virtually all of the earliest crucks were converted out of whole trees, and are square in section.[2] They generally retain the natural taper in the tree, reducing in section upwards. Examples include Mill Farm, Mapledurham (MDM-A, 1335), where both elm and oak blades were used in the same truss (in T2, Fig. 4.1b). By the fifteenth century, boxed-heart and halved conversion were being used about equally for cruck blades, but after 1500, many more examples of halved blades are found. These were almost always used together in pairs in the same truss, giving a symmetrical appearance to the truss, even though the crucks themselves may not been evenly curved. The halved trees were generally pit-sawn, since see-sawing (trestle sawing) is difficult for cruck blades, because of the large size and awkward shape of the trees. However, some see-sawning marks were noted on smaller members, as at SOU-A (1418/19). Thus, we can see a gradual progression from large, square-sectioned blades in the earliest surviving crucks to thin almost plank-like ones for the latest. In the later 1400s we have several examples of blades about 6in thick (NWL-B, 1454/5; CAD-A, 1472/3; HAL-A, *1465–83*), with the thinnest being the 4in thick blades at Radley (RAD-A, 1522/3).

The average width of the cruck blade seems to be about 12in throughout the entire period, but some halved blades are of exceptional width. Tudor House, Steventon (STE-B, 1355/6, Fig. 4.2) has blades about 30in wide, and the Leopard, Bishops Tachbrook (BIT-A, 1413/4, Fig. 4.3) and ALC-A (*1398–1407*, Fig. E) have blades approaching 24 and 19in wide.[3] The other extreme is represented by

Paradise Cottage, Newton Longville (NWL-C, Fig. Q), Low Thatch, Weston on Avon (WOA-A, *1655–87*, Fig. P) and the wing at 26 Manor Road, Didcot (DID-A, *1517–28*, Fig. N), where the boxed heart blades are little more than 6in across.

Some of the earlier cruck trusses are far from being matching pairs, no doubt because of a lack of access to better quality timber. This is carried to the extreme at Mill Farm, Mapledurham (1335, Fig. 4.1b) where the blades in the open truss are so differently shaped that the front purlin has had to be tenoned into the blade (butt-jointed) while the rear purlin rests more conventionally on the back of the blade. Occasionally also, the cruck blades had to be extended. Thus, at BIN-A (1474/5, Fig. K), one blade reaches to the apex, but the other stops short and is set into the packing piece. This treatment is particularly common in the earlier buildings, with ten of the 24 crucks dated to pre-1350 having one or more blades extended. This is significant given that from the later examples, only a couple have extensions.[4] Very unusually, at WAL-A (1384/5, Fig. C), the feet do not reach the ground, but are supported on the cruck studs.[5]

Use of timber: a case study

During the re-roofing in 2004 of Mill Farm, Mapledurham (MDM-A, 1335), the roof structure was briefly exposed (Fig. 8.6.3 and Ch. 8.6), allowing the roof timbers to be examined, establishing the numbers and size of the timbers used and their conversion (Table 5.1). By studying the circumference of surviving sapwood and bark edges, it was possible to work out the diameter of the trees used.[6]

The largest trees were those used for the crucks and the saddles. The saddles were halved from sections of a tree which must have been 24in in diameter. As they are quite short, they probably came from the butt end of one of the trees felled for the cruck blades. The crucks themselves are all boxed heart, thus requiring six trees in all, one for each blade, ranging in diameter from 15in to 24in. Their upper branches would have been ideal to form the arch braces of the open trusses (T1 and T2; Fig. A). They would also have provided other smaller members such as the ten windbraces, most of which were halved. These trees would have been large with crooked trunks and forking branches, and one of them was an elm. It is likely that they grew not within a dense woodland, but around the edge of a wood or in a hedgerow, so that the lower branches could spread out.

Taller medium-sized trees were used for longer elements that need to be relatively straight, including tiebeams, wall plates, purlins, and ridges. These all used boxed heart conversion, and they measured 5 by 7in for the wall plates, 5–6 by 8–9in for the purlins, 5–6in square for the ridges, and 6 by 7in for the tiebeams. For these elements,

Table 5.1. Dimensions of trees used at Mill Farm, Mapledurham (MDM-A, 1335).
For the definitions of Tree class and Units, see the text.

Element	No of trees	Diameter	Tree class	Units	Conversion
Cruck; 2 saddles, 6 windbraces, 2 arch-braces	1	24in	4	8	Whole/Halved
Boards, riven laths and staves	1	18in	4	8	Riven/sawn
Cruck; 4 wind braces	1	18in	4	8	Whole/Halved
Cruck, king post	1	17in	3	4	Whole
Cruck, soulace arch braces	1	16in	3	4	Whole
Crucks	2	15in	3	8	Whole
Collars, hip yokes, cruck spurs, wall braces	1	12in	2	2	Whole
Purlins	3	12in	2	6	Whole
Purlins	3	11in	2	6	Whole
Collars, small sectioned timbers for smoke louvre	1	10in	2	2	Whole
Wall plates, hip yokes & collars	6	10in	2	12	Whole
Tiebeams to hip ends	2	9in	2	4	Whole
Corner posts, 2 from each timber	2	8in	1	2	Whole
Rafters, louvre plates	3	8in	1	3	Riven
Ridges, end purlin; tiebeam	4	8in	1	4	Whole
Rafters, louvre posts, spurs	3	7in	1	3	Halved
Ridge	1	7in	1	1	Whole
Rafters	20	6in	0	10	Whole
Studs, 2 from each log	15	6in	0	7.5	Whole
Rafters	20	5in	0	10	Whole
Rafters	20	4in	0	10	Whole
Totals	111			122.5	

a total of 19 trees with base diameters ranging from 12in down to 7in were required. Other components such as the three collars, would have required one or two trees with a diameter of 10in to 12in. As they are relatively short, two collars could probably have come from one tree. The upper parts of these trees would also have provided smaller and shorter timbers such as hip yokes, cruck spurs, wall braces, and small-sectioned timbers for the smoke louvre.

A total of about 30 studs were needed for the external walls and the infill of the closed truss (T3). These measured on average 4 by 5in and were about five feet long.[7] These were all boxed heart with much waney edge, and would have probably required 15 trees of about 6in in diameter, with two studs cut from each tree. Similarly, the four corner posts (for trusses T4, Fig. V, and T0 (removed)), measuring about 6in square, would have required two slightly larger trees (8in diameter). The roof was composed of about 80 rafters measuring 3–6in wide by 2½–4in thick, each about 15ft long. The majority of these were boxed heart and they would have required 60 trees ranging from 4 to 6in in diameter at the butt end. Six rafters were halved, for which an additional three 7in diameter trees were needed. Finally, about 14 rafters, many on the hip ends, were probably riven from three 8in diameter trees. Thus the roof was constructed of very young trees, some having grown for only 12 years, and at the tops they could be as little as 2in in diameter.

Finally, small components such as some thatching laths and pegs, would have probably been cleft from the smaller-diameter upper portions of the trees, rather than produced from the wood left over after squaring up the timbers. This material would have been removed with a side axe in the form of chippings, rather than being sawn off, so it would be useful only for firewood. It is likely, however, that one good straight-grained tree of, say, 18in diameter would have been converted by sawing or riving, solely to provide most of the thatching laths (riven) and other riven or sawn boards for the louvre, the shutters and doors.

In all, approximately 111 trees would have been felled to construct Mill Farm, Mapledurham. Two-thirds of these (75) came from immature trees of 6in diameter or less, grown in woodland that produced tall and relatively straight trees. Of the remainder, 30 originated from small to medium sized trees, again from woodland settings, the largest one being about 18in diameter, chosen to be straight grained for easy conversion into boards, laths, and staves. Only about six large trees (5% of the total) were from hedgerows or woodland edges that provided bent and branching trees suitable for crucks and other curved members such as arch braces and windbraces.

Very few similar analyses to this have been carried out. Oliver Rackham established that Grundle House, a substantial double-crosswing Suffolk house of about 1500, required 332 trees.[8] Rackham assigned classes to the trees

used to establish the total amount of wood needed, and his procedure has been followed here. The classes start with those of 4½ to 6in diameter (class 0), and increase so that each class has twice the cross-sectional area of the previous one, with timber units in proportion to the area (starting at 0.5 units for class 0); this assumes that the useable length of every tree was constant. It is not surprising, in view of its size, that Grundle House required three times as many trees as at Mapledurham (572 timber units, 4.5 times as many), excluding its floor boards which seem to have made of imported oak of exceptional quality. Similar studies have examined a small three-bay Cambridgeshire house of c. 1600, which needed only 79 trees, and a 2½ bay Sussex house of c. 1570 for which 36–39 trees were used.[9] In both these cases, larger trees (a minimum of 12in diameter in the Sussex house), were used, sawn into multiple components rather than used whole, corresponding to 134 and about 250 units of timber respectively. Thus, their carpenters had a far more commercially-oriented approach to their timber than in Mapledurham, utilising substantial and no doubt valuable timbers, rather than the gleanings of the locality.

Rackham estimated that an acre of woodland would produce 100 units of timber in 50 years. Thus, Mill Farm could be built from the growth of 1¼ acres in 50 years. This remarkably modest woodland resource would have been easily satisfied in Mapledurham, where the houses were surrounded by copses and wooded enclosures (see Fig. 8.6.11). Indeed, the tree-ring dating indicates that even the largest trees in the house had only grown for about 50 years before being felled. Croppings of small stuff could have been made every 10 years or so, especially poles from coppice stools.

Pegs and holes

Pegs tend to be square, driven home and cut off in the more elegant structures, but often projecting on one or both sides in the plainer frames (see Fig. 5.5). The head was occasionally trimmed to an octagonal shape and left projecting (e.g. at IVI-A, *1288–1323*). Pegholes were round, typically ¾ to 1¼in diameter. The specialised technique of *skew-pegging* used for securely attaching halved transverse timbers to cruck trusses is discussed below.

At COS-A (undated), the pegging shows an unusual technique not seen elsewhere. On the face side of the timber, the start of the hole has been scalloped out about ½in wider than the peg hole and almost this deep. The ¾in diameter pegs have a thickened head which wedges into the cup, thus making a tight fit. It is not known why such a wide cup should be gouged out, as a less tapered hole would grip the peg more tightly. Another very unusual pegging arrangement was seen in one truss at DIS-A (undated; not drawn). A peg pins the two cruck blades together immediately below the ridge. Where this emerges on the back of the cruck, the peg is fox-wedged (with a wedge driven into the end of the peg) to prevent withdrawal; this technique has not been observed elsewhere during the project.[10]

At HUG-A (undated), rafter holes were found: holes drilled partly through the sides of the rafters towards their outer end. During restoration, these were erroneously interpreted as evidence for lost sprockets. However, it is now generally thought that such holes were used for aligning the rafter couples during construction on the ground, placing them on a template with a pair of pins projecting upwards, which were matched to the holes drilled in the side of the rafter feet. This technique is more commonly found in higher-status buildings and has been recorded in churches, crown-post roofs, and aisled halls.[11]

In some Buckinghamshire and Oxfordshire houses, 'collar holes' were noted, where the collar has a large diameter hole in it, on the centreline of the truss and usually drilled right through (e.g. EAH-C, 1421, Fig. E). The suggested explanation for these holes is that they were used for alignment, as with the rafter holes in common-rafter couples. During assembly, each truss could be laid either over a template or over the preceding truss, and during erection, the carpenter could sight through these holes to ensure that all the trusses were aligned correctly. Other examples are at STE-C (*1312–46*), WEE-A (*1446–50*), BIF-A (1454), LON-D (*1494–1506*), LON-A (*1506–30*), LON-F (*1551–9*), and MOU-A (1559).

Carpenters' marks and setting-out marks

The most usual marking up system for truss components comprises a series of Roman numerals scribed with long strokes on the face side of the frame on each side of a joint, or sometime with a single Roman numeral scratched across the joint. A 'tag' often distinguishes the two sides of the frame. Good examples have been recorded at ROW-A (*1383–1408*), HAR-C (1399/1400), SOU-A (1418/19), HAR-B (1420/1) and ROT-D (*1492–9*), and this system continued well into the sixteenth century. Other assembly marks were gouged rather than scribed, as at CAD-A (1472/3). At STE-C, the assembly marks were gouged over a set of scribed marks, confirming the re-use of the trusses (original felling date and range 1365/6 and *1317–46*, with re-use probably in the fifteenth century). Sometimes, compass-scribed marks were used to create a series of different truss identifiers; these include half circles and circles, some of the latter with dots in the centre and some with strokes through them. These are found from the fourteenth century (LOW-B) to as late as 1472/3 (CAD-A). In the latest buildings, chisel marks were used, as LWH-A (*1558–62*) and COS-B (*1566–77*). Plumb-and-level marks were used on many of the crucks including ROW-A (1383–1408; Fig. 4.2), WOE-A (1426–30, Fig. F), CAD-A (1472/3, Fig. K), LON-F (*1551–9*, Fig. O), LWH-A (*1558–62*, Fig. P), and LEW-A

(undated, Fig. T).[12] At BIL-A (Fig. R) a centreline mark for the truss was scratched on the triple saddle. An extremely interesting scribed line for setting-out was found at NWL-D (1492, T2, Fig. 4.3) in the form of the arc of a large circle of 5ft 8½in radius, scribed over the crucks, collar, and arch braces, corresponding precisely to the top edge of the braces. Other marks unrelated to assembly or setting out include a series of overlapping 3in diameter circles found at ROT-B (1444–8).

The cruck trusses and the frame

In a cruck truss, the two cruck blades are linked at the apex, though not necessarily directly attached, and are connected by one or more elements (tiebeams and collars), forming a truss. They are sometimes strengthened by arch braces, particularly in the open trusses spanning the centre of two-bay halls.

The blade shape

The majority of the cruck trusses have parallel-sided blades, shaped to smoothly curved profiles. It is noticeable that the earliest crucks tend to be somewhat elbowed (e.g. SUC-A and MDM-A, Fig. 4.1), although only one truss (STE-B2, 1355/6, Fig. 4.2) shows the expansion at the elbow found in some heavy crucks from Herefordshire and the Marches. By contrast, later plain crucks are often irregular, sometimes extremely so (e.g. HBY-C, Fig. 4.2, LOX-A, Fig. 5.2), while by the end of the period, the better-formed blades tend to be nearly straight.

Arch braces

The braces are usually close to semicircular in profile, as at Haselor (WAL-A, 1384/5, Fig. C), but may be somewhat flattened, as at Steventon (STE-B, 1356, Fig. 4.2) and Oxhill (OXH-A, *1450–6*, Fig. I). Braces with rather more two-centred shapes were used at Erdington (ERD-A, 1400, Fig. D) and MDM-C (1458, Fig. J). A variant was found at Bishops Tachbrook (BIT-A, 1413/14, Fig. 4.3) where the missing braces appear to have crossed to form ogee scissors.[13] At Woodhouse (WOE-A, 1426–30, Fig. F), an end truss has downward tension braces to the middle of the tiebeam. This is typical of the framing of gables and closed trusses in south-east England, but is rare in cruck trusses.

At MDM-A (1335, Fig. A) the truss between the lower bay of the hall and the service end has interesting convex braces (both ogee and cranked) performing the same role as arch braces. In contrast to the carefully shaped and chamfered arch braces of the central open truss, which are tenoned into the cruck blades and the collar, these braces have notched-lap joints with refined entries (see below).

Supporting the cruck blades

The cruck blades are supported in a variety of ways, although it can be difficult to identify the primary arrangement, since the bottoms of the crucks and the original sill beams have often rotted, resulting in one or more phases of underpinning. In what was presumably the earliest method, although it is now the rarest in standing buildings, the blades are set into the ground, i.e are *earth-fast*. None of the buildings included in the study has evidence for earth-fast crucks, but the early cruck from Upton Magna, Shropshire, dating from 1269 is thought originally to have used this technique.[14] A few crucks are supported on padstones (NOS-C, *1447–54*; POL-A, 1509, Figs. I, 5.6), and sometimes the blades stand on padstones within the external wall frame (HAR-E, *1294–1324*; COS-B, *1566–77*; LOX-A; NEW-A, Figs. A, P, 5.2, S).[15] Most often, the crucks are jointed into a sill beam, itself supported by padstones or a continuous foundation wall (ROT-B, 1444–8; MDM-B, 1455; MOU-A, 1559, Figs. G, J, P). In mass-walled buildings the blades often stand on timber pads part way up the wall, but in the only such building included in the survey (OXH-A, *1450–6*), the cruck feet are concealed.[16]

Cruck apexes

One of the most striking features of cruck trusses is the variety of forms by which they are connected at the apex. The principal types found in our study are illustrated in Figure 5.1 and characteristic examples are shown in Figure 5.2. Table 5.2 defines the different types, Table 5.3 lists their occurrence in individual houses, and Table 5.4 summarises their distribution by date and county. The mapping of common apex types in Fig. 5.3 includes both project and non-project houses, to avoid any bias from the sampling strategy.

Apex forms have been suggested as a dating indicator,[17] and they do show some chronological dependence, but this research demonstrates that most of them were in use concurrently and their usage seem largely to depend on local carpentry styles. We can, however, use apex types to glimpse, even if faintly, some of the ways in which carpentry traditions developed and were transmitted. In Mapledurham, Pithouse (MDM-B, 1455, Fig. J) has type C apexes with a square-set ridge, whilst Three Chimneys (MDM-C, 1458, Fig. J) has the more unusual type E apex with a diagonally-set ridge. Given that it is probable that both buildings were constructed by the same carpenters, it is interesting to see these different designs being used almost simultaneously.

The most frequent apex types are C and its common variant F1, where the blades are connected by a saddle which directly supports the ridge (usually square-set) (C) or carries it on a short king post (F1). These types are very often found together (e.g. at LOX-A, undated, Fig. 5.2) and it seems clear that F1 was used when one pair of cruck blades was slightly shorter than another. Types C and F1

occur in all the project counties (Fig. 5.3a), though they are least common in Buckinghamshire, and they are found at all dates from the fourteenth to the late sixteenth century. Four examples of type C date from before 1350 (SUC-A, 1317/18; LOW-C, *1323–49*; HAR-D, *1305–57*; MDM-A, 1335), and the earliest F1 apex is at Mapledurham (MDM-A, 1335). An interesting variant of apex C has the underside of the saddle scalloped out to continue the line of the cruck blades, forming an elegant arch (STE-B, 1356 (Fig. 4.3); LOW-C, *1323–49*, Fig. B). Truss T3 at STO-B (*1444–57*, Fig. 4.3) is especially elegant, 17in deep and finished with a 1in chamfer which runs out where it meets the top of the cruck blades.[18] As an alternative to type F1, a few houses have saddles greatly enlarged by placing two or three blocks together, as at Oxhill (OXH-A, 1450–69) and BIL-A where three timbers are pegged vertically together form the saddle (Figs. I and R).

The rare F3 and F2 apexes are similar to F1, but have principal rafters either in addition or instead of the king post, presumably to provide additional strength. Two early crucks with F2 apexes need special consideration. Both Tudor House, Steventon (STE-B, T2, 1356, Fig. 4.2) and the fragmentary central truss at Tibberton Cottage, Harwell (HAR-E, T2, *1294–1324*, Fig. A) have open trusses with collars carrying heavy upper principals. These were elaborately cusped at Tudor House and the removed principals at Tibberton Cottage may possibly have been similar. Both have previously been described as base crucks, but are here classed as true crucks since they lack any of the characteristic features of base-cruck houses, such as aisled closed trusses and square-set plates instead of diagonally-set purlins. However, it seems likely that this apex type was chosen both for its decorative potential, and to allow both an increased span (as for base crucks).

Almost all of the less common apex types are first recorded in the fourteenth century, but only A, D, and W/V continued in use after 1500. What might seem to be the simplest form, D, in which the blades just cross, is surprisingly rare. It is found in the earliest Leicestershire house, one of the latest and three undated ones there (HBY-C, 1380; CAS-B, 1553/4; BIL-A, DIS-A; HAL-B, Figs. C, O, R, R and S), but otherwise only in one Buckinghamshire and one Oxfordshire house. Some of the rarest types, such as H and L2, with only a couple of examples each, are more common outside the project counties; they are relatively common in Devon and Wales respectively.[19] We can only speculate that their carpenters had encountered these forms while working away from the Midlands.

The dominance of apexes C and F1 is only challenged by the type W or *truncated cruck*, in which the blades extend no higher than the collar and the upper roof is carried only on the common rafters (STC-A, Fig. 5.2). We can associate with this the type V apex which is structurally identical, but is used specifically as the end truss of a half-hipped roof.[20]

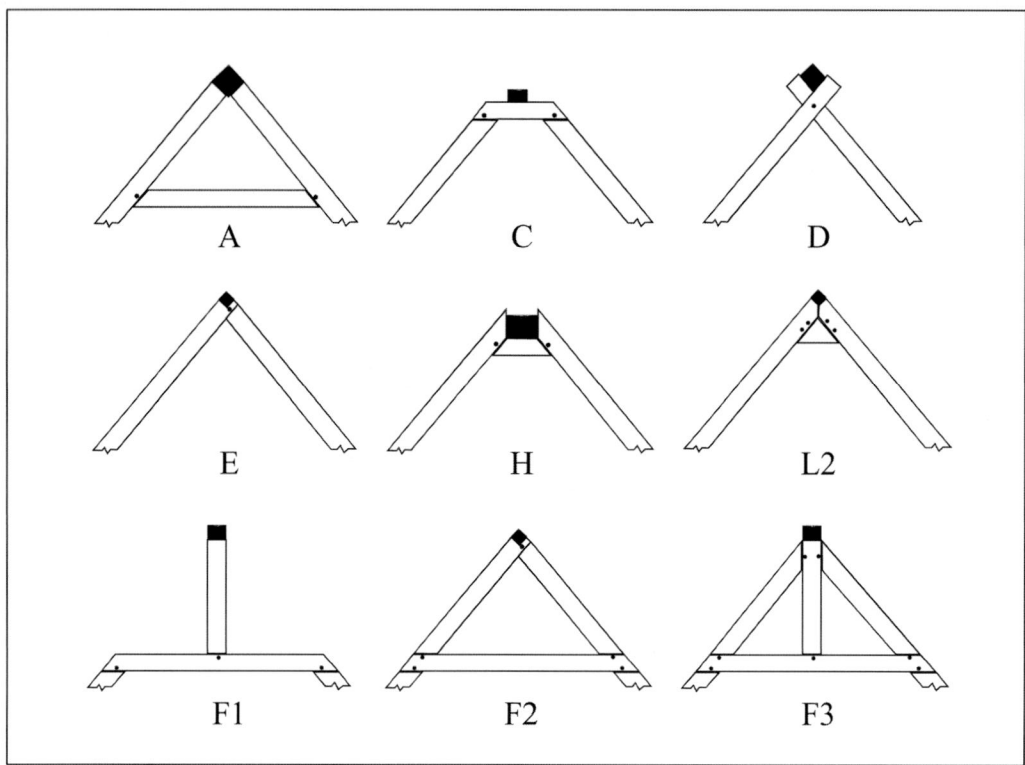

Fig. 5.1. Types of cruck apex recorded in project houses. Redrawn from Alcock, *Cruck construction*. For types W and W1 (and V, identical to W), see Fig. 5.2.

Table 5.2. Description of cruck apex types.

Types B and L1 have not been recorded in project buildings.

A	Blades hardly meet and are not jointed at the apex, being held together by the collar
B	Blades meet on a vertical line, with a collar below the apex
C	Blades held by a saddle or yoke carrying only a ridge-piece (usually but not necessarily square-set)
D	Blades cross
E	Blades jointed together diagonally
F	Blades held by a saddle (sometimes set very low) carrying extra structure F1: Carrying a short king-post (possibly with braces) (contrast *W2* with long king post rising from collar) F2: Carrying two rafters F3: Carrying two rafters meeting on a kingpost rising from the saddle
H	Blades held by a yoke, rising to clasp the ridge-piece, with a gap between the blades (ridge usually but not necessarily square-set)
L	Blades held together by a (triangular) block just under the apex L1: blades hardly meet above block (compare A) L2: blades meet on vertical line below ridge (compare B)
V	Half-hipped or full-hipped cruck truss in an end wall
W	Blades truncated above collar, passing the collar but with no upper structure (contrast F) W1: As W, but with *long* king post rising from collar (contrast *F1* with short king post)

Type W is principally found in Buckinghamshire with the only Oxfordshire examples clustered in the south of the county (Fig. 5.3b).[21] Virtually all the examples are relatively late, from the later fifteenth and the sixteenth century, although two are from the fourteenth century (MDM-A, 1335, Fig. A and STE-C, 1365/6, Fig. B). Although the first of these is an internal truss, it is in effect at the end of the house (i.e. type V), since it was originally set part-way up a fully-hipped roof, with a lean-to beyond it (now removed). The frame structure of STE-C was apparently

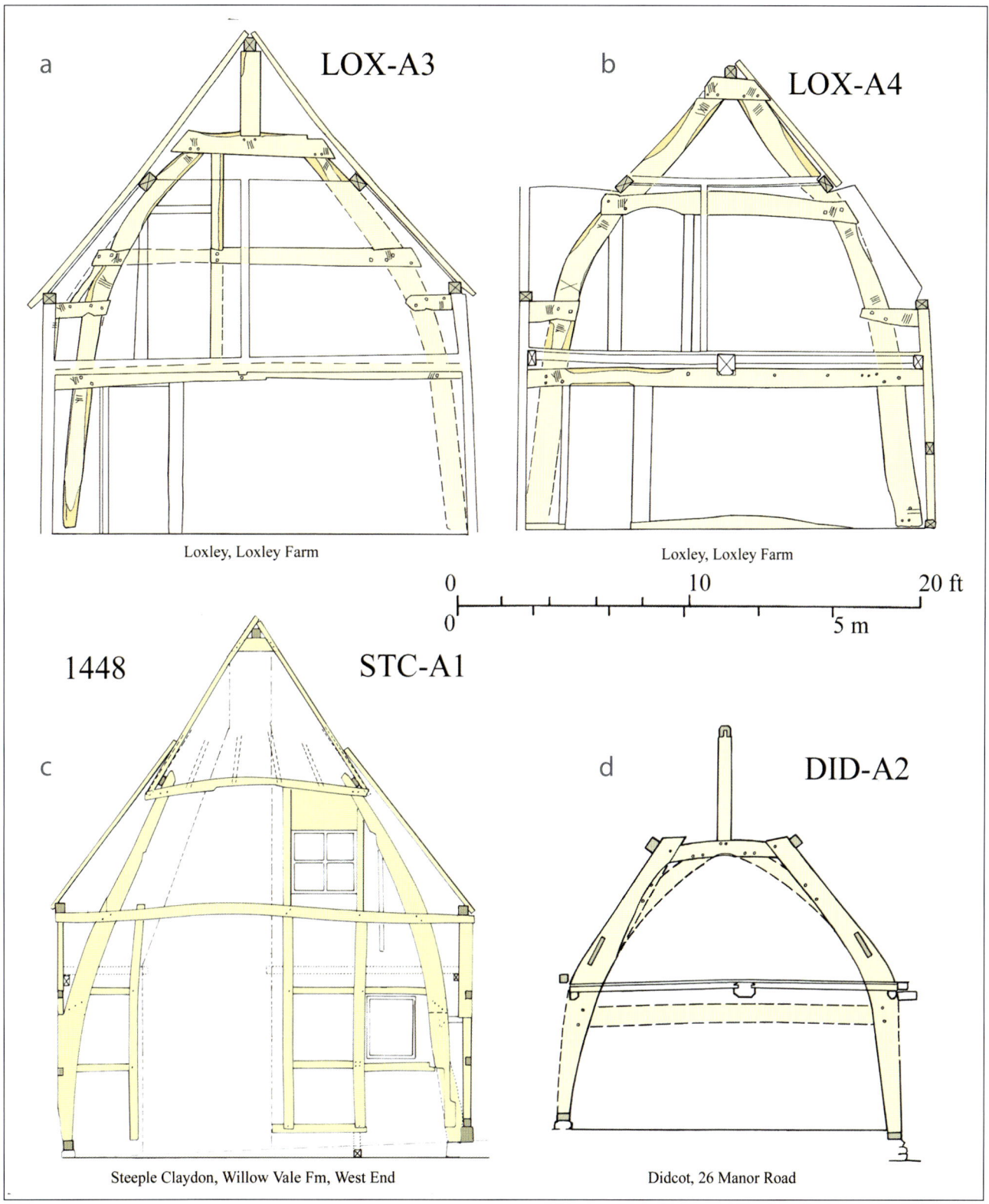

Fig. 5.2. Examples of the major cruck apex types: (upper) (a) apex C; (b) apex F1, both at Loxley Farm, Loxley, Warwickshire (LOX-A, undated); (lower) (c) Apex W at Willow Vale Fm, West End, Steeple Claydon, Buckinghamshire (STC-A, 1448). (d) Apex W1 at 26 Manor Road, Didcot, Oxfordshire (DID-A, T2, undated). Apex V (not illustrated) is identical to Apex W, but forms the end truss of the building and carries a half-hip.

Table 5.3. Cruck apexes and dates.

Code	Cou	Apex	Date
ALC-A	WA	L2	*1398–1407*
ANS-A	LE	C	1449/50
ASH-A	WA	A	*1464–75*
BIL-A	LE	C D	
BIN-A	WA	A	1474/5
BIT-A	WA	C	1413/14
BOT-A	BU	W1 V	1507–9
CAD-A	LE	A F1	1472/3
CAS-A	LE	A	*1512–35*
CAS-B	LE	D F1	1553/4
COS-A	LE	C	
COS-B	LE	C F1 H	*1566–77*
COU-A	WM	C	
DID-A	OX	B C W1	
DID-A	OX	L2	*1517–28*
DID-B	OX	W	*1549–60*
DIS-A	LE	A D	
EAH-A	OX	W	1553/6
EAH-B	OX	E	
EAH-C	OX	C	1418/20
ERD-A	WM	E F1	1400
FOS-A	GL	E	1496/7
FOS-B	GL	C E V	
FRI-A	OX		*1550–65*
HAL-A	LE	C F1	*1465–83*
HAL-B	LE	C D	
HAR-A	OX	C	
HAR-B	OX	F1	1420/1
HAR-C	OX	C F3	1399/1400
HAR-D	OX	C W1	*1305–57*
HAR-E	OX	F2 V	*1294–1324*
HAR-F	OX	W W1	1504/5
HBY-C	LE	D	1380
HIW-A	WA	C	1470–8
HOB-A	LE	C	1440/1

Code	Cou	Apex	Date
HUG-A	BU	W	
LEW-A	WA	C	
LON-A	BU	W	*1506–36*
LON-B	BU	W V	
LON-C	BU		*1466–97*
LON-D	BU	W	*1494–1506*
LON-E	BU	C	1447
LON-F	BU	W V	*1551–9*
LON-G	BU	W	
LON-H	BU	C	*1441–51*
LON-I	BU	F1	
LON-J	BU	W	
LON-K	BU	W	*1430–58*
LON-L	BU	E	
LOW-A	OX	C V	
LOW-B	OX	D F1 V	
LOW-C	OX	C	*1323–49*
LOX-A	WA	C F1	
LWH-A	LE	C	*1558–62*
MDM-A	OX	C F1 W	1335
MDM-B	OX	C W V	1454/5
MDM-C	OX	E V	1458
MOU-A	OX	W1	1559
NEB-A	WA	F1	
NEW-A	LE	C	
NEW-B	LE	C	1437/8
NOS-C	NT	A	*1447–54*
NWL-A	BU	W V	1536–8
NWL-B	BU	C	1454/5
NWL-C	BU	W V	
NWL-D	BU	C V	1492
OXH-A	WA	C	*1450–6*
POL-A	WA	C	1508/9
RAD-A	OX	D F1	1522/3
RAD-B	OX	C	1513/14

Code	Cou	Apex	Date
ROT-A	LE	A F1 F2	
ROT-B	LE	C	1444–8
ROT-C	LE	C	
ROT-C	LE	C F1	*1576–1610*
ROT-D	LE	C F3	1492–9
ROW-A	WA	A	*1383–1408*
SKI-A	BU	W	*1444–74*
SOF-A	WA	C	1409+
SOU-A	WA	C F1	1418/19
STC-A	BU	C V	1448
STC-B	BU	C V	*1431–6*
STC-C	BU	F2 V	1444/5
STE-A	OX		
STE-B	OX	F2	1355/6
STE-C	OX	F1 W	1365/6
STE-E	OX	C	1350/1
STO-B	WA	C	*1444–57*
STO-C	WA	C	
STO-D	WA	C F1 H	*1496–1515*
STO-F	WA	C F1	1480–2
STR-A	WA	A	1462/3
STW-A	BU	D	
SUC-A	OX	C	1317/18
SUF-A	WA	C	*1480–92*
SUT-A	WM	C	1442–4
SYS-A	LE	C	
WAL-A	WA	C	1384/5
WEE-A	BU	C	1446–50
WEL-A	WA	C F1	1430
WEN-A	BU	W	
WOA-A	WA	A	*1655–87*
WOE-A	LE	C F1	1426–30
WOE-B	LE	C	1455/6
WOR-A	WA	F1	1398/9
WOS-A	WM	C	

rearranged in the fifteenth century, and this truss may also have originally been at the end of the house.

Both the date range and distribution of apex type V are virtually identical to those of type W, with just one early example identified (HAR-E, *1294–1324*, Fig. A). Indeed, it seems likely that it was the choice in Buckinghamshire and south Oxfordshire of a half-hipped (or fully hipped) roof profile, instead of the ubiquitous gable ends of the more northern counties, that led to the use of truncated crucks.[22] They were then adopted as an economical form for internal trusses by carpenters familiar with their use as end trusses. By the sixteenth century, it had become apparent that type W crucks were less limited in height than other forms, and we find them in use at, for example, MOU-A (1559, Fig. 5.6) and HUG-A (undated, Fig. Q), to provide exceptionally tall buildings. A handful of crucks are of type W1, in which the collar of a truncated cruck carries a king post (e.g. DID-A, undated, Fig. 5.2). Most

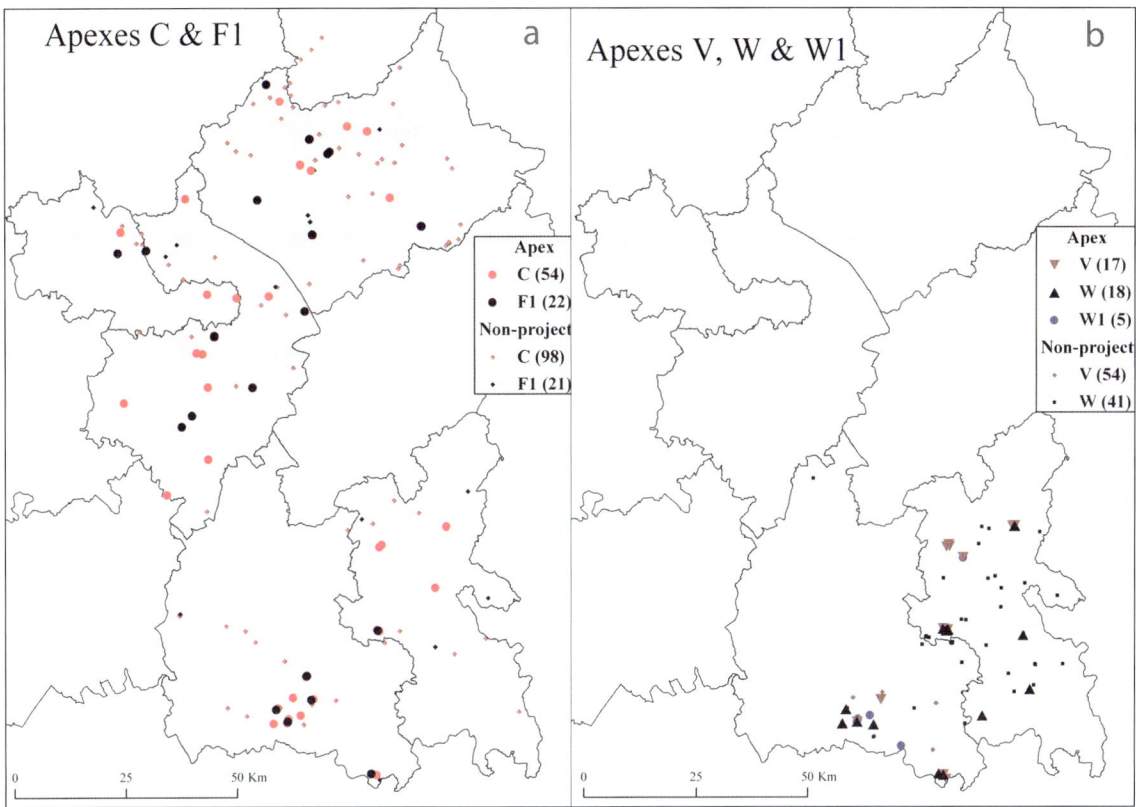

Fig. 5.3. Distribution of the major apex types: (a) (left) C and F1; (b) (right) W, V and W1. Larger and smaller symbols indicate project and non-project houses respectively. In (b), many symbols overlap as they are located in the same villages. Most V (end truss) apexes are found in houses that also have W-apex trusses.

Table 5.4 Dates and distribution by county of common cruck apexes.

Apex	A	C	D	E	F1	F2	F3	W	W1	V
Date range	*1383–1408 to 1655–7*	1317/8 to 1566–77	1380 to 1553/4	1400 to 1496/7	*1335 to 1576–1610*	*1294–1324 to 1444/5*	1399/1400 & *1492–9*	1335 to 1553/6	*1305–57 & 1559*	*1294–1324 to 1551–9*
Number	10	54	8	6	22	4	2	19	5	17
14th century	1	7	1	1	3	2		2	1	1
15th century	5	28		2	9	1	2	4		6
16th century	1	4	2		5			7	3	3
17th century	1									
Undated	2	15	5	3	5	1		6	1	7
Buckinghamshire		7	1	1	1	1		12	1	11
Leicestershire	4	16	5		8	1	1			
Oxfordshire		12	2	2	5	2	1	7	4	5
Warwickshire & WM	5	18		1	8					
Glos/Nott	1	1		2						1

Also (one or two occurrences): H: *1496–1515* (Warwickshire); *1566–77* (Leicestershire); L2: *1398–1407* (Warwickshire); *1517–28* (Oxfordshire).

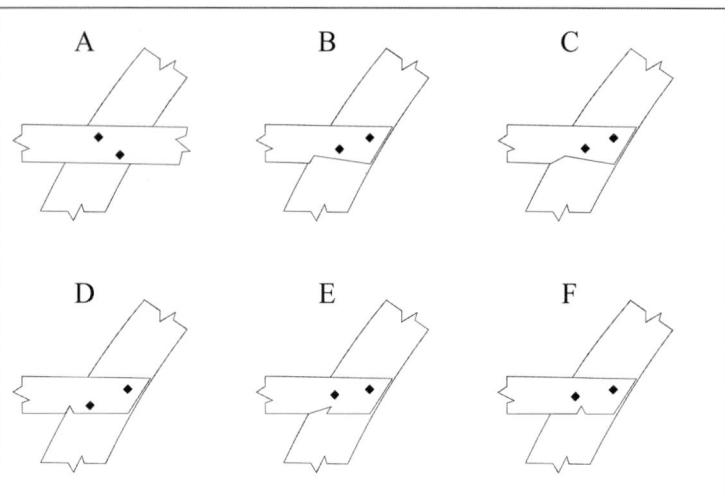

Fig. 5.4. Halved joints.

A   basic halving
B   bare-faced dovetail
C   bare-faced dovetail with refined profile
D   notched-lap joint with simple entry
E   notched-lap joint with refined entry
F   notched-lap joint with central notch

The nomenclature follows Alcock, Meeson *et al.* (1996).

of them are minor variants on type W, but at DID-A, and HAR-D (*1305–57*, Fig. B), the king post seems to be used to enhance the impressive character of the arch-braced open truss.

The jointing of transverse truss members

Halved joints. Cruck trusses carry a variety of transverse members, including tiebeams, collars, arch braces, spurs and saddles. These are either held by mortice-and-tenon joints or, more commonly are halved, essential if the transverse member extends past the cruck blades, as is frequent for tiebeams and collars. Four main types of halving joints have been found in cruck trusses. The simplest is the basic halving, without either dovetailing or notching (Fig. 5.4A). Examples were found at HBY-C (1380), FRI-A, DIS-A (collar only), SYS-A, STO-B (*1444–57*), LON-A (*1506–36*), LON-C (*1466–97*), POL-A (1508/9), COS-A, NWL-C and RAD-A (1522/3).

The most common halved joint is the bare-faced dovetail (Fig. 5.4B), where a dovetail is cut on one side of the timber to prevent withdrawal. At least 34 houses use this joint, sometimes together with basic halvings. They are principally of the fifteenth century, but their dates range from 1398/9 (WOR-A) to *1512–35* (CAS-A) and *1566–77* (COS-B). The next stage of development involves dovetails with refined profiles, where two cuts in the matrix improve their resistance to withdrawal (Fig. 5.4C). BIL-A (undated) has both plain and refined bare-faced dovetails, whilst nine other refined examples were recorded, ranging from ROW-A (*1383–1408*), NEW-B (1437/8), WEL-A (1430), and ROT-D (*1492–9*). None dated to the sixteenth century.

In notched-lap joints, the edge of the crossing timber continues across the cruck blade or post, with a V-shaped notch cut into it, to prevent withdrawal. These are typical of thirteenth century carpentry before mortice-and-

tenon joints came into general use, and a chronological development has been suggested.[23] Those with simple entries, in which one side of the notch is cut parallel to the edge of the post or cruck blade (Fig. 5.4D), are considered to be earlier than those with refined entries, in which the notch is at an angle to the edge of the other timber Fig. 5.4E). Examples of both types were recorded, though they are rare. At LON-G (1205), the notched-lap joints have simple entries, as would be expected at this early date (Fig. 5.5a; at AST-A, they have refined entries (Fig. 5.5b). The notched-lap joints at Church Farm, Harwell (HAR-B, 1420/21) have simple profiles with very narrow notches. Two houses, CAD-A (1472/3; and FOS-A (1496/7), use very steep notch laps with acute angles. A variant was also noted, in which the notch is set centrally rather than starting

Fig. 5.5 (opposite page). Joints and pegging.

a   Notched-lap joint with simple entry at LON-G (1205) on a reused arcade plate, with the matrix of a similar joint.

b   Notched-lap joint with refined entry and splayed and tabled scarf with key at AST-A (1282/6); the end of the dragon tie is also visible

c   Halved joint between collar and cruck in truss T1 at Mill Farm, Mapledurham (MDM-A, 1335).

d   Notched-lap joint (refined entry) between cruck and brace in truss T1 at MDM-A.

e–f   Front and side views of the apex joint at 28 High Street North, Stewkley (STW-A).

g   Halved joint between the (missing) windbrace and the reused purlin at Church End Farm, Nether Whitacre (NWH-A, *1423–46*). The first peg was driven straight through the centre of the halving, and the second peg ran obliquely through the windbrace into the purlin (at the bottom of the picture). The upper peg probably held a rafter.

h   Arcade post head at LON-G (1205). The tiebeam is a replacement, probably of the fifteenth century.

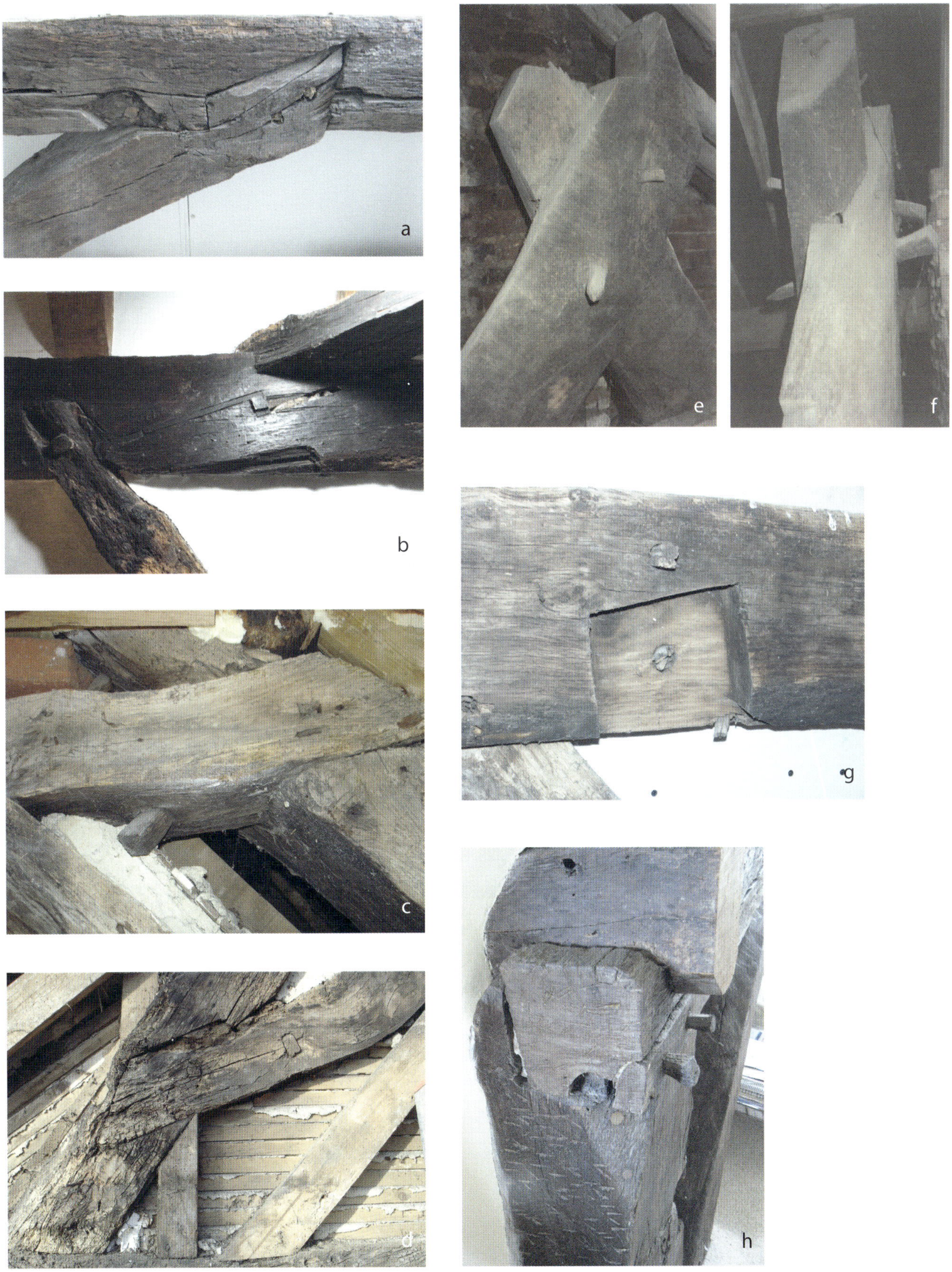
a
b
c
d
e
f
g
h

at the edge of the timber. This *central notch lap joint*, found at LOX-A (undated) (Fig. 5.4f), seems not previously to have been recorded.

Cruck spurs, which extend out from the blades to engage with the wall post, or more commonly support the wall plate directly, might be expected to be tenoned into the blades. However, they usually have bare-faced dovetails (with the upper edge running through), sometimes with notched-lap joints, although in some of the smaller, simpler frames, a halving with no dovetailing at all is used. In contrast, on collars and tiebeams the lower edge generally runs through (e.g. CAD-A, 1472/3, Fig. K). This systematic difference suggests that the carpenters had a clear view of the likely direction of the stress on these joints. An unusual spur joint was found at Hallaton (HAL-A, *1465–83*), where the spur is slotted into a tapering, dovetail-shaped groove in the side of the cruck blade. This would have provided exceptional resistance to the spur becoming detached from the cruck.

Skew-pegging. The pegging of lap joints is crucial to their stability. Whilst the half-dovetails and the more refined notched-lap joints prevent the timbers from withdrawing along their length, they do not do much to prevent the trusses twisting or the tiebeams and collars coming off the face of the crucks. The technique of skew pegging was utilised to keep these joints tight. The two pegs in each joint were driven in from the face of the longitudinal member into, and through, the cruck blade, angled to each other, usually at about 30°. Judging from the available evidence, skew-pegging seems to have been introduced after about 1300. It was not used at Sycamore Farm, Long Crendon (LON-G, 1205), where the notched-lapped arcade braces are either single-pegged or have two parallel pegs.[24] At Tibberton Cottage, Harwell (HAR-E, *1294–1324*), the pegging of the halved joints is not visible.

Standard skew-pegging seems to have been preceded by a form in which one peg was driven through the face of the joint, with the other one perpendicular to it, passing through the sides of the timbers. At the Royal George, Cottingham, Northamptonshire (1262), the single-pegged halvings of the collars are reinforced by long pegs driven into the joint through the cruck blade in the plane of the collars.[25] Similar jointing is used at Quaintree House, Braunton (BRN-H, *1305–9*), where a few of the notched-lap joints are not pegged from the face, but from the side, through the thickness of the lapped timbers. This was perhaps an experimental technique that can surely not have proved very satisfactory, particularly for the relatively thin braces and rafters to which it was applied. At Mill Farm, Mapledurham (MDM-A, 1335), this perpendicular pegging is used between the collar and the cruck of truss T1 (Fig. 5.5c), but the notched-lap joint between the cruck and the brace has standard skew-pegging (Fig. 5.5d).[26] Skew-pegging is seen at its most dramatic in the apex joint at Stewkley (STW-A, undated, probably early fifteenth

century), where the simple halved joint was secured by two markedly angled pegs (Figs. 5.5e–f). An exploded example is seen in the purlin-windbrace joint at Nether Whitacre (NWH-A, *1423–46*), where the windbrace has been removed (Fig. 5.5g).

Mortice-and-tenon joints. The more elegant trusses (especially those dating from the fourteenth to early fifteenth centuries) generally employ mortice-and-tenon joints. Crucks with arch-braced collars usually have tenoned joints, even when halved joints were used elsewhere in the same building. Most of these braces were fixed with smallish pegs of ¾ to 1in diameter, usually round rather than square, with the number of pegs to each joint varying between two (STW-A and DID-A, both undated, Figs. R, S) and six or seven (HAR-D, *1305–57*; BIT-A, 1413/4, Figs. B, 4.3).

Collars in other trusses normally have bare-faced dovetail joints, and they are generally extended to support the purlins. However, exceptions to both patterns have been noted. Most of the plain Oxfordshire houses show a distinctive carpentry trait, with mortice-and-tenon joints rather than halvings used for the collars. By contrast, at NWL-D (1492, Fig. 4.3) the collar in the arch-braced open truss is halved over the cruck blades rather than tenoned. It is probably relevant that this is the latest recorded truss using arch braces.

Joggled halvings. Most remarkably, some trusses in which the arch braces are halved into the face of the cruck blade use what can be called 'joggled' joints, as at Water Orton (WOR-A, 1398-9, Fig. 4.2). Simpler halved joints between the arch braces and the collar and cruck blades were used at Walsgrave (WOS-A, probably fifteenth century, Fig. U) and on the reused blades at Nether Whitacre (NWH-A, *1423–46*, see CD-report), both in Warwickshire.[27] The reused cruck blades at Binfield Heath, Oxfordshire (BIF-A, 1453–5) had both tenoned and halved joints to the arch braces. Mill Farm, Mapledurham (MDM-A, 1335) has conventional tenoned arch braces with multiple pegs to the main open truss, but on the truss at the lower end of the hall (T1), the braces take the form of convex soulaces with open notched-lap joints (Fig. A).

Longitudinal timbers

The cruck trusses are connected by a number of longitudinal members including sill beams, wall plates, purlins, and ridge pieces. The wall plates are supported in a number of ways. Most directly, the plates rest on the cruck blades themselves, if these are elbowed or exceptionally cranked or bent, as at Sutton Courtenay (SUC-A, 1317/18, Fig. 4.1) and Steventon (STE-B, 1355/6, Fig. 4.2). Normally, the cruck blades are set within the line of the wall plates and the walls include 'cruck studs', the studs in the plane of the truss that help support the plate, while also forming part of the wall framing. These studs may be tenoned into the sill beam independent of the cruck blades, but they are often

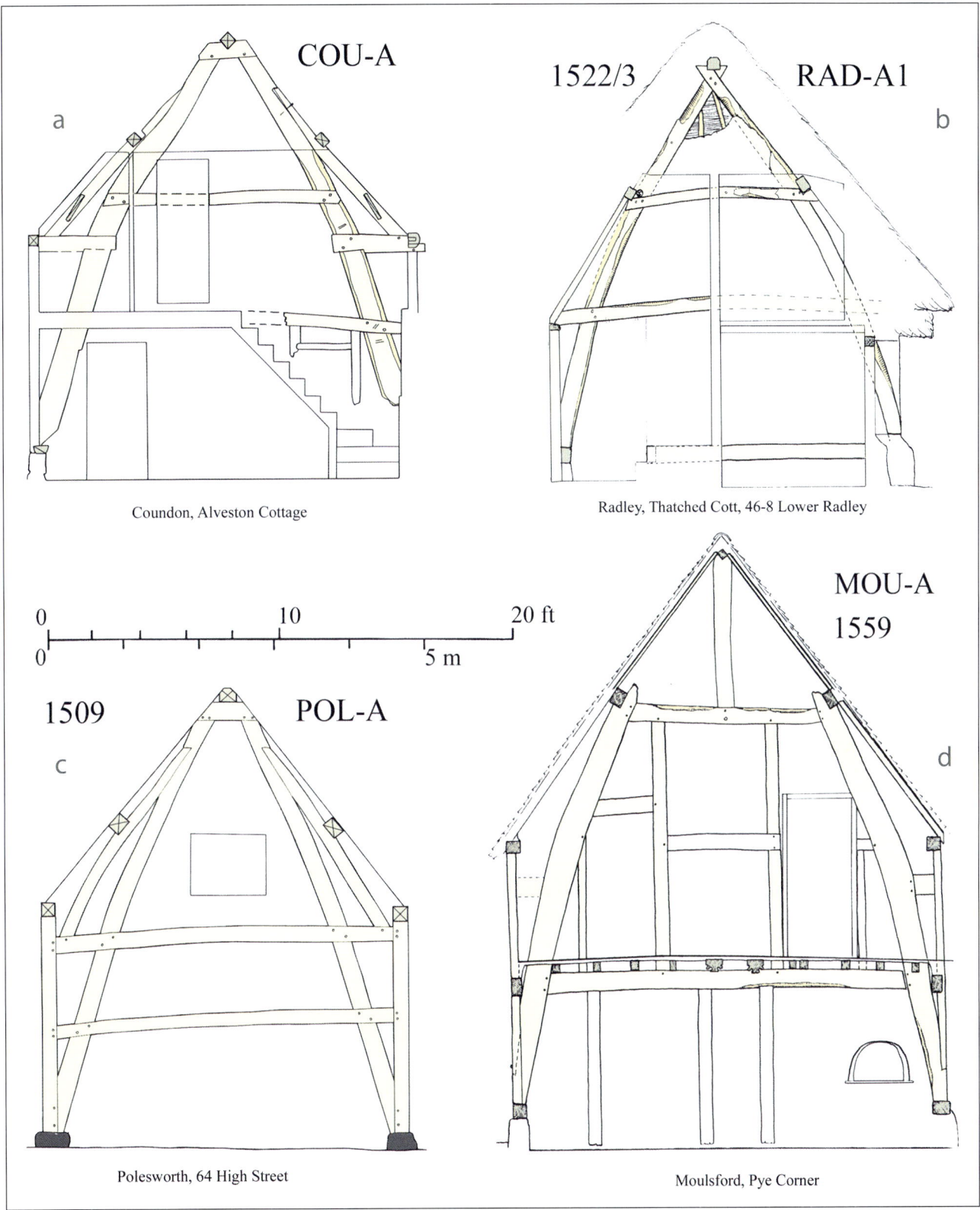

Fig. 5.6. Cruck trusses showing different methods of supporting the wall plates. (a) Alveston Cottage, Coundon, West Midlands (COU-A); (b) Thatched Cott, 46–8 Lower Radley, Oxfordshire (RAD-A); (c) 64 High Street, Polesworth, Warwickshire (POL-A); (d) Pye Corner, Moulsford, Oxfordshire (MOU-A). For other support methods, see Figs. 4.1–3.

carried by the bases of the cruck blades, being pegged to them (often with very substantial pegs), or set in V-notches in the back of the blades (e.g. STO-F, 1480–2, and SUF-A, *1480–92*). At Moulsford (MOU-A, 1559), three different techniques were used at this position. For truss T1, the blade runs down to the sill beam, with the cruck stud joined to the back of the blade about 2ft 9in above the bottom of the cruck, with an offset tenon 15in long with three pegs. At truss T2, the cruck blade is joined to the stud with a double-pegged free tenon about 1ft 6in below the mid-rail. The cruck is let into the inner face of the post with an under-squinted abutment. Finally, at truss T3 (Fig. 5.6), the cruck studs are seated on the back of the blades as in T1, but are face pegged rather than tenoned. It is interesting to find such a wide variety of jointing at this position, probably reflecting the ways in which the carpenter has had to make the most of the available timbers.

The lateral support of the studs and plates is most often provided by spurs, jointed into the cruck blades and extending out to the wall plates. The spur usually carries the wall plate directly, or occasionally is tenoned into it (e.g. COU-A, Fig. 5.6). This is the almost invariable pattern in open trusses, but even when the truss has a tiebeam, it quite often does not extend as far as the cruck studs, as at ROW-A, which has a proliferation of transverse members with a tiebeam, spurs, two collars and a yoke (*1383–1408*, Fig. 4.2). In other houses, the tiebeam is attached to the cruck stud, below the spur. An alternative was to carry the wall plate directly on the tiebeam (e.g. at NWL-D, 1492, Fig. 4.3). This is the reverse of the normal assembly in box-framed trusses, where the tiebeams are set above the wall plates; surprisingly, one truss uses this normal arrangement (RAD-A, 1522/3, T1, Fig. 5.6). At STC-A (1448, Fig. H), one truss uses spurs and the other a tiebeam to carry the plate. In later buildings with taller walls, the cruck studs sometimes carry the plate directly, with tiebeams or spurs set below this, as at POL-A, with two tiebeams engaging the studs (1508/9, Fig. 5.6) and MOU-A, with spurs only (1559, Fig. 5.6).

Purlins and packing pieces

Most often, these cruck houses have just one set of purlins, but better-built examples use two tiers, as at Bishops Tachbrook (BIT-A, 1413/4) and OXH-A (*1450–6*). The purlins are supported in a variety of ways. They can be pegged into the back of the blades (e.g. MDM-A, 1335, truss T3); surprisingly, at COS-B (*1566–77*), the purlins are supported only by the substantial 2in pegs underneath them. More satisfactorily, trenches in the back of the crucks provide a seating to prevent their sliding down the blade, as at Erdington (ERD-A, 1400) and Harwell (HAR-B, 1420/1). With truncated (type W) crucks, the purlins often sit in a notch cut in the tops of the blades as at East Hagbourne (DID-B, *1549–60*, Fig. O). Positive support

can also be given by a halved collar extending beyond the blades and providing a notched seating to carry the purlins, as in RAD-A (1522/3, Fig. 5.6). Often the crucks are not close enough to the roof line to support the purlins directly. This is remedied by introducing *packing pieces* (sometimes called secondary rafters) which are tenoned into the cruck spur or tiebeam at the base and fixed to the back of the cruck blade at the top, sometimes engaging with the end of an extended collar (e.g. COU-A and POL-A, Fig. 5.6). These are then trenched to support the purlins as if they were the crucks themselves, as at Normanton-on-Soar (NOS-C, *1447–54*) and Stoneleigh (STO-F, 1480–82). The latter also shows a variant where the packing piece is used as a strut set under the bottom of the purlin (truss T1; also at HAL-A, *1465–83*). Butt-purlins, which have the purlin tenoned into the side of the cruck blades, were very rarely used, although they are found at Steventon (STE-B, 1355/6, Fig. 4.2) and in one truss at Mill Farm Mapledurham (MDM-A, 1335, Fig. 4.1). At the latter house, the blades of the open truss (T2) have such different profiles that one purlin is carried in a trench and the other tenoned into the blade. NWL-D (1492) also has butt-purlins in its end truss, with the others carried on the ends of the collars.

Scarf joints

Wall plates, purlins, and ridges are rarely long enough to span the entire length of the building, so the sections have to be scarfed together; wall-plate joints appear to be similar to those in purlins, but they are often difficult to record, and we have little direct evidence for them. Figure 5.7 shows the commonest types of scarfs, together with some unusual or unique examples, but the number of variations in design and pegging pattern makes it impossible to illustrate them comprehensively.

The earliest buildings employ splayed and tabled scarfs (*trait-de-Jupiter*) (Fig. 5.7A). Some have under-squinted abutments (upper face in Fig. 5.7A), when they could be strengthened with central keys (driven in to push the two sides of the scarf against the abutments) (Fig. 5.5b). As well as being used in the early aisled and base-cruck houses, such as IVI-A (*1250–77*), this form is also found at Aston Tirrold (AST-A, 1282/6) and Sutton Courtenay (SUC-A, 1317/18). The Aston Tirrold examples are interesting in that the scarf in one wall plate has an under-squinted abutment on the top only, whilst the other wall plate has them on both top and bottom, with the added refinement that the notch matrix for the lap joint of an adjacent wall brace is provided by the pointed end of the scarf abutment (Fig. 5.5b). Another ingenious *ad-hoc* refinement of a wall plate scarf is seen at TIL House (CLI-B, 1466 phase), where the joint is locked together by the tenon of a wall brace, passing through both halves of the scarf as a key.

The simplest and most frequently found form, the splayed (or through) scarf, was recorded in fifteen houses with

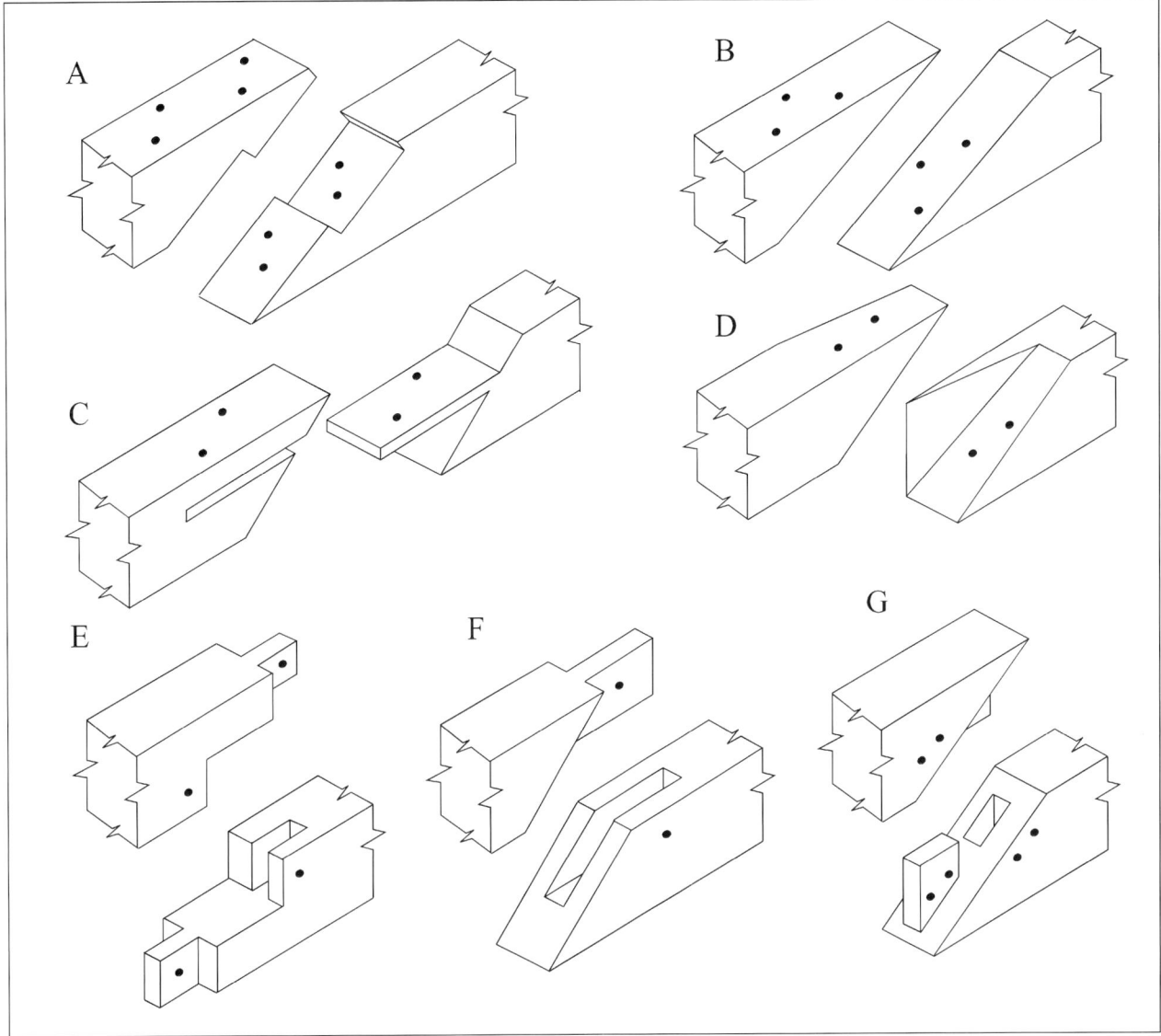

Fig. 5.7. Scarf joints.

A   Splayed and tabled scarf (trait-de-Jupiter). The upper face only
    is shown with an undersquinted abutment, but in reality both
    or neither face would use this refinement.
B   Simple splayed scarf
C   Splayed and tongued scarf (ROT-A)

D   Double-splayed scarf
E   Side-halved and bridled scarf. Unusually, the scarf of this type
    at HAR-C, also has two pegs driven down from the face.
F   Splayed and bridled scarf
G   Splayed and counter-tongued scarf at EAH-C (1418/20)

Based on drawings from Alcock, Meeson *et al.* (1996) and site records (redrawn to uniform dimensions).

dates ranging from 1335 (MDM-A) to *1536–8* (NWL-A)
(mainly fifteenth century) (Fig. 5.7B). A variant at SUT-A
(1442–4) has a steeply splayed scarf with a free tenon set
into a slot in the upper face, double pegged on each side
(similar to Fig. 5.7F, but with the tenon extending in both
directions). Similarly, at STO-E (1537) the splayed scarf
has a double-pegged free tenon or key (passing transversely
through the purlin, rather than longitudinally as at SUT-
A). A somewhat similar scarf was used in the diagonally-set
ridge at ROT-A, with a thin tongue projecting from one

part of the scarf into the other and pegged through the
tongue rather than the splay (Fig. 5.7C).

A double splayed scarf (Fig. 5.7D) was used for the
purlins at Skirmett (SKI-A, *1444–74*) and three other
houses: NWL-B (1454/5), WEE-A (*1446–50*), and LON-
F (*1551–9*). It seems to be a regional variant, as all these
are Buckinghamshire houses. The unique scarf found at
STE-E (probably of 1365/6) is similar to this, but has the
feather-edge of Figure 5.7D enlarged into a 1–2in thick
bare-faced tongue.

Side-halved and bridled scarfs are found at LOX-A and HAR-C (1399/1400) in the ridges and wall plates (where the purlins use simple splayed scarfs); this scarf became standard in post-medieval houses, and these are exceptionally early examples. (Fig. 5.7E).[28] It is similar in its function to the splayed and bridled scarf at WAL-A (1384–5), a type which was also common in the sixteenth century (Fig. 5.7F).

Other scarf joints noted include a splayed scarf with bridled abutment on the top, with one edge peg through the tenon and face pegs through the splay (BIF-A, 1453–5 and SOF-A, 1409+). A classic example of a scissors scarf was found in the ridge piece at STE-C (1365/6). At RAD-B (1513/14) a side-halved scarf with square abutments was used to join the ridge pieces.[29] A very unusual scarf was used for both the purlins and the ridge at EAH-C (1418/20) which is splayed and counter tongued, with four edge pegs (Fig. 5.7G).

If nothing else, the variety of these designs illustrates the ingenuity of the medieval carpenter in designing improvements to the simple splayed scarf, which could easily come apart under stress.

Windbraces

Windbraces are used to brace the roof frame against longitudinal racking. The more sophisticated examples are tenoned into the sides of the cruck blades or packing pieces (as in most of the early houses). Alternatively and more simply, they are trenched into the back of the blades or packing pieces. Occasionally they overlap on the back of the crucks and are pegged through each other, as at ROT-B (1447) and SOF-A (1409+). They rise to the purlins, where halved joints are much more frequent than tenons (see below). In this respect cruck framed structures are very similar to box-framed roofs of the same period. Very rarely, the windbraces descended from the cruck blades to the purlin, as in one truss at Castle Donington (CAS-B, 1554) and at STO-C and BIL-A.

A good indicator of age is given by the thickness of the windbraces. Like the cruck blades, they progress from thick, almost square-sectioned, braces to thin planks by the 1500s. Early crucks with windbrace thicknesses of 3 to 4 inches or more include SUC-A (1318), MDM-A (1335) and BOT-A (1366–1398, re-used). By the end of the 1300s, the windbraces are usually about 2 inches thick (ROW-A, 1383–1408; BIT-A, 1413/14), and by the end of the following century, 1 to 1½ inches is common (NWL-D, 1492). These later windbraces are often missing, as their decreased thickness makes them likely to deflect and fall out over the course of time. Exceptions to the trend can be found, however, as at Anstey, Leics (ANS-A, 1450) where the windbraces are a massive 4½in thick.

An interesting method of windbracing for a fully-hipped roof was seen at Mill Farm, Mapledurham (MDM-A,

1335). Here a brace is mortised into the top of the wallplate, which is cranked into the plane of the roof and then rises to carry the purlin just before it reaches the line of the hip. This effectively provides a windbrace without the need for a truss. Similar evidence in the form of empty mortices was also noted in the box-framed chamber block at Aston Tirrold (AST-A, 1282/6).

The jointing between wind braces and purlins has only been recorded in a few examples, when access to the upper side of the purlin was possible. At MDM-A, the lap dovetail is of archaic form (Fig. 8.6.7), as also seen at SOU-A (1418/19). Those at LOX-A, BIT-A (1413/14), ROT-B (1444–8), and BIN-A (1474/5) have tapering lap joints which, rather than forming a half-dovetail, are reduced to a triangular form. At COU-A a similarly-shaped lap joint is used for one windbrace, while another has a lap joint with a shallow refined entry.

Apart from windbraces, other longitudinal bracing is very rare, although at The Old Post Office, Oxhill (OXH-A, 1450–6), the square-set ridge piece is braced down to the king strut, an arrangement of which few other examples are known (see report).

The roof

Common rafters

With the structural frame erected and adequately braced, all that remains to finish the roof is to place the common rafters on the frame. Many common rafters still survive in the houses surveyed, although complete examples, such as the Leopard at Bishop's Tachbrook (BIT-A, 1413/4) and Mill Farm, Mapledurham (MDM-A, 1335) (Fig. 8.6.3) are rare. Rafters were usually small diameter trees halved and almost always fairly roughly finished with a side axe, with some just riven from larger trees (as at DIS-A and LWH-A, 1560), having much waney edge left exposed and hardly if ever chamfered. As well as oak, elm was often used for rafters, as at LON-I, with other species occasionally found, including beech at MDM-C (1458), and birch poles at POL-A (1509). Often the rafter feet have been lost, but at LNG-M (1339–40) the original hollow-shaped rafter feet with chamfers are preserved, measuring 3 by 5in, typical of higher-status carpentry.

The primary fixing points for the rafters were the purlins, with pegs that could be as large as 1in diameter. Secondary fixings at the wall plates usually used simple bird-mouthed joints, which might or might not involve a triangular notch to seat the bottom of the rafter. On some early buildings, as at Aston Tirrold (AST-A, 1282/6) and Mill Farm, Mapledurham (MDM-A, 1335), the outer edge of the wall plate has a heavy chamfer of 1 to 1½in wide, on which the rafters were laid (apparently unpegged).[30] At the ridge, they might be in line with the opposing rafter (NWL-B, 1454/5), or staggered, with the rafters on the two sides of the roof offset by a few inches (MDM-A, 1335; SKI-A, *1444–74*). The rafters are rarely pegged to the ridge and are only bridled together in the few buildings that lack a ridge piece, such as DID-B (*1549–60*).

Rafter Size. The rafters varied considerably in thickness from as little as 1½–2½in at NWL-B (1455) to 3–4½in thick at Tudor House, Steventon (STE-B, 1356). While Tudor House is a well-carpentered higher-status building, another house of similar status, Manor Farm, Stretton on Fosse (SOF-A, 1415+) had rafters only 2½in thick, although between 6in and 7in wide. Other exceptionally wide rafters were found at LWH-A (*1558–62*) where the 2in thick rafters were 4 to 8in wide. Generally most rafters averaged between 2 and 3in in thickness, and 4 to 6in in width, usually tapering to the apex, following the natural shape of the tree. The rafters were always set with their widest dimension on the flat, as with medieval joists, and usually at 16 to 18in centres, although one house (BOT-A, 1507–9) had rafters set at 11in centres, while at the other extreme RAD-A (1522/3) had them at 22in centres.

Smoke louvres

Evidence for former smoke louvres was sought with particular care, since the smoke louvre is expected to coincide with the position of the open hearth, and thus helps interpret the original plan. In houses of peasant status, the smoke louvres were generally set or 'planted' on top of the rafters, which were not trimmed or framed out, as found in higher-status houses. Notable soot encrustation near the louvre (³⁄₈/in thick) was noted on the underside of the ridge at RAD-B (1513/14), and at LON-I (undated), with a ¼in thick layer on the rafters and the thatch. Surviving smoke-blackened thatch was also seen at STC-A (1448) and LON-I.

Almost invariably, the only evidence of a former louvre position is given by a few peg holes in the common rafters, 18 to 24in below the ridge, sometimes with the tapered ends of pegs remaining, as at The Leopard, Bishops Tachbrook (BIT-A, 1413/4), and Kingsholm, East Hagbourne (DID-B, *1549–60*). Other examples were seen at HAL-A (*1465–83*), and LON-I (undated). Evidence for other variants of smoke louvres was occasionally found. At Pithouse, Mapledurham (MDM-B, 1454/5), a set of inclined mortices part way down from the ridge probably received the corner framing of the louvre. At the nearly contemporary Three Chimneys, Mapledurham (MDM-C, 1458), evidence survives for a primary smoke louvre in the form of two peg holes in the first two rafters on the service side of the open truss.[31] On the north side of the same truss a secondary smoke louvre was positioned off-centre from the ridge, indicated by two mortices in the purlin, one partially over the open truss cruck blade and the other some 3 feet away. These evidently received the two lower corner posts of the louvre with the other side presumably supported by the ridge. This louvre

was open to the weather for some time as the cruck blade adjoining it was washed clean of soot.

The base-cruck hall at LNG-M (1340) had a more elaborate smoke louvre than any of those so far described. It was positioned adjoining the open truss, with two rafter couples carrying pairs of uprights morticed into the collars; the rafter apexes are rebated for horizontal timbers, probably the 'tiebeams' of the louvre roof (Fig. 8.3.4). At another base-cruck house, Quaintree House, Rutland (BRN-H, *1306–9*) the absence of framing above the end truss suggests that the smoke escaped through a gablet opening.

A staple was found at BIT-A (1413/4), adjacent to the louvre position, perhaps for some form of shutter controlling the louvre opening, that might have been operated by a rope passing through the staple. At WOE-A (1426–30), three rafters in the rear slope and one surviving rafter on the front slope have oblique peg holes for a base plate, placed 2ft 5in down the roof slope from the ridge. The adjoining rafter on the front roof slope carries an iron hook set about 3ft 9in down from the ridge, which may also have been related to some form of shutter. EAH-B (undated) has a hinge pintle set off-centre 2ft below the ridge, and WOR-A (1398/9) and ANS-A (1449/50) have wrought iron staples in the ridge beam, which may indicate the positions of their louvres.[32] However, these staples may also (or alternatively) have been used for hanging meat or bacon in the roof space. A massive wrought-iron nail driven into one of the windbraces at Pithouse, Mapledurham (MDM-B, 1454/5) must surely have served this purpose.

The smoke louvre at Mill Farm, Mapledurham

Only one example of a louvre base plate remains in situ, at Mill Farm, Mapledurham (MDM-A, 1335), and this house provides enough evidence for a tentative reconstruction of the louvre (Fig. 5.8c). The triangular base plate is 3ft 7in long, and about 3½in wide on the top and side (Fig. 5.8a). As the plate has no housings or mortices for a framed superstructure, the sides of the louvre were probably of timber boards, nailed to the roughly vertical side of the plate, where one nail remains near its upper edge, projecting about an inch. Two mortices in the ridge piece, immediately above the louvre plate, held posts which must have risen to support the ridge of the louvre, the stub of the southern post still remaining in situ (Figs. 5.8a–b). The shouldered tenons measure 2 by 4–5in, the post section probably being 3–4 by 5in. These mortices were not pegged, so the posts must have been kept in place by the weight of the structure, and by the nailed boarding. The mortices were crudely made, with 1in holes drilled at each end and the middle roughly chopped out, in contrast to the neat mortices used in the trusses themselves. This rather crude treatment suggests that the louvre may have been an afterthought, or that it was constructed by someone other than the master carpenter.

The posts presumably carried a small ridge beam,

Fig. 5.8. The louvre at Mill Farm, Mapledurham (MDM-A, 1335).

a   View of the louvre base plate. The fractured tenon of the ridge post can be seen behind the right-most front rafter, and the empty mortice is concealed behind the left-most rafter

b   View of the ridge at Mill Farm, showing the empty mortices of the louvre post

c   Reconstruction drawing of the louvre at Mill Farm, Mapledurham (watercolour by Lynn Courtenay based on a sketch by Nat Alcock)

perhaps a foot above the top of the thatch, which probably had sloping boarding nailed to it, extending down to meet the side-boards. For their support, we can infer the existence of plates at the junction between the top and side-boarding, bevelled to receive the boards. These plates would themselves be carried on horizontal ties halved across the posts. As well as the vertical boarding on the sides of the louvre, the lower parts of the ends must also have been boarded, protecting the surface of the thatch from both rain and sparks and embers. The sloping roof boards were needed to keep rain off the hearth below, and so the smoke must have escaped through the upper parts of the gable ends. The suction caused by the Bernouilli effect in even a modest breeze would have pulled the smoke out through the louvre very effectively.

The only complete examples of smoke louvres at this social level have been discovered in Devon, probably as a result of the re-thatching technique there, which involved replacing only the outermost layer of old thatch. Louvres have been found at one probably fourteenth- and one fifteenth-century house, Leigh Barton, East Leigh, Coldridge, and West Clatworthy, Filleigh.[33] Both are similar, triangular in form, constructed with light-weight struts covered by boards. In the first, the ridge of the louvre runs parallel to the ridge, projecting above the thatch, while at the second house, the louvre is set across the line of the roof, providing openings through the side of the thatch (and it was described as a 'smoke-tunnel').

Smoke bays and smoke hoods

One apparently original smoke bay has been identified, at Sutton Coldfield (SUT-A, 1442–44). An intermediate collar for the smoke hood is birds-mouthed between the purlins, and this carries stave holes on the bottom face, and a stave groove above, with signs of the fixings for the upper ends of the staves on the adjacent rafter couple. The next two common rafters to the east have peg holes 1ft 6in down from the ridge, indicating the position of the smoke louvre within the bay.[34] The rafters immediately below this are weathered, but those on the other side of the intermediate collar are perfectly clean, showing that this partition was original. An original smoke hood was found at NWL-C (probably sixteenth century), although others at AST-A (1620 phase) and LOX-A (sixteenth century?) were later insertions. That at NWL-C is supported by two front corner posts carrying a mantel-beam. Above this rise slanting posts, with several crosspieces. The hood is infilled with hazel staves with cleft laths for wattles to receive the lime-rich daub.

Upper floors

In all, thirty cruck and box-framed hall ranges and all of the nine wings or chamber blocks are believed to have had original upper floors in at least one bay, although for ten houses the evidence is inconclusive, since the floor is concealed or has been removed or completely replaced. The single-storey service range at DID-A is the only unfloored wing. Floors in the box-framed houses (ASH-A, STE-D, STO-G) are similar to those in the cruck houses and they are considered together. Characteristically, the floor joists are plain and either square in section, or rather wider than they are high (dimensions in Table 5.5). In the box-framed wings and chamber blocks, the joists of the earliest floors (AST-A (1282/6), STE-E (1356/65) and WOR-A (*1415–53*)) all run transversely. The latter two have axial beams held on samson posts giving additional support. Exceptionally, HAR-C (probably of 1400, the date of the cruck range) has unsupported axial joists. The lodged joists are clamped in place by rails above them at STE-E and WOR-A, and also at ROT-B (1444–8) (floored chamber bay), where the bottoms of the upper studs are tenoned into a clamping beam which sits on top of the joists.

The earliest floored chambers in hall ranges are dated to the 1440s, although some earlier houses may have had original floors.[35] The joists are lodged in all but five of these houses, and a majority (twelve) have their joists oriented axially, resting on the mid-rails of the end truss, often with additional support from a transverse beam in the middle of the bay (seven houses). The earliest dated floors of this type are at ROT-B (1444–8) and NOS-C (*1447–54*). In floors with transverse joists (seven), the earliest are STC-A (1448), ASH-A (*1464–75*) and HIW-A (*1470–8*). All these also have axial beams for additional support. Framed stair openings were used in a number of houses, including HAL-A (*1465–83*), HIW-A (*1470–8*); ROT-B (1444–8);

Table 5.5. Joist dimensions. Not all the centre-to-centre spacings have been recorded.

(a) Lodged joists.

Site	Date	Width (in)	Height (in)	Centres (in)	Direction
AST-A	1282–6	8–9	4½	18	Transverse
DID-B	*1549–60*	4–6	5	18	Longitudinal
HAR-C	1399/1400	6–8?	5	20½	Longitudinal
HIW-A	*1470–8*	9–12	5	25–9	Transverse
HUG-A	Undated	6–8	6		Longitudinal
NOS-C	*1447–54*	5½–7	4½	17	Longitudinal
ROT-B	1444–8	6½	6	15	Longitudinal
SKI-A	*1444–74*	5½–7	5½	21	Longitudinal*
STE-E	1364/5	5½–6	4–5	19	Transverse
SUF-A	*1480–92*	8–11	4–5	16	Longitudinal
WEN-A	Undated	7	6		Longitudinal
WOR-A	*1415–53*	7–11	4	7–11	Longitudinal

*Notes: SKI-A. The joists may be tenoned or notched into the tiebeam, where the joint is obscured.

(b) Tenoned joists

Site	Date	Width (in)	Height (in)	Centres (in)	Direction
HAL-B	Undated	8½	5	20	Transverse
LON-A	*1506–36*	7	6		Transverse
LON-I	Undated	6½	4½		Transverse
MOU-A	1559	4½	6	20	Transverse
NWL-A	*1536–8*	6		16	Transverse
STC-A	1448	6	4½–5	19	Transverse*

* STC-A. The joists are tenoned into the spine beam, but lodged on the outer rails.

STO-C (undated); STO-G (1490doc). Apart from the floor at WOR-A mentioned below, the joists are usually spaced at 16 to 20in centres. They range from the exceptionally narrow at SUF-A, with 8-11in joists at 16in centres, to an extreme of 25–29in centres at HIW-A (*1470–8*), where the joists themselves are some of the widest encountered (9–12in across).

The earliest chamber floored with tenoned joists is at SKI-A (*1444–74*, Fig. H); unfortunately, the joist joints are hidden. Four late houses, three dated (LON-A, *1506–36*; LON-F, *1551–9*; MOU-A, 1559) and one undated (LON-J, probably *c*.1530), have the joists tenoned into the axial or transverse ceiling beams, as would be expected for flooring by the mid-sixteenth century. The joist joints at MOU-A have diminished haunches above housed soffit shoulders.

The most remarkable floor surveyed is that in the wing at Water Orton (WOR-A, *1415–53*). The flat joists 4in thick by 7–11in wide, are butted against one another like floor boards (Figs. 8.12.8–9). They are supported by an axial beam in the centre and a mid-rail on the outside walls where the joist ends are clamped by a second rail immediately above them. This type of construction is most unusual, the only other example known being the Old Rectory, Clifford Chambers, (X-CLI, 1433/4) The axial beam is a

massive timber, 13in wide and supported front and back by substantial posts rising to the first floor mid-rail and in the centre by a samson post.

A floor type frequent in Leicestershire and occasionally found elsewhere is made of lime ash or gypsum plaster, usually supported on close-spaced reeds, which provided a vermin-proof flooring for a room storing corn or other valuables. It is found in the cross-wings at WOE-A (1426–30) and CLI-B (1466), carried on the medieval joists (Fig. 5.9). Other such floors have been recorded at BIL-A and LWH-A (1560). These floors have been considered to be post-medieval, and certainly they were being constructed in the seventeenth century. However, it is difficult to suggest why those at WOE-A and CLI-B should have replaced earlier boards, so they may have been used considerably earlier than has previously been supposed.

Wall framing and decoration

Wall framing

A variety of framing patterns have been found during the survey. The most common arrangement is of large panels generally between 3 and 5 feet in width, and extending from sill to wall plate. If the walls are relatively high, they may also have a middle rail. Thus, a typical arrangement has the side wall of a bay divided by a centre stud and a horizontal rail. This arrangement is found, for example, at BOT-A (1507–9), STO-D (*1496–1515*), and STO-F (1480–82). Framing of this type has been found in buildings dating from the fourteenth to the sixteenth centuries. For a floored bay, if the joists run transversely, the mid-rail may be moved up to allow the floor joists to be lodged on it, as found at NWL-A (1454/5).

In the earliest house with evidence of wall framing, at MDM-A (1335) the side panels seem to have had central studs only. At Manor Cottage, Sutton Courtenay (SUC-A, 1317/8), large panels without middle rails were used but, surprisingly, peg holes show that the side walls did include long steep braces from the cruck studs to the plate.[36] These seem to be the only identified side-wall braces in cruck ranges although such braces are invariably present in the box-framed structures (below). The absence of such braces presumably caused the severe racking occasionally seen in houses such as STO-C.

Some examples of close studding were found in Leicestershire, at Cadeby (CAD-A, 1473) and April Cottage Rothley (ROT-B, 1444–51), although CAD-A only has close studding in the gable end, with a middle rail and large panels in the one surviving bay of side-framing. At ROT-B, the close-studding is used internally, in the partition between the hall and the floored chamber, but the exterior framing is not visible. Close-studding is also used in the side wall of the box-framed house, STO-G (1490doc).

Fig. 5.9. The eighteenth or nineteenth century lime-ash floor in the wing at TIL House, Clifton, Nottinghamshire (CLI-A, 1466) from the underside, showing the reed support.

The wall-frames in the chamber blocks, cross-wings and box-framed ranges also have large panels, but they include bracing, typically in both the gable ends (Figs. V, W) and the side walls. The earliest surviving wall framing, at Aston Tirrold (AST-A, 1282–6), comprises large panels the whole width of the side-wall bays (11–12ft), with only a single mid-rail (4in high by 6in) to support the lodged floor joists. The diagonal corner braces are generally notch-lapped to the posts and plates. The gable end is only subdivided above the mid-rail, where two vertical studs (morticed into the tiebeam) frame a decorated window. This has a projecting sill extending extended all the way to the corner posts forming an upper rail, halved across the vertical studs (Fig. 8.1.5). At ROT-C the fragmentary side frame of a box-framed cross-wing (1290–99) has steeply pitched wall braces tenoned to both the wall plate and the central post (Fig. P).

A characteristic somewhat later example is the wing at 39 The Causeway, Steventon (STE-E, 1356/65), with saltire bracing in the gable and rather irregular arch/ogee braces in the long walls. The gable of the cross-wing at WOR-A (*1415–53*) has arch braces to both the tiebeam and the mid-rail. The box-framed range at 71 The Causeway, Steventon (STE-D, 1463/7) has large arch braces in the side walls, with mid-rails in each bay, but apparently no other divisions. At Motslow Cottage, Stoneleigh (STO-E, 1537), the panels are divided by both mid-rails and studs, and have short arch braces from posts to plates. The box-framed end wall of MDM-A (1335, Fig. V) has a single curved brace, but further braces were apparently not considered necessary.

Panel infill

The standard method of infilling the walls between the structural timbers is by wattle-and-daub. This usually consists of a series of staves set vertically between horizontal members, with the tops located in purposely-cut mortices in the underside of the tiebeams, rails, and wall plates, and the bottoms of the staves slid into V-grooves set in the top surface of the lower horizontals, usually the rails or sill beams. Staves were almost universally riven but, exceptionally, at MDM-B (1455) sawn oak was used. Hazel withies were then woven between the staves to form wattle-work on which a daub of mud, straw, and other aggregate was applied, giving a panel about 4 inches thick. The size of the stave holes varies from 2½ by 1in at 12in centres (BOT-A, 1509), to 1 by 3in at 13½in centres (RAD-B, 1514), but they sometimes just consist of single large holes, such as at FRI-A (1550–75) where 1¼in diameter holes were drilled at 13in centres.

Different arrangements are seen in the earliest building with surviving infill, AST-A (1282/6). Here, the primary panels have riven oak staves with riven oak laths nailed onto the outer faces of the staves at 3–4in centres (Fig.

8.1.8). A chalk/lime daub mixed with chopped straw was applied on this framework, finished flush with the inside face of the staves and with the outer surface of the wall, covering the laths externally by about an inch. Overall, the panels average about 2½ to 3in thick. The only substantive variation is that the west end wall had the laths nailed on the inside instead of the outside. Externally, the panels may have been finished with a lime-rich lime/hair finish coat while the inner surface was coated with a fine silty/sandy coat over the daub. Nailed laths were also found in the much later COS-B (*1566–77*).

The internal truss at ROT-B (1447) shows traces of having had a very unusual infill – thin stone slabs. The edges of the studs are grooved to allow the stones to be inserted between the studs which would then have been plastered on both sides.[37]

Doorways and windows

Relatively little evidence survives for either the positions or the character of doorways and windows. The simplest form of external doorhead would have been no more than a horizontal rail, as seen at STO-F (1480–2, Fig. 8.11.2). A similar opening at WAL-A (1384/5) is chamfered on the jamb and lintel, but is not otherwise decorated. Although internal doors might be expected to survive more frequently, very few have been identified, perhaps because they have generally been enlarged. At WOR-A, doorways with shallow ogees cut into their head beams lead from the hall (1398/9) both into the lower end bay and into the later cross-wing (*1415–53*). More remarkable is the framed first floor doorway in the truss between the hall and the floored chamber bay at SUF-A (*1480–92*, Fig. L), which would have required a ladder from the hall for access.[38]

Windows in the cruck houses probably normally had diamond mullions. One four-light window of this type survives in the hall at MDM-B (1455), measuring 2ft 6in across by 2ft 9in high. A more substantial window at WAL-A (1384/5) also has four lights, but with a transom, measuring internally 4 by 5ft; the mullions are of square rather than diamond section (Fig. 5.10a). More sophisticated windows might have decorated heads. At EAH-C (1418/20), the elaborately carved cusped head of a five-light window is set between two full height wall posts on the front elevation (Fig. 5.10c). The rear wall contains the jambs of a smaller window, but the nature of its head is unknown. An elaborate and sophisticated mullioned window existed in the gable wall of the chamber block at Aston Tirrold (AST-A, 1282/6). It had four lights, and the mullions appear to have been octagonal, with moulded capitals. Its headboard is lost, but cusping is suggested on the analogy of contemporary stone window openings.

One most remarkable window has survived, also at Aston Tirrold, of a third type, that may perhaps have been very common. This is set entirely within one of the

a

b

Fig. 5.10. Early windows

a   Internal view of the lower half of the window at Cruck Cottage, Walcote, Haselor, Warwickshire (WAL-A, 1384/5)

b   'Wind-eye' in the north wall of the chamber block at AST-A (1282/6)

c   Cusped head of the hall window at Godfrey's Farm, East Hendred, Oxfordshire (EAH-C, 1418/20)

c

frame infill panels, and so all evidence for it would have disappeared if the panel had been replaced. It consists of a small quatrefoil opening (7in across) cut out of a thin board (9 by 15in) nailed to the staves (Fig. 5.10b). Furthermore, the opening retains most of the original internal shutter, which is harr-hung from projecting ears at the top of the panel. This is a unique survival of a feature that may once have been common.

Decoration

Some of the lesser houses seem to have no decoration at all, but the majority at the least have some frame elements chamfered. Arch-braced central trusses are usually chamfered, though sometimes only on the arch-braces themselves, as at MDM-A (1335, Fig. 4.1). Often the cruck blades have simple chamfers of ½ to 1½in width, which may be carried through on the arch-braces if they are of the same thickness as the blades themselves (e.g. EAH-C, 1418/20; ROW-A3, *1383–1408*, Figs. E, C). More sophisticated are the hollow chamfers, as at HAR-D (*1305–57*) and the double chamfers, of which one component runs onto the braces, the other continuing on the blades, as at Manor Farm, Stretton-on-Fosse (SOF-A, 1409+) and BIT-A (1413/14, Fig. 4.3), WAL-A (1384/5), LOW-B (fourteenth or early fifteenth century), and WOE-A (1426–30). Only at LOW-B, is the curve of the arch brace extended onto the collar, although at STE-B (1355/6, Fig. 4.2), the collar was given an ogee nick. Surprisingly, the blades there have only a single chamfer, though the cusped upper principals are also chamfered. Purlins are usually unchamfered, with a few exceptions, including STR-A (1463) and NWL-D (1492), both of which have relatively wide chamfers (1½ to 2in).

Most of the chamfers end in simple run-out stops, but the crucks at SOF-A (1409+) have pyramid stops, and STC-A uses a stepped ogee stop, shown by the dating to belong to the primary phase (1448). A double chamfer with pyramid stops is also found on the wall posts of the cross wing at ERD-A (1461). CUB-A (1318) has shallow stepped stops to its chamfers, a form that continued through the fifteenth century (e.g. STW-A) and at least until *1551–9* (LON-F).

Octagonal crown posts with good moulded bases and capitals are found on most of the early base crucks, including IVI-A (*1288–1323*), BRN-H (*1306–9*), CUB-A (*1313–41*) and LNG-M (1339/40). The early box-framed cross-wings (X-WHA, 1284/5; STE-B, 1299; SUC-A, 1317/18; HAR-C, 1400(?)) also use crown posts, but these are all plain, as indeed are those of the lesser base-cruck houses (CLI-B, 1319/20; LON-O, 13–14th century; X-MIL, 14th century). Even so, these plain crown posts seem to have carried prestige. This can be seen at STE-E (1356/65), where what appears in the gable to be the end of a crown post roof, was in reality purely for show, since

the remaining trusses are totally plain (see Fig. V). The very crude crown post inserted in *1301–28* to stabilise the roof at Sycamore Farm, Long Crendon (LON-G), a century after the house was originally built (1205), is entirely undecorated (Fig. 8.5.4–5).

A number of trusses in higher-status houses include decorative struts and braces above the collar, as at Oxhill (OXH-A, *1450–6*) and Stretton-on-Fosse (SOF-A, 1415+). Collars are occasionally cambered (HAR-D, *1305–57*; WAL-A (T3, not drawn), 1385; ROW-A, *1383–1408*; OXH-A, *1450–6*), or cranked (LON-J, undated). Some open trusses have tiebeams as well as arch-braced collars, of the type known as mantel beams (see p. 44). The more striking examples have a chamfered strut rising from the tiebeam to the collar, as at Erdington (ERD-A, 1400, Fig. D), and STW-A (undated, probably early fifteenth century, Fig. R). These are perhaps emulating crown posts, but neither is very sophisticated.

Purely decorative elements are very rare, though Oxhill (OXH-A, *1450–6*) has carved blocks applied to the collar of the open truss, serving as finials to the ridge braces. At Quaintree House, Braunston (BRN-H, 1306–9), the underside of the spere-truss tiebeam carries a boss, sharply carved with a hexagonal rosette (Fig. 5.11). The base-cruck blades at Bathley (BAT-A, 1294/6) and Clifton (CLI-B, 1319/20) both have mouldings imitating capitals, composed of a series of shallow rolls and a row of pellets.

Moulded and decorated beams and similar features have been recorded in a number of houses. However, they are not often associated with the primary structure, being either reused, like the elaborately moulded joists of fourteenth century date at MOU-A (1559), or later insertions, like the outstanding c. 1500 fireplace at WOE-A (1426–30), with a cranked and embattled mantel beam with triple mouldings. This is of considerable interest as an indication of the status of the house a century after it was built.

Aisled and base-cruck halls and box-framed ranges

Posts and tiebeams

The most significant carpentry details in these buildings not also present in the cruck ranges appear in the treatment of the arcade and wall posts, and the use of passing braces and of dragon ties. All the posts dating from 1300 or before are unjowled, as are those in the framed truss at MDM-A (1335, Fig. V). Later principal posts have a variety of head forms (Figs. V–W), the earliest being jowled (STE-E, 1356/65; HAR-C, 1400?; also STO-G, 1490doc), though splayed heads are commoner (EAH-C, 1418/20 to STO-E, 1537).

The posts at Sycamore Farm, Long Crendon (LON-G 1205, Fig. 5.5h) have external bevelled upstands and tenons set into the arcade plate itself (the only tenons used in the

Fig. 5.11. Decorative boss at Quaintree House, Braunston, Rutland (BRN-H, 1306–9), on the soffit of the spere truss.

primary frame). Other houses with unjowled posts have upstands on the inside of the posts (IVI-A, *1250–77*; STE-B, 1299), while the posts at AST-A (1282/6) are tenoned into the plates. The later houses have standard three-way joints between post, wallplate and tiebeam. Generally, the tiebeams are dovetailed onto the arcade plates, but at Sycamore Farm an archaic cogged joint was used. A portion of the originally rounded plate was left standing proud with the rest of the timber cut down to fit the groove in the end of the tiebeam. The rafter foot is also grooved to fit over the cog (Fig. 8.5.8).[39]

Sycamore Farm uses timbers of consistently smaller scantling in its upper roof than any of the other houses, with the rafters and braces of only 3–4in section (as against 6–8in), and it is notable for the simplicity of its joints, consistent with its being the earliest of the houses studied by more than 50 years. Its roof timbers have simple lapped joints throughout, including the junction of rafters and tiebeams, notched-laps with simple entry being used only at the lower ends of the passing braces and for the arcade braces (Fig. 5.5a). As noted previously, the arcade plates have been reused, apparently rotated through 90° from their present setting; a cogged tiebeam joint and two notched halvings survive on one plate (with traces on the other). The halvings were apparently for dragon ties, stabilising the tiebeam, as in the north transept at Salisbury Cathedral.[40] Notched-lap joints are also used for some of the wall-frame braces at AST-A (Fig. 5.5b. At Pendyce House (IVI-A) and

Lime Tree House, Harwell (X-HA1) the rafters are tenoned to the tiebeams, and these frames have dovetail halvings for most of the collar and passing-brace joints.[41]

Base-cruck trusses

The simplest way of supporting the arcade plates in a base-cruck hall was to carry them on the bearer trusses comprising base-cruck blades, tiebeams and arch-braces. This was no doubt the reason why doubled tiebeams were retained at BAT-A (1294/6), BRN-H (*1306–9*), CUB-A (*1313–41*) and LNG-M (1339/40), even though these houses were built with base crucks, rather than being converted from aisled halls. The blades are usually tenoned into the horizontal soffits of the tiebeams, but curiously at BAT-A, the end of the tiebeam (only one survives) is cut off obliquely (Fig. Y).

In the earliest houses with single tiebeams, West Hagbourne (X-WHA, 1284/5, not drawn) and Ivinghoe (IVI-A, *1288-1323*, Fig. Y), a more daring solution to supporting the arcade plates was used, gripping the plate in a birdsmouth joint at the top of the base-cruck blade, apparently relying on the braces alone to link the blades to the tiebeam. The form of this joint that developed later is structurally more satisfactory and is more or less the same as the three-way jointing at the top of a post in a box-framed structure. Here, the base-cruck blade clasps the plate and is also tenoned into the tiebeam. This form is used at Clifton, Milton and Stokenchurch (CLI-B, 1319/20, X-MIL and STK-A).

Passing braces

In the aisled halls, the passing-brace system was standardised, combining a high collar with braces running from the rafters down to the arcade posts. Pendyce House (IVI-A) has doubled braces on truss T1, but the number of redundant halvings on its collar suggests that single braces may have been doubled when the upper roof was reconstructed (c. 1298).[42] The end trusses at Lime Tree House, Harwell (X-HA1) were simpler, with collars and small ashlar pieces, braced only below the tiebeams. At Long Crendon Manor, probably the latest of the halls that were originally aisled, with base crucks inserted later, the passing braces only reach the collar, as also seen at Bathley (BAT-A, 1294/6, Fig. Y). As here, several of the later base-cruck trusses continued to use passing braces. Quaintree House, Braunston (BRN-H, *1306–9*, Fig. Z) has full passing braces with unrefined notched-lap joints to the arch-braces. It also has up-braces from the tiebeams to the rafters, and Cubbington has similar up-braces, forming St Andrew's crosses with the down-braces from the crown post.[43] Though the evidence is sparse, it seems that passing braces were retained later in the north of the region, as indicated by the contrast between West Hagbourne (X-WHA, 1284/5, not drawn), Bathley (1295/6) and Braunston (1306–11).

Crown posts and collar plates (purlins)

The simplest crown post identified is that at Sycamore Farm, Long Crendon (LON-G), which was originally considered to be primary, some 70 years earlier than any firmly dated examples. However, radiocarbon dating has shown that it was inserted soon after 1300 (*1301–28*) (see Ch. 8.5). The post is totally plain, braced only to the collar plate, as also are the crown posts at York Farm, West Hagbourne (X-WHA, 1284–5). Most of the other crown posts have four-way up-braces, with Harwell, Ivinghoe and Braunston (X-HA1, IVI-A, BRN-H) being the most decorative, each with a series of roll mouldings at head and foot. The carpenters of Milton, Clifton and Long Marston (X-MIL, CLI-B, LNG-M, Fig. ZZ) used plain crown posts with down bracing on their closed trusses, a structurally less demanding type, because four brace mortices did not have to be cut at the same position on the post. Similar bracing is also found on the base cruck truss at CLI-B, and on the central box-framed truss at HAR-C.

In several houses (X-WHA, 1284/5; STE-B, 1299; BRN-H, *1306–9*; SUC-A, 1317–18), the collar plates are not continuous but in sections, each length tenoned into the head of the crown post, which is itself tenoned into the collar.[44] Surprisingly, though Bathley had a collar plate, it lacked crown posts. Quaintree House (BRN-H, *1306–9*) uniquely provided extra support for the collar plate, with the collar of the central couple in each bay curved and passing under the plate, thus holding it firmly against the other collars.

Dragon ties

Dragon ties have only been found in eight buildings, generally being restricted to the end trusses, rather than used on all of them. At Sycamore Farm, Long Crendon (LON-G, 1205, p. 190f), what appear to be housings for dragon ties are present on the re-used arcade plates, but, perhaps for this reason, are not present in the existing building. Dragon ties are used in particular on the aisled trusses either preceding or associated with base crucks in four houses: IVI-A (*1250–77*), LON-O (on both central and end trusses), CUB-A (*1313–41*) where the dragon ties are moulded, and LNG-M (1340) where they are curved, these superior details indicating the quality of carpentry in these houses. The remaining four examples are in box-framed chamber blocks and crosswings: AST-A (1282/6, Fig. 5.5b), STE-B (1299, removed, probably during the 1448/9 reconstruction of the roof), SUC-A (1317/18), STE-E (1356/65). Generally, dragon ties ceased to be used

by about 1350, so this final example falls at the very end of their range.

Problems and mistakes

Inevitably, not all the carpenter's work was entirely successful. It is remarkable how well these buildings have survived during the 500 to 700 years since they were built, but we can see some signs of defective workmanship although mistakes are often only visible when a structure has been dismantled or extensively opened up. As mentioned above, the thin windbraces of the later fifteenth and sixteenth century houses have often buckled and sometimes cracked or fallen out. The lack of side-wall bracing led to racking of the crucks in one house (STO-C) to the extent that the end cruck fell out – admittedly not until 1910!

The frequent simple splayed scarfs were prone to coming apart. Perhaps because the timbers being joined were in-line rather than perpendicular, skew pegging seems not to have been used for these joints. We can see from the variety of alternative scarf types, each used once or twice, that the carpenters were exploring solutions to this problem before bladed scarfs became standard in the sixteenth and seventeenth centuries.

The selection of timber seems often to have been less careful than might have been expected. For example at ROT-D (1492–9) (Ch. 8.8), the supporting beam for the chamber floor is well-finished at one end, but degenerates into an extraordinarily waney and knotty shape at the other (Fig. 8.8.4). The elm crucks at STO-B (*1444–57*, Fig. 4.3(d)) which have their feet patched with pieces of oak cruck blades can hardly be regarded as high points in the carpenter's art. Similarly, at STE-B (1355/6, Fig. 4.2a), one side of the highly-finished open truss has a massive plank applied to it, although whatever problem this was intended to remedy remains hidden.

Perhaps the most striking example of the problems the carpenters might encounter can be seen at LNG-M (1339/40) (Ch. 8.3). When the carpenters were drilling the pegholes in the tiebeam for one of the arch brace mortices, part of the base of the tiebeam split off, revealing a large shake and a cavity. The holes were abandoned, and the end of the brace was secured to the tiebeam with an iron strap. Confirmation that this occurred during the original construction is demonstrated by the smoke-blackening inside the split in the tiebeam (Figs. 8.3.5a–c). On the other end of the tiebeam, the problems were almost as bad. The pegholes were completed, but when the pegs were being driven, the soffit of the tiebeam again split and had to be repaired with another strap.[45]

6

Documentary Evidence

In this chapter, the first section presents an overview of documentary evidence and historical approaches to peasant houses, mainly from the Midlands. It explores the historical significance of peasant buildings, under the headings of peasant economy, domesticity, their place in communities and in the social hierarchy, and finally their chronology. Attention is particularly focussed on the implications of the sample of buildings dated during the project. The three following sections examine the documentary evidence county by county, both generally and though case studies of villages with exceptionally good survival of both documents and early buildings. The aim of these studies is to establish the economic context in the medieval period, either of specific houses or of the community as a whole. A short final section examines the social background to the base cruck houses included in the survey.

6.1 Medieval Peasant Buildings 1250–1550: Documents and Historical Significance

Chris Dyer

Introduction

The term 'peasant house' was coined in the early days of the study of smaller rural buildings by such authors as S. O. Addy, and was given a new impetus in the late twentieth century by architectural historians, such as J. T. Smith and Jane Grenville, and particularly by the archaeologist J. G. Hurst. Similarly, the title of one of the most important contributions by a documentary historian to the subject, by R. K. Field, uses the phrase 'peasant buildings'.[1] Recent studies have more often characterised buildings according to their construction, such as 'timber framed' or 'cruck' buildings, or their layout and form, as 'Wealdens' or 'hall

houses' (as indeed was the genesis of the present project). The advantage of the phrase 'peasant house' is that it commits us to think about buildings in their social and economic context. The term 'peasant' leads to a focus on the countryside, and on the lower ranks of society, people with limited resources.

Historians have been increasingly reluctant to use the word 'peasant', though not for very good reasons. Some claim that the definition of 'peasant' is too imprecise, but that does not stop them using words such as 'merchant' (which covers every trader from an upmarket shopkeeper to an international tycoon), or equally broad categories such as 'culture'. The main reason for sensitivity is their dislike of a term which is associated with a 'class' analysis of society, but in expressing their prejudice against a particular approach to the past they are putting obstacles in the path of a clear analysis of social differences. 'Peasant' is a very useful word, and no-one has devised an adequate substitute. The term 'villager' is not appropriate for the inhabitants of hamlets and isolated farms. Contemporary words such as 'villein', 'husbandman' and 'yeoman' apply only to sections of rural society categorised by legal status or wealth – they are not generic terms. The word 'farmer' in the middle ages meant a leaseholder, who belonged to a minority of superior tenants. Its modern sense describing an occupation, or the owner or tenant of hundreds of acres is hardly analagous to the much smaller holdings of the past.

Peasant is a convenient term for the holder of land on a small scale, in the case of medieval England only occasionally exceeding 30 acres before 1350 or 70 acres in the period 1380–1540. They gained their main living from agricultural production on their holding, but they often also pursued such occupations as mining or fishing, or they worked as artisans or traders.[2] Smallholders (especially those with no more than a cottage) in particular needed additional income, and they often found employment as wage earners in agriculture. Tenants with 15 acres of arable could feed their families from their own resources, but if they had more, they would have had a surplus of grain to sell. Thus, many peasants engaged to some degree with the market both as buyers of basic food and drink (the smallholders) and as sellers of produce. At all levels they bought some foodstuffs, clothing, tools and utensils, and the services of specialists such as building craftsmen. Peasants might hope to find the labour for working the land from their own resources, with the head of the household receiving support from his wife and children. If they consistently needed extra help, they commonly took a servant or two into their household. As small-scale landholders, peasants occupied a subordinate position in society, paying rents to their lords and taxes to the state. Although weak and vulnerable as individuals, they gained strength from their association with others in a community. Their culture tended to be based on oral communication, but they were closely involved in religion at parish level, which again required them to act collectively in support of the church and in attending its ceremonies.

How does the term 'peasant' add to our understanding of the small rural house or, to put it more directly, what peasant characteristics can be seen in the peasant house? When the phrase was being used in the 1950s and 1960s it could justify preconceptions, even myths, about peasants. As they were assumed to be miserably poor, the structures were thought to have been temporary and insubstantial, which required repeated and frequent rebuildings. As peasants were regarded as being locked into a self-sufficient economy, it was believed that they were only able to use materials obtained in the immediate locality, which would not have been of the best quality, and that the builders were the tenants themselves. Each holding, it was said, was served by a single building, which often combined accommodation for animals as well as people, so the 'longhouse' of the highland zone, combining a dwelling and a byre, represented a survival of a type once found throughout England, and the 'farm', with a number of

separate agricultural buildings set around a yard (or in a line) developed gradually and sometimes did not emerge until the end of the middle ages.[3] The 'vernacular threshold' (the date after which houses could survive to the present day) was supposed to have been crossed at quite a late date. Thus, most standing timber-framed buildings with their relatively sturdy and sophisticated standards of construction belonged to the sixteenth and seventeenth centuries, and had been built only for superior peasants, if those who occupied them could be described as peasants at all. For those who believed that the standing buildings were associated with people akin to peasants, such as yeomen, romantic notions could be entertained about the closeness to the soil of the occupants, and their simple and honest values. Just as houses built to high standards by specialist craftsmen were thought to have been impossibly expensive for a peasant, so their furnishings were dismissed as few and of low quality.[4]

Peasants and their houses

The account given here of the connections between peasants and their buildings will be based on documents as well as on the results of excavation and the study of standing buildings, informed by recent writings on late medieval rural society. Peasants took advantage of the local materials available to them as much as possible, such as clay and wattles for wall panels, or earth for mud walls. They would have obtained timber from the local wood if they had rights of housbote, and if the wood contained suitable trees. Many villages, however did not have access to woods, either because none existed (or they had only small groves which lacked an abundance of large trees), or because the lord reserved the timber for his own use and profit. When lords encouraged tenants to repair and rebuild in the period of housing decay after 1350 they sometimes offered to supply the timber, which implies that normally tenants did not have free access to these materials. The best indication that peasants bought timber comes from those occasions when lords paid for buildings. They presumably then followed the normal practices of peasants arranging their own building work. At Murcott in Northamptonshire, for example, in 1432–3 the lord bought spars and laths from Lutterworth (Leicestershire) in two loads at a total cost (including carriage) of 16s 4d.[5] Those undertaking building throughout the villages of south Leicestershire and north-west Northamptonshire, where woods were scarce, would go to Lutterworth to buy timber and wood which had originated in the Forest of Arden. Similar markets where timber could be obtained are known in other towns, such as Stratford-upon-Avon in Warwickshire and Woodstock in Oxfordshire, which acted as gateways connecting woodland with regions without plentiful timber.[6]

As the standards of buildings rose, peasants needed

to find more money for materials. At Thorner in west Yorkshire in 1423–7 the lord paid for roofs of stone slates, presumably because this expensive roofing had become customary among the tenants. This meant not only paying for the slates, their carriage, and the slater's wages, but the robust timber frame (at increased cost) that a heavy roof also required.[7] Stone slates have been found in excavations of rural settlements in Sussex and Warwickshire.[8] Ceramic tiles were also bought (at some distance – from Coventry) for a Murcott house in 1430–1, probably to provide a fire-proof section of the roof near to the louvre by which smoke escaped.[9]

Peasants could themselves make a contribution to building work, by digging foundations and removing earlier structures, and presumably by using their cart or wain to haul materials. However, the role of the peasant should not be exaggerated, as even the least skilled jobs might be done by specialists. Mud walls at Hoby in Leicestershire in 1452–3 for a barn in the tenancy of John Grene were made by William Friseby 'and his associates' for 4s 4d. For more highly skilled work, carpenters could be hired within

a few miles by lords, and presumably also by peasants if they were arranging the work; examples include Thomas Boye of Ashby St Legers who worked on one of the Murcott buildings for 13s 4d, or the carpenter from Bocking in Essex, John Seburugh, who worked on a building at Stisted in Essex in 1390.[10] Any list of rural occupations, and especially the poll tax lists of 1379 and 1381, demonstrate that there were large numbers of carpenters in England. Taking a sample of a hundred villages in five counties in 1381, sixty carpenters were named, which if replicated across the 14,500 taxation vills would give a total in excess of 8,000 carpenters – and there were many also living in towns.[11] They could make a living in such numbers only if they worked on a wide range of building projects, which included houses and farm buildings commissioned by and for peasants.

An analysis of sources of building materials fits then with our earlier characterisation of the peasant economy. In general, they combined a degree of self-sufficiency with an engagement with the market. Their use of labour indicates that peasants made some contribution to building work,

Table 6.1. Costs of peasant building in the fifteenth century.

Place	Date	Building	Construction	Cost	Source
Bishop's Clyst, Devon	1406	4 cottages of 2 bays each	stone foundations, cob wall, thatched roof.	£12 15s 18½d (est.)	Alcock (1965)
Thorner, W. Yorkshire	1423–7	house	slate roofs	£4 8s 3d	Le Patourel (1991), 863; Leeds Archives, WYL156/MX/M10/3/11, /13
Thorner, W. Yorkshire	1423–7	house and barn	house with slate roof, barn thatched	£7 13s 1d	Ibid.
Bedale, N Yorkshire	1429–30	house	stone foundations, timber frames, stone slate roof	£11 3s 9d	Harrison and Hutton (1984), 4–5
Bedale, N Yorkshire	1442–3	house	as above	£4 15s 6d	Ibid.
Fulstow, Lincolnshire	1429–30	house with chamber annexed, and new barn	timber frame, thatched roof.	£3 9s 3d	Lincolnshire Archives, LMR 16/2
Murcott in Watford, Northamptonshire	1430–1	messuage	timber and thatched roof; tiles for part of roof, earth walls	£4 3s 4d	Dyer (2008), 69
Murcott	1432–3	messuage	earth walls, timber and thatched roof.	£4 7s 0d	Ibid.
Murcott	1436–7	messuage	as above	£2 8s 6d	Ibid.
Durrington, Wiltshire	1436	house	stone foundations, 3 doors, 4 windows	£6 18s 9d	Hare (2011), 144
Tillington, Staffordshire	1437–8	house of 3 bays, and barn of 3 bays	foundation, timber frame and thatched roof	£3 18s 2d	Dyer (2008), 28–9.
Brassington, Derbyshire	1440–1	house of 4 bays, and barn of 3 bays	stone walls to eaves on house, half-height on barn. Thatched roofs.	£8 9s 2½d	Le Patourel (1991), 864–5; TNA, DL 29/369/6180
Rolston, Staffordshire	1444–6	barn of 3 bays		£7 5s 2d	Birrell (1979), 40
Chevington, Suffolk	1457–8	house	stone foundations, timber framed, thatched roof.	£2 2s 10d	Suffolk R. O., Bury St Edmunds branch, E3/15.52/2.1a
Hargrave, Suffolk	1457–8	new barn	timber frame, roof of reed, sedge and straw thatch.	£3 18s 7½d	Ibid.
Sidbury, Devon	1460–2	house	stone foundations, cob wall, thatched roof.	£8 4s 3d	Exeter, Cathedral Library, D&C 5055–6; Fox (1991), 171; Alcock (personal communication)

but a greater proportion was undertaken by hired artisans. A shift towards the employment of artisans came in the thirteenth century when the market in general expanded, and a division of labour increased the numbers of those with specialist skills. Expenditure on a number of peasant houses and barns which were built by lords has been recorded in manorial documents, mainly in the period 1400–60. The examples in Table 6.1 show that the total cost could range between about £2 and £11, with a median figure around £4. Lords would probably have incurred higher costs than would a peasant commissioning a building, but the figures do not entirely misrepresent the level of spending incurred by a peasant embarking on a building project. A check is provided by the valuation put on the deterioration of buildings suffering from neglect by manorial juries, which could rise to £2, £3 or £4. An unusual statement of costs from before 1350 comes from Holbrook in Derbyshire in 1312, when a marriage agreement was disputed, and a new house was said to be worth £2.[12] An indication of the value attached to rebuilding also comes from the penalties imposed by courts on tenants who did not build as required, like the sum of £5 placed on the failure to build a house at Stoke, near Coventry in 1365, though as a punitive sum it may have exceeded the expected cost (see p. 143).

Regional differences

The landscape in which peasants conducted their farming activities is believed to have had a strong influence on their economy, notably in the balance between arable and pasture in the land that they farmed, and in the different types of animal and crops on their holdings. This same generalisation can be applied to their buildings. The materials varied from one type of countryside to another, so we find in the later middle ages flint used as the foundation material in Sussex, chalk in the Yorkshire wolds, oolite in the Cotswolds and granite on Dartmoor. The choice was not always determined by the most convenient local supplies so, for example, timber building predominated in parts of Wales, even though building stone was locally available. Builders in areas with abundant stone, such as Dartmoor and the Cotswolds, did not begin to use it for foundation walls until the thirteenth century. Walls of earth were not confined to those regions, such as parts of the Midlands, where alternative materials were relatively scarce.

The region to which peasant houses belonged had a profound effect on their siting, whether within villages, in the central province running through the Midlands and including parts of the south-west and north-east, or in smaller hamlets or isolated farms in the areas of dispersed settlement in the east, south-east and west.[13] Houses belonging to hamlets and farms were sometimes spread out along roads, often with an enclosed field separating one house from another, or they were strung at intervals on the edge of commons or upland pastures. We find 'cruck villages' such as Stoneleigh and Rothley, in the Midlands, but surviving cruck houses are also plentiful in areas of dispersed settlement such as the counties on both sides of the Welsh border. The documents show that crucks were once the normal method of construction throughout a county with contrasting landscapes such as Warwickshire, both in the villages of the south and east of the county, and in the hamlets and farmsteads of the Arden to the north-west.

Houses, households and the peasant economy

The most distinctive feature of peasant houses, which clearly separates them from buildings belonging to the aristocracy, is their role in production. The word 'house' (Latin *domus*) can be applied to any building, and the court records which complain about decay often mention the 'messuage'. This term refers to the structures built on a plot of land, which might include three, four or five buildings, together with yards, garden plots, manure heaps and other features which served as the centre for the exploitation of a holding; they were summed up in the frequent description of tenancies as a 'messuage and a yardland' or 'a messuage and 13 acres of land'. The great majority of houses stood alongside an agricultural building (usually a barn) and accommodation for animals, such as a byre, stable, sheepcote or less often a cart- or wainhouse, maltkiln, horse mill, hay house, cheese house, pigsty or poultry house. Another building commonly found in documents and excavated sites, though rarely in standing buildings was a bakehouse or kitchen, which was often also used for brewing. Dovecotes occasionally figure as a structure on a peasant holding, which should not be surprising because although most such buildings belonged to the lords of manors, keeping doves was not a seigneurial monopoly. A full description of the structures on a single holding comes from Sutton under Brailes in Warwickshire in 1507, which lists a dwelling house, barn, stable, sheepcote and dovecote.[14] Farm buildings were regarded by the lord's officials as important parts of the productive capacity of peasant holdings, and therefore were singled out when they required a tenant to repair or rebuild. On the Ramsey Abbey estate (mainly in Huntingdonshire) 199 buildings were mentioned in entries extracted from their court rolls, dating between 1399 and 1458. A total of 107 (54 per cent) were dwellings or parts of dwellings (halls, chambers and solars), and 51 (26 per cent) were barns.[15] In Gloucestershire, on the manors of the Archbishop of York in the fifteenth century, 42 (53 per cent) of the total of 80 buildings recorded as in need of repair were barns.[16] Tenants of Evesham Abbey around 1500, also in Gloucestershire, were reported in 31 (28 per cent) cases to have defective barns, and 39 were ordered to undertake the upkeep of buildings designed for animals or birds: horses, cattle, sheep, pigs and doves.[17]

Excavations on village sites shows that these buildings usually stood close together, often around a yard. A manorial complex, like that at Chalgrove in Oxfordshire, would have two groups of buildings, with some separation between residential accommodation and farm buildings.[18] In a peasant messuage the productive activities practised in the barn, byre and sheepcote were integrated with the food preparation and consumption in the bakehouse and the dwelling. The combination of functions was famously demonstrated in some regions, notably Devon and Cornwall, by the longhouse with animals and humans living under the same roof. More commonly, as the earliest probate inventories of the fifteenth century show, rooms in houses designed primarily for living, might be used to keep implements such as sickles and scythes, and the dwelling was also used for supplementary storage, not just of the conventional sides of bacon, but also for grain.[19] At Wharram Percy in one house, the barn was used to store coal which would be burnt on the domestic hearth.[20] The idea of separating living and working space would probably not seem a meaningful concept to members of a peasant household. Those who slept in the chambers and ate in the hall would also work on the land or in the dairy or brew house. In the 1381 poll taxes, we find the phrase 'son and servant' and 'daughter and servant' which makes plain the role and status of teenage children (they had to be aged fifteen or older to be included in the tax). The servants who were not close relatives still shared in meals at the table and slept somewhere in the premises, perhaps in the hall or in farm buildings. Meals and accommodation formed part of their pay, so the house was contributing to the labour supply on the land. It is difficult to draw a sharp line between domestic and farm buildings, as their function could change. There is good documentation for the conversion of bakehouses, carthouses, and stables into dwellings for retired peasants who had relinquished the main house to a new generation. A standing building at Norwell in Nottinghamshire, now called the Auld Cottage, was built as a barn in 1512, and subsequently converted into a dwelling.[21]

The close association between dwellings and farm buildings leads us to another conclusion about the nature of buildings in the peasant economy. The quality of the construction of some farm buildings was comparable with the dwellings, which explains the ease with which they could be converted from one use to another. A barn at Scropton in Derbyshire was to be built using 24 trees, which would not be very different from the quantity needed for the basic frame of a cruck house.[22] Paying for such buildings to be constructed or repaired represented an investment by the peasant, who expected to gain a return in terms of crops stored safely. Animals would be well sheltered from the elements, and fed conveniently from nearby stores of hay, oats and legumes. Carts and ploughs would last longer if kept under a roof. It was worth spending the money, which would probably have been borrowed in the active credit market well documented in some villages.[23] The improvements in the efficiency of farming would bring financial returns to pay off the debt and to justify the expenditure. The sheep sheltered in the sheepcote would yield heavier and higher quality fleeces that would command a better price; livestock and grain could be kept in good condition in preparation for sale. If a peasant had a malt kiln, he could dispose of the surplus barley crop as malt at enhanced prices in the urban market. Birds from a peasant dovecote would be sold in towns or to the local gentry or clerical households, rather than being consumed by the peasant family, which was unaccustomed to such luxuries. In other words, buildings brought in income, and constructing them was well worth the expense. Peasants became involved in profitable crafts as well as agriculture, and the structures on the messuage could include pottery kilns, tile kilns, forges and smithies.[24]

The word 'domestic' has already crept into the analysis of the use of buildings, but it has been suggested that domesticity is an inappropriate word to describe medieval houses in general. It is said that they were too sparsely furnished to be regarded as comfortable places, and the presence of non-family members prevented private family life.[25] This makes the buildings seem cold and functional, but documents imply that domesticity of a specific kind could be found in peasant households. It resembles our own in the sense that each generation on marriage formed its own household. Young married couples did not generally share houses with their parents, because they were likely, especially in the period after 1350, to have married in their twenties, after a period of working and saving, which gave them resources and experience necessary to run a household and acquire a house and land.[26] At Halesowen in Worcestershire, younger sons and daughters, who could not inherit the main holding, were sometimes provided by their father with dwellings at the rear of the messuage.[27] This practice might explain some of the evidence for buildings in such a position on well-preserved deserted village sites, which are normally interpreted as accommodation for the elderly.[28] When old people retired they were allocated space, whether the converted farm buildings already mentioned, or separate rooms, with access to the hall or garden carefully specified.[29] On the Titchfield estate in Hampshire in the fourteenth century a widow was assigned a third share of a dwelling, or a chamber.[30] The sense of privacy did not extend to a strict separation between family and servants, but the presence at the meal table of non-relatives, such as lodgers, was a commonplace of homes until very recently. Nor were peasants oblivious to comfort, as their inventories include cushions and 'bankers' which were long cushions to soften the hardness of a bench. A high proportion of the value of peasant household possessions was represented by bedding – sheets, blankets, coverlets and mattresses, which suggests that the chamber was not so austere.[31] Nonetheless, we should not exaggerate the 'homeliness' of the peasant house. It was organised on hierarchical principles, with a father in charge who sat in the only chair at meals and was regarded in law as responsible for the behaviour of the household members.

Peasant families and communities

It was once believed without question that peasant families and their holdings were connected by a close bond, which would have been focussed on the house as well as the land. In the midlands and the south in the thirteenth and fourteenth centuries, much land passed on the death of a tenant to a family member, who was often a son and heir, though this was not so common in commercial East Anglia. This practice diminished in the two or three generations after the Black Death, and the attachment of a family to a particular house was weakened. With increasing frequency, young people left the family and found their own holding and house elsewhere. Retired peasants seeking security in their old age were willing to trade their holding to a non-relative for a promise of an annuity or a share in land for the rest of their lives. Tenants making their wills contemplated without apparent sentiment the sale of their home to provide money for their heirs. When the houses that we are studying here were built, their builders and owners had no strong expectation that their children and grandchildren would in future inhabit them, though they may have hoped that this would happen. They must have thought that, sooner or later, a durable house would enhance the value of the holding when it was sold.[32]

The assumption that a male dominated the house ought to be qualified by the recognition of the special role of women. They were of course expected to manage the household, prepare food, and clean, but they also had important agricultural and horticultural responsibilities, as they had charge of the garden, poultry, pigs and beehives. They milked cows and ewes, and made butter and cheese. They also brewed and baked, and it was they who went out to fetch water and fuel. They either took grain to the mill, or milled it at home on a hand mill. These activities contributed not just to the food and drink consumed in the households, but also to its cash income, as ale, cheese, butter, eggs, honey and garden produce were sold by them, both to neighbours and in urban markets. They were also expected to work on the land when necessary, specifically to help with such tasks as weeding and harvesting. This not only made them important contributors to the well-being and income of the household, but also heightened their status and gave them some independence. At important stages of the family life-cycle a woman was in charge, acting as executrix of her husband's will, sole tenant in the

time when she held free bench after her husband died, and having some influence over the transmission of the house and land to the next generation.[33] Male peasants seem to have regarded their wives as partners, as indicated by the increasingly common custom from the fourteenth century of husbands and wives holding land as joint tenants. The courts behaved as if they were tender of the rights of women as property holders: if a woman had inherited land in her own right, usually as a daughter, her husband could not sell it until she had been 'examined sole', that is asked by the court if she gave her consent, in the absence of her husband.[34] Space in and around the house should be seen as being run by women, and for periods of time, women were managing the whole property, and would have commissioned repairs and new buildings.

Peasant households formed part of a community, which in its physical arrangements could be a congested grouping of houses in a nucleated village, or an association of scattered holdings in an area of dispersed settlement. The collective dimension was represented by certain spaces: a village green, roads and a pond or well for example. The churchyard often served as an important public open space, and a few villages had a market place.[35] Buildings that served the community included the church, a church house for the holding of church ales, a guild hall for parish fraternities (mostly in East Anglia), and the mill and bakehouse which everyone was expected to use. Ale houses would not usually have been purpose built, but customers drank in the hall of an otherwise conventional dwelling, and an ale stake outside showed that drink was being sold. A material culture which was common to all of the villagers would be evident in the materials and architectural style of the houses.

While accepting the importance of the village community in peasant life, we notice, as would a visitor in the later middle ages, that each house was separate and was protected from unwanted intrusions. The messuage or toft would be surrounded by a ditch and bank surmounted by a fence or hedge (or a dry stone wall in some districts); access would be by means of a gate leading on to the street, and once this had been passed the visitor would find that they gained entrance to the house (or were denied it) by a door with a lock. Space within the house was divided between the hall where visitors were welcomed, and the chamber which was more private. Peasants had possessions which they wished to protect from theft, and they clearly feared that they would be the victims of crime. Houses had small shuttered windows, secure doors, and once entry had been effected, chests containing valuables had their own locks. Peasants protected their privacy through the manor court, which might deal with anti-social offences which included eavesdropping – that is standing by the walls of houses to listen to conversations within. Individuals and families valued their reputations, and were concerned that the public gossip (*fama* or 'fame') might be hostile to them.[36]

Peasants belonged to communities, which therefore might be regarded as having an egalitarian dimension in the sense that they all shared in common assets. By-laws which were announced in the manor court were often said to have been agreed by all tenants, or the whole community, or the whole homage. The stratification of village society however has implications for understanding their buildings. We have already seen that most definitions of peasants include both cottagers and substantial tenants with 60 acres of land, those who held land as freeholders and those who held by customary (originally unfree) tenures, those who depended entirely on agriculture, and those who practised trades and crafts. These differences did not necessarily divide them into mutually hostile groups. They depended on one another because the better-off employed the smallholders on the land, sold them grain, and probably lent them money. The poorer villagers might hope to receive patronage, such as support in the proceedings of the manor court, from their wealthier and more influential neighbours. They were bound together by their shared responsibilities to higher authorities, the lord, the church and the state. They did not always co-operate with their superiors, and could mount collective resistance against their lord.

Some archaeological evidence points to distinctions between the housing of smallholders and more substantial tenants. A thirteenth-century settlement at Coton in Warwickshire, the name of which means 'cottages', consisted of a number of small buildings based on earthfast posts, reminiscent of houses of the pre-Conquest period.[37] They do not resemble in size or construction the many excavated houses of the thirteenth century, which often measured 15 by 30–45ft and had some form of stone foundation. On sites dating mostly from the fourteenth and fifteenth centuries, such as West Whelpington in Northumberland and Caldecote in Hertfordshire, a few inferior buildings interpreted as cottages are found among the 'regular' village houses.[38]

Sometimes it is said that the surviving houses are socially unrepresentative: that they belonged to the village elite, and mislead us about the standard of housing as a whole.[39] Of course numerous rural timber-framed buildings are now called cottages, but many of these were originally attached to a yardland or half-yardland holding (about 30 or 15 acres of land). A surviving building which really was a cottage at the time it was built at Stoneleigh (STO-F, see pp. 146, 248ff), seems neither smaller nor notably inferior to the other cruck houses in the village.[40] The same phenomenon has been noted at Steventon where surviving houses can be shown to have been attached to holdings of 8 acres and even 1 acre (see p. 141). The buildings do not help us to make clear distinctions between different layers of society and neither do the documents. A high proportion of the buildings which were subject to agreements between lords and tenants for replacement were specified to be of three

bays, which included those attached to smaller holdings of a quarter yardland (8 acres).[41] A cottage was occasionally said to stand alone, without an outbuilding, but a cottager commonly possessed a barn, and sometimes another building. Messuages attached to larger holdings invariably contained a number of buildings, including specialist animal houses.

The houses of wealthy peasants might be thought to have had an advantage in their rate of survival, but our admittedly incomplete knowledge of the people associated with particular buildings does not support this view. Extending our focus from individual holdings to the distribution of existing rural cruck buildings in general, they do not coincide with areas of wealth as reflected in tax payments. The west midland counties to the north and west of the Cotswold edge, including the Severn valley and south-west Shropshire, where the cruck buildings are clustered in special abundance, contributed to the 1524–5 lay subsidy at a rate of below 20s per square mile, when parts of the south-east, including such counties as Kent and Sussex, with concentrations of surviving substantial and well-built Wealden houses, were rated at above 40s per square mile.[42] The houses that survive did not belong to people of unusual wealth, nor were they always situated in prosperous regions.

Housing culture

Surviving buildings cannot easily be linked with the individuals who built and lived in them, and even if we know their names their wealth and status are not always easily judged. On the other hand, peasant buildings are usually markedly different from those built for occupation by the aristocracy, and those found in the streets of towns. A much discussed problem is the extent to which peasants were motivated in planning their houses by a desire to emulate aristocratic and urban models. It could be said that any similarities arose from the common culture shared by all sections of society, rather than imitation by the lower orders of their lords. The issue is full of complexities, as peasants seem to have had their own culture. They did not practise or idealise lordship as did the gentry and the peerage. The authority of the peasant head of household, a man or woman who worked alongside his older children and servants, can scarcely be compared with the power, titles and grandeur claimed by an esquire or knight. An apparently similar material culture might have different meanings: both lords and peasants displayed weapons on the walls of the hall, but for the aristocracy the lances and swords represented their claim to be a military elite, whereas the peasant's axe or bow was showing that he had a military role, as part of the armed force available to rulers in the event of disorder or invasion, and also for his own self defence.[43] Nonetheless, they sought to express their sense of worth and to indicate the small-scale social hierarchy within each household. The arrangement of their halls and the occasions (especially meals) held in them resemble the practices in a lord's manor house. That was the model available to them in a society over which the aristocracy extended a cultural hegemony. In the same way peasants recognised that towns had a distinctive way of life, and did not seek to become townspeople, but they admired urban sophistication, and were happy to have their houses provided with jetties, just like those in towns. The jetty had been a response to the lack of space in towns, and was unnecessary in the country, but gave the house a desired urban style. The tendency for peasant houses to acquire upper storeys, which is apparent by c. 1300, and which developed most strongly in the east and south-east, may also owe something to urban models (e.g. Aston Tirrold (AST-A, 1282–6) and York Farm, West Hagbourne (X-WHA, 1284–5)).

Peasant houses had a distinct character of their own, and should not be regarded only as pale imitations of manor houses and urban buildings. The outward appearance of their houses expressed the self confidence of their occupants. Cross wings, upper storeys, and the display of timbers, such as closely set studs must all have conveyed messages about the wealth and status of the tenant. A detail with the same purpose might be a door studded with large-headed iron nails. The tenants who commissioned these buildings were part of a community, and their common culture, often regional rather than that of a particular village, formed part of their identity. Houses might display various signs and symbols: the ale stake to advertise the sale of drink, or a timber feature of unknown form 'the sign of the heriot', showing that the holding was liable to pay heriot to the lord, as recorded at East Bergholt in Suffolk.[44] At Dassett Southend, Warwickshire, the name of a tenant, Gormand, was cut into the stone jamb of a doorway, which may reflect a more normal practice of painting the name.[45] The interlocked circles which are frequently seen incised on accessible timbers are conventionally thought to have been apotropaic signs, warding off the forces of evil.[46]

The dates of project buildings, and their historical implications

The peasant economy, although influenced by the market, did not fluctuate in the same way as a modern capitalist economy. The rise and fall in the size of population determined the overall number of peasant houses – there were about half a million rural households in England in 1100, rising to a million around 1300, falling again to a half million by 1400, at which the total remained until the second quarter of the sixteenth century. That is not to say that population was the sole explanation of change. While, throughout England, half a million houses fell into ruin in the fourteenth century and continued as empty plots after

1400, some districts and settlements were acquiring new houses and households, especially where industry created a new demand for employment.

The higher reaches of the economy, represented by the fluctuations of the incomes of great landed estates and the ups and downs of international trade, were depressed after about 1375 and went through a profound recession in c.1440–80. Features of economic slump included low prices, notably for grain, and reduced rents, because holdings lacked tenants, or because the annual dues were reduced to attract and keep tenants. These circumstances did not necessarily spread gloom and poverty in rural society. This was a period when the size of holdings increased; their exploitation shifted from arable to a mixture of arable and pasture. The 'great rebuilding' theory set out by Hoskins linked new houses in the period 1570–1640 with the prosperity of yeomen farmers in an age of rising prices of agricultural produce, but we can identify an earlier phase of rebuilding in the fifteenth century in completely different social and economic circumstances.[47]

The project dates for cruck buildings in Leicestershire and Warwickshire are summarised in Figure 6.1. They show that all but three of the houses were built between 1380 and 1510, with a high proportion in the fifteenth century, reaching a peak between 1430 and 1480. Though the sample is small, it is very much in accord with the dates from Buckinghamshire and Shropshire for cruck buildings, and from Kent for all timber buildings, most of them Wealden houses.[48] Oxfordshire has a relatively high proportion of earlier and later buildings, but a substantial minority belong to the fifteenth century.

These dates present a striking paradox, because they coincide almost exactly with the evidence from documents for the decay and destruction of tenant buildings, mostly in the period 1370–1480, though on some manors beginning in the 1350s and 1360s, and sometimes continuing well after 1500. Tenants were ordered to carry out repairs, often under threat of paying a penalty, after their buildings were presented as being in a ruinous state. If the order was not carried out – the usual case – it was repeated under a stiffer penalty. Some records give the type of building, and the part requiring repair – the roof of a barn, the wall of a chamber, or even occasionally identifying the decayed timbers. Less common presentments refer to acts of deliberate destruction rather than neglect. A tenant is said to have 'made waste' in a holding, or to have removed timbers for use elsewhere, or even to have sold a building or its materials. At Bishop's Tachbrook (Warwickshire) in 1350, John Tewyng and his wife were accused of carrying off old and decayed timber from a holding that was in the lord's hands (meaning untenanted), and burning it, presumably as firewood.[49] Reports of ruinous buildings sometimes tell us that a house or barn is 'prostrated to the ground'. Total disappearance of buildings is implied by the description of the holding as

Dates of cruck houses: Leicestershire and Warwickshire

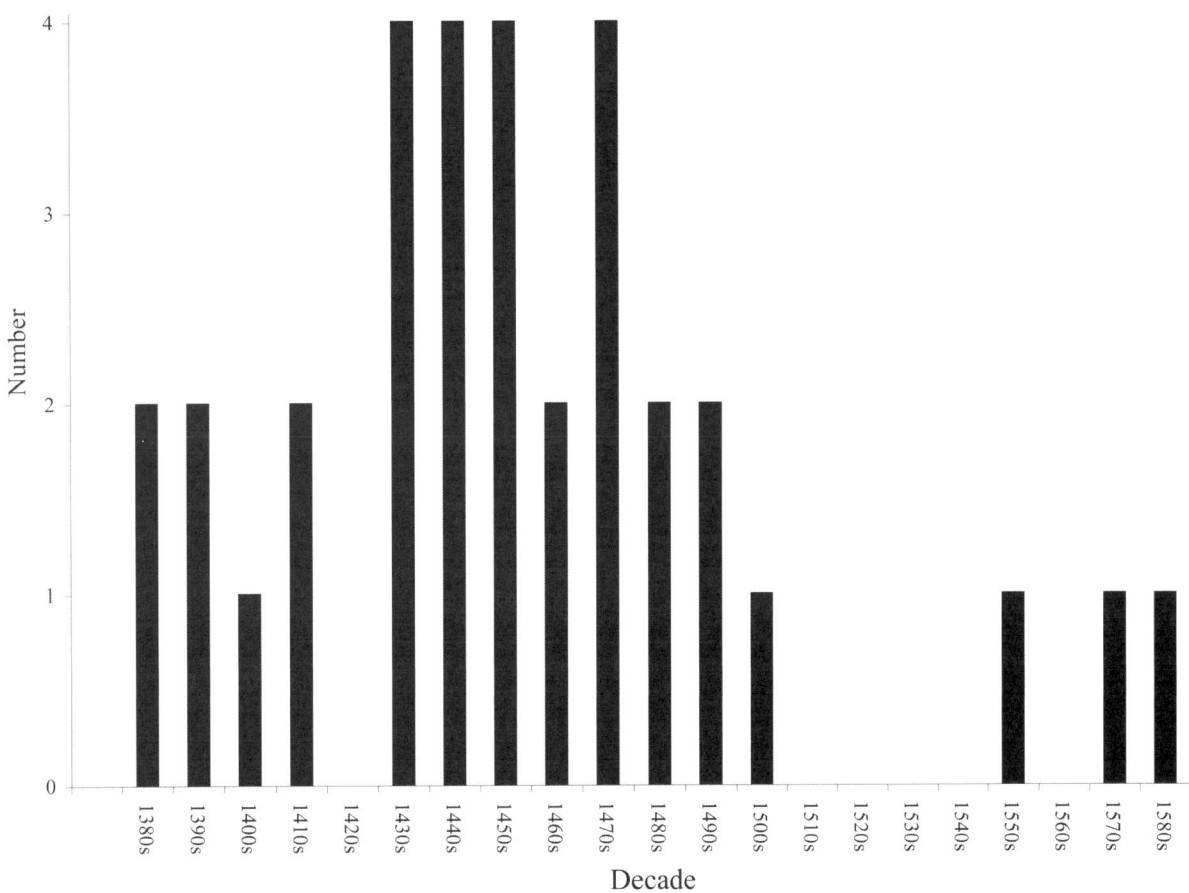

Fig. 6.1. Dates by decade of cruck houses in Leicestershire and Warwickshire. The probably urban crucks in Alcester, Warwickshire (ALC-A) and Castle Donington, Leicestershire (CAS-A; CAS-B) are excluded, as is the late and probably non domestic example at Weston-on-Avon (WOA-A). An earlier version of this figure, based on the then available dates, is in Dyer, *Age of transition*, 153.

a toft rather than a messuage. In many villages half of the former messuages and cottages were described as tofts in records of the mid-fifteenth century. New buildings appear in the records, such as those that incoming tenants agreed to build in a specified period – a three-bay dwelling within two years, for example. Subsequent records may complain that the agreement was not carried out. Lords attempted to push tenants to carry out the work by relieving them of rents for a year or two, cancelling arrears of rent, or granting materials. Lords who despaired of cajoling tenants paid for the work themselves, lest their assets waste yet further. At least we can be sure, when the details of building work appear in the accounts, that the new building came into existence.

The idea of a 'peasant housing crisis' can be linked readily to general conceptions of the economic trends of the period.

Population had fallen, so half of the housing stock was made redundant. Individual peasants had accumulated multiple holdings, and the houses and buildings which were surplus to their requirement were not worth repairing. Sometimes the tenants were falling into poverty, and their houses decayed, especially if their children had moved away and had no strong desire to inherit the holding. These were times of low land values, low prices for agricultural produce, and a general contraction in the rural economy.

How are we to reconcile the contradictions in our evidence? The standing buildings tell us of new construction, but the documents of houses falling down. Is this an example of two types of evidence giving irreconcilable information? In fact the sources are not as diametrically opposed as at first appears. The material evidence from the excavation of village sites reflects the written evidence very closely, because they reveal over the whole country hundreds of foundations of houses that were abandoned between the mid-fourteenth and early sixteenth centuries. Deserted villages might be thought to be extreme cases, a minority of ill-favoured settlements that disappeared completely, but there is abundant archaeological evidence of shrinkage in surviving villages, which cumulatively amount to a larger number of lost houses than can be found in the totally deserted sites. It is not necessary to use the arguments either that the standing buildings are a small and unrepresentative sample, which were unusual because they were built to a higher standard than the normal houses of their period, or that they are special cases because they have not been demolished in subsequent centuries.

In answer to the first allegation, the size and construction of the houses that still exist seem similar to those that appear in the documents. There is no reason to think that they belonged to some special tenant elite, or were built by exceptionally talented carpenters. On the second point it is true that only a tiny proportion of the houses that once existed have survived, and this was very much a matter of chance affected by the later policies pursued by landed estates, or by local economic variations.[50] The fact that they were built at a particular time is an important piece of historical information, and we must accept that the few dozen buildings that have been dated are a sample of the many thousands being erected at the time. The dates of reused crucks are equally relevant, because each tree felled presumably related to a new building.

Historians of this period are accustomed to reconciling contradictory tendencies. There has been a long running controversy over the 'economic decline' of the later middle ages.[51] An example of an argument put forward by those who see recession or decline as the main characteristic of the period relates to the supply of timber. After the Black Death, they say, the cultivated area diminished, and the woods expanded. The demand for timber also fell, as the number of major construction projects, such as castle or cathedral building, diminished. The combination of the increased supply and reduced demand caused a fall in timber prices, and therefore peasants found that building new houses became more affordable. Unfortunately for this line of reasoning, under-used agricultural land is known to have reverted to scrub, but not so often to productive woodland; we have little reliable data on changes in the price of timber; and the wages of carpenters and other workers, which accounted for a high proportion of building costs, certainly rose in the late fourteenth and fifteenth centuries, so the expenses of building are very unlikely to have fallen.

The resolution of the debate has come from the recognition that decay and new growth coexisted in late medieval society. For every symptom of decline, some related and opposite trend can be identified. As the population fell, the sum total of economic activity slumped; yet individuals increased their incomes, whether because they acquired larger holdings of land, or because their wages rose. Global production of foodstuffs and raw materials was reduced; but the productivity of individuals rose with the decline in underemployment. Cultivated land was abandoned – to be used as grazing for animals, which produced good returns because wealthier consumers demanded more meat. Villages decayed and were deserted; their empty fields were converted into productive pastures run by yeomen farmers and butcher graziers. Rents declined, which was bad for the revenues of landlords, but this made land cheap for those enterprising peasants who wished to expand their holdings. Some towns declined; others remained much the same size, and a few expanded, and so did rural industries and new market centres.

The sources need careful interpretation. We are dependent for much of our information on the records of the manorial courts, and at this time the manor was losing some of its authority. Perhaps it was a futile and unrealistic gesture for the courts to attempt to maintain control of holdings, at a time when the tenants, because of their scarcity and general resistance to the claims of lordship, were in a strong bargaining position. The courts were attempting to restore the old order, in the expectation that the situation would take a turn for the better, and tenants would come back to reoccupy the decayed messuages. While the lord's officials were busily engaged in this resistance, they ignored new developments which were taking place outside the manorial organisation. For example, the cloth industry of the Stroud valley in Gloucestershire, has left only small traces in the manorial records, though hundreds of artisans were employed in an industry serving a European market.[52]

If we turn to another type of source material, wills, which reflect the world of the tenants, especially the better-off tenants, the whole picture is transformed. The largest collections of wills before 1500 are found in the East Anglian archives, and are abundant there at the height of the peasant housing crisis, in the mid-fifteenth century. Their references to buildings give the opposite impression of that gained from the court rolls. William Clerk of Stratford St Mary (Suffolk) in 1458 left his son John 'my new house'; at Icklingham in the same county in 1474, Thomas Schercroft bequeathed to Joan, wife of Richard Smyth, 'all that tenement and croft ... that I built anew', and so on.[53] When the court rolls tell us of the neglect of buildings, the will makers specified that their buildings be maintained, and even allocated sources of income for that purpose. To some extent the wills are focussing our attention on the new activists and decision-makers in late medieval society – the yeomen, the farmers, and the cloth makers, but they include a large number of middling and better-off peasants – people with as little as 10–20 acres of land – and so are not entirely unrepresentative of the manorial tenants who played such a prominent role in the housing crisis revealed in the court records.[54] New buildings actually receive mention in the manorial records. Sometimes they are implied because a court was satisfied that a repair order or an agreement to build had been carried out; on occasion a grant of land or a rental will mention the rebuilt state of a messuage. Take the Warwickshire manor of Sambourn, which had its share of presentments of ruinous buildings in the 1470s and 1480s, including a barn of cruck construction (its *forkleggs* are mentioned). Here the lord even consented to the reduction in the building stock – in 1487 a tenant leasing part of the demesne was given permission to allow six bays to decay. The problem continued into the 1490s and early 1500s, but in 1497 we are told that William Bovy was taking a holding with a house 'newly rebuilt'.[55]

Building new houses

What then were the occasions for new buildings at the time of the peasant housing crisis? A number of special categories of building can be readily identified. These were firstly those connected with industrial expansion – not just the obvious industrial buildings like the tile houses and fulling mills, but also the dwelling houses integrated with workshops, warehouses, dyeing houses, and the other structures of the expanding cloth industry. A unique record tells us of the forty-seven houses mainly for cloth-making artisans built at Castle Combe in Wiltshire in 1409–59. In other textile districts, such as south-western Suffolk, the architectural evidence, gives a strong impression of extensive new building.[56] Another feature of the late medieval economy lay in the development of new informal centres of trade. Though often small, they attracted groups of traders, craftsmen and inn-keepers. Their growth at this period is sometimes marked, as at Stourbridge, Worcestershire, and Knowle, Warwickshire by surviving timber-framed buildings of an urban type.[57]

Buildings with public functions such as halls for parish fraternities, were especially numerous in East Anglia, but are found further west, for example at Aston Cantlow in Warwickshire. Church houses proliferated towards the end of the middle ages, and occur most frequently in the south-west, but some still survive in the Midlands. They were centres for church ales, and were often located in or near a churchyard. Almshouses were occasionally established in a similar location. These new public buildings reflect both the strength of communities, at a time when they are sometimes thought to be in decline, and the existence of surplus cash in the hands of some villagers.

Changes in agricultural management that followed the leasing of demesnes by lords could lead to new building, if the lands were divided. The separate parts were equipped with dwellings, barns and animal houses, for example at Hanbury in Worcestershire where the former manor house on the main manor was abandoned and lessees built new

farms on at least two of the new scattered subdivisions. In the same parish, the Cistercian grange of Holeway was split into two farms in about 1480, and two new houses were built. This echoed the subdivision of large monastic granges throughout the country.[58]

At the opposite end of the social spectrum of the late medieval countryside, houses and cottages were appearing on new sites towards the end of the fifteenth century, as populations were growing or families were relocating in response to economic changes. This was a phenomenon of areas of dispersed settlement, both woodlands and uplands, where wide roadsides and the edges of greens and common pastures provided sites for encroachment. This new wave of settlement dispersal is often regarded as a characteristic of the early modern period and early industrialization, but was clearly a significant context for new house building well before 1500.

Only one of the sample of dated Midland buildings is likely to belong to the categories of new construction detailed here. This is the house at Sutton Coldfield (Warwickshire) which has timbers felled in 1432. It lies beside the main road between Birmingham and Lichfield, a developing trading centre characteristic of woodland districts of the west midlands. Manorial records show Sutton to have contained many retailers of food and drink, presumably serving both its local rural hinterland and the travellers passing on the road. There were also a number of craftsmen, such as a weaver, named because he was accused of theft in 1434. While the manor was not immune to the usual problems of a declining land market and in 1434 the lord spent 22s on 'houses in the vill', it shows little sign of the decay found in most contemporary records. Ultimately Sutton's potential as a small town was recognised: it was incorporated in 1528 and benefitted from a deliberate policy of improvement.[59]

Most of the other 30 dated cruck buildings in the Leicestershire/Warwickshire sample stand in or near to nucleated villages which had been continuously inhabited for at least three or four centuries before the period 1380–1510. They were not new farms on outlying demesnes, or cottages encroaching on roadsides and wastes. They seem to have been built as private dwellings or barns, not as halls for community use. We cannot rule out the possibility that some of their builders had some craft or by-occupation in addition to agriculture, but the villages in which they stand were not especially noted as industrial centres. In order to investigate the background to their construction, we can use surviving records from a number of places where cruck buildings have been dated.

These places were undergoing many of the changes outlined earlier. They exhibit many symptoms of contraction and decline. At Haselor (cf. WAL-A, 1384/5), a rental of 1396 lists 24 messuages and cottages: these had once been held as separate holdings, but were now in the hands of

21 tenants. A century and a half later the manor contained only 10 messuages and 4 cottages.[60] The familiar story of shrinking arable farming is reflected in the rents paid for the tithe sheaves of Stretton-under-Fosse (cf. SUF-A, *1480–92*). In 1411 the farmer had bargained to pay £9 for these (suggesting a total grain crop worth £90, from perhaps 400 acres), but some difficulty in either production or sale is implied by the pardon granted by the lord for £1 of this sum. By 1444 the farmer was paying only £5.[61] This may partly be attributed to lower prices, but most likely resulted from a reduction in the sown acreage. A reeve's account of 1464–5 for Old Stratford, the manor in which Shottery lay (cf. STR-A, *1472/3*), tells a familiar story of difficulties in rent collection. A toft and half-yardland (the toft indicating that the building of the messuage had collapsed) for which a tenant had once paid 13s 4d per annum had recently been rented for 3s 4d, but in the current year yielded nothing, 'because there were no buyers'. Another toft and yardland had its rent reduced from 13s 4d to 10s. The names of successive tenants show the instability of land holding and the tendency for holdings to pass between tenants who were either unrelated or at least fairly remote relatives. One building had its tenants described as 'once Richard Folewelle, and afterwards John Irmonger and Thomas Garette, and now let to John Wytheleye'. Arrears represented a major problem at Stratford, partly because tenants were reluctant to pay even the relatively low official rents, and by 1464 the reeve and various other former reeves and officials owed a total of £70 17s 10¾d, more than the total annual revenue from the manor.[62]

The buildings of these villages were suffering from the usual problem of decay, and the lords were taking a range of counter-measures. At Oxhill (cf OXH-A, *1450–6*) in June 1394 three tenants were presented for the ruinous state of their buildings. Each had been previously ordered to carry out repairs under penalty of paying £1. Payment of this sum had been levied, and a new penalty of £2 was imposed. In the following October, two of them had still not complied, the £2 was levied and a further penalty of £3 was to be paid if they still failed to do the work. These were unusually tough sanctions – most lords were content to threaten, but not actually to levy, a penalty, and most penalties were rated in shillings rather than pounds. We must doubt whether the tenants paid these large sums, but they put sufficient pressure on one of the offenders, William Tounesend, to surrender his holding. He was said to be disabled ('impotent') and in arrears with his rent, so he was not a tenant much to be valued by the lord – but his departure held dangers for the manor's rent roll. If the lord pursued too draconian a policy on repairs, he was liable to drive tenants away, and lose both the building and the rents. In fact new tenants were forthcoming at Oxhill, but when granting lands in 1396 the court roll carefully noted the number of buildings on each messuage, in order to

check that the tenant kept them in good repair. The grange (this was a manor of the Cistercian abbey of Bordesley) had the largest number of structures – a dovecote, barn, byre and sheepcote, as well as a hall and chambers. The messuages of yardland and half-yardland holdings were each provided with four buildings, and a 3-acre smallholding had three.[63]

Another Cistercian monastery, Stoneleigh Abbey, at its manor of Stoneleigh inserted specific requirements into its grants of land, to maintain buildings. As at Oxhill, the court roll entry of the grant also might contain a description of the buildings. In 1438 Thomas Beele received a large holding of 2½ yardlands at Crulefield with a three-bay house and a four-bay barn. Other grants like one at Ashow (cf. ASH-A, *1464–75*) in 1438 included a threat of forfeiture if repairs were neglected. The lord also offered help, not just the major timbers, but also straw, and rods for wattles in one case, and in 1478 at Ashow, spars, laths and studs. In 1438 Roger Nottynge took a toft and two crofts, so this was land devoid of any building, and he agreed to erect a house of three bays at his own expense, though this would have been much reduced by the lord's grant of 'sufficient timber' and 40s in cash. A remarkable campaign against deteriorating buildings was launched in 1481. Four holdings at Stoneleigh were reported to be in disrepair, and the buildings itemised (Table 6.2). They all had halls and chambers, barns and byres (called 'oxehouse'). Three had kitchens and one was also provided with a bakehouse. All of the holdings lay vacant, two of the tenants having died in poverty; another had left with two other people to wander begging 'from village to village'. The repairs were valued at a total of £8 16s 4d, omitting 'the great and small timber'. As part of the contract for the sale of a coppice on the estate the buyer was to supply £5 towards this cost.[64]

The dated standing buildings clearly belong to the same type as those recorded in our documents. They were comparable in size – three or four bays, and were of similar construction, with crucks, timber frames, wattle and daub panels, and thatched roofs. The documents show that each house once stood as part of a group of between three and five structures in an enclosed plot. They might have been built by lords, or by tenants ordered or encouraged by their lords. Most buildings, however, came into existence because tenants decided to build them on their own initiative, using their own resources to buy materials and to hire craftsmen.

Between 1380 and 1510, houses were being rebuilt, and the siting of the dated houses along village streets makes it very likely that they succeeded earlier structures. Indeed many of them may have been preceded by houses erected in the thirteenth or early fourteenth centuries, for which there is good archaeological evidence. Abandoned houses with substantial stone foundations have been excavated at Bascote and Goldicote in Warwickshire, which would no

Table 6.2. Repair presentments in the Stoneleigh manor court, 1481 (SCLA, DR 18/30/24/17).

Tenant	House
William Reve, villein (*nativus*)	Hall, chamber, kitchen, barn, oxhouse, bakehouse (*Le Bakhous*)
John Colin	Hall, chamber, barn, oxhouse
Roger Warner, villein	Hall, chamber, kitchen, barn, oxhouse
Thomas Frankelyn, villein	Hall, chamber, kitchen, barn, oxhouse

doubt (in view of extant examples in the vicinity) have supported timber frames based on crucks.[65] Some of the houses built before 1350 have survived until the present day in Oxfordshire, and there is no reason to believe that Warwickshire lacked houses which had the capacity to survive. The generations of peasant buildings from before 1350 were threatened by falling population and economic changes which eventually led to the desertion or severe shrinkage of villages. The problem was felt in all settlements, like Blackwell or Hampton Lucy, where court rolls show holdings changing hands frequently, and sometimes lying without a tenant for months or even years.[66] The houses on those holdings were endangered by the unbalanced nature of the land market, which seems to have had more sellers than buyers. Breaks and gaps in tenancy posed obvious dangers that buildings would be vulnerable to ruin if roofs were not maintained. Deliberate neglect accompanied accumulation of tenements by tenants seeking to expand the size of their holding. At Old Stratford in the late fifteenth century we find multiple holdings of 1½, 2, 2½ and 3¼ yardlands, each of which involved a single tenant having two, three or four messuages – or rather tofts, because in such circumstances only one messuage was maintained.[67]

The house which emerged from this process of potential decay as the one selected to serve as the main messuage of a multiple tenement would probably have been rebuilt. It is likely to have suffered from some earlier period when it had passed from one tenant to another, or when it had been the secondary holding in an earlier unstable combination. Just as the decay of houses was a natural accompaniment of the fluid tenurial transfers of the period, so were replacement buildings. A further incentive to rebuild lay in the changing structure of land holding. At the apex of village society a minority of yeomen and farmers accumulated so much land that they had no choice but to build on a larger scale. Quite apart from questions of status, their houses needed to be large enough to accommodate a number of servants. The few probate inventories that survive from this period, many of them relating to this agrarian elite, such as that of Roger Heritage of Burton Dassett compiled in 1495, refer to between seven and eleven rooms and buildings.[68] Such houses will not appear in the dated sample because they were unlikely to have used cruck construction. But more modest accumulators of land, those with 1½ to 3 yardlands, who may well be included in the tenants of our dated buildings, might still have felt pressure to replace

a house built for a single yardland because of the need to increase living and storage space, and perhaps even to reflect their newly acquired standing in village society. An example might be the house at Goldicote built around 1400 which had the unheard of luxury of a window with stone mullions and glazing.[69]

The accumulators of multiple holdings enjoyed the opportunity for greater prosperity than their predecessors. Holdings of forty or sixty acres offered a better living than had twenty acres, especially if a proportion of the land was given over to feeding stock, which gave higher returns than grain. But those with single yardlands, who in Warwickshire formed perhaps a fifth of the manorial tenants of the late fifteenth century, and even smallholders, who gained the higher earnings available from either agricultural or industrial employment, shared to some extent in the prosperity of the period. How would a peasant gaining extra income from the sale of stock to the butchers, or a smallholding craftsman with increased wage earnings use the cash? An improved diet would absorb some of these resources, as would more and better quality clothing, but only a limited range of consumer goods was available. Housing represented an area of expenditure which would give the family more comfortable living space and make a visible statement of the builder's status. New agricultural buildings might contribute to the efficiency of farming; and better building would enhance the value of the holding if the tenant or his heirs wished to dispose of it.

The sample of dated buildings is too small to identify with any certainty any peaks or troughs of building activity within the period when cruck buildings were being constructed, but general evidence suggests a degree of recovery in demand for land around 1500 when rents rose a little, and holdings were passed between members of the same family more frequently. The dates obtained, however, do not suggest that the main phase of new building came during this gentle upswing, but rather that it reached a peak within the 'depression'.

The new information from dated cruck buildings makes an important contribution to our knowledge. It helps to correct the bias of our written sources, which give a very one-sided account of the history of houses in the period 1380–1510. The 'great peasant housing crisis' is a correct historical description of the period – but to concentrate entirely on the decaying buildings, and on the struggle between lords and tenants over the repair and reconstruction of decayed houses, shows only one side of a complicated picture. Renewal, new ventures, confidence for the future, high-quality craftsmanship, and investment were a feature of the period, not just of housing, but of society as a whole.

6.2 Buckinghamshire and Long Crendon

Nat Alcock and (the late) John Chenevix Trench

BUCKINGHAMSHIRE

Documentary sources for medieval houses in Buckinghamshire have been little studied, but books of extracts from the court rolls of the St Albans' manor of Winslow for 1327–1377 and 1423–1460 provide some useful information.[70] The court for this small market town between Aylesbury and Buckingham also covered two rural villages. Entries mentioning buildings mostly relate to the town, but its inhabitants were clearly principally involved in agriculture, suggesting little if any difference between housing in the town and the villages. The court rolls include a number of admissions which required the recipient to erect a house, most often on empty or subdivided plots. However, in 1327 John le Shoemaker and Amabilia his wife received a cottage lying between the market-place of Wynselowe and the land of John Mayn, and had to build a solar there.[71] In a particularly interesting entry in 1368, Walter Brasiar was required firstly to maintain a chamber in the holding formerly Thomas William's (that he had apparently just acquired), and also to construct anew a new house, with 2 pairs of *seules* and 2 *cuttes*, before the following Christmas.[72] The *seules* must surely be siles, i.e. crucks, and the *cuttes* were perhaps lean-to bays at each end of a one-bay building (see below).[73] The text does not make clear whether it was for domestic or agricultural use, but the mention of the chamber suggests that it represented the rebuilding of the hall and other parts of the house.

More commonly, the entries refer to the reservation of part of a house for the life of the previous tenant. Thus, in 1360, Christina Ward surrendered a holding comprising a messuage and 12 acres on condition that she could have all the buildings from the door of the hall up to the entry-gate of the said messuage for her life (and could keep eight cocks and hens).[74] In 1424, William Evresdon surrendered a messuage and yardland for his son, keeping his lodging within the aforesaid messuage, a high chamber called the

Soler in the lower part of the hall, and a brewhouse in the western part of the same messuage.[75] In the following year, John Est surrendered into the lord's hands a substantial holding including two messuages to William Perkyn, who had to plough and sow 9 acres for John and his wife. He also had to allow them a high chamber at the end of the hall, the use of the hall with William Perkyn and his wife, and a house called Litulberne [little barn] together with a stable at the end of the great grange. If they quarrelled, then William had to make a respectable hall for them in the Bakhows [bakehouse?], at his own expense.[76] In 1458, in a similar entry the use of two chambers and the path to the latrine [*latrina*] was reserved.[77]

One group of medieval Buckinghamshire deeds, for Wotton Underwood, includes three maintenance agreements, similar to those found in the court rolls.[78] In the first (1347) a widow, Juliana Rokeleye, received the solar and 'celer', with the chimney on the east side of the hall, and with free right of access, presumably through the hall. In 1358, another widow could use a chamber beside the door of the hall, and in 1379, Letice Webbe had an easement (access and use) in a 'seler' at the north end of the hall, and in a chamber between the kitchen and the dovecote. She had the same two rooms as Juliana Rokeleye, but they were physically separated and the space was shared rather than exclusive.

The court rolls for Long Crendon, discussed below, contain a considerable number of presentments of decayed buildings and their repair, as well as various items concerning easements and surrenders, similar to those at Winslow; no doubt other groups of court rolls and deeds include similar information. However, the references just considered show that by the mid-fourteenth century, village houses might be quite sophisticated, in particular including high chambers or solars, sometimes heated. They also suggest the possible dual use of a bakehouse as a dwelling, albeit after conversion. The 1368 reference to the use of siles is particularly significant, since it predates by almost 100 years the earliest dated cruck house in Buckinghamshire, corresponding more closely to those dated in Oxfordshire.

LONG CRENDON AND ITS CRUCK HOUSES[79]

Long Crendon is notable as containing no less than 23 buildings of cruck construction, more than any other village in England,[80] and extensive documentation has also survived, making it possible to delineate the social and economic background to these buildings with some precision.[81] This throws light on the circumstances underlying both their construction and their survival. For individual houses, the map made at enclosure in 1827 (Figs. 6.2–3) and the associated documents provide identifications at this date, which can often be traced back to the sixteenth century.

The village (SP 69 08) stands at a crossroads on one of the hummocks of Portland stone that punctuate the vale of Aylesbury. Historically, the landscape was typical of 'champion' country, with a nucleated village completely surrounded by open fields, apart from some areas of old enclosure to the north of the village and around Notley Abbey to the east. Its economy was essentially agricultural until the late seventeenth century, when needle-making was introduced, which enabled more people to find employment.[82] The number of households was about 85 in the 1660s, rising to 205–280 in the early nineteenth century.[83] The increasing population (particularly of extremely badly-off needle-makers) was accommodated by dividing farmhouses into cottages, by infilling between the older houses, particularly with stone and wichert (mud) cottages, and by building on roadside verges (e.g. on the roads leading south in Fig. 6.3c and north in Fig. 6.3d). However, twentieth century improvements in housing standards have resulted in the disappearance of many of both the older and the newer cottages.

The manors

The complex manorial structure of Long Crendon is important for understanding the documentary evidence. In 1086, the manor was held by Walter Giffard, from whose family it passed to William Marshal (later Earl of Pembroke) in 1191. In 1275, the manor was divided between the three co-heiresses of Eva de Braose, sister of Anselm Marshal.[84] One third was obtained by Lord Ferrers de Groby, descended to Thomas Grey, Marquis of Dorset, and was bought in 1520 by Michael Dormer. It remained in that family until sold in 1759 to George Grenville of Wotton Underwood, whose son became Marquis of Buckingham.[85] The second part belonged for a period to the Hastings family and then to John Barton of Thornton, Buckinghamshire, and in 1442 was granted by Isabel Barton to All Souls College, Oxford.[86] The last third came

Fig. 6.2. Key map of Long Crendon: 1880 Ordnance Survey 1:2500 map with location of maps 6.3(a)–(d) and cruck houses (A–U).

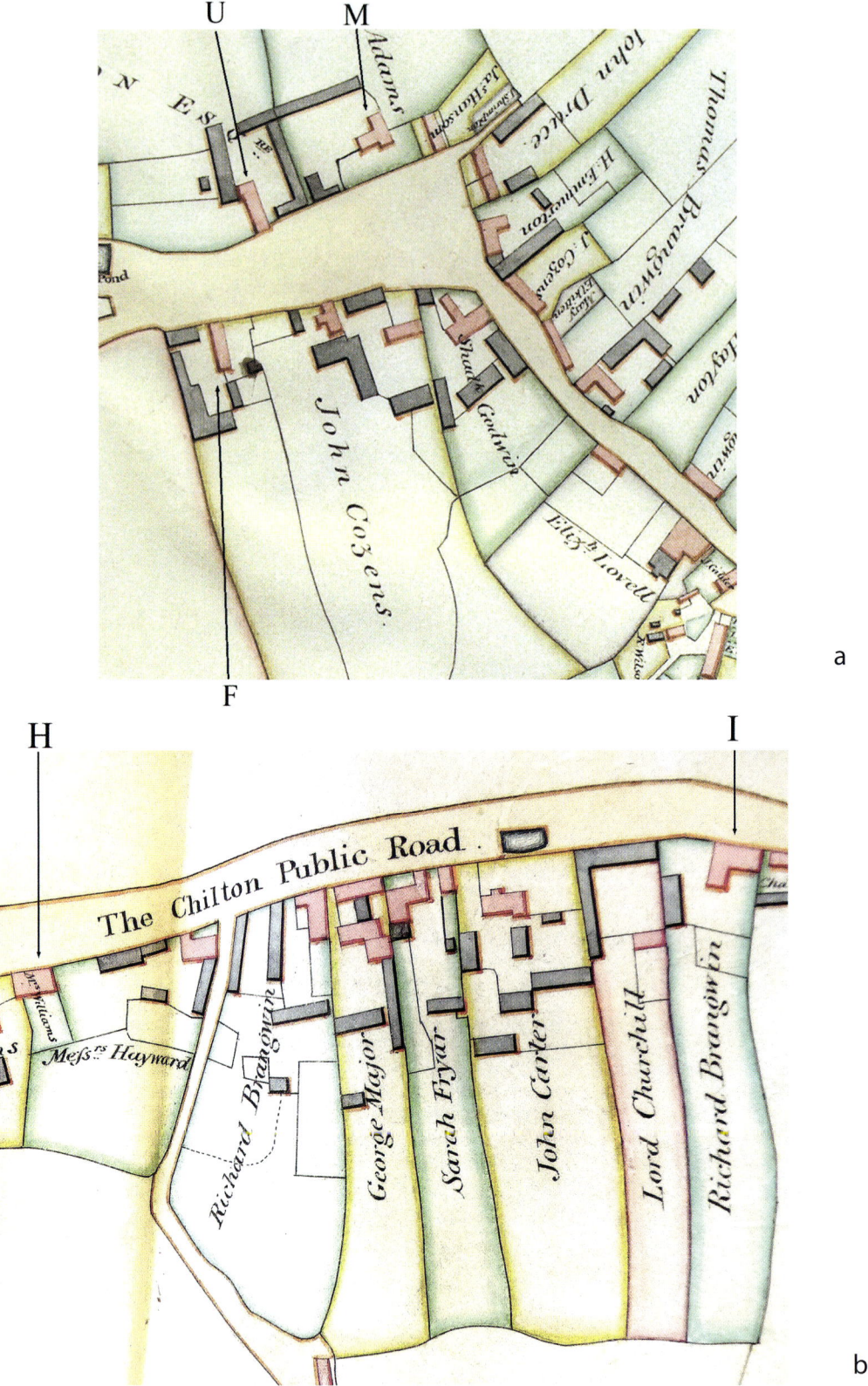

Fig. 6.3. Sections of the 1827 map of Old Enclosures at Long Crendon: (a) north-west of village: Lower End; (b) centre of Bicester Road. The letters A–U identify the cruck buildings (CBS, IR/95/Q).

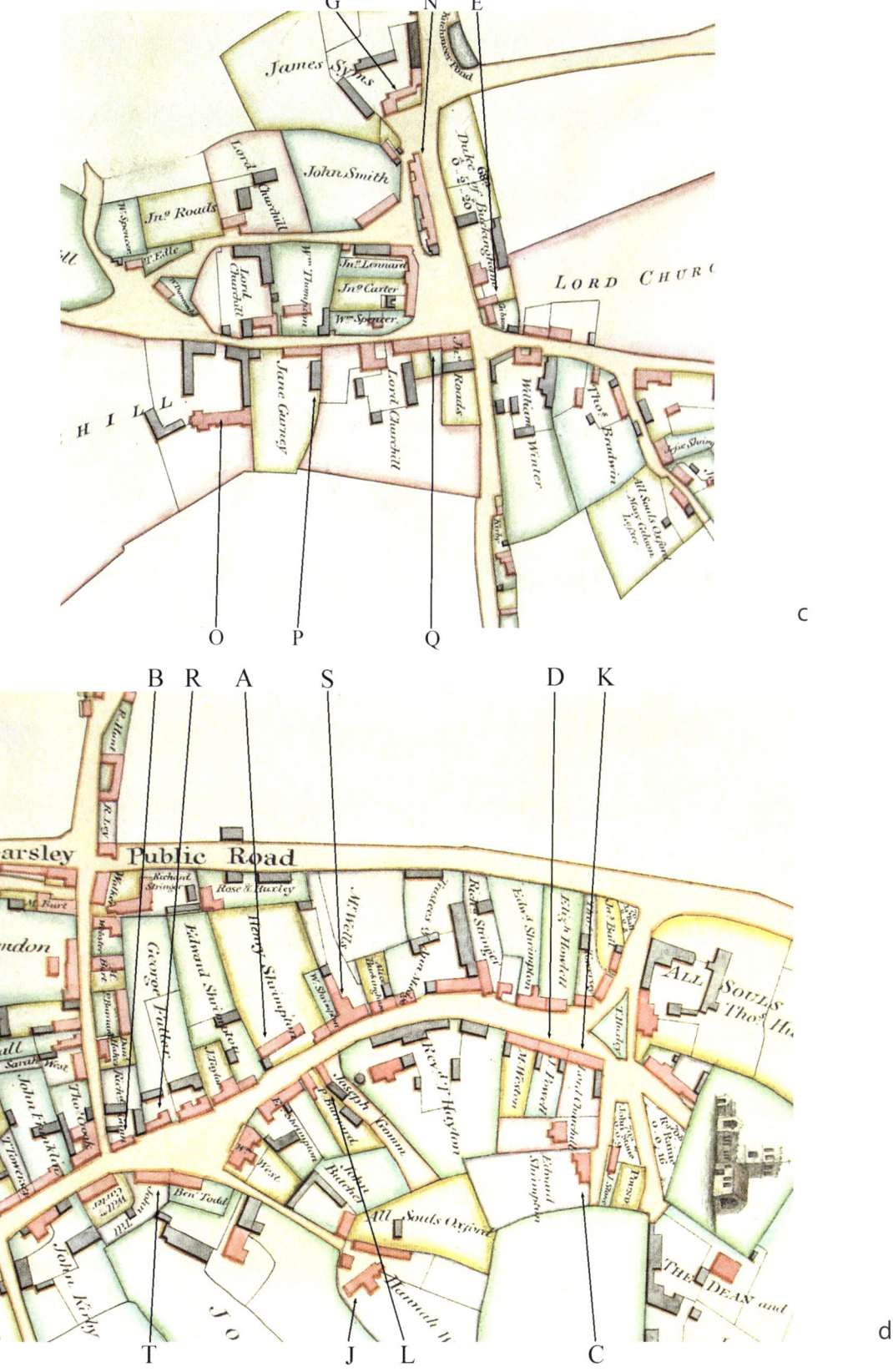

Fig. 6.3 (continued). (c) The Square and Frogmore Lane; (d) east end of High Street.

by marriage to the de Bohuns, and was inherited by Henry V as co-heir to Humphrey Bohun in 1419. It was granted to his queen, Katherine de Valois, and returned to the crown on her death in 1437; it was briefly held in dower by Edward IV's queen, but in 1479 became part of the endowment of St. George's Chapel, Windsor.[87] During the Commonwealth, the chapel's property was confiscated and the manor was bought by Captain Henry Cannon, whose father had been the tenant of the manor.[88] It was recovered at the Restoration and remained with St George's until taken over by the Ecclesiastical Commissioners in 1867.

The division did not result in three separate manors. Long Crendon remained a single manor with a single court, but the three lords physically divided both the demesne and the copyhold lands, and shared the quit rents of the free land.[89] Very numerous court rolls and books survive, from 1343 to the twentieth century (with few substantial gaps).

Notley Abbey

Besides the divided lordship of the main manor, a second substantial manor (known confusingly in the nineteenth century as the Manor of Crendon) was created by the foundation of Notley Abbey in 1162 by William Giffard, grandson of the first Norman lord of Long Crendon.[90] The site of the abbey was the Earl's park, which lay to the east of the village This formed part of its original endowment, together with some 15 appropriated churches, those standing on the Earl's demesnes, including that at Crendon.[91] In the village, the abbey's original endowment only included a garden and the site of a *coquina* where the Earl's dogs played.[92] However, it later received many gifts of property in the village and became a full-fledged manor, complete with its own court.[93] At the Dissolution, the site of the Abbey and its Crendon land came into the possession of Sir John Williams, later Lord Williams of Thame. It passed by marriage to the Bertie family, later Earls of Abingdon, and was sold in 1764 to the Duke of Marlborough, passing on his death to his second son, Francis, Lord Churchill of Wychwood. A broken series of court rolls from 1720 onwards survive for this manor, with a few from the seventeenth century, supplemented by some rentals.

Lovedens, Revels and Sperlings

Sub-infeudation gave rise to three substantial freeholdings that were sometimes described as manors. *Lovedens* took its name from Thomas de Loveden, who is recorded as holding half a knight's fee in 1330; as the 'Manor of Lovedens', it was bought by Michael Dormer in 1517.[94] Another sub-manor originated in a very early grant. Robert, son of William Revel held land of William Marshal in 1185, and somewhat later Benedict Revel received a grant of 10 virgates from William Marshal's son Richard. This estate

appears under the name of *Revel's Place* in 1390, when a court was held for it; it then passed to the Pepir family and in 1350 to William FitzWater; it also later came into Dormer ownership, when it was known as FitzWaters.[95] A grant of 2½ virgates made by Earl William Marshal to Matthew de Lucy, his butler, for a bezant at Michaelmas was acquired by Andrew Spurling and after his death in 1440 became part of the endowment of the chantry of St Christopher in Thame Church; at the dissolution, this estate was granted to Sir John Williams and was united with the Notley Abbey manor.[96]

Landholding

In 1086 the settlement was assessed at 20 fiscal hides and 25 ploughlands.[97] By the eighteenth century, the open fields of the parish were recognised as containing 112 yardlands, each of 30 customary acres, divided between the demesnes, the copyholds and the freeholds.[98] Before any boundary changes, the total acreage of Long Crendon was 3,120 (1,295ha).[99] The common fields as allotted at enclosure in 1827 occupied 2,821 acres (1,143ha), with the balance, 299 acres (121ha), made up of 'old enclosures'. Thus, the average Long Crendon yardland contained 25.2 statute acres, i.e. each customary acre was about three-quarters of a statute acre.[100] The yardlanders also had rights to meadow plots, chosen by lot every year.[101] Pasture on the fallow was regulated by grazing rights according to the size of each holding.

The Demesnes

The arable demesnes of the various lordships lay dispersed in the common fields,[102] and the sources indicate that each lordship of the main manor had ten yardlands in demesne.[103] The original Notley Abbey demesne probably comprised the Earl's park, corresponding in 1827 to the old enclosures around the abbey site, but the estate also included eight yardlands in the common fields, which may have originated as freeholdings acquired by the Abbey in the medieval period.[104] Thus, the demesnes of the main manors comprised 38 yardlands in the open fields (including the Notley open field land): 34% of the village total. Of demesne old enclosures, only Notley, with 137ac (57ha) seem to have had significant amounts.[105] The demesnes were let at farm throughout the period covered by this study, often to local men, but increasingly during the eighteenth century to outsiders.[106]

Copyhold/villein land

In the sixteenth century, all three main lordships had 13½ yardlands in copyhold tenure, paying a standard rent of 14s per yardland.[107] The same 13½ yardlands (*virgates*) held by 14 tenants are listed explicitly, in a survey of the Bohun third of the manor (later St George's Chapel) in 1336, and again as a summary in 1390.[108] In addition, each lordship included a number of cottages, paying rents ranging from a few pence to a few shillings. By the sixteenth century, some of the yardland holdings had been combined, though only one exceeded two yardlands (Table 6.3).

For the Notley Abbey manor, the earliest evidence comes from rentals of about 1635 and 1728 which list three one-yardland and one two-yardland holdings, accompanied by 13 or 14 cottages; many of the latter were associated with three to seven acres of open-field land, a total of almost 40 acres, perhaps derived from the disintegration of about two other yardlands.[109] Thus, the copyholdings comprised about 47 yardlands (42% of the open-field land). Copyholders also had their tofts – backsides, gardens and orchards, generally ranging from about half an acre to two acres in size (0.2–0.8ha).

The copyholdings remained stable from the mid-sixteenth to the eighteenth century, but thereafter in an increasing number of cases, the land was split off from the house.[110] The separated cottages were frequently acquired by prosperous villagers and let to the less prosperous, often divided between several tenants.[111]

Freehold land

Freehold land was an important element in the Long Crendon landscape. After allowing for the demesne and the copyholdings as above, we can estimate that in the sixteenth century, it amounted to about 27 yardlands (24% of the total). All these freeholdings would have been created originally by grants from the lord of the manor, apparently before the division of the manor in 1275 (since the divided lordships had equal amounts of demesne and copyhold land in the sixteenth century); indeed, a few of the grants survive as original deeds. The freeholdings paid quit rents and these were presumably also divided when the manor was partitioned; we have some information about these rents, but little evidence of what they represented in terms of land-holding. In 1549, the Dormer manor received about 9s, and in 1586/7, the All Souls College rental recorded 'for quyt rent as muche as I cold fynd owt 6s 3d'.[112]

More than half of the freehold can be identified with the three sub-manors mentioned above. In 1552, William Dormer sold to Nicholas Bethom a capital messuage and 8½ yardlands called Lovedens, and in the next year 6 yardlands and 5 closes called FitzWaters.[113] The size of Sperlings is uncertain. The original grant to Matthew de Lucy was of 2½ yardlands, but it seems likely that it had increased by the sixteenth century, when its tenants paid rents totalling £8 16s.[114] Many references to the remaining freeholdings are found in deeds and wills, but it is not possible to produce a full list and they can only be identified occasionally.[115] One such is a holding comprising a messuage, toft and about eight acres of arable which was sold by Henry Burt of Chilton to All Souls College in 1523. This became known as Mortimer's tenement, after its sixteenth century tenant, and remained as a leasehold from the College (lower right on Fig. 6.3c). The 1549 Dormer rental includes 1½d quit rent from the College for 'Land lat Henry Byrtt'.

Enfranchised copyhold and dispersed freehold

From about 1550 on, the amount of freehold land was greatly increased through the process of enfranchisement, by which land held by copy of court roll was sold as freehold by the lord of the manor, usually to the copyhold tenant. For the Dormer copyholds, the disposal of all 13½ yardlands and three of their four cottages can be identified from counterpart deeds dating from either 1554–1614 or 1704–8.[116] Curiously, one cottage (53 High Street, 'Alice Buckingham' on Fig. 6.3d, next to LON-S) remained as copyhold and was only enfranchised in 1928.[117] The five messuage-and-yardland holdings enfranchised in 1704 can all be identified on the ground, but this is not possible for most of the earlier sales.[118]

Neither All Souls College nor St George's Chapel seem to have enfranchised their holdings until this became unavoidable at the end of the nineteenth century, but one St George's property was enfranchised during the Commonwealth.[119] In 1658, when the manor was in the hands of Henry Cannon, he made a grant to James Reynolds, of two messuages and 1½ yardland, to hold for ever at a rent of 22s.[120] However, following the Restoration, this must have been rescinded, since in 1667 the same James Reynolds surrendered as copyhold what must be these messuages with their 1½ yardlands.

Table 6.3. Sizes of copyholdings at Long Crendon (yardlands).*

Manor	Date	3 ydl	2 ydl	1½ ydl	1 ydl	½ ydl	Cottages
Bohun (Windsor)	1336				13	1	6 + 2*⅓
All Souls	1587	Unstated (13½ ydl)					3
Dormer	1549		2		9	1	4
Windsor	c. 1560	1	2	1	5	1	[abs]
Windsor	1720		3		6	1	6
Notley	1728		1		3		14

* Sources: see text footnotes. Windsor = estate of St George's Chapel.

As well as the additions by enfranchisement to the pool of freeholding land, the holdings associated with Lovedens and FitzWaters were dispersed in the seventeenth century.[121] After the sale by William Dormer in 1552–3, they were acquired in 1564 by James Braybrooke.[122] They passed through various hands before reaching Henry Allnutt in 1652, who sold them off piecemeal, the capital messuage being acquired by William Cannon in 1658. Several deeds survive for these sales, and they are also referred to in various wills.[123]

Summary

In 1798, almost half the land (both copyhold and freehold) was still owner occupied, in the hands of 34 owners, while the tenanted property had 41 owners. However, two-thirds of the whole parish was in the hands of only 15 proprietors.[124]

The process and effects of enclosure

It is a commonplace that, by extinguishing rights of common, enclosure had a devastating effect on the economy of cottagers. However, at Long Crendon, these rights were very sparse. The infilling cottages undoubtedly had no common rights. Most of the smallholdings had originated through the dismemberment of yardland holdings, as is seen from example after example (Table 6.4b), and had lost their common rights at the same time. In other villages, landholdings were burdened with both the costs of the enclosure itself and of hedging and fencing. By contrast, at Long Crendon, before any land was allotted to copyholders and freeholders, not only had the tithe owners to be compensated, but the commissioners' expenses were defrayed by withdrawing a proportion of the land. 550 acres went to the tithe-owners, chiefly Lord Churchill, and 442 acres was sold to pay the commissioners. In addition, allotments totalling 24 acres went to the manorial lords, to compensate for their 'right of soil'. Thus, 955 acres, 36% of the total was withdrawn, so that the owners received only 64% of their open-field holdings, although they no longer had to pay tithes and they benefited from having enclosed fields.

Tracing the histories of the standing buildings

Many of the case-studies (in reports LON-A – LON-U) follow the same pattern, starting from the identification of the property at enclosure in 1827, when necessary tracing ownership (and sometimes occupancy) onwards to the 1910 'Domesday', and then working back through earlier records, particularly the admissions listed in the court rolls.[125] Disappointingly, although Long Crendon is covered by four of the magnificent All Souls College Hovenden maps (1590s), only a small part of the village is shown on them; it seems likely that a fifth map has been lost since the later seventeenth century.[126]

The Land Tax assessments, which survive for almost every year from 1782 to 1832 have been less useful than hoped for tracing ownership through this crucial period. Although the total paid remained unchanged at £306, the number of payers varied erratically: 94 in 1782; 101 in 1795; 90 in 1801; 96 in 1825.[127] The number increased substantially to 130 in 1826, and at the same time the individual assessments, which had previously been unchanged from year to year, were all altered. This discontinuity undoubtedly reflects a re-valuation associated with the enclosure. The alterations involved, firstly, 'The Commissioners' Land' – the land taken to pay the expenses of enclosure, with the larger assessments correspondingly reduced. Secondly, many new entries appear, that can be identified as cottages and crofts not associated with farmland, which previously had not paid the tax.[128] Unfortunately, these properties cannot therefore be traced backwards through the assessments.

The standing medieval buildings

The surviving cruck buildings range in date from the mid-fifteenth to the mid-sixteenth centuries (by dendrochronology); they comprise all but three of the oldest secular structures in the village, the exceptions being Long Crendon Courthouse,[129] the aisled hall at Long Crendon manor that was converted into a base-cruck (*LON-O*, later thirteenth century?), and the bay of an aisled hall within Sycamore Farmhouse (LON-G, 1205). Moreover, the 1827 map of the village shows the cruck buildings randomly and fairly evenly distributed among the houses then standing (Fig. 6.2). This distribution is what would be expected if all or most of the village houses had been cruck-framed in the fifteenth century.

The documentary evidence for the history of the standing cruck buildings is set out in the reports on the individual houses, and is summarised in Table 6.4b. Through this detailed analysis, a substantial majority of the houses (16 from 21) have been traced back to the early seventeenth century or before.[130] The process was onerous though relatively straightforward for the eleven houses that remained as copyhold until enfranchisement in about 1900 (Table 6.4a).[131] Although the court rolls survive with few gaps to before 1400, they have not been fully transcribed for the later fifteenth and earlier sixteenth century, and it has only been possible to trace the copyholdings at best to the 1540–50s.[132]

Three freeholds can be linked to Dormer copyholdings enfranchised in either the 1550s or 1704, using deeds and wills, and this is also a probability for two others. One house, Long Crendon Manor, can be shown to have been the 'capital messuage' of the large freeholding or sub-manor called *Lovedens*. It is unclear whether the remaining three freeholds had once been copyholdings. Whether the remaining three freeholds had once been copyholdings.

In view of the tenurial structure of Long Crendon, discussed above, it is not surprising to find that half or

Table 6.4. Summary of resources associated with early Long Crendon houses.

(a) Earliest tenure established

Earliest tenure	Manor	Number
Copyhold All Souls College	ASC	3
Copyhold Windsor	W	5
Copyhold Notley	NOT	3
Freehold (former Dormer copyhold)	F [DOR]	3 +2(?)
Freehold (former Notley copyhold)	F [NOT]	1
Freehold (not identifiable as copyhold)	F	4

(b) Individual houses*

Use: M: Messuage; C: Cottage; D: Domestic/outbuilding; Ag: Agricultural building. *Resources*: ydl: yardland. *Hearths*: ex: exempt

Code	Building	Use	Manor	Traced to	Earliest Tenure	Earliest Resources	1827 Resources	Reduced in	Hearths
LON-A	Abel's Cott, 43 High Street	C	F [DOR?]	1809	freehold	½ acres	½ acres		
LON-B	Woodpecker's, 25 High Street	C	F [DOR]	1543	Copyhold	4 acres	Garden	1801	2?
LON-C	Church Green Cott, 104 High Street	C	NOT	c. 1600	copyhold	½ acres	½ acres		
LON-D	96 High Street	C	NOT	c. 1595	copyhold	3 acres	Garden	1789	
LON-E	Cordwainers, 2 Bicester Rd	C	W	1559	copyhold	1 ydl	Garden	1699?	(3)
LON-F	Dragon Farm, 121 Bicester Rd	M	F [DOR]	1536	Copyhold	1 ydl	1 acres	c. 1775	3
LON-G	Sycamore Farm, 9 Bicester Rd	M	ASC	1553/1556	copyhold	1+1 ydl	1 acres	1815	3
LON-H	Old Bakehouse, 61 Bicester Rd	C/Ag?	F	1645 (1618?)	freehold	Garden	Garden	By 1669	–
LON-I	Warwick Fm, 31 Bicester Rd	M	ASC	1615	copyhold	1 ydl	1 ydl	1838	2
LON-J	Wapping, 66 High Street	C	W	1536 (1423)	copyhold	toft	Orchard		1 (ex)
LON-K	98 High Street	C	F [NOT]	c. 1730	freehold	Garden	Garden		
LON-L	82 High Street	C	NOT	c. 1635	copyhold	1 ydl	Garden	1805	
LON-M	Lower End Ho, 72 Bicester Rd	M	F	1630	freehold	2 ydl?	60 acres		5
LON-N	Harfield Cott, 7 Bicester Rd	M	ASC	1533	copyhold	1 ydl	Garden	1810	2
LON-O	Long Crendon Manor	M	F	14th cent.	freehold	c. 250 acres	340 acres		5
LON-P	'Manor Garage' (at Manor House)	D/Ag	W	1728 (1539/1546)	copyhold	1 ydl	1 ydl		–
LON-Q	2 The Square	M	W	1544	copyhold	1 or ½ ydl	Garden	1709	2
LON-R	27–29 High Street	M	W	1600	copyhold	1 ydl	Garden	1792	2?
LON-S	Eight Bells, 51 High Street	C	F [DOR?]	1827	freehold	Garden	Garden		
LON-T	58–60 High Street	C	F	1777	freehold	10 ac?	2 acres	1795	
LON-U	Northend Farm [demolished 1965]	M	F [DOR]	1554	copyhold	1–1½ ydl	4½ ydl		

* LON-A to LON-K form part of the main project. *LON-L* to *LON-U* have been examined primarily from documentary sources.

more of the houses are first recorded with one yardland in the open fields. What is also notable, and perhaps less expected, is that almost all of them lost their land in the later eighteenth or early nineteenth century. Thus, their characteristic trajectory involved construction as farmhouses in the fifteenth or early sixteenth century, continuing with moderate prosperity in the occupation of a yeoman or husbandman to around 1750 (but at dates as early as 1699 and as late as 1838), until the land was added to a larger farm or split up between several owners. The house was generally then surrendered to a new owner, and subdivided into cottages (the process examined in more detail below).

Indeed, it is clear that this change in ownership often only placed on a formal basis changes in occupancy that might already have taken place many years earlier. Thus, for Holly Farm in Jesse's Lane, an All Souls copyhold messuage with a half-yardland holding, the house was disposed of in 1786, but it was already recorded with two occupants in 1735.

Not all the cruck houses originated as yardland holdings. Two copyholds from the main manors (LON-B and J) and two from Notley manor (LON-C and D) were undoubtedly associated with only their gardens or a few arable strips, as early as the sixteenth century. Indeed, the court rolls show that Wapping (LON-J) was built shortly before 1536, on what had been a vacant croft. This corresponds to the evidence from other counties (p. 143ff) that the size and character of medieval village housing generally did not vary greatly with the size of holding.

The status of the owners of these smaller holdings is not very easily established, but Rowland Edmunds (96 High Street, LON-D) was a husbandman in 1619, though he held only the three acres that accompanied this cottage; Edmund Nicholls (c. 1595) (104 High Street, LON-C) was a carpenter. The original copyholder for Wapping (LON-J) also held two other messuages and two yardlands, and probably rented them all to sub-tenants. We have no information about the status of the holders of the fourth of these cottages.

Manorial Dues

The outgoings of medieval peasants have been studied in detail by Christopher Dyer.[133] The following section examines those specific to Long Crendon, depending on manorial custom and the will of the lord. Copyhold rents remained unchanged from 1336 or earlier until enfranchisement. It was through entry fines and heriots that the lord kept pace with inflation, and the former in particular were not fixed by custom and could be onerous. The standard heriot up to the Civil War was the tenant's best beast, later commuted to a money payment. On the All Souls lordship in the early nineteenth century the standard heriot was £5 per yardland.[134] Entry fines varied widely. The custom was that if an estate descended by inheritance to the eldest son, the fine was one to one-and-a-half years rent; if it passed to another descendant or by sale, the incoming tenant had to reach agreement with the lord.[135] Two such fines in 1819 show the range at that period: £42 for one yardland, and £50 for two.[136] Two court-book entries, in 1810 and 1812, note 'fine not paid as consideration considered too high'.[137]

For cottages and small holdings, some rents and fines are recorded. Rents of 3s 4d plus a cock and a hen at Christmas were common on the Notley manor for landless cottages, though two paid only 2s after they were detached from the few acres of land they had previously held.[138]

On the main manor, rents in the eighteenth and early nineteenth centuries were closely comparable with those of the fourteenth. Three All Souls cottages commanded 2s, 1s 3d, and 6d, while two St. George's copyholds were rented at 4d and 6d.[139] Comparable rents for 1336 were 1s 2d for an acre of land; 5s plus a cock and a hen for a cottage with four acres.[140]

Housing

Messuages and cottages

The sixteenth-century court rolls distinguish carefully between messuages, held with at least half a yardland, and cottages with little or no land. However, from the eighteenth century onwards, this distinction became increasingly obscured, as the yardland holdings were combined into larger units and the houses converted into labourers' cottages. As a result, the proportion of entries relating to cottages in the court rolls increased. In the sixteenth century, 50 transactions involving cottages are recorded (out of 115); in the seventeenth, 33 out of 96, in the eighteenth, 96 against only 89 for messuages.

The beginnings of the process can be seen in the reaction to growing population in the Tudor period. Nine men who had built cottages on the waste were in 1588 allowed to keep them on copyhold tenure.[141] Self-help was indeed encouraged: in 1586 a man who had built himself a cottage was not only admitted as customary tenant but had his entry fine pardoned.[142] The Act calling for every new cottage to have at least four acres of land seems largely to have been ignored, but strenuous efforts were made to enforce the statute against taking in lodgers for more than a year, which would give them a 'settlement' in the parish. The court rolls record a stream of presentments for keeping 'inmates'. Although the threatened penalties were severe – £6 per inmate – several men were presented more than once.[143] The outcome was a proliferation of cottages. In 1618 the homage complained that poor people were putting up buildings on the waste.[144] A little later eight men were fined £10 for erecting cottages 'against the statute'.[145] Another cottage on the waste was occupied by the builder's daughter and a man not her husband; when the daughter died the man left the village, and the inhabitants petitioned that they might have the cottage to house the poor.[146]

Sometimes the process can be traced in more detail. The 1777 plan of a holding (Fig. 6.4a), shows two cottages that had been built between the farmhouse and the road.[147] In 1836 five cottages had been 'lately erected on part of Charles Lennard's homestall';[148] by 1856 they had become six.[149] In 1864 there were four cottages on the site of, or converted from, a barn; four years later a malthouse was being used as cottages.[150] This list could be greatly extended, and no doubt something similar was happening on freehold land.

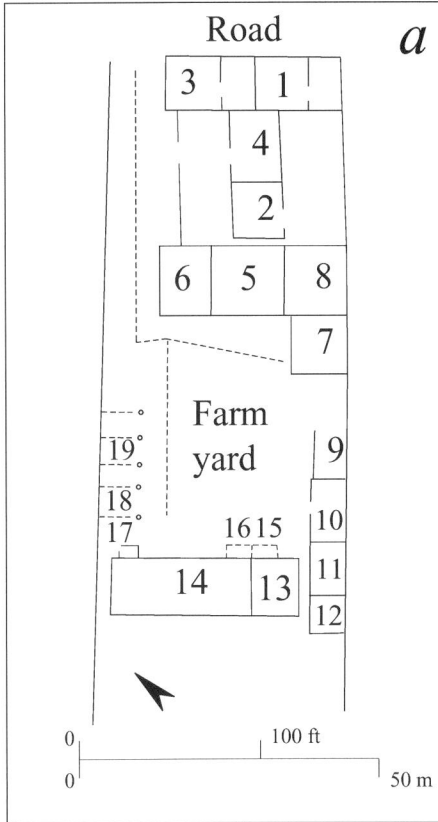

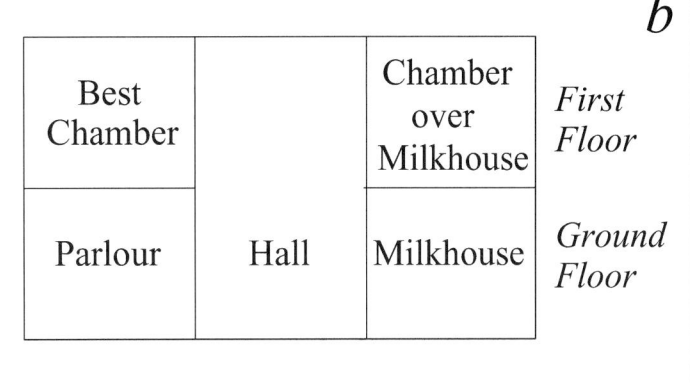

Fig. 6.4. (a) Plan of a Long Crendon farm in 1777, the later Bakers Close, 43 Bicester Road, the house of George Major in 1827 (Fig. 6.3b). (Redrawn from CBS, D-X727/1, a copy of the original at the Museum of English Rural Life, Reading, D81/4).

1 Cottage	7 Kitchen	14 Barn
2 Woodhouse	8 Dairy	15 Chaff House
3 Cottage	9 Cart House	16–17 Sty
4 Woodhouse	10 Woodhouse	18 Cart Stall
5 House	11 Cow House	19 Cow stalls
6 Parlour	12–13 Stables	

(b) Reconstruction of the plan of the home of Richard Towersey, from his inventory of 1695 (Bodl, Ms.ch.Bucks 800).

Some of the cottages were stigmatised as 'bad' or even 'miserable'.[151]

At the same time houses were being divided. In 1732 we read for the first time of 'a messuage lately divided in two'; in 1792 a messuage has been divided in three.[152] In 1803 a copyhold messuage was described as 'a good house let in tenements',[153] and thereafter it becomes common to read of a 'tenement lately divided in two', 'a messuage now occupied as three tenements', 'a messuage occupied as four tenements'.[154] A count of such references for copyhold properties identifies six divided houses in the last quarter of the eighteenth century and the addition of eighteen extra dwellings. In the first quarter of the nineteenth century four houses were divided and nine dwellings added. These eighteenth century cottages were built in simpler (and presumably cheaper) materials than the historic timber-framing, either rubble masonry or wichert (the local name for clay/mud mass-walling). They no doubt accommodated farm labourers, but their main purpose was undoubtedly to house the extremely badly off needle-makers; it is these later houses rather than the better-built timber-framed houses which tended to disappear during the later nineteenth and twentieth centuries.

St. John Priest in 1810 reported that there were 25 farmhouses and 100 cottages at Long Crendon.[155] The first figure agrees well enough with the enclosure award, which lists 21 holdings of a yardland or more, and five of half a yardland.[156] However, the second was an under-estimate, as the 1801 census abstract identifies 205 houses occupied by 241 families. It was clearly difficult, though, to estimate just how many different dwellings were represented by some of the subdivided houses.

The Hearth Tax

The Hearth Tax returns catch the creation of cottages at an intermediate stage. The only surviving return lists 57 people paying the tax, and takes no account of those exempt, whose names are given in three certificates, the longest list comprising 29 names.[157] Assuming that this largest number gives the best estimate of their numbers, and that they each had only one hearth,[158] the distribution of hearths can be plotted (Fig. 6.5).

The numbers of hearths range from Norris Lenton's substantial twelve at Notley Abbey down to the 51 with one hearth(59% of the total; 34% exempt); analyses of other Midland counties show broadly similar figures (e.g. 62% and 30% in Bedfordshire).[159] Eleven of the occupiers of the cruck houses can matched with hearth tax names (though doubtfully in a few cases) (Table 6.4b). Of these, one only comes from among the exempt, John West at Wapping

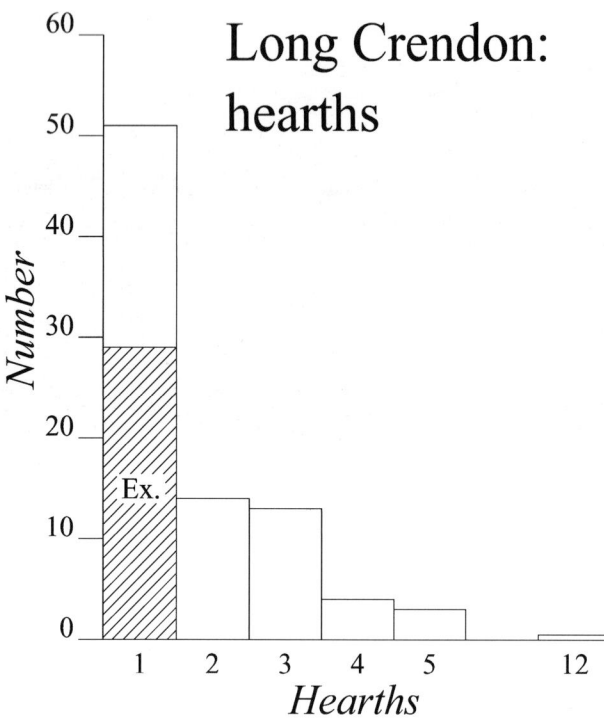

Fig. 6.5. Distribution of hearths at Long Crendon, 1662, paying households (from TNA, E 179/80/354) and 1672, exempt households (shaded). The exempt are added from the 1672 list (E 179/80/362/36), and assumed each to have had one hearth.

(LON-J), but our lack of knowledge of later seventeenth century Notley manor tenants may conceal others. The remaining identified examples match the distribution as a whole, having two to three hearths, apart from two five-hearth houses. One of the latter was Long Crendon manor (*LON-O*, the Lovedens capital messuage), no doubt then as later a large and rambling farmhouse. The other can be identified as Lower End House (*LON-M*), where the original cruck house was considerably extended in about 1600, perhaps adding several hearths to the one previously inserted in the original hall.

Rooms in the houses

Documents shed some light on the use of rooms. The 1777 plan of a farmstead, referred to above (Fig. 6.4a), labels the rooms in the farmhouse as: parlour, hall and dairy (in-line) and the kitchen in a wing at the rear. This arrangement for the main house can also be suggested from other sources. The probate inventory of Richard Towersey, a yardlander who died in 1695, lists 'the best chamber', 'the chamber over the milkhouse', the hall and the parlour.[160] It may have been laid out as shown in Fig 6.4b, which assumes that 'the best chamber' was over the parlour. Similarly, the 1673 inventory of James Reynolds, also a yardlander, lists a parlour and a chamber over it, a milkhouse and a chamber

over that, and the hall – which has no chamber over it – apparently between them. But it has a puzzling additional feature: a 'passage between the chambers', large enough to have a 'corn whitch [chest],' 8 bushels of wheat and 30 of malt stored in it.[161] Perhaps the hall was part-floored, with a gallery linking the end chambers.

Two of the twelve inventories known from Long Crendon list only a hall and a chamber; both are of smallholders with only two acres under crops (dated 1601 and 1604).[162] A third, that of a wood-worker who died in 1607, names no rooms at all but lists goods in groups that make it clear that his house also had only a hall and chamber.[163] For another, of 1618, also naming no rooms, a hall, chamber and buttery can be deduced.[164] The most elaborate of the houses, inventoried in 1699, indicates a house with two cross-wings.[165]

Some further evidence for the rooms in the houses comes from incidental mentions in wills. In 1559, Thomas Witmell left boards for flooring over the 'chamber in the head of the hall and the chamber where he lyeth', indicating a house then only of one storey, but with two ground-floor chambers. Several sixteenth-century wills refer to lofts, rather than to upper chambers, suggesting relatively low buildings.[166] However, by the early seventeenth century, we find an 'upper chamber', a house with a 'coffer at the stairhead' (so clearly more substantial), and a chamber over the milkhouse.[167] This last matches the inventoried houses described above.[168]

Kitchens are rarely named, and what evidence we have suggests that they were separate buildings; four such appear among the presentments for decay (below).[169] There was one on the Windsor lordship as late as 1803, which describes the kitchen as 'detached, composed of wattle daubed & thatched';[170] the structural evidence suggests that a fragment of a detached kitchen may survive at 11 Frogmore Lane (*LON-P*).

Both wills and court rolls indicate how widows and those retiring from farming could be provided for. The will of Peter Nicholls in 1694 sets out the manorial custom, that his wife should hold, according to custom, one of the best rooms in his copyhold messuage, and a place in the chimney by the fire, and one space or bay in the barn.[171] In 1755, Mary, the wife of William Randolph, was to have 'a room called the hall and the use of the kitchen and the little cellar and the room over the kitchen and the closet and the far room and the room over the parlour for her life'.[172] Similarly, in the court rolls, when Thomas Cannon surrendered his messuage and virgate to the use of his son James in 1617, James was allowed to grant his mother a lease for life of a chamber and 'one baie of buildinge' in his barn.[173]

Agnes Doorle, on surrendering her messuage and a half virgate in 1425, reserved for herself as dower *una camera bassa*, and another widow kept two rooms at the east end of the house.[174] The *camera bassa* probably indicates a ground-floor room, implying also the presence of an upper floor, while the two rooms at one end of the house might also have been in a floored bay. In 1547, Henry Baldwin surrendered his cottage called *Baldwyns* to the use of Thomas Witmyll, with Henry and his wife Joan retaining *unum le bay et unum le Cutende* for life.[175] The latter may well have been a lean-to end-bay, as suggested for Winslow.[176] This may have been the same house that Thomas Witmell floored over in 1559 (above), but he had also acquired a messuage and a yardland in 1547, that is perhaps more likely to have become his home.

Decay and repair of houses

The court rolls indicate that both messuages and cottages suffered from neglect. For the 110 years between 1437 and 1547, presentments survive of 26 people for having their houses out of repair.[177] Usually the buildings are designated simply as 'tenements'; most appear to have been cottages, but at least two of those presented were yardlanders, and one of the houses *in decasu et ruinosa* was described as a *domus mansionalis* – the house of a substantial holding.[178] The incoming tenant of another messuage and yardland paid no entry fine in 1533 because the house was ruinous.[179]

Often the roll does not specify the respect in which a house was *ruinosam*. When it does, the defect may be only in thatch or tiles. But one house was so bad that the bailiff was ordered to seize it – walls, sill-beams and roof were all defective.[180] Another was *ruinosam in omnibus* and ten were *valde ruinosa in omnibus* (totally ruinous in all respects).[181] Despite this activity, it was not easy for the court to get action and the same men were presented year after year.

These statistics may understate the problems. Many of the presentments were made in the court of the little 'reputed manor' of St Christopher's Chantry, where in 1520 nine tenements in Crendon were totally ruinous.[182] This must have been the chantry's entire Crendon tenantry, since the homage and the defaulters combined never numbered more than nine. For St Christopher's, a common outcome was a gift of timber to the tenant, but there is no record of such generosity on the part of the main Crendon lordships.[183] This is perhaps sufficient explanation of Crendon's record in the matter of neglect appearing better than the chantry's.

Crucks are not mentioned in any of the presentments, but neither are posts, so both types were probably subsumed within the term *maeremia*. Wall-plates, groundsills and rafters are mentioned, so when these occur with *maeremia*, it seems likely that the word was being used specifically for the main structural timbers, rather than with its usual meaning of 'timber in general'. We may note, for example, a presentment that *Johannes Edmundes permittit unum cottagium esse ruinosam pro defectu le wallplate, groundcylleing, maeremia et coopertura*, and another house needed *groundpynning et meremia*.[184] Ten of the surviving cruck houses in Long Crendon now have outer walls of

Fig. 6.6. Demolished house adjoining Wapping, Long Crendon (LON-J on Fig. 6.3d) (c. 1945 photo, Joyce Donald Collection, 46A, in possession of Gill Donald).

rubble; but these are probably replacements for timber framing. When dilapidated walls occasionally make their appearance in the rolls, they seem to be boundary walls.[185]

On the tenant's side, we find in 1545 a requirement for John Rygge to build a house of two and a half bays within a year, on one of two closes called *Sangwen* and *Wardenweke* that he held from the Dormer manor.[186] Since this is before smoke bays or half bays for chimneys became general in the county, this too probably referred to a lean-to end bay. In fact, this very cottage can probably be identified with one demolished in the mid-twentieth century, that stood north of Wapping (LON-J), for which a photograph does indeed show two full bays and a half-bay (Fig. 6.6).

6.3 Medieval peasant houses in the Vale of White Horse, Oxfordshire

Christopher Currie

The Vale of White Horse (Fig. 6.7) runs from east to west between the north-facing chalk escarpment of the Berkshire Downs, and the Thames on the north. It includes a clay vale north of the Downs, a low ridge of Corallian sandstones and limestones between the clay and the Thames, and an area of gravel and alluvium at its eastern end where the Thames winds southwards to pass through the escarpment. Four historic farming countries have been identified: the sandy Corallian Heights in the north, the Central zone of clay and alluvium, the Icknield zone including a strip of fertile Upper Greensand immediately below the escarpment,

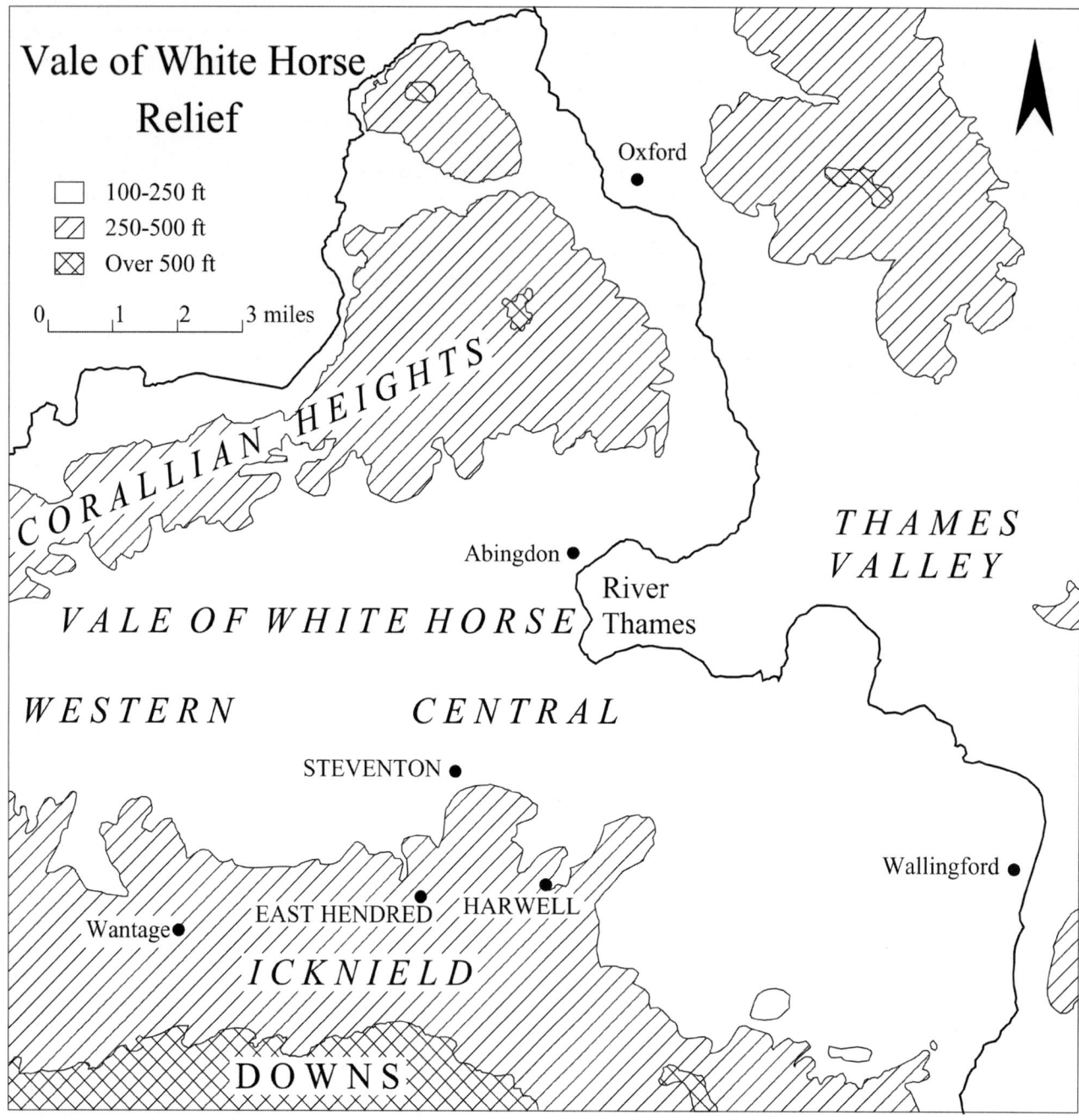

Fig. 6.7. Relief map of the Vale of White Horse showing the main agrarian regions and the locations of the villages discussed. (Redrawn from Currie, 1976).

and a Western zone where the soils are formed from the underlying clays. The eastern area has a high proportion of Grade 2 and a low proportion of grade 4 soils; in the west the ratios are reversed.[187]

The timber-framed buildings sampled for this project lie in the eastern part of the Icknield and in the Central zones. Woodland, which by 1086 was limited to the Corallian zone, later survived mainly in the north-east corner round Cumnor. Oak timber was usually brought in from south of the Downs or sometimes from Oxfordshire; elm, however, was locally available in fields and closes,[188] and the project has shown that it was often used in smaller medieval houses, sometimes combined with oak. Such a mixture of timber types was prescribed in a contract for a peasant building probably at East Hendred in 1421. The lord was to provide 'great timber' (*grosso merem*, presumably implying oak) for the couples (probably crucks) and elm for wallplates and 'sideresons' (either cruck tiebeams or middle rails).[189]

The scarcity of woodland reflected the early arable development of the region. Charters hint at extensive open field in the later 10th and early 11th centuries at least in the Icknield zone.[190] The open field was accompanied by a settlement pattern of nucleated villages. By the thirteenth century the eastern Vale was marked (within the inevitably mixed medieval farming system) by predominantly arable production and high corn yields, particularly of barley. In 1334 the core area of the eastern Vale, south of Abingdon, was one of a half dozen richest rural areas of England: 'it is likely that these very high assessments reflect exceptional local agricultural prosperity'.[191] Despite some decline after 1350, yields remained high in the fifteenth century:[192] the area's medieval yields of barley were not widely surpassed before the eighteenth century.[193] There was probably some shift to pasture, and a reduction of arable, in the fifteenth century, though the evidence has never been investigated in detail. In the sixteenth century, however, the eastern Vale was again mainly arable.[194] About then the western farming zone began to shift towards a more pastoral husbandry and after 1700 overtook the others in wealth,[195] but in the Middle Ages it was more marked by relative poverty than by any particular specialization.[196] Those diverse experiences reflect, besides differences in soils, differences in transport and access to markets, both favouring the east over the west.[197]

In contrast with its agrarian prosperity, there is little evidence of industrial activity in the medieval Vale. A large-scale kersey-cloth-finishing industry flourished briefly in a few villages on Ginge brook in the late fourteenth century and early fifteenth, but thereafter seems to have declined and to have become concentrated at East Hendred, leaving a legacy of Lollardy.[198]

Documentary evidence for late medieval peasant housing in the region

Few court-roll contracts or manorial building accounts for peasant houses have been found.[199] Among larger freehold houses, one at Farthing, East Hendred, in 1361 had hall, solar and cellar, kitchen, bakehouse, ox-house, and sheephouse, and another at Harwell in 1393 had a hall with a chamber at the north end, and a kitchen and stable annexed. A lease of a small plot at Steventon in 1402 required the tenant to build a new house of three couples, and another of a 19-acre holding at East Hendred in 1421 also specified a three-couple house, the lord providing timber for the three couples, and four elms for wallplates and 'syderesons'.[200] At Steventon in 1483 Henry Winchester was reported to have broken and carried off one *bayewindowe*. He had also carried off a pigsty (*domum porcinum*) and six planks and two doors. Furthermore,

part of his house, *le Parlor*, encroached on the lord's land by three feet, and his longhouse (*domus longa*) and barn (*orreum*) encroached by two feet, but no rent was being paid for them.[201]

The character of peasant building at the end of the Middle Ages is reflected in a presentment of 1556 reporting on houses 'decayed' at Fyfield and its hamlets between 1534 and 1554, covering both cottages and farmhouses of a yardland or more. Six had three bays, but two cottages had only two bays each. Most farmhouses had barns of two to five bays; four had detached kitchens, one combined with a stable and another with a millhouse. One had a detached two-bay chamber. At Long Wittenham at the same period, four of fourteen surveyed holdings had barns. This pattern of housing is confirmed by the evidence of a 1607 survey of part of East Hendred, which gives the size in bays of 21 tenant houses. They ranged in size from one to ten bays, and one also had two *le cuttinges* and another a *sher'*, both probably indicating lean-to bays (cf. p. 118). Significantly also, they included seven detached service buildings: two kitchens (*coquina*), one kitchen with a malthouse, one malthouse, and three *culina*, a word also generally translated as kitchen, but presumably here with a different nuance, perhaps referring to a back kitchen or brewhouse.[202]

Tenures

The tenure and size of peasant holdings was related to the pattern of manorial landholding. At one extreme were the large manors of long-established ecclesiastical institutions, with few freeholders and with customary tenements arranged in a hierarchy of standard sizes and subject to relatively heavy dues and services. At the other extreme small gentry manors often had many freeholders and light services, and show the early development of peasant leasehold.

In the later Middle Ages demesne leasing provided opportunities for enrichment (despite the risk of bankruptcy) for the better-off husbandman. Little is known of twelfth-century manorial leasing in the area. The late-medieval form of demesne leasing began in the later thirteenth century, but most demesnes were not let until the earlier fifteenth century.[203] Sometimes, as at Steventon, small pieces of demesne were let first, but the bulk of the farm was usually kept in one piece, and parts leased earlier were sometimes reabsorbed in the main part.[204]

Of 35 parishes in the eastern zones, in about 1300 only eleven contained a single manor or formed part of a manor extending over more than one parish.[205] From before 1066 small manors had been commonest in the Icknield zone, East Hendred parish having six manors in c. 1300; by contrast, in the Corallian zone, Cumnor manor included three parishes and many settlements. Most large manors were held by Benedictine houses or by members of the nobility. Abingdon abbey was the only great landowner with extensive estates in the Vale; other great lay and religious estates had one or two outlying manors each. Several alien priories held lands in the area. Local gentry families typically held one or two manors each; several combined a manor in the Vale with one in the wooded area south of the Downs.[206]

Freehold tenure was a post-Conquest development in the Vale. The Icknield zone, with its small manors and numerous lay lords, had many freeholders by the thirteenth century and retained the highest concentration in the seventeenth,[207] partly because, in the thirteenth century, corporate manorial lords elsewhere had been buying up large freeholds or recovering them by escheat.[208] As the market in freeholds developed in the thirteenth and early fourteenth centuries, some became very fragmented, with many tiny plots selling at up to £5 an acre.[209] In the fourteenth century much freehold was engrossed into large holdings; some of these came to be reputed manors, even where they began as peasant accumulations, and their successful owners might become gentry, while the estates of others became targets for upper-class acquisitions. Thus freehold became scarce in the land market, and between c. 1300 and c. 1500 there was a large rise in the effective cost (calculated as the number of years' rent income needed to repay the purchase price) of buying freehold, even where the price in cash terms fell.[210]

Outside the Icknield zone freeholders were greatly outnumbered by customary tenants.[211] The standard holdings were, as elsewhere, yardlands, half-yardlands, and cottages; as in Oxfordshire, and in contrast to eastern England,[212] the yardland was apparently the modal holding on most manors. Yardlands in the eastern Vale varied in size but appear to have been relatively small, 11 to 25 acres of arable at Harwell, for example,[213] and 24 acres at Steventon.[214] Their terms of tenure varied greatly. Week-work, at least for the whole year, seems to have been relatively unusual even in the thirteenth century, but labour services were quite heavy on some manors. In about 1300, even for the more heavily burdened tenants, the combined weight of rent and labour due was nevertheless generally only a half to two thirds of that endured by episcopal tenants in Worcestershire and Warwickshire (despite their poorer soils).[215] Instead landlords attempted to claw back the tenants' surpluses by charging high entry fines, which reached £10 per yardland, and occasionally much more, as at Bishop's Harwell and South Moreton; such high fines were, however, not universal even for good quality holdings. Even these fines were far below the market rate, as indicated by purchase prices for freeholds and the rents paid by sub-tenants. With luck and good management, the less heavily burdened of customary yardlanders could therefore make large profits.

On some gentry manors, the changed economic con-

ditions of the fourteenth century encouraged the conversion of customary tenements to leaseholds for lives.[216] More often they continued as copyhold. Holdings of more than one yardland are rarely recorded before the late fourteenth century; in the fifteenth, standard holdings were often combined, but these accumulations were temporary. On some manors standard holdings were allowed to fragment, making the land market more flexible, despite the loss in administrative convenience and of income from fines,[217] but on others, probably the majority, such fragmentation was rare before the seventeenth century.[218] Though entry fines fell dramatically in the late Middle Ages, they remained relatively high by national standards on good soils (£4 to £6 a yardland at Bishop's Harwell, for example). Relative depopulation, as elsewhere, made life easier for labourers and allowed many peasants to enlarge their holdings, although the successful peasant with a multiple holding often became a demesne lessee, and thus may have had no need to enlarge the house on his own farm. Not until the sixteenth century did such multiple holdings become relatively stable, allowing the development of an established yeoman class. Not until then, too, did gentry rather than husbandmen figure frequently as demesne lessees, though even then they might in reality be middlemen between the lord and rack-rented yeomen or husbandmen. Because of the relative rise in the cost of freehold land,[219] copyholdings, where they had sufficient security, became attractive to gentry buyers, and thus they appear as copyholders on some manors. By the seventeenth century leaseholds or copyholds held for lives were usual, but manors held by colleges, churchmen, and corporations often had copyholds of inheritance,[220] with rents and entry fines fixed and immune to the inflation that plagued tenants of copyholds for lives.[221] Paradoxically, therefore, where tenants' conditions had been harshest before the Black Death they were often the most favourable by 1600.

Tenurial conditions and the background to housing

To identify the owners or occupiers of specific peasant houses when they were built involves establishing a complete descent to recent times. Yet descents of houses other than manor houses can seldom be traced from the middle ages. In this area, unlike some areas of scattered settlement, houses cannot be readily identified by location and rarely retained their names for long periods, so that a succession of owners must be established. Tracing freeholds depends mainly on access to, and the survival of, title deeds, but those rarely extend back before the seventeenth century at best. Lime Tree House, Harwell, a yardlander's house whose descent can be traced back to the time of its construction in the thirteenth century, is a rare exception.[222] For copyholds, the survival of a continuous series of court rolls or the equivalent from the time of building to the

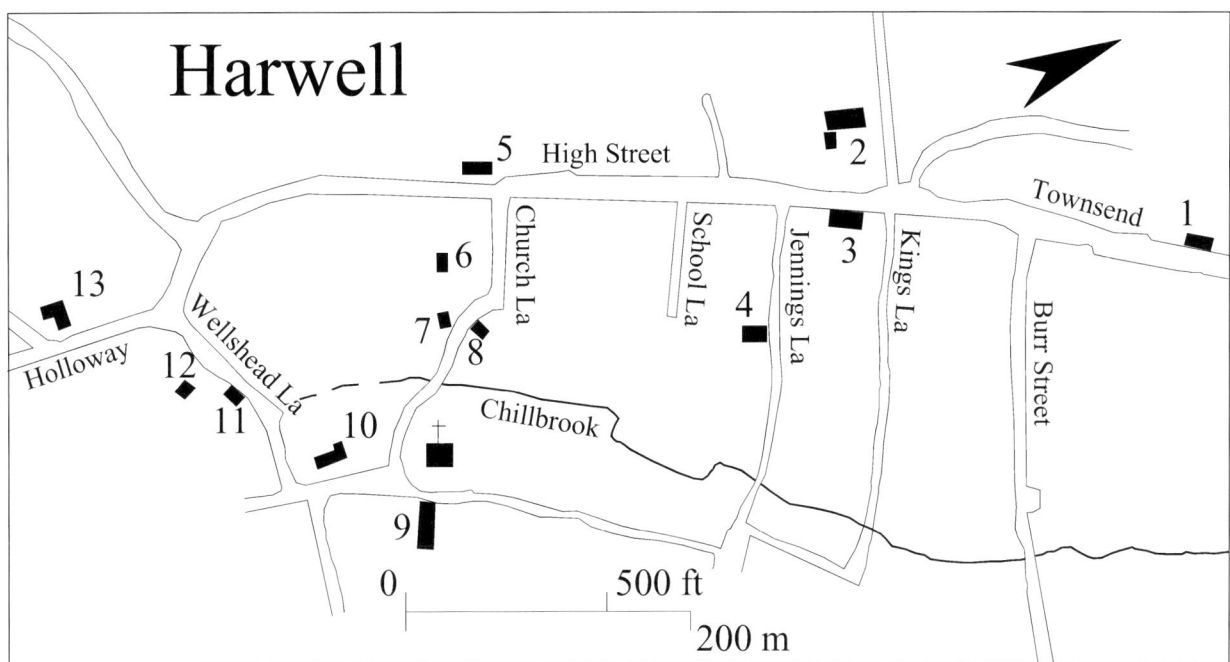

Fig. 6.8. Outline map of Harwell, showing the location of the village lanes and early houses.

1 Pomander House (HAR-D)	6 Lockton Farm outbuilding	11 Holywell Cottage (HAR-F)
2 Middle Farm (X-HA2)	7 The Dell (HAR-A)	12 Tibberton Cottage (HAR-E)
3 Adnams Farmhouse	8 Church Farm (HAR-B)	13 Abbey Timbers (HAR-C)
4 Seymour House	9 Prince's Manor Farm	
5 Lime Tree House (X-HA1)	10 Wellshead Farm	

date of the earliest deed or detailed map is required. Even where such material is extensive, as at Bishop's Harwell and Steventon, a gap of two or three decades may interrupt descents (but see below for Steventon). Moreover where a house is found – as is usually the case – to have formed part of a composite holding at some period it may well not be identifiable with a particular earlier component. Family names cannot be relied on: although the Woodleaf (Woodliff, Woodley) family remained in Harwell from King John's to Queen Victoria's reign and the Lyford family in Steventon from 1280 to 1900, they did not retain the same holdings throughout and several family members were often found as contemporaneous tenants.

It is, however, possible to establish the approximate standing of the original builder of a house: if the manor it belonged to can be identified, if the type of tenure is known, and if medieval evidence exists of the conditions of tenure and size of holding on that manor, or sometimes if the house's descent can be traced back to a date before holdings were allowed to fragment. Manor-wide information on the size of holdings may set a maximum holding size for each of a group of surviving houses. It may be moreover possible to identify any exceptional tenements with their modern successors, whether or not the surviving houses are old. If the medieval houses do not belong to that group it follows

that they were on standard holdings. This comparative and eliminative approach is applied to the first two parishes examined. For the third, Steventon, the discovery in 2010 of previously unknown manorial court books has allowed a more detailed treatment of the village, although, because holdings fragmented earlier there than elsewhere, the date back to which an early house must be traced to understand the likely size of its original holding is also earlier than elsewhere.

Harwell

From 1086 to the nineteenth century Harwell (Fig. 6.8) had two main manors. One was held by the bishop of Winchester and later by the Ecclesiastical Commissioners.[223] The other resulted from Roger D'Ivry's union of two pre-Conquest estates and was held by a succession of lay lords; it was later known as Prince's manor. Between 1361 and the Dissolution it belonged to St. Nicholas's college, Wallingford.[224] A third reputed manor, Brounz's, developed in the fourteenth century by amalgamation of the largest freeholds on each of the main manors with other property. Extensive manorial documents exist for Bishop's manor, but no court rolls are known to have survived for Prince's manor, while Brounz's manor apparently never held courts.[225]

Prince's manor included at least one large freehold by the 1190s and from the early thirteenth century its lords were selling land to create smaller freeholds.[226] In 1300 the 11 smaller freeholders held 10½ yardlands, 5 houses, and a 'plot' in units varying from 1 croft to 2½ yardlands, for an average burden for rent and works of 4s 6d per yardland. There were also apparently 13 yardlands held in villeinage in two groups, ten averaging 5s 11d for rent and works and three averaging 8s 0½d; tallage averaged 3s 1d a yardland.[227] Villein holdings also owed entry fines: in the 1290s fines of 5s to 20s for half-yardlands and 53s 4d for a yardland were recorded.[228] By 1370 some of the earlier freeholds had been absorbed into Brounz's Manor and the Catewy's Farm (later Lime Tree House) estate.[229] The active land market of the late thirteenth and early fourteenth centuries which preceded such absorption had seen very high prices, up to 40 marks for a yardland or £5 for a single acre.[230] In the mid sixteenth century the remaining customary tenants still owed over £11 altogether in rents,[231] but by the early seventeenth no houses were held by copy.[232] Some former copyholdings had been sold off on very long leases, but some were probably enfranchised directly.[233]

Most holdings on Bishop's manor, on the other hand, were in villeinage, later becoming copyhold. Of its two large freeholds in the mid thirteenth century, one later became part of Brounz's manor and part of the other was incorporated in Catewy's farm.[234] The 32 customary yardlanders paid rents of 6s and owed works valued apparently at 5s, 15 customary half-yardlanders had obligations about half of the yardlanders', and the manor had a few smallholders and cottagers.[235] Although Harwell yardlands and half-yardlands seem to have varied in size, there was no difference in average land quality between the two manors, since strips were intermingled in the same open fields. Nevertheless entry fines were much higher on Bishop's than on Prince's manor, and by 1258 had already reached £13 13s 4d for a yardland and (exceptionally) £10 6s 8d for a half-yardland.[236] Fines in the earlier fourteenth century were at similar levels or a little lower, but 40 marks was paid for two yardlands (the only holding of that size) in 1326.[237] Though the Black Death in 1348–9 had no lasting effect on entry fines,[238] after the 1361 plague, fines fell somewhat and composite holdings are sometimes recorded; by the mid fifteenth century £4 to £6 fines for a yardland and 6s 8d to 10s for a half-yardland were typical.[239] In the sixteenth century, when customary tenure had become copyhold of inheritance and fines for particular tenements became fixed, farms still consisted of standard holdings, though they were often grouped in larger units.[240] Only from the mid seventeenth century was division of standard holdings, with proportional division of entry fines, allowed.[241]

As far as house-building is concerned it is clear that between c. 1250 and 1350 the freeholders and customary yardlanders of Prince's manor were better able than customary yardlanders on Bishop's manor to have accumulated the necessary capital, because they enjoyed cumulatively far lower rents, services and fines. After 1400, still more after 1500, the differences in tenure should have made little difference to available building capital. Nevertheless the only documented case of pre-1350 building expenditure concerns a peasant whose father had a large customary tenement on Bishop's manor, and who spent at least £169 on buying freeholds, and after that, in 1316, agreed to pay the large sum of 27 marks (£18) to build a new timber-framed house.[242]

Though estate maps covering the two main manors are lacking, and a firm boundary between them in the village cannot be drawn, the Inclosure Map of 1804 shows which houses were copyhold, and therefore held of Bishop's manor, and which freehold and leasehold. The great majority of the freeholds and leaseholds (apart from some Brounz's manor properties) were held of Prince's manor, originating either as medieval freeholds or as copyholds enfranchised in the sixteenth century. High Street and Church Lane were areas of intermingled holdings. The area east of High Street and north of Church Lane, where tenements are laid out in a grid of parallel lanes, was almost entirely copyhold and presumably results from a twelfth-century expansion of the village plan by the bishops. The south end of the village evidently belonged to Prince's manor.

The surviving medieval houses include Prince's Manor Farm (the former manor house, of about 1500) and the putative rectory house (Willowbrook, later Wellshead Farm), of which a fourteenth-century cross wing survives. The hall of Brounz's manor (Middle Farm, X-HA2) uses base crucks as does the capital messuage of Catewy's estate (Lime Tree House, High Street, X-HA1), the latter an improved yardlander's mid-thirteenth century aisled hall (see pp. 36, 49, 151). Of lower status houses, the most numerous are cruck-built.[243] Medieval box-framed wings accompany three of the cruck halls,[244] and probably also existed at Pomander Cottage (HAR-D) and Tibberton (HAR-E). Other surviving late-medieval houses are box-framed.[245]

Those wholly box-framed houses were all copyhold of Bishop's Manor. So were five of the cruck buildings including Pomander House and The Dell (HAR-A). Those two belonged to composite holdings in 1804 and their earlier descent cannot be traced, though Martha Thomas, the owner of The Dell and two other houses in 1804, had little field land and The Dell may therefore have originated as a cottage. The remaining cruck halls were freehold in 1804 and therefore held of Prince's Manor. Church Farm seems to be on the site of a house held by the wealthy atte Hall family in 1303, but that family's estate had been broken up long before the present house was built.[246] The owner of Abbey Timbers was allotted 11 freehold acres at inclosure.[247] The owner of Tibberton Cottage had no field land in 1804. It may have been one of the Prince's Manor copyholds enfranchised in the sixteenth century.[248] Holywell Cottage also had no field land in 1804 and was built on the roadside on a small triangular plot which had clearly been carved out of Tibberton Cottage's curtilage. It was presumably therefore created as a cottage in the fifteenth century.

East Hendred

Medieval landholding in East Hendred (Fig. 6.9) was exceptionally complex, and it already included several manors by 1086, of which five can be identified later, a sixth emerging before 1300; the later descent of other substantial medieval estates cannot be traced.[249] The largest Domesday holding, a ten-hide estate later known as King's manor, was held by the count of Evreux who gave it to the alien priory of Noyon. After the suppression of alien

priories in the early fifteenth century it passed to Sheen Priory and, after the dissolution of that house, remained Crown property until 1833.

Outside the boundaries of King's Manor was what became the Abbey Manor, a five-hide estate held by the King in 1086 and given by the Empress Maud to Reading Abbey. After the Dissolution the manor passed to the Norreys family in 1544, being sold in 1623 to William Eyston, already lord of the small manor of Arches. Though the Abbey manor house was in the village, the tenantry were in a separate tithing from the rest of the parish and the manor had a self-contained set of fields.[250] The manor houses of King's and Abbey manors occupy a plot surrounded by roads, and the straight boundary between them should date from before 1066.

Three smaller manors lay within the boundaries of King's manor, but were feudally independent.[251] Of them, Frampton's, allegedly of 7 hides, was held by the alien priory

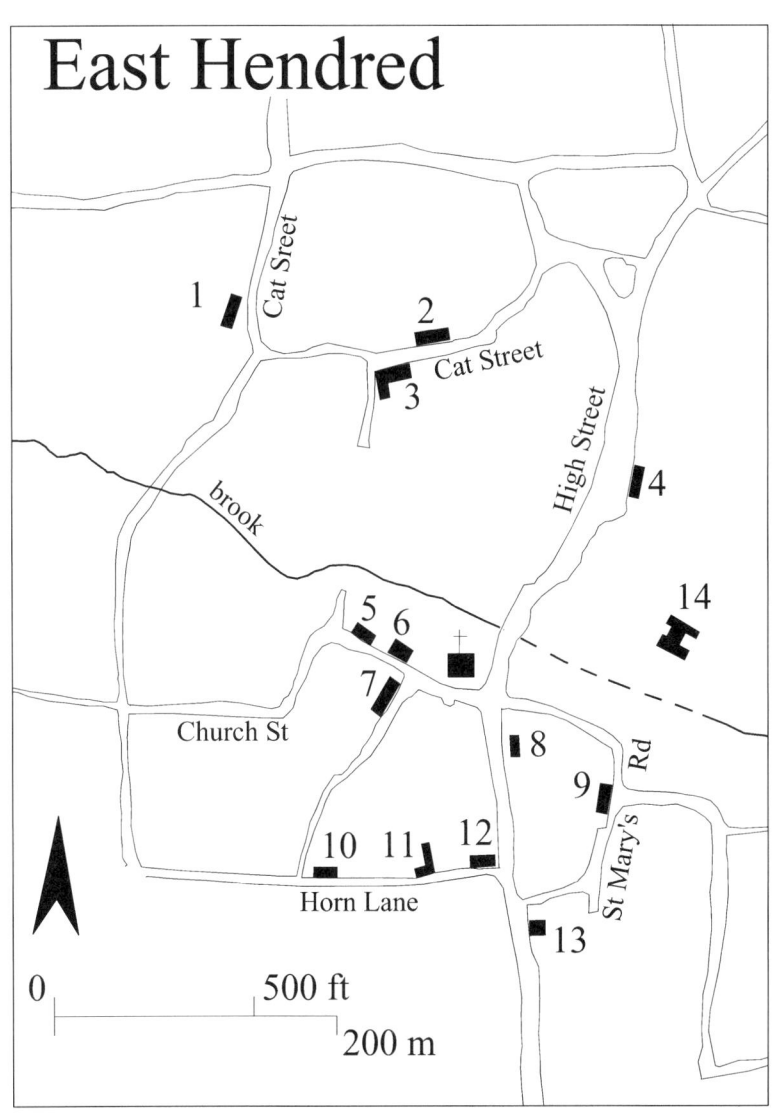

Fig. 6.9. Outline map of East Hendred, showing the location of the village lanes and early houses.

1   Hickman's Cottages
2   Inglenook-Penny Green (EAH-B)
3   Briar Cottages
4   The Stores & Wisteria Cottage (X-EAH)
5   Wythe Cottage
6   Church Street cottages;
7   Old Forge/Forge Cottage (EAH-A)
8   2 Newbury Road
9   Godfrey's Farm (EAH-C)
10 The Cottage, Horn Lane;
11 Windyridge-Dunelm
12 Meadow Cottages
13 Featherbed Cottage
14 Hendred House (thirteenth century and
    c. 1500 manor house of Arches manor)

of Frampton, passing after 1410 to the Duke of Bedford, whose heir was Henry VI, and before 1516 to Bradenstoke priory (Wilts.). In the seventeenth century it belonged to the Sherwood family.[252] The manor of Arches passed by inheritance from the Turberville family (mid twelfth to late thirteenth century) to the Arches (early fourteenth to early fifteenth century), and the Eystons, lords from 1453 to the present. It was said to be of one hide at Domesday,[253] but may have been enlarged later, since many tenements in the village appear to have been in the purview of its court in the eighteenth century.[254] A one-hide estate, held from 1232 by Littlemore priory, is thought to have become New College's manor, but the Oxford college may also have acquired all or part of a manor belonging c. 1300 to Tristan of Padhale.[255]

The tenancies on King's and Frampton's manors as indicated by surveys of 1294, 1324, and 1551 are summarised in table 6.5. On King's manor in 1294 and 1324 the tenants' labour services were trivial. The freeholds may have been converted to customary land after 1324, since the manor included 30 customary yardlands altogether in 1551. Nevertheless the full yardland or a multiple of it was much the commonest holding, and in contrast to Steventon (below) little land was held in irregular parcels. Moreover, though some houses had evidently decayed, the only landless houses were cottages and no large holdings lacked houses. By 1607, when there were 31 tenants, the pattern of holdings had begun to break up but was still recognisable.[256] At Frampton's manor, on the other hand, mention of reliefs in the later fifteenth century suggests that the conversion to freehold evident from the table had

taken place by then. Entry fines on the manor were then low, the highest recorded in proportion to holding size being 13s 4d for a house and half-yardland in 1461.[257]

The other manors already included several freeholds in the thirteenth and fourteenth centuries, some with as much as a hide of land, though it is often impossible to know from which manor they were held.[258] On the manor of Arches, customary holdings were being let on leases for lives from the 1350s, and by 1453 at least 12 of 21 manorial tenants were life leaseholders, the others comprising one freeholder, one tenant at will, and seven with unspecified tenure. Though some tenants held standard holdings, other such holdings had clearly been fragmented.[259]

Besides income from farming, East Hendred villagers profited from a cloth-finishing trade, which, as at Steventon, developed in the later fourteenth century. A market and fairs were established in the early fifteenth century, and in contrast to Steventon the village remained a clothing centre at least until the late fifteenth century.[260]

Generally, the descent of the early non-manorial houses in East Hendred has not been traced. Nevertheless by the time of inclosure in 1802 all the smaller medieval houses of the village were no more than cottages, with little or no field land.[261] They had thus either originated as cottages or had been reduced to cottages by 1802, and most owe their present-day survival to the conservative management of the Eyston estate.[262]

Hickman's Cottages, Cat Street, is notable as the widest cruck house yet found in the Vale, with an internal span of 21 ft, and the largest floor area and volume within a single range.[263] It was allegedly built as a cottage by or

Table 6.5. Tenancies on King's and Frampton's Manors, East Hendred, 1294–1551.

K and F refer to King's and Frampton's manors respectively. (From Currie, 'Smaller Domestic Architecture', 60–1, 81, summarising TNA E106/2/6, rott 3, 8 (1294); E179/73/5, rot 18d (1322); E106/8/5, rot 7d (1324); LR2/187, ff 296–9, 300v–301v (1551)). The 1607 survey is not directly comparable with the four earlier surveys and is excluded.

Date		1294			1322	1324			1551		
Tenure	Size (ydl)	K	F	Both	F[a]	K	F	Both	K[b]	F	Both
Free	Over 2										
Free	1–2	2		2		2		2		3	3
Custom	Over 2								7		7
Custom	1–2	}19		}31					3	3	6
Custom	½–1		}12			24	5	29	3		3
Custom	½						9	9	1		1
Custom	Under ½	2				2	3	5	2	1	3
Total tenants		21	12	33	35	28	17	45	16	7	23
Total yardlands		28.5	8	36.5		28	9.5	37.5	30	>7	>37
Total houses									21	10	31

a   For Frampton's Manor in 1322, the total given is the number of named villeins, probably including under-tenants.

b   For King's manor in 1551, the holdings of each tenant are combined, even if more than one property is listed.

for Laurence Rushbrooke between December 1595 and October 1596, when he sold it to Thomas Hickman. Its character, however, is archaic in comparison to all late sixteenth-century Oxfordshire houses, whether cruck-built or not. This suggests that it was a much earlier building that had stood elsewhere and had been dismantled and re-erected in 1597. Furthermore, its size and sophistication indicate that when originally built it was a house of significant status, far more than that of a simple cottage. In 1607 it was a cottage, without associated farmland, held by Henry Hickman.[264] In 1802 it was a copyhold with a large close and no field land, but its owner had a larger farm centred on a different farmhouse.[265] At that time, the Eyston estate included three cruck buildings, Old Forge, Church Street (EAH-A), Godfreys Farm (EAH-C), and 2 Newbury Road, one other certainly and one possibly medieval house, the Stores and Meadow Cottages.[266] Of the other cruck houses in the parish, one in 1802 was part of a row of cottages,[267] and another was attached to a smallholding for which 4 acres was allotted at inclosure.[268] Two other cruck cottages,[269] and one small box-framed medieval house,[270] had no field land. Another box-framed house appears to have belonged in 1802 to a large farmer who lived elsewhere.[271] Both the last two were part of the Eyston estate by 1970, as was the remaining cruck house,[272] whose ownership in 1802 is obscure.

Documentary evidence for early houses in Steventon

Manorial structure and tenure

Steventon was unusual among Vale parishes in that it had but one manor conterminous with the parish, and the exceptionally complete manorial documentation has allowed more detailed study than elsewhere of the historical background to its medieval houses.[273] From the twelfth century the manor belonged to the Norman priory of Pré, a cell of Bec, which established a non-conventual cell at Steventon with a prior and (in peacetime) another resident monk. During the French wars, from 1294 onwards, it was repeatedly taken into Crown hands. In the late fourteenth century the manor passed through the hands of Sir Hugh Calveley, John Waltham, Bishop of Salisbury, Roger Walden and then Richard II, who gave it to Westminster Abbey. The abbey and its ecclesiastical successors held it until the nineteenth century, except during the Commonwealth and for a brief period after the Dissolution.[274]

Though substantial freeholds had existed in the thirteenth century, the two largest had been sold or escheated to the prior before 1281, and were let to tenants at will. In 1324, two freeholders with undertenants and three smaller freeholders are listed. Freehold rents of 48s recorded in 1400 may have included those paid by undertenants of

Farthing in East Hendred, which had passed with Steventon to Westminster Abbey. Two substantial freeholds survived through the fifteenth and sixteenth centuries, but in the mid sixteenth century only two or three houses were freehold, though 16 tenants had some freehold land.[275] Most peasant farms in Steventon were therefore held by customary tenure (later copyhold). The customary tenants were sokemen of ancient demesne, a status that supposedly limited increases in their services, and from 1399 the copyholds were always heritable.[276] Altogether 77 customary tenants were named in a lawsuit of 1281, besides 11 tenants at will who held on the same terms as the others. In 1294 there were said to be 63 customary tenants holding 77 yardlands, owing an average of 12s 4d a yardland for rent and works, while, in 1324, 33 yardlanders owed rent and works totalling 9s 6d a yardland, 22 half-yardlanders owed rent and works totalling 5s 3d each, and there were 9 cottagers.[277] The development of composite holdings of more than a yardland, which the 1294 figure of 77 yardlands appears to suggest, is not borne out by late fourteenth-century evidence. Despite any effects of the plague, of 36 tenements changing hands between 1382 and 1399 only four were composite, and of those the largest consisted of two messuages and half-yardlands; though a holding of three messuages and 2½ yardlands is recorded in 1404 and one of two messuages, a toft, and three yardlands in 1426. Population had been sustained at a relatively high level by the growth since c. 1350 of a cloth-finishing industry.[278] In about 1300, Steventon tenants had to pay entry fines of £4 to £6 6s 8d for a yardland; by the late fourteenth century £4 for a yardland or £2 for a half-yardland was normal, corresponding to six years' rent.[279] For complete holdings comprising a messuage and a yardland or half-yardland, fines at those rates continued to be charged until the 1530s.[280]

Nevertheless, most Steventon copyhold conveyances had long been subject to a different tariff. Exchanges of small amounts of field land between tenants had been allowed since the 1380s for fines of 12d an acre, but in 1406 two tenants exchanged their houses, and from 1428 to 1441 exchanges of messuages, or of a messuage for a single acre, were common, again usually for a 12d fine.[281] Following also an outburst of apparently collusive pleas of debt in the subsistence crisis of 1438–9,[282] from 1439 Westminster Abbey, contrary to its normal policy elsewhere, began to permit tenants to buy and sell houses and small parcels of land rather than complete holdings,[283] again usually for fines of 12d an acre or two years' rent.[284] Thus standard holdings became fragmented, and large irregular holdings, including groups of houses or house-plots, could develop; their owners also sometimes held the lease of the demesne or the rectory. Before the late fifteenth century, however, these large holdings were mostly broken up in the tenant's old age or at his death.[285] The unfettered land market and defined costs drew outside investors to Steventon. Two

London mercers had dealt in copyholds there in the 1430s, but probably as trustees.[286] From about 1470 absentee owners became prominent, and several built up large estates, notably the Spicers of Ilsley from the 1490s,[287] the Yates of Charney and later Buckland from 1489,[288] Michael Dormer of London (who bought and extended the Spicer estate) in the 1530s,[289] and Oliver Wellesbourne of Hanney from 1528.[290] The largest copyholding of all, however, was created by the resident Richard Doo from 1430 to the 1470s; he also built the most substantial house in the village.[291]

From the 1550s, stewards began to increase entry fines, which sometimes reached 3 years' rent in the late 1570s,[292] but the tenants repeatedly insisted that two years' rent was customary,[293] and in the mid 1580s several refused to pay more.[294] An agreement in 1590 set all fines permanently at twice the cash rent but required the tenants to pay malt rents in addition.[295] These stable rents (13s 4d for a 24 acre yardland or 6d per acre for parcels of land) and fixed fines at a time of inflation brought a number of resident yeoman families to prominence by about 1600.[296]

Economic background to the early houses

Steventon shared the general agricultural economy of the eastern Vale. Its soils, graded 3 and 4, were wetter and poorer than those of Harwell and Hendred,[297] but its fourteenth-century copyholders were partly compensated by the lower entry fines. A Steventon merchant, Robert Holway, is mentioned in 1349 as a creditor.[298] He was one of a group of Steventon men who leased the manor and priory from the Crown in 1357; from 1369 to 1377 Steventon men were the prior's pledges for the lease.[299] Whether Holway was a cloth merchant is not clear, but John le Folere, a debtor in 1361,[300] may have been a fuller, and plenty of evidence survives for the cloth-finishing trade in the late fourteenth and early fifteenth century.[301] Its decline was apparently accompanied by decreasing population. From the 1380s to the 1420s, 15 to 25 men paid chevage to reside in the village as non-tenants, but in the early 1430s numbers fell and after 1447 no payments are noted.[302] Clothiery decline may have been accelerated by pollution of watercourses by tanners, which also may have encouraged the abandonment of houses backing on the brook. Two tanners were presented in West End in 1433, and three in East End in 1440 for fouling the stream;[303] two of those probably worked from their tenements on

the brook south of the Causeway.[304] Tanners continued to be presented until 1522.[305] Although inventories of a roper in 1544 and apparently a mercer in 1556 (below) suggest some industry, Steventon was thereafter primarily an agricultural parish with barley and malt the principal output. In 1524 and 1525 William Hopkins, the demesne farmer, was the largest taxpayer, assessed on £20 in both years. Of the 30–31 other men assessed, few were worth over £5 (Table 6.6).

Village topography

Our recent work has drastically revised our understanding of Steventon's medieval topography (Fig. 6.10). It had two tithings, usually known as East End and West End, possibly indicating an origin as two settlements,[306] and it clearly includes elements of an irregular green village and a medieval planned village. The church stands at the west end and the manor house, later Manor Farm, immediately south of it; from the twelfth to the fourteenth century the alien priory was located there. East of the church was an area of rectorial glebe and a tithe barn, which survived into the eighteenth century. The raised and paved causeway that is Steventon's most striking feature runs from the church and manor house eastwards along the south side of the green,[307] at its east end veering further northwards to cut across the green. On its south side is a long row of rectangular north-south tofts (TM2–TM137), evidently the fruit of deliberate planning; on them stand most of the surviving medieval and early modern farmhouses, with their crofts behind. This row, and therefore the Causeway (and Milton Lane, its eastern section), existed by 1299 as a street, the date of the earliest known surviving house aligned with it;[308] the raised path itself, however, is not documented until 1404.[309] Lanes and streets ran southwards from the Causeway between the houses, from Mill Street in the west to High Street (called Highway Lane in the seventeenth century) in the east. South of the crofts lay a further row of closes, and south of that the Mill Brook. Beyond the Mill Brook and its adjacent closes ran a series of east-west back streets: Cat (later Castle) Street in the west, mentioned in 1420,[310] Pugsden Lane in the east, and an intermediate street (not named in the Middle Ages, and partly diverted in 1839 for the railway) from Stocks Lane to Highway Lane. The area south of those streets was in 1842 occupied by large closes apparently already present in the late-medieval

Table 6.6. Steventon subsidy assessments 1524–5.

Source: 1524, TNA E 179/73/134; 1525, E 179/73/128.

Year	Goods £20	Goods £10–£13	Goods £5–£9	Goods >£2–<£5	Goods 40s	Assessed at 20s on Wages	Total
1524	1	3	1	10	10	7	32
1525	1	2	0	7	5	15 (+one at 26s 8d)	31

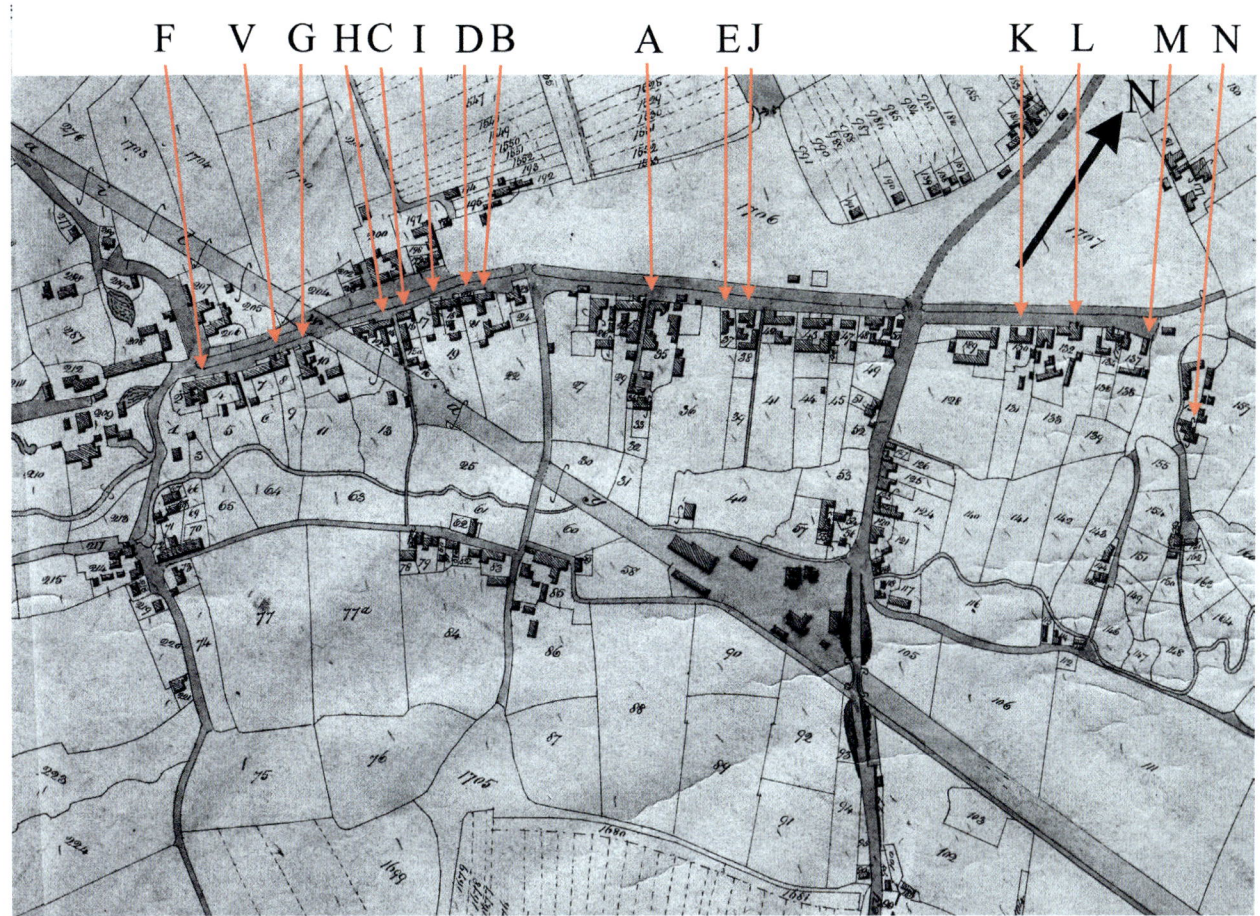

Fig. 6.10. Steventon in 1842, as mapped for the Tithe Apportionment (Berks RO). Letters identify the medieval houses discussed in the individual reports (STE-A-N); V marks the Old Vicarage. Mill Street is the prominent north-south road at the west (left) and Highway Lane that at the east (starting below letter L), with Stocks Lane midway between them. Milton Lane is the eastward extension of the Causeway (houses K–M) with Sheepwash and Kennel Lane running south from it (house N). Pugsden Lane runs south of the stream, between Kennel Lane and Highway Lane. Little Lane runs south from beside house C.

period.[311] The scattered post-medieval houses along Cat Street and Pugsden Lane seem to have been mainly cottages or smallholdings (and it had formerly been assumed that all the medieval cottages also lay there).[312]

Although all but one of the surviving medieval houses lie along the Causeway, it has now become clear that the farmhouses of many of the medieval customary yardland and half-yardland holdings lay away from the Causeway, as did most of the twelve 'burdewes' or cottage holdings.[313] In particular, the East End included, besides houses on the planned row in Milton Lane (with several medieval and early-modern survivors), numerous houses on irregular plots, along the path to Milton, round the Lower Green, and on Sheepwash, Kennel, and Pugsden Lanes. Most of those were derelict by 1560, and Old Farm House (STE-N) is apparently the only medieval survivor. Plots at either end of Pugsden Lane show continuity of occupation, but between them several houses had disappeared by the late sixteenth century.

Moreover, behind the crofts of the houses on the Causeway, from Little Lane in the west to Highway Lane, what in the nineteenth century was still an almost continuous hedge line marked the position of a narrow lane, the Twychen or Twychens (see Fig. 8.10c.1), on whose south side, in what were later pasture closes, were the frontages of more houses between the lane and the brook. Those in Cook's Close (TM 40) included at least three former farmhouses, two of yardland and one of half-yardland size; one of the yardland house sites seems to have been the main-house of Vowcylles or Foushulls, a two-and-half yardland combined holding recorded in 1404; one or more of Foushulls' two other houses many have adjoined it; and other houses are recorded in this area.[314] The lane extended east of Highway Lane, probably as far as Sheepwash Lane, with further houses there.[315] The repeated problems of encroachment, draining and fencing along the Twychens[316] probably underlie the abandonment by 1560 of all the houses there.

In Cat Street, medieval houses seem to have lain on its north side, but by the late seventeenth century a row of houses was developing on the south side, probably on former field land (TM 78–83). Stocks Lane Farm (TM 86) was built in that period, possibly on a new site. Renewed development also took place from about 1560 onwards on previously unoccupied areas north of the Causeway and the Green, although the site of Causeway Farm, (TM 200) which existed by 1571, may be medieval.[317] The adjoining houses (TM 197–199) were built before 1600.[318]

These changes in the topography of the village have also influenced the survival of houses. Overall, at most 10 per cent of the houses standing in 1400 still survive. Much of this loss is the result of post-1350 demolition without replacement; this would broadly be expected simply because of the 50–70 percent decrease in population, and is reflected specifically in the abandonment of house sites in back streets and the East End, as discussed above. By contrast, of houses standing on The Causeway/Milton Lane in 1560, mostly built in the preceding century, nearly half have survived all the later vicissitudes to which they have been subjected.

General evidence for Steventon houses

A few documents throw light on the character of the medieval houses in Steventon. The copyholders had an obligation to repair their houses, but information on this is rarely recorded in the court rolls, usually in relation to a failure by the guardians of minor heirs to maintain property. Thus, in 1480 the guardians of two imbeciles were to keep their tenements in repair.[319] In 1493, the court ordered two tenants by the curtesy to repair buildings they had allowed to decay, in each case on a double holding.[320] Conversely, the manor court ignored, presumably because they did not affect minor heirs, two complete demolitions and evictions alleged in 1517 to have been made in 1498 and 1499.[321] A number of probate inventories can be associated with the medieval houses studied in detail, but generally do not give particularly early descriptions of them. In all, only eight inventories are dated before 1560, including two for the manor farm, William Hopkins (1528) and Thomas Smalbone (1558), and one for the vicarage, Edward Haylett (1557).[322] Some, probably most, still had open halls, with bacon and sometimes beef at the roof,[323] a chamber, not necessarily upstairs (though Smalbone had a loft over 'the mayden's chamber'), and sometimes a kitchen, buttery, or brewhouse. Ellys Cox (1556) of Stocks Lane had a hall, two chambers, a kitchen, and a shop; his 46 debtors from over 22 places and a reference to 'pieces sold' suggest that he was a draper or mercer.[324] Occasionally an early inventory, such as that of David Luckyns in 1561, appears to fit the medieval phases of a house very closely, even though it does not name the rooms (see STE-G).

Tracing the houses

The earliest maps identifying the owners of all the houses in Steventon are of 1839 and 1842 (Fig. 6.10), although a map from 1835 shows those parts of the village affected by the construction of the Great Western Railway.[325] Since the great majority of village houses were copyhold, it is the manor court rolls that provide the crucial evidence for tracing ownership. When these were studied in the 1970s,[326] the latest court roll known to exist dated to 1800, and it proved impossible to bridge the period between then and 1842. Thus, the holdings described in the individual copyhold admissions could not be located on the ground. In 2010, in the course of research on other aspects of Steventon houses, it was discovered that the complete series of court books from 1664 to 1925 had been deposited since 1980 by the Church Commissioners at Westminster Abbey, but had not been catalogued as such.[327] Including this material, the court rolls survive in a largely unbroken sequence from 1382 to 1925.[328] Survival is patchy from 1382 to 1399, and there are large gaps in the seventeenth century: 1602–36, and 1641–61.[329] At some periods, precise dating of some courts is difficult, notably between 1483 and the 1530s, when spring courts were often dated in relation to Hock Tuesday.[330] Occasionally a court seems to have been simply misdated by the clerk, probably because its record was engrossed from paper minutes long after the event.[331]

The major undertaking of linking the nearly 3,000 admissions into sequences for the individual properties has provided the successions of names of individual owners, associated with descriptions of the property held.[332] Particularly in and before the seventeenth century some of the holding descriptions include the names of the adjoining tenants, sometimes making it possible to identify the sequences of owners even when some admissions are lost.

Some rentals and surveys also survive, although they are of less use than might have been expected, because of the active land market in Steventon which reduces the continuity between successive documents, and because of diverse methods of compilation. For the period after 1664, the linkage has been greatly helped by the work of the contemporary stewards of the manor, who seem to have been confronted by precisely the same problems of property identification. They compiled a numbered summary of all 800 admissions from 1664 to 1800, and identified many links between successive admissions, noting when properties were divided or combined. Similarly, in about 1800 and again in 1890, they compiled indexes by property, listing the successive admissions.[333] In the 1870s-80s, many of the property descriptions were rationalised, including their identification on the tithe and enclosure maps, but often omitting any correlation with the earlier description.

The result of this very detailed study has been that, with very few exceptions, the 110 houses or cottages identified on the tithe map can be linked to their manorial holding and followed back to the first admission after 1664. For the period before 1664, work has concentrated on the 16 known medieval houses (Table 6.7). The prevalence of multiple holdings causes some problems, particularly in the fifteenth century, and in the mid sixteenth century stewards revised many property descriptions, making identification of holdings with their predecessors difficult.[334] In addition, from 1432 until c. 1560 the term 'messuage' was regularly used for derelict as well as for standing houses. On the other hand, some late sixteenth and early seventeenth-century abuttals, unchanged descriptions, and persisting tenement names, have helped us bridge the large seventeenth-century court-roll gaps. Other holding sequences have been reconstructed by combining the evidence of stable quit rents with that of wills, parish registers, and a few published pedigrees.

The freeholdings and the vicarage

Freeholds are normally mentioned in the court rolls only at the death of a tenant in fee and only a handful of intermediate conveyances were recorded. Many of the freeholds recorded in the court rolls and surveys consisted of arable land only. Court presentations suggest that some copyholdings were passed off as freeholds in the sixteenth century and later reverted to copyhold. Conversely one medieval freehold messuage was treated as copyhold after 1601 (STE-A), as was another after 1660.[335] Incomplete post-medieval deed sequences have been found for two freehold houses, and Chancery suits relate to one of those.[336] For the Old Vicarage, which can be regarded as equivalent to a freehold, the secularization deed of 1841 confirms its identity, and published lists of vicars and incidental references to them give the names of earlier incumbents.[337] Wills and/or inventories of at least four vicars from the sixteenth and seventeeth centuries survive.

Steventon house owners

We have been able to trace the ownership of all but one of the medieval houses back to before 1500, the exception being one of the two freeholdings (summarised in Table 6.7). Still more significantly, the ownership of eight of the medieval houses has been traced to the period of their first surviving phase. Thus we can confidently place them in their economic milieu. For the other medieval houses, the

Table 6.7. Summary of resources associated with early Steventon houses.

STE-A to STE-E form part of the main project. The reports on *STE-F to STE-N* are mainly based on the documentary research.
The *Tenure* column indicates whether the holding was copyhold or freehold. The six following columns indicate the holding size at the stated dates, the final ones showing the earliest date at which the property and its owners or tenants can be directly identified. Acreages are rounded to the nearest whole numbers. After 1590, acreages given in virgates are rough estimates; although they were conventionally equated to 24 acres as for the medieval virgates, in reality they might contain 20 acres or less. For STE-I, the acreage in 1477, close to the building date of the house, is also included.

Code	Address	Tenure	Later 17th cent		Mid 16th cent		Earliest	
			Date	Size	Date	Size	Date	Size
STE-A	Folly House, 53 The Causeway	copy	1670	4 v	1563	43 a	1490	19 a ^
STE-B	Tudor House, 67 The Causeway	copy	1686 (1657)	1.5 v	1571	44 a	1413	1 v ^
STE-C	83 The Causeway, Steventon	free	1665	0	1548(?)	1.5 a	1548(?)	
STE-D	71 The Causeway (with STE-B)	copy					1413	0.5 v ^
STE-E	39 The Causeway	copy	1661	12 a	1559	[2 a]	1467	0.75 v*
STE-F	The Priory, 123 The Causeway	copy	1664	1.5 v	1564	56 a	1463	3.5 v*
	Priory Cottages, 125–7 The Causeway	copy	1677	2.5 v	1564	56 a	1386	0.5 v ^
STE-G	99 The Causeway [Botleys]	free	1686	43 a/2 v	1551	43 a^	1477	40 a
STE-H	87 The Causeway	copy	1696	70 a*	1546	72 a*	1499	8 a
STE-I	79 & 81 The Causeway	copy	1676	2.25 v	1559	2.5 v 6a	1406 (1477)	1 v (0.5 v + 23a)
STE-J	35–7 The Causeway	copy	1661	1 v ^	1563	1.5 v 4 a	1459	1 a
STE-K	12 Milton Lane	copy	1677	10 a	1554	25 a	1477	27 a
STE-L	Home Fm, 14–16 Milton Lane	copy	1681	4 v	1546	50 a	1463	1.5 v*
STE-M	Green Fm (I), 1 Milton Lane	copy	1670	24 a	1548	28 a	1461	8 a
STE-N	Old Farm, 5 Kennel Lane	copy	1686	2 v	1545	41 a*	1413	0.5 v
(V)	Old Vicarage, 103/7 The Causeway	free		Small tithes		Small tithes		Small tithes

* acreage of a larger holding of which the messuage and others were part
^ holding apparently associated with a house that was part of a larger composite holding.

ownership at the time of early but secondary construction phases can be identified.

Holding sizes

The distribution of holdings by size in about 1700 is plotted in Fig. 6.11, which reveals no close correlation between the size of holding and survival of medieval houses. Table 6.7 shows the farmland associated with surviving houses at various earlier dates. Several formed part of larger estates, and the acreage may not give an accurate indication of the resources supporting the house. Because of the very flexible copyhold land market in Steventon from the 1430s to after 1800, farm sizes were neither stable nor standardized, but very fluid, and the exchanges of 1428–40 separated many messuages from their original holdings.

These factors may have been more significant for the types of surviving houses rather than their number. In

contrast to Harwell, East Hendred, and Long Wittenham, and indeed to the other villages examined during this project, Steventon has only two single-range cruck houses, STE-C, which appears to be an unusual survival of a small freeholder's cottage, and STE-A, enlarged in the 1560s to become a substantial farmstead with 43 acres (and still more later). The earliest evidence shows it with 19 acres, but is more than a century after it was built, so may well not reflect its original farm size.

The other medieval houses are more substantial than these, mostly including cross-wings. They fall into two main groups, those at least partly built before 1428, and those built from the 1460s onwards. The houses with the earliest surviving structure (STE-B, STE-E, STE-F, STE-L, STE-N and the Old Vicarage) have a subtle feature in common. Each formed part of a site associated with a holding with a component, one yardland (STE-B) or a half-yardland (STE-E, STE-F, STE-L, STE-N) – that had *not* been separated from its messuage between 1428 and the 1460s.[338] We can only suggest that the surviving structure was associated with that component, but this continuity would provide continuing resources to maintain a substantial house.

By contrast, the later houses, stone or box-framed structures incorporating open halls, belonged to reshuffled holdings that showed frequent variations in size.[339] Thus they could well have passed through periods when the house became run-down, later being rebuilt when the available resources had increased. No 99 The Causeway (STE-G) is a partial exception to this correlation, as a freeholding that did not change in size, but the late-medieval house was built when it formed part of a larger, mainly copyhold, estate.

One house, The Priory (STE-F), in effect falls into both categories. It contains a storeyed cross-wing, part of a house of 1340, but this was vastly extended by Richard Doo in the 1440s–1460s, after he had amalgamated the original half-yardland with 3½ yardlands acquired from a number of earlier tenants. With additional resources from shares in the leases of the manorial demesne and the rectory,[340] he was able to enlarge the earlier house to create what can only be called a 'gentry house', even though it was still held by peasant tenure and he was described as a husbandman.[341]

Conclusion

The case studies illustrate the variety of peasant experiences in a region distinguished by the survival of many more early houses than elsewhere in the Midlands, with numbers of them dating from before the Black Death. Many have proved to have very modest economic backgrounds at the earliest time when this can be established. It may be that the loss of the substantial holding which allowed a house to be built has in itself made its survival more likely. At Steventon, survival of early houses seems to be associated with the retention of their original holding, whether enlarged or

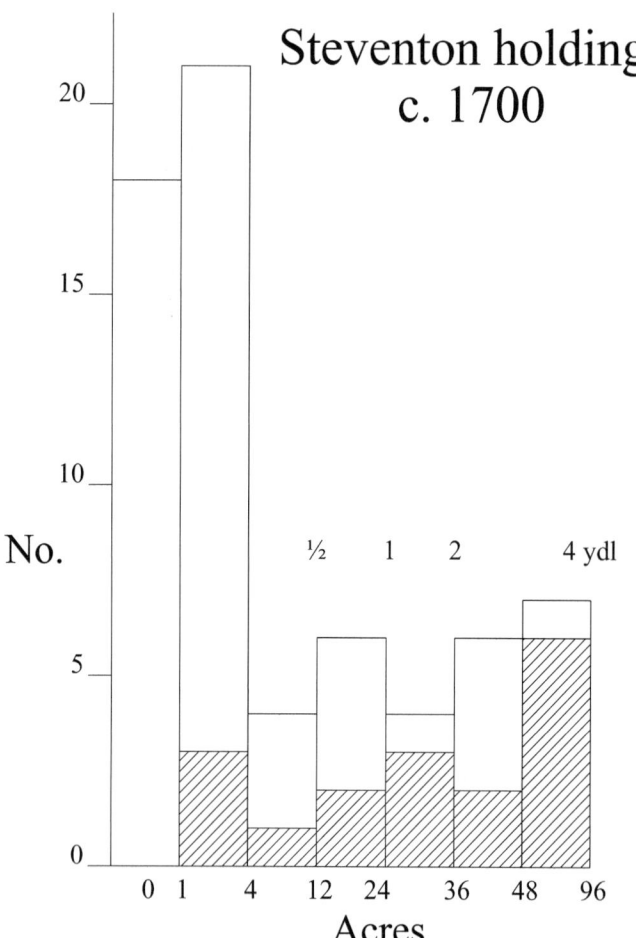

Fig. 6.11. Holding sizes in Steventon, c. 1700. Based on the earliest admission to each holding in the post-1664 court books (additional land-holdings ignored). Shaded holdings have standing medieval houses. One yardland is equated to 24 acres.

not, through the disruptive land market of the fifteenth century. Unfortunately, the evidence to establish similar patterns does not survive for the other villages.

In the earliest period, from c. 1250 to c. 1360, some peasants with no more than the standard yardland holding could afford strikingly large houses, while smaller surviving houses range much further down the social scale, including, it seems, at least one freehold cottage. Large houses on standard holdings can be explained by the region's high arable productivity, perhaps enhanced by entrepreneurship. Nevertheless that does not explain the survival of houses of half-yardlanders and smallholders who were, if anything, in a less favourable economic position than their counterparts in regions with more extensive pasture rights.

The more uniform scale of cruck houses of the sixteenth and probably the fifteenth century may have been determined by lower profits for the wealthy or middling peasant.[342] The purchasing power of the agricultural surplus of the larger peasant farms, in relation to building costs, was much smaller per acre, and perhaps absolutely, then than earlier, though that must have been partly counterbalanced by the growth of composite holdings. The most successful peasants could lease manor-houses instead of rebuilding their own, although at least one (Richard Doo of Steventon) chose to build his own gentry-style house instead. From the 1460s onwards, too, some certainly built tall, wholly box-framed, houses of four or more bays, larger in scale than most contemporary crucks; smaller box-framed houses also survive whose date and relationship to the cruck ones remains uncertain. Moreover some of the biggest peasant houses of the period may have been replaced by post-medieval yeoman farmhouses, misleadingly leaving only the smaller houses. The great majority of the cruck houses discussed above had little or no field land at the earliest date from which evidence has been found. They survive in villages where the more substantial farms had by c. 1800 acquired larger post-medieval farmhouses. Some of the cruck houses may have descended the social scale but, in at least one case (Inglenook-Penny Green, East Hendred, EAH-B), any such decline must have taken place within a century of the Reformation.

6.4 Warwickshire and Leicestershire: Stoneleigh and Diseworth

Nat Alcock

For Warwickshire, extensive documentary evidence for medieval peasant building has come to light, both through systematic research and by chance discovery. Furthermore, the best 'cruck village' in the county, Stoneleigh (with

evidence of eight cruck buildings), is also covered by outstanding documentary sources.[343] These both establish the social background to the houses and provide a view of the peasant lifestyle within them. By contrast, the general sources for Leicestershire peasant building have been much less thoroughly investigated. For its most notable cruck village, Rothley, with ten recorded cruck houses, the surviving documents, though extensive, have proved insufficient to reconstruct even the post-medieval tenurial structure.[344] However, for Diseworth, where new discoveries have also brought the number of cruck buildings to ten (though three are agricultural buildings) the documentary evidence is sufficient to establish the pattern of holdings at the end of the medieval period, though it only provides limited information on individual houses.

Documentary references to Warwickshire and Leicestershire cruck buildings

A number of references relating to medieval houses can be recognised as describing cruck construction (see p. 7) using the Latin term *furca* (and occasionally *sylys* or siles, a dialect term for crucks). These, coupled with the evidence of the standing buildings, confirm that cruck construction was the norm for rural peasant houses in these counties. Most notably, they include by far the earliest mention yet found of cruck construction for a house of peasant status, rather than for a building forming part of a manorial demesne. In 1232, a dispute was resolved between Worcester Cathedral Priory and the lord of the manor of Little Packington, Warwickshire, one Gilbert Picot, over the latter's refusal to pay tithes due to the monks.[345] By their agreement, Gilbert would give the monks the tithes of hay and provide 12 cartloads of wood each year. In addition he would erect and maintain a house for the chaplain there with six forks (*cum sex furcis*), i.e. a simple two-bay house with three pairs of crucks. Only a little later, in 1240 at Blackwell on the Warwickshire/Worcestershire border, the villagers were required to provide Worcester Priory with posts, forks (*furcas*), rafters, and other timber, to be used for the hall, chamber, barn, oxhouse, and kitchen of the priory grange. As this obligation formed part of their villein services, it had probably already existed for a considerable time.[346]

In the next century (1346–7), as a condition for the granting of a 60 year lease, the new tenant of a two virgate holding in Long Itchington, Warwickshire was required to build a house of five pairs of forks (*unam domum de v per' forkes*) within two years. It is interesting to see that a relatively large, four-bay, house was specified for this substantial holding, which was apparently formed by combining two vacant virgate holdings as it included two tofts.[347] In about 1365, John Ellis had made a grant for life of a messuage and half-virgate at Stoke, near Coventry to William Bittlesby, on condition that William should build a house of four 'forks' and two 'stanchions' before the following Easter (subject to a penalty of 100s); this suggests a partly cruck, partly box-framed, house of three bays.[348]

In the fourteenth century, crucks are also recorded in Coventry itself. In 1348, one house in Spon Street had a pair of *furcae* in a gable wall, while in 1370 a new tenant was to build a house of four adjoining crucks (*quatuor furcis contigue*) in Friary Lane within two years; this apparently stood between two other houses, so might have had three bays rather than the one apparently described. In the following year, a new tenant for a holding in Cook Street belonging to one Simon Coupere was to rebuild a house with six forks, so presumably of two bays (*unam domum ibidem de novo cum sex forkes*), the landlord providing sufficient timber but not laths or nails.[349]

None of the many medieval Coventry houses that survived to be recorded in antiquarian drawings used crucks and it is probably significant that these examples were in minor streets. Some of the surviving fifteenth century houses in the city are no larger than those described in the documents, but their structures clearly reflect distinctive urban carpentry traditions.[350]

In the fifteenth and early sixteenth centuries, further references to *furcae* have been located. For Leicestershire, the court rolls for the Merton College manor of Kibworth Harcourt in the 1430s contain many references to village houses and barns needing repairs to their timbers and thatching, but give no details. However, in 1434, one William Bron, smith, became tenant of a house lately in the tenure of John Smyth; he was to have 8s from John's goods together with a pair of forks (*unum par' furcarum*) and all timber from a certain old sheephouse (*antiq' barcaria*), and was to build a house of two bays at his own expense.[351] In Wigston in 1405, the lease of a holding for 100 years required the tenant to build a house with three pairs of forks (*tribus paribus de forkes*).[352]

In Warwickshire, at Wilmcote in 1468, a presentment was made of a broken *forklegge* in the house of William Phippes;[353] At Stivichall in 1453 and 1479, forks were mentioned, in one case in a granary, in the other, two *hovelforkes* were taken from a house.[354] At Leek Wootton in 1529, the costs of repairing Thomas Frankeleyn's house were:

> Furst the [*word lost but probably* oxe] house byneth the hall in tymber 6 sylles, 6 walleplates, 6 syde peses, a peyre of forkes, 3 *oreswarte* [athwart?] sylles, tymber for studdes for the same [*margin* 40s]. Item for the halle, 2 sylles, 2 walleplates. Item in thakchyng for all maner of howsying in stree [*straw*] 8 lodes and yn yardes for the said howes 3 lodes. Item in cley 24 lodes [*margin* 8s]. Item in grunselyng [*blank*].[355]

This suggests the complete rebuilding of three agricultural bays, though replacing only one pair of crucks and three of the four transverse sill beams, coupled with re-framing the side walls of a two-bay hall. This is followed by a similar presentment for Roger Barner's house including four sills for his ox house and *tiling* his hall.

Medieval houses in Stoneleigh

The place

Stoneleigh and its small neighbour Ashow stretch around the south-west quarter of the city of Coventry, extending some 7½ miles south-east to north-west, with a greatest width of 3½ miles, and covering between them almost 11,000 acres. The river Avon and its tributary the Sowe run through their southern end, and along the rivers, the land is alluvial, but to the north-west very mixed soils are found, including heavy clays (used by medieval potters). The land there rises to over 400 ft (120 m), but most of the south-east end is at 200–250 ft (60–75 m). They span the two geographical regions of Warwickshire, the Felden, dominated by open-field villages and almost without woodland, and the Arden, heavily forested, with enclosed fields and isolated farmsteads predominating over nucleated villages, and concentrating on pastoral farming, in contrast to the arable husbandry of the Felden. This wide tract contains some dozen settlement centres. The largest of these survive as nucleated villages, all at the southern end: Stoneleigh (45 houses in 1597), Ashow (25 houses) and Stareton (13 houses). Medieval houses survive only in Stoneleigh village, apart from one cruck (ASH-A) and one probably early box-frame house in Ashow. Apart from one monastic grange, no early houses remain in the outlying parts of the parish.

Ownership

In the Anglo-Saxon period, Stoneleigh appears to have been the centre of a large royal estate, including several adjoining parishes.[356] In about 1155, Henry II made an important grant of land in Stoneleigh to provide a new site for a Cistercian Abbey, founded some fifteen years earlier at Radmore in Cannock Chase. Although it was probably intended to include the manor of Stoneleigh, this was only clearly confirmed to the abbey in 1204.[357] The monks also acquired the adjoining small manor of Ashow in the thirteenth century.[358] In the course of the fourteenth and fifteenth centuries, Stoneleigh Abbey came to own almost all the property within the two parishes, apart from land already in the possession of other religious houses, notably a number of houses belonging to Kenilworth Abbey.

After the dissolution, the manor and the bulk of the tenanted land at Stoneleigh was bought in 1562 by Sir Thomas Leigh, a successful merchant in the Levant trade (and Lord Mayor of London); he also obtained the Kenilworth Abbey properties at about the same time. The abbey estate has remained the property of his descendants, and this continuity has led to the preservation of post-medieval estate documentation of exceptional quality. Pre-dissolution material is sparser, but some fifteenth and early sixteenth century rentals and court rolls have survived.

Land tenure

The most significant feature of tenure in Stoneleigh was its informality. Admissions for tenure by copy of court roll are rare, with some recorded in the fifteenth century, but only a few after 1500. Some tenants, described as 'sokemen of the manor of Stoneleigh', were virtual freeholders with minimal obligations and their inheritance fines fixed at a year's rent. Apart from them, the major freeholdings were created by Crown land sales after the Dissolution, and their only burden was attendance at the manor court. A few of the tenants had written leases, but even by the eighteenth century these made up less than 10% of the total number. Most tenants held at will, which in reality implied life tenure at a fixed rent. This seems to have been controlled by custom, accepted without controversy by both lord and tenant. A heriot of the best beast or possession was taken, and the succession of a widow seems to have been automatic. William Farr in his will (1564) left to his son 'the interest of my house according to the custom of the lordship'. Although rents were generally constant for an individual and his widow, after the Dissolution increases on change of tenant were common.

In the sixteenth century in Stoneleigh itself, a legal distinction was made between the 14 main tenants and the 27 cottagers. The former held significant amounts of open field land (a half yardland or more),[359] while the cottages had only a few strips or none at all; each had a right to common pasture for two cows and one horse. It was the tenant's tenurial status rather than the character of his house that decided whether it was a cottage.[360]

Tracing the houses

In Stoneleigh and Ashow, tracing houses and holdings back to the mid-sixteenth century is straightforward, starting from the map of 1597 (Fig. 6.12) and its associated survey.[361] Frequent rentals survive back to the acquisition of the Stoneleigh Abbey estate by Sir Thomas Leigh in 1562; the former Kenilworth Abbey properties are included from

Fig. 6.12. The village of Stoneleigh, Warwickshire in 1597. STO-J is just off the map to the north, and STO-G is considerably further to the north. (SCLA, DR671/3)

Table 6.8. Summary of resources associated with early Stoneleigh houses.

ASH-A and STO-A to STO-G form part of the main project. *STO-H* to *STO-J* have been examined primarily from documentary sources.

The *Status* column indicates whether the holding was a messuage (Mess) (with significant open field land) or a cottage (Cott). The *Traced to Date* column gives the earliest date at which the property and its tenant can be identified. The *Hearths* column gives the number of hearths in the 1670 Hearth Tax return (Arkell & Alcock, 2010); 'E' indicates a household exempt from the tax.

Code	Location	Status	1597			Traced to	Hearths
			Croft	Ydl	Field		
ASH-A	Trinity Cottage, Ashow	Mess	1r	¼	12 ac	1566	1
STO-A	10 Vicarage Road	Cott.	3r 30p	–	1 ac	1468	–
STO-B	3 Birmingham Road	Cott.	30p	–	–	1488	1E
STO-C	8–9 Vicarage Road	Cott.	2ac	–	–	1468	?
STO-D	22–5 Birmingham Road (holding size increased after 1575)	Cott.	1r 20p 3r 36p	–	2 ac	1488	1E
STO-E	Motslow Cottage	(Free)	1 ac 2r	1	28 ac	1250	2
STO-F	1 Birmingham Road	Cott.	2r 24p	–	–	1533	1E
STO-G	Pypes Mill	(mill)	1 ac	–	–	1490	2(1)
STO-H	2 Church Lane	Mess	1ac 3r	½	14 ac	1522	2
STO-I	Bridge Cottage	Mess	3ac 1r	1	28 ac	1551	–
STO-J	Croom Cottage, Birmingham Road	Cott	3r 16p	–	–	1572	1

Table 6.9. Summary of early Stoneleigh probate inventories: 1532–1560.

Inventories for all parts of Stoneleigh parish and also Ashow are included. The acreage is given when the holding can be identified. *Rooms*: number of rooms listed, excluding farm buildings (included in the *Rooms named* column)

Date	Name	Acres	£	Rooms	Rooms named
1538	William Convey	15	9	2	Hall and Parler
1538	Thomas Hobley		8	2	Hall, Bedchamber
1547	Thomas Gekoc		15	2	(Hall), Chamber; Barne
1553	John Sotherne	78	41	2	Halle, Kechen; Barne
1556	Wyllyam Nycolles		8	2	Haull, Parler
1559	Margaret Ball, widow	59	13	2	Hall, Chamber; Barne
1556	Humfrey Hylles, husbandman	38	21	3	Halle, Parler, Kechen
1557	John Lorde	3	12	3	Haull, Parler, Kechen
1558	Thomas Couper	88	17	3	Haull, Bakehousse, (Chamber)
1558	Thomas Tuter, husbandman	29	8	3	Haull, Chamber, (Kitchen)
1559	John Gesse		18	3	Haull, Chamber, (Kitchen)
1537	John Allyt, weaver	4	7	4	Hall, Chamber, Kychin, Shop
1549	James Gaundy (fuller)	9	85	4	Hall, Chambers, Kechen
1552	Robert Dene	16	56	4	Halle, Chamber, Seler, Kechen
1556	Edmund Hudson	28+	7	4	Halle, Chamber, Chechyn, Buttere
1556	William Powres	10	2	4	Halle, Kechyn, Botter, Chamber
1558	George Kockes	71	45	4	Haull, Parler, Kechen, Celer; Werkehousse (farm tools)
1559	Godfrey Parton	3	15	4	Haull, Chamber, Other chamber, Kechen
1547	Richard Hyll, yeoman		71	5	Halle, Parler, Other Chamber, Buttyre, Kechen
1553	Ralph Gressold, yeoman	77	50	5	Hall, Chamber, Nether Chamber, Third Chamber, Kytchyn; Barn
1551	Thomas Roweley, yeoman	59	115	6	Hall, Parler, Chambre, Nether Chambre, Kechyn, Boltynge House
1557	William Pyppe (fuller)		16	6	Haull, Kechen, Bruehousse, Chamber, Celer, Other Celler
1558	Thomas Dadley		259	7	Hall, Parler, Chamber, Bedchamber, Servants Chamber, Kychyn and Buttrie
1556	Jane Wynter	47	57	8	Hall, Parler, Chamber over the Parler, Other Chamber, Kychen, Day Howse, Yelding Howse, Menes Chamber

a year or two later. Earlier rentals survive for 1550, 1551 and c. 1559 (Crown ownership, including Kenilworth), preceded by ones for 1533 and 1536; before this is a gap until 1501,[362] with others then running back to 1466 (Stoneleigh Abbey property only).[363] All but one of the early houses can be traced continuously back to between 1550 and 1533, taking into account the rental order, the rents and the names of the tenants (Table 6.8). Despite the preceding gap in which virtually all the names change, about half of all the entries in the 1533 rental can recognised in the 1497 rental, including four of the five houses traced to 1533. These can be followed back to 1484–8, and indeed two can be identified in 1468, the first complete rental. The ability to establish these links illustrates the conservatism of the rent administration on the Abbey estate. One other house (*STO-J*, Pypes Mill) does not appear in the later sixteenth century rentals because it did not then belong to the Leigh estate. However, it can be traced through deeds and leases from its building in 1490.

Economic background to early houses

The distribution of holdings by size in Stoneleigh village in 1597 is shown in Figure 6.13. The majority of the holdings were 'cottages' (30 of the 45 houses), at most with four acres of land; of the substantial holdings, the largest had

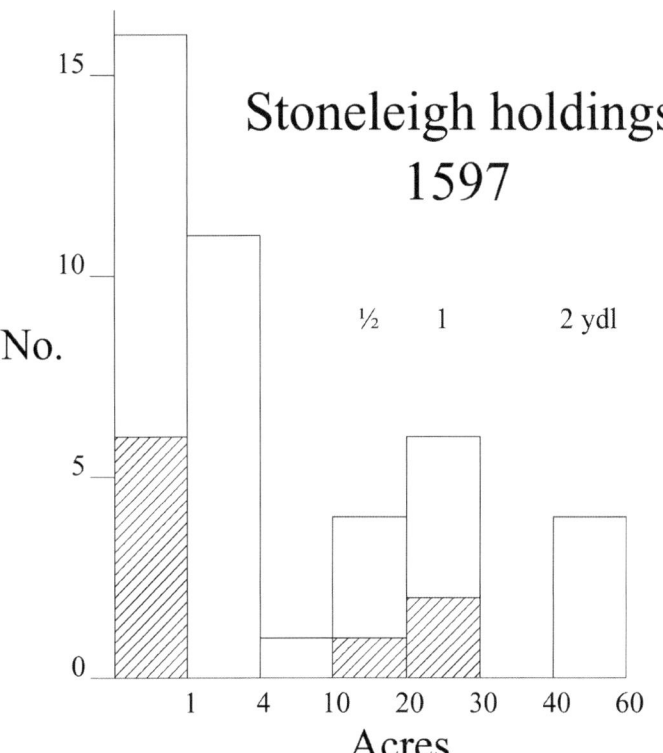

Fig. 6.13. Land-holding sizes in Stoneleigh village in 1597. Holdings listed in Table 6.8 are shaded (omitting ASH-A, which was held with 18 ac).

two yardlands (56 acres). The surveyed buildings (shaded) show essentially the same pattern, though none had more than one yardland. This range in their economic status contrasts notably with the houses themselves, which are very similar in both construction and size. Apart from the one freeholding (STO-E), the four houses that can be traced back before 1500 were all cottages with at most a couple of acres in the open fields; they paid rents of 3s to 6s a year, unaltered until the later sixteenth century. As far as the evidence goes, the status of most of the tenants matches their small landholdings. The tenant of one house (*STO-H*) also held a fulling mill in 1522; another (STO-G) was a miller's house. For a third (STO-D), the 1559 inventory includes considerably more crops and stock than could have been supported by its small land-holding, and it seems that the tenant must have held other land outside the parish.

Inventory descriptions

We can add considerably to the evidence for the early houses in Stoneleigh from the probate inventories, which survive from as early as 1537 and regularly include room names (Table 6.9).[364] Despite this being the very end of the medieval period, these inventories can be seen as describing medieval houses still furnished in medieval style, for two reasons. The first is obvious, that change is a slow process. Probate inventories, made after a person's death, usually document the belongings of elderly people. So, the last change to the house and its main furnishings might have been twenty to thirty years earlier. Secondly, and more important, these inventories show a distinctive pattern of lifestyle in comparison to the changing material culture found in the later sixteenth century.

Most notably, the size of the house and its economic status show almost no correlation, just as is found for the standing buildings. Of the twenty-four inventories with room names dating from before 1560, only five relate to houses with more than four rooms, and four-room houses (the commonest) were associated with anything between three and 71 acres.[365] The two-room houses had *Hall* and *Parlour* or *Chamber*, apart from one with *Hall* and *Kitchen*, where the owner's bed was in the hall, a room that others might have called the *Parlour*. The three-room houses added a kitchen (or in one case a bakehouse), while those with four rooms generally had another chamber or *Solar* (*Celer, Seler*), the name used for a subsidiary sleeping room; judging from the inventories of Robert Dene and William Pyppe, these were upstairs.

None of the lowest-status tenants of the surviving cruck houses left inventories, but two of the four-room inventories can be linked to standing cruck buildings: Robert Dene (*STO-H*, 1552) (see p. 157) and Godfrey Parton (STO-D, 1559). These fit exactly with their three-bay houses, assuming that the *Seler* and the *Other Chamber* were upstairs; each had a *Hall, Chamber* and *Kitchen* on the ground floor. A second inventory for *STO-H*, taken in 1607, shows that the *Kitchen* had become a buttery and an extra room (or separate structure) had been added as a *Boulting House*. The 1610 inventory for 8–9 Vicarage Road, Stoneleigh (STO-C) matches the same pattern, though it is complicated by the original division of the inner room into two little chambers, which are reflected in the *Little Chamber next the Yarde* and the *Street Chamber* of the inventory; by this date an extra room had also been added at the other end.

The two-bay house of William Pyppe (STO-G), that had been built in 1490, had already undergone improvements by the date of his 1557 inventory. What had been a large hall (accompanied by a chamber and solar) had been subdivided into a smaller open hall and a kitchen, and a brewhouse had been added in a detached building. The new kitchen had a chimney and was floored, with the *Other Celer* above it.

Repair presentments

The small group of presentments made in the manor court in 1481, of holdings whose buildings needed repair (already mentioned above, p. 116 and Table 6.2) are the only such document surviving for the manor. The descriptions of the buildings match precisely the pattern identified in the inventories. All four houses had a hall and chamber, accompanied for three of them by a kitchen, and for the largest by a bakehouse (or backhouse), which was clearly detached since it was listed after the barn and oxhouse.

Cruck houses in Diseworth

The place

Diseworth is a moderate-sized parish (1,900 acres) in north Leicestershire, predominantly on heavy clay soil; an 1831 valuation notes that 'The lands in Diseworth are very cold and wet generally'.[366] It contains only the single village, and the later history indicates that the parish was divided between two manors which were combined in the 16th century in the ownership of Christ's College, Cambridge. The early manorial history is obscure, and the information given by Nichols is not consistent with a series of deeds in the college archives.[367] These show one manor in the hands of the Duke of Norfolk in 1441–2 when it was sold by him to Roger and Phillipa Ratclyff. From their descendants, it passed by 1480 to Richard, Duke of York, and then in 1485 to one Thomas Jenney, who sold it in 1487 to Sir Henry Colet.[368] In 1505, it was acquired by Lady Margaret Beaufort and became part of the endowment of her foundation of Christ's College. The second manor was held by Langley Priory until the dissolution; in 1544,

it was granted by the Crown to Edward Elryngton and Humphrey Metcalf, and immediately acquired from them by the College.[369]

Tenurial structure

The parish was entirely in open fields until the 1795 enclosure, when it was mapped and surveyed.[370] It was stated in the eighteenth century to contain 72 yardlands, which averaged 24 acres each.[371] The college tenants held 50–60 yardlands, with the remainder being freehold.[372] In the sixteenth century, tenure (apart from the freeholdings) was by copy of court roll, initially administered directly by the college, but in 1560, a head lessee was established, holding the manor from the college. In 1588, John Hawford, the then chief tenant, persuaded the sub-tenants to convert their copyholds into 21-year leaseholds; this proved to be greatly to their disadvantage since what was apparently the former custom, that rents and fines were fixed, was abandoned, and the tenants failed in a Chancery suit to prevent this.[373] It is reported that the frequent renewals of their leases and the substantial entry fines imposed a great burden on them.

A pair of rentals taken in 1494/5 and 1522 for the Colet manor are particularly significant because of their early date and because they include both copyhold and freehold property.[374] Both describe 25 houses holding 32 virgates (yardlands) of land, relatively evenly distributed (Fig. 6.14a), with six houses holding no land, and the remainder ranging up to 3 virgates; most of the eleven freeholdings comprised land without houses, but they also included four messuages, two with three and one virgates, and two new-built, with 11 and 1¾ acres of land. Rents were somewhat variable, but on average 11s was paid for each virgate. For the Langley Priory manor, we have only a rental, probably taken just before the 1544 sale. It lists nine tenants, whose rents would correspond to about nine virgates rented at 11s each, and it includes seven chief rents (from freeholders).[375] It seems unlikely that the Langley freeholders could make up the deficit between the overall total of 72 yardlands for the parish and those accounted for in the rentals. Thus it is probable that the demesne lands of both manors are omitted from the rentals.

The structure of the estate was very different by the later seventeenth century, judging from the hearth tax returns and the 1698 terrier of the college estate (Fig. 6.14b–c). The tax return for 1670–1 lists 79 households, ranging down from Mr John Marshall with seven hearths. In all, 32 households had two or more hearths and 47 had one hearth, of which 25 were certified as exempt from payment. In 1698, the college property included 63 houses, five of them 'little tenements standing upon common or waste ground', while the 1795 map and survey identifies 54 college and 30 freehold houses.

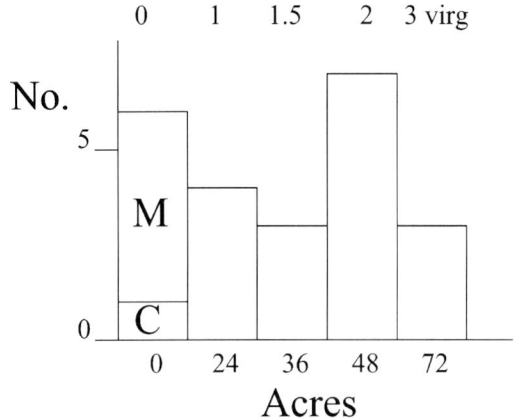

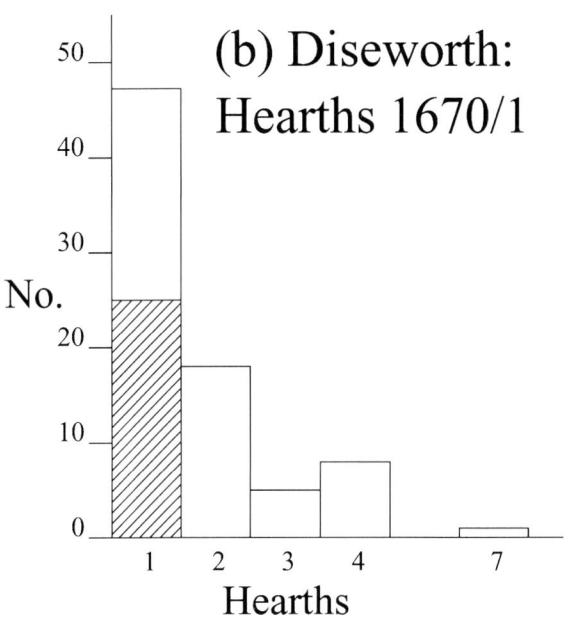

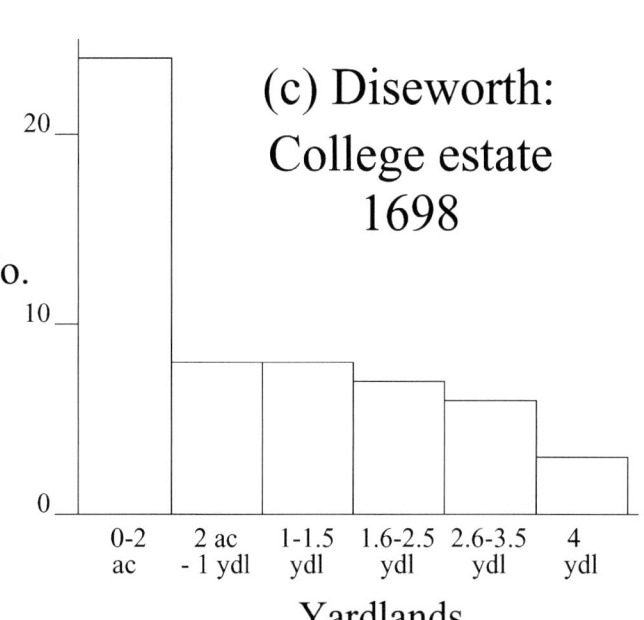

Fig. 6.14. Holdings in Diseworth.

(a) Distribution of holding sizes in 1494/5 on the Colet manor (ignoring small open-field and enclosed land holdings). The acreage equivalent is based on the correlation between yardlands and statute acres established from the 1795 enclosure award. Of the landless holdings, four are distinguished as messuages (M), one as a cottage (C). (CCC, Ad (4)).

(b) Distribution of hearths in Diseworth, 1670/1 (TNA, E179/240/279, r. 11–12). Households 'Discharged by certificate' are shaded; two of the three-hearth households also had forges.

(c) Distribution of holding sizes in 1698 on the Christ's College estate.

Documentary evidence of housing

A few late fifteenth-sixteenth century court rolls survive from both the Colet and Langley Priory manors, which include some presentments of building defects. Thus, in 1493, the barn of John Pope needed two *silles* and two *walleras* [wallplates?] and all his buildings required thatching; in 1518, the tenement of William [*blank*] required an *entertyse* [tiebeam], a *syll, studdes* and *sparres*; however, in 1498, Henry Fellez assumed responsibility for all the repairs to his tenement.[376] A significant mid-fifteenth century deed reveals one Diseworth house of considerable sophistication. In 1454, Thomas Blount leased to William Blakewell his tenement in Diseworth which he had recently bought from Reignold and Margaret Bromelaye, reserving *the chambor and the parler with the housyng att the over end of the hall, and a lytle haye house of ij bayes with an hovell standyng att the shepen end.* The former owner and his wife were given leave *to bak* [bake] *and brew within the kechen, bakehous and brewhous theer*, and they could keep two cattle, two sheep, a cock and four hens with William's own stock; the landlord was to pay 4s to the Duke of Norfolk and 5d to the prioress of Langley (no doubt as chief rents).

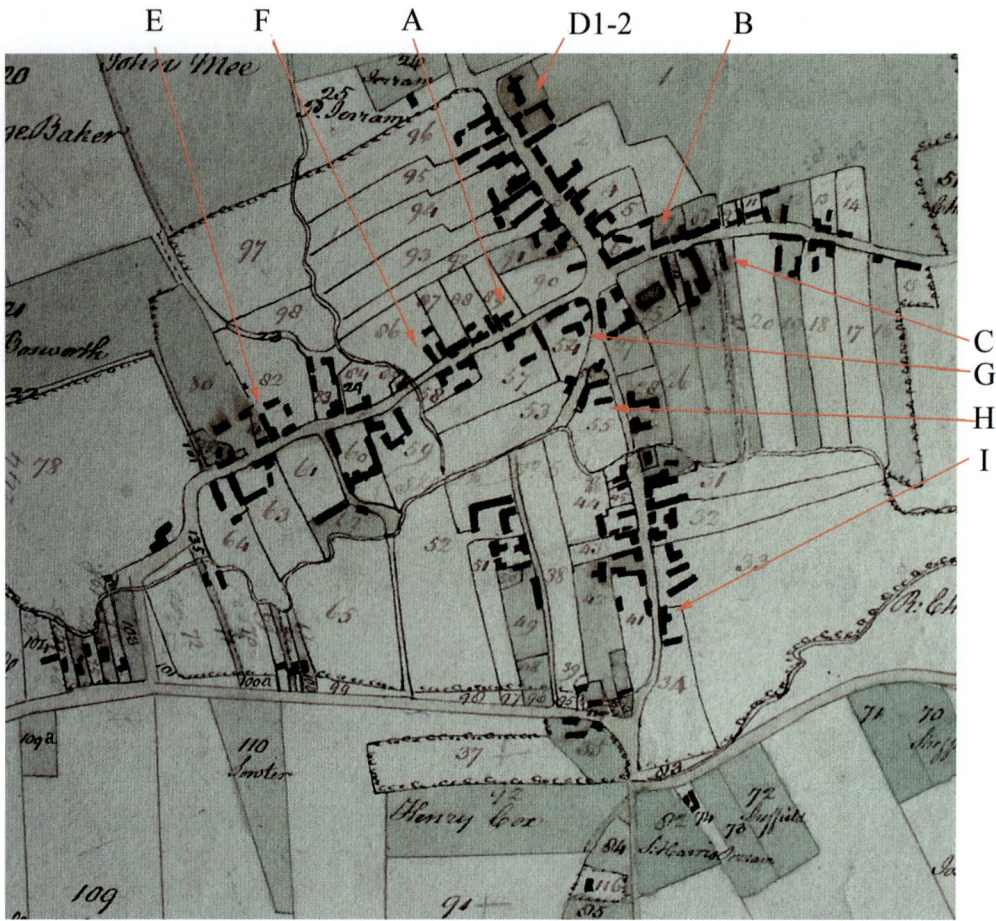

Fig. 6.15. The village of Diseworth, Leicestershire in 1795. The deeper green tone represents freehold property, the lighter tone that belonging to Christ's College. (CCC, Diseworth, Agg(1)).

Presumably, Blount had agreed to allow the retiring owner to continue to live in part of the house, as part of his purchase agreement.[377]

Tracing the houses

The cruck buildings can be located on the 1795 enclosure map of the parish (Fig. 6.15), and the land allotted to their holdings identified. For the college tenants, a detailed terrier made in 1698 of the open field lands of each holding includes abuttals (one side only) for the house tofts but freeholdings are omitted, so not all the 1795 holdings can be located.[378] Almost 150 counterpart leases also exist, dating from the 1680s to 1836, some of which can be related to the cruck houses, providing some further information about the college properties.[379] For the freeholdings in Diseworth, some deeds exist but none relate to the properties of particular interest. Hardly any relevant documents survive for the period between 1522 and 1698, and none of the college properties in the earlier surveys can be related to

the later terriers. Thus, detailed tenurial histories could not be compiled.

Economic resources

In 1795, the cruck houses were associated with the smaller holdings, from a few acres up to one yardland (Table 6.10). The two holdings which still retain cruck-built farm buildings (D, E) were among the largest in the village; their farmhouses date from the 17th and 18th centuries. To the limited extent that they can be identified, the size of holdings associated with the cruck houses in 1698 was similar to that a century later.[380] On a longer timescale, the relatively even distribution of holdings in 1494/5 had changed substantially by 1698, through the formation of larger holdings, and particularly through the creation of a much larger number of cottage holdings. However, it is important to remember that the 1494/5 survey only relates to a half or less of the village so this change may have been less extensive than appears.

Table 6.10. Resources associated with early Diseworth buildings in 1795.

Only DIS-A forms part of the project. *Letter* identifies the building on Fig. 6.15. CCC = Christ's College estate. F = Freehold

Letter	*Letter address*	*1795 status*		
		Own	*occupier*	*Enclosure allotment*
A (DIS-A)	Plough Inn	CCC	Thos Upton junior	1¾ acres
B	1, 3 Clements Gate	F	John Hall	14 acres (1 ydl?)
C	[12] Clements Gate	F	John Cotton	3¼ acres
D1–2	Old Hall Farm, barn; stable	F	Thos Cheslyn	14 acres old enclosure; 54½ acres, fields
E	13 Hall Gate [barn?]	CCC	George Baker	98 acres
F	25 Hall Gate	CCC	Robert Jaques	16 acres (1 ydl)
G	Lilly's House	CCC	Ruth Draper	3¾ acres
H	6 Lady Gate	CCC	John Hood/John Litherland	½ acres
I	11 Lady Gate	CCC	George Sowter	10¾ acres

6.5 The social setting of the base-cruck and aisled halls

Nat Alcock

The base-cruck halls

The documentary evidence for the base-cruck houses included in the project has given some surprising results. The original expectation was that they would all be of manorial or gentry status, previously recognised as being characteristic of these buildings;[381] although potentially useful for comparative dating, they would thus be of little direct relevance to our study of peasant houses. This assumption has had to be modified. The four principal counties do indeed all contain substantial high-status base-cruck buildings, including: Buckinghamshire: Huntercombe Manor; Leicestershire: Nevill Holt Hall; Oxfordshire: The Abbey (former rectory) and Manor House, Sutton Courtenay; Warwickshire: Maxstoke Castle.[382] However, of the buildings considered here (Table 6.11), only two definitely had the manorial (or equivalent) status normally associated with base crucks. Quaintree House, Braunston was a small manor house and Pendyce House, Ivinghoe a substantial rectory. The Hollies, Bathley may also have served a sub-manor, although direct evidence for its status is lacking and by the eighteenth century it was a 50-acre freehold farm. One step down in status was Long Crendon Manor (LON-O). It was once described as a manor in a fourteenth century document, but was in reality a very substantial freeholding, with a capital messuage and 8–9 yardlands (about 250 acres) in 1550–60; it was held of the All Souls Crendon lordship.

By contrast, of the two Warwickshire houses recorded,

which are of similar size and quality of construction to these examples, Cubbington (CUB-A) was a freeholding and Long Marston (LNG-M) either a freeholding or an enfranchised copyholding. The earliest direct documentary evidence relating to Cubbington shows it in 1640 as a two-yardland farm, held from the Crown in socage, for the rent of a rose, and it probably corresponds to a freeholding held of Coventry Priory by this rent in 1279–80. By the late sixteenth century, Long Marston was a three-yardland freeholding, although it may have been a copyholding enfranchised when the manor was broken up after 1565. Similarly, although the argument from size is dangerous, it is difficult to see TIL House, Clifton, Nottinghamshire (CLI-B) as more than a freeholder's house.

Detailed work by Currie has shown that several Oxfordshire base-cruck houses were originally of even more modest status, small freeholdings or even villein copyholdings.[383] Lime Tree House, Harwell (X-HA1) was a freehold with one yardland (21 acres) until 1316, although by 1329 it had been acquired by someone who achieved considerably higher status than its earlier owners, Walter Catewy, from 1341 serjeant-at-arms to Edward III.[384] Middle Farm, Harwell (X-HA2) (sometimes known as Bayllol's Manor) was in the later fourteenth century the capital messuage of a substantial estate belonging to Richard Brounz, later regarded as having manorial status. However, this had been acquired piecemeal from several previous owners. The construction of the base-cruck hall in 1367–71 may well have signalled the enhanced status of its owner; an earlier wing survives (dated to 1323), and the hall associated with it must have been more modest.[385] The smallest Oxfordshire base cruck, at Milton (X-MIL), was undoubtedly a copyhold, since a rental of 1538–9 lists thirteen customary tenants, two tenants at will, and only one freeholder, who is known to have held a different property; the historic

Table 6.11. Dating and status of aisled and base-cruck halls.

Sources for the non-project houses (X-) are given in Appendix II, Table A2.1b.

Code	Location	Cou	Date	Type	Status
BAT-A	Bathley, The Hollies	NT	1294/6	Base-cruck	Unknown, possibly sub-manor
BRN-H	Braunston, Quaintree House	RU	*1305–9*	Base-cruck	Manorial
X-BUR	Burmington, Burmington Manor	WA	1159+	Aisled	Manorial
CLI-B	Clifton, TIL House, 56 Village Rd	NT	1319/20	Base-cruck	Unknown, possibly freehold
CUB-A	Cubbington, Old Manor House	WA	*1313–41*	Base-cruck	2 yardland freehold
X-HA1	Harwell, Lime Tree House, High Street	OX	1243–7 1294–1306	Aisled l Base-cruck	1 yardland, copyhold
X-HA2	Harwell, Middle Farm, south range hall and north range	OX	1323 1367–71	Box-framed wing Base-cruck	Sub-manor by 1360
IVI-A	Ivinghoe, Pendyce House, 6 Station Road	BU	*1250–77* *1288–1323*	Aisled Base-cruck	140 acre rectorial estate/manor
LNG-M	Long Marston, Hopkins, Wyre Lane	WA	1339/40	Base-cruck	3 yardland freehold or enfranchised copyhold
LON-G	Long Crendon, Sycamore Farm, 9 Bicester Rd	BU	1205	Aisled	1 yardland copyhold
LON-O	Long Crendon, Manor House, Frogmore Lane	BU	13th century?	Base-cruck	8–9 yardland freehold
X-MIL	Milton, 4–42A High Street	OX	Mid-14th century?	Base-cruck hall & box-framed wing	1 or ½ yardland Copyhold
STK-A	Stokenchurch, Kensham Farm	BU	Late 14th century	Base-cruck	Freehold
X-TEM	Temple Balsall, Old Hall	WA	1176–1221	Aisled	Hall of Templar preceptory
X-WHA	West Hagbourne, York Farm	OX	1284/5	Base-cruck hall & box-framed wing	40(?) acres, freeholding

holding size of the base-cruck house is not known, but all the 1538–9 tenants held combinations of what had originally been either one or half-virgate properties.[386] York Farm, West Hagbourne (X-WHA) was a freeholding, apparently of 40 acres when the house was built, though increased later to 80 acres.

Kensham, Stokenchurch, was also a yeoman freeholding, though this is less surprising in view of its probable late fourteenth-century date. By this time, base crucks seem to have passed out of use for manor houses and in those areas where they were still being used, they are associated with substantial yeomen.[387] Kensham is of particular interest as late base-cruck halls have not hitherto been discovered in Buckinghamshire.

These thirteenth and fourteenth century base-cruck houses span the social range between the substantial peasant or yeoman and the minor manorial lord. Thus, they

seamlessly extend our evidence for the range of housing to which peasants might aspire in the thirteenth and early fourteenth centuries.

The aisled halls

Most of the aisled halls have survived because of their later conversion to base crucks (X-HA1; IVI-A; LON-O), with the range of status described above. The three aisled halls which remained unconverted all date to the years around 1200. The Old Hall, Temple Balsall (X-TEM) was the hall of a Templar preceptory, and Burmington Manor (X-BUR) was manorial in status. The third, Sycamore Farm, Long Crendon (LON-G), was a one-yardland copyholding in the sixteenth century, and nothing suggests that when built it was any more significant. Thus, these halls also spanned a wide social range.

7

Conclusions: The Medieval Peasant House in Midland England

Dating

The great majority of the 118 houses recorded during this project satisfy both the criteria necessary for them to be identified as standing medieval peasant houses: they are medieval, and they were built by or for people of peasant status. Some of the householders and their houses have been shown to be of very modest status, although alongside them we see a few houses, such as Tudor House, Steventon (STE-B), whose builders must have had both greater aspirations and more resources that most of their neighbours. That the peasant houses in the Midlands were invariably cruck-built has proved to be broadly, though not precisely true. From the later thirteenth century onwards, the standing buildings are indeed dominated by crucks. Starting in the earlier fifteenth century we see them gradually superseded by box-framed houses. The cruck tradition outlived the medieval period, with cruck houses still occasionally constructed until the end of the sixteenth century, before changing carpentry preferences and perhaps the lack of suitable timber led to their final abandonment. Indeed, at the end of the medieval period, design changes (the W-apex, p. 83ff) allowed for better headroom upstairs, and made it easier to build completely two-storeyed cruck houses.

In relation to the actual dates obtained, Dyer (p. 112) points to the apparent contradiction between the documentary evidence of decay and the evidence for new building in Leicestershire and Warwickshire from the end of the fourteenth century onwards. The resolution of this paradox lies, he suggests, in the co-existence of decay and new growth – one man's economic decline against another's new prosperity. In Oxfordshire we see an even more remarkable manifestation of optimism triumphing over adversity. No less than five structures are dated to the fifteen years after 1350, the period in which it is generally

considered that building work would have been completely halted by the Black Death and its aftermath: STE-E, 1350/1 (hall); 1356/65 (wing); LOW-A, 1352–62; STE-B, 1355/6; STE-C, 1365/6. The clustering of these buildings in Steventon is primarily a consequence of our sampling strategy, but we have no reason to suppose that the pattern elsewhere in this region would be different.

The ability to date the majority of the houses precisely or to within a few years has allowed us to identify the date ranges for some features that might otherwise appear to be arbitrarily chosen alternatives. We have been able to use this information to suggest the age of those houses for which tree-ring dating failed. The great majority of these typologically dated buildings appear to be of the later fifteenth to sixteenth centuries, which raises the possibility that buildings of this period are less amenable to dendrochronology than earlier ones. It is not clear why this should be so, although it can possibly be connected to the increased survival of lower-status houses, with less access to good quality (more easily dateable) timber.

The examination of box-framed structures was not one of the original objectives of the project, because of our belief that crucks were the dominant structural type in the region. However, the present survey and other recent studies have shown that box-framing formed a significant component in the medieval carpenter's repertoire.[1] The association between the two carpentry traditions was much closer than expected and, as a result, a number of completely or partly box-framed houses were recorded. In particular we can see, for example in the chamber blocks at Steventon and the integral box-framed wing at Manor Cottage, Sutton Courtenay, the choice of box-framing for two-storey ranges as against crucks for the single-storey hall.

In combination with some dates reported independently,

an outline chronology can now be identified for the replacement of cruck by box-framed houses at village level in the region. Apart from the early box-framed crosswings, this development started in the fifteenth century, with the first examples often of manorial or similar status (e.g. X-CHA, X-CLI, X-FRI), working its way gradually down the social scale. One fully box-framed Warwickshire house (STO-E) proved to date from 1537. It was clearly medieval in form with a large open hall and had a similar linear tripartite plan to those of the cruck houses, but lacked any dateable decorative detail. Taking this example with those just mentioned, cruck construction in Warwickshire was clearly dying out by the early sixteenth century. The last dated crucks (STO-D and POL-A) are of *1496–1515* and 1508/9, though it is reasonable to suppose that some of the simple undatable (or rejected) examples might be somewhat later.[2] For Buckinghamshire and Leicestershire, dating evidence for early box-frame houses is more limited but suggests the same pattern, though crucks persisted considerably longer. In Oxfordshire, box-framed chamber blocks appear as early as any crucks, and one relatively early single-range house (EAH-C, 1418/20) uses box-framing, apart from the impressive cruck truss spanning the two-bay hall – a clear case of the technique chosen reflecting function. Despite this early appearance of innovative technology in the county, crucks continued until at least 1559 (MOU-A).

At the other end of the date range of our standing buildings, the earliest house identified, Sycamore Farm, Long Crendon (LON-G, 1205) was unexpectedly discovered to be not a cruck but an aisled hall.[3] Does this indicate that aisled halls were the normal peasant house at this period, to be replaced by crucks later in the thirteenth century? Were this correct, it seems unlikely that we would have only three or four known examples of aisled halls, all dating from the early to mid-thirteenth century, after which aisled trusses are only found as subsidiary components of base-cruck halls.[4] Rather, they should be seen as the alternative to crucks for those who, for whatever reason, wanted a hall 24 feet or so wide, rather than the 15 to 18 feet usual for crucks – a need that would later be satisfied by a base-cruck hall. The four identified aisled halls are only of slightly higher status than the better cruck houses, comprising two one yardland holdings, one certainly and the other possibly held by customary tenure, a rectory and a substantial freeholding (later of 200 acres) (see Table 6.11).

Even though in our region, the first fragmentary survivals of crucks date only to the later thirteenth century, we can reinforce their evidence from standing thirteenth-century buildings in adjoining counties, notably Cottingham, Northamptonshire and Upton Magna, Shropshire.[5] At the same period, documentary references are found to *furcae*, notably at Little Packington, Warwickshire in 1232, and Blackwell in 1240 (or earlier), as well as at Cound,

Shropshire (1242), and in Berkshire, Buckinghamshire, Rutland and elsewhere.[6] Thus, thirteenth-century crucks, though sparse within the project region itself, are widely distributed around it (Fig. 7.1). The forthcoming detailed analysis of excavated medieval houses by Mark Gardiner should show whether aisled or unaisled plans were the norm before the early thirteen century, even if this evidence cannot easily distinguish crucks from other unaisled structures.[7]

Survival and survivability

The pattern of dates for the buildings studied also invites consideration of the linked questions of *survival* and *survivability*. A seminal paper by Currie examined the survival of individual or grouped houses.[8] He showed that this depends on many factors, most involving such chance occurrences as fires or campaigns of improvement. Two circumstances that seem to encourage survival can be suggested from the present work. The first is the association by the eighteenth or nineteenth century with small or very small land-holdings. Thus, at Long Crendon, following the consolidation of holdings, the early houses that survive are systematically those that were stripped of their land in the eighteenth century and converted into cottages (usually in multiple occupation), for which no doubt both landlords and tenants had low expectations of housing standards. Similarly, in Stoneleigh by 1800, the cruck houses were occupied as cottages. Another, less easily quantified factor can also be suggested, notably at Stoneleigh and East Hendred, that romantically- or historically-minded owners in the eighteenth and nineteenth centuries seem to have encouraged the preservation of early houses, either directly for their own property, or through their influence on others.

Survivability (also discussed by Currie, though not under this name) identifies the systematic trends which control whether groups of houses of a particular type and date remain in use or are replaced completely. It is clear that medieval peasant houses can survive to the present day, but what is less obvious is why the earliest cruck houses in Oxfordshire date from before 1300, but in Leicestershire and Warwickshire from the 1380s and in Buckinghamshire from no earlier than 1430. The dates of surviving houses do not fit well with a model of gradual attrition extended backwards indefinitely, but require differential factors to have operated on houses of different types (the 'differential attrition' examined by Currie). As a result, there seem to be thresholds beyond which no houses survive, in contrast to extensive survivals of buildings dating from after the threshold.[9] Of course, those houses which have disappeared comprise not only those replaced by the existing medieval houses, but also those that coexisted with them, to be demolished later.

Inevitably, it is difficult to decide how such vanished houses might have differed from those now standing.

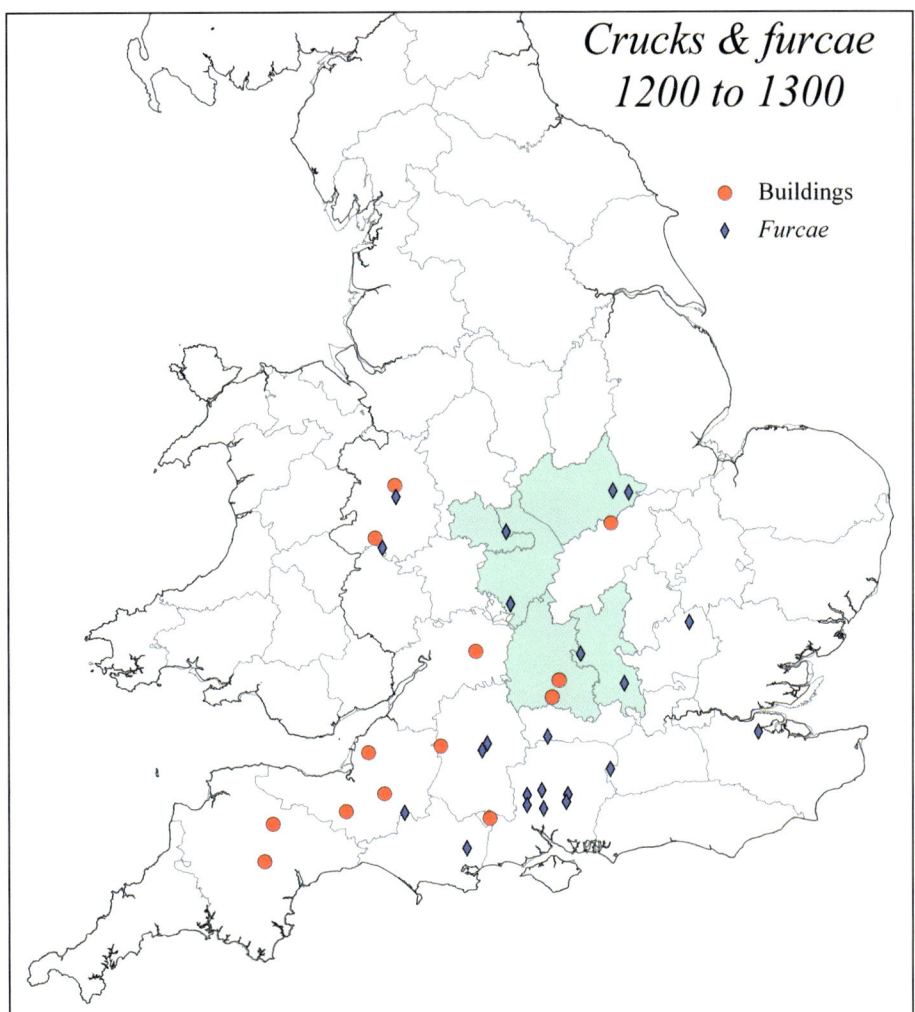

Fig. 7.1. Map of standing cruck buildings and of references to *furcae*, 1200 to 1300. For sources, see text.

However, two suggestions can be put forward. The first possibility is of constructional weakness, in particular having the principal timbers set in postholes rather than standing on sills or padstones. This technique was undoubtedly used in houses of the eleventh and twelfth centuries, but seems largely to have been relegated to secondary or minor structures after about 1200–50, too early to explain the thresholds observed.[10] Indeed, if earth-fast crucks were used, as has been suggested for a few buildings (pp. 82–3), it is far from clear that they would *ipso facto* not have survived; it would have been entirely possible to have later underpinned them with padstones or a sill beam. We also have indications, for example from the mud-and-stud buildings of Lincolnshire which use earthfast posts, that buildings using this technique can survive indefinitely.[11]

Consideration of some of the earliest Oxfordshire crucks points to a second possibility. Both SUC-A (1317/18) and MDM-A (1335) are notable for having wide but relatively low cruck trusses (widths 22.2 and 19.8ft; height, 18.9 and 17.1ft; eaves height 7.5 and 6.7ft; Fig. 4.1). If more modest early houses had the same proportions but widths of 12 to 16 feet, they would have measured no more than 12–14 feet to the ridge. An upper floor inserted in such houses would be hardly useable.[12] Equally, the survival of early chamber blocks (Steventon and Aston Tirrold) whose original halls have been replaced suggests that the latter were too small to be convenient, even in the medieval period. It is obvious that a valuable asset, such as a well-built house, would only be replaced when this became necessary. Thus a house which was too small to modernise could survive either until replaced by a larger medieval house, or until an upper floor was needed, when it would have had to be rebuilt. The difference between the counties can then be explained by variation between the expectations of housing standards in the different areas. With sufficient excavation evidence, it should be possible to test this model, at least to the extent of determining typical widths for thirteenth and fourteenth-century houses in the counties studied.

Status

The second criterion for peasant houses, that of status, has been directly confirmed for project houses in the villages where good documentary evidence exists. Some of these villages have a relatively uniform economic structure, with full and half-yardland holdings predominating, as at Long Crendon, Buckinghamshire, and Diseworth, Leicestershire. In Stoneleigh, Warwickshire, by the mid-sixteenth century and even before, many of the holdings associated with the surviving houses were small, two acres or less. Steventon, Oxfordshire, in 1324 had a uniform yardland and half-yardland structure with a few cottages, but from the 1430s onwards an extremely active land market developed, producing multiple holdings, sometimes with more and sometimes less land associated with individual houses. All but one of the early houses can be traced back to 1500, but not generally for more than 50 years before then. However, since most of the houses are known or believed to be earlier than this, they can be associated with the uniform holdings typical of the pre-1400 period. Thus, there as elsewhere, we can identify these houses as belonging to ordinary 'peasant' villagers ranging down the social scale from yardlanders and half-yardlanders at least to one cottager. This said, it does seem that for one house (Tudor House, STE-B), which is identified with a one-yardland holding in about 1400, the size and quality suggest that for at least two generations its owners and builders may have had access to greater resources than would be usual for someone with this size of holding.

In contrast to these homes of villagers, one outstandingly well-finished Warwickshire cruck house (SOF-A, 1409+) can plausibly be identified as manorial, showing that crucks were occasionally used above the peasant level.

The houses

The archetypal peasant house in our region is cruck-built, of three bays. The earlier houses have one-bay inner rooms (chamber or parlour) and two-bay halls, with the hall open truss generally though not always arch-braced, and sometimes spanned by a low beam (p. 34). A substantial minority have a fourth bay, presumably for service and storage, and it seems that several apparently three-bay houses also had service lean-tos (which have all since been removed; p. 25).

Houses built after the mid-fifteenth century differed from the earlier ones in two ways. The open trusses were replaced by closed ones, giving one-bay halls with adjoining service rooms. Secondly, the chambers began to be floored over, either as part of the original structure, or as insertions. This process was more drawn out than the division of the hall. It started in the 1440s and by, for example 1474, a tenant building a new three-bay house was expected to include a solar with stairs.[13] The process was not complete for at least a century, since the early Stoneleigh inventories of the 1530s–40s (Table 6.9) show that most houses were still single-storeyed. In 1555, the lease for a house there included a covenant for the tenant to 'make a chamber flower over one parler ther'.[14] He also had to 'build and set up … one chymney of stone', an improvement that would have taken him beyond a medieval style of living.

The open arch-braced trusses are generally well-finished, sometimes notably so, as at BIT-A (1413/14, Fig. D). In the houses that lack arch-braced trusses, refinement is conspicuously absent and the carpentry is purely functional. Their disappearance, largely by the mid-fifteenth century, seems to mark the point at which village yeomen who expected their homes to be of some quality might select a fully box-framed building in preference to a cruck house. For example, in Warwickshire, BIT-A (1413/4) and SUT-A (1442–4) each has have an elegant arch-braced cruck in their open hall. However, a house built in 1449 by an upwardly mobile yeoman, Hall House, Sawbridge (X-SAW), has an exceptionally elegant moulded open truss of post-and-rafter, rather than cruck, form.[15] In the following 50 years, box-framed houses clearly became an accepted alternative to crucks. Other Warwickshire examples include a three-bay house at Knowle (X-KNO), tree-ring dated to 1478–9, and one with a firm documentary date of 1490 at Stoneleigh (STO-G, Fig. W).[16] In Nottinghamshire, at NOS-C, the close-studded bay added in *1475–92* to the cruck range of *1447–54* fits the same chronology.

Plan development

The disappearance of the two-bay hall marks one stage in a much longer development, starting well before the date of any of our surviving buildings. We can infer from excavations that houses, of not very different dimensions to those still standing, were physically undivided, although the identification of light-weight partitions is not always reliable. The first step forward involved the creation of a separate sleeping space. This might involve dividing off one bay as a chamber or, with rather more sophistication, creating a detached chamber block, as in a few of our earliest houses.[17] In one of these (AST-A, 1282/6) the low space under the solar must surely have been used for storage, as, possibly though less certainly, were the ground floors of some of the other chamber blocks. Later, they seem to have become purely private rather than service space, with good quality carpentry detailing. Integration of these blocks with the halls, as crosswings, was the normal practice after about 1300, though the development was not straightforward as evidenced by the frequent differences in date between the wings and the halls.

In the earliest cruck-built single-range houses with one end divided off for the chamber, the rest of the house should not be seen simply as unstructured space. Rather, we have evidence for its differentiation. This comes particularly from houses like Bishops Tachbrook (BIT-A, 1413/14) which had two louvres, one in each bay of the house – clearly for two hearths, one for heat and the other for cooking. Similarly, in houses such as Stewkley (STW-A, undated) and Erdington (ERD-A, 1400), the low beams spanning their open halls must have helped mark the functional division into space for living and space for cooking, 'hall' and 'kitchen', and it is suggested above that these beams could have carried curtains to define the spaces further. Only after 1450 was the final step taken in the long development of the once unitary house into partitioned and specialised rooms by physically dividing the hall bays.

Although it is very rare that such direct evidence for the differentiation of use in physically undivided space in these medieval houses can be recovered other than

by excavation, similar multi-functional spaces have been observed in later houses. Notably, within living memory the 'single-pen' houses in North Carolina, USA, contained such multiple functions. The single space might be used for sitting, sleeping, entertaining, cooking and eating. It could be divided by furniture, or sometimes by blankets thrown over cords.[18] Rooms in Welsh cottages are also known to have been partitioned by furniture.[19]

The home of a medieval peasant

It is appropriate to conclude this survey of medieval peasant houses by visiting one of them, as it might have been lived in. Robert Dene rented a cruck house, the later 2 Church Lane in Stoneleigh (*STO-H*, undated but similar in structure to STO-F, 1480–2), with a croft and half yardland (15

Table 7.1. Probate inventory of Robert Dene (1552).

Thys ys the inventore indentyt of all goodes & cattells of Robart Dene of the parysche of Stoneley late decessed, valued, pressed & taken by Thomas Burbere, Thomas Donton, Wyllyam Ferre, the 8th day of June [1552] [Source: Lichfield Record Office].

In the Halle
A folden tabull, a halmere, a coffer, 2 cherys; 6 quyscions, 2 fourromes, pentyt clothes | | 11 | 4

In rement
A gowne, 2 dublettes, 3 jackettes; 2 pere of housse, 2 scurttes | 1 | 0 | 0

In the Chamber
A beddestyde, 2 coffers, a wyche, a chere; a halmere, a lyttell fourm | 1 | 0 | 0

In the Seler
3 Bedstyddes, 2 coffers and a lettell sprusse coffer | | 2 | 4
In maslen [brass] 2 basons, a laver, 14 candelstykes, a morter of brasse, 2 salttes, 3 peutur pottes, a chafyng dysche,
 a iron pannar, and 3 leden wyghttes | | 14 | 0

In the Kechen
15 Pecys of putur, 4 pottes, 3 posnettes, a chafin; 4 brasse pannys, a scellet, a scymmer, a pere
 of pottehoukys with a chene, a grydyron, a pere of tonnges, 5 spittes, 5 gouberttes | 2 | 11 | 0
3 Lomys, 2 fattes, 4 payllys, dyschys, trenchers with oder implementtes | | 2 | 0

In Beddyng
2 Feturbeddes, 2 matreys, 2 coveryngs, 2 coverlettes, 2 twylly schettes, 6 pere of schettes,
 4 bosturs [bolsters], 3 pylloys | 2 | 7 | 8
3 Bagges, a feu pentyt clothes, 2 heggyns[hangings?], 3 yron wegges; 2 axys, a hachet,
 2 byllys, 2 nougars [augers], a pere of pynssouns; a brodde bordde, 2 lyttell borddes | | 4 | 0
2 Stolys, a strycke, 2 maltte syffes, a hoppe | | 2 | 0
5 Towelles, 4 bordeclothes | | 3 | 0
6 Selver spones | | 12 | 0
12 Quartar of maltte, 2 quartar of rye | 7 | 0 | 0
4 Oxon, 2 sterys, 6 kyne, a heryng [yearling] calffe; a mare and a coltte | 16 | 0 | 0
5 Score and 10 scheppe | 12 | 0 | 0
6 Swyne, 4 pygges, 2 hennes and a kocke | 1 | 2 | 0
13 Acurres of rye, 9 acurs of wottes | 6 | 0 | 0
A iron bounde wayne, 3 youckes, 3 touys, 6 hokes | 2 | 0 | 0
A pere of scleddeyrons, 2 ploys, 2 scharys, on cultur; a oxe haro, 2 smalle haroys | | 13 | 4
In wodde | | 1 | 6 | 8

| | | | Sum | 55 | 12 | 2 |

Fig. 7.2. Re-creation of the home of Robert Dene, based on his probate inventory of 1552 (Table 7.1), and his house, 2 Church Lane, Stoneleigh. *Drawing*: Pat Hughes.

acres in all), probably inheriting the tenancy from his father in the 1530s.[20] He must have leased other land from his neighbours, since he had crops on 22 acres when he died in June 1552 (and presumably another 11 acres or so in the fallow field), and he also had 110 sheep and 13 head of cattle. Fortunately, his inventory (Table 7.1) is sufficiently detailed for us to re-create how his house might have looked (Fig. 7.2). It reveals a typical late medieval lifestyle, with none of the improvements in living standards and furnishings that began in Stoneleigh in the following half-century.[21]

Robert Dene's four rooms were named as *Hall*, *Chamber*, *Seler* (i.e. solar) and *Kitchen*, corresponding to the three bays (one floored) of the surviving house.[22] The inventory shows the separation of functions characteristic of the period: living (hall), sleeping (chamber and solar), cooking and service (kitchen). The *Hall* had the standard table (*folding*, probably implying trestles), benches, chairs and cupboard (*halmere*), while painted cloths, cushions and a *bordcloth* (tablecloth) provided decoration and a touch of comfort. It must have had an open hearth, just for warmth so without any fire-furniture.[23] At other times of year, haunches of bacon might well have been hanging from the roof beams, smoking above the fire.

The *Chamber* had one bedstead, no doubt the best one, used by Robert and his wife. It was also used for storage, with two coffers, a *wych* (whitche, a wooden chest, often used for meal) and, unusually, another cupboard, a chair and a little bench. The rest of the family, his younger son and daughter, who were probably living at home, with any farm or house servants, must have slept in the *Solar's* three beds.[24] It also housed three coffers, and one of these may well have held the maslen (brass alloy) basins, laver, candlesticks (no less than 14), mortar and lead weights, listed next in the inventory. The bedding was listed separately and is graded in quality, with only two featherbeds but also two mattresses (stuffed perhaps with straw or flocks), two coverlets and two *coveryngs*, sufficient sheets for everyone and four bolsters, but only two pillows.

The *Kitchen* had all the cooking utensils and fire fittings, including the pots and pans, pothooks and chain, gridiron, spits and *gouberts* (cobirons, supporting the spits).[25] The kitchen also held several vessels (*loom*, *fats* and pails), the pewter, dishes (earthenware?) and trenchers (wood). Apart from the vessels on the floor, these items were presumably kept on shelves, although these are not mentioned, perhaps because they were considered to be part of the house. What the kitchen most obviously lacks is either a table or chairs, and this is typical of all the earlier sixteenth-century inventories from Stoneleigh.[26] Although this furniture might occasionally have been omitted by accident, their systematic absence implies a rather different pattern of use for the kitchens than more modern practice would suggest. It seems likely that when a table was needed, as it often must have been, the table in the hall was used. We can perhaps see in this a carry-over from the earlier style of house with a two-bay hall but no separate kitchen. The more fluid movement that this undivided space would allow may have continued in houses with separated rooms, before the functions of hall and kitchen became more distinct.

Earlier houses

For the peasant homes of earlier generations, we sometimes get telling glimpses, although we cannot examine them systematically. The occasional inventories of household goods show us not dissimilar furnishings to those of Robert Dene. For example, those of Richard Slatter of Elmley Castle, Worcestershire, in 1475 included kitchen containers, bed and bedding, chair, trestle table, benches and chests.[27] In the thirteenth and fourteenth centuries, coroner's inquests show us the dangers in the house, revealing incidentally the life being led there.[28] Thus, we see children scalded by water in pots on the open hearth, and chickens wandering around setting fire to the straw on the floor. A candle placed on the tiebeam by a girl going to bed (upstairs, presumably) fell down and set fire to her bedding. A thief fell off the ladder he was climbing to steal a ham hanging from a beam. Brewing vats had a fatal attraction, as did wells, for mothers using the oven in the yard and for children watching them. Although these events were out of the ordinary, the houses in which they took place must have been typical of those in Midland England.

PART II

Examples of Medieval Peasant Houses

8

Selected House Reports

The following case studies present examples both of the most typical and the most remarkable houses examined as part of our project. The documentary history of STE-B and STE-D is examined following their architectural description, a study which illustrates in particular the important documentary resources available for Steventon houses. The reports for all the project houses are included on the CD-ROM.

House reports in Part II

No	Code	Address	Dates	Structure	Pages
8.1	AST-A	Aston Tirrold, The Cottage, Aston Street, Oxfordshire	1282/6 1517/19 1620	Box-framed chamber block Hall & chamber block re-roofing Addition of wing	163
8.2	HBY-C	Harby, Home Farm, Leicestershire	1380 1657	Cruck house Ceiling	174
8.3	LNG-M	Long Marston, Hopkins, Warwickshire	1339/40	Base cruck hall	178
8.4	LON-C	Long Crendon, Church Green Cottage, 102–104 High Street, Buckinghamshire	1466–97	Cruck house	184
8.5	LON-G	Long Crendon, Sycamore Farm, 9 Bicester Road, Buckinghamshire	1205 *1301–28*	Aisled hall Crown post	190
8.6	MDM-A	Mapledurham, Mill Farm, Oxfordshire	1335	Cruck & box-frame house	200
8.7	RAD-B	Radley, Baker's Close, 104 Lower Radley, Oxfordshire	1256–88 1513/14	Reused cruck blade Cruck house	210
8.8	ROT-D	Rothley, 91 Town Green Street, Leicestershire	*1492–9*	Cruck house	214
8.9	STC-B	Steeple Claydon, Rhenold's Close, 28 North End Road, Buckinghamshire	1431–6	Cruck house	218
8.10a	STE-B	Steventon, Tudor House, 67 The Causeway, Oxfordshire	1299 1355/6 1448/9	Box-framed wing Cruck hall Reconstruction of crosswing	222
8.10b	STE-D	Steventon, 71 The Causeway, Oxfordshire	1463/7	Box frame house (same ownership as STE-B)	235
8.10c	STE-B & STE-D	Steventon, Documentary history of 67 and 71 The Causeway, Oxfordshire			239
8.11	STO-F	Stoneleigh, Phoenix Cottage, 1 Birmingham Road, Warwickshire	1480–2	Cruck house	248
8.12	WOR-A	Water Orton, The Chestnuts, Church Lane, Warwickshire	1398/9 *1415–53* 1579/80	Cruck hall Box-framed wing Replacement of lower end	254

8.1. AST-A: Aston Tirrold, The Cottage, Aston Street, Oxfordshire

Grid reference: SU 5565 8578   *Survey date*: 1990–1993   *By*: D. Miles
Note: Since the house was originally surveyed, it has been re-named Tirrold House.

Fig. 8.1.1. View of the house in 1993, after restoration.

ARCHITECTURAL DESCRIPTION

SUMMARY AND HISTORICAL DEVELOPMENT

The Cottage, Aston Tirrold (Fig. 8.1.1–2) is a multi-phase building consisting of a chamber block (bays I–II) dated by dendrochronology with felling dates from 1282 to 1286 (indicating construction probably in 1286), an early sixteenth century box-framed hall (bay III), with felling dates from spring 1517 to winter 1518/9, and a seventeenth century wing (bays IV–V) probably of about 1620, the date inscribed on the inserted floor in the hall (Fig. 8.1.10).[1]

PHASE 1: The two-storied chamber block of 1282/6 is probably the earliest building retaining complete external framing yet identified in England, as well as the earliest timber-framed free-standing chamber block (almost identical in date to the integral chamber wing at York Farm, West Hagbourne, Oxfordshire, X-WHA, 1284/5). It is thought that the block abutted an early hall. Evidence for the precise position of the hall has not been obtained, but the presence of a late twelfth/early thirteenth century hall near the position of the 1517/19 hall has been demonstrated by excavation. The hall was not of earthfast-post construction but had ground sills, with padstones under the truss feet.[2]

The chamber block is of two bays with large wall panels (Figs. 8.1.3–4). In plan, the west end is at a slight angle to the side walls, with the north side about a foot shorter than the south. It seems likely that the block was built square-on to an existing hall, and extended to the front of the toft, which was not quite perpendicular to the side walls. The block

---

[1] The significance of the building was initially recognised by Dr C. R. J. Currie and it is discussed in detail in Currie, 'Larger medieval houses', 103–7.
[2] Richmond, 1993.

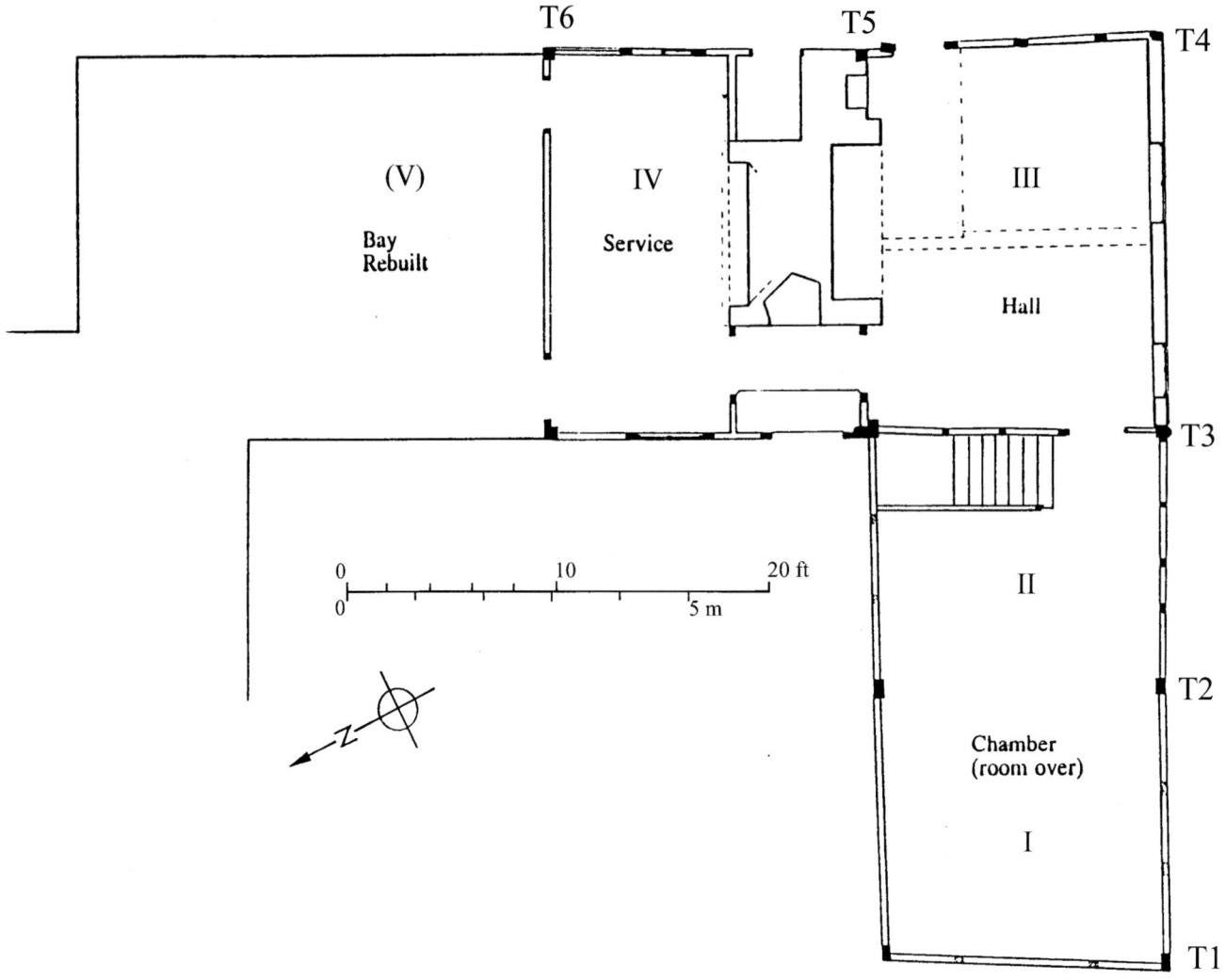

Fig. 8.1.2. Plan, showing truss and bay numbering.

was entered by a door at the east end in the position of the present doorway. Immediately inside, a staircase rose to the north, on the site of the present stair. The ground floor would have been little more than an undercroft, as the floor level (established by excavation) was only five feet below the level of the joists. Upstairs would have served as a chamber or solar and it was lit principally by a four-light window at the west end (Figs. 8.1.4–5), with one small 'wind-eye' on the north side just off centre of the panel to the north of the staircase (Fig. 8.1.6). There may have been other window openings of this type in the side walls, but the only other surviving original large panels are in the east end.

The roof was replaced in 1519, at the same time as the hall to the east was built. This later roof appears to have been fully hipped at one end, but its structure is uncertain since it was largely destroyed in a fire in 1956. The evidence for the form of the thirteenth-century roof is difficult to interpret. The top outer edges of the plates have heavy chamfers without original rafter fixings, but the bird-mouthed rafter seatings in the longitudinal wall plates are clearly secondary.

PHASE 2: In about 1519, a single bay (III) was built in-line with the east end of the chamber block, apparently adjoining a pre-existing structure to its north. It has jowled wall posts, tiebeams and a queen-strut roof. It was single-storeyed, from the evidence of a mullioned window remaining in the east wall, which is bisected by the floor inserted in 1620. Soot encrustation on the northern wall plate indicates that this was either an open hall or a kitchen. The close proximity to the chamber block suggests that a hall is more likely. Otherwise, access between the solar and a hall to its north could only go through the kitchen.[3] The elaborately moulded mantel beam now reset in bay IV (Fig. 8.1.9) may have originally related to a smokehood in this bay.

---

[3]   The opposite view is taken in Currie, 'Larger medieval houses'.

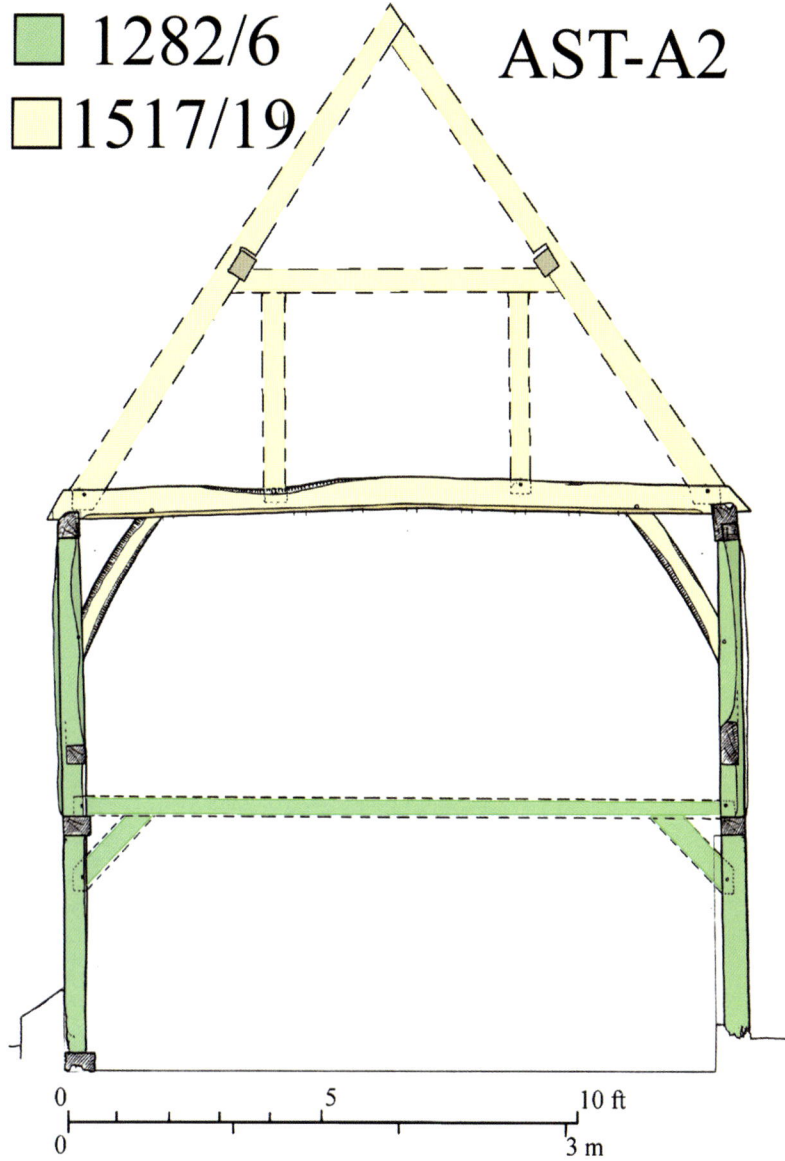

Fig. 8.1.3. Section of truss T2. The approximate profile of the destroyed later roof timbers is dashed.

PHASE 3: In 1620, a floor was inserted into bay III. This contained a smokehood which extended between the inserted transverse beam and the east wall. The upper chamber in bay III was accessed both from the chamber block, through a door cut through the east wall, and from the north range. Probably at the same date, a two-bay range was added, extending northwards at right angles to the hall block (bays IV–V). This was floored over from the start and its chambers evidently superseded those in the phase 1 solar block.

LATER PHASES: Later in the seventeenth century, the central chimney stack was built just to the north of the smoke bay, giving the house a lobby-entry plan. The smokehood was dismantled and infilled, and bay IV (and presumably V) took on the role of a kitchen, with a bread oven and a copper added to the east and west of the chimney. Bay III, once the hall, now became the parlour, with a good fireplace. During the seventeenth century the original floor in bays I–II was partially replaced, with posts supporting an axial beam carrying small joists, and two windows with diagonally-set mullions were inserted upstairs on the south elevation. The staircase may have been reconstructed at this time.

Probably in the nineteenth, century, bay (V) was removed, apart from a small single storey lean-to which may have served as a pantry and scullery for the kitchen. In the 1930s, the first floor was removed in bays I–II and a door and

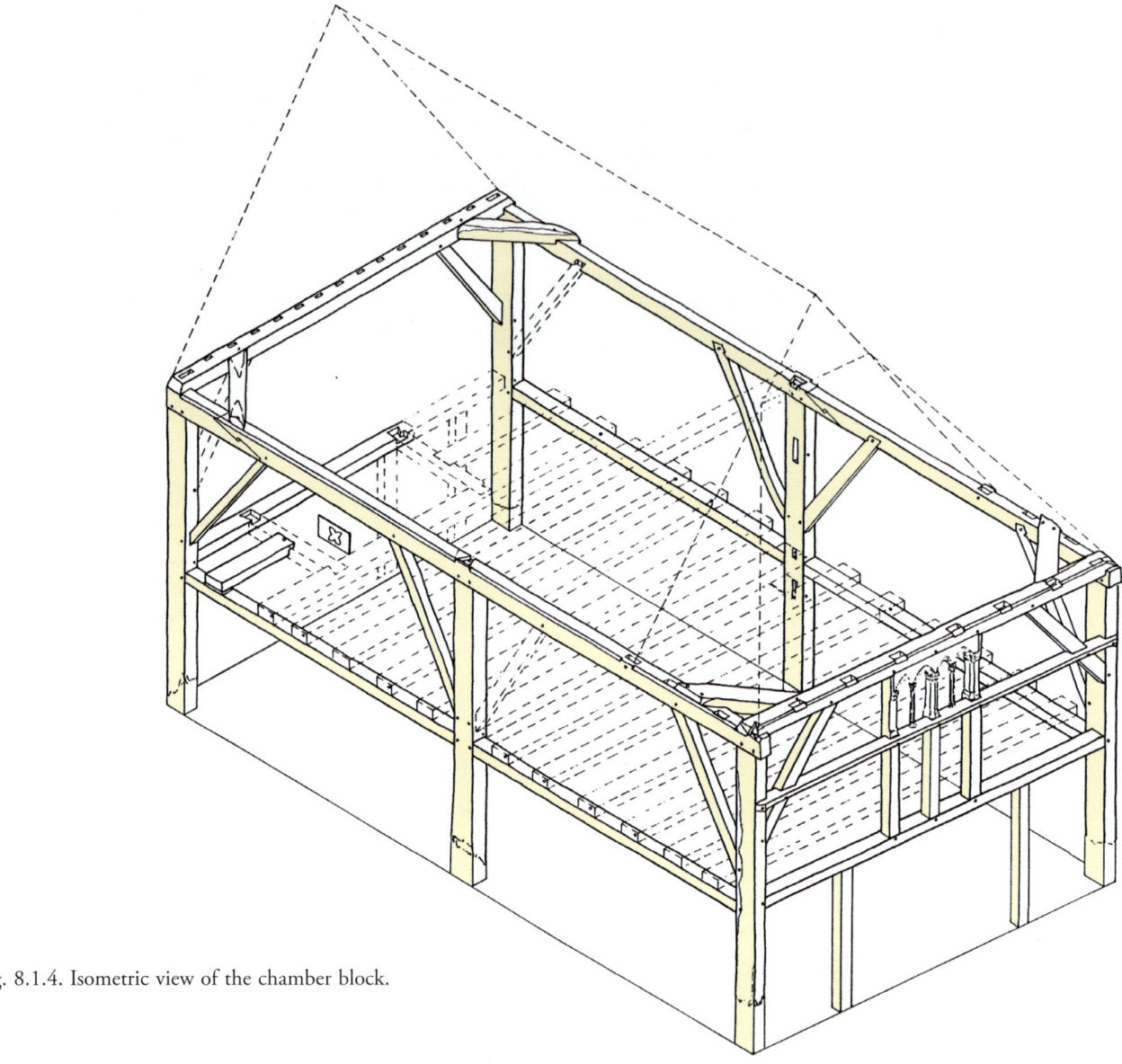

Fig. 8.1.4. Isometric view of the chamber block.

chimney inserted on its south wall. On 5th November 1956, the house was severely damaged by fire; the thatched roofs of all ranges were largely destroyed but most of the walls remained intact. The roofs were all reconstructed in softwood with cedar shingles. In the 1960s, the lean-to north of the kitchen was demolished and a modern single-storey brick extension built. In 1990–91 the roof over the south-west block was reconstructed in oak to the 1519 form; the north wing gable end was similarly restored and the roofs all re-thatched. In 1992 the wall-framing to the south-west block was repaired and the thirteenth century fenestration to the west elevation restored.

STRUCTURAL FEATURES

PHASE 1: CHAMBER BLOCK: The two storied chamber block was built as a free-standing structure, presumably abutting a hall range to the east, communicating with it through an internal door at ground level. It contains two box-framed bays. Significant features are the very wide panels (approx. 11–12ft wide by 5ft high) on the side elevations, and the slenderness of the storey girts and braces. Nothing remains of the original roof except the uncambered end tiebeams and the dovetail lap joints for the replaced central tiebeam. A pair of mortices in the upper face of the wall plates most probably held the tenoned ends of an intermediate truss set back about five feet from the western hipped end; this would

Fig. 8.1.5. Gable end framing, viewed upwards under the eaves.

Fig. 8.1.6. 'Wind-eye' in the north wall of the chamber block.

have consisted of a pair of principals rising to a gablet above a hipped end. A piece of unpegged tenon, with the grain slightly oblique to its length, was found in the southern mortice. It is probable that the gablet rafters had curved feet (explaining why the grain ran almost vertically in this tenon). A similar arrangement, but with a tiebeam at this point, exists in the chamber block at nearby York Farm, West Hagbourne (X-WHA, 1284/5). An alternative interpretation is that these mortices held windbraces rising to purlins at the hip end of the roof, as found at Mill Farm Mapledurham (MDM-A, 1335; Chapter 8.6). However, the position of the mortices towards the outer face of the wall plate, where they interrupt the outer chamfers, would cause such windbraces to run into the rafters. The fact that the grain of the tenon in the southern mortice is perpendicular to the wall plate also makes this interpretation less likely.

The top outer edges of the wall plates and on both the north and south sides of the western tiebeam carry heavy chamfers. These are uninterrupted except where the tiebeams are lapped on and at the positions of the mortices for the intermediate truss. These chamfers might be for fixing rafters, but contain no peg or nail holes. A similar chamfer was found at Mill Farm, Mapledurham (MDM-A, 1335). The birdsmouth housings for the rafters along the north and south sides are clearly secondary, since they conflict with the intermediate wall plate.

A much decayed 3 × 5½in timber was reused externally as a cleat at the bottom of the central post on the south side. It had complete sapwood (although the last 20 rings had to be counted rather than measured), and tree-ring dating (sample

Fig. 8.1.7. Wall plate scarf in the chamber block.

13) shows that it is from the primary phase. It was almost certainly a rafter, as no other removed first phase member is likely to have had such dimensions.

PHASE I CARPENTRY: A combination of advanced and archaic carpentry features was used in the thirteenth century structure. The wall posts are totally unjowled and without upstands. The wall braces, mostly straight, are joined to the wall plates with notch-laps having 'refined' entry profiles on the inside along the north and south longitudinal walls and externally on the east (Fig. 8.1.7). However, the bases of all the braces and the wall-plate ends at the west are tenoned, indicating more care and consideration in the appearance of the structure there. The tiebeams have secret half-dovetails with single pegs. Dragon ties at the corners are tenoned into the tiebeams and jointed with half-dovetails into the wall plates. The only scarf joints in the building are in the wall plates. Adjacent to the centre post, the south wall plate has a tabled scarf with a undersquinted abutment to the top side only, face pegged with a transverse key (Fig. 8.1.7). The north wall plate scarf has undersquinted abutments both top and bottom. On the south wall plate, the bottom abutment was omitted, clearly because that wall plate is only 6in high compared to 8in to the north. A delightful subtlety is shown in the positioning of the northern scarf joint; it is placed at the east end of the wall plate just to the east of the last brace, so that the lower undersquinted abutment also forms the notch in the lap joint to the wall brace. The storey girts are 6 by 4in, laid flat, and (apart from the infill panels) are supported only by tenons at each end into the main posts; surprisingly, this optimistic approach has remained reasonably intact.

The original first floor joists ran transversely and were lodged on the storey girts. They were occasionally pegged on, but many simply rested in place. Half-lapped dovetails for two stair trimmers can be seen in the eastern storey girt.[4] The trimmers have been removed but one joist remains *in situ* under the present stair landing and, indeed, the staircase still occupies its original position. This sole remaining joist measures 3 by 8in and was probably thinner than the others, as it only carried the landing; it is raised on a packing block and the whole is surrounded by what appears to be undisturbed thirteenth century daub. The other joists probably measured 4 to 4½in high by 8 to 9in wide, as evidenced by the storey girts at the ends and the mortices for the central beam. This was fixed and braced into the centre posts (Fig. 8.1.3).

No evidence was found for primary samson posts, but archaeological investigation in 1990 found a small padstone under the central truss.[5] This probably related to a replacement floor arrangement using smaller joists; one of these, about

---

4   Currie, 'Larger medieval houses', 115 suggested a stair at the west end from the absence of pegs in this area and by analogy with York Farm, West Hagbourne, where the staircase still rises in the end bay under to the gablet, but this has been superseded by the discovery of the actual stair position.

5   Richmond, 1993.

Fig. 8.1.8. Original stave and daub infill.

4in square, remains adjacent to the staircase, with the truncated end of an axial beam with a post below it next to the staircase, which aligns with the padstone found beneath the floor. Upstairs, a cleat was found nailed to the lath and daub panel in the east wall directly above the position of the stair trimmer. This probably received a handrail.

The mortice for a door post and a portion of run-out chamfer remain just to the north of the existing doorway, below the east end of the truncated storey girt. These must relate to the original entry position. During the underpinning operation, archaeological excavations found a deep depression running through this door way towards the foot of the stairs. This trench contained pottery dating from the late 12th to early thirteenth century, probably relating to an earlier hall range to the east.[6] It is likely that the entrance to this earlier building was on the site of the present doorway and that, when the chamber block was built in 1286, the same entry position was retained.

Although no original infill panels survive below the storey girt, several of the upper ones remain. The two panels on either side of the west window are primary and intact, as is the large panel at the east end. This panel has only been damaged by the insertion of the doorway (presumably in 1620) leading into the upper part of the chamber block adjacent to the south-east corner post (which had been replaced during the reconstruction of the hall in 1519). The panel in the eastern half of the north elevation also survives intact, including the 'wind-eye' described below. These primary panels comprise riven oak staves with riven oak laths *nailed* onto the outer face of the staves at 3 to 4in centres (Fig. 8.1.8). A chalk/lime daub mixed with chopped straw was applied on this framework, finishing flush with the inside face of the staves and with the outer surface of the wall, covering the laths externally by about an inch. Overall, the panels average about 2½ - 3in thick. The only main variation is that the west end panels had the laths nailed on the inside instead of the outside. Externally, the panels may have been finished with a lime-rich lime/hair finish coat, whereas internally the panels had a fine silty/sandy coat over the daub.

During the careful removal of modern hard cement render over the surviving thirteenth-century daub panel on the north side, a small area of infill daub, 12.5in below the underside of the wall plate, was revealed. The removal of this infill revealed a small quatrefoil 'wind-eye' cut out of a solid ½in thick plank of oak (Fig. 8.1.6). This measured 9in high by 15in wide, and was nailed to the outside of the vertical staves. Externally, riven oak laths were nailed around the plank, and the lime/chalk daub was applied to a thickness of 4in, forming a slightly bevelled reveal measuring approximately 8½in square. Centred within this was a pointed quatrefoil opening set in a 7¼in diameter circle which, together with the horizontal and vertical setting-out axes, had been scribed into the external face of the plank. The arris of the opening was finished with a fine $^5/_{16}$in hollow with a quirk similar to the setting out lines, while internally the opening has a plain ¼in

6   Richmond 1993.

flat chamfer. Equally remarkably, the major portion of the original internal harr-hung shutter survives *in situ*, pivoting on wooden ears or pintles let into sockets on the inside of the staves and retained by small cleats of riven oak lath, the latter with bevelled edges nailed top and bottom to the staves. This flap originally covered the whole of the inside of the opening and when opened would have been hooked or tied to the underside of the wall plate.

In the west end wall, evidence for an elaborate and sophisticated mullioned window was discovered behind the reveals of the nineteenth-century window (Fig. 8.1.4). The sill and jambs survived, with remains of moulded capitals on each jamb and a rebate for a face-fixed plank headboard, which was also rebated into the tiebeam. Mortices remained in the tiebeam and sill for a central king mullion as well as intermediate 'colonnettes', all of which presumably were octagonal and decorated to match the jambs. A chamfered window sill runs across the whole end wall, with run-out chamfer stops just before the curved ends. The 7¼in diameter of the small quatrefoil on the north side provides a module which fits the framework of the west window. The headboard was 1 module high by 5 wide, while below the imposts, the window is 2½ modules high by 5 wide. The spacing between each of the four lights is 1 module and the cusping as restored is geometrically derived from this. This window has been reconstructed at the suggestion of the owners to a design by David Brock and Paul Woodfield of English Heritage. Whilst the elements described above had reasonably clear evidence for their restoration, the cusping of the headboard

Fig. 8.1.9. Mantel beam in bay IV (probably from the 1517/19 range).

as well as the bases are conjectural, based on the few remaining examples of thirteenth century windows (principally in stone). Thus, the window as reconstructed may not correspond precisely to the original, but is important none-the-less in that it shows that houses, even of such modest size as this, could have sophisticated fenestration. When lime-washed, as it probably would originally have been, the capitals with the plank headboard and the projecting sill would have echoed stone construction. By contrast, the small quatrefoil 'windeye' has far-reaching implications, in that many smaller houses which were apparently without much fenestration, may have had similar openings incorporated into their daub infill, leaving no evidence if the panels were replaced.

Later wattle and daub panels survive on the western part of the north elevation and the eastern part of the south elevation. These are of a cruder nature and probably date either from the rebuilding of the south-east block (1519) or from the 1620s. One panel in the south-east corner of the south wall, shows the shadow of a shutter rail which would have served the mullioned window inserted centrally in this bay. Another inserted mullioned window (blocked but now re-opened) survives at the west end of the same elevation, tucked in beside the corner brace. The south and north elevations include a number of later studs inserted both above and below the storey girt. The sill beam for the eastern half of the south wall (bay II), was replaced in or immediately after 1508. This beam was morticed to receive the foot of the central post, but its association with the replaced south-east corner post is obscured by the extensive decay at this point.

PHASE 2: The south-east block was rebuilt in 1519, sharing the east wall of the 1286 range rather than having an independent frame. The east tiebeam (T4), the roof above it, and the whole of the south wall frame, were replaced after the 1956 fire. The north wall plate survives and is thickly encrusted with soot along the whole of its length. This member has no mortices or stave holes below which indicates that the range abutted an earlier building to the north.[7] The east wall frame contains two jowled corner posts and a centre stud, adjacent to which is the head of a window about 3ft below the tiebeam, with the mortice for a sill 3ft below this. This window had three diagonally-set mullions and clearly served the south-east block while it still functioned as a open hall. In 1620, the window sill was removed and another rail inserted a foot further up, at the level of the inserted floor, serving a new ground-floor window. Consequently much of the remaining wattle and daub in this wall probably dates from 1620. A short fragment of the south wall plate remains

Fig. 8.1.10. Beam and bracket in the 1620 block.

in the south-east corner but was severed immediately to the west when the wall was rebuilt in brick after 1956. All of the timbers on the east face are very heavily weathered.

The chamber block was re-roofed at the same time as the south-east block was built. All of this later roof was destroyed in 1956 except the lower part of truss T3 which consisted of the original 1286 tiebeam but with later principal rafters, collar and queen struts. The principals had been severed just above the clasped purlins, short sections of which remained after 1956. Mortices in the replaced tiebeam for truss T2 indicated that exactly the same arrangement had existed there. The principal rafters have windbrace mortices. Rafter seatings in the wall plates, to the east of the gablet mortices, presumably relate to the 1519 re-roofing since one conflicts with the north gablet mortice; each has a thin scribed assembly mark (on the top of the wall plate), using Roman numerals (I–XX) running consecutively anti-clockwise from the southern to the northern gablet mortice. They indicate that the 1519 roof contained ten rafter couples with the westernmost carrying a gablet to which the hip rafters were fitted.

In 1990–91 the principal rafters to truss T3 were repaired and extended, and a similar truss was constructed and fitted into the existing mortices of the truss 2 tiebeam. The hip was reconstructed with hip rafters set into existing notches and fixed to a flying collar (as usual with roofs of this period in the locality). Both common and jack rafters were fitted into the existing birds-mouthed seatings on the wall plates. The only conjectural aspects were whether there was a ridge piece and whether the principals were diminished above the collar. It is not known if the roof was originally hipped or gabled at the east end, as the T4 tiebeam was destroyed in the fire.

At some date between 1519 and 1620, the open hearth in this bay was apparently superseded by a smoke hood, and the very decorative mantel beam (Fig. 8.1.9) (now reset in bay IV) was probably associated with this hood; its mouldings resemble those on beams dated to the later sixteenth century.[8]

PHASE 3: Only one bay survives of the two-storey north wing, which probably dates from close to 1620. The framing members are of small scantling, some of elm. Evidence for two diagonally-set mullioned windows, one above the other, was found on the east side, as well as evidence that it extended further north. It seems to have been truncated prior to 1875.[9]

---

[8]   Linda Hall (2005) *Period house fixtures & fittings: 1300–1900*, Newbury: Countryside Books, 158f.

[9]   Not shown on the first large-scale OS map.

A floor was inserted in 1620 in bay III. The ceiling beam and applied half-beams are decorated to a very high standard, with ovolo moulding on the transverse beam accompanied by chiselled zigzag patterns and scalloped carvings with ornate floral brackets (Fig. 8.1.10). The transverse beam has clear evidence for a smokehood with a corner post and stave holes. The eastern half beam stops at the line of the smokehood, with the incised 1620 date centred in the remaining section. The smokehood was subsequently replaced by the existing brick chimney stack which also serves the north wing, and the mantel beam, which is presumed to have been associated with it, was reset in bay IV, as the lintel of the new chimney.

DENDROCHRONOLOGY

For dendrochronology abbreviations see page facing Introduction.

Sampling Comments: In all, 26 samples from 24 timbers were taken over a period of three years. The first ten samples (AST-A01–10) were cores taken on 15th December 1989 by Robert Howard. In an initial study, samples AST-A07–09 produced a felling date range of 1260–1285 (*VA* **23** (1992) 58–9). During repairs e during 1990 and 1991, samples (AST-A11–13) were taken by D Miles for English Heritage Ancient Monuments Laboratory (AML). All three of these had complete sapwood and the first two produced precise felling dates of spring 1282 and spring 1284. The third sample (AST-A13) had such narrow ringed sapwood that the last 20 rings could not be measured or even counted with absolute certainty, therefore a felling date range of 1278–1284 has been given for this sample.

During repairs during 1992, a further thirteen samples (AST-A14–20 and AST-A51–6) were obtained and processed by D Miles for AML. Five of these produced precise felling dates, ranging from late spring 1284 to early spring 1286; AST-16, although it had complete sapwood could only be given a range of 1280–4. These results indicate that the building was under construction during or immediately after 1286. Another sample (AST-A56) from a replacement sill beam produced a felling date of late summer 1508. A further seven samples from the south-east block matched together with the tiebeam (Truss T2) of the replacement roof over the north-west wing and were combined to form the site master ASTON2, although they could not initially be dated (and did not match with sample AST-A56, which on archaeological grounds might have been coeval). On re-examination in 2011, these were successfully matched to give felling dates from spring 1517 to winter 1518/19.

Tree-ring Sample Record and Summary of Dating

Sample Code	Sample Location	Total Rings	Sapwood Rings	FMR Date	LHR Date	LMR Date	Date Cat
Phase 2: South Block							
AST-A01	Principal rafter truss T3 S side	74	28C	1445	1490	1518	1
AST-A02	Collar truss T3	NM	—	—	—	—	—
AST-A03	Principal rafter truss T3 N side	NM	—	—	—	—	—
AST-A04	Queen strut truss T3 N side	NM	—	—	—	—	—
AST-A05	Queen strut truss T3 S side	NM	—	—	—	—	—
AST-A06a	Tiebeam truss T2	56	28C	1463	1490	1518	1
Primary Phase – Chamber Block: West Wing (A10 of repair phase; A13 reused)							
AST-A07	Tiebeam T3	82	2	1168	1247	1249	1
AST-A08	Principal post T2 N side	55	—	1135	—	1189	1
AST-A09	Principal post T1 N side	58	—	1183	—	1240	1
AST-A10	Principal post T3 S side	74	12	1438	1499	1511	1
AST-A11	Corner post NE, T3	150	54C	1132	1227	1281	1
AST-A12	Wall plate SW, T1–2	110	31C	1174	1252	1283	1
AST-A13	Reused timber (rafter? see text)	94	18+22NMC	1167	1237	1260	1
AST-A14	NW wall plate T3	113	30¼C	1171	1253	1283	
AST-A15	S jamb west window T1	39	13¼C	—	—	—	—
AST-A16	N & S centre posts T2	134	11+15NMC	1136	1258	1269	
AST-A17	N NE girt T2–3	128	31¼C	1156	1252	1283	
AST-A18	NW & SW corner posts T1	113	32¼C	1171	1251	1283	

Sample Code	Sample Location	Total Rings	Sapwood Rings	FMR Date	LHR Date	LMR Date	Date Cat
AST-A19	Joist, NE corner T2–3	142	29¼C	1143	1255	1284	
AST-A20	W girt T1	77	19¼C	1209	1266	1285	
Phase 2: South Block							
AST-A51	N purlin T3	88	15¼C	1429	1501	1516	1
AST-A52	S purlin T3	68	7	1435	1495	1502	1
AST-A53	SE corner post T4	85	34½C	1433	1483	1517	1
AST-A54	NE corner post T4	81	29½C	1436	1487	1516	1
AST-A55	N wall plate T4	89	22C	1430	1496	1518	1
Repair Phase: West Block							
AST-A56	Sill plate T2–3 S side	127	33½C	1382	1474	1508	1

Site sequences: AST-A (samples 7, 9, 11, 12, 13), 152 rings long dated to 1132–1283 with *t*-values of 6.9(E.MID), 6.4(S. ENG). Sample 8 dated with *t*-values of 6.5 (OXFORD), 6.3 (E. MID). ASTON2 (ast01, ast06a, ast10, ast51, ast52, ast53, ast54, and ast55) 90 rings long dated to 1429–1518 with *t*-values of 6.87 (BSNGSTK1); 6.39 (KLBASQ03);.6.37 (WHBASQ01); 6.14 (THEVYNE2).

Felling dates of samples with complete sapwood and identified final rings:

	Phase 1		*Phase 2*
AST-A11	Spring 1282	AST-01	Winter 1518/19
AST-A12	Spring 1284	AST-A51	Spring 1517
AST-A14	Late Spring 1284	AST-A53	Summer 1518
AST-A17	Early Summer 1284	AST-06a	Winter 1518/19
AST-A18	Early Summer 1284	AST-A54	Summer 1517
AST-A19	Early Spring 1285	AST-A55	Winter 1518/19
AST-A20	Early Spring 1286	AST-A56	Late Summer 1508

DOCUMENTARY HISTORY

The deeds survive from 1753; the first deed recites back to 1666, when William Sadler, Alice his wife, and Jacob Sadler granted the house, then or previously occupied by Richard Tirrold, to Joseph Tirrold on a 2,000–year lease. After that time the property included only the adjoining orchard, with no field-land. In the eighteenth and nineteenth centuries it was owned by local labourers and tradesmen, and occupied by labourers. The east part of the curtilage was separated from it in 1745, and the orchard to the south sold off as a separate house, apparently in 1946. Further ownership details are given by Currie.[10]

Presumably the Sadlers must have been entitled to the freehold in order to grant the original lease, but the fact that three of them were vendors may indicate that they had recently enfranchised a copyhold held on three lives (normal in the 17th century in this area), and were selling the house separately while retaining the farmland; it is also possible that it formed part of a marriage settlement. The phrasing of the recital of the lease suggests that the Sadlers owned other houses in the village. The modest size of the curtilage suggests that in the medieval period this was no more than an ordinary peasant copyhold or freehold.

No court rolls appear to survive, but Crown surveys made between 1547 and 1550 cover all but one of the manorial estates in the parish.[11] Six houses and three cottages were freehold, and at least 15 (perhaps as many as 22) houses and four cottages, were held by copy. They were attached, or had been attached, to holdings of which about 12 were yardlands and 15 half-yardlands, besides two larger holdings. At least eight members of the Sadler family were current or recent tenants, ranging from Sir Ralph Sadler, the former owner of one of the manors, to Joan Sadler with a half-yardland, Richard Sadler with two freehold cottages, and Richard Dewe alias Sadler with a copyhold cottage. Thus, the original holding of William, Alice and Joseph Sadler could have been anything between a yardland and a cottage. Examination of seventeenth-century Sadler wills has failed to provide any relevant information.

---

[10] Deeds in the owners' possession. Currie, 'Larger medieval houses'.
[11] TNA, LR 2/187, ff. 306–313.

8.2. HBY-C: Harby, Home Farm, Leicestershire

Grid reference: SK 7438 3116   *Survey date*: 1984   *By*: Mr Dove

Fig. 8.2.1. View of the house from the south.

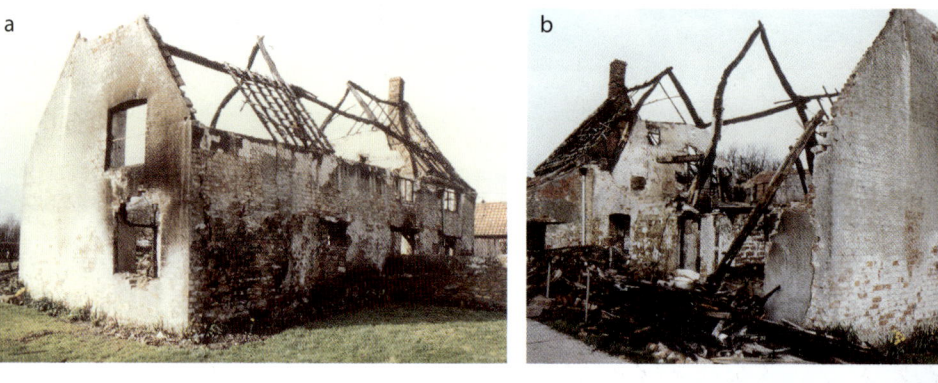

Fig. 8.2.2 (a–d). Views of the house after the fire.

ARCHITECTURAL DESCRIPTION

SUMMARY AND HISTORICAL DEVELOPMENT

Home Farm, Harby was destroyed by fire in 1984, and this report is based on the evidence of eight photographs taken after the fire, a roughly scaled ground floor plan and a tree-ring dating report by the Nottingham University Tree-ring Dating Laboratory. As a consequence, information about the building is less complete than for other houses studied. The general view (Fig. 8.2.1) shows the house in relation to the long farm-building/cottage range to its north, and Figures 8.2.2a–d show details of the structure. Its precise site can be identified in relation to this range on early maps. A photograph of *c.* 1900 shows the eastern end of the range.[1]

Home Farm was a three-bayed cruck structure dated through dendrochronology to *c.* 1380. It had two cruck trusses with type 'D' apexes in the centre of the building (Fig. 8.2.3). The trusses are numbered C1 and C2, as shown on the plan.

The original house appears to have been a three-bay full-cruck structure, most probably with a service bay, hall and chamber (most likely at the west end) (Fig. 8.2.3). The date of the floor in the chamber bay is unknown. It may well have predated the hall floor, though it is unlikely to be primary. In the seventeenth century (*c.* 1657), the hall was floored over. A chimney was inserted under the hall truss (possibly preceded by a fire hood), and a winder staircase built immediately to the north. The lower parts of the timber-framed side walls were probably replaced in ironstone at about this time. Probably in the nineteenth century, the rest of the external walls were replaced in brickwork and the roof covered in pantiles.

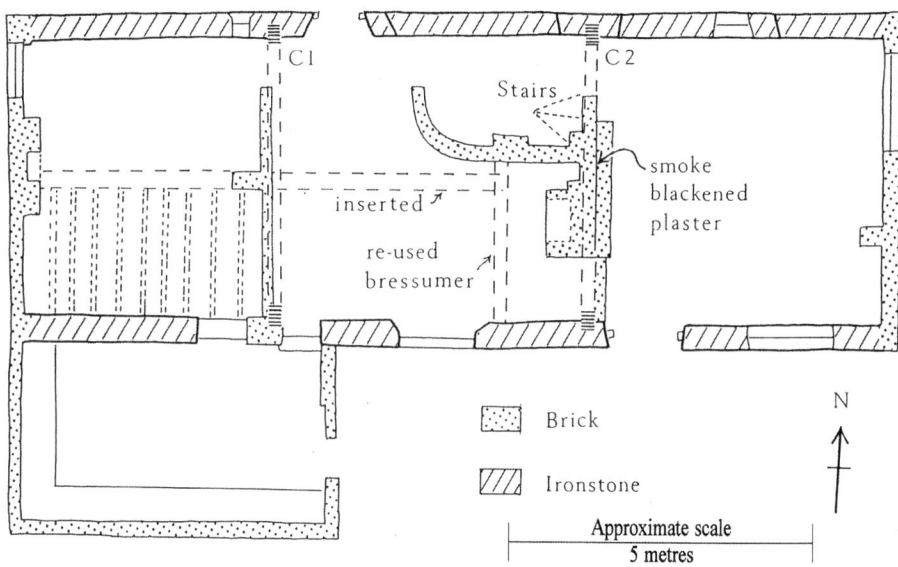

Fig. 8.2.3. Ground floor plan, showing truss and bay numbering.

STRUCTURAL FEATURES

PHASE 1: The external dimensions (measured from the foundations) were about 45 ft by 19 ft, which is somewhat wider than for most Leicestershire cruck houses. The building appears to measure about 10 feet to the eaves, and another 10 feet to the apex to the ridge (estimated from a count of 40 brick courses on the eastern gable end). The cruck blades themselves were whole trees, roughly squared with a gentle bend at eaves level (Fig. 8.2.4). They were, however, exceptionally irregular in form (notably the southern blade of truss C2); this suggests that suitable trees for crucks were not readily available to the builders. The cruck blades crossed at the apex to form a type 'D' apex, and this supported a diagonally set ridge. The cruck spurs were half-lapped onto the west face of the cruck blades. A collar was similarly halved across the blades about half way up the roof slope. Both trusses had tiebeams which were presumably also halved across the blades (though neither joint is visible in the photographs). The presence of these tiebeams makes it most likely that both trusses were closed; plastered infill remained in the upper part of truss C1. If the chimney was inserted in the characteristic hearth-passage

---

[1]   Harby Village website, http://www.harby.co.uk/0279.htm, accessed on 21 Dec 2011.

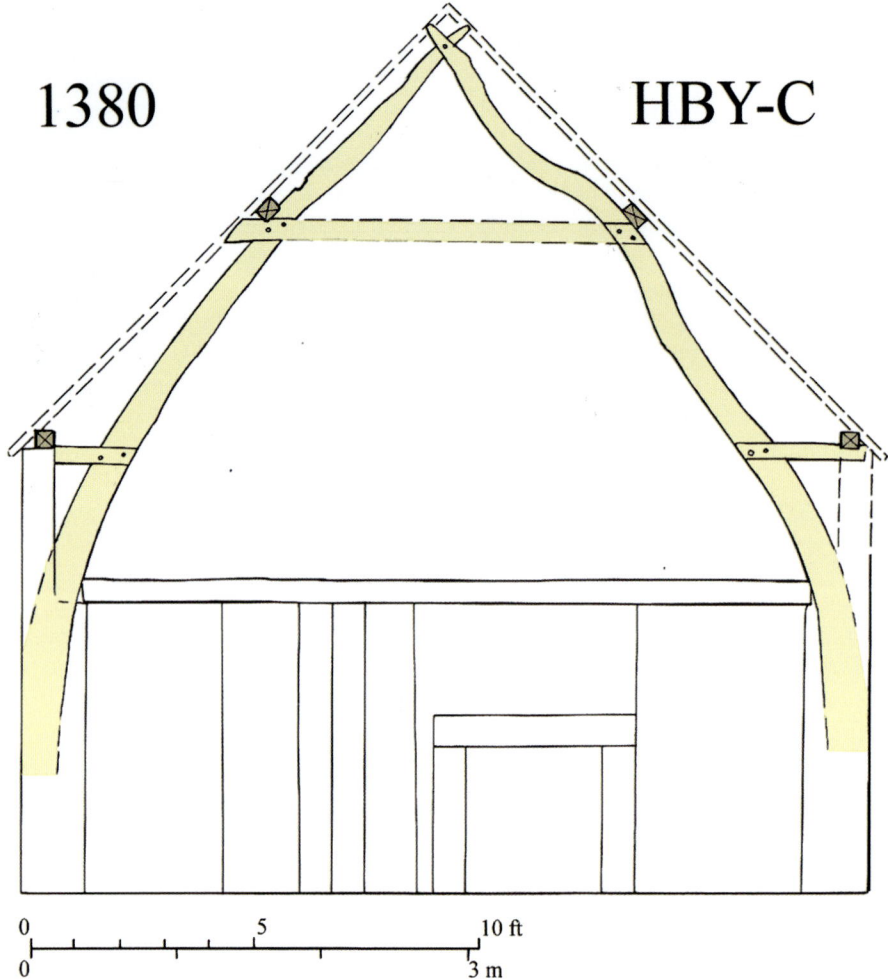

Fig. 8.2.4. Section of Truss C2.

position (consistent with the entry position in the south wall), then the eastern bay (I) was presumably the service end.

The extended ends of the collars supported the purlins. These appeared to have been scarfed at the trusses, possibly with plain splayed scarfs. The rafters, a few of which survived the fire in the westernmost bay, were cleaved and very uneven in section and form. No windbraces were visible in the post-fire photographs. The house was obviously thatched originally. A single section of wallplate appears in the photographs, on the south side of the easternmost bay. This had fallen off the cruck spur to truss C2, but was still suspended at eaves level at the gable end. There appear to be mortices in this member, strongly suggesting the walls were originally timber framed.

LATER PHASES: The only available information is included in the summary (above).

DENDROCHRONOLOGY

For dendrochronology abbreviations see page facing Introduction.
Sampling Comments: Thirteen sawn samples were obtained from the various surviving timbers, by the Nottingham University Tree-Ring Dating Laboratory, in March 1984. Precise sampling locations are not known.

TREE-RING SAMPLE RECORD AND SUMMARY OF DATING

Sample Code	Sample Location	Total Rings	Sapwood Rings	FMR Date	LHR Date	LMR Date	Date Cat
HBY-C01	Principal beam, SE bay	58	—	—	—	—	—
HBY-C02	Lintel	72	HS	—	—	—	—
HBY-C03	Not known	37NM	—	—	—	—	—
HBY-C04	Tiebeam	65	14	—	—	—	—
HBY-C05	Cruck blade (pair with C06)	68	12	1308	1363	1375	2
HBY-C06	Cruck blade (pair with C05)	73	18C?	1307	1361	1379	2
HBY-C07	Cruck blade (pair with C08)	67	14	1313	1365	1379	2
HBY-C08	Cruck blade (pair with C07)	60	HS	—	—	—	—
HBY-C09	Ridge piece	56	—	—	—	—	—
HBY-C10	Purlin	71	13	1587	1644	1657	weak
HBY-C11	Floor joist	92	17C?	1564	1638	1655	1
HBY-C12	Cruck spur	48	13	1332	1366	1379	2
HBY-C13	Floor joist, middle bay	89	—	—	—	—	—

Site sequence: (composed of samples 5, 6, 7, 12) 73 rings long dated 1307–1379 with *t*-values of 6.5 (E.MID), 5.1 (OXHASQ4, site sequence of OXH-A, VA20.89).

Sample 10 dated 1587–1657 with *t*-values of 4.7 (E.MID), 5.1 (FORBSQ010) 4.2 (ARN-H1, Trans. Thoroton Soc, 1979) 4.1 (BLI-C1, Trans. Thoroton Soc, 1982) and 3.8 (BRA-T1, Trans. Thoroton Soc, 1979); Sample 11 dated 1564–1655 with *t*-values of 6.7 (E.MID) and 5.6 (MGB-E01); the match for sample 10 is relatively weak, but it corresponds to the stronger match for sample 11.

When originally examined, sample C08 was matched with C10–C11 and dated to *c.* 1657 (VA15.84), but on re-evaluation, this match is no longer supported.

Estimated felling dates: c. **1380** for samples C05–C07, C12, (VA15.84). (Sample 6 with the last dated ring probably with complete sapwood).

c. **1657** for samples C10, C11; (sample 11 probably with complete sapwood).

8.3. LNG-M: Long Marston, Hopkins, Wyre Lane, Warwickshire

Grid reference: SP 1554 4865   *Survey dates*: 1990–6   *By*: N. Cooper; N. W. Alcock

Fig. 8.3.1. View of Hopkins, Long Marston from the south.

ARCHITECTURAL DESCRIPTION

SUMMARY AND HISTORICAL DEVELOPMENT

PHASE 1: The house stands away from the main village street, facing south. The original structure consists of a two-bay hall with a central base-cruck truss and aisled end trusses, which has been tree-ring-dated to 1339/40. It possibly had a cross-passage in the position of the later stair. The upper roof structure includes a four-way braced crown post. The original house did not extend to the west beyond truss 1, and it probably had a crosswing on the site of the later east wing. Sooting at the junction with the hall and the wing and the latter's soot-blackened rafters suggest that this wing may have been a kitchen.

LATER PHASES: A post inserted half way along bay II at first floor level (supporting a tiebeam) appears to be part of a late medieval division, pre-dating the later internal partitioning. The wing has a queen-post roof and perhaps dates from around 1500. The main modernisation of the hall took place in the early seventeenth century, with the insertion of the fireplace and ceiling, and the partitioning of the ground first floors; a number of original door frames and doors survive. Probably at this date also, a tall chimney was constructed for the wing. The replacement of most of the exterior walls in stone with mullioned windows may be of the same date, but could be rather later. A new stair was added in about 1700. In the early to mid-eighteenth century, the walls of the wing were rebuilt in brick.

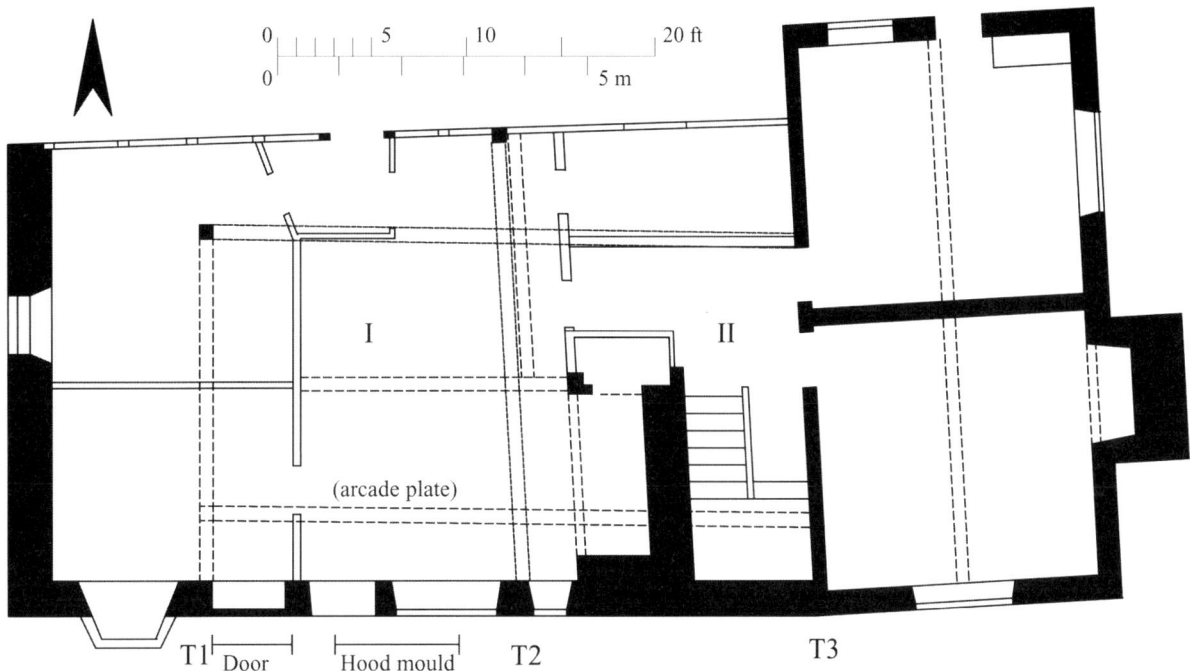

Fig. 8.3.2. Plan, showing truss and bay numbering.

STRUCTURAL FEATURES

PHASE 1: The original hall was approximately 33ft long by 25ft wide (rather irregular in shape), and measures 13ft 8in between the arcade plates. Original framing survived (concealed) in the rear hall wall until recently (now partly replaced/restored). Truss T1 is set 8ft within the present west wall. It includes two 9in square aisle posts; these lean towards the east (the tops displaced by about 8in) and the lower end of the southern post has been removed. The northern post (but not apparently the southern one) has an open notched-lap halving for a down-brace across the aisle. The slightly curved square-section arcade braces have small chamfers with small step stops at the top and pyramid stops at the base. The west sides of the posts are heavily weathered and the arcade plates terminate 8in to the west of the posts, indicating that this was the original end of the house. The mid-rail joining the posts survives, with a series of mortices for studs in its soffit. The tiebeam and upper roof were replaced in the seventeenth century.

Truss T2 is of base-cruck form (Fig. 8.3.3). Its main tiebeam carries either a complete upper tiebeam, or clasping pieces locating the arcade plates (mostly concealed in the ceiling). The north side blade survives almost complete, but the other has been removed below first floor level, presumably when the front wall was replaced in stone. The truss is chamfered in a smooth curve up the lower part of the blade, the arch braces, and across the collar. The blades and braces are halved timbers, with the waney side facing east; the upper face of the brace on this side is extraordinarily irregular and it was masked by a plank set in a rebate. The tiebeam carries an octagonal crown post with moulded octagonal cap and base. The upper part is chamfered with four-way up-braces (Fig. 8.3.4).

The original carpenters clearly encountered problems when making the tiebeam. On the south side, the brace mortice was cut and the pegholes in the top of the arch brace were drilled, but those in the tiebeam go only half-way through, because at this point a chunk of the base of the tiebeam split away, revealing a massive shake and cavity in the beam. The holes were abandoned and the end of the brace was then secured to the tiebeam with an iron strap held with square-headed nails, which is a most remarkable fourteenth century survival; the split is smoke-blackened inside, demonstrating that the damage is medieval. The strap and the un-drilled west side of the tiebeam are illustrated in Fig. 8.3.5a. On the other side of the truss (Fig. 8.3.5b), the split tiebeam and the rebate for the plank that was intended to conceal the waney edges of the brace and the blade can be seen. The pegholes in the brace are just visible in the photograph; the upper sides of the pegholes in the tiebeam remain on the broken soffit.

The north side of the truss gave almost as much trouble (Fig. 8.3.5c). Here, the pegholes were drilled through but,

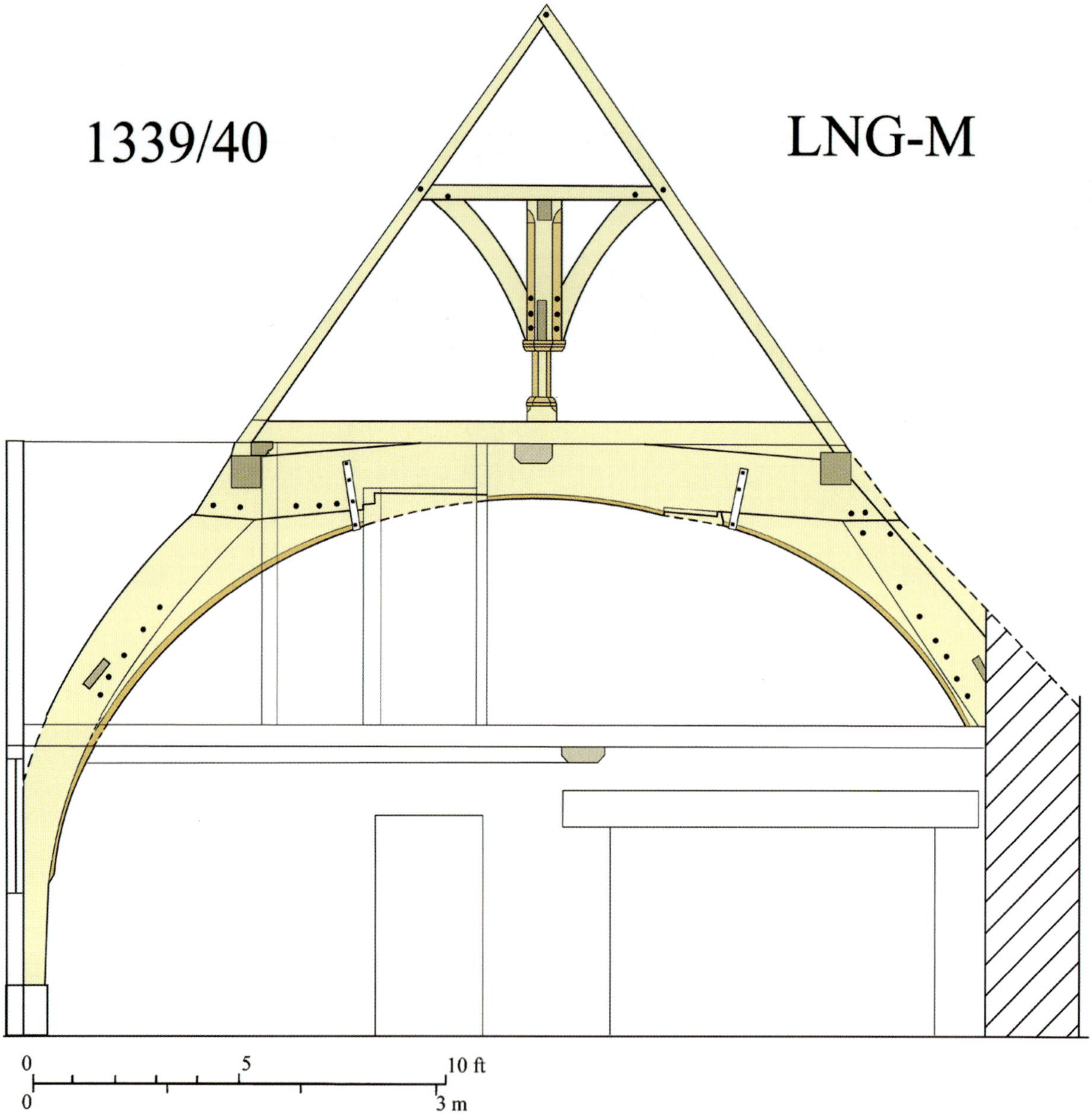

1339/40   **LNG-M**

Fig. 8.3.3. Section of Truss T2. The cornice is shown, though it only survives on the far side of this truss.

probably when the brace was being pegged (since only one peg of the three is in place), the tiebeam split along the line of the pegholes. Again, the brace was repaired with a strap, identical to that on the other end. The other side of this brace is concealed, so we do not know if it also had a plank to cover the waney edges.

Truss T3 is of aisled form, similar to T1, and carries a down-braced crown post. The collar purlin terminates just to the east of T3. The east side of the truss is heavily sooted over daub and batten infill (also sooted); one of the battens is nailed onto the rafter with a heavy round-headed nail, clearly medieval. The soot-blackening indicates that the medieval crosswing included an open hearth, thus may well have been a kitchen.

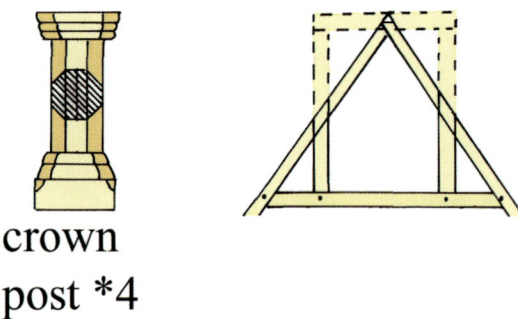

crown post *4

Fig. 8.3.4. Crown post detail and suggested louvre structure.

Fig. 8.3.5. (a) Tiebeam and strap, south end, west side. Note the absence of pegholes for the tenon of the brace.
(b) Tiebeam and strap, south end, east side. Note the pegholes in the brace tenon (just visible), and the waney edge of the top of the brace, with the rebate for the masking plank. The upper sides of the pegholes in the tiebeam (where the soffit has split away) can be seen by looking obliquely upwards into the cavity.
(c) Tiebeam and strap, north end, west side.

The arcade plates have trait-de-Jupiter scarfs just west of truss T2 and a small length of hollow-moulded cornice survives in bay II. Curved dragon ties link the plates and the tiebeam of T3; any evidence for their use at T1 is concealed. Ten common rafter couples survive in Bay I (concealed in Bay II); the rafters are set flat and measure 3 by 5in, with tenoned collars and halved apexes. The louvre was positioned between the first and third couples west of T2; these couples carry a pair of uprights, and their apexes are rebated for a horizontal timber (suggested form in Fig. 8.3.4).

LATER PHASES: The wing roof has queen-post trusses, possibly of around 1500, with clasped purlins having splayed and bridled scarfs. It includes six reused sooted rafters similar to those over the hall, but with the collars halved rather than tenoned. Two other reused rafters are un-sooted and retain their chamfered and scalloped lower ends (which had projected beyond the wallplate); they have rafter holes.

The inserted fireplace has a fluted lintel, similar to one of 1604 from Surrey.[1] The side of the fireplace contains a latticework door (cf. Hall Farm, Loxley, Warwickshire, LOX-A), giving access to a small space that may have been a smoking chamber. The ceiling is supported on chamfered but unstopped beams. The stonework of the walls and the octagonal mullioned windows are probably early seventeenth century, as is the tall brick chimney to the wing, which has stone quoins. The ground-floor fireplace in the wing has a Tudor arch with ovolo moulding and pumpkin stops (probably of the same period).

---

[1]   Hall, L. and Alcock, N. W. (1994) *Fixtures and Fittings in Dated Houses: 1567–1763*, Council for British Archaeology, York); an iron fireback dated 1626 is probably a modern replica.

In the years around 1700, a dog-leg stair with turned balusters was inserted behind the chimney; this space may well have previously been the position of a cross-passage, though direct evidence for this is lacking. In the early/mid-eighteenth century, the crosswing walls were rebuilt in brick with segmental-arched windows, though the earlier chimney was retained.

DENDROCHRONOLOGY

For dendrochronology abbreviations and master sequence references, see page facing Introduction.

Sampling Comments: 9 samples were obtained through coring by Robert Howard on 22nd April 1991. Dating was funded by the Royal Commission on Historical Monuments (England).

TREE-RING SAMPLE RECORD AND SUMMARY OF DATING

Sample Code	Sample Location	Total Rings	Sapwood Rings	FMR Date	LHR Date	LMR Date	Date Cat
LNG-M01	Tiebeam truss 2	30	—	—	—	—	—
LNG-M02	Front (S) blade truss 2	101	31C	—	—	—	—
LNG-M03	Front brace truss 2	51	11	—	—	—	—
LNG-M04	Front arcade plate	63	18C	1277	1321	1339	2
LNG-M05	Rear arcade plate	50	15c	1289	1323	1338	2
LNG-M06	Rear brace truss 2	49	01	—	—	—	—
LNG-M07	Rear blade truss 2	39	HS	—	—	—	—
LNG-M08	Rear plate bay 2	28	—	—	—	—	—
LNG-M09	Aisle post truss 3	21	—	—	—	—	—

Site sequence: (composed of samples 4 and 5), 63 rings long dated 1277–1339 with *t*-values of 6.5(MGB-E01), 6.6(READING).

Felling date (sample 4 has complete sapwood, with the 1339 ring complete and sample 5 is virtually complete): **1339/40**.

DOCUMENTARY HISTORY

A map of 1776 by W. Sollis (in the house) identifies the property as an estate called The Lower Farm, the property of John Haynes, gentleman.[2] The map includes an elevation of the house, corresponding closely to its present appearance. In the 1774 Enclosure Award, John Haynes received 110 acres for Lower Farm and 67 acres for Upper Farm.[3] The latter is identified as a 2½ yardland farm in the will of John Haynes (1772; proved 1774), suggesting that Lower Farm comprised about 4 yardlands.[4] It passed to his son, another John (the 1776 owner), presumably by settlement since it is un-named in his will. Components of Upper Farm comprising 1 and 1½ yardlands were purchased by the Haynes family in 1713 and 1729;[5] no earlier documentation has been located for Lower Farm and it may have belonged to the Haynes family for many years before 1774; members of the family were living in the parish as early as 1637.[6] Sale particulars of 1812 indicate that Lower Farm paid a chief rent of 8d to the Lord of the Manor; however, lists of chief rents show that these rents were paid solely for encroachments.[7] The house is named for Thomas Hopkins who bought the farm in 1813 and whose family held it until 1879.[8]

---

2   Photostat at WCRO.
3   WCRO, CR631/6.
4   SCLA, ER5/145.
5   WCRO, CR2028/Box 3.
6   WCRO, DR326/15.
7   WCRO, CR2028/Box 8; Boxes 1 and 6.
8   Deeds in possession of Mr P. Hodges, The Goodwins, Long Marston.

The manor of Long Marston belonged to Winchcombe Abbey before the Dissolution. It was held by Robert Dudley in 1566 and was acquired by Ralph Sheldon from Ambrose Dudley, Earl of Warwick, in 1589. The Sheldon family retained it until about 1780, although the manor site and its buildings had been sold off by 1578.[9] A Winchcombe Abbey survey of 1355 lists four freeholders (with one, two, two and three yardlands), seventeen customary tenants holding 20 yardlands for fairly substantial rents (typically 16s 2d per yardland), and four cottagers. Two post-dissolution surveys list three freeholders (holding only three yardlands altogether) and eleven copyholders holding 27 yardlands and paying 13s 4d per yardland (mostly with several messuages and corresponding numbers of yardlands).[10]

From the later history, it appears that the copyholdings were sold off piecemeal between 1550 and 1600; one sale deed of 1567 for five messuages and five yardlands survives. There is no indication that Lower Farm formed part of the Winchcombe Abbey manorial demesne. An undated memorandum (probably late sixteenth century) lists properties being rented, with 'one messuage … called the Lower House with a barne and a stable and thre yardes lande and the closse thereundo belongeing' being rented to one Thomas Yeate for £12 per year; it is listed with other rented meadows and closes. This may have been drawn up by whoever had acquired the properties on the break-up of the manor.[11]

It seems likely that, as a substantial pre-Black Death house, Hopkins can be identified with one of the three freeholdings listed in 1355, perhaps indeed the three-yardland holding. However, we have insufficient evidence to confirm this and we cannot exclude it being an enfranchised copyholding.

---

[9]   Rental at Longleat House (1566); BAH, Ms 328771 (1589); WCRO, CR2028/box 4 (1578).
[10]   Gloucestershire Archives, D678/1 M4/3 (1355; information from Professor C. Dyer); TNA, SC2/175/1, f.467ff (1545); E164/39, f.150 (1550 x 1565).
[11]   SCLA, ER3/2838 (1567); WCRO, CR2028, box6/1.

8.4. LON-C: Long Crendon, Church Green Cottage, 102–4 High Street, Buckinghamshire[1]

Grid reference: SP 6979 0901   *Survey date*: 1989   *By*: D. Miles

Fig. 8.4.1. View of Church Green Cottage, Long Crendon from south.

ARCHITECTURAL DESCRIPTION

SUMMARY AND HISTORICAL DEVELOPMENT

PHASE 1: 102–4 High Street is a three-bay house of cruck construction, with felling date range of *1466–97*, notable as the only house in Long Crendon with an exposed cruck (Fig. 8.4.2). It is aligned along Church Green, at right angles to High Street (Fig. 8.4.5). The walls are mostly timber-framed with plastered infill and rubble stone plinths, but bay I has been partly rebuilt in limestone rubble. The roofs are thatched with half-hipped gables. The timbers have all been painted over, so that the identification of smoke-blackening is difficult. However soot encrustation was thought to be present in bay II, adjacent to truss T2. Thus, a hall can be suggested in bay II, perhaps with service in bay I and chamber in bay III. The roof space is inaccessible, making it impossible to confirm this. The original entry appears to have been into bay II, adjacent to T2.

PHASE 2: Sometime, probably in the sixteenth century, bay IV was constructed as an extension to the north-east of bay III, with a cruck gable end. It probably provided an additional parlour with sleeping accommodation. The floor in bay III is of a similar date. These changes lend weight to the suggestion that the service room was at the other end of the house.

---

[1]   This report has been compiled with the help of notes kindly provided by Catherine Murray. Documentary history by Nat Alcock and Eric Sewell, building on the work of John Chenevix Trench†.

Fig. 8.4.2. View of Church Green Cottage, Long Crendon, from east.

Church Green Cottage, Long Crendon

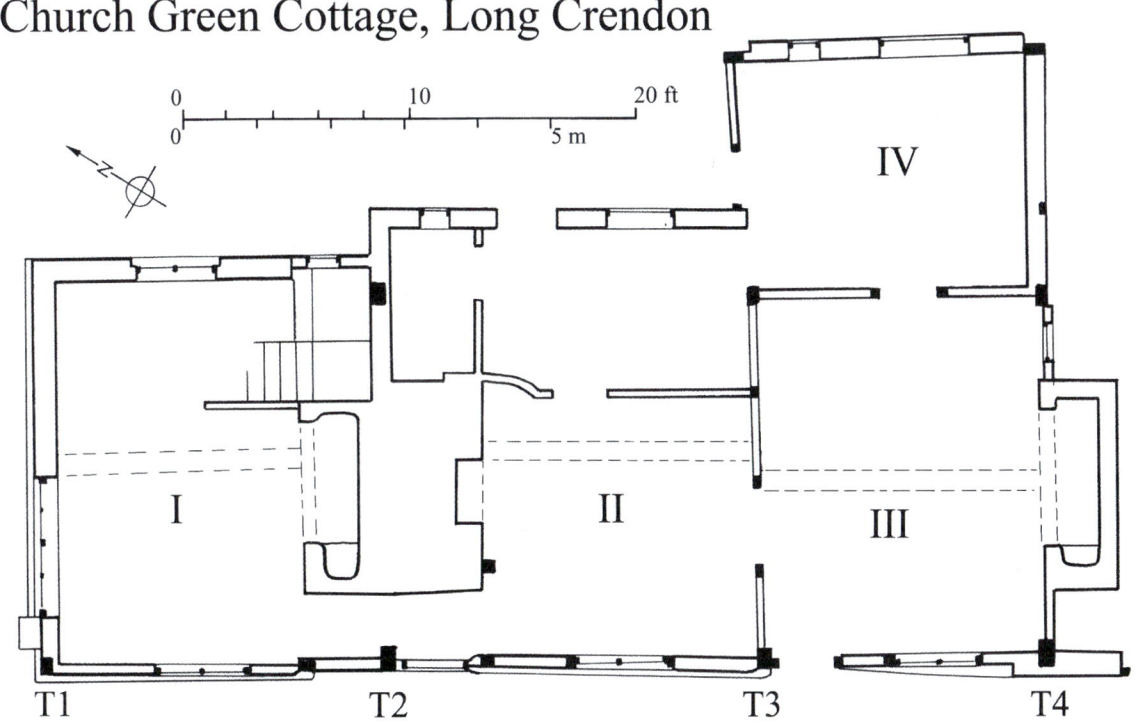

Fig. 8.4.3. Ground floor plan, showing truss and bay numbering.

PHASE 3: In the seventeenth century, bays I and II were floored over, a gable-end chimney inserted for bay III and a central chimney stack built adjacent to truss T2. Access to the house at this time was possibly in front of this central stack, with a stair on the other side of the stack. Truss T3 had the tiebeam severed for a door to connect the first floors of bays II and III. Also at about this time, the gable and back wall of bay I were rebuilt in limestone rubble.

LATER PHASES: During the twentieth century, the ground floor wall to the rear of bay II was demolished and a new partition inserted to divide bay II from the shallow brick extension with pentice roof at the back.

STRUCTURAL FEATURES

PHASE 1: All the cruck blades survive, except the rear blade of truss T1, but they are not visible above collar level. Trusses T2 and T3 appear to have been closed originally, as both have tiebeams. However, these tiebeams have undergone considerable alteration: they have been cut through to provide first floor doorways, and their ends are covered by clasping timbers. Truss T2 is now obscured by the seventeenth-century chimney stack. Truss T3 contains a stud partition, probably seventeenth century but with possibly original studs flanking the ground floor doorway.

The ends of the main tiebeams extend to connect with the wall-framing and to support the wall plates. The trusses also have lower tiebeams, but it is not entirely certain that these are original and they may relate to the insertion of the first floor doorways. The collars support the purlins on the backs of the cruck blades. The roof retains original purlins except to the rear of bay I. The front purlin of bay I has a roughly curved windbrace to the gable end. Most of the main structural timbers are boxed heart, and were converted with a combination of axing and pit-sawing.

Original walling survives to the rear of bay III. It is timber-framed with plaster infill on a low rubble plinth. The front wall of all three bays is also timber-framed but was altered in the seventeenth century when the plinth and sill were raised. However, the cruck stud of T2 remains, with a peg-hole indicating the probable position of a doorhead.

PHASE 2: REAR WING: The gable end of the extension has a cruck truss of similar type to the earlier ones in the main range but of smaller scantling. It has tiebeams at first floor and wall plate levels, the upper one possibly re-used. The walls are timber-framed but have been partly rebuilt in rubble stone and brick. The extension seems to be tied to the earlier structure with spurs to the earlier cruck blades. The structure of the first floor is concealed but is probably original, judged from the position of the lower tiebeam. The floor in bay III has a 10in axial beam and 5½–6in wide joists, all chamfered with shaped stops. This might be primary, but is more likely to be a later sixteenth century insertion. The joist ends are carried by half-beams attached to the inside of the wall rails. The front half-beam is chamfered, the rear boxed in. The front joists also have later cleats.

LATER PHASES: In bay III, the gable chimney has a large ground-floor fireplace with a heavy timber lintel. This is chamfered with a stop at the left end. The inner reveals of the fireplace have recesses, the left with an armrest and old wooden seat, the right altered with a higher plastered sill. There is no evidence for a fireplace at first floor level. The chimney shaft has been rebuilt in brick, probably in the eighteenth/nineteenth century.

The front wall of the house may have been partly rebuilt at this time, with raised plinth and sill. The ground floor windows in bays II and III are in their original positions as indicated by chamfers in the rail above. The rail above the window in bay III also indicates the position of a central mullion.

The inserted floor in bay II has a 9in axial beam and 3½–4in wide joists, all chamfered with ogee stops. As in bay III, the front joists have later cleats and rest on a chamfered half-beam, now plastered over. The seating for the rear joists is concealed. The central chimney stack has been completely plastered and the shaft rebuilt in eighteenth/early nineteenth century brick. The large ground floor fireplace to bay II has been altered and filled in. It has a rough timber lintel with the left end supported on a timber post, but this does not provide convincing evidence for an earlier smoke hood. Adjacent to the right end, in the side wall of the room, is a plastered recess with an old timber sill, possibly the blocked opening to a former oven. The ground floor fireplace to bay I has a timber lintel with narrow run-out chamfer, and side recesses. The lobby to the front of the chimney stack has traces of two blocked doorways, one either side of the cruck blade of truss T2. The lobby ceiling has plain square-cut joists. In bay I, the floor consists of a rough 7in wide axial beam with concealed joists.

Most windows have modern wooden casements but the first floor window to front of bay II is a c. 1700 three-light window with diamond leaded glazing. The ground floor window in the gable end of bay I incorporates the wooden frame of a former two-light window of similar date. The house has several blocked doorways, some probably arising from its multiple tenancy in the nineteenth century. The lobby entry doorways between bays I and II and the gable end entry next to the chimney in bay I are possibly of earlier origin.

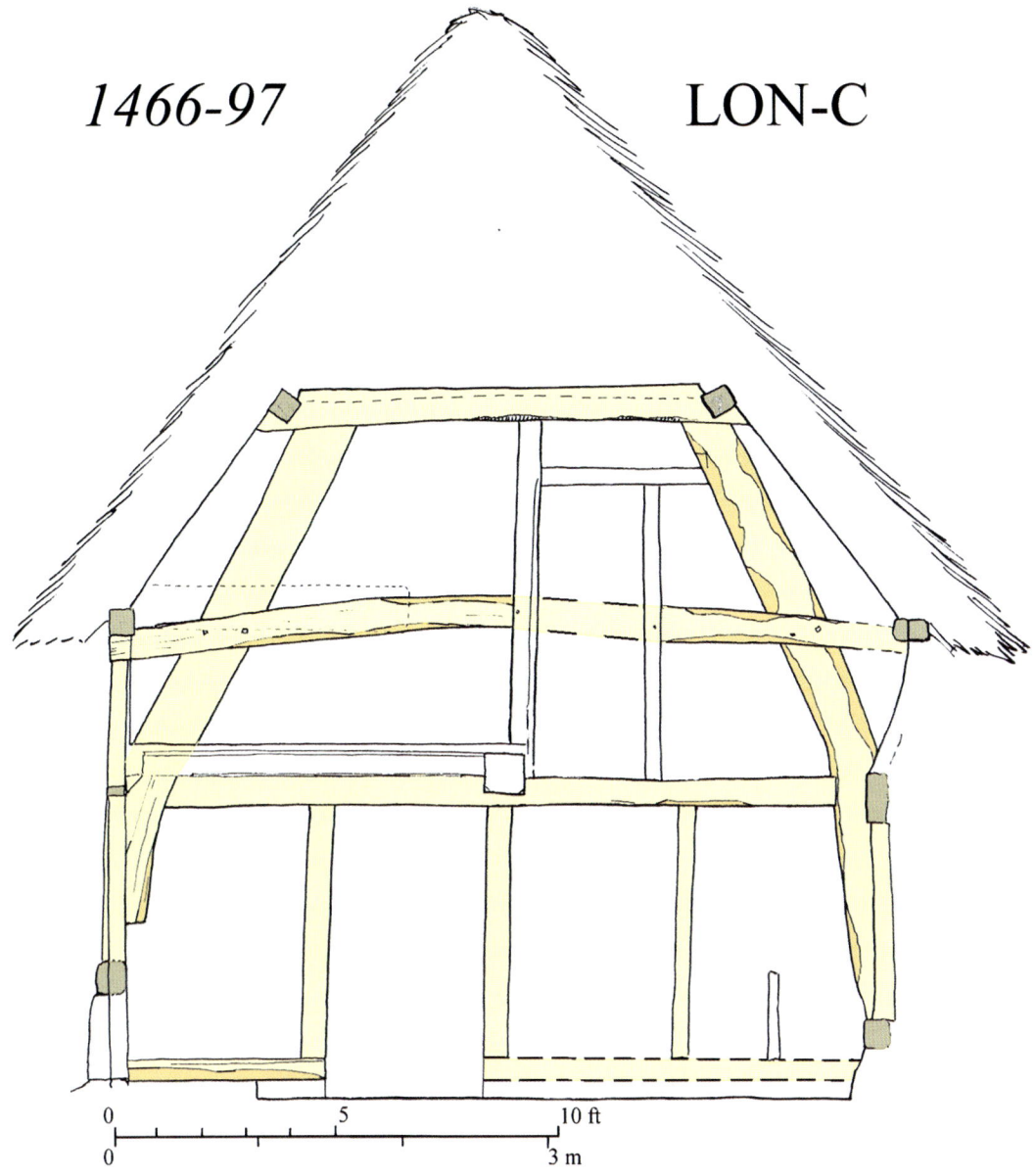

1466-97   LON-C

Fig. 8.4.4. Section of truss T3 from the south.

DENDROCHRONOLOGY

For dendrochronology abbreviations see page facing Introduction.

Sampling Comments: Eight samples were obtained through coring by Robert Howard on 13 January 1989. One of these, the rear purlin bay III, was not oak, and five others had less that 50 rings.

TREE-RING SAMPLE RECORD AND SUMMARY OF DATING

Sample Code	Sample Location	Total Rings	Sapwood Rings	FMR Date	LHR Date	LMR Date	Date Cat
LON-C01	Rear cruck blade truss 2	70	HS	1386	1455	1455	2
LON-C02	Collar truss 2	35NM	—	—	—	—	—
LON-C03	Front cruck blade truss 2	47	04	—	—	—	—
LON-C04	Rear cruck blade truss 3	51	—	—	—	—	—

Sample Code	Sample Location	Total Rings	Sapwood Rings	FMR Date	LHR Date	LMR Date	Date Cat
LON-C05	Rear purlin bay III	Not oak	—	—	—	—	—
LON-C06	Front purlin bay III	37NM	—	—	—	—	—
LON-C07	Wind brace truss 4	26NM	—	—	—	—	—
LON-C08	Front cruck blade truss 3	42	02	—	—	—	—

Site sequences: (sample 1 only), 70 rings long dated to 1386–1455 with *t*-values of 5.0(OXFORD), 7.9(WICK). 95% felling date range: **1464–1496** (previously 1468–1493). OxCal refined felling date range: *1466–97*

DOCUMENTARY HISTORY

This was a Notley Abbey copyhold, comprising a cottage and orchard (¼ acre) paying a rent of 3s 4d. It can be followed back in the court rolls to 1786 and through the Notley manor rentals to about 1600. It was held by the Nicholls family from the earliest date at which it is recorded until 1786. They were followe by the Way and then Shrimpton families. It was enfranchised in 1892.

Court rolls and rentals

The court roll entries are summarised in Table 8.4.1. The earliest identified admission is only in 1786; the rolls that would have contained the admissions of Edward Nicholls in 1760 and his father, perhaps in 1738, are lost. The Notley manor rentals for both 1761–4 and 1728 list Edward (Mr) Nichols paying 3s 4d, with the succession of Richard Way annotated against the entries. In 1728, it is recorded as having only its ¼ acre croft and no arable land. This makes the identification with the holding of Edward Nicolls in the rental of *c.* 1635 and that of Edmund Nicholes in *c.* 1595 (both paying 3s 4d) very plausible, since the former also had no extra land.[2]

None of the copyholders from the later eighteenth-century onwards lived in the cottage,. Richard Way, gentleman of Thame, was succeeded by his son, a clergyman who later held the living at Lapworth, Warwickshire.[3] The John

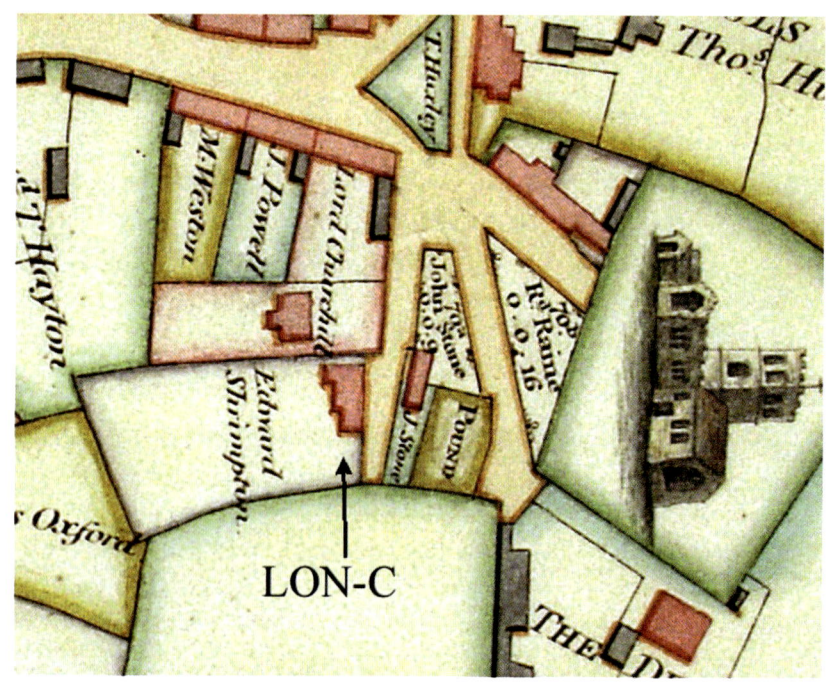

Fig. 8.4.5. Part of the 1827 map of Long Crendon (CBS IR/95/Q).

Shrimpton acquiring the cottage in 1794 cannot be identified with certainty, though he was probably the father of Edward Shrimpton, who was a baker living in Tetsworth, and is the copyholder named on the 1827 map (Fig. 8.4.5).[4]

---

2   The identification is not entirely certain, since two other landless cottages paid the same rent; the *c.*1595 rental gives rents but no descriptions. Bodl., Ms top.gen.e.64: p. 116; Ms dd.Bertie.c.27/5.

3   He also owned 23 acres in the open fields probably inherited from his father, which were bequeathed to trustees in 1817 (TNA, PROB 11/1588). The Way interest in the village arose from the marriage of Richard Way and Ann Randolph (of a Long Crendon yeoman family) in 1773.

4   He is probably the Edward Shrimpton baptised on 30 September 1774, son of John and Mary; a second Edward, baptised on 19 October 1778 (son of Thomas and Sarah) would not have been of age in 1797. He had a son, John Kirby Shrimpton, baptised in 1799, who later lived at 54 High Street, Long Crendon, and whose son, James Webster Shrimpton, was baptised on 9 October 1822.

The earliest identified copyholder, Edmund Nicholls was the son of Edward Nicholls (d. 1591), a carpenter, as probably was his son, since he was left his father's tools; Edmund's son, another Edward was born in 1607.[5] However, Edward Nicholls, dying in 1738, was a labourer. Two of the landless cottages on Notley Manor were held by carpenters in the seventeenth century (Thomas Burnham and John Gynckes) and a third was held by William Goodwin in the eighteenth.[6] Thus, this relatively substantial cottage may well have been regularly owned and lived in by craftsmen.

Table 8.4.1 Admissions to 102–104 High Street, Long Crendon.

1786:	Richard WAY, gent, of Thame, admitted on surrender of Edward NICHOLLS (admitted 1760) to a messuage divided into three with orchard and gardens, then occupied by John NICHOLLS, Thomas GRANT, Samuel ALNUT and widow WEST situated near Church Green.
1786:	James WAY admitted on death of Richard WAY his father, to the above tenement, fine 3s 4d. Rent 3s 4d
1794:	John SHRIMPTON admitted on surrender of James WAY, to a messuage divided into three with orchard and gardens, occupied by Thos GRANT, Geo MORTIMER & Joseph BELSON situated in Church Green, fine £2 15s. Rent 3s 4d
1797:	Copy Court Roll (Duke of Marlborough). John Shrimpton surrenders to Edward Shrimpton, a messuage formerly three, near Church Green, now in tenure of Thomas Grant, George Mortimer, Sarah Belson, widow. rent 3s 4d. (CBS, P134/1/22)
1849:	John Kirby SHRIMPTON, eldest son of Edward Shrimpton, decd. '[who was admitted in 1797 and 1824]. Messuages occupied by (a) John BRUCE & Solomon HAWKES (b) Thomas WARNER, Spencer SEWELL & John WARNER. Rent 3s 4d
1860:	John Webster SHRIMPTON elder son of John Kirby Shrimpton deceased [who was admitted in 1849], 2 tenements occ (a) John BRUCE & Solomon HAWKES (b) Spencer SEWELL, Thos WARNER & Chris HOLLIMAN. Rent 3s 4d.
1879ff:	[Survey book]: Messuage formerly divided into three with orchard & garden occupied by Thos WARNER, Spencer SEWELL & Chas HOLLIMAN. Copyholders: J K SHRIMPTON 1849, Jas Webster SHRIMPTON 1860, J E LOOSLEY 1879. Enfranchised 1892. Rent 3s-4d (CBS, D78/box 6, Notley manor survey, p. 154)
1879:	J. E. Loosely admitted
1892:	Enfranchised

Deeds

The earliest deed is of 1925, the sale of the cottages by Rev. Elwell to Miss R. E. S. Elwell.[7] This confirms the previous occupation by Thomas Warner, Spencer Sewell and Charles Holliman.

Building Evidence

The only member of the Nicholls family listed in the Hearth Tax is John, with two hearths. However, he is firmly associated with a Dormer copyhold messuage and yardland (the later 66 Bicester Road), so presumably the cottage was listed in the return under the unknown tenant's name.

1910 valuation: hereditaments 542–4. Owned by Rev. Claude Simeon Elwell, occupied by George Webb and Mark Blinco, described as cottages with two rooms up and two down.

---

5   CBS, D/A/Wf/11/303; PR 134/1/1. The Nicholls are represented spasmodically in the parish registers between 1592 and 1741; other family members named Edward were baptised in 1685 and 1691 (sons of Edward and Dorothy), 1687 (son of John and Mary) and 1741, son of Jonathan and Alice.

6   Ginkes and Burnham are listed in the *c.* 1635 Notley rental, paying 3s 4d. William Goodwin was admitted in 1740 (CBS, D/BASM/23a). Ginkes must have prospered, as in 1631 he also acquired the cottage built in the late 16th century standing on *Wardeynwyke*, a one acre plot on Wapping Lane (CBS, D-X34; see fig. 6.6). In 1736, this cottage was bought by William Butcher, wheelwright.

7   In the owner's possession.

8.5. LON-G: Long Crendon, Sycamore Farm, 9 Bicester Road, Buckinghamshire[1]

Grid reference: SP 6931 0870   *Survey date*: 16 February 1990   *By*: D. Miles

Fig. 8.5.1. View of the house.

ARCHITECTURAL DESCRIPTION

SUMMARY AND HISTORICAL DEVELOPMENT

Sycamore Farm, Long Crendon is identified as a two-yardland copyhold farm held from All Souls College, Oxford from 1555. It is a complex linear building, with its length aligned south-west to north-east, involving at least five major phases and with much alternate rebuilding.

PHASE 1: The first phase comprises an aisled hall dated by dendrochronology to 1205. One complete bay (III) survives (Fig. 8.5.3), with one nearly intact roof truss (T4a) (Fig. 8.5.4) and the posts of a second (T3). The arcade posts have external upstands, and the tiebeam is joined to the plates with an inclined cogged joint; the truss has passing braces from the apex down to the arcade posts with notch-lapped joints (Figs. 8.5.6). The original house certainly included the present

---

[1]   Documentary history by Nat Alcock and Eric Sewell, building on the work of John Chenevix Trench†. The radiocarbon dating was supported by the Vernacular Architecture Group. This report includes some material drawn from Feltbower, I. J. and P. V. (1984) 'A First Survey of Sycamore Farm House, Long Crendon', unpublished report, for which we are grateful.

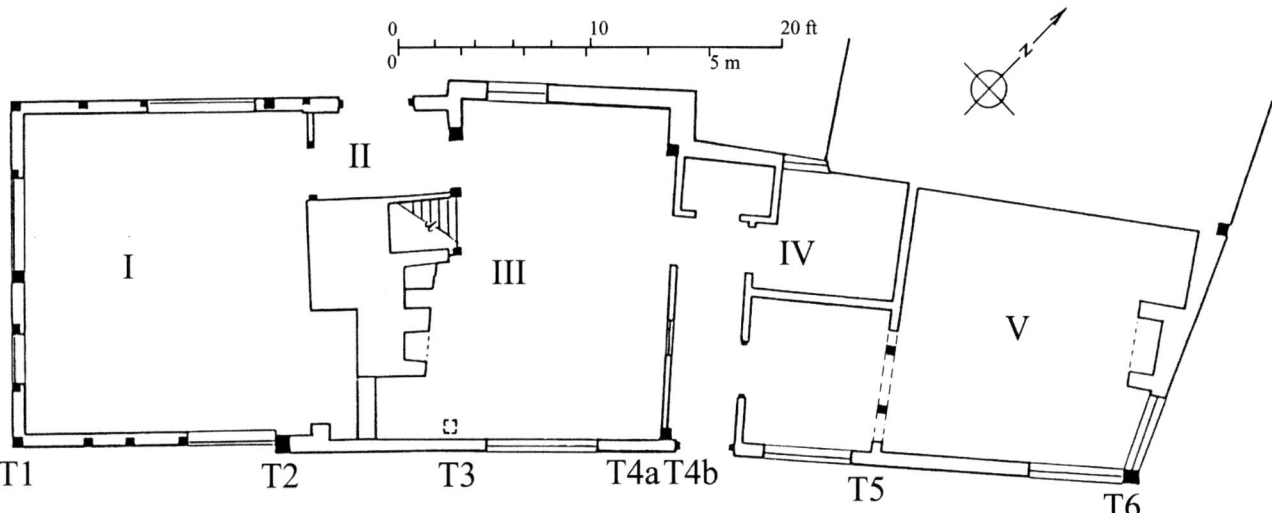

Fig. 8.5.2. Ground floor plan, showing truss and bay numbering.

bays III and IV and it probably continued into bay II as well, though no clear evidence is visible on the arcade posts of truss T3. It is likely that the hearth was located in bay III, as the smoke blackening is heavier on this side of the truss. The front aisle has been removed, possibly in Phase 2, but the rear aisle still survives at the rear of bay III, though it has probably been reduced in width.

The arcade plates have been reused, as the existing curved arcade braces (notch-lapped onto the face) partially obscure even earlier notch-lap joints (Figs. 8.5.4 and 8.5.6). The plates were sampled but had too few rings to date; however, the similarity between the later and earlier joints suggests that their reuse was not very long after they were originally employed.

A notable feature of the truss is an undecorated crown post, braced only to the collar purlin, which is tenoned into the tiebeam and into a short surviving section of collar purlin. It was initially considered that this crown post must be primary, since it seemingly could not have been inserted later, despite its being some 50 years earlier than any other known crown post. Neither the crown post nor the collar purlin have enough rings for tree-ring dating, but radiocarbon dating has given a felling date range of *1299–1324* for the crown post, conclusively demonstrating that it is secondary. Further consideration has also shown that dismantling and re-assembling the scissor-braced rafters would have been comparatively easy, since they are simply halved and pegged together. Indeed, their falling apart may have been the reason for strengthening the truss with the crown post and purlin.

PHASE 2: At sometime in the fifteenth century, judging from the general style of the roof carpentry (narrow tiebeams with collars and clasped purlins), bays II and III were rebuilt, probably involving the removal of the front aisle and most of the Phase 1 framing except for the arcade-plates in bay III. At T2, a new truss was presumably inserted (removed in Phase 4), while at T3 the earlier truss was entirely replaced except for the arcade posts; T4b was erected against the south-east side of T4a, carried on the original arcade plates. T4a was left intact, probably because it still supported the bay IV roof structure.

PHASE 3: Bay IV was rebuilt in the sixteenth century, when the original truss T5 was replaced with a cruck or raised cruck with a type 'W' apex (blades terminate immediately above the collar). The wall alignment suggests that this rebuilding included bay V as well but no structural evidence now remains in this bay. Neither of these later phases have given tree-ring dates.

LATER PHASES: Judging from the style of the timber framing, bay I was probably added to the south-west end of the house in the seventeenth century (Phase 4). This is a well-built two-storey chamber block with an attic room. In Phase 5, later in the seventeenth century, the end of bay V was rebuilt on the skew to align with the Bicester Road, the end truss (T6) having a slightly cambered tiebeam. During the eighteenth and nineteenth centuries, the front of the house was faced in brickwork. A new roof structure was added above the earlier roofs of bays II to V and the front wall raised about 18in.

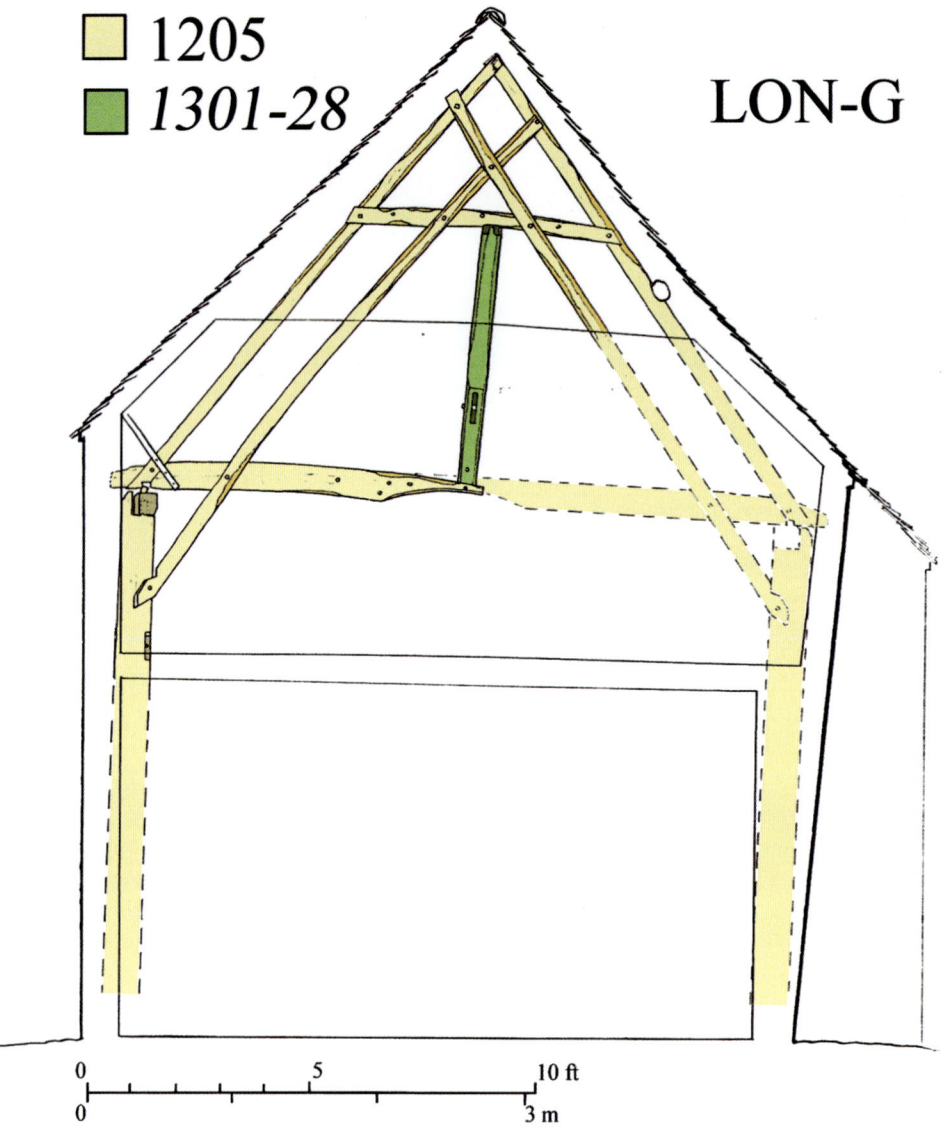

1205

1301-28

LON-G

Fig. 8.5.3. Section of truss T4a, from the east.

STRUCTURAL FEATURES

PHASE 1: This is the most significant part of the house and, although much altered, what remains allows a reasonably clear picture of the basic arrangement. The dimensions of bay III within the arcade posts are 12ft from truss to truss and about 15ft from front to back. The rear aisle is about 3ft wide, but this provides relatively high eaves. An original height of about 6ft seems more likely, implying 5ft aisles within an overall internal width of about 24ft. Much of the structure of truss T4a is intact (Fig. 8.5.3). Of truss T3, only the two arcade posts remain, though the front (south) one has been severed at first floor level, retaining only the upper part. The arcade posts are straight with bevelled off upstands on the outside of the arcade plates. These posts measure 9 to 13in square and carry notch-lap joints for arcade and tiebeam braces (though none are visible for braces across the aisles). Three of the four posts have tree-ring dates consistent with felling in 1205.

In addition to the two arcade posts of T4a, the tiebeam survives, though it has been gouged out below for a low door and was eventually cut through for the present door frame. The rafters of this truss are strengthened by a pair of passing braces (Fig. 8.5.5) which continue past the tiebeam to the arcade posts where they have notch-lap joints. A collar is

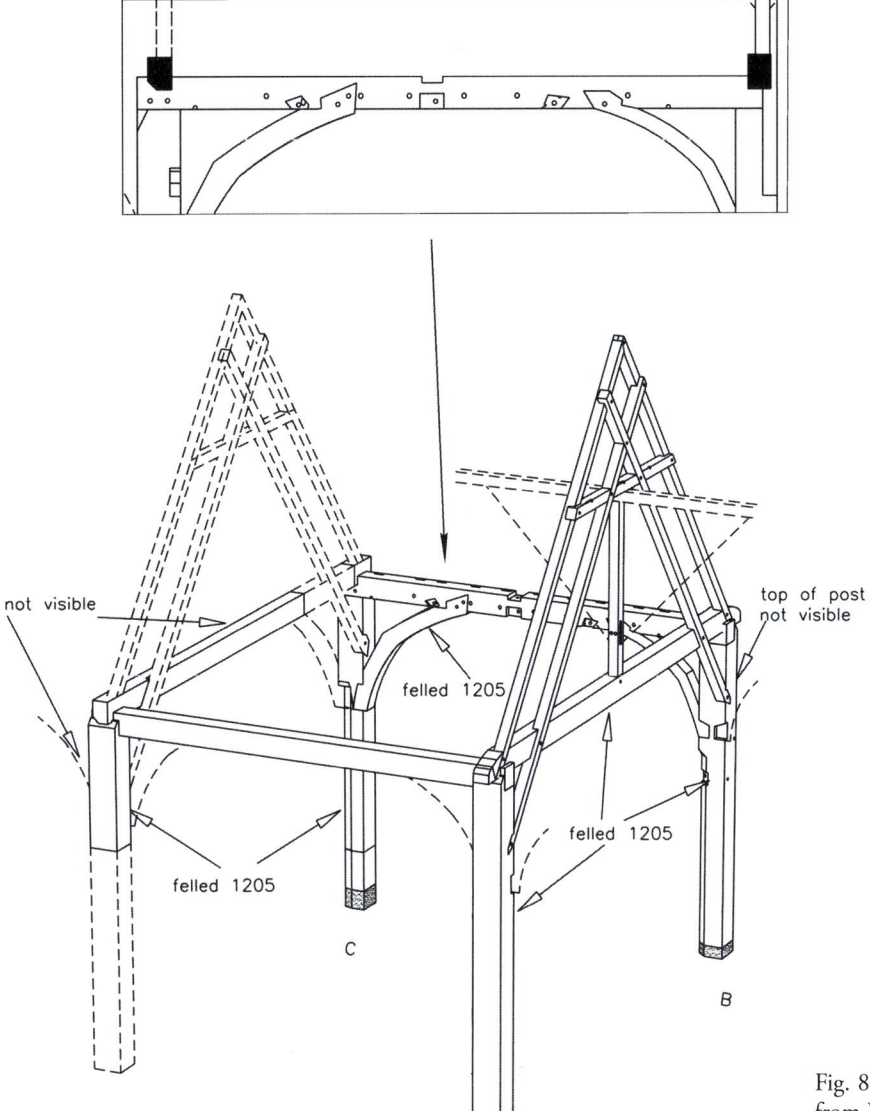

Fig. 8.5.4. Isometric view of bay III (amended from Walker(1999)).

Fig. 8.5.5. The passing braces of truss T4a. The top of the inserted crown post and the severed collar plate can be seen below the collar, and the yoke and ridge of truss T4b are also visible.

Fig. 8.5.6. Notched-lap joint with simple entry on the reused arcade plate, showing the matrix of a similar joint.

Fig. 8.5.7. Arcade post head, T3 (north). The tiebeam is a replacement, probably of the fifteenth century.

Fig. 8.5.8. Cogged joint of arcade plate, tiebeam and rafter (south side of truss T4a)

threaded in between the rafters and the passing braces with pegs at all the intersections, and with three extra peg-holes on its north-east side, angled slightly downwards. Although these might have secured hip rafters for an end aisle, their placing and character suggests rather that they were used for hanging such items as hams. The rafters and passing braces are of very small scantling, averaging 3–4in squared boxed heart in section. The timbers are all heavily smoke blackened. The truss was later strengthened by a crown post with the remains of a collar purlin (discussed below).

In the front wall and along the rear arcade of bay III, both arcade plates are preserved, although the front one was severed by the insertion of the front window, probably in the seventeenth century. Arcade braces are notch-lapped to the plate and to the posts (Fig. 8.5.6). The arcade plates are clearly reused, since the rear plate has notch-lap joints for braces which are partially obscured by the present arcade braces (themselves dated to 1205); the plate is also cut away for a cogging, but on the side rather than the top face. This indicates that it has been rotated through 90° and suggests that the empty halvings were for dragon ties on each side of a tiebeam (suggested by D Stenning).

The junctions of the posts, tiebeams and arcade plate are of considerable interest. The posts have external bevelled upstands and tenons set into the arcade plate (the only tenons used in the primary frame) (Fig. 8.5.7). Instead of a lap or secret lap-dovetail on the tiebeam and plate, as found later in the 13th century (as at AST-A, 1282/6, Chapter 8.1), the upper surface of the arcade plate is cogged, (i.e. cut away to leave a projecting inclined tongue of timber which here measures approximately 1½–2in square). Unfortunately only one of these joints could be inspected, and the plate has been severed about an inch away from the tiebeam. At truss T4a, the outer rafter is notched to sit over the cog (Fig. 8.5.8). Another interesting feature is an inch-wide chamfer on the outer top arris of the plate. This could only be seen in the joint, but it does seem to have been cut deliberately, though its purpose is not understood; a similar feature was noted at AST-A.

The crown post. The crown post was initially considered to date from 1205, making it of exceptional interest. It is firmly fixed into the 1205 structure, its foot tenoned and pegged into the top of the tiebeam, whilst the top is tenoned into the underside of the collar purlin, held firmly under the collar. However, this use of mortice-and-tenon-joints is more consistent with a later date. It is also relevant that both the crown post and the collar purlin are of elm, complete with waney edge and bark, in contrast to the well-finished oak of the aisled hall. The radiocarbon dating has confirmed that they are secondary, dating to the early 14th century. For their insertion of the crown post, the most obvious method would be the removal and re-pegging of the collar and the top ends of the passing braces.

PHASE 2: This comprises the rebuilt roof over bays II and III (now heavily altered) and the inserted truss T4b on the west side of T4a, presumably to strengthen it. This truss has a collar and tiebeam of slender dimensions with clasped purlins and a yoke carrying a ridge beam. The principal rafters are 6 by 3in tapering to 2in, laid flat with a collar 7in high by 4in thick. The yoke is 5in high by 3in, and both collar and yoke are tenoned into the principals. The purlins are approximately 4–5½ by 6in and the ridge beam is 5½in square. At one time, wind braces were present, whose steeply pitched diminished halvings on the upper surface of the purlins are still evident. At T3, the whole upper roof was replaced, with a new tiebeam (chamfered on the lower edges) spanning between the original arcade plates.

As part of the Phase 2 alterations, wattle and daub was fixed to the original timbers of T4a and some upright staves were fitted in between trusses T4a and T4b. This wattle and daub is heavily smoke blackened, on the bay III side particularly, as are all the Phase 2 timbers. The tiebeam of T4a has stave holes drilled underneath at 11in centres (noted by the owners); these may well have been added in Phase 2 for a partition at this end of the hall.

PHASE 3: The only identified feature is the cruck truss at T5, which is mostly hidden by plaster. The crucks measure about 7½in square and are of elm. They survive only at first floor level, being supported by a boxed ceiling beam. They appear most likely to have been full crucks with a type W (truncated) apex, but the possibility of upper crucks (originally carried by this beam) cannot be excluded. The cruck blades have spurs which are about 18in lower than the present eaves, lining up with the original Phase 1 arcade plates. A second spur runs from the front cruck blade to the present eaves level and probably dates from the last phase of alterations during the eighteenth/nineteenth centuries, when the front wall was raised. This phase may also have included bay V, though little timber framing is evident here except for the first floor girts and the tiebeam; the wall studs were probably removed in the late eighteenth century alterations. Sometime in the seventeenth century, the end of bay V was rebuilt parallel to the road.

PHASE 4: This wide extension (bay IV) measures approximately 18 by 14ft and has the most complete timber-framing in the building. It has 7in square corner posts with jowled heads and the gable end has a substantial central stud. Smaller studs and rails divide the wall into three-panel high squares. These lack wattling stave holes,[2] suggesting that the brick

---

2   Observed by the owners.

infill panels, many in herringbone fashion, are the original infill. The front elevation of bay I contains a window with ovolo moulded mullions; this is secondary, as a brace had to be removed to accommodate it.

The roof trusses at T1 and T2 have queen struts with princess struts and interrupted collars with clasped purlins. In the first floor room of bay I some painted decoration was noted consisting of ochre coloured shapes with a black border. The floor to this room consists of joists tenoned into an 11in square axial beam with simple chamfers.

DENDROCHRONOLOGY

For dendrochronology abbreviations see page facing Introduction.

Sampling Comments: In all 22 samples have been taken from this building (cores, apart from LON-G16). Samples 1–12 were taken by Robert Howard of the Nottingham University Tree-Ring Dating Laboratory on 9th February 1989. Almost all of these timbers were of elm or had less than 45 rings and could not be dated. However, the sample from the arcade post with 50 rings gave a felling date close to 1203. This engendered considerable interest and D. Miles returned on 16 November 1990 and obtained another 8 samples (from Phase 1, apart from sample 20, a Phase 2 tiebeam which proved to be of elm). These samples gave three precise felling dates in the spring of 1205 (*VA* 23.58). Samples LON-G21–22, of the crown post and collar purlin, were taken for radiocarbon dating on 26 July 2009. Samples LON-G12 and G18 are from the same timber; samples LON-G01–G05 and G20 are from later phases. 'Front' = SE side.

TREE-RING SAMPLE RECORD AND SUMMARY OF DATING

Sample Code	Sample Location	Total Rings	Sapwood Rings	FMR Date	LHR Date	LMR Date	Date Cat
LON-G01	Front rafter of clasped purlin truss T4b	28 NM	12	—	—	—	—
LON-G02	Rear rafter of clasped purlin truss T4b	21 NM	10	—	—	—	—
LON-G03	Ridge beam clasped purlin truss T4b	20 NM	3	—	—	—	—
LON-G04	Yoke clasped purlin truss T4b	25 NM	5	—	—	—	—
LON-G05	Collar clasped purlin truss T4b	10 NM	5	—	—	—	—
LON-G06	Front passing brace truss T4a	23 NM	5	—	—	—	—
LON-G07	Rear passing brace truss T4a	20 NM	—	—	—	—	—
LON-G08	Front rafter truss T4a	10 NM	10	—	—	—	—
LON-G09	Arcade plate bay III rear	43	11	—	—	—	—
LON-G10	Rear cruck blade truss T6	Not oak	—	—	—	—	—
LON-G11	Front cruck blade truss T6	Not oak	—	—	—	—	—
LON-G12	Arcade post truss T3 rear	50	20c	1154	1183	1203	1
LON-G13	Arcade post truss T4a front	78	—	—	—	—	—
LON-G14	Tiebeam truss T4a	40	06	1147	1180	1186	3d
LON-G15	Arcade post truss T4a rear	124	33C	1082	1172	1205	3d
LON-G16	Arcade plate bay III front	39	11	—	—	—	—
LON-G17	Arcade post truss T3 front	90	HS	1082	1171	1171	3d
LON-G18	Arcade post truss T3 rear (as G12)	43	22C	1162	1182	1204	1
LON-G19	Arcade brace bay III rear	154	22C	1052	1183	1205	1
LON-G20	Tiebeam truss T3	Not oak	—	—	—	—	—
LON-G21	Collar purlin beside truss T4a	25 elm	C [radiocarbon dating sample]				
LON-G22	Crown post, truss T4a	10 elm	C (bark)				

Site sequence 1 (composed of samples 14, 15, 17), 124 rings long dated 1082–1205 with *t*-values of 5.0 (E.MID), 4.9 (OXFORD)
Site sequence 2 (composed of samples 12, 18, 19), 154 rings long dated 1052–1205 with *t*-values of 6.2 (OXFORD), 5.1 (S.ENG).
Felling dates: **1205** (sample 15 and probably 19 were felled in the spring of 1205, while 18 has the beginning of the 1205 ring (March felling?).

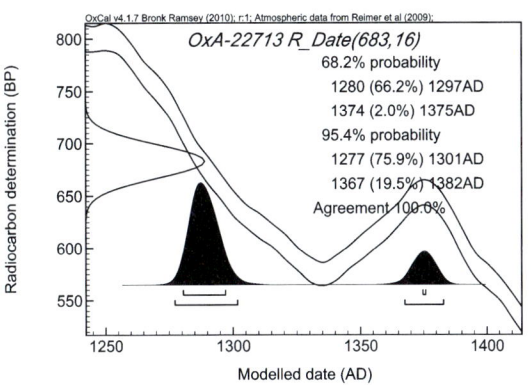

Fig. 8.5.9. Calibration of the radiocarbon date for the first five rings of sample LON-G21.

Radiocarbon dating

A radiocarbon sample comprising the first five rings from core LON-G21 was submitted to RLAHA, Oxford for radiocarbon dating by accelerator mass spectrometry. This gave the calibrated date (Fig. 8.5.9): OXA-22713 *Cal AD 1276–1303* (76%); *1366–1384* (20%) (95.4% probability range). Since the sample was 25 rings long, complete to the bark edge, the corresponding felling date ranges are: *1299–1324* (76%) or *1390–1405* (20%). The simplicity of the carpentry strongly indicates that the first range is much the most likely. This demonstrate that the crown post was not part of the primary 1205 structure. Dating of a second sample, comprising the final five rings from the core was not considered necessary, though it would probably have resolved the date range ambiguity.

DOCUMENTARY HISTORY

Summary

The name of this farm (first documented in the 1891 Census) is probably a metathesised form of Ketchmere (Kyttsmere, 1455), the name of the now filled-in pond at the centre of the village, beside which the house stands (Fig. 8.5.10). The farm was a two-yardland holding, formed by the amalgamation of two single yardlands in 1555, which may previously have been in a single ownership. It was held by copyhold tenure from All Souls College, Oxford, in the hands of the Syms family from the 1550s until 1815, when the land was sold. In 1835, the house was transferred to Thomas Dodwell, and it remained with this family until the twentieth century. The house was one of the larger ones in the village, with three hearths in 1662.

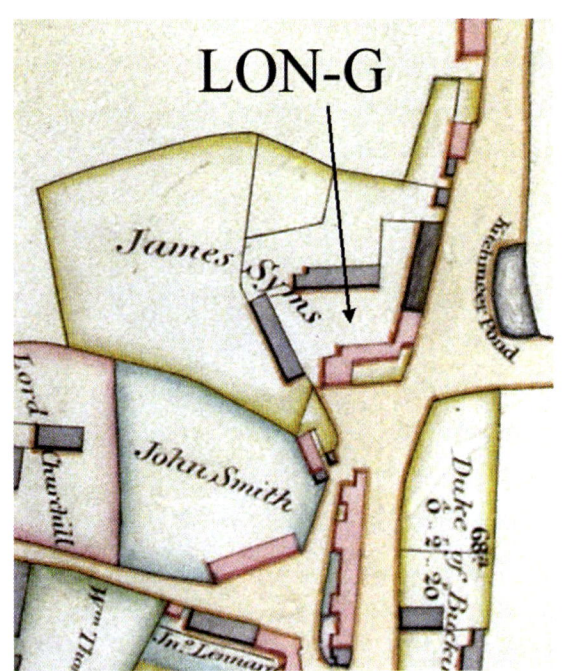

Fig. 8.5.10. Part of the 1827 map of Long Crendon (CBS IR/95/Q).

Court References

The Syms family had a very long tenure of the farm. It first definitely appears in the Long Crendon court rolls in 1553–5, when John Syms was admitted to an All Souls yardland (1553), and to a second messuage and yardland in 1555 on the surrender of Richard Stokes.[3] This was probably one of the two yardlands Stokes had acquired from John Appulford in 1541 and indeed, since Stokes is not mentioned elsewhere in the rolls, the yardland Syms obtained in 1553 may well have been the other Stokes/Appulford yardland. John Appulford had received them in 1531 and 1536, the first by surrender from Thomas Appulford his father, and the second on the latter's death.[4]

---

[3]   The former tenant of the first yardland is not given. It probably had a messuage with it, although this is not stated (information that was often omitted at this period); the admission of Stokes in 1541 makes no mention of messuages, although one of the admissions of John Appulford was to a tenement with a yardland. No other admissions involving John Syms are recorded before his death in the largely complete series of rolls for this period (only 1552, 1556 and 1563 missing between 1520 and 1570). The Syms family is recorded in an isolated court roll reference in 1359, but there are no Syms in the Muster Roll of 1522 or the Subsidy Roll of 1524, so they probably moved to Long Crendon in the 1550s.

[4]   Thomas Appulford's will (proved 25 Jan 1535[/6]; CBS, DAWe: 3 145) names sons John, Richard, Thomas and Henry, but gives no

On John Syms's death in 1564, his son, Thomas, inherited these two houses and two yardlands (subject to the life interest of his mother, Juliana), and they passed in 1615 to William and in 1640 to Henry Syms. When described in 1687, only one messuage accompanied the two yardlands; the second messuage had probably been subsumed into the farm complex. In the seventeenth century, Henry Syms bought 29 acres of freehold arable land and three acres of lot meadow, and most of this then descended with the farm.[5] However, in 1796 James Syms mortgaged both the freehold and copyhold land to Robert Eeles, a Brill maltster;[6] in 1798, James had 5 horses, 1 wagon & 2 carts.[7]

In 1815, the whole estate was put up for auction, and almost all the land bought by Benjamin Eeles, Robert's son. James retained only the house, a close at Writs Hill and 1 acre at Waterside or Naggotts, for which he was allotted 1¾ac at enclosure.[8] On his death in 1832, the property was divided between five of his children.[9] His son, William was admitted in 1834, but Thomas Dodwell (husband of another beneficiary, Mary Syms) bought the property from him (or from the legatees jointly) in 1835. Thomas Dodwell seems to have moved away, and in 1838 sold it to his elder brother, Christopher, in whose family it descended until the twentieth century.[10] By 1851 (and probably considerably earlier), it had again become the centre of a substantial farm, although it was divided into two houses, one of which was occupied by Christopher's son, James Dodwell, the farmer.[11] The final admission was in 1918, of Bertram Harold Dodwell, and it was enfranchised in 1931.[12]

Table 8.5.1. Court references to Sycamore Farm, Long Crendon

Year	Details
1531	John APPLEFORD admitted to messuage & 1 virgate (ASC) late in tenure of Thomas APPLEFORD senior
1536	John APPULFORD admitted to 1 virgate late in tenure Thomas APPLEFORD his father (probably following his death)
1541	Richard STOKES admitted to 2 yardlands (ASC) late in tenure of John APPULFORD
1553	John SYMS admitted to 1 yardland (ASC)
1555	Richard Stokes surrendered messuge & 1 virgate (ASC) to use of John Symmez.
1564	John SYMS died holding 2 messuages & 2 yardlands (ASC), Thomas SYMS eldest son, aged 14; Juliana, widow, claims during her life; admitted. [will CBS, DAWe 15/37].
1615	Thomas SYMS died holding 2 messuages & 2 yardlands (ASC), surrendered to William SYMS, son, admitted.
1640	William SYMS died holding 2 messuages & 2 yardlands (ASC), heir is Henry SYMS, son.
1687	Henry SYMS died holding messuage & 2 yardlands (ASC), surrendered to Henry SYMS, heir.
1706	Henry SYMS died holding messuage & 2 yardlands (ASC), surrendered to Henry SYMS, son, admitted.
1738	Henry SYMS died holding messuage & 2 yardlands (ASC), surrendered to James SYMS, junior, son & heir, admitted. [*Henry's son James, senior, died almost immediately after his father, and this James was Henry's grandson.*]
1785	James SYMS surrendered messuage & 2 yardlands (ASC) to which he was admitted as son of James SYMS senior, to use of his son, James SYMS junior

---

information about his copyholding.

[5] CBS, AR 42/51, P134/1/2a, /7a–b, /4.

[6] CBS, AR 42/51, P134/1/21, /2/3.The mortgage was increased from £400 to £1,100 in 1805. The house with the remaining land was surrendered in 1818, to one Robert Staples of Thame, cooper, probably as a mortgage, since James Syms was still the owner in 1827.

[7] *Posse Comitatus.*

[8] In 1818, he surrendered the property to Robert Staples of Thame, cooper, probably as a mortgage (ASC, C21/64h). This was never entered into the court book, so was probably quickly cancelled.

[9] CBS, DA/Wf 118/56. The 1818 surrender given in the table was probably a further mortgage.

[10] Mary was the eldest daughter of James Syms. The 1835 and 1838 purchase prices are given as £220 and £299, respectively. Bertram Harold Dodwell (1884–1968) still lived at Sycamore Farm in 1959. He was the great-grandson of Christopher (1798–1844), grandson of James (1809–86) and son of John Christopher(1852-1916).

[11] The censuses from 1841 to 1881 record James and Deborah Dodwell as the occupiers of the farm, farming between 140 (1851) and 330 (1881) acres.

[12] TNA, MAF 13/1 (391).

1796	James SYMS, yeoman, holding messuage & 2 yardlands (ASC) to which admitted in 1785 as son of James SYMS: conditional surrendered for £100 to Robert EELES the elder maltster of Brill.
1811	Jas SYMS, strip of land part of messuage & 2 yardlands (ASC) to which admitted in 1785, surrendered for £3 to Chas SPENCER, shepherd.
1815	James SYMS auctioned his copyhold and freehold estate totalling 88a.
1816	James SYMS, 2 yardlands (ASC) to which admitted in1785, descended from James SYMS senior occupied by Jas SYMS, surrendered for £1100 to Ben EELES, maltster of Brill. Except messuage occupied by Jas SYMS, close at *Writs Hill* & 1a at *Waterside* or *Naggotts*, Eeles admitted 1818.
1817	*James SYMS, land (ASC) next to that of James SYMS, by house late Thomas HOWLETT at NW, house late William DRURY at NE, surrendered to Charles SPENCER..*
1827	Enclosure: James SYMS
1834	James SYMS, messuage, passes to William SYMS
1835	William SYMS baker, son of James SYMS (d.1833), messuage divided into 2, surrendered for £220 to Thomas DODWELL baker.
1839	Thomas DODWELL late of LC, baker, 2 messuages formerly 1 (ASC), lately occupied by Sylvanus SHRIMPTON & Thomas DODWELL then James DODWELL & Samuel CAPORN, surrendered for £299 to Christopher DODWELL of LC, yeoman.
c. 1863	Survey of ASC copyholds: Messuage divided into two, with barn and stables. Previously occupied by Sylvanus Shrimpton and Thomas Dodwell, but in 1838 by James Dodwell and Samuel Caporn. [CBS, D/78]
1869	All Souls Copyholds: Messuage now 2 messuages, barn, stables & other bldgs, yard & garden, used by [Sylvanus] SHRIMPTON & Thomas DODWELL, copyholders James SYMS 1795, William SYMS, 1834, Thomas DODWELL 1835.
1888	Joshua & John DODWELL admitted to 2 messuages (ASC) formerly occupied by Sylvanus SHRIMPTON, Thomas DODWELL, lately Jas DODWELL & Sam CAPORN now Deborah DODWELL and ~JORDAN.
1931	Enfranchised (plan): Bertram Harold DODWELL, 2 messuages formerly 1 with barns, stables, other buildings & gardens also adjacent orchard (1a) of Jas DODWELL to which Bertram Harold DODWELL admitted1918–19, occupied by Sylvanus SHRIMPTON & Thomas DODWELL lately Jas DODWELL & Sam CAPORN then Deborah DODWELL and ~ JORDAN.

Building References

In the Hearth Tax listing (*c*. 1662), Henry Symms paid for three hearths.

1910   Valuation: hereditament 238.

Owner: James DODWELL, Crendon Villa, Benjamin Road, High Wycombe, occupier John Christopher DODWELL. Part freehold, part copyhold ASC & W. House of brick & tile, 4 bed, 2 sitting, kitchen, scullery. 4-bay shelter, coach house with loft, old stable of brick & thatch with loft, 3-bay shelter of stone & slate, loose box, barn with dirt floor, piggeries of brick & tile, shed of brick & thatch, stable for 3, loose box, stable for 5 with loft. woodshed of stone & thatch, barn of witchert & thatch with dirt floor, 7-bay cart shed of witchert, stone & tile. 129 acres.[13]

---

[13]   TNA, IR58/2152.

8.6. MDM-A: Mapledurham, Mill Farm, Oxfordshire

Grid reference: SU 6764 7777   *Survey dates*: 1992 and later   *By*: D. Miles

Fig. 8.6.1. View of Mill Farm, Mapledurham, from the east.

ARCHITECTURAL DESCRIPTION

SUMMARY AND HISTORICAL DEVELOPMENT

PHASE 1: Mill Farm stands on an isolated site, facing east (Fig. 8.6.1, 8.6.11). The house is of three bays, although as built it had an additional lean-to half-bay at the south end (partitioned off in 1445/6 and later removed). Samples from trusses T2 and T3, plus the roof structure, have been tree-ring dated to 1335. As well as this early date, the house is of particular interest due to its mainly unaltered state. The original house was fully single-storeyed, the two southernmost bays (bays I and II) being the open hall, bay III (north) the chamber and the removed bay 0 a small service space (not divided from the hall). The chamber was partitioned off from the open hall by truss T3, a closed truss. It is not possible to determine the original door position, but the house now has external doors into bay III just north of T3 and bay I just south of T2. Both these doors were probably in position by the eighteenth century. The drawing of the house in 1587 (Fig. 8.6.11) shows a door towards the southern end of the house, in either bay 0 or bay I.

Three cruck trusses remain. The arch-braced open truss (T2) has a short king post standing on a saddle (type 'F1' apex) and the closed truss (T3) has a saddle apex (type 'C'). Cruck truss T1 is now at the end of the house but was previously internal. It is half-hipped and was originally open below the collar which carried the lean-to rafters of the removed bay 0. The other end truss (T4) is box-framed, with posts and a tiebeam in reversed-assembly, giving a fully hipped end to the house. The end truss of bay 0, beyond T1, was no doubt of the same form as T4, giving an overall fully-hipped profile to the house.

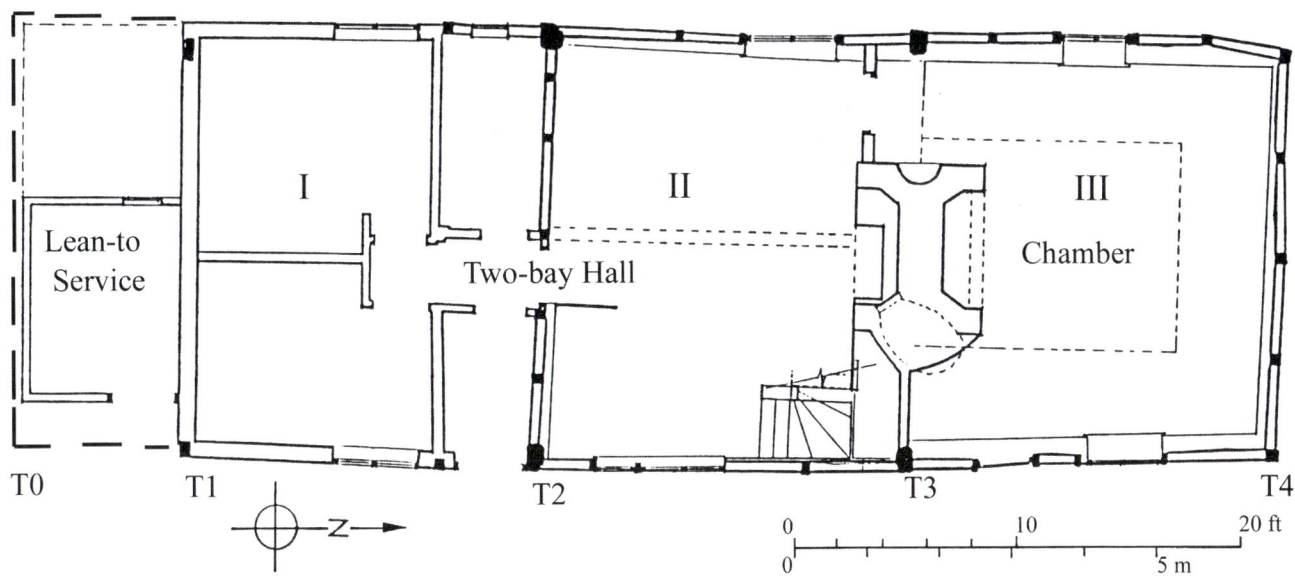

Fig. 8.6.2. Plan, showing truss and bay numbering.

Fig. 8.6.3. View of the roof of Mill Farm during re-thatching in 2004.

Elements of the smoke louvre survive, just south of T2. Soot blackening is present in all areas of the roof, including the chamber end. It is particularly heavy on the upper faces of the purlins adjacent to the smoke louvre, although the ridge at the other end of bay I was almost clean.

An analysis of the use of timber in the house is presented in Chapter 5.

LATER PHASES: In 1446, the tiebeam was inserted in T1, and the lower part of the truss was probably infilled. In the late fifteenth to the early sixteenth century, a chimney stack was inserted just inside the chamber, serving two fireplaces back

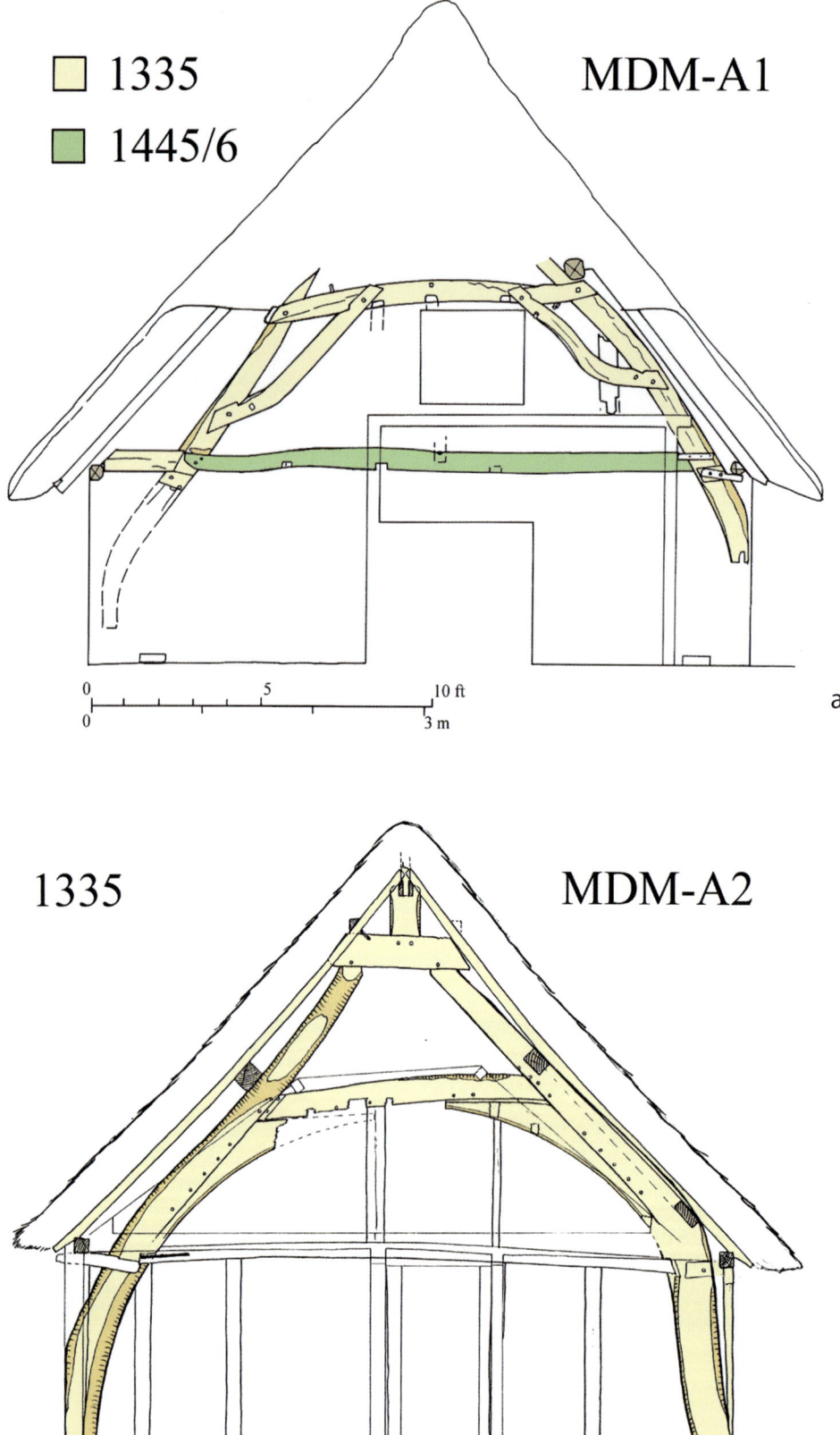

Fig. 8.6.4. Sections of trusses: (a) T1, from south; (b) T2, from south.

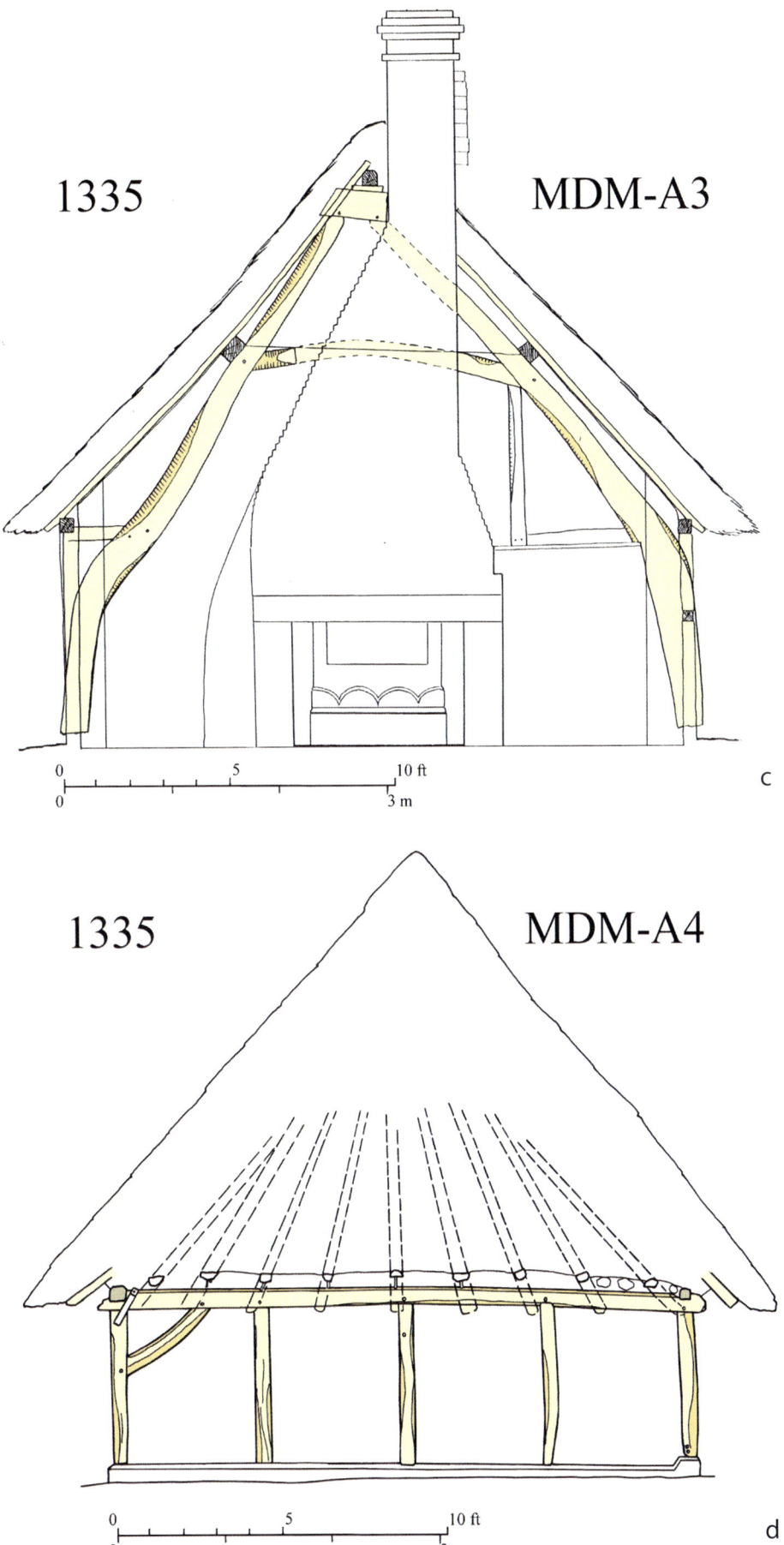

1335   MDM-A3

0   5   10 ft
0   3 m

c

1335   MDM-A4

0   5   10 ft
0   3 m

d

Fig. 8.6.4. Sections of trusses: (c) T3, from north; (d) T4 from north.

to back.[1] Later, probably in the seventeenth century, the northern half of the hall (bay II) was floored over. The chamber was also floored at some stage, as the brick stack contains beam sockets averaging about 5–6in wide. This upper floor would have been very dark and low, essentially only a loft, and by the seventeenth century it had been removed and this bay was plastered up to purlin level. The southernmost bay (I) has always been of one storey, with the smoke-blackened roof rafters only plastered over in the twentieth century. Possibly as late as 1900, the lean-to bay 0 was removed and a brick and tin outhouse constructed on part of its footprint; truss T1 was then covered in weatherboarding. The cottage was re-thatched in 2004, and the opportunity was take to photograph the surviving roof timbers (Fig. 8.6.3 and other detail photographs).

STRUCTURAL FEATURES

PHASE 1: The structure consists of three bays with three cruck trusses, the northernmost truss being boxed framed (Figs. 8.6.4a–d). Each bay measures approximately 15ft 6in long between the trusses, and externally the building is 18ft wide. The southern truss, T1 carries a half hip, whose profile was almost certainly continued by the rafters of the lean-to bay 0. As it exists now, it would be classified as a type 'V' cruck (truncated end truss), but originally it would have been of type 'W' (truncated internal truss). The truss carries a primary collar, strengthened by straight braces, and the crucks terminate above this. The collar is attached with an early type of skew-pegging and the braces use notched halvings (Figs. 8.6.5a–b); the present tiebeam was added in 1446. The whole roof structure at this end is deformed, with this truss particularly affected, as a result of the western corner subsiding by almost two feet. The rafters of the half-hip are now supported by an early twentieth century strut.

Truss T2 is an open truss with the rear blade being of elm and the front one of oak. Both have been dated and are coeval. The blades are 10in deep at the bottom, tapering to 6in at the top. They are joined by a saddle carrying a king-post to support the ridge (type 'F1' apex). The saddle measures 6 by 10–11in, and the king post is 10in wide by 4½in deep, with run-out chamfers on all four arrises. The two arch braces have 1¼in chamfers, and the western brace has been mutilated at some stage. The collar is tenoned into the cruck blades and measures 8in wide by 4in deep. The crucks have cruck studs outside them which are notched into the back of the crucks and rise to meet the short cruck spurs (halved onto the blades).

Truss T3 is a closed truss with a collar and tiebeam, both jointed into the cruck blades with half-lapped joints. Most of this truss is now incorporated into the chimney stack. At the front, it retains a similar cruck stud to that in T2.

The end truss T4 is box-framed with a full hip and is clearly part of the 1335 work. The roof in this bay is smoke blackened although the soot deposits are considerably lighter than in bays I and II. The truss has two 5½ by 6in corner posts and uses reversed assembly, the elm tiebeam resting directly on the corner posts with the wall plates, again of elm, being trenched into the top of the tiebeam. This end wall has the best preserved of any of the original framing (Fig. 8.6.6). The framing comprises three studs, the sill beam and one brace which

Fig. 8.6.5 Joints in truss T1 (a) notched-lap joint (refined entry) between cruck and brace (b) halved joint between collar and cruck.

---

[1]   The date is assigned from the brick sizes. Nathaniel Lloyd (1925) *History of English brickwork*, London, H. G. Montgomery.

Fig. 8.6.6. Framing of the north end of the house.

is slightly ogee in shape and is flush with the external face of the truss. The studs are 5½in wide, the tiebeam 6½in square and the brace is about 4½in square. The panels still retain what may be their original wattle-and-daub infill.

Little can be discovered of the front and rear wall-frames. Although the wall plates exist for the entire length of the house, they are either obscured by plaster, or by the brickwork which replaces most of the external walls in bay I. Bay III has two studs in the rear wall frame which may be original. Immediately above these is a secondary wall plate fixed to the outside face of the rear wall plate. This appears to be a reused rail or tiebeam with rectangular stave holes in the underside; it measures 4½ by 5½in and is unlikely to come from the present structure.

Most of the primary roof structure survives intact (Fig. 8.6.3). The ridge is 5in square in section, with the top inch being chamfered to give a seating to the rafters. It is in three lengths, with face-pegged splayed scarfs immediately to the north of trusses T2 and T3. These joints, combined with a similar scarf in the front wall plate immediately north of T2, indicate that the order of erection was from south to north. The purlins are of substantial section, averaging about 6 by 8in. They are lodged on the backs of the crucks, either on packing pieces or housed into the backs of the blades. A notable exception is that the purlins are butt-jointed (with bare faced soffit tenons) into the eastern blade of T2. Windbraces are still in place on the east side of bay I. They are ogee in shape, measuring 6 × 3in, and have notched lap joints into the top of the purlins (Fig. 8.6.7). The wind braces on the western side of the bay have been removed, as have those in bay III, if they ever existed. The purlins and rafters in bay II are plastered, concealing any windbraces which might exist.

Fig. 8.6.7. The windbrace-purlin lap joint, on the east side of bay I.

Fig. 8.6.8. The louvre: (a) View of the louvre base plate. The fractured tenon of the ridge post can be seen behind the right-most front rafter, and the empty mortice is concealed behind the left-most rafter; (b) View of the ridge, showing the empty mortice of the louvre post.

An interesting roof feature is the pair of mortices in the wall plates to the south of the hip end wall (T4). These received diagonal braces which rose to meet the ends of the purlins which extend into the hip-end bay from T3. Thus, they supported a fully-hipped roof without the need for an intermediate truss, as was used at AST-A (p. 163).

The roof seems to have been almost completely stripped and rethatched in the late medieval period, when many of the original rafters which measured approximately 3–4 by 2–2½in were replaced with much larger ones (about 7 by 2½in). Although the east and west sides of bay III were spared this rebuilding, the north hip and the whole of bays I and II were overhauled, resulting in only about ten original rafters remaining in bay II, and twelve in bay I. A number of smoke blackened thatching laths also remain over bay III. For the fully hipped roof of the northern end, the rafter pair at the top of the hip carries *two* yokes, one clasping the ridge piece, and the other set about 10in below it, on which the hip rafters are fixed. The present hip rafters, most of which are probably late medieval replacements, are hooked over the lower yoke.

Fig. 8.6.9. Reconstruction drawing of the louvre (watercolour by Lynn Courtenay based on a sketch by Nat Alcock).

A particularly intersecting feature is the substantial evidence for the original smoke louvre.[2] The louvre is located immediately to the south of the open truss (T2) and, as in other houses where we have evidence of the louvre position (cf. Pithouse Farm, Mapledurham, MDM-B; Kingsholm, East Hagbourne, DID-B; The Leopard, Bishop's Tachbrook, BIT-A), it was fixed to the rafters, about 18–24in down from the ridge (Figs. 8.6.8a–b). The evidence for its reconstruction is examined in Chapter 5, and Fig. 8.6.9 shows its suggested form.

LATER PHASES: The principal later work comprises the reconstruction of truss T1 in 1446, discussed above, and the insertion in about 1500 of the chimney at T3, which severed the tiebeam and collar, and truncated the saddle (Fig. 8.6.4c). This chimney is built of narrow bricks (9½ by 4½ by 2in), and it serves back-to-back fireplaces in bays II and III. That in

---

2   Although a number of other houses have evidence for the position of the louvre, this is the only building in over a hundred inspected for this project in which a louvre base plate survive, and the only one with evidence for ridge posts.

Fig. 8.6.10. The fireplace in bay III.

bay II is closed in, but in bay III the fireplace has been opened up to reveal a fine scalloped shaped fireback in moulded brickwork (Fig. 8.6.10). The jambs are splayed and the chimney breast is supported on a reused timber beam (inserted in the 1980s). A short section of the original timber mantel beam is visible to the side of the bay II fireplace. The chimney stack has an unusual protruding vertical band of bricks at the position of the dividing wiff (flue partition). To the west of the stack was a semi-circular recess for a copper, and to the east a bread oven, probably early nineteenth century, which collapsed in 1979 and was removed.

Bay II was floored rather late, probably in the seventeenth or eighteenth century, judging from the 7in wide axial beam with 1in chamfer and run-out stops. The joists are of elm, 3 to 4in deep. Perhaps at this stage (possibly earlier) the open truss (T2) was infilled with wattle and daub, both above and below an inserted tiebeam. Above the collar, only the side facing bay II was finished, with the space above the wall plates in bay I sealed off.

Most of the panels in the longitudinal walls were replaced in brick in the eighteenth and nineteenth centuries save for one rear panel immediately to the south of T3 which retained its wattle and daub until 1984. The walls of bay I were reconstructed in 9in brickwork in the early twentieth century.

DENDROCHRONOLOGY

For dendrochronology abbreviations see page facing Introduction.

Sampling Comments: Seven samples were taken by D Miles in March 1990, all as cores from timbers considered to be original. One sample was of elm and the others had fairly short, wide ring sequences. Despite the unpromising nature of the samples, these were processed in the usual manner at the Ancient Monuments Laboratory of English Heritage and all the samples were matched together visually, with the elm sample matching the others particularly well. This site master was then cross-matched against other local and national reference curves and a single strong date was found at 1335. The shortness of the individual samples combined with the resultant low *t*-values for matches with each other here illustrates the importance of visual cross-matching as an adjunct to matching by computer. Since this building has been dated in a different laboratory by somewhat different methods to the main project sites, no confidence level is given, but the quality of the match corresponds approximately to category 2. Sample MDM5.01 is of elm and it was not possible to distinguish heartwood from sapwood on seasoned timber, therefore no value is given for Sapwood Rings or LHR Date. This sample matched very well with the other samples and was included in the site master. Sample MDM5.08 was taken in Summer 2010 from the inserted tiebeam in truss T1.

TREE-RING SAMPLE RECORD AND SUMMARY OF DATING

Sample Code	Sample Location	Total Rings	Sapwood Rings	FMR Date	LHR Date	LMR Date
MDM5.01	Rear cruck blade T2 (Elm)	43	C	1292	—	1334
MDM5.02	Collar T2	24	9	1310	1324	1333
MDM5.03	Front cruck blade T2	33	0	1284	1316	1316
MDM5.04	Rear cruck blade T3	51	14¼C	1284	1320	1334
MDM5.05	Collar T3	40	15¼C	1293	1319	1334
MDM5.06	Front (East) purlin bay III	30	10	1304	1323	1333
MDM5.07	Rear (West) purlin bay III	34	2	1291	1322	1324
MDM5.08	Inserted tiebeam T1	83	17C	1363	1428	1445

Site sequence MDM5: (composed of samples 01–07), 51 rings long dated to 1284–1334 with t-values of 7.08 (Oxford Mean), 6.27 (Lewknor), 6.26 (Zacharias*), 5.83 (Queen's Head*), 5.1 (Reading). (masters included in Oxford Mean marked with *.) Sample MDM5.08 83 dated to 1363–1445 with t-values of 7.17 (HALL); 5.53 (KLYNN_SG); 5.42 (SHALFORD).

Felling dates: **1335** (samples with last measured rings complete to bark: MDM5.01 October 1334–March 1335; MDM5.04 about March 1335; MDM5.05 between April–May 1335); **Winter 1445/6** (sample MDO5.08 with last measured ring complete).

DOCUMENTARY HISTORY

The documentary history has not been extensively investigated, although the Mapledurham archives undoubtedly contain much information about the house. It is clearly shown on the Blagrave map of the Mapledurham estate in 1587, in a bird's-eye view from the west, when it was in the tenure of Richard Page (Fig. 8.6.11).

Fig. 8.6.11. View of Mill Farm on the Blagrave map of 1587 (at Mapledurham House).

8.7. RAD-B: Radley, Baker's Close, 104 Lower Radley, Oxfordshire

Grid reference: SU 5328 9874   *Survey date*: 14 Dec. 1989   *By*: D. Miles

Fig. 8.7.1. View of Baker's Close, Lower Radley from the east.

ARCHITECTURAL DESCRIPTION

SUMMARY AND HISTORICAL DEVELOPMENT

PHASE 0: The cruck blade from the north truss (T1), which was reused and extended in the existing structure, gave a felling date range of 1256–1288, making it one of the earliest crucks found in the country.

PHASE 1: The existing house at Baker's Close, Lower Radley is a three-bay cruck-framed house orientated north/south with its gable end to the street. The southern bay (III) is the chamber (possibly floored), and the other two bays make up the open hall (Fig. 8.7.2). Truss T1 is heavily weathered on the north face, indicating that the original structure never continued beyond it. Smoke-blackening is visible on the original roof timbers in all three bays, heaviest in bays I and II. Bay III appears to have been partitioned off originally, although the roof timbers are somewhat sooted. The three surviving cruck trusses have saddle apexes (type 'C'). A tree-ring date of 1513/14 has been obtained from the tiebeam of T1 (the same truss whose west blade dated to 1256–1288).

PHASE 2: BAY IV: Probably in the late sixteenth century bay III was substantially reconstructed, extending it about 8 feet southwards and partitioning it off into two bays, the present bays III and IV. The inserted floor is slightly sooted adjacent to bay II, suggesting that the hall open fire was still in use at this stage.

LATER PHASES: In the first half of the seventeenth century, judging from the size and style of the joists, bay II was floored over. Probably at this time the chimney stack just north of T2 was inserted. It was not possible to inspect the underside of the inserted floor in bay I but it is likely to have been floored over at about the same time. In the 1950s,

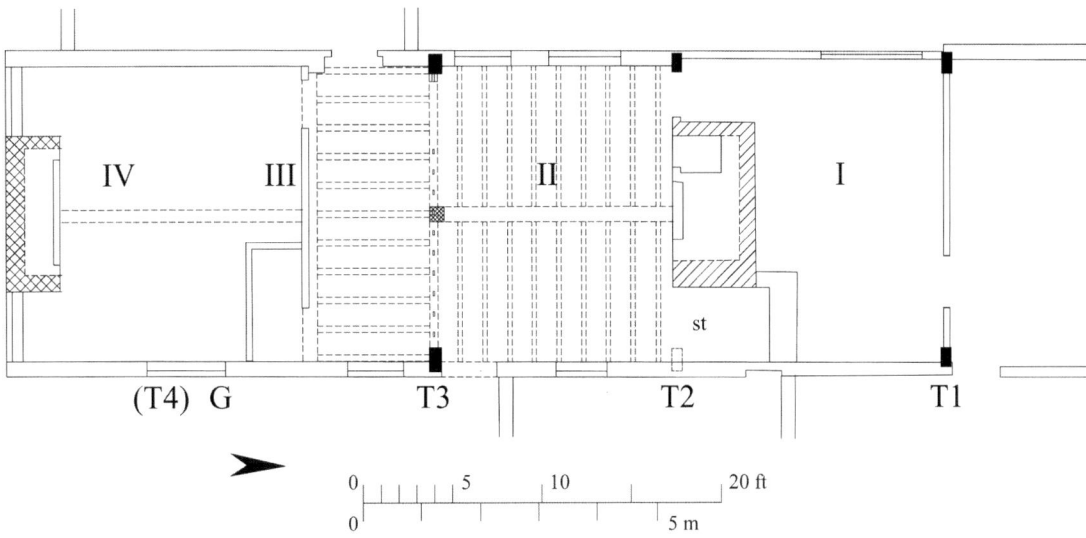

Fig. 8.7.2. Plan, showing truss and bay numbering. The position of T4 (removed in Phase 2) is approximate.

the house was very substantially enlarged with large brick extensions to the north, east, and west. In March 2011, it was seriously damaged by fire.[1]

STRUCTURAL FEATURES

PHASE 1: The crucks are visible on the ground floor apart from the eastern blade of T2 which has been severed at first floor level adjacent to the staircase. Upstairs, most of the cruck frames and purlins have been plastered over, and are only visible in the roof space. All three cruck trusses have the blades joined by saddles which supports the ridge piece (type 'C' apexes). Both T1 (an external truss) and T3 have tenoned collars and tiebeams with skew-pegged bare-faced dovetail joints to the cruck blades. In T1 and possibly T3, the wallplate was supported on the extended ends of the ties.

The western cruck blade in T1 (Fig. 8.7.3) differs from the others, being very accurately cut and finished, with a sharp crisp crank rather than the more gentle curved elbow used elsewhere. Dendrochronology has shown that this cruck blade was reused, and that it dates to the later part of the 13th century. The top of this blade was extended, presumably when reused, to reach the roof apex. A splayed scarf with undersquinted abutments was used for the junction and the extension piece has a tongue with two pegs set into the main part of the cruck. The collar to this truss has unused pegholes, so is probably also reused, perhaps from another cruck blade, but in its present position is part of the 1513/14 truss; it was sampled but had too few rings to give a date. The sill beam and the studs below the tiebeam are presumably part of the original infill, although they could be later replacements.

Truss T2 has a collar but the tiebeam is not visible. There were no peg holes for arch braces, but it has a mortice for a cruck spur on the west side of the cruck blade. This truss appears to have been open, as it has thick soot encrustation on the underside of the cruck blades and saddle. However, the infill daub is unsooted as are the nailed-on staves. A notch on the underside of the saddle to receive a central stave is unsooted and therefore secondary. The staves appear to follow the line of the crucks much more closely than in T3, confirming that they are of a different period. Soot deposits of almost ½in thickness were noted on the upper surface of the ridge beam in bay II, about 4 feet to the south of T2.

The T3 tiebeam has a series of stave mortices, 3 by 1in, with rounded ends. These run in an unbroken sequence at 13½in centres, from the east cruck to about four feet from the west cruck where they are interrupted by what appears to be a doorway; a mortice for a door post is visible next to the cruck blade. The tiebeam measures 7 by 5½in, with soot encrustation up to ⅛in thick on the soffit. Some of the wattle and daub infill in T3 is clearly original, as the northern side also has soot encrusted to the same thickness. The positions of two staves either side of the centre of the truss are indicated by two nails, but the next staves have been pegged to the inside face of the crucks, an unusual feature. The pegs are ½in diameter and are clearly primary as both they, the staves, and the underside of the cruck blades are sooted. Such soot deposits (passing through the truss) do not necessarily prove that the infill is later than the truss. Three Chimneys,

---

[1]   Oxfordshire Buildings Group, Report 131 was compiled after the 2011 fire, and key information from this has been incorporated here.

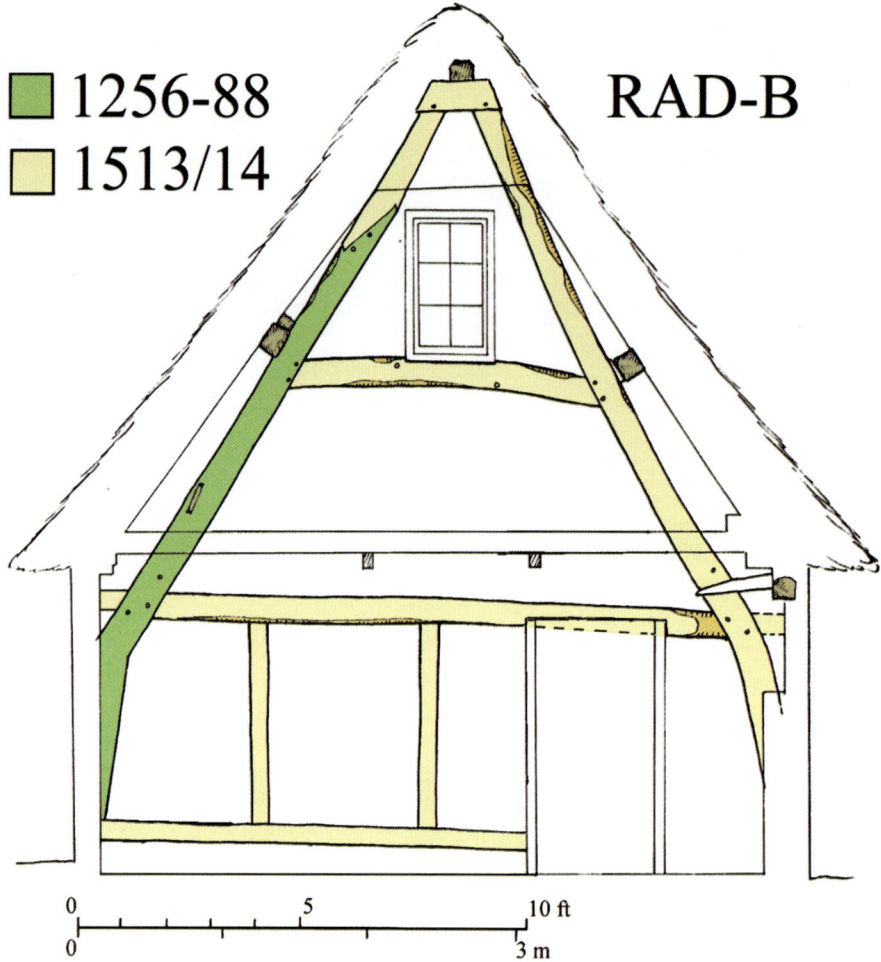

Fig. 8.7.3. Section of truss T1, viewed from south (as recorded in 1989).

Mapledurham (MDM-C) showed a similar soot pattern, but the infill stave (which was presumed to be later) proved to be of precisely the same date as the cruck. What has obviously happened in these cases is that the daub panels shrank and smoke leaked through it, thus depositing soot within the gap.

The original roof ends at a pair of gablet rafters (G on Fig. 8.7.2). These are joined at the top with a 3in thick yoke, which supported the ridge piece (terminating at this point). It had a single common rafter pegged in the centre of its south face and, to either side and a few inches below this, are peg holes for hip rafters. The building would therefore originally have extended some feet further south to the removed truss T4; this would most likely have had crucks rising only to collar level (type 'V'). These crucks and the rafters to the south of the gablet were removed during the sixteenth-century rebuilding of bay III. On the east side, the wall plate is scarfed to the southern extension with a splayed scarf finishing about 3ft 6in to the south of T4. This confirms the position of the missing end truss.

Only two assembly marks could be found; the north face of the T3 cruck blade carries a scratch mark /// tag and a similar mark, but with four strokes, was found on the north face of the cruck blade of T2. It seems likely that the assembly marks did not run in sequence, as has been observed elsewhere, even for trusses. The crucks have all been heart-sawn (halved) with the other faces adze-dressed. The collars and purlins are similarly heart-sawn, and the ridge piece appears to be sawn boxed heart. The rafters, with the exception of the large reused members, were riven, either into halves or quarters, with the other faces adzed. The cruck blades, ties, collars and saddles are of oak, but the rafters, ridge, and some of the purlins are of elm.

The purlins measure 5½ by 7½in and are trenched onto the backs of the cruck blades although in at least one place the purlin is held away from the back of the blade by a block. Windbraces were either morticed into the cruck blades or pegged onto the backs of the blades and were trenched into the back of the purlins. These purlins trenches are found on either side of T2 but apparently not beside T3. On the north side of (G), the trenches are inset 1ft on the east and 2ft on the west side; this suggests that the missing hip was very steep. The ridge is 6in square with 2in chamfers on its top edges. It is made up of two pieces, one being over 25 feet long, scarfed just north of T2 with a simple side-halved joint. The purlins have been scarfed to the south of T2 with vertically splayed scarfs with 2in square abutments. On the west side the wall plate is scarfed to the north of T3, with a side-halved joint similar to that in the ridge. The rafters measure 2–3 by 3–5in, although some reused rafters in bay III (and one in bay II) measure 4 by 6–7in. They are individually pegged to the ridge, alternating in position, and all are soot encrusted. No evidence could be found for a louvre position despite all the rafters being *in situ* in bays II and III. Peg holes further down on the large reused rafters probably relate to an earlier purlin fixing. The most probably position for the louvre is therefore in bay 1 at the present chimney position, where the rafters have been removed for the chimney, apart from the pair nearest to T2. One of these has a peg hole 3–4in below the ridge which might relate to a louvre plate but is more likely to be the fixing for the rafter to the ridge, exposed through the rafter slipping down.

PHASE 2: BAY IV: The reconstruction of bay III was radical, extending the building southwards by about eight feet. A floor was inserted, supported by a transverse beam (9 by 8in) set about 7ft south of T3, the joists tenoned into the north side of the beam (diminished-shoulder tenons) and lodged on top of the T3 tiebeam. The joists measure 4–4½ by 4in and have ½in chamfers with stops formed by saw cuts; finished with a run-out or bevelled stop; the transverse beam has a 1½in chamfer. To the south of this transverse beam, an axial beam 8in wide runs the length of bay IV. The joists either side of it are plastered over. The difference in character between the joists on each side of the transverse beam, and the position of this beam (close to the original end of the house) suggests that the north side joists may be those of the phase I floor, reset when bay IV was extended. In the roof, the purlins have been extended. The ridge has also been extended to the south gable, joined at the yoke at (G). None of the rafters in bay IV show any smoke blackening.

LATER PHASES: The inserted floor to bay II has an axial beam (9in square) lodged over the fireplace lintel, and halved under the T3 tiebeam, where it is supported by a brick pier. This beam has a heavy chamfer with a scroll stop at each end. Joists (3 by 4in) are jointed into the main beam with diminished-haunch tenons. Each joist has a small ¼-½in chamfer with simple scroll stop and the joists are set at 16¾in centres. The floor in bay II is about 5 in lower then in bays III and IV. A staircase stands just inside bay IV on the east side of the axial beam. This has a short run of eighteenth-century turned balusters, of either elm or chestnut.

DENDROCHRONOLOGY

For dendrochronology abbreviations see page facing Introduction.

Sampling Comments: Eight samples were obtained through coring by Robert Howard on 14 December 1989. Of these one had only 39 rings and the another had even fewer and was not measured. None of the samples matched each other but two of the samples were dated individually.

TREE-RING SAMPLE RECORD AND SUMMARY OF DATING

Sample Code	Total Sample Location	Sapwood Rings	FMR Rings	LHR Date	LMR Date	Date Date	Cat
RAD-B01	W cruck blade truss T3	39 NM	15	—	—	—	—
RAD-B02	E cruck blade truss T3	62	07	—	—	—	—
RAD-B03	W cruck blade truss T2	92	08	—	—	—	—
RAD-B04	E cruck blade truss T2	58	—	—	—	—	—
RAD-B05	E cruck blade truss T1	53	17	—	—	—	—
RAD-B06	W cruck blade truss T1	77	04	1175	1247	1251	1
RAD-B07	Tie beam truss T1	88	25C	1426	1488	1513	3a
RAD-B08	Collar truss T1	22 NM	08	—	—	—	—

Site sequences: (sample 6 only), dated 1175–1251 with *t*-values of 6.4(OXFORD), 5.9(S.ENG). (sample 7 only), dated 1426–1513 with *t*-values of 5.6(S.ENG), 4.7(MOU-A, the site sequence of Pye Corner, Moulsford, VA22.45)

95% felling date range: (sample 6), **1256–1288** (revised from 1262–1297, VA22.46, due to new sapwood estimates). Felling date: Sample 7 with complete sapwood: **1513/14.**

8.8. ROT-D: 91 Rothley, Town Green Street, Leicestershire

Grid reference: SK 5811 1232   *Survey date*: 14 June 1989   *By*: D. Miles

Fig. 8.8.1. View of 91 Town Green Street, Rothley from the south-west.

ARCHITECTURAL DESCRIPTION

SUMMARY AND HISTORICAL DEVELOPMENT[1]

PHASE 1: No. 91 Town Green Street Rothley is a three-bay cruck house of one main constructional phase. In the original house, bay III was probably the chamber, and the middle bay (II) served as the hall, partially divided from the service area in the east bay (I). Further study of the soot distribution is needed to confirm this interpretation. However, it appears that the hall and service bays were open to the roof, whilst the chamber end may have been floored originally; its floor is carried on a heavy transverse beam rather than the axial beams of bays I and II. Two cruck trusses (T2 and T3) are complete to the apex, one carrying a king post with braces on the collar (apex type 'F3') and the other having a saddle apex (type 'C'). Both the other cruck trusses survive but are incomplete. A tree-ring felling date range of *1492–9* has been obtained.

---

[1]   The house has previously been described in Webster, V. R. (1954) 'Cruck-framed buildings of Leicestershire', *Leicestershire Archaeol Hist Soc Trans*, **30,** 26–58, p. 40.

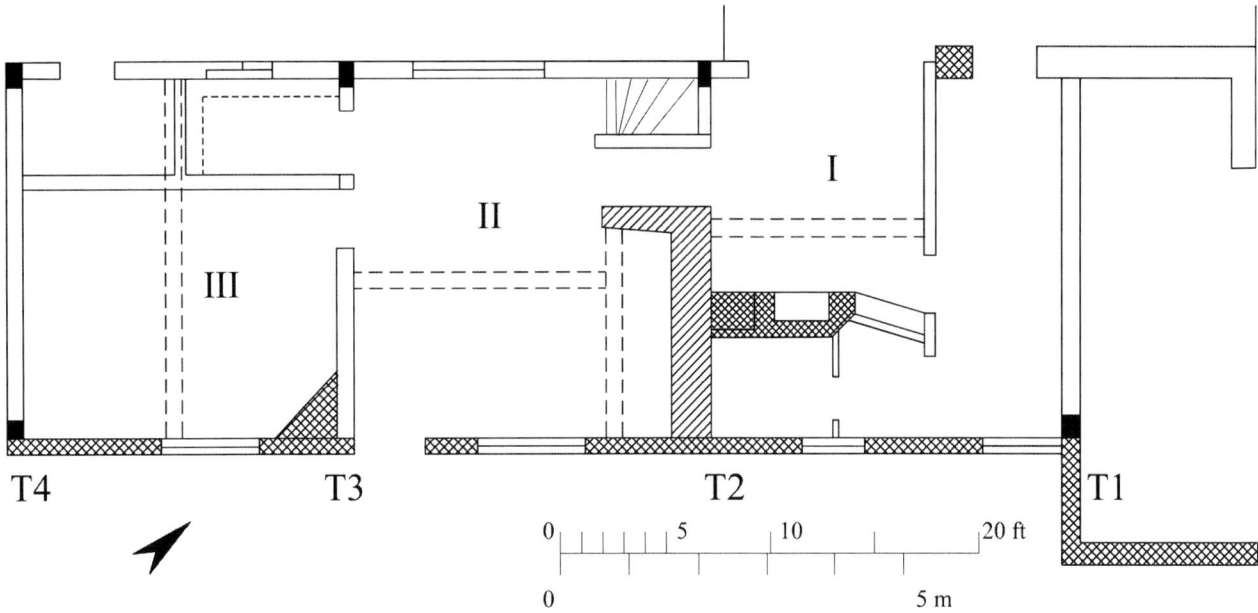

Fig. 8.8.2. Plan (prior to 1980s alterations) showing truss and bay numbering.

LATER PHASES: In the seventeenth/eighteenth century, the hall and service bays were floored over with axial beams and joists, over which a lime-ash floor was constructed. A ceiling was inserted upstairs and the inside of the rafters lined with plaster supported on reeds. In the nineteenth century, the front wall was rebuilt in brick, the level of the eaves raised, and the front wall plate and purlin removed. A dairy with thralls and a coal-hole were cut off from the inner room.

STRUCTURAL FEATURES

PHASE 1: Truss T3 is the best preserved of the internal trusses. The cruck blades are joined by a long saddle with a superstructure comprising a king post and two curving braces carrying a square set ridge piece (removed) (type 'F3' apex). The collar has been cut through by an inserted doorway. Evidence for the tiebeam is hidden behind plaster, but two pegholes by the side of the door to the dairy indicate its probable position. The truss is been infilled with studs or staves with reed lath fixed to the south-west side and plastered. It was not possible to inspect the underside of the saddle or collar to check for the existence of stave holes.

The purlins are trenched into the back of the cruck blades, and no evidence was visible for windbraces. The front purlin has been removed. The wall plates are carried on cruck spurs which are fixed to the south-west side of the truss with bare-faced dovetail halvings. The outer end of the rear spur was originally supported by a cruck stud, as indicated by an empty mortice just visible under the wall plate; this shows clearly that the outer walls were originally timber-framed. On truss T2, the apex is missing, but it has both a collar and a tiebeam, the latter extending to support the wallplates. The pegs to the joints in this truss are strongly skewed, each being driven in at 45 degrees to the surface of the truss. Relatively little of truss T4 is visible. Its cruck blades are longer and carry a saddle which supported the ridge directly. It has a collar and cruck spurs, set about five feet below the collar. Of truss T1, only the front foot of the cruck remains.

Assembly marks on truss T2 comprise two strokes, with a tag on the front side of the truss. The marks are scribed across the half-dovetail joint with the collar, and below the joint with the tie. A plumb-and-level mark is also visible on the blade between the tiebeam and collar.It is likely that the trusses were numbered sequentially, with T1 being I and T4 being IIII. All the timbers were converted from whole trees, boxed heart, and were shaped with an axe. The trees were relatively fast growing and were under 100 years old when felled.

The transverse ceiling beam in bay III (Fig. 8.8.4) is notable for having one extremely waney end (south), although the north end is neatly squared and chamfered with run-out stops; it is probably of elm. The joists are light, with small chamfers and run-out stops. It is clear that this bay was floored before the others, but the presence of a mortice on the underside of the south end of the beam suggests that it may have been an early insertion rather than a primary feature.

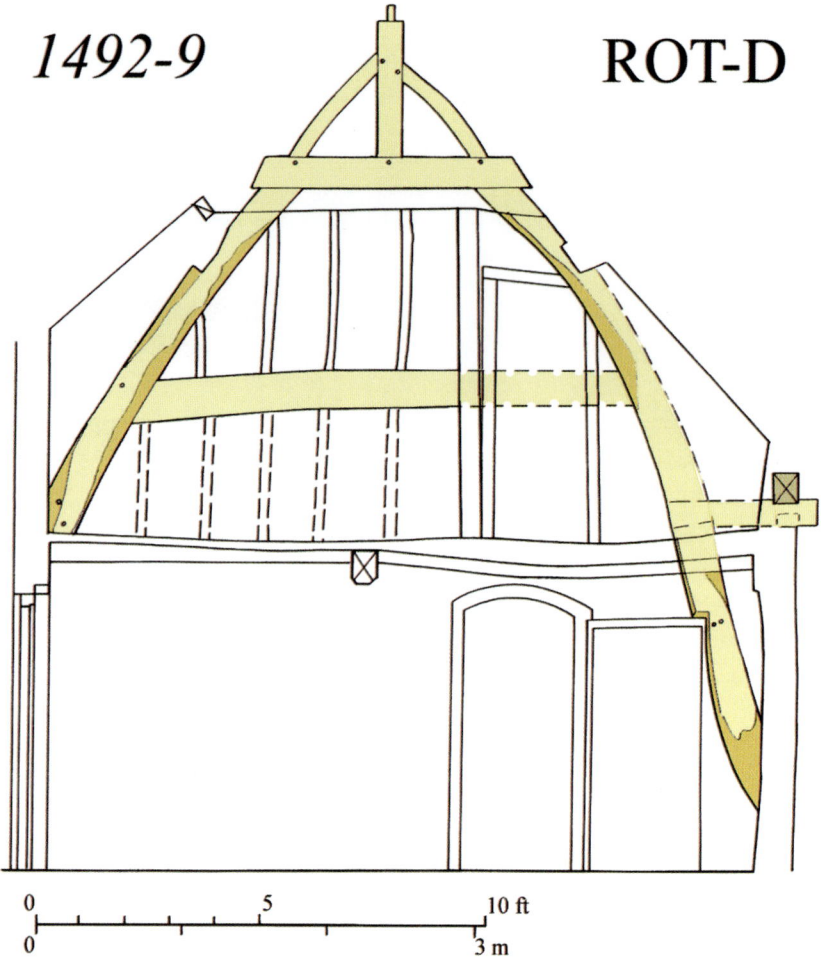

1492-9   **ROT-D**

0   5   10 ft

0   3 m

Fig. 8.8.3. Section of truss T3.

Fig. 8.8.4. The ceiling beam in bay III, showing the transition from the regular chamfered part to the waney end.

DENDROCHRONOLOGY

For dendrochronology abbreviations and master sequence references, see page facing Introduction.

Sampling Comments: Eight samples were obtained through coring by Robert Howard on 14 June 1989. Six cruck blades, as well as the collar of T3 and the tie of T2 were cored. The two cruck blades from T2 matched together and were combined to form a sequence of 80 rings. A sample from the rear cruck of T4 gave a last measured ring date of 1484.

TREE-RING SAMPLE RECORD AND SUMMARY OF DATING

Sample Code	Sample Location	Total Rings	Sapwood Rings	FMR Date	LHR Date	LMR Date	Date Cat
ROT-D01	Rear cruck blade truss T2	80	27	1412	1464	1491	—
ROT-D02	Front cruck blade truss T2	62	22	1430	1469	1491	—
ROT-D03	Rear cruck truss T3	45	04	—	—	—	—
ROT-D04	Front cruck truss T3	NM	—	—	—	—	—
ROT-D05	Rear cruck blade truss T4	58	08	1427	1476	1484	3a
ROT-D06	Rear cruck spur truss T3	NM	—	—	—	—	—
ROT-D07	Collar truss T3	80	28	—	—	—	—
ROT-D08	Tiebeam truss T2	32 NM	3	—	—	—	—

Sample 5 matched at 1427–1484 with *t*-values 5.0(E.MID), 2.6(OXFORD), 4.8(HAG-C1), 4.7(LEI-C1), 3.9(CADASQ01), 3.6(CASBSQ03). A weaker fit for a site sequence composed of samples 1, 2, 80 rings long at 1412–1491 is consistent with this date and has been confirmed by later analysis.

Estimated 95% felling date reange: 1492–1511 (previously 1492–1508). OxCal refined felling date range *1492–9*.

8.9. STC-B: Steeple Claydon, Rhenold's Close, 28 North End Road, Buckinghamshire

Grid reference: SP 6992 2738 *Survey date*: 1990 *By*: D. Miles and C. Murray

Fig. 8.9.1. View of Rhenold's Close from the south-east.

ARCHITECTURAL DESCRIPTION

SUMMARY AND HISTORICAL DEVELOPMENT

PHASE 1: Rhenold's Close is an unusually small thatched house, originally of only two full bays. It lies parallel to the street, on the south-east side. Bays II and III of the present house formed a two-bayed open hall, probably functionally divided at ground-floor level. It is possible that the south-west end continued as a lean-to half bay, as at Mill Farm Mapledurham (MDM-A), although no structural evidence for this has been found. The central open truss has a saddle apex (type 'C'), and both end trusses were half hipped (type 'V' apexes). Both bays are smoke blackened, indicating that the centre truss (T2) was open at least above the tiebeam, although it has a tiebeam as well as a collar. Most of the original roof structure survives above purlin level. The house has no evidence of any original flooring. The original structure has been dated through dendrochronology to **1431–6**.

PHASE 2: In the seventeenth century, truss T3 was removed and an in-line extension was added to the south-west end, of two-storeys plus attic. A large rubble-stone chimney stack was built in the position of T3 and a lobby entry formed. This bay evidently served as a parlour. At the same date or possibly later in the seventeenth century, the medieval hall was partitioned and floored over. A partition was built within the central cruck truss (T2) with two doorways, and bay II was partitioned along the axial beam. The house contains much original detailing from this period (although some features may be antiquarian restorations).

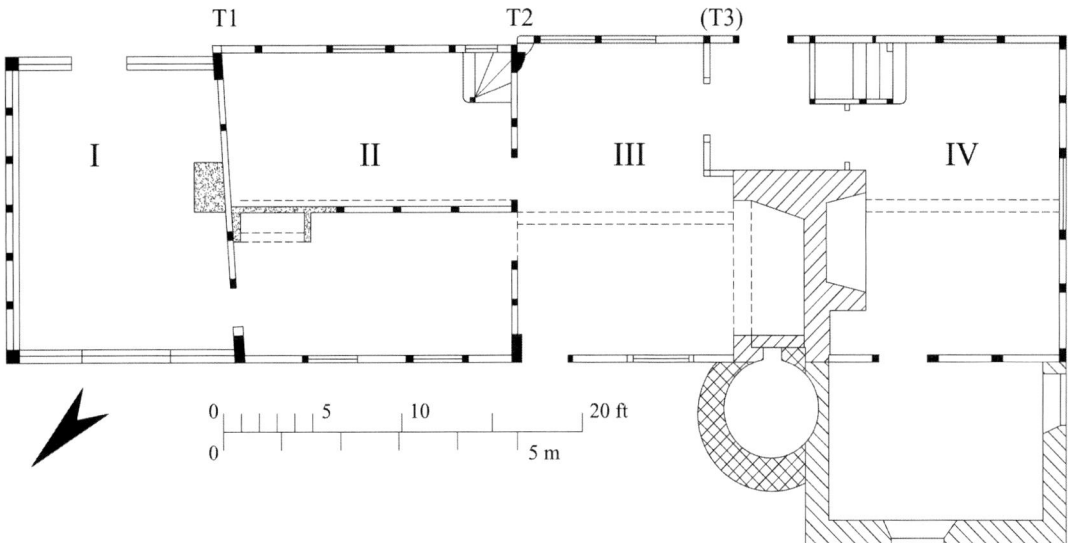

Fig. 8.9.2. Plan, showing truss and bay numbering.

LATER PHASES: In the eighteenth century, a rubble-stone lean-to extension was built to the NW of bay IV. Later in the same century an oven projection was added to the stack, blocking an opening in the lean-to. During the nineteenth/early twentieth century a chimney stack was inserted in bay II and bay I was added, using much second-hand timber.

STRUCTURAL FEATURES

PHASE 1: Truss T1 is a cruck truss with collar and tiebeam. Other timbers visible at ground floor level appear to be comparatively modern or reused. The cruck blades terminate just above collar level for the half-hipped roof (type 'V' apex). The north-east face of this truss is heavily weathered, indicating that it was certainly the end of the house. At the apex of truss T2, the blades support a saddle for the ridge (type 'C' apex). The north-west blade is extended, with a joint above the collar. This appears to be an early repair for although it is smoke blackened it is not chamfered, as are the blade below the joint and the saddle which it partly obscures. A raising notch was noted near collar level on the south-west face of the opposite blade. Both cruck trusses have their horizontal timbers halved and pegged onto the north-east face. None of the infill timbers below the tiebeam of T2 appear to be primary. A removed lean-to half-bay at the south-west end is possible, but had this existed, T3 would be expected to have been gabled rather than half-hipped.

All the roofs are thatched. The medieval bays retain the original purlins resting on the backs of the cruck blades. The ridge is supported on the saddle of T2 and on yokes at each end; the north-east yoke is set on the second couple in from T1, and the south-west one is similarly placed in relation to the start of bay IV, indicating that the original end truss stood exactly at the junction between bays III and IV. The ridge and the purlins are scarfed on the north-east side of T2. Original rafters survive above purlin level but have been cut off below this (except for two rafters in Bay II). The rafters are substantial in scantling, with flat soffits and roughly shaped upper surfaces supporting the thatch. Large single wooden pegs attaching the rafters to the purlins can be seen in the dormer window bays. The windbraces are long and curved, and mortices and peg holes in the purlins show the position of the removed windbraces at the south-west end of the building.

PHASE 2: The seventeenth-century roof to bay IV has double trenched purlins with long diagonal windbraces and original rafters. The wall-framing of the medieval bays was reconstructed, independent of the cruck trusses; the garden front (south-east) shows a building break at T2, perhaps the result of a misfit between the irregular original plan and the new frame. Bay IV has rectangular wall panels with long diagonal braces to the tiebeam and wall plates. The wall between bay IV and the north-west lean-to has an exposed rail with stave holes indicating that it had originally had lath and plaster infill. Much infill was replaced in the eighteenth/nineteenth century with brick. One panel above the door on the north-west side has seventeenth century herringbone brick infill.

The seventeenth-century main chimney stack is built of coursed rubble stone with roughly squared, coarsely-tooled

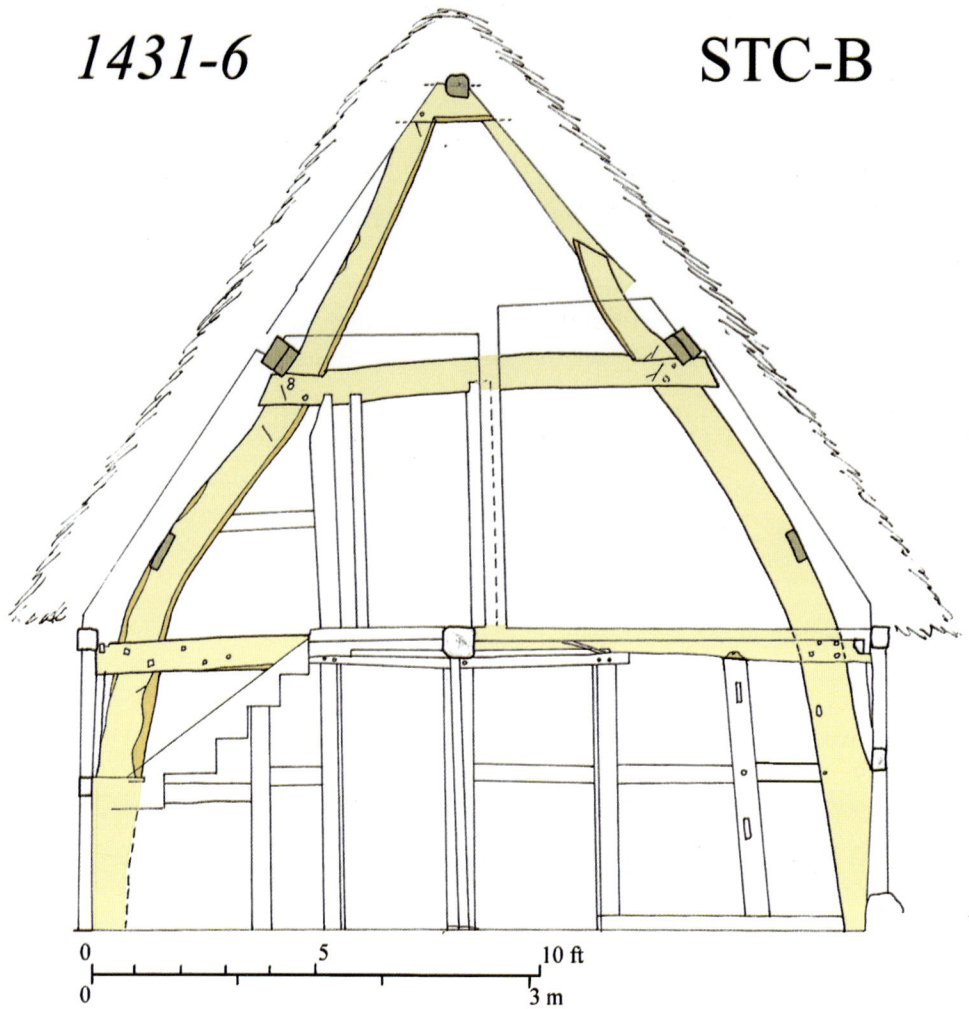

1431-6   **STC-B**

Fig. 8.9.3. Section of truss T2, from the south-west.

blocks, and is capped by a brick chimney retaining some narrow seventeenth-century brick at its base. The ground-floor fireplace in Bay III has a roughly chamfered timber lintel, a salt niche and a later opening to a domed brick oven that projects on the outside of the building. On the floor above, the stack has been altered and has a shallow plastered projection. This contains a length of reused timber, possibly a lintel for a now-blocked fireplace, but it is most unlikely to have been an original seventeenth-century feature. In bay IV, both ground and first floors have fireplaces whose very slightly arched timber lintels have narrow run-out chamfers. The first floor lintel rests on brick jambs that appear to be an addition to the main stack. This suggests that both fireplaces could be late seventeenth/eighteenth century rather than earlier. The brick firebacks have been rebuilt. The side of the stack facing the lobby entry has a long shallow niche with a timber lintel.

Bay IV has an original seventeenth-century ceiling with axial spine beam and joists. These have narrow chamfers with ogee stops. The upper room has a similar spine beam but the joists are concealed. Both this room, the attic, and the upper rooms in bays II and III, have floors of old wide boards. The lobby has plain joists, one chamfered in part. The position of this chamfer and the adjacent trimmer suggests the site of a former staircase in the corner between the chimney and the entrance to the centre bay. Bay III has a narrow spine beam with narrow chamfer and run-out stops on square-cut joists. These could well be of late seventeenth- or even early eighteenth-century date. Bay II has a very irregular ceiling with bent joists and two trimmers exposed in the north half. The ceiling in the south half is concealed. Bay IV has a framed winder staircase from ground floor to attic, with chamfered newel post and many seventeenth/eighteenth century treads. The winder stair in Bay II is probably eighteenth century.

The house contains a number of plank doors with nailed battens and hook-over strap hinges, apparently late seventeenth/eighteenth century in date, but in suspiciously good condition. The doorway to the first floor of bay IV has a chamfered frame with ogee stops. The doorways between bays II and III on the ground floor have run-out chamfers. The windows are generally eighteenth-century or later imitations. All have leaded glazing with either rectangular or diamond type panes, some with old glass. The opening lights have iron frames, some with good eighteenth-century catches and restrainers (e.g. bay II ground and first floor windows on the north-west side). The window mullions are mostly chamfered but Bay IV and the lean-to also have mullions with narrow ovolo mouldings. There are three oriel windows, each of three lights with curved wooden sills and lintels Although those in bay III and bay II might be eighteenth century, that in the lean-to is certainly modern, and it is likely that all these windows are twentieth-century insertions.

DENDROCHRONOLOGY

For dendrochronology abbreviations see page facing Introduction.

Sampling Comments: Eight samples were obtained through coring by Robert Howard on 10 March 1989. Four of these matched together to form a 74 year sequence which dated with a last measured ring of 1430.

TREE-RING SAMPLE RECORD AND SUMMARY OF DATING

Sample Code	Sample Location	Total Rings	Sapwood Rings	FMR Date	LHR Date	LMR Date	Date Cat
STC-B01	Rear cruck blade truss T2	50	20	1380	1409	1429	1
STC-B02	Rear purlin bay II	20 NM	—	—	—	—	—
STC-B03	Front purlin bay II	43	08	—	—	—	—
STC-B04	Collar truss T1	74	28	1357	1402	1430	1
STC-B05	Ridge piece bay II	34 NM	—	—	—	—	—
STC-B06	Rear cruck blade truss T2	50	02	1379	1408	1428	1
STC-B07	Rafter 1 from truss T2 front	55 +2NM	23+2NM	1374	1405	1428	1
STC-B08	Rafter 4 from truss T2 rear	12 NM	2	—	—	—	—
	Average date of last heartwood ring				1406		

Site sequences: (composed of samples 1, 4, 6, 7), 74 rings long dated 1357–1430 with *t*-values of 5.5(E.MID), 5.6(S. ENG).

95% felling date range: 1431–1447 (revised from 1433–1456, VA21.90, due to new sapwood estimates), probably close to the beginning of the range, in view of the surviving sapwood. OxCal refined felling date range: *1431–6*.

8.10a. STE-B: Steventon, Tudor House, 67 The Causeway, Oxfordshire

Tudor House, 67 The Causeway, Steventon (STE-B) and the adjoining 71, The Causeway (STE-D) are closely integrated in structure, and also were in the same ownership from the fifteenth century until 1897. They are therefore presented together, in three sub-sections: architectural history of STE-B and STE-D in Chapters 8.10a and 8.10b; documentary history of both houses in Chapter 8.10c.

Grid reference: SU 4676 9174   Survey dates: 1988; 2010   By: D. Miles; Oxfordshire Buildings Record

Dating and recording in 2010 were supported by the Vernacular Architecture Group and the Oxfordshire Buildings Record. We are very appreciative of permission to use their information.

Fig. 8.10a.1. View of Tudor House from the north.

ARCHITECTURAL DESCRIPTION

SUMMARY AND HISTORICAL DEVELOPMENT

Tudor House is a substantial house of hall and crosswing plan, with the hall oriented east-west, facing north onto the Causeway (Figs. 8.10a.1, 2); its size is perhaps most dramatically indicated by Figure 8.10a.3, showing Robert Howard in the roof of the hall. Sections of the roof trusses are shown in Figure 8.10a.4. The historical development and structural details of both ranges have been well described in previous work, although the dating and development have been refined and further structural details have been observed.[1] The size and quality of the house suggests that the builders of its two earliest phases must have had access for at least two generations to unusually extensive resources.

---

[1]   Currie, C. R. J. (1976) 'Smaller domestic architecture in North Berkshire, *c.* 1300 – *c.* 1650', Unpublished D. Phil thesis, Oxford; Currie, C. R. J. (1992) 'Larger medieval houses in the Vale of the White Horse', *Oxoniensia*, 57, 81–244, pp. 199–203. Oxfordshire Buildings Report 67, 2010.

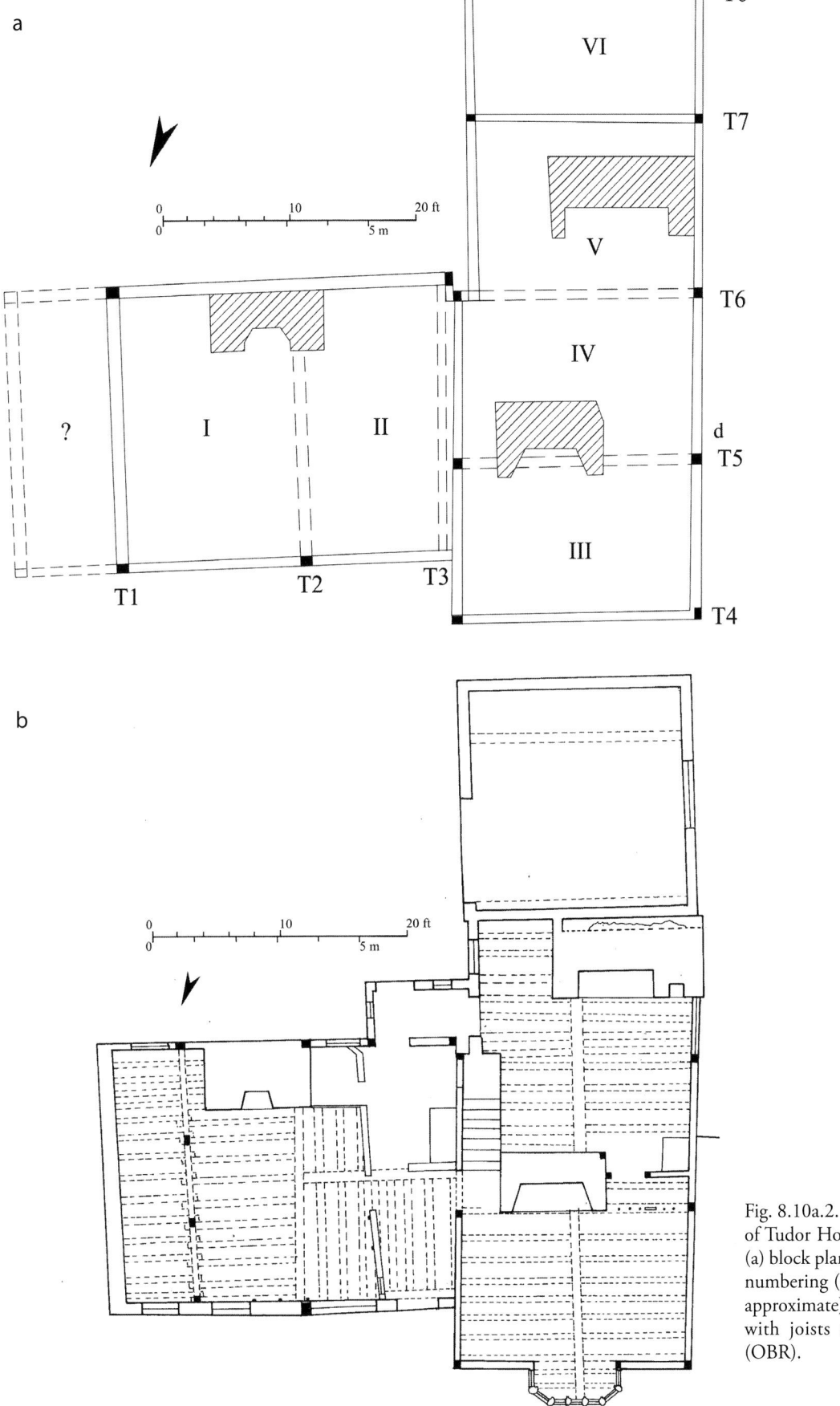

Fig. 8.10a.2. Ground floor plans of Tudor House
(a) block plan with bay and truss numbering (positions of T7, T8 approximate); (b) detailed plan with joists and beams shown (OBR).

A notable and previously unexpected feature is the close relationship between Tudor House and the adjoining 71 The Causeway (STE-D, 1463/7; see Chapter 8.10b), separated from it by no more than 12–18in and with doors between the buildings on both floors. Although 71 The Causeway is apparently an independent late-medieval house (dated to 1463/7), it was in common ownership with Tudor House from the early 1400s until 1897 (Chapter 8.10c).

PHASE 1: The earliest part of the house is the tall box-framed crosswing, originally containing at least two bays. Since the hall extends slightly further to the south than truss T6, a further bay is likely, though this may have been a short staircase bay, as at York Farm, West Hagbourne (X-WHA, 1284/5). The wing was presumably associated with a hall, the predecessor of the present one, but it is not known whether the hall was free-standing or attached to the wing. One timber from this range has given a felling date of **Spring 1299**, and others are consistent with this date. Only one truss (T4) of the original roof survives, with replaced principal rafters and purlins;[2] it has a crown strut carrying the mortice for a collar purlin (Figs. 8.10a.4(d), 5). The posts are down-braced to a heavy mid-rail and the truss originally had scissor-bracing below the tiebeam. Much of the side wall framing survives, incorporating steep arch braces.

PHASE 2: The two-bay cruck hall range has been tree-ring dated to **1355/6**. The central open cruck truss (T2) is particularly notable for its massive and elegantly chamfered timbers, whose cusps form an ogee pointed arch under the collar (Fig. 8.10a.6). Short upper principals form a cinquefoil arch above this. This truss has previously been described as a base-cruck,[3] but the range lacks the features, such as square-set arcade plates associated with base-crucks and the truss is now regarded as a true cruck with F2 apex (collar carrying upper principals). The end truss (T3) against the wing is a light arch-braced truss carried on the wall-plates. That at the other end (T1) has short inner principals, carried on a dropped tiebeam, supporting the purlins and secondary principals((Figs. 8.10a.4(a, c). A further bay, suggested as a lean-to service end, has been removed beyond this truss. Its very unusual form can perhaps be explained as an ad-hoc solution to the structural problem posed by a difference in height between the wallplates of the hall, supported directly by the posts, and those of the lean-to end bay, which would have been supported on the dropped tiebeam.

PHASE 3: The southern bay in the wing (IV) and the whole wing roof were reconstructed in 1448/9. The new roof has clasped purlins with queen posts to T5 and T6. In T4 and the adjoining roof, it is probable that the principal rafters, collars, purlins, windbraces, and clasped ridge all belong to the 1449 phase.

LATER PHASES: The hall was probably floored and provided with a chimney in about 1600, and a chimney with fireplaces on ground and first floor was also inserted into the cross wing. By this period (and perhaps considerably earlier), the house had a cross-passage at the west end of the hall (Fig. 8.10a.2(b)). An oriel was added to light the hall chamber, probably when the floor was inserted. A two-storey bay was added to the front of the crosswing in 1657 and, somewhat later, the front ground-floor room was panelled and both it and the hall were given painted overmantels.

   A 1½ storey two-bay range with a substantial fireplace was added to the south of bay IV, probably in the mid/later seventeenth century. Bays IV and V were then combined on the ground floor to produce a large kitchen, and, following later fire damage, the first floor rooms in bays IV and V were also combined.

STRUCTURAL FEATURES

PHASE 1: *The crosswing.* Bays III and IV form the early crosswing, now of two bays with T4 a gable truss, T5 an open truss and T6 closed. Since the present hall projects slightly to the south of T6, a third (perhaps short) bay almost certainly existed, extending the wing beyond the side wall of the present hall; without this third bay, the un-filled hall truss T3 would be partly open to the outside. From this phase, most of truss T4 survives. Its principal posts have upstands on their inner (east and west) sides, but their outward-facing (north) sides are jowled, supporting the projecting ends of the wallplates, and the north-west jowl is pegged into the wallplate. These wallplate projections would probably have carried heavy bargeboards, birdsmouthed onto them. As well as the straight tiebeam, the truss includes a heavy mid-rail supported on arch braces (now concealed). The framing above the rail had scissor-bracing flanking a window with diamond mullions; the bracing was similar to that at 39 The Causeway (STE-E), but only the post braces now survive, the others presumably removed when the bay window was added. In T5, the thin un-jowled west post is original. The east post here has a gunstock jowl, and it, both posts in T6 and the tiebeams of T5 and T6, are replacements of 1449.

   Much of the original side-wall framing survives, particularly in the north bay. Both wallplates are original, in single lengths from T4 to T6, with halvings for dragon ties against these two trusses (but not against T5); no traces are visible of

---

[2]   The principal rafters are aligned to the opposite side of the tiebeam to the crown strut and braces, proving they are secondary.
[3]   Currie, 'Larger medieval houses'.

Fig. 8.10a.3. Robert Howard in the roof of Tudor House in 1988.

scarf joints to extend the plates, despite the inference that the wing did have a third bay. Some early ranges in the region have dragon ties against closed internal trusses, so these ties do not imply that T6 was the end of the range.[4] In the north bay, both first-floor side wall-frames are similar with central studs and steep arch braces to the wall plates. A horizonal spandrel strut spans between the north-east post and the adjoining brace. Since this brace is slightly longer than that on the west side, the strut may have served as the sill of a small window. A series of diagonally-aligned pairs of pegholes survive on each of the four arch braces in the north bay, at different levels on the two sides. Their function is unclear, but they do not seem to have held a window-sill rail (one suggested explanation). They also do not align with the spandrel strut.

The large infill panels are supported on staves that are visible internally; they were probably similar to the panels at Aston Tirrold (AST-A, Ch. 8.1), with laths nailed to the outside face of the main members and solid daub infilled between the staves. The ground-floor front framing is concealed by the panelling, but in the rear bay on the west side, what appears to be the original mid-rail survives, tenoned into the replaced post of T6. At first floor level here, a fragment of the brace survives. The first-floor framing in bay IV, beside the present stairs, has been removed, but the wall-plate contains mortices corresponding to the bay III framing. Some of the ground floor framing probably survives but is concealed. The first-floor joists in the north room are medieval but reused, with their ends cut back where they are jointed into the later N-S beam.

PHASE 2: The central hall truss (T2) is a full cruck of massive and elegant construction (Fig. 8.10a.4b). The blades are capped by the collar, which has a small notch in the centre giving an ogee form to the arch braces (Fig. 8.10a.6). The latter are chamfered, as are the blades below the arch-brace seating. The upper principals are also chamfered and cusped, with a similar notch in the saddle. This carries the square-set ridge piece. In bay I, the heavily-sooted ridge is a reused wall plate with mortices and stave holes apparently for giant wall panels (perhaps derived from the original hall). It is jointed to the next section with a through splayed scarf with two angled pegs. The ridge and purlins are substantial, 6 by 6½ in, and 8½ by 6½ in respectively; the latter are of elm, butt-jointed to the blades just below the collar. A reused rail has been used as a strut between the purlins in bay I, and further smoke-blackened frame elements are found as purlins for the added gable carrying the oriel. One cranked windbrace survives, similar to but more substantial than those in the wing. The rafters range from 3 by 4½in to 4 by 7in, and are of both oak and elm.

At the west end of the hall, truss T3 is set about 1ft within the line of the side wall of the wing, although the corner

---

4   E.g. the 1320s wing at Middle Farm, Harwell (X-HA2).

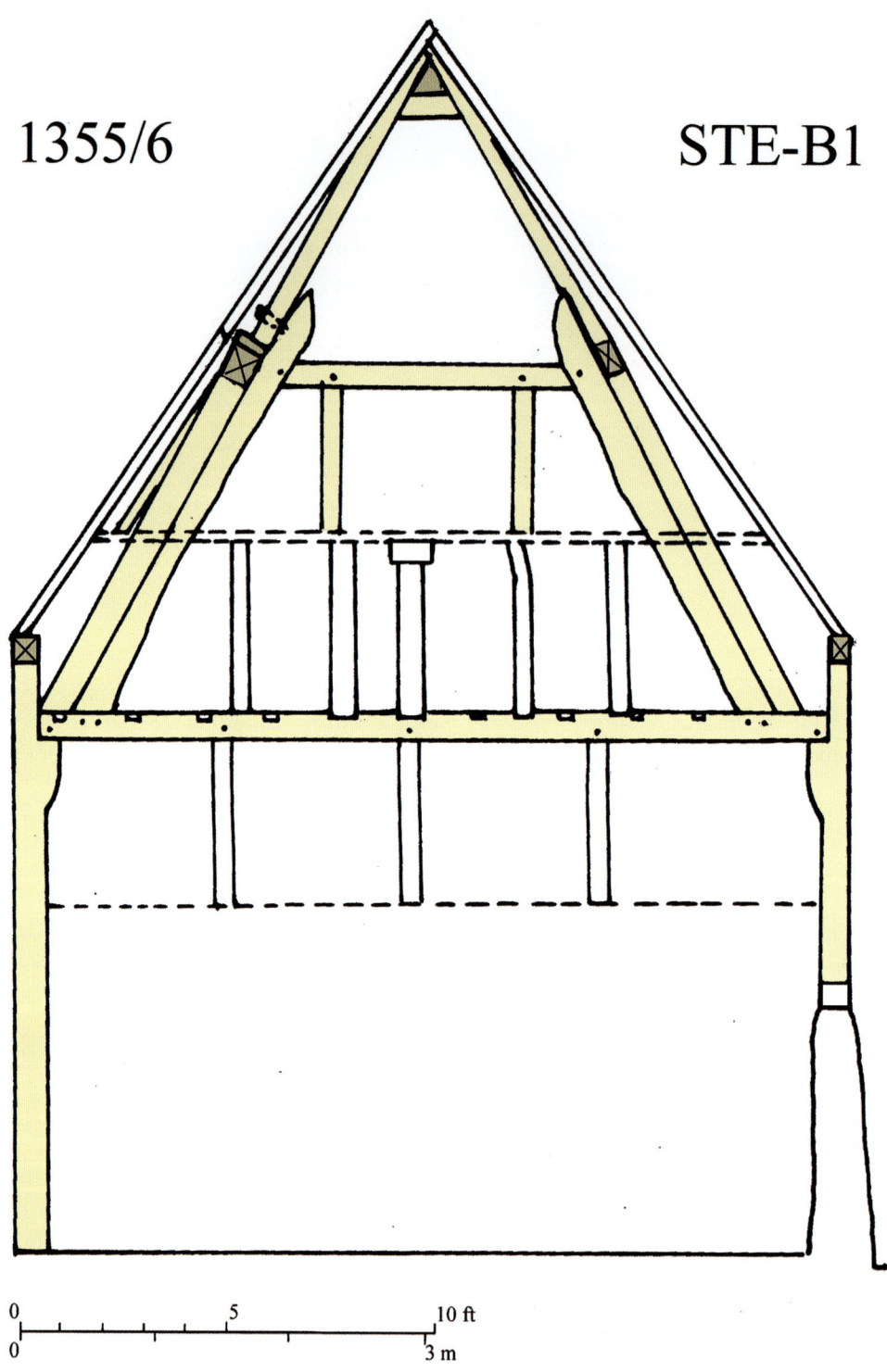

1355/6   STE-B1

Fig. 8.10a.4(a). Section of trusse T1.

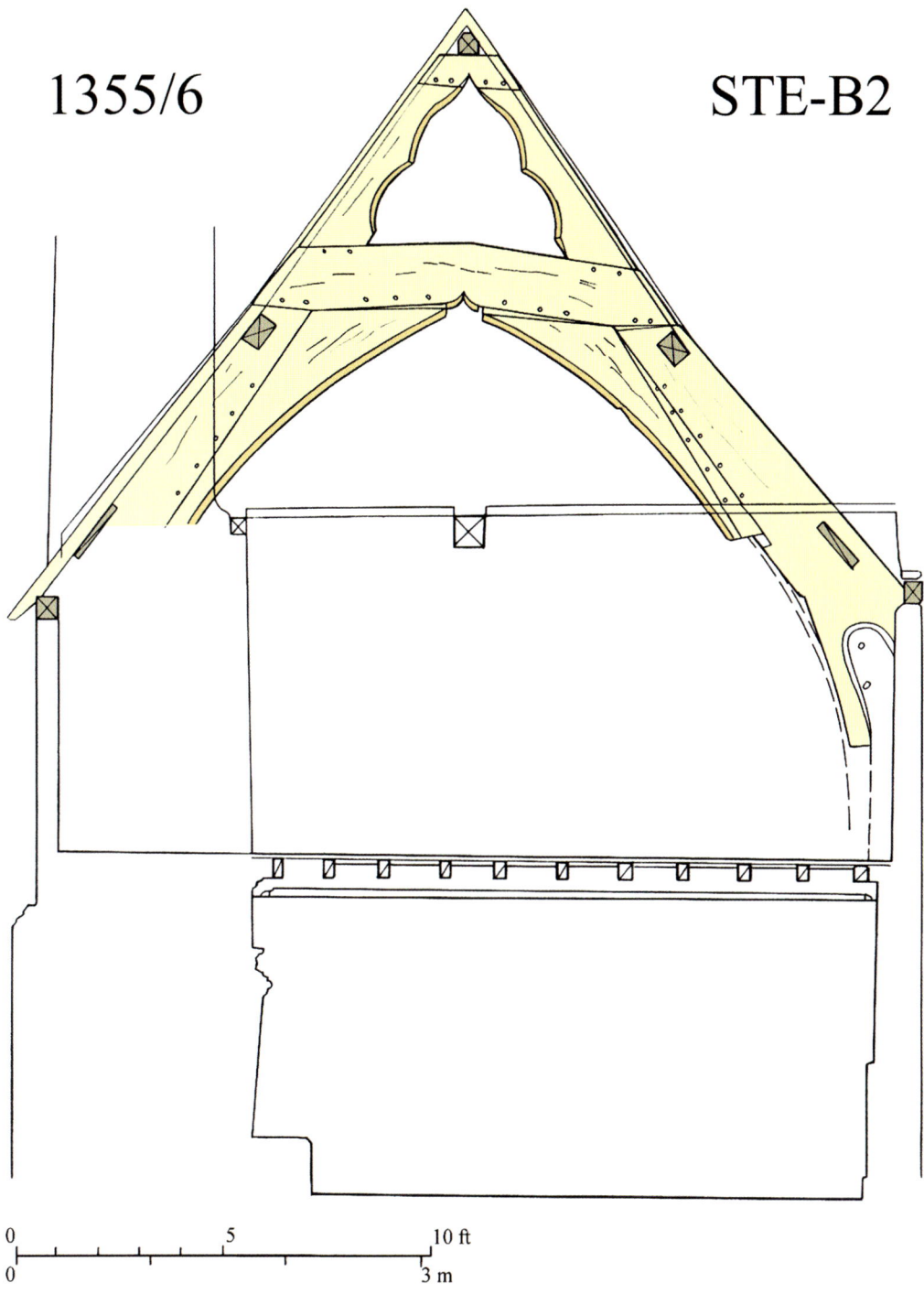

Fig. 8.10a.4(b). Section of truss T2.

post abuts directly on the wing. This is an intermediate truss, with relatively light arch-braced principal rafters carried on the wallplates, clasped purlins, and a yoke holding the ridge (Figs. 8.10a.4c). This truss is clearly a contemporary part of the roof, as it has a mortice for a lost windbrace on the east side, is smoke blackened, and the apex is similar in form to that of T1. It also clearly terminated this range. The purlins are cut off a short distance beyond the truss, but the ridge extends approximately six feet towards the crosswing, where it is cut with a bevel; this section is all sooted, including the cut end. The western side of the principals and the ends of the purlins are also sooted. Evidence of stave grooves in

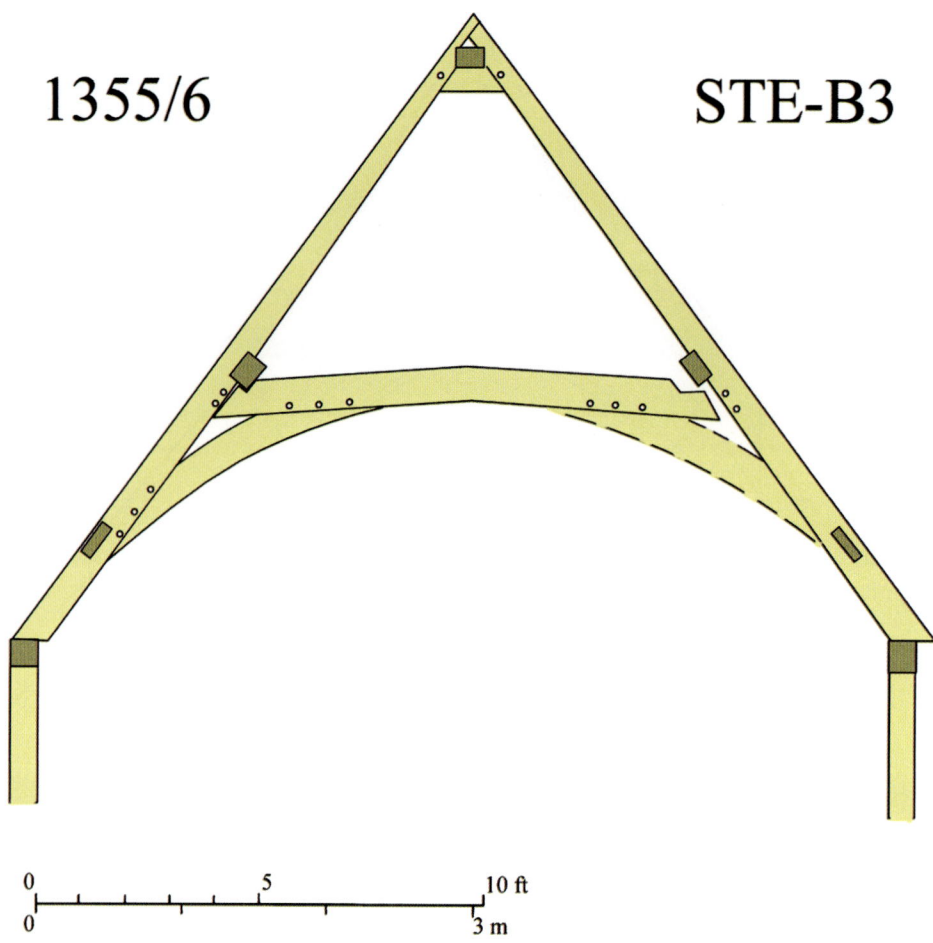

1355/6   **STE-B3**

Fig. 8.10a.4(c). Section of truss T3.

the top of the collar show that this truss was closed above the collar, but it was open below. It has no windbraces on the west side.

The truss at the east end of the hall (T1) was a closed truss, but was not the end of the building, as both purlins are scarfed just within the line of the truss; it is heavily sooted in the roof space. The truss has short principal rafters which rise to just above the collar, from an anchor beam set 2ft below the wallplate. The collar is pegged into the principals and is also supported by pegged queen struts; both the collar and struts are covered with daub which was apparently thickly sooted, though much of this sooting has later flaked off. This truss originally had no windbraces but post-medieval ones have been added. Doubled outer rafters rise from the beam to the purlins, and single rafters rise in separate lengths from the purlins to the ridge. The upper part of the truss is similar to T3, with the ridge held in a yoke. All these timbers are very heavily sooted.

The anchor beam is square-sectioned and is supported on integral brackets set below the tops of the wall posts. The series of studs below the ceiling are later additions and the original queen struts are concealed by the plaster; the central stud is chamfered and stopped and has apparently been extended to raise the central ceiling beam by about 12in. The beam also has a series of notches (plaster-filled) which can only have carried joists. Since the north end notch is blocked by the sooted rafters of the truss, the joists must have run to the west, providing a floor or ceiling pre-dating the insertion of the hall floor (as they would be have been about 4ft over this floor). They possibly supported a ceiling for the cross-passage.

PHASE 3: Most of the roof of the crosswing was replaced in this phase, dated to 1448/9. The new roof has clasped purlins, with a central cambered tiebeam. The ridge is trapped by a small yoke, and steep windbraces rise to the purlins. Although the crown post, collar and braces of T4 remain from Phase 1, the principal rafters, collar, purlins, windbraces, and clasped ridge are probably all of Phase 3. This is consistent with presence of a diagonal clasped ridge, as used in the

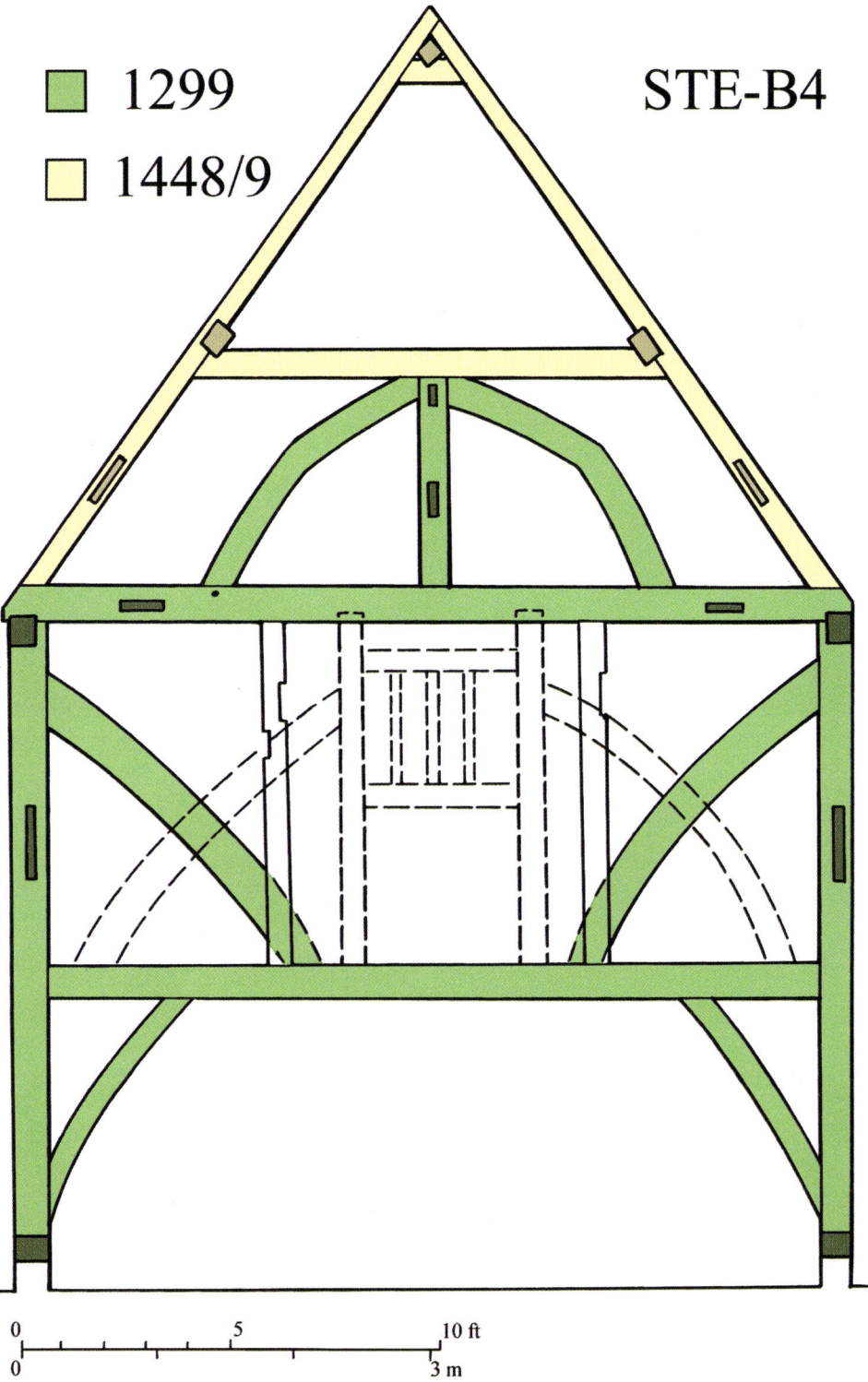

1299
1448/9

STE-B4

Fig. 8.10a.4(d). Section of truss T4.

Fig. 8.10a.5. The crown strut of truss T4, with the primary tiebeam and braces and the secondary collar, principal rafters and clasped purlin (Photo: OBR).

Fig. 8.10a.6. The apex of cruck truss T2.

Fig. 8.10a.7. The 1657 date and initials of Richard Smalbone and the Sun fire insurance plaque of Sarah Bosley.

Fig. 8.10a.8. Painted panels above the parlour fireplace.

north-west block of The Priory, Steventon (STE-F) (of the 1440s) rather than a flat clasped-ridge, as found, for example, at 39 The Causeway (STE-E). Truss T6 (tiebeam dated to 1448/9) was a closed truss, probably forming the south end of the crosswing in this phase. This tiebeam is heavily charred on its south underside, from a fire in bay V, up to the line of the stud mortices.

LATER PHASES: *Sixteenth and early seventeenth century.* This phase saw the insertion of the ceiling and the stack in the hall, the latter set against the rear wall (unusual in the region). The hall joists have step stops, suggesting a date of around 1600 for this ceiling. The principal beams have a T-shaped layout, with a transverse beam at the chimney and a main- and half-beam arrangement at the west end. A cross passage was present at the east end, clearly marked by a beam now supported on posts; the studs and infill have been removed, but the mitre for one side of the central doorway can be seen. Before the hall was ceiled, this partition presumably extended upwards, carrying the joists running west from T1. The brick fireplace on the ground floor has a flat three-centred moulded arch and is likely to be original to the stack, i. e. around 1600, although it has been suggested that it is an 'Arts-and-Crafts' replacement. The ground and first floor front crosswing fireplaces are also of this period. They have stone jambs and, from the depth of the stack, the existence of ground- and first-floor rear fireplaces (in bay VI) is possible.

Later seventeenth century. A two-storey gabled bay window was added to the front of the crosswing, carrying the initials RS (Richard Smalbone) and date 1657 on the gable bressummer (Fig. 8.10a.7).[5] It has chevrons and dentils on the principal timbers and ovolo-moulded secondary mullions; the uppermost window is of bulls-eye form. An oriel window added to the chamber over the hall is putatively also of 1657, but its mullions have a complex cavetto moulding that suggests an earlier date; it clearly cannot pre-date the flooring of the hall.

Panelling The front ground floor room of the crosswing is finished with fielded panelling with painted false quartered marquetry, which appears to have been made for the room. The downstairs fireplaces have heavy bolection-moulded surrounds with pulvinated friezes above, of the late seventeenth or early eighteenth century; they may perhaps be associated with the acquisition of the house by Edward and Elizabeth Weston in 1695 (see Chapter 8.10c). Both hall and crosswing fireplaces have painted overmantels, which were discussed by Dr Evans, a previous owner of the house, in an article for *Country Life* and dated by him to 1657 (Fig. 8.10a.8).[6] However, more recent consideration suggests a late seventeenth-century date (Andrea Kirkham, personal communication). The panelling, fireplaces and paintings are prerhaps all of the same date

Some anomalies to the panelling appear in the south-west corner where a former doorway connected with no. 71 and the panelling changes in style. The work seems to date the early twentieth century, aimed at exposing the post while trying to complete the room in a similar style to the original. The present south wall at this point may be made up of the panels previously forming the lost partition. The insertion of this wall presumably dates from the separation in ownership of Tudor House and no. 71 in 1897. A similar blocked doorway exists on the first floor, at the north end of the chamber.

Kitchen: Bays V–VI and the building extending southwards from it are of 1½ storeys, the roof with queen struts and clasped purlins. Presumably when they were added, the ground floor end wall of the wing was removed to create a kitchen, served by the fireplace in bay V; prior to this, this room may have been heated by a smaller fireplace at the back of the parlour chimney. The axial elm spine beam in bays IV–V and the joists have small chamfers and step/scroll stops. The fireplace has a wooden mantelpiece with scratched inscriptions, including one reading 'T H 1717'. This probably refers to Thomas Hayward, son of Elizabeth Hayward, the then owner. Above this fireplace, and probably contemporary with it, is a mantel shelf and two spit supports, all decorated with an incised diaper design. To the right of the fireplace are two cupboards, one retaining its original wooden door and surround; these were probably for salt and spices respectively. All this kitchen equipment seems to date from the mid- or later seventeenth century. At the back of the chimney is the projection for a bread oven and a copper, indicating service use for bay VI.

The fire damage to the tiebeam of T6 clearly destroyed the partition below the truss and probably the gable above it, and patches of burning are also seen on the purlins in bay VI. As part of the reconstruction following this fire, possibly in the mid-nineteenth century (from the character of the replacement timbers), the first floor room in bay IV was extended up to the bay V chimney.

---

[5]   Above this is a Sun Insurance firemark numbered 270999, relating to a policy dated 24 June 1769 insuring the dwelling house of Sarah Bosley.

[6]   Evans, E. B. (1957) 'Seventeenth-century painted overmantels' *Country Life*, **122** (Nov. 28, 1957) 1138–9.

DENDROCHRONOLOGY

For dendrochronology abbreviations see page facing Introduction.

Sampling Comments: Seven samples were obtained through coring by Robert Howard on 2 July 1988. Five of these were from the cruck range, while another two were taken from the front frame of the crosswing. Despite the samples having as many as 160 rings, they proved difficult to measure and only two shorter samples, 3 and 4, matched together. In May and October 2010, further cores from the crosswing were taken by D Miles (Oxford Dendrochronology Laboratory [ODL] (samples THS1–6; THS11–13).

Tree-ring Sample Record and Summary of Dating

Sample Code	Sample Location	Total Rings	Sapwood Rings	FMR Date	LHR Date	LMR Date	Date Cat
Cruck hall							
STE-B01	Arch brace open truss T2 S side	103	—	—	—	—	—
STE-B02	Collar of open truss T2 (moulded)	160	—	—	—	—	—
STE-B03	Principal rafter open truss T2 N side	88	30C	1268	1325	1355	3b
STE-B04	Principal rafter open truss T2 S side	47	—	1273	1319		3b
STE-B05	Cruck blade open truss T2 N side	36 NM	—	—	—	—	—

Site sequence (composed of samples 3, 4 from the principal rafters) 88 rings long matched at 1268–1355 with *t*-values 4.9(OXFORD), 4.3(S.ENG), 3.3(E.MID), 5.8(JMF-102).

Felling date:(sample 3 with complete sapwood) **1355/56** (VA20.89).

Crosswing primary phase

Sample Code	Sample Location	Total Rings	Sapwood Rings	FMR Date	LHR Date	LMR Date	Date Cat
STE-B06	Brace NE corner, cross wing, T4	36 NM 2	—	—	—		
STE-B07	Main post NW corner, cross wing, T4	110	HS	1175	1274	1284	1
THS1b	ditto (ODL sample)	84	H/S	1201	1284	1284	
THS1	Mean of STE-B07 + THS1b	110	H/S	1175	1284	1284	
THS2	Front RH (W) brace to corner post	56	27				
THS3	Front stud to RH (W) side of bay window	30	17C				
THS4	Front (N) tiebeam, T4	87	H/S+9NM	1190	1276	1276	
THS5	LH (E) wall plate, bay III	101	2+13 NM	1164	1262	1264	
THS6a	RH (W) wall plate, bay III	109	22¼C	1190	1276	1298	
THS6b	ditto	102	20¼C	1197	1278	1298	
THS6	RH (W) wall plate, bay III	109	21¼C	1190	1277	1298	

THS4: A total of 25mm of sapwood were lost in sampling. By taking mean ring width of end of core, 18 rings of sapwood can be estimated. This has been halved to 9 rings for minimum number of rings lost to allow for possible variable ring width, giving a felling date range of 1285–1317.

THS5: A total of 30mm of sapwood were lost in sampling. By taking mean ring width of end of core, 21 rings of sapwood can be estimated. This has been halved to 13 rings for minimum number of rings lost to allow for possible variable ring width, giving a felling date range of 1275–1303.

Site sequences: sample 7 from crosswing dated 1175–1284 with *t*-values 6.0(S.ENG), 6.2(READING); Site sequence CAUSEWY3 (THS1, THS4, THS5, THS6) dated 1164–1298 with *t*-value 12.6 (HANTS02) and other matches with *t* > 10.0.

Felling date (sample THS6 with complete sapwood and spring growth rings) **Spring 1299**. (previous felling date range 1285–1315). All dated timbers are consistent with this felling date.

Crosswing reconstruction phase

Sample Code	Sample Location	Total Rings		Sapwood Rings	FMR Date	LHR Date	LMR Date	Date Cat
THS11	T6 tiebeam	112	20C	1337	1448	1428		Winter 1448/9
THS12	T6 RH (E) wall post	104	29C					
THS13	T5 tiebeam	136	19C	1313	1448	1429		Winter 1448/9

Despite some growth irregularities in the ring sequences, the two tiebeams (THS11, THS13) matched together and were combined to form the 136-year site sequencemaster CAUSEWY4. This is dated to 1313–1448 with *t*-values 6.47 (OXON93), 5.95 (NORWICH), 5.81 (STHELEN1).

Felling date (both timbers retained complete sapwood) **Winter 1448/9**. Despite having 104 rings, the rear cornerpost failed to match conclusively.

8.10b. STE-D: Steventon, 71 The Causeway, Oxfordshire

Grid reference: SU 4674 9173   *Survey date*: 2010   *By*: Oxfordshire Buildings Record

Note: This house was formerly known as 69–75 The Causeway. It has been added to the project after its tree-ring date was reported, and the close relationship with the adjoining Tudor House (STE-B) became apparent. It has been surveyed by Oxfordshire Buildings Record and dated by Dr Andy Moir, Tree-ring Services, who have generously allowed their work to be used.

Fig. 8.10b.1. View of 71 The Causeway, Steventon, with Tudor House (67 The Causeway) beyond.

ARCHITECTURAL DESCRIPTION

SUMMARY AND HISTORICAL DEVELOPMENT[1]

PHASE 1. No. 71 The Causeway immediately adjoins Tudor House, 67 The Causeway (STE-B) for which it was a subsidiary house, in the same ownership until 1897. It is box-framed, with four bays of almost equal size, of which bays I and II originally contained a two-bay chamber on the first floor, and either a two-bay or two one-bay ground floor rooms. At both ground and first floor levels, doorways (now blocked) gave access from Tudor House. The position of the original front door is unknown. The rafters of bay III are smoke-blackened, identifying this as the former open hall, and bay IV, also apparently floored, was presumably for service. The roof is of queen-post construction with clasped purlins. Precise tree-ring dates have been obtained from seven samples, dating between Winter 1463/4 and Spring 1467, suggesting that the house was built in 1467, or perhaps a year or two later.

LATER PHASES. Bay I was given a front gable, perhaps in the seventeenth century. This was possibly intended to echo the gable crosswing of Tudor House. Perhaps at the same time, bays I and II were subdivided on both floors, bay III was floored, and chimneys were inserted in all four bays. By the nineteenth century, the house had been converted into four

---

1   The house is described in: Currie, 'Smaller domestic architecture', 314; Currie, 'Larger medieval houses, 205; Oxfordshire Buildings Record (2010) '71 The Causeway, Steventon', Unpublished report, OBR.87.

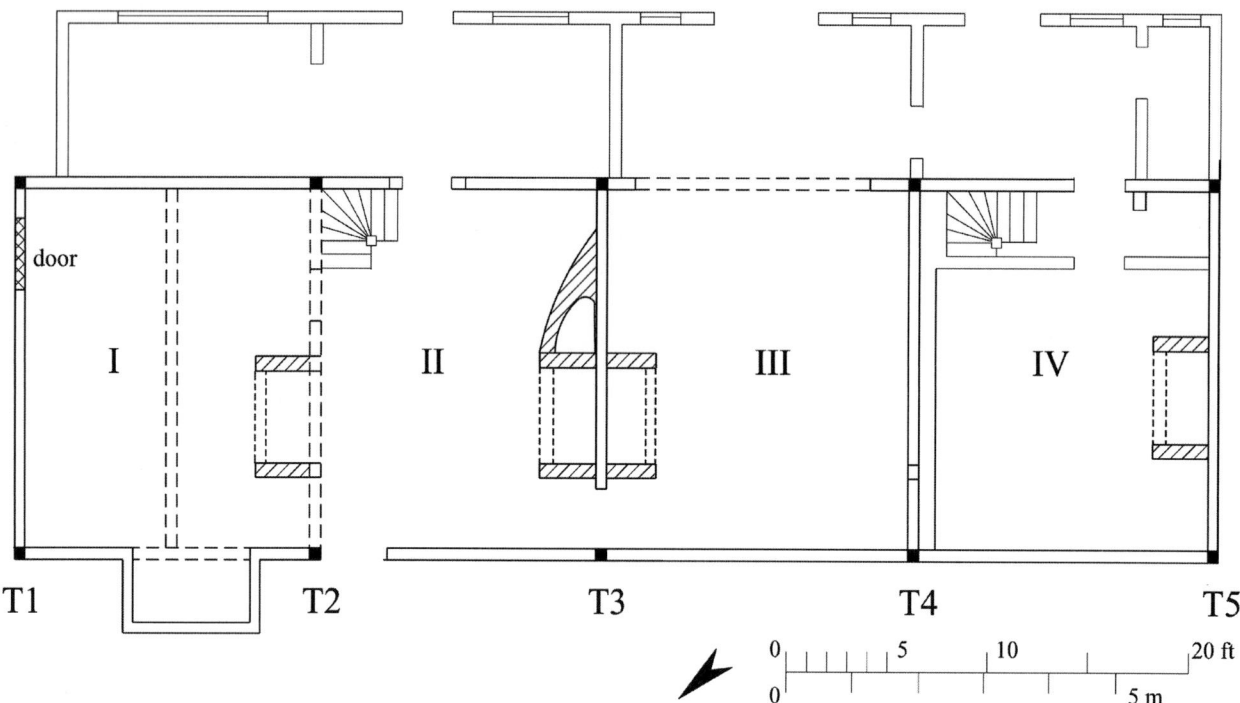

Fig. 8.10b.2. Ground floor plan, showing truss and bay numbering. Inserted wall filling is cross-hatched, and inserted chimneys are shaded diagonally.

cottages. Perhaps as part of this conversion, a lean-to was added across the back of the house, and the front wall of bay IV was rebuilt in brick (this bay now partly used as a garage).

STRUCTURAL FEATURES

PHASE I. The external wall-framing is visible on the north side in bays II and III, with large primary panels divided by mid-rails and with large flattened four-centred arch braces between the posts and the wallplate. Truss T1 contains what appears to be an original chamfered doorhead, leading to Tudor House (presumably tenoned into hidden studs). The north wall plate in bay II has evidence of a shutter groove, although it is not clear if the present window position is original.

Truss T1 is largely covered by modern materials, but a mid-rail is visible. T2 has a mid-rail and cambered tiebeam (Fig. 8.10b.3). The posts of truss T2 have splayed heads, with short angle-braces connecting them to the tiebeam. The braces and tiebeam (though not the posts) are chamfered. There are numerous assembly marks, with each joint numbered individually in scribed Roman numerals. Above the tiebeam are queen struts to the collar, with clasped purlins. The infill below the tie-beam is secondary, apparently with a central window. Truss 3 has a straight tiebeam, again with queen-struts above. The apex of this truss has *in situ* soot-blackened wattle-and-daub infill. The ground-floor infill of both T2 and T3 is concealed, but the mid-rail of T2 shows no indication of it having been closed below. Thus, it seems likely that this truss was open, and that T3 was closed. Truss T4 is similar to T3 and sits above a stone partition wall, which appears to be relatively modern; truss T5 is concealed.

There are windbraces from the principals to the substantial purlins, which have bridled scarfs with straight abutments. The common rafters (eight per bay) are oak, half-lapped and pegged at the apex, with no ridge. Where visible, the timbers appear to have been trestle-sawn. In Bay I, the rafters at the north appear to have been re-set, perhaps when the gable was added, as all have redundant peg holes visible below the purlin. The timbers in bay III are smoke-blackened. What might appear to be a louvre trimmer, spanning between the rafters in the centre of Bay IV is entirely clean, so perhaps it related to an early chimney that has since been removed. The small studs infilling the gable of truss T5 have a number of pegs in them, set in rows, probably for cheese shelves.

Bay I has a transverse ceiling beam with wide chamfers and step stops, with massive axial joists laid flat (6–8 by 4in) tenoned into it using plain soffit tenons. Their other ends are lodged on the mid-rails of trusses T1 and T2. These joists

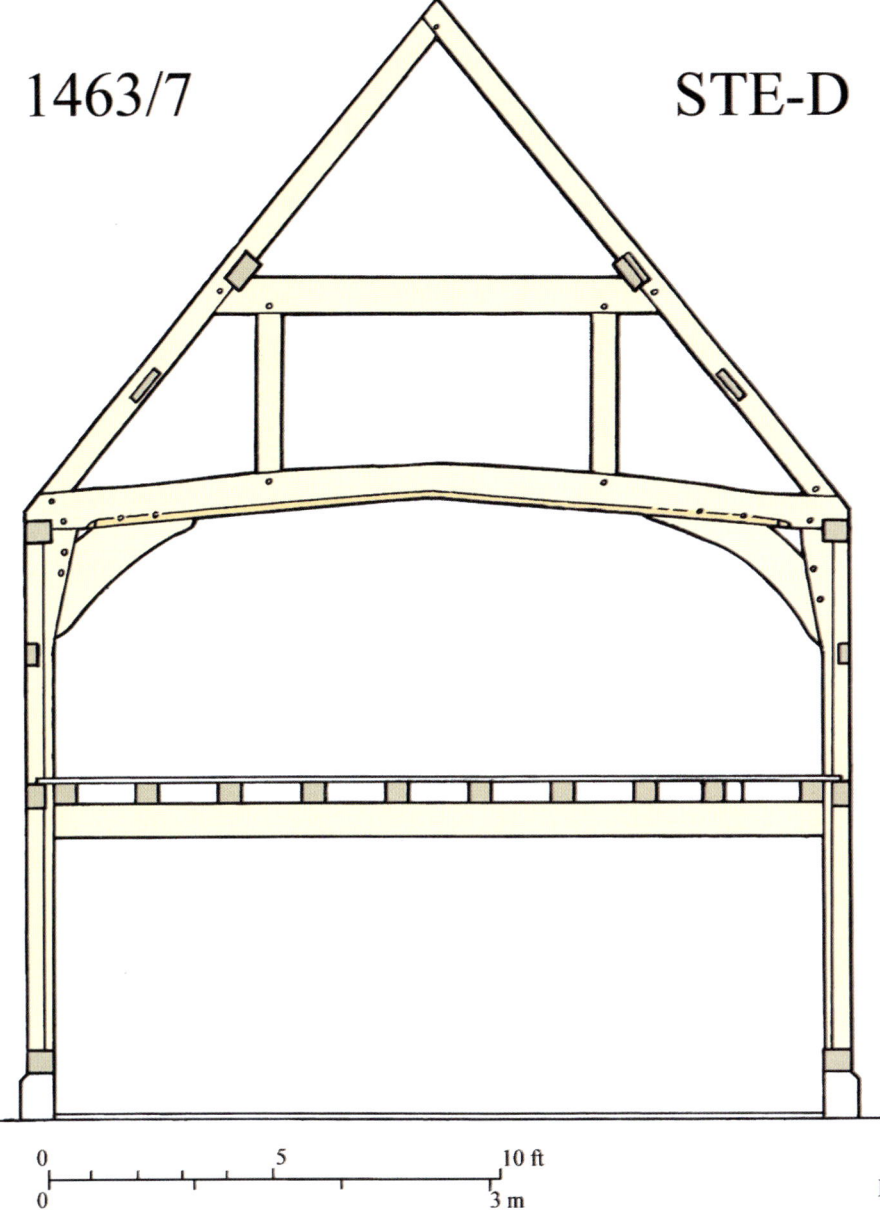

1463/7   STE-D

Fig. 8.10b.3. Section of truss T2.

Fig. 8.10b.4. The post head and tiebeam of truss T2, also showing the secondary infill.

are mostly of beech and some have obvious marks of trestle-sawing. Bay II has no central beam but the joists are similar. A trimmer on the south side relates to the present stair, but it is not clear if this was the original stair position. In bay III, the joists are secondary, supported on a axial chamfered elm ceiling beam with scroll stops. Bay IV is reported to have an original floor, although the evidence for this is not obvious.

DENDROCHRONOLOGY

For dendrochronology abbreviations see page facing Introduction. This summary is extracted from the report by Dr A. Moir.[2]

Sampling comments. Eleven core samples were taken by Dr Moir on 16th March 2009. Most of the timbers were identified as oak; however, the purlins in the end bay at the south-west end were elm, and many of the rafters in this bay have been replaced or reinforced using elm. Sample 10 was of beech. Sample 11 showed blocks of narrow rings indicating wood management. Apart from the two short sequences, all the sequences could be matched together. The truss letters (A-E) in the original report have been replaced by the truss numbers (T1–T5) used here. See also *Vernacular Architecture*, 41 2010, 87. Because of the different methodology used by this laboratory, no date category has been assigned.

Tree-ring Sample Record and Summary of Dating

Sample Code	Sample Location	Total Rings	Sapwood Rings	FMR Date	LHR Date	LMR Date
ABC-A01	Rafter, bay IV, 1st north of T5	67	32¼C	1400	1434	1466
ABC-A02	Principal rafter, T5 (south)	100	16Cw	1365	1448	1464
ABC-A03	Tiebeam, T5	111	30Cw	1356	1436	1466
ABC-A04	Tiebeam, T4	117	30¼C	1350	1436	1466
ABC-A05	Wallplate, bay II (south)	59	1	1383	1440	1441
ABC-A06	Tiebeam, T3	126	34¼C	1341	1432	1466
ABC-A07	Wallplate, bay II (north)	120	22Cw	1345		1464
ABC-A08	Principal rafter, T2 (north)	30				
ABC-A09	Ceiling beam, bay I	85	24Cw	1379	1439	1463
ABC-A10	Ceiling joist, bay I	29				
ABC-A11	Mid-rail, bay I (north)	103	h/s 1335	1437	1437	

(w = winter bark)

Site sequence: (composed of samples 1–7, 9, 11) 132 rings long dated to 1335–1466 with *t*-values of 7.65 (CAPEL-10); 7.11 (TCKNHM1X); 6.88 (WCOTT-LF).

Estimated felling dates (samples 1, 2, 3, 4, 6, 7, 9 have complete sapwood): Winter 1463–4 (sample 9); Winter 1464/5 (samples 2, 7); Winter 1466/7 (sample 3); spring 1467 (samples 1, 4, 6)

---

2   Moir, A. (2009) 'Dendrochronological analysis of oak timbers from 71 The Causeway, Steventon, Oxfordshire, England', Unpublished report, Tree-ring Services, ABCA/10/09

8.10c. Documentary history of Tudor House, 67 The Causeway (STE-B) and 71 The Causeway, Steventon (STE-D)

The documentary history has been compiled by Nat Alcock and Chris Currie with the assistance of Heather Horner and Catherine Lorigan.

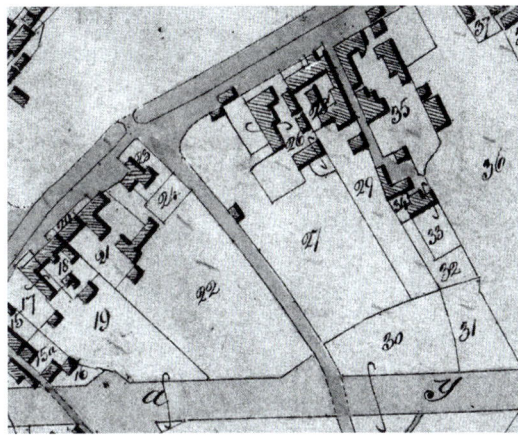

Fig. 8.10c.1. Extracts from the 1842 and 1839 maps of Steventon: (a, left) the 1842 Tithe Map; (b, right) the 1839 map.

Tudor House is plot 21 (1842) or 23; 71 The Causeway is plot 20 or 22; the North Star is plot 23 or 25. On the 1839 map, the added faint numbering matches the Tithe Map numbers. The Twytchen is represented by the field boundary parallel to the brook.

SUMMARY

Tudor House and no. 71 were copyholdings held from Westminster Abbey (followed by the Ecclesiastical Commissioners) until the 1920s. They were owned together by the Smalbone family from 1570 onwards, with 2 (later 1½) yardlands, passing to Edward and Elizabeth Weston in 1695 and to the Hayward family in 1713. From 1767, they belonged to the Bosley family, who sold off the land in 1834, and the house in 1861. Tudor House and no. 71 were finally separated in 1897. Before 1571, they were among a number of houses belonging to the estate assembled by Michael Dormer, and they can be identified as having been acquired as two separate houses, associated respectively with a half and one virgate. Both had originally belonged to a Cristina Smith who married Thomas Berton in about 1413. They were split up by his descendant's widow in 1519, before being reunited in Dormer ownership in 1535.

The history is examined in sections: 1664 onwards; from 1535 to 1664; before 1535. Each section is accompanied by tables of court entries. A pedigree of the Smalbone family is included (Fig. 8.10c.2). A final section examines building evidence and probate records.

LOCATION AND IDENTIFICATION

Tudor House is numbered 21 on the Tithe Map and 23 on the 1839 map (Fig. 8.10c.1a–b). It was owned by William Bosley, occupied by Hannah Bosley. The adjoining house, 71 The Causeway, was then and had been for some four centuries subsidiary to Tudor House, in the same ownership although no doubt different occupation (number 20 or 22). In 1842, it was also owned by William Bosley and comprised five cottages, occupied by James Brewer, William Slatter and others. They are identified in the 1897 admissions as the properties numbered 154 (Tudor House) and 153 (71 The Causeway) on the 1884 altered tithe apportionment.

HISTORY AFTER 1664 (*Table 8.10c.1*)

Tudor House was copyhold until enfranchised in the 1920s, and it is identified as holding 80 in the c. 1800 and c. 1890 indexes to Steventon copyholds. It can be followed in the court books from 1686 when it belonged to Richard Smallbone (III) (see the family tree, Fig. 8.10c.2). It was then held with 1½ yardlands, paying a rent of 14s 1d, and it also included 71 The Causeway, although this is not mentioned explicitly in the court entries. The initials RS 1657 carved on the bressumer of the bay window can be identified as those of Richard Smalbone (III). It appears to be this Richard Smalbone who in his will of 1687 recites his surrender of his copyhold property to trustees (as recorded in the court book for 1686), for the benefit of the children of his four sisters and his brother. Following a case in Chancery, the property was sold to

Fig. 8.10c.2. Smalbone family tree.
Bold type identifies the holders of Tudor House. * Discussed further in the notes.

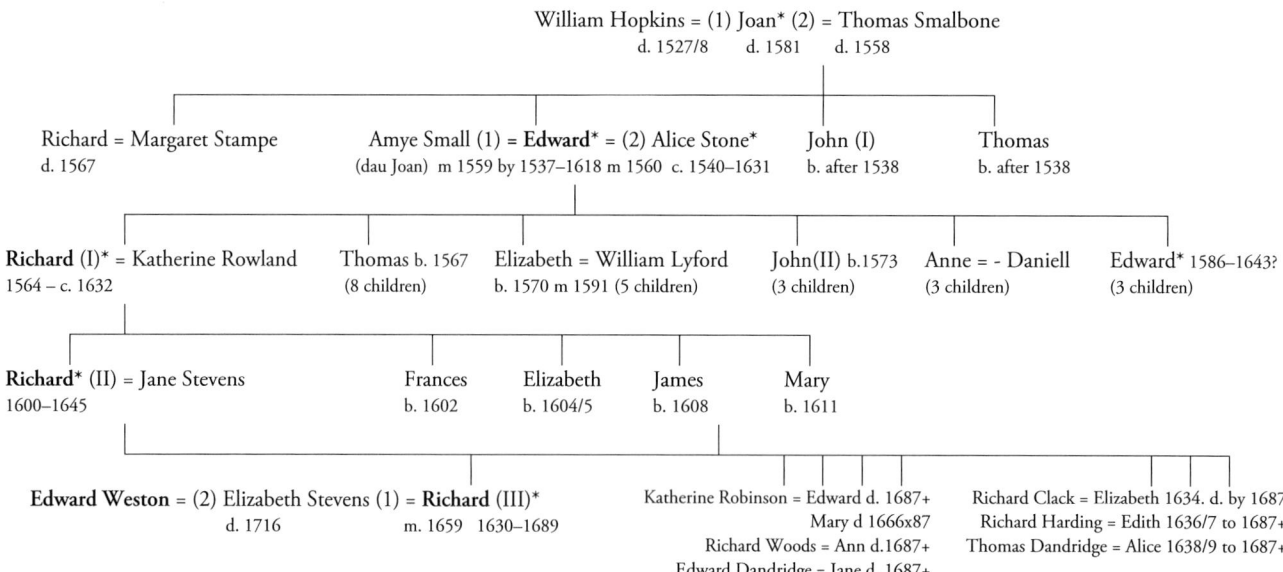

Notes: This tree shows only the descent from Edward Smalbone, son of Thomas and Joan, and the children of the successive eldest sons, omitting the many other branches of the Smalbone family; for the descendants of John (I), see STE-F. The tree is based on wills, register entries and court records and a pedigree certified by Richard Smalbone (III) included in the Berkshire 1665–6 Heralds' Visitation (Rylands, W. Harry (ed.) (1907–8) *The Four Visitations of Berkshire*, Harleian Society, vols. 56–7).

Joan (d. 1581) must have been about 80 when she died, since her first child was born in 1519–20 (her son John Hopkins was aged about eight in 1527/8 on the death of her first husband; WAM 7412, rot 22).

Edward (d. 1618) was born not later than 1537, since he was apparently already of full age and therefore provided for by the time of his father's death in 1558. Thus, he was not mentioned in Thomas's, will although he was left household goods by his mother. His first marriage and daughter Joan are given in BL Harleian 2395. He died aged about 80, and his wife Alice lived to be 90 or more; Edward, apparently the youngest child of Edward and Alice, was baptised in 1586, suggesting that Alice was no more than 20 when she married.

Richard (I) (1564–c. 1632). A gap in the registers, 1629–35, probably held the burial of Richard (I), the marriage of Richard (II) and the baptisms of most of his children. The Bishops' Transcripts (also incomplete) supply the baptism of Elizabeth. The age of Richard (III) in 1665–6 is given in the Visitation.

Table 8.10c.1. Sequence of admissions: 1686–1897.

In the admissions tables, Mess = messuage (house); a r p = acres rods perches; d. = died. s. = surrendered. The reference numbers in these tables are for identifying the entries only. For the North Star, only the 1669 and 1693 admissions are included (italics).

Date	Ad	To	From	Property
1669	*48*	*Adjoining holding (later North Star) described as having Stocks Lane (N), Richard Smalbone (S)*		
1686		Rental: Richard Smalbone paying 14s 1d rent		
1686	141	Tho Groves et al., trustees	s. Richard Smalbone	Messuage & 1½ virgates, rent 14s 1d
1695	1/267	Edward Weston in trust for wife, Elizabeth	Surrender Thomas Grove, Edward Weston, Walter Doe	messuage & 1½v, surrender authorised by decree in Chancery. rent 14s 1d
1693	*201*	*Elizabeth, wife of Edward Weston*	*s. Nicholas King*	*4 Oct 1692. Mess & barn etc, Stocks Lane (E) (North Star), 2d*
1696		Rental: Elizabeth Smalbone [Weston] paying 14s 3d rent		
1713	338	Elizabeth Hayward	Surrender Edward Weston & Eliz, w	messuage & 1½ virgates, rent 14s 1d
1713	339	Elizabeth Hayward	Surrender Edward Weston & Eliz, w	3 bays barn, orch, arbutus (hopgarden), rent 3d
1746	509	Thomas Hayward	Surrender Elizabeth, mother	Reversion. Messuage & 1½ virgates; barn, orchard & gdn with Stocks Lane (E), rents 14s 1d & 3d
1767		Sarah Bosley	Death Thomas Hayward	3 rents, 14s 1d; 3d, 6d
1773		John Anns	Surrender John & Sarah Anns (late Bosley)	Messuage, 1½ yardlands, 3 bays barn etc, rent 14s 1d & 3d
1818		Joseph Bosley	Death Sarah Anns	Same
1834		Thos Holford	Conditional surrender by Joseph Bosley	Mess, homestd, orch, gdns surrender for £350. (rent apportioned as 3s 9d)
1834		Barrett; Goodman	Surrender Joseph Bosley	(remainder of holding)
1852	5/40–2	Wm Bosley	Death Joseph Bosley	
1861	5/198	Ric Tyrrell	Death Wm Bosley	
1861	5/207	Ric Tyrrell	Surrender Jos Bosley (heir)	
1874	5/401	Geo Tyrrel Lay etc	(trustees of Tyrrell)	
1897		Wm Belcher	Geo Tyrrel Lay etc	Altered tithe map 153, rent 3d [71 The Causeway]
1897		Wm Smith	Geo Tyrrel Lay etc	Altered tithe map 154–155, rent 1s [Tudor House]

Edward Weston and his wife Elizabeth, who was Smalbone's widow.[1] The Smalbone family were lessees of the manor of Steventon from Westminster Abbey, and Richard and Henry Smalbone are recorded jointly in the 1664 Hearth Tax for 'the farm'. Richard then has another entry, probably included out of sequence to bring his two assessments together, with either four or two hearths, which might relate to Tudor House.[2]

In 1713, the holding was enlarged by incorporating the rear part of the small property (a house and four acres) that stood to the east of Tudor House on the corner between The Causeway and Stocks Lane, most of which later became the North Star public house; this acquisition included three bays of a barn, and paid 3d in rent; by 1767, further field land paying 6d rent had also been bought.

The holding was acquired by Elizabeth Hayward in 1713, and passed to her son Thomas in 1746. The latter's will includes a request for him to be buried in Marcham, Berkshire beside his parents.[3] With this evidence, he can be identified as the Thomas, son of Charles and Elizabeth Hayward baptised there on 17th Nov 1699 (*IGI*). It also follows that the Charles Hayward, who was of Steventon in his 1731 inventory, but was not buried there, must be Thomas's father.[4] Since the family owned no other property in Steventon, this inventory presumably relates to either Tudor House or 71 The Causeway.

---

[1]   TNA, C5/637/65 and /286/72. The case was brought to allow Richard's trustees to sell the property, despite his widow's outstanding dower rights, which could in principle have been exercised against the trustees, even though she was the wife of the purchaser.

[2]   TNA, E179/75/381, m. 7; /76/460, r. 21; /243/25, ff 527–8; f 538. Although the lists are broadly topographical, they are not easily interpreted, since no substantial house is listed where Tudor House would be expected in the sequence.

[3]   TNA, PROB 11/929.

[4]   Berks RO, D/A1/198/152. Administration granted to his son, Thomas.

In 1767, Thomas left his copyholding to his servant, Sarah Bosley (a surprising bequest that must surely conceal a human story!); it remained with her family until 1861. In 1834, Joseph Bosley sold off the open field land and the rent was reduced to 3s 9d, and in 1861 his heir sold the house to Richard Tyrrell, a substantial Steventon land-owner. In 1897, the two houses were separated, with Tudor House acquired by William Smith and no. 71 by William Belcher.[5]

HISTORY 1535 TO 1664 (*Tables 18.10c.2 and 3*)

The 1686 and 1696 rentals show Richard and then Elizabeth Smalbone paying 14s 1d and 14s 3d respectively.[6] In the 1645–6 rental Richard Smalbone paid £1 1s 2d, but the sequence is not precise enough to be certain that this corresponds to Tudor House. Taken together, however, the evidence strongly suggests that this house was acquired by Edward and Alice Smalbone in 1571 and descended to Richard Smalbone (III) by inheritance in this branch of the Smalbone family. None of the earlier descriptions include abuttals, and all three inheritances in the first half of the seventeenth century (1618, c. 1635 and 1645) fall in gaps in the surviving court rolls, but the proposed succession fits well with all the sixteenth and seventeenth century references, and no likely alternatives have been identified.

Edward and Alice Smalbone first appear in the court rolls when they were admitted in 1570/1 to two messuages, an adjoining close and about 48 acres of land at a rent of 22s 4d, on the surrender of John and Isabella Stamp (C494); they received a further 12 acres (with common of pasture for ½ virgate) in 1575 by surrender from Joan Smalbone, Edward's mother (C550). In 1601, the main holding was settled on Edward for life, with reversion to his son Richard (C693), and in 1632, Richard Smalbone, senior, leased all his messuages and some specific land for 60 years after his death, to Richard, junior (they must be Richard (I) and Richard (II), since Richard (III) was then only two years old).[7]

Tudor House and the Dormer estate

The property acquired by Edward Smalbone had been part of the large Steventon estate of Michael Dormer, a London mercer, that was inherited by his son Thomas in 1545. Thomas died in 1550, leaving his daughter Isabella, aged 2 to inherit.[8] Soon after she came of age, in 1571, she and her husband John Stamp appear to have systematically sold off the Dormer estate.[9]

Table 8.10c.2. Admissions and survey entries: 1571–1664

Year	Adm	Admitted	Previous	Property	WAM
1570/1	C494	Edw Smalbone, Alice his w, & heirs of Ed	John Stamp & Isabella his wife [identified in preceding entry as dau & heir of Thos Dormer decd.]	2 mess; one close adj now in tenure of Edw Smalbone sen; 44 a arable; 3 a meadow; parcel of land near le shepehouse in S field; 1 a called ley land in Short mead, pasture 5 cows 6 horses 100 sheep. Rent 22s 4d	7418, rot 13; 7524
1575	C550	Edw Smalbone [her son]	s. Joan Smalbone	12 a late of Lawrence Chisselde and Sibill his w (details of land), and common pasture for horses & sheep acc to old rate for ½v of land. Rent 6s [or 6s 7d]	7418, rot 20d; 7523
1599		Rental: Edward Smalbone paying £1 8s 4d			
1590		Rental: Edward Smalbone paying £1 8s 4d			
1601		Edw Smalebone for life then Ric his s	Edw Smalebone	1 mess 2v, rent 22s	7419, rot 16
1641		Ric Smalebone sen	Ric Smalebone jun. Lease for 60 years exhibited	All mess in Stev and lands belonging, after Ric sen's death, remainder to Richard, junior	7420, rot 3
1645–6		Rental: Richard Smalbone paying £1 1s 2d			

---

5   It is worth noting that William Bosley was only admitted in 1852, though his father had died in 1837; probate administration, Berks RO, D/A1/226/93.

6   Although by the latter date, she was the wife of Edward Weston.

7   This was probably a device to prevent dower rights being exercised on the leased property.

8   Thomas was living in Burghfield, Berkshire at his death (TNA, PROB 11/33); cf. STE-A.

9   WAM 7418, r. 13–13d; WAM 7524, [ff 8–9, list of fines]. In the redistribution during these sales, holdings previously rated in yardlands, rented at 13s 4d per yardland, were described by their number of acres, rented at 6d per acre (12s for a 24 acre yardland), so the process apparently led to a loss of rent for the Abbey.

Table 8.10c.3. Selected admissions relating to the estates of Thomas and Michael Dormer

Date	Adm	To	From	Property	WAM
1534	C1014	Michael Dormer citizen & mercer of London	Thos Spycer	[messuages only] 3 mess in the Estend near land of Ric Waynelond & parcell of 1 mess called Datyngtons, from Ric Rycott or Carpenter; 1 mess & 1 parcel of 1 mess from Joan late w of Andrew Collyns; 2 mess from Ric Hobbes	7412, rot 29d
1535	C1018	Michael Dormer of London, mercer	s. Edw Burley and Katherine his w, John Mylle and Alice his w, Edw & John held in right of said Kath & Alice	1 mess 1 v land with meadow belonging & pasture of 2 cows as coheirs of late John Morres clerk as by court 26 Hen VIII	7412, rot 30
1535	C1020	Michael Dormer	s. John Trewlocke	1 mess, 1/2v land and meadow & pasture belonging thereto, which he had from the surr of Thrustan Asheley	7412, rot 30
1545	C1075	Thomas Dormer son & h	d. Michael Dormer kt	[includes properties above]	7412, rot 38d
1551	C343	Isabella dau & h aged 2	d. Thomas Dormer	[includes properties above]. By Isabella wife of Hen Jusse, her mother	7414, rot 3

PRE-DORMER HOLDINGS (*Table 8.10c.4*)

The Dormer estate contained eight or nine messuages, whose descriptions are given in the court rolls and in the surveys. By close examination of the earlier and later evidence, most of these can be excluded from identification with Tudor House. Two possibilities remain, the former properties of the Rawlyns and the Berton families, and these are examined next.

(a) Rawlyns

A large block of property was bought by Michael Dormer from Thomas Spycer in 1534 (C1014), which included six houses (and two parts of houses), and extensive land. Earlier and later evidence allows all these houses to be approximately located and eliminated *except* the two houses obtained from Richard Hobbes. These can be followed back to 1495 (Table 8.10c.4a), when Richard Rawlyns surrendered two messuages to his son; these reached Richard Hobbes in 1512 and Spycer in 1515. Although the description as two messuages matches Tudor House and 71 The Causeway, for the whole of this period they were associated only with ¾ acre land, paying a rent of no more than about 6d (judged from the fine in 1495). It seems highly unlikely that this modest holding could have supported two substantial houses, and it is most probable that the Rawlyns houses stood on one of the back lanes in the village, and they may well have been derelict or demolished by1495.[10]

(b) Thomas Berton family houses

Two houses, associated respectively with one and one-half virgate, were acquired by Michael Dormer from John Trewlocke and the heirs of John Morres in 1535 (C1020; C1018). These were apparently jointly held by one William Palmer in 1562–4, and so could represent 71 the Causeway and Tudor House, although their independent acquisition would seem to make this unlikely. However, examination of their history reveals that both Trewlocke's and Morres's holdings originated as part of the property of Thomas Berton, and that this can be followed back to before 1400.

Cristina Smyth, who held two houses and 1½v, married Thomas Berton, and in 1413 (entry lost) she settled this property on him, as recorded in 1416 (C2204, C2204a, C2129, Table 8.10c.4(b)); presumably one house was associated with one and the other with a half virgate. In 1445, he resettled the two properties on his wife (un-named, but presumably a second wife) (C1677), and in 1448 it passed to his son and heir, another Thomas, who settled it on his own marriage to Alice the same year (C1704, C1706).

It would have been during the ownership of this second Thomas that 71 The Causeway was built on the subsidiary holding (1467d). Perhaps this development can be connected with the offences for which he was reported to the manor

---

10 Most messuages recorded in pairs or larger groups at this period, and not individually described, can be shown to correspond to empty closes by the mid-sixteenth century.

court at almost the same time: encroaching on the 'Twytchen', the narrow lane that ran behind the Causeway houses (C1432).[11] This Thomas died in 1495 (C1240), and his widow Alice married Robert Feld (C844). She died apparently in 1519, having sold one house with a virgate, to Robert Seaston (C844) and the other, with a half-virgate to Thomas Paradyse (C854). The former also died in 1519, and was succeeded by his widow Margery (C853). The court refused, however, to confirm the ownership of Paradyse and Seaston, because the 1448 settlement had not disinherited Thomas Berton's heirs, who were unknown. A string of proclamations delayed a settlement until the mid 1520s.

(c) Messuage and virgate bought by John Morys

Margery Seaston surrendered her house to the bailiff of the manor (C896), but was eventually re-admitted to it in 1525 (C915). However, next year she sold it to the vicar, John Morys, (or Morris, DCL or BCL) (C918). He died in 1531, and his coheirs (who took some finding) sold the property to Michael Dormer in 1535 (C978, C987, C999, C1018).

(d) Messuage and half-virgate acquired by Richard Trewlocke

As with Margery Seaston's sale to William Yong, Paradyse 's acquisition of the half-virgate and its messuage was not ratified, and it was instead granted in 1525 to Thurstan (or Christian) Asteley (or Asheley), a Westminster Abbey servant, who sold it to Richard Trewlocke in 1533. John Trewlocke (presumably Richard's son) sold the holding to Michael Dormer in 1535.

Table 8.10c.4. Pre-Dormer admissions

(a) Rawlyns holding (later Spycer)

Date	Adm	To	From	Property	WAM
1495	C1236	Wm [Rawlyns] his son	s. before death Ric Rawlyns	2 mess 3r land (fine 1s)	7411, rot 14d
1509	C760	Alice his w, 5 yrs, then Ric Baker sen, then John Baker his son	s. before death Wm Rawlyn	2 mess 3r land	7412, rot 1
1512	C790	Rob Sesson	s. Ric Baker & John Baker his son	Reversion of 2 mess and 3r after 5 yrs	7412, rot 4
1512	C791	Ric Hobbys	s. Rob Sesson	Reversion of 2 mess and 3r after 5 yrs	7412, rot 4
1515	C822	Thos Spycer	s. Ric Hobbys	2 mess, 3 r land	7412, rot 7d

(b) Berton property (later Morres and Trewlocke)

Date	Adm	To	From	Property	WAM
1400	C2204	Order to do fealty	[tenants include Thomas Barton]	For lands held [unspecified]	7262, rot 2
1405–12?	C2204a	Unpaid fine	Thomas Berton	Fine for 1½ v [houses not named in list]	7352
1416	C2129	Thomas Barton	s. Cristina Smyth, later w of Thomas Barton	[s. in 14 Hen IV (1413)] 2 mess 1½ v	7263, rot 10
1445	C1677	To wife for life then Thomas Berton son & h	s. before death of Thomas Berton (died in April)	1 m 1½ v	7409, rot 7
1448	C1704	Thomas Berton jun, son & h	d. Thomas Berton	2 m 1½ v	7409, rot 14
1448	C1706	Thomas and Alice his w	s. out of court Thomas Berton	2 m 1½ v	7409, rot 14
1468	C1432	Purprestures [encroachments]	Thomas Berton & Wm Mersh; Rob Smarte & Henry Cooke	Both pairs made purprestures (different) in the high road at the lane (venella) called le Twychen.	7410, rot 10

---

[11] This survived as a nearly continuous field boundary, seen on Fig. 8.10c.1b as the hedge running behind fields 21 (partly interrupted by the railway) and 24 (black numbers).

Date	Adm	To	From	Property	WAM
1495 (Nov)	C1240	Alice his w	d. Thomas Barton Aug last	Alice has status in lands	7411, rot 15
1518	C844	Rob Seaston	s. Alice Feld out of court	1 mess 1 v as by court [1448]	7412, rot 11
1519	C853	Margery Seaston his w. Adm delayed	s. before death Rob Seaston	1 m 1v with meadow & pasture, late Alice Feld	7412, rot 11d
1519	C854	Thomas Paradeyce. Adm delayed	s. Alice Felde	1 mess ½ v late Thomas Bertons	7412, rot 11d
1520	C859	Rob Seaston decd	s. before death Alice Feld, recited	1 mess 1v, parcel of 2 mess 1½ v with meadow & pasture of 1 2/ v as by court [1448], held jointly with Thomas Berton decd. She surr by court [1518]	7412, rot 12d
1520	C860	Margery Seaston his w.	s. before death Rob Seaston decd, recited	1 mess 1 v as above. Proclamation.	7412, rot 12d
1520	C861	Thomas Paradyece. Proclamation ordered	s. before death Alice Feld, recited	1 mess ½ v; parcel of 2 mess 1½ v with meadow & pasture of ½ v, court [1448], joint with Thomas Berton decd. Proclamation.	7412, rot 12d
1520	C864	Proclamation for heir	Thomas Berton [and Alice]	2 m 1½ v land with meadow & pasture belonging	7412, rot 13
1521	C866	Margery Sesson	Formerly Thomas Berton, by lord's special grant	1 m 1v parcel of 2 m 1½ v; long preamble about Thomas Berton, Alice, and courts decision; orig copy 26 Hen VI	7412, rot 13d
1521	C867	Proclamation	Thomas Berton	1 m ½ v	7412, rot 14
1522	C877	First proclamation	Alice Feld & heirs of Thomas Berton	Mess & ½ v	7412, rot 14d
1522?	C880	Second proclamation	late Thomas Berton	Mess & ½ v	7412, rot 15
1524	C886	Third proclamation	Late Thomas Bertons	1 mess ½ v	7412, rot 15d

(c) Morys property (Seaston after Berton)

Date	Adm	To	From	Property	WAM
1523	C896	Wm Yong[er], bailiff, and his heirs	s. Marg Seaston out of court	1 m 1 v late Bertons and afterwards Alice Felds	7412, rot 17
1525	C915	Alice Seaston [for Margery?]	Formerly Alice Feld and Thos Berton	1 m 1v, parcel of 2 m 1½ v as by court [1520], third proclamation	7412, rot 18d
1526	C918	John Morys DCL	s. Margery Seaston	1 mess 1 v late Thos Bartons as by court [1519]	7412, rot 19
1531	C978	Unknown heirs, to seize	d. John Morres, vicar	2 mess and 1 v with pasture of 2 cows late Alice Felds, court [1526]	7412, rot 24d
? 1533	C987	Retain in lords hands	[d.] John Morryce or Morres, clerk	1 mess, 1v and pasture of 2 cows; 9 a	7412, rot 26d
1532	C999	To inquire	John Moryce clerk	1 mess 1 v	7412, rot 28
1535	C1018	Michael Dormer of London, mercer	s. out of court Edw Burley and Katherine his w, John Mylle and Alice his w, held in right of said Kath & Alice	1 mess 1 v land with meadow belonging & pasture of 2 cows as coheirs of late John Morres clerk as by court [1534]	7412, rot 30

(d) Trewlocke property (Asteley after Berton)

Date	Adm	To	From	Property	WAM
1525	C916	Grant to Thurstan Asteley, lords servant	Formerly Alice Feld and Thos Berton	1m ½v	7412, rot 18d
1533	C1000	Ric Trewlock	s. Christian Asheley	1 m ½ v late Thos Berton as by copy [1449] [*sic*]	7412, rot 28d
1534	C1011	To distrain	John Trewlocke & Michael Dormer	Divers lands	7412, rot 29d
1535	C1020	Michael Dormer of London, mercer	s. John Trewlocke	1 mess, ½v land and meadow & pasture, received by surr of Thrustan Asheley	7412, rot 30

BUILDING EVIDENCE AND PROBATE RECORDS

Tudor house carries a Sun Insurance firemark numbered 270999, relating to a policy dated 24 June 1769 insuring the dwelling house of Sarah Bosley (spinster) for £240 and her household goods for £60. The house is described as being of stone and timber with a slate roof.

A series of early wills and inventories also relate to the house.

EDWARD SMALBONE THE ELDER OF STEVENTON YEOMAN: 1618. Berks RO, MWB 117.
Will: 13 Apr 1614 [recte 1618]. Proved 2 June 1618.
Sons Richard, Thomas and John Smalbone £3. Daughters Anne Daniell [d 1639] and Elizabeth Lyford (d. 1645, see STE-N), 40s. To Joan Draker, servant, 20s at age 21 or marriage. Remaining goods to wife Alice Smalbone. Neighbours Wm Simpson & Rob Weston overseers. Codicil dated 15 May 1618, reciting will 13 Apr 1618. Richard Smalbone my eldest son to have table … in the hall, and the pott hangers fastened in the chimney wall next the entry door there, and the stable door chain on the south side. Son Thomas Smalbone to have cupboard in hall. John Smalbone my son to have bedstead in chamber where I now lodge. Edward Smalbone my son best bedstead. Alice my wife shall have use of all the said premises during her life. Witnesses Richard Kirfoot, William Lyford.
Inventory: dated 20 May 1618. £227 11s 10d. appraisers Thomas Stevens, Richard Hopkins, John Smalbone, William Stevens, Robert Weston.
    Rooms named:
    Chamber, Hall, another Chamber, another Chamber [beds etc], then brass & pewter, silver, linen, barells etc, beam & scales, potthooks etc, cheese press, various tools.

ALICE SMALBONE, WIDOW: 1631. Berks RO, MWB 118
Will: 30 Jan 1631.
To son Richard Smalbone all pales gates & mounds in backside, doors locks & keys about house, benches & glass in house, cupboard standing in my hall, besdstead wherein I now lie, being the best bedstead in my best chamber. Also brass furnace, salting trough, churne (*a local dialect word for a bacon frame*) to hang bacon, and the gates of iron and two iron dogs in the hall chimney, and lesser of three spits which hangs up and my shuttels of windows. To each of said son Richard's children, being five in number, Richard and James his two sones and Frances Elizabeth and Mary his three daughters 20s each. To Thomas Smalbone my son £5. To eight children of my son Thomas 20s a piece. To Son Thomas my best fetherbedd..[other furnishings] and my russet cloak which was his father's. To my daughter Lyford, £5 and [linen]. To my dau Lyford's five children £5, 20s apiece. To my daughter Daniell £5; to her 3 children £3, 20s apiece. To my son John Smalbone's three children £3, 20s apiece. To Edward Smalbone, son of my son Edward Smalbone, to Mary & Mabel the daughters of my son Edward, 20s apiece.
    To Joan my maid £5. To said Joan ..[much furniture etc]
    To my four goddaughters Mary Smalbone Jane Smalbone Alice Smalbone Mary Smalbone being all four the daughters of my four sons to each 1 platter 1 pottenger & 1 great saucer. To son Edward's daughter my coffer called the big coffer. To Mabel my son Edward's daughter my little box. To Elizabeth Lyford, my god-daughter [kitchen items]. To god-daughter Mary daughter of my son Richard one little coffer. To god-daughter Jane Smalbone my son Thomas's daughter one other little coffer. To Thos Smalbone my grandchild my late servant my coffer. To my son Edward my best coverlett ..[more]. To son John Smalbone [kitchen items] and I forgive him a debt of £20 and upwards which he oweth me by bonds. To Alice, my son John's daughter my best chest.

Residual legatees sons Thomas Smalbone and Edward Smalbone, execs. William Sympson & Robert Weston overseers.

Inventory: 8 Nov 1631, praised by Richard Trewlocke Robert Weston William Simpson. Total £153 7s 10d. Rooms named:

> Hall; Buttery within the Hall; a Little house behind the chimney; Kitchen; Boulting house; Milkhouse; Apple loft; Chamber over the Hall; Chamber where she did lodge; Chamber at the stair head; Wheat house; Barley barn; over the cow house.

RICHARD SMALBONE, 1687. Wiltshire & Swindon Archives, P1/S/544.

Will: 29 January 1686[/7]. Proved 1689.

To brother Edward, £10. Sister Jane, Edith, Alice, £5 each. Anne, daughter of brother-in-law James Stevens, £1; Thomas, his son, £4; rest of his children £10 each. Has surrendered his messuage & 1½ yardland to use of trustees: to sell after death of him and his wife Elizabeth, the profits in five parts to go to the children of his deceased sister, Anne and of his three other sisters, and the children of Mary, daughter of his brother Edward. Wife, Elizabeth to be executrix.

Inventory: dated 11th September 1689. Total £946. Rooms named:

> Hall; Little room adjoining to hall; Parlour; new Chamber; Chamber over Parlour; Little chamber adjoining; Little chamber over hall; Chamber adjoyning and the Closett; Pantry; Cheese Chamber; Buttery; Roome behind the Buttery; Kitchen; Mault House; Barne; Granary (parcell of beanes); Milkhouse.

CHARLES HAYWARD, 1731. Berks RO, D/A1/198/152.

Administration: To his son, Thomas.

Inventory. Total. £130 3s. Lists only 'goods' within each room:

> Chamber over the hall; Room; Chamber over the Parlour; Hall; Parlour; Buttery; Kitchen; Malt house; Brew house (listed after backside, so probably detached).

THOMAS HAYWARD, 1767. TNA, PROB 11/929

Will: 13 June 1767. This recites the surrender in 1746 of the property to the uses of his will, and the bequest of the property to his servant Sarah Bosley (executrix and residual legatee). He also made various small monetary bequests to Hayward relatives, and Joseph Bosley of Steventon received £10.

Interpretation

Only the inventory taken after Richard Smalbone's death in 1689 gives a reasonably full listing of rooms. Of those named, the first three:

> Hall, Little room adjoining the hall, Parlour

seem likely to represent the main ground floor rooms in bays I–III. The new chamber (named next) was perhaps in bay IV on the ground floor, although it seems more likely to have been upstairs. Andirons are listed in the hall and parlour, confirming that they were heated. The specific mention of a 'picture' in the parlour may refer to the painted overmantel.

The upstairs rooms presumably correspond to those on the ground floor, though starting with the first room reached at the head of the stairs, a chamber in bay IV:

> New Chamber over the parlour, Little chamber adjoining, Little chamber over the hall, Chamber adjoining (heated and with a closet).

He had extensive service rooms which seem to have been on the ground floor and presumably occupied bays IV–VI (and the suggested service room at the east end of the house, if that still existed):

> Pantry, Cheese chamber, Buttery, Room behind the buttery, Kitchen, Malthouse.

8.11. STO-F: Stoneleigh, Phoenix Cottage, 1 Birmingham Road, Warwickshire

Grid reference: SP 3295 7280   *Survey dates*: 1967–1992   *By*: N. W. Alcock, J. G. Braithwaite & M. W. Jeffs

Fig. 8.11.1. View of Phoenix Cottage from the south.

ARCHITECTURAL DESCRIPTION

SUMMARY AND HISTORICAL DEVELOPMENT

This is an exceptionally well-preserved cruck house, with virtually complete wall-framing, which has been tree-ring dated to 1480–2. The three bays comprised floored inner room & solar; hall; entry and service/kitchen. In the seventeenth century, the hall and kitchen were floored, and a chimney inserted. Later, the floor of the inner room was removed and it was used as a small barn.[1]

---

[1]   The house has previously been described in Alcock, N. W., Braithwaite, J. G. and Jeffs, M. W. (1971–1973) 'Timber-framed buildings in Warwickshire: Stoneleigh village', *Trans Birmingham Archaeol. Soc.* **85**, 178–202; Alcock, N. W. (1993) *People at home: Living in a Warwickshire village, 1500–1800*, Chichester: Phillimore.

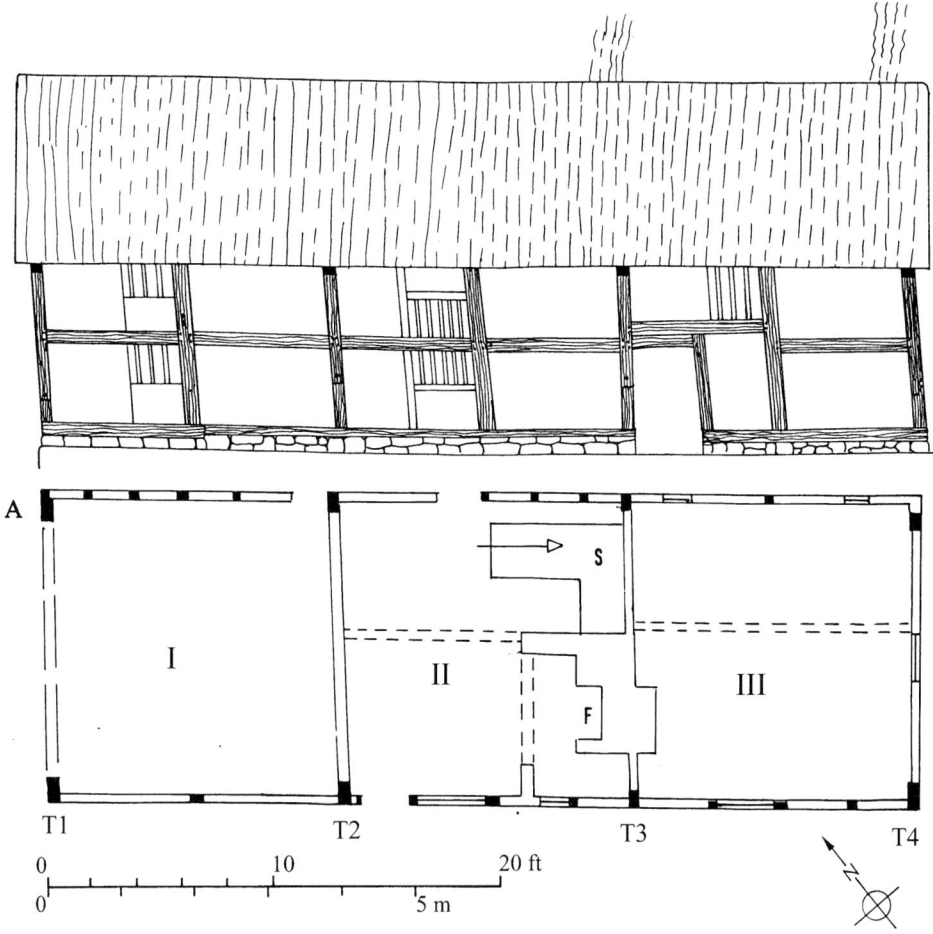

Fig. 8.11.2. Ground floor plan, showing truss and bay numbering (lower); reconstructed elevation (upper).

STRUCTURAL FEATURES

PHASE 1: Four complete closed cruck trusses define the three original bays. The blades are boxed heart with notably irregular unmatched profiles; the trusses have saddle apexes (type 'C') or type 'F1' (saddle with short king post, T1) (Fig. 8.11.3–4). They include halved collars, spurs and tiebeams (removed on truss T1), and they carry packing pieces. None of the trusses have any decorative features, but well-shaped long curved windbraces are present. The sill beams are carried on low sandstone walls.

The original simple wall-framing is virtually complete (Fig. 8.11.2). Each cruck blade has a wall-stud ('cruck stud') on its outside, carried in a V-cut and splay on the cruck and secured by a face-peg (or on T1a free tenon, Fig. 8.11.5); the cruck spurs are halved across these studs, projecting beyond them. Plank-like studs (8in across) are set in the centre of each bay, and 8in mid-rails span from stud to stud. The large panels defined by these elements appear originally not to have been subdivided, although some bays have had additional lighter studs inserted. The presumed wattle-and-daub infill has been entirely replaced in brick. The door position in bay III is indicated by the mid-rail being at a slightly higher level, with a stud for a door jamb at the centre of this rail, and pegs in this and the cruck stud for a door-head. The sill wall is interrupted at this point. Neither the window positions nor the framing elements for them have been identified, and they were perhaps defined by light studs set into un-pegged mortices in the rails.

Evidence for an original floor in bay I comes from the slot in its central wall stud. This can be recognised as being a through mortice for a transverse ceiling beam which would have carried heavy square joists running axially, similar to the beams and joists in three of the other Stoneleigh cruck houses (STO-C, STO-D, STO-H). Soot-blackening is present in

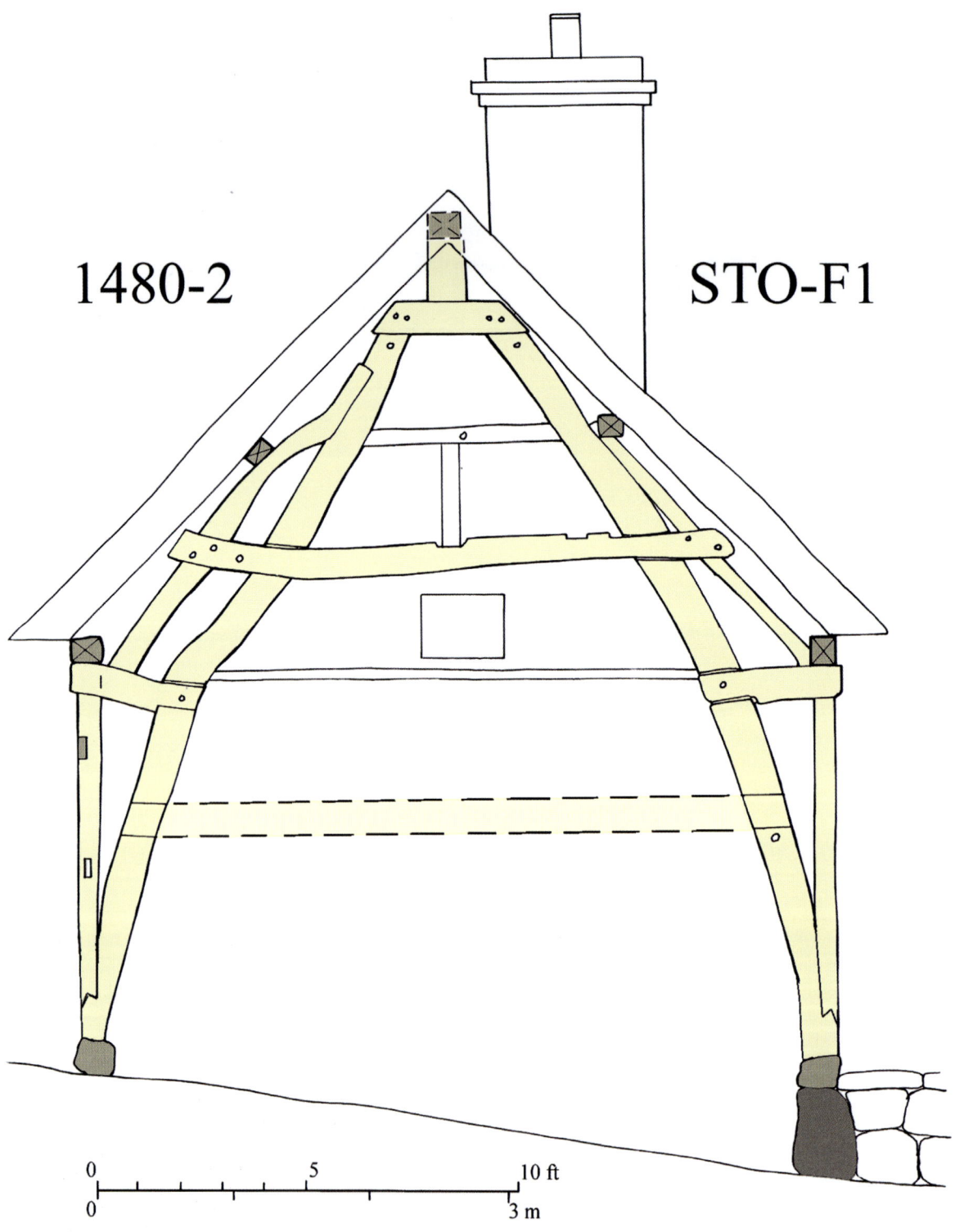

1480-2   STO-F1

Fig. 8.11.3. Section of truss T1.

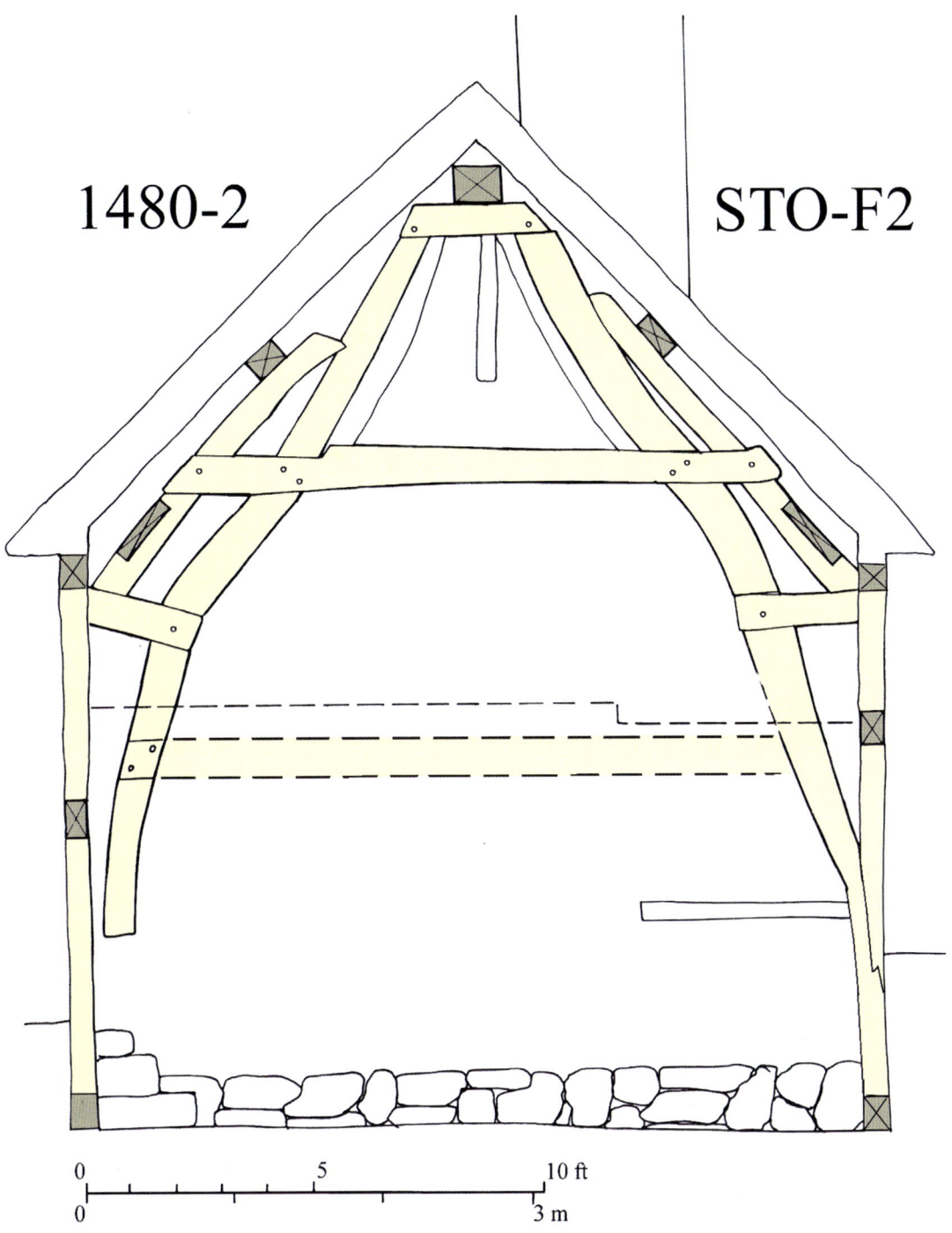

1480-2   STO-F2

Fig. 8.11.4. Section of truss T2.

Fig. 8.11.5. The cruck foot of truss T1 (north-east), showing the V-cut and the free tenon.

both bays II and III. This leads to the identification of room use as: bay I, inner chamber with solar above; bay II, open hall; bay III, entry and kitchen/service.[2]

LATER PHASES: In later work, upper floors were inserted in bays II and III, with a chimney in bay II. The ceiling beam in bay II and the fireplace lintel have chamfers and scroll stops, indicating a seventeenth century date for this work. At some period, bay I was converted into a small barn by the removal of the floor (reinstated in the 1980s).

DENDROCHRONOLOGY

For dendrochronology abbreviations see page facing Introduction.

Sampling comments: nine samples were obtained through coring by Robert Howard and one slice was obtained from timber removed during renovation (STO-F10).

Tree-ring Sample Record and Summary of Dating

Sample Code	Sample Location	Total Rings	Sapwood Rings	FMR Date	LHR Date	LMR Date	Date Cat
STO-F01	Front (SW side) purlin T3–T4	84	12	1387	1458	1470	2
STO-F02	Brace purlin/cruck T3 front	20	—	—	—	—	—
STO-F03	Front cruck blade truss T4	45	—	—	—	—	—
STO-F04	Rear cruck blade truss T2	67	09	1409	1466	1475	2
STO-F05	Rear purlin bay I	76	14c	1402	1463	1477	2
STO-F06	Front cruck blade truss T2	48	03	1426	1470	1473	2
STO-F07	Front cruck spur truss T2	48	05	—	—	—	—
STO-F08	Front purlin bay I	60	—	—	—	—	—
STO-F09	Rear cruck blade truss T3	51	—	1403	—	1453	3d
STO-F10	Mid-rail	59	13NM	—	—	—	—
	Average date of last heartwood ring					1464	

---

[2]   Cf. Alcock, *People at home*, 23f.

Site sequence: SEQ 3 (composed of samples 1, 4, 5, 6), 91 rings long dated 1387–1477 with *t*-value 5.3 (E.MID), 5.2 (HIW-ASQ01, site sequence of Thatched Cottage, Hill Wootton, VA20,89)

Sample 9 dated 1403–1453 with *t*-values of 5.5 (E.MID), 4.7 (S. ENG).

Felling date: (sample 5 with last dated ring of 1477 lost about 3 or 4 rings in coring) **1480–2**.

DOCUMENTARY HISTORY

Phoenix Cottage is identified on the 1597 map with the name Elizabeth Jenkens (Fig. 8.11.6). It can be traced continuously through the estate rentals and surveys for Stoneleigh Abbey and then the Leigh estate, from 1533 onwards, held as a cottage with only a ½ acre croft, occupied by people of low status (Table 8.11.1). From 1533 to 1551, its tenant was John Hogkyns (sometimes Hogekynson), and he was succeeded (by 1559, the next surviving rental), by his widow Joan. He is regularly recorded in the court rolls from 1540 to 1546 as a juror and was tithingman in 1546; in 1539, he had two unringed pigs, and in 1546 was assaulted by one William Edwards. For her, they note the heriot paid as a cottage tenant on her death; her best possession was a *broach* [spit], valued at 4d (although her common rights would have allowed her to pasture two head of cattle). She was succeeded by John Jones and he in his turn by his widow, Elizabeth (tenant 1589–1606). Their occupations were as brewers and sellers of ale, typical of the poorest cottagers. 'John Jones' wife' (later Widow Jones or Elizabeth Jones *alias* Jenkyn) was presented at virtually every court for breaking the assize of beer. In 1585 John was fined 1s for allowing four villagers to play cards in his house. No probate records relate to the house.

STO-F

Fig. 8.11.6. Section of the 1597 map of Stoneleigh (SCLA, DR671/3).

Richard Heyllworth, the tenant before 1533 can probably be recognised as the Richard Eylward fined 2d in 1529 for failing to appear at the court, but he is not among those named in the 1522 listing of tenants.[3] Although the 1497 rental is broadly in the same order as that for 1533, and the latter's entries 10–18 and 25–32 can be matched from the sequence of rents, the six intervening entries (including this cottage, entry 19) do not correspond to the four entries listed in 1497, all of which have larger rents. It is therefore possible that the holding had been reduced in size in the intervening period.

Table 8.11.1. Rental entries for Phoenix Cottage, Stoneleigh

Date	Rent	Name	Notes
Pre-1533	5s	Richard Heyllworth	Replaced in Lady Day 1533 rental by John Sawyer
1533	5s	John Sawyer	Lady Day rental only [then in a different cottage]
1533–1551	5s	John Hogkyns, for a cottage	Replaces John Sawyer in Michaelmas 1533 rental
1559–71	5s	Joan Hogkyns	1559 Goodwife Hoggkynes
1575–88	5s	John Jones	
1589–1606	5s	Elizabeth Jedkin alias Jones	1597 Map (Fig. 8.11.6): Jenkens 266 (correctly 260) Survey: 260 Elizabeth Jedkin, widow 2 r 24p; common for 2 beasts & a horse (SCLA, DR18/30/24/279)

---

[3] SCLA, DR18/30/24/126.

8.12. WOR-A: Water Orton, The Chestnuts, Church Lane, Warwickshire[1]

Grid reference: SP 1765 9139   *Survey dates: 8 March 1990 & 2006*   *By: D. Miles*

Fig. 8.12.1 (*above*). The Chestnuts in 2006 from the north (composite photograph).

Fig. 8.12.2 (*right*). The Chestnuts in 2006 from the south.

ARCHITECTURAL DESCRIPTION

SUMMARY AND HISTORICAL DEVELOPMENT

PHASE 1: The Chestnuts is a substantial house facing north onto Church Lane in Water Orton but set back from it (Figs. 8.12.1–2). The overall arrangement is of a hall flanked by crosswings (Fig. 8.12.3), but dating shows that both wings are later than the central block, which has been tree-ring dated to 1398/99. This two-bay hall range now retains

---

[1]   For further details, see Alcock, N. W. (2008) 'The Chestnuts, Water Orton', unpublished report (copy at WCRO).

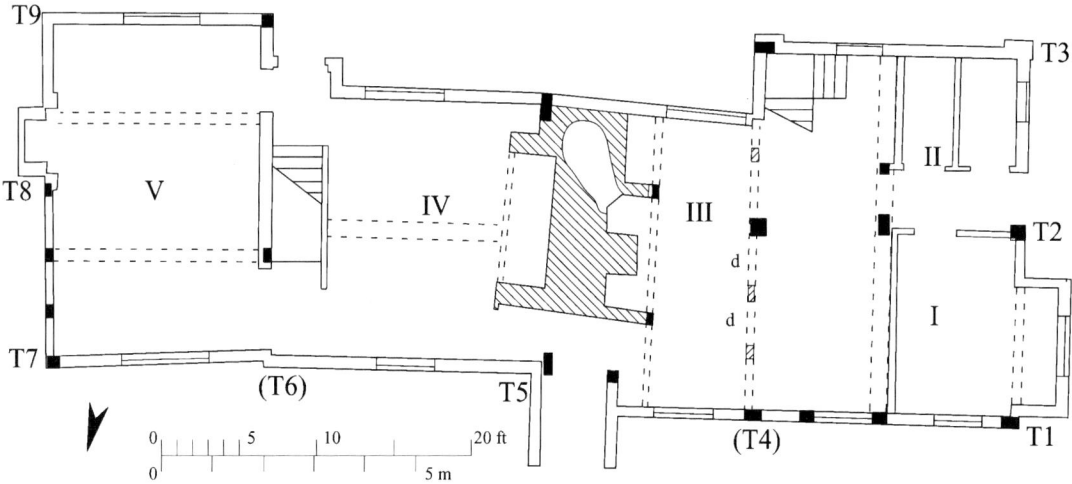

Fig. 8.12.3. Plan, showing truss and bay numbering.

only the arch-braced open central cruck truss (T5, Fig. 8.12.4) and the purlins; the wall plates may survive in part but cannot be examined closely. The range is unsymmetrical, the eastern bay being 18 feet long compared to 13 feet for the western bay, perhaps the result of the latter having been truncated when the west wing was added. The truss has a saddle apex (type 'F1') and is most noteworthy for the jointing of the arch braces. Instead of being tenoned into the crucks and collar as is normal, they are let into the face with 'joggled' halvings. No trace remains of either of the original end trusses of the hall. It is probable that the original building had in-line bays at each end, since if there had been predecessors of the present wings, it is difficult to see why the hall end trusses should not have been retained.

PHASE 2: The *western crosswing* was originally thought to be of the 1350s, from apparently archaic features, such as the samson post supporting the first floor axial beam. However, close structural study showed that it could not pre-date the hall, though it was not possible to establish if they were contemporary or if the wing was later. Tree-ring dating samples failed to provide a satisfactory match, but a sample from the principal post of T2 has given a radiocarbon felling-date range of *cal AD 1415–53*, demonstrating that it post-dates the hall by some 20–40 years. Double doorways facing the hall show that it was divided at ground floor level, presumably for paired service rooms. Since the fair face of the hall truss is to the east, this must be a low-end service and solar wing. Presumably it replaced a service bay, and the inferred chamber at the other end may then have been relegated to service use. The roof of the wing is of standard clasped-purlin construction. This range is of particular interest for its solid wooden first floor composed of joists butted together. These joists are clamped between two rails on the outside wall and are supported by a massive axial beam carried on a samson post. The radiocarbon date matches closely with the date of the only other example of a touching-joist floor known to us, at The Old Rectory, Clifford Chambers, Warwickshire, of 1433/4 (X-CLI).

PHASES 3–4: The two-bay *eastern crosswing* has been tree-ring dated to Winter 1579/80. It is narrower than the west wing but has a similar roof structure, with clasped purlins and queen struts below the collar.

Flooring the hall. Probably in the late 16th century, the hall was floored over and a chimney stack serving two fireplaces, and with a bread oven was built just west of the central truss. This dating is based on the chamfers on the mantel beam and axial beam and the size of the bricks in the stack. This may well have taken place at the same time as the eastern crosswing was constructed. Probably at the same date, large timber-framed cross gables were added to both the front and back of the eastern bay of the hall, probably to improve the lighting of the inserted upper room.

LATER PHASES. Late eighteenth or nineteenth century renovation is seen in the brick infilling of the frame, and also in the decorative ironwork window of the west crosswing. The east wing chimney is probably also of this date. A large window appears to have been inserted in the east wing rear gable, that has since been removed.

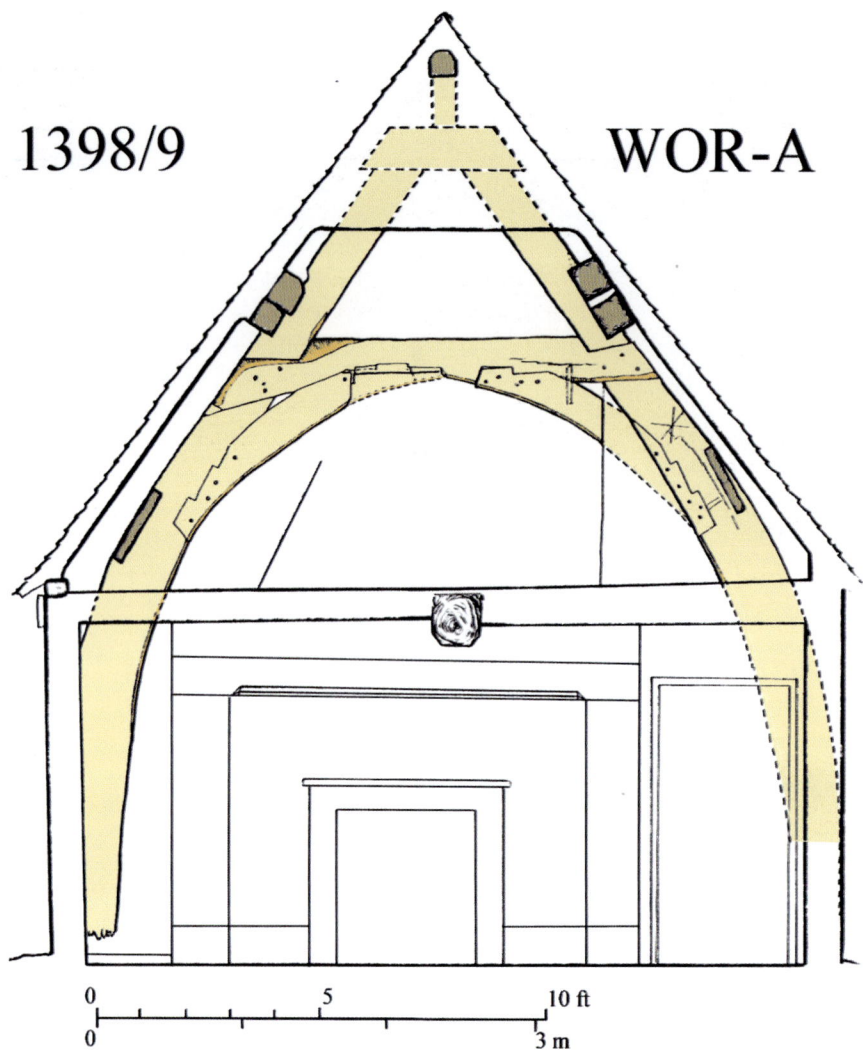

Fig. 8.12.4. Section of truss T5, from the east.

STRUCTURAL FEATURES

PHASE I: *Hall range*: The front blade of the central cruck truss has been deeply cut away for a later doorway. It was not possible to gain access to the roof space to the east of the chimney stack to survey the cruck above purlin level. However, a saddle and king strut (apex type 'F1') were visible through a small hole behind the front cruck blade (Fig. 8.12.5) (sketched on the section of T1). A heavy staple is set into the ridge beam, just east of the cruck apex. Soot blackening is evident on the crucks and purlins. The undersides of the braces and cruck blades carry ¾ in chamfers. The arch braces are face-lapped with joggled halvings into the collar and cruck blades (Figs. 8.12.4, 6). This method of jointing is most unusual, the only near parallels being at 1–2 Ufton Fields, Ufton (X-UFT) and 14–16 Hinckley Road, Walsgrave-on-Sowe (WOS-A) (1407d and probably early fifteenth century). The former is closely similar to The Chestnuts, but in the latter, the arch braces are very simply halved into the face of the crucks and collar, a much less refined arrangement than at The Chestnuts. The fair face of the cruck truss faces east, and a 'square' mark is evident just above the windbrace mortice on the northern blade. Apart from a II on the same cruck blade at the foot of the arch brace, no assembly marks are evident on the visible timbers.

Both purlins survive and the separate sections for each bay are lodged one above the other on the central truss. The only windbrace pegs are for those adjoining the open truss. The purlins measure up to 8½ by 10in and are boxed heart. The

Fig. 8.12.5. The apex of truss T5.

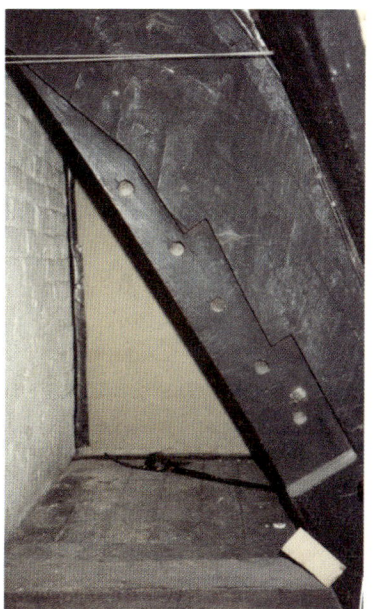

Fig. 8.12.6. The joggled halving of truss T5. The remainder of the brace has been cut away for access past the chimney.

Fig. 8.12.7. Truss T2 in the west crosswing.

windbraces measure 3 by 10–12in and are jointed to the purlins with barefaced dovetails. The rafters are concealed by plaster. The ends of the purlins are supported by the crosswing wall plates at both ends. At the west end, the ridge beam continues past the wall line and is simply cut off against a rafter, consistent with bay III having been shortened when the wing was built. The rear wall of the hall here joins up awkwardly with the wing, at a slight angle to the other hall bay, and the purlins of the hall are notched onto the crosswing wall plate.

At the east end, the hall purlins are carried on the wall plate, as at the other end of the hall, but the ridge beam terminates on the wall-line, suggesting that the original end truss might have been a 'portal frame' (as at The Old Crown House, Skirmett, Buckinghamshire (SKI-A)), with two aisle-posts carrying a tiebeam supporting the purlins, and with a central king-post.

No framing is visible in the walls of the hall below wall plate level, with the exception of the cruck blades. However, the rear elevation has sandstone footings running apparently continuously along the whole of the hall range. The front wall has been built out as a lean-to, between the present front door and the west wing.

PHASE TWO: *Western crosswing*: All three trusses have clasped purlins and cambered collars with queen struts (Fig. 8.12.7); the front tiebeam is almost straight. In contrast to the other wing, the east end of the central wing tiebeam is cut to the line of the roof slope rather than squared off. The principal rafters of truss T2 are bridled together, with

Fig. 8.12.8. The continuous joist floor of the west crosswing.

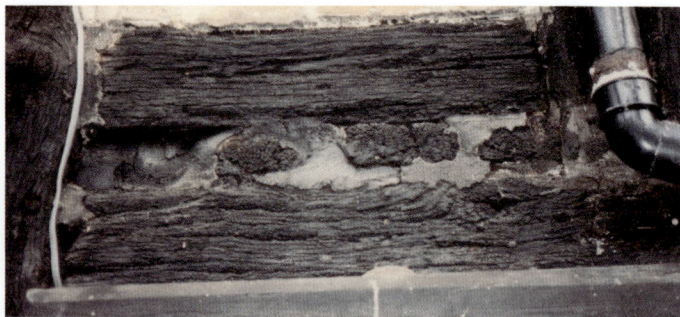

Fig. 8.12.9. Joist ends and mid-rails of the west crosswing.

Fig. 8.12.10. The samson post and ceiling beam of the west crosswing.

expanded heads. At the front, the heavy corner posts (9 by 14–16in) have very slight jowls and up-braces to both the tiebeam and the first floor girt (Fig. 8.12.1). The centre posts along the sides measure 12–14in square and are arch-braced to the wall plate. The north-west corner post is carried on a sandstone block (rather than a continuous plinth), apparently lapping over a removed sill beam on the west elevation.

Probably the most notable feature of the wing is the first floor construction which consists of flat joists 4in thick by 7–11in wide, laid butted against one to serve as floor boards, and presumably originally infilled to produce a level floor (Fig. 8.12.8). They are supported by an axial beam in the centre and a mid-rail on the outside walls where the joist ends are clamped by a second rail immediately above (Fig. 8.12.9). The axial beam is a massive timber 13 in wide, decorated by a simple 1–2in flat chamfer with stepped run-out stops. This beam is supported front and back by substantial posts rising to the first floor mid-rail and in the centre by a samson post which is similarly chamfered and stopped (Fig. 8.12.10).

The eastern wall of the wing, fronting onto the hall, retains segmental heads in the mid-rail for two doors, one on either side of the centre post. Smoke blackening is visible along the hall side and underside of these rails (and also in the wing roof, indicating that this was not sealed off from the hall). The panel to the north of the northern door into the hall has a central rectangular mortice in the underside of the rail, quite unlike the four stave holes in the last panel to the north. There was presumably a partition running from between the two doors into the hall, westwards to the samson post; only the head beam of this remains. The stairs at present rise from the south-east corner of the wing but it is not known if this is the original position, as the joists are not exposed on the east side of the axial beam.

PHASE 3: *East crosswing*: This wing is of two storeys with the gable again fronting the road. The tiebeam at the back has been severed and plated on top, probably for the insertion of a very large window (since removed) (Fig. 8.12.2). Little framing remains at the back or on the east side. The trusses have collars with raking queen struts on trusses T7 and T8, but one strut to the collar and a raking strut either side on T9; the wind braces are short and straight. The west end of the central tiebeam is cut vertically, confirming that this end has always been internal. The first floor is carried on two 8in wide transverse beams; these are supported on 6 by 10in posts at each end, the beams and the posts carrying them being chamfered with scroll stops. The wall posts of the central truss are 8–9in wide,. A later chimney stack stands to the east just beyond the centre post. The west wall side rail retains a door head cut into a shallow ogee, leading into the hall.

LATER PHASES: The two inserted cross gables of the hall chamber each contain an upper and lower collar with raking struts above. The rear principals are of very crooked timber, probably the same tree cut in half. The inserted hall chimney stack is to the west of the open truss and is in line with the kink in the rear wall. The stack is built of early bricks (9¾ by 4¾ by 2¼in), and on the west side rests on two oak posts some 9–10in square. The stack is most unusual, as the top finishes with a very elaborate shaft which includes a saw-tooth band below a number of pilasters. Strangely, these start below the roof line. The fireplace lintel on the east side of the stack is decorated with a 2in chamfer with ovolo and hollow mouldings with angled stops. The axial beam is chamfered but with no visible stops (apparently cut off at the eastern end).

DENDROCHRONOLOGY AND RADIOCARBON DATING

For dendrochronology abbreviations see page facing Introduction.

Sampling Comments: Seventeen samples were taken through coring by Robert Howard on 8 March 1990 and later. Of the nine samples taken from Phase 2, the cruck open hall, only three dated: the two purlins to the east of the open truss and the front cruck blade. Both the front purlin and the cruck blade retained complete sapwood giving a firm felling date of 1398/9. Samples 10 to 17 from the western cross wing were all short, and none could be cross-matched with each other, or matched consistently with master sequences. Further cores were taken by D. Miles on 7 Oct 2006, of the east post of truss T2 (sample A12b), the east wing and the inserted hall floor. Of these, two samples from the east wing dated to 1579/80 (probably winter) and to a range including this date; those from the west wing could not be matched. In 2010, two five-ring samples taken from sample A12b were submitted for radiocarbon dating. The radiocarbon dating was supported by the Vernacular Architecture Group.

TREE-RING SAMPLE RECORD AND SUMMARY OF DATING

Sample Code	Sample Location	Total Rings	Sapwood Rings	FMR Date	LHR Date	LMR Date	Date Cat
Hall							
WOR-A01	Front purlin, W side of T5	30	12	—	—	—	—
WOR-A02	Rear purlin, W side of T5	53	12	—	—	—	—
WOR-A03	Front purlin, E side of T5	43	11C	1356	1387	1398	2
WOR-A04	Front cruck blade, T5	60	19C	1339	1379	1398	2
WOR-A05	Front arch brace, T5	41	—	—	—	—	—
WOR-A06	Rear purlin E side of T5	71	14c	1324	1380	1394	2
WOR-A07	Collar, T5	56	—	—	—	—	—
WOR-A08	Rear windbrace, E side of T5	34	11	—	—	—	—
WOR-A09	Rear cruck blade, T5	NM	—	—	—	—	—
West wing							
WOR-A10	Truss T1 E side post	37	HS	—	—	—	—
WOR-A11	Truss T1 W side post	38	HS	—	—	—	—
WOR-A12	Truss T2 E side post	58	21C	—	—	—	—
WOR-A12b	Truss T2 E side post, additional	94	22C [radiocarbon samples]				
WOR-A13	Truss T2 W side post	38	HS	—	—	—	—
WOR-A14	Wall plate truss T2–3 E side	54	17C	—	—	—	—
WOR-A15	Wall plate truss T2–3 W side	58	07	—	—	—	—
WOR-A16	Tiebeam truss T1	37	—	—	—	—	—
WOR-A17	Tiebeam truss T2	22 NM	—	—	—	—	—
WOR-A18	West wing, joist	NM					
WOR-A19	W front wall plate	57	-09				

Sample Code	Sample Location	Total Rings	Sapwood Rings	FMR Date	LHR Date	LMR Date	Date Cat
East wing							
WOR-A20	E crosswing, E rear windbrace	133	24C?	1447	1555	1579	—
WOR-A21	E crosswing, centre tiebeam, T7	130	H/S	1416	1545	1545	—
Hall floor							
WOR-A22a	Hall inserted axial beam	50	—	—	—	—	—
WOR-A22b	ditto	114	06	—	—	—	—
WOR-A22c1	ditto	20	—	—	—	—	—
WOR-A22c2	ditto	31	21½C	—	—	—	—

Site sequence I (composed of samples 3, 4, 6), 75 rings long dated 1324–1398 with *t*-values of 5.3(E.MID), 5.8(OXHASQ04, site sequence of Post Office, Oxhill, VA20.89). Site Sequence II (WORA20–21) (composed of samples 20, 21), 99 rings long dated 1416–1579 with *t*-values of 7.7(FORESTR1), 6.6 (SMMRSFRM), 6.4(PENIARTH).

Estimated felling dates: sequence I (samples 3, 4 with last dated rings have complete sapwood) **1398/9**. Sequence II (sample 20 with probable complete sapwood) Winter **1579/80** (sample 21 with heartwood-sapwood boundary, felling date range 1556-86)

Radiocarbon dating
Radiocarbon samples comprising the first and last five rings from core WOR-A12b were submitted to RLAHA, Oxford for radiocarbon dating by accelerator mass spectrometry. This gave calibrated dates (Fig. 8.12.11a): OXA-22712 (first five rings) *Cal AD 1287–1326* (39%) or *1343–1395* (56%); OXA-23077 (final five rings to bark edge) *1414–1447*. The combined felling date range is *1414–53* (Fig. 8.12.11b). Even within this range, tree-ring dating gave no tentative matches.

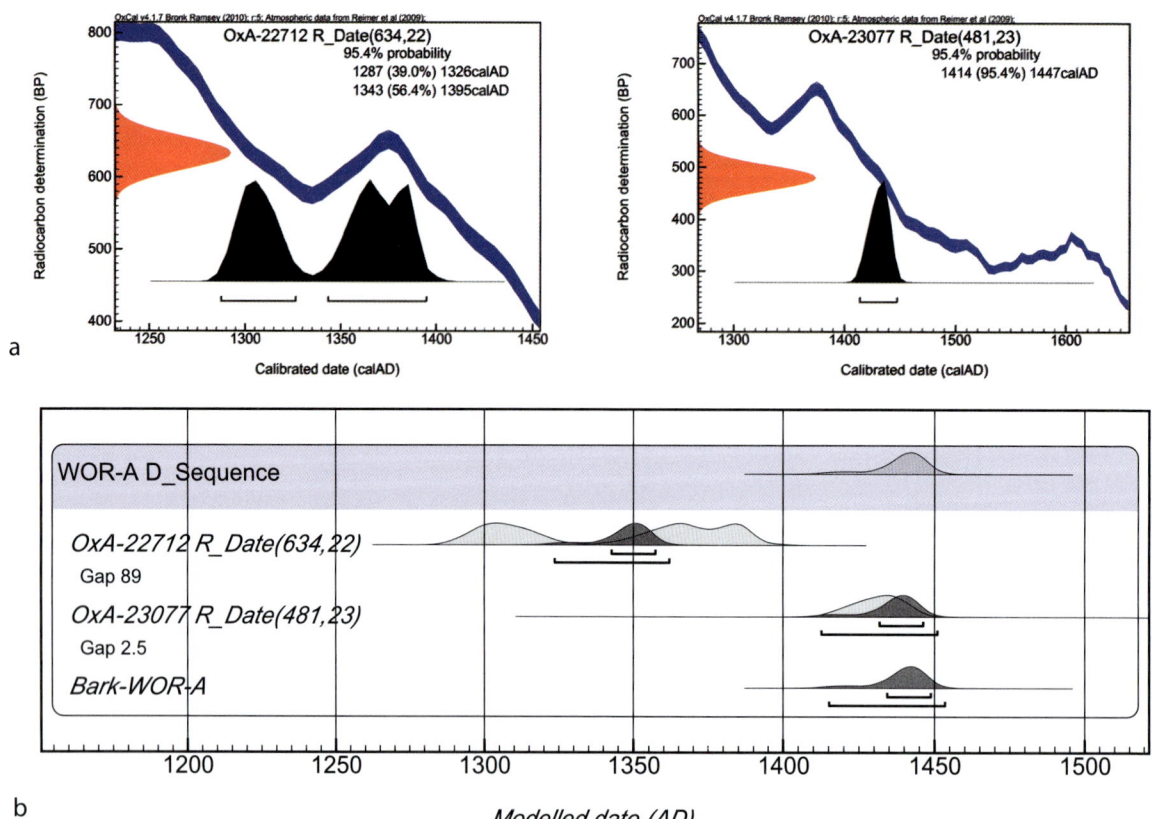

Fig. 8.12.11. Radiocarbon dating of timbers from the wing: (a) Calibration plots; (b) joint calibration.

DOCUMENTARY HISTORY

VCH Warwickshire IV, 262 suggests this is the former manor house of Water Orton, but without citing any evidence other than its position near the site of the original chapel. A full study of the documentary history is included in Alcock (2008) and is summarised here. In the sixteenth and seventeenth centuries, the house appears to have been one of several substantial freehold farms in Water Orton. From the eighteenth to the twenty-first century, the house was owned by the Hargrave family and their descendants (sometimes incorrectly called *Hargreaves*) (Fig. 8.12.12). It became known as The Chestnuts in about 1890, before then not having an individual name. For convenience it is referred to below under its modern name.

It is shown on the Aston Tithe Map (1848) as e29–30, owned and occupied by Jane, Julia, Elizabeth and Frances Hargrave, whose property also included Hall Croft (e195–6), the adjoining field to the east (Fig. 8.12.13).[2] In the '1910 Domesday' Field Book (surveyed in 1914), the owners of The Chestnuts are given as Hargraves Trustees, and the occupier as W. S. Willday.[3] This trust was established by the wills of Frances and Julia Hargrave who died in 1887 and 1888, and a bundle of deeds relating to this trust clarifies its later history.[4] It was finally sold in 2005 by the descendants of the Hargrave family.

In the nineteenth century, The Chestnuts can be traced through a series of family wills. The first is that of Thomas Hargrave (II) of Water Orton, proved in 1838 by his sons Thomas of Lea Marston and Abraham (II) of Water Orton.[5] He left his

Fig. 8.12.12. Hargrave family Tree. Bold type indicates owners of The Chestnuts.

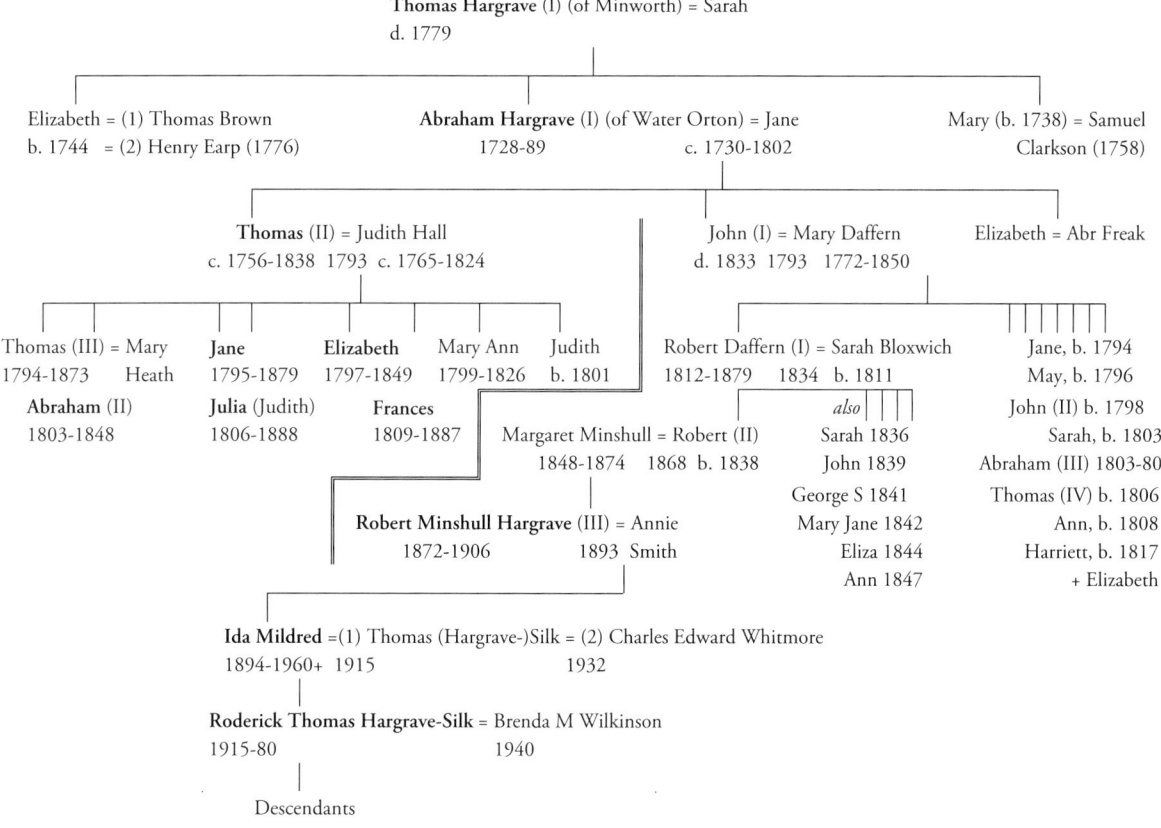

Sources: Parish registers (WCRO & IGI); FreeBMD (on-line); Curdworth Inscriptions (WCRO).

---

2   Map: TNA, IR30/36/10; apportionment: IR29/36/10.

3   TNA, IR58/60726 (hereditament 7736).

4   These were kindly produced for examination by Paul Kimberley of Young & Lee, Birmingham (successors to Haynes Duffell, the Hargrave-Silk solicitors in 2002).

5   Lich, Thomas Hargrave, proved 6 Oct 1838; the will is dated 13 July 1833.

four daughters, Jane, Elizabeth, Julia and Frances, 'my messuage in Water Orton', together with various fields; they were to have this for live while they remained unmarried, and eventually it was to go to his son Abraham. The latter died in 1848 when he was living in Water Orton, probably in The Chestnuts; he left all his property to his cousins Abraham and John Hargrave, as trustees for his four sisters.[6] Of them, Elizabeth died in 1849, and Jane in 1879,[7] and their shares in the estate passed automatically to Julia and Frances. The wills of the latter were identical, leaving their substantial estate (some ten houses and at least 50 acres of land) to each other, in trust for Robert Hargrave (III) (grandson of their cousin Robert Dafforn Hargrave) and then to his heirs.[8]

Before 1838, the Hargrave family can be traced to Abraham (d. 1789), of Water Orton, father of Thomas (II), and to his father Thomas Hargrave (I) (d. 1779), of Minworth (adjoining Water Orton to the north). Thomas (I) is listed in the earliest poor rate levy book for Aston Church (1768), paying for 'The Hall Crofts'; corresponding entries cannot be recognised in the earlier assessments (1696, 1700, 1736).[9] This suggests that Thomas (I) acquired The Chestnuts in the mid-eighteenth century. His predecessors cannot be identified from the rate lists.

A few references to the Hall Crofts (which may include The Chestnuts) are found among the sparse early documents relating to Water Orton. The manor belonged to the Arden family of Park Hall, Castle Bromwich from before 1452 until 1583, when Edward Arden was executed for high treason, and his lands confiscated.[10] Water Orton, Park Hall and other Arden properties were granted to Edward Darcy in 1586 but surrendered to the Crown in 1609 and re-granted to the Arden family.[11] A summary of rents formerly belonging to Edward Arden, paid from the manor of Curdworth, includes a rent from 'Halecroftes' in Water Orton.[12] This rent is

Fig. 8.12.13. Part of the Aston parish Tithe Map of 1848, covering Water Orton, showing some of the property then owned by the Hargrave family (including The Chestnuts and its croft, e29–30 and Hall Croft Meadow (e196, immediately above e29). (East is to the top; TNA, IR30/36/10).

listed in a 1552 Arden rental, as 13s 4d payable at Martinmas (11 Nov), but the name of the payer is not given.[13] The Arden connection is confirmed by a document of 1701, by which Richard Wilcox of Minworth assigned a lease of Halls Crofts to William Barnes.[14] The original lease had been granted in 1677 by Edward Darcy, who still owned the former Arden family property in Curdworth. Barnes was the husband of Elizabeth Darcy, one of the co-heirs of Edward Darcy, so this assignment probably cancelled the lease.[15] The Barnes family seem to have sold off some of their Curdworth property in 1756, so Hall Crofts may have passed to Thomas Hargrave then. The Chestnuts may well have belonged to them as well, though this cannot be confirmed.

A rental of the Arden manor in Water Orton, taken in 1563, lists only four tenants, only one apparently with a farmhouse, and makes no mention of a manor house or the demesne lands that would go with it. It does, however, include nine freeholders paying 'chief rents'.[16] Thus, the manor mainly consisted of these independent farms, and The Chestnuts can probably be identified as one of them.

---

6   Abraham (III) and John (II) on the family tree.
7   Aston Registry Office, Sept 1849 (vol. 6d, 151) and Jun 1879 (vol. 6d, 515).
8   BAH, Birmingham Probate Office records. Both were dated 11 June 1883.
9   BAH, EP/41 [1] 1768–75; BAH, 21228, 21233, 21253.
10   *VCH Warwickshire*, IV, 262.
11   TNA, LR15/148/1–2.
12   TNA, E367/1851, particulars of rents reserved on a lease of chief rents formerly belonging Edward Arden, leased to Edward Darcie in 1609; the amount of the rent is unstated.
13   BAH, Norton 382.
14   Stoke-on-Trent Record Office, D4842/12/1/6. There had originally been no house on Halls Crofts, but one had been built since 1677.
15   *VCH Warwickshire*, IV, 60f.
16   BAH, Norton 155. Staffordshire Record Office, D1287/G34 and G81 are lists of chief rents for 1656 and 1717.

Appendix 1

The Application of Scientific Dating in the Project

Nat Alcock, Cliff Litton, Dan Miles and Bob Laxton†

This appendix describes the tree-ring and radiocarbon dating procedures used. Some technical aspects of the results of the application of dendrochronology in the project are then considered, making particular use of the substantial number of buildings studied, one of the largest coherent groups of buildings examined in a British dating project. The majority of the tree-ring dating was carried out by Robert Howard at the Nottingham University Tree-ring Dating Laboratory with the methodology described below. Some later dating has been undertaken by the Oxford Dendrochronology Laboratory.

Date Presentation

Felling dates and felling-date ranges

Estimated felling dates were originally presented as 'circa' dates, corresponding to the most probable number of sapwood rings, and some such dates have been published in *Vernacular Architecture*. However, it appears from experience that this procedure can give a false impression that the date estimates are more precise that they are in reality, and such dates have frequently been mis-quoted.[1] Following accepted current practice, *felling-date ranges* are now quoted, which have been recalculated using the best current sapwood estimates (see below). Where multiple samples with incomplete sapwood are derived from a single phase, the OxCal computer program has been used to improve the precision of the felling-date range; the unrefined dates are

also included in the reports. Following the proposals of Tyers, these dates are given in italics, indicating that they are interpretative dates.[2]

Table 2.2 (p. 15) lists all the main and subsidiary dates obtained. For plotting and analysis purposes only, 'central felling dates' are used to assign dates to centuries and to place them in chronological order. These correspond to the precise felling date when this is known (final year), or to the mode of the sapwood distribution appropriate to the geographical region (or the first year of the felling-date range if this is later than the modal year). For *terminus post quem* dates, the 'central felling date' is taken as 25 years after the *tpq* date (unless strong indications for a longer period have been identified).

For the conventions used in citing dates in the text, see the table on p. 2.

Tree-ring dating

In much of Britain the major influence on the growth of a species like oak is the weather conditions experienced from season to season, controlling the amount of new wood and thus the width of the annual ring. Trees of the same species growing at the same time in similar habitats are thus expected to respond to climatic conditions by producing similar sequences of ring-widths. The basis of tree-ring dating is that these sequences can be matched from one timber to another and, in particular from one sequence of unknown date to another for which the years that correspond to each ring have been identified (a 'master' or 'reference' chronology).

Naturally, the ring widths of an individual tree are influenced not only by the basic climatic 'signal', but also by genetic variations controlling its response to external stimuli, by its own local environment, by competition, damage, disease, management etc. By taking several samples from the same building phase, it is often possible to cross-match the ring-width patterns, and to average the values for the sequences, so maximising the common signal between trees. The resulting 'site chronology' or 'site sequence' may then match more closely with existing master chronologies.

Sampling

The project tree-ring samples were normally cores, taken with a 12–16mm hollow corer which produces a core approximately 10–12mm in diameter; visible holes were plugged with dowels, stained to match the surrounding surface. Occasionally offcuts from repair work were available. The *sampling strategy* for an individual building was normally established by the project architectural historian and the dendrochronologist working together. As well as carrying out a preliminary examination to discover if sufficient suitable timber could be found, the different phases were identified and timbers original to the phase located. Normally, eight core samples were taken from each phase to be dated, if this number of suitable timbers could be found. This is a standard tree-ring dating procedure, the multiple samples compensating for the relatively low probability that any one sample can be dated.

Suitable cores need to have at least 50, and ideally 100 rings. Therefore, the best samples are from large, slow-grown timbers, without distortions, and retaining their bark edge. Unfortunately, the Midlands cruck houses frequently use small, often fast-grown, trees, converted as boxed heart, only partly squared (see p. 79). This conversion method minimises the loss of timber and so allows smaller trees to be used. However, even the largest timbers (usually the crucks) may have less than 50 rings and, indeed, subsidiary structural timbers, such as collars, sometimes have as few as 10 growth rings.

To determine the precise felling date for a timber, it is necessary to date the final growth ring of the tree. However, in oak the outermost rings are of sapwood. Compared to the heartwood, this is soft and readily suffers insect attack and general degradation over time. Thus, medieval carpenters often removed as much sapwood as possible. Despite this, the need to achieve timbers of a uniform size frequently led them to leave some sapwood at the corners of squared beams or, especially with cruck blades, to leave them entirely in the round, with complete sapwood over part or much of their length. Even if the sapwood is not complete, the number of sapwood rings is relatively constant (see below), so that

if some sapwood is present, an estimate of the felling-date range can be made.

In sampling, particular care was taken to include sapwood out to the bark edge (waney edge) whenever possible. For a few samples, although the bark edge was present, the outer rings were very soft and could not be preserved during coring, so that the number of sapwood rings is slightly uncertain. Overall, this care in sampling sapwood has been well rewarded. Of the 84 tree-ring dates obtained for primary phases, 53 were precise (or had only slight uncertainty about the last few sapwood rings), while for only one house do the dated timbers lack even the heartwood/sapwood boundary.

The use of timber other than oak posed a particular problem in the survey. Although tree-ring dates have been reported for elm, by cross-matching with British oak chronologies, no independent chronologies have been established to confirm their validity.[3] Elm, in particular, was used very frequently in the Midlands for all except the highest quality work, and it tends to be even faster-growing than oak, and have still fewer rings. Some buildings were rejected because they appeared to be entirely of elm; other samples proved to be of elm when examined in the laboratory, although this was not immediately apparent in the building. Elm samples were deliberately taken at two buildings (WAL-A and LON-I), the first of which was believed to be completely of elm, to see if they could be dated. However, great difficulty was found in measuring the ring widths accurately and no dates could be obtained; paradoxically, during the sampling of WAL-A, oak purlins were identified, that dated satisfactorily.

Analysis

The first stages in sample analysis are the sanding and polishing of one surface of the core, followed by the measurement of ring widths using a travelling microscope linked to a computer, so that the individual ring positions can be recorded by pressing a key. Each core is measured twice and the values averaged.

Cross-matching between two sequences can be done visually by comparing plots of the ring-widths, but this needs a trained eye for any comparisons other than the most obvious. The Nottingham procedure for matching is to use a computerised comparison of the two sequences, sometimes with a visual check of the apparent match, which also serves as a check on measuring procedures. This is a statistical process, and requires sufficiently long sequences for confidence in the results. The minimum length of a tree-ring series that can be cross-matched is not defined, but sequences of less than fifty rings are hardly ever used.

Filtering. Before cross-matching is attempted, the *growth-trend* needs to be removed. In general the younger, inner, rings of a tree tend to be wider than the outer rings. This trend is removed to produce ring-width *indices* and it is standard practice to cross-match with these indices rather than the raw ring widths themselves.[4] These long-period trends are removed by dividing each ring width by the five-year moving average centred on this ring. After this, taking logarithms ensures that the filtered sequence has an approximately normal distribution (positive and negative values with a mean of 0). Specifically, let

$$x_1, x_2, \ldots, x_{i+2}, \ldots, x_n$$

be a sequence of raw ring widths from a sample of timber, then the filtered index for the year $i + 2$ is defined as:

$$y_{i+2} = \ln[(5x_{i+2})/(x_i + x_{i+1} + x_{i+2} + x_{i+3} + x_{i+4})].$$

Here ln denotes the natural logarithm. Note that the first index is for ring three and the last is for $n–2$, so two widths are lost from each end in changing from raw ring widths to ring-width indices and instead of n ring widths there are only $n–4$ index values for comparison.

The statistical comparison of two sequences is based on programs by Baillie & Pilcher and uses the Student's t-test, which is an established statistical technique for determining the significance of matching between two datasets. It is based on the correlation coefficient measuring the agreement between the two tree-ring sequences.

The calculation of t-values. Consider two sequences of indices. Let the first have $n–4$ indices denoted by $y_3, y_4, \ldots,$ y_{n-2} and the second have $m–4$ indices denoted by $z_3, z_4,$ $\ldots, z_{m-2}$. Suppose that these two sequences of indices are compared at a given offset k so that index $k+2$, represented by y_{k+2}, in the first sequence is aligned with the first index in the second sequence, represented by z_3. This is seen diagrammatically as:

$$y_3, y_4, \ldots, y_{k+2}, \quad y_{k+3}, \quad \ldots, \quad y_{n-2}$$
$$z_3, \qquad z_4, \quad \ldots, \quad z_{(n-2)-(k-1)}, \ldots, z_{m-2}.$$

The correlation coefficient, denoted by r, between these two sequences at this offset depends only on those indices they have in common; viz. the pairs

$$(y_{k+2}, z_3), (y_{k+3}, z_4), \ldots, (y_{n-2}, z_{(n-2)-(k-1)}).$$

It is defined as:

$$r = \{(y_{k+2} - \bar{y})(z_3 - \bar{z}) + (y_{k+3} - \bar{y})(z_4 - \bar{z})$$
$$+ \cdots + (y_{n-2} - \bar{y})(z_{(n-2)-(k-1)} - \bar{z})\}/$$
$$\left\{ \sqrt{(y_{k+2} - \bar{y})^2 + \cdots + (y_{n-2} - \bar{y})^2} \times \right.$$
$$\left. \sqrt{(z_3 - \bar{z})^2 + \cdots + (z_{(n-2)-(k-1)} - \bar{z})^2} \right\}$$

where $\bar{y}$ is the mean of $y_{k+2}, \ldots, y_{n-2}$ and $\bar{z}$ is the mean of $z_3, \ldots, z_{(n-2)-(k-1)}$ (the two sets of overlapping indices).

The correlation coefficient r always lies between +1 and –1, and the nearer r is to +1, the greater is the correlation between the two sequences at this offset. In tree-ring dating terms this means that at this offset, the two sequences of indices are very similar (as are the underlying sequences of widths).

The t-value for the two sequences at this offset is defined as

$$t\text{-value} = r.\sqrt{\{((n - k - 3) - 2)/(1 - r^2)\}}.$$

Thus, t depends not only on the correlation, r, between the two sequences at this offset but also on how many indices are being compared ($n–k–3$ in this case). For a given positive value of the correlation coefficient, the more indices that are being compared, the greater the value of t, which is a reasonable thing to demand. The t-value can have any value positive, negative, or zero, and large positive values of t correspond to values of r which are positive and for which $n–k–3$ is large. Therefore in practice, dendrochronologists search for offsets which have large values of t. This is carried out by varying the offset and calculating the t-value at each offset.

Master chronologies and site sequences

Long reference chronologies have been developed by cross-matching the innermost rings of modern timbers with the outermost rings of older timbers successively back in time, adding data from numerous sites. Data now exist covering many thousands of years and it is, in theory, possible to match a sequence of unknown date to this reference material. However, the chances of matching a single sequence are not as great as for matching a tree-ring series derived from many individual sequences, since the process of aggregating the sequences removes or reduces variation unique to an individual tree, and reinforces the common signal resulting from widespread influences such as the weather. Long site sequences (200+ rings) are likely to contain sufficiently distinctive climatic patterns that they can be readily matched against several national master chronologies. However, for the short sequences often obtained from cruck buildings, we have found that more local masters are essential, since regional or national master chronologies did not provide as good matches as specific site sequences. This presumably arises because the variations suppressed in the construction of a master chronology are common to a number of trees in a locality although not to the majority of trees making up the chronology. Thus, the East Midlands chronology matches well with those site sequences that reflect the general climatic conditions of the region but less well with those influenced by microclimates.

The likelihood of successful dating is considerably improved if site sequences can be constructed by cross-matching and averaging the individual samples from a building. This has the same effect for individual buildings as the averaging used in the construction of master chronologies: the removal of individual random variation and the enhancement of systematic climatic effects.

Initially, of course, our samples were matched against previously available master sequences and site sequences for other Midlands buildings. A number of local Oxfordshire chronologies by J. M. Fletcher and D. Miles were made available by the Ancient Monuments Laboratory of English Heritage, which proved useful for the southern part of the survey area. During the course of the project, a working master chronology was built up, based on the project sequences as they were obtained. However, this did not prove as useful as had been hoped, and failed to provide dates that could not be established from other chronologies. This contrasts with the experience of the Nottingham Laboratory in dating Kentish houses, where the creation of the chronology KENT-88 made a major contribution to successful dating.[5] In the present project, the well-replicated East Midlands master chronology provided the initial match for many sequences.[6]

During the course of the project, a substantial number of dated site sequences were produced, which proved to be particularly useful for further dating. Several re-evaluations have been carried out as additional dated sequences have been established, leading to the matching of previously undated sequences, and the replacement of tentative by firm dates.[7]

Sequence matching and criteria

Matching of samples is undertaken in two stages, firstly the creation of site sequences by cross-matching between individual samples, and secondly the matching of site sequences and unmatched samples against master chronologies and dated sequences from other sites. Only sequences or individual samples with at least 50 rings were deemed to be suitable for dating. However, because of the initial presumption that samples from one building phase are likely to be of the same date, it is possible to accept rather shorter samples and matches at lower significance levels for incorporation into site sequences than are appropriate for dating against master sequences. Thus, occasionally a sample with as few as about 40 rings was considered usable, if it cross-matched exceptionally well with a longer sample from the site and so could be incorporated into the site sequence; the dependence of t-value on sequence (overlap) length has the automatic effect of requiring extremely good agreement between ring-width indices before a short sequence matches with acceptable t-values. About two-thirds of the dates obtained were based on site sequences, the remainder depending on the matching of individual samples.

In the Nottingham procedure, all matching is assessed by the calculation of 't-values' and no dependence is placed on visual matching; other laboratories use visual matching to confirm the validity of statistically-indicated matches and this additional procedure was applied to a few of the supplementary dates included in the project.

The minimum t-value which is considered acceptable has been the subject of debate. Originally values above 3.5 were accepted (with at least 100 years of overlapping rings) but now 4.0 is often taken as the base value. It is possible for a random set of numbers to give an apparently acceptable statistical match against a single reference curve – although the visual analysis of plots of the two series usually shows the trained eye that the match is unsatisfactory. When a series of ring-widths gives strong statistical matches in the same position against a number of independent chronologies, we can be extremely confident that it has been correctly dated.

With the generally short site sequences found within this project, the need to avoid spurious matches has indicated the importance of matching against *relevant* master sequences, or against local site sequences. This has

Table A1.1. Categories and Numbers of Dates.

Date Category	Matches with		Number of dates	%
	Relevant national/ regional master sequence	Local site sequence (including second sequence from same house)		
1	Two *t*-values > 5.0		39	41
2	One *t*-value > 5.0	One *t*-value > 5.0	20	21
3(a)	One *t*-value > 4.5	One *t*-value > 4.5	8	8
(b)	One *t*-value > 4.0	One *t*-value > 5.0	8	8
(c)	One *t*-value > 3.0	One *t*-value > 6.5	2	2
(d)		Two *t*-values > 4.5	3	3
4(a)		One *t*-value > 5.0; one *t*-value > 4.0	1	1
(b)		Two *t*-values > 5.0	2	2
5	Several concordant matches; lower *t*-values but several > 4.0; OR alternative matches at higher *t*-values		12	13
		Total	96	

led us to quantify the criteria for acceptable dates as listed in Table A1.1.

In all cases, a match with more than one sequence is considered essential. For categories 1, 2 and 3, matches with *t*-values exceeding 4.5–5.0, including at least one regional or national master sequence, provide excellent replication.[8] The great majority of the dates obtained in the present project fall into these categories. If *only* matches with local site sequences are found, but these include some with *t*-values of 5.0 or greater (category 4), the date is judged to be acceptable, but a slight possibility of a spurious match is felt to exist; only three of our dates fall into this category.

When the maximum *t*-value is no more than about 4.5, the matches are most often with local site sequences only. Sometimes, it is clear from other information that samples have been correctly dated at such levels. As an example, for CAD-A, a site sequence could be constructed from five of the eight samples, which dated to 1472/3 (maximum *t*-value 7.1; category 1). The three remaining samples did not match acceptably with the site sequence, but could be individually matched. Sample 1 matched two national masters (maximum *t*-value = 5.6) and was assigned to category 3d, but samples 4 and 5 respectively had maximum *t*-values of 4.7 and 4.5, with only four local site matches for the former (including a match at t = 3.8 with the main site sequence). However, the indicated final ring dates were 1472 and 1469, and it is clear that these samples have also been correctly matched.

Not all dates at this level are so satisfactory, and the possibility of the match being spurious becomes greater. At a *t*-value of 5 (or sometimes even higher), a few sequences also show alternative matches. Thus, the site sequence for BIT-A (129 rings long) matches several sequences at 1171–1299, with a maximum *t*-value of 6.1 against one master chronology (READING), but also at 1285–1413 with a maximum *t*-value of 5.2 against another (DROITWICH); both would be classified as category 2 on their own.[9] The architectural evidence lends strong support to 1413 and makes a 1299 date implausible, but the existence of the alternative match inevitably reduces the certainty that the dating is correct.

The dating of a number of samples with maximum *t*-values below 4.0 was also evaluated. It was apparent that several of them were probably spurious because they did not match the general architectural pattern of the survey, while others gave more than one possible date. We have concluded that, for the relatively short samples encountered in this work, matches at this level unsupported by higher *t*-values cannot be considered reliable, and they are not normally reported.

In the dating procedure used by the Oxford Dendrochronology Laboratory, individual sequences or averaged site sequences are compared to a large number of dated sequences and *t*-values are calculated for a long range of potential final sequence years. All *t*-values above a pre-set threshold are cumulated, and the results are presented graphically, so that a any possible dates appear as peaks on a year-by-year graph. A sample is considered to be dated if a sufficient number of high values are found for a single year, and possible alternative dates can immediately be seen. Although this is a qualitative procedure, and the results depend on precisely which dated sequences are used, for a successful match, the contributing *t*-values can be listed and evaluated in the same way as previously described (and these are listed in the reports, as for other dates). It is also possible with this procedure to identify potential matches, even if the individual *t*-values are relatively small.

Sapwood Estimates

As stated above, only if the bark edge is present on the sample, can dendrochronology give a precise felling date. When some but not all of the sapwood is present, it is essential to have statistical information about the likely number of sapwood rings, in order to estimate the *felling-date range*; this applies also to radiocarbon dating although that method always gives a range, even if all the sapwood survives. The number of sapwood rings varies both with region and with the size and age of the tree. Some dendrochronologists have viewed the actual width of the sapwood as being the determining factor, estimating the number of sapwood rings by dividing the mean sapwood

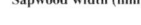

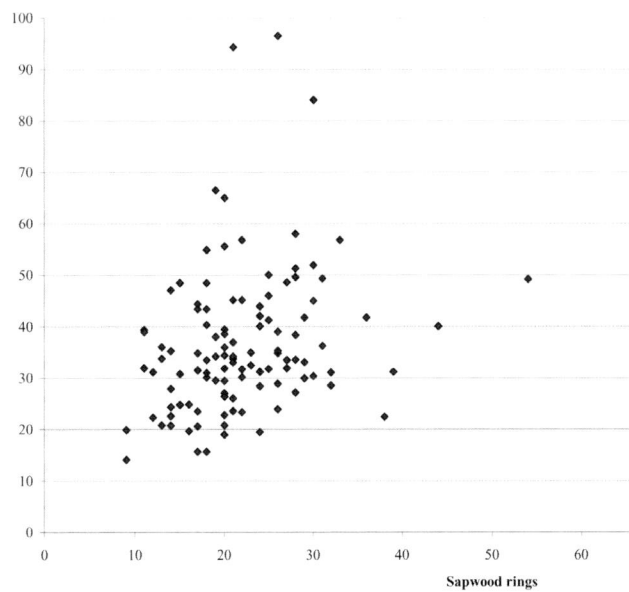

Fig. A1.1. Correlation of total sapwood width with mean ring width, for samples with complete sapwood. Note: the total sapwood width is calculated from the number of sapwood rings multiplied by the mean ring width.

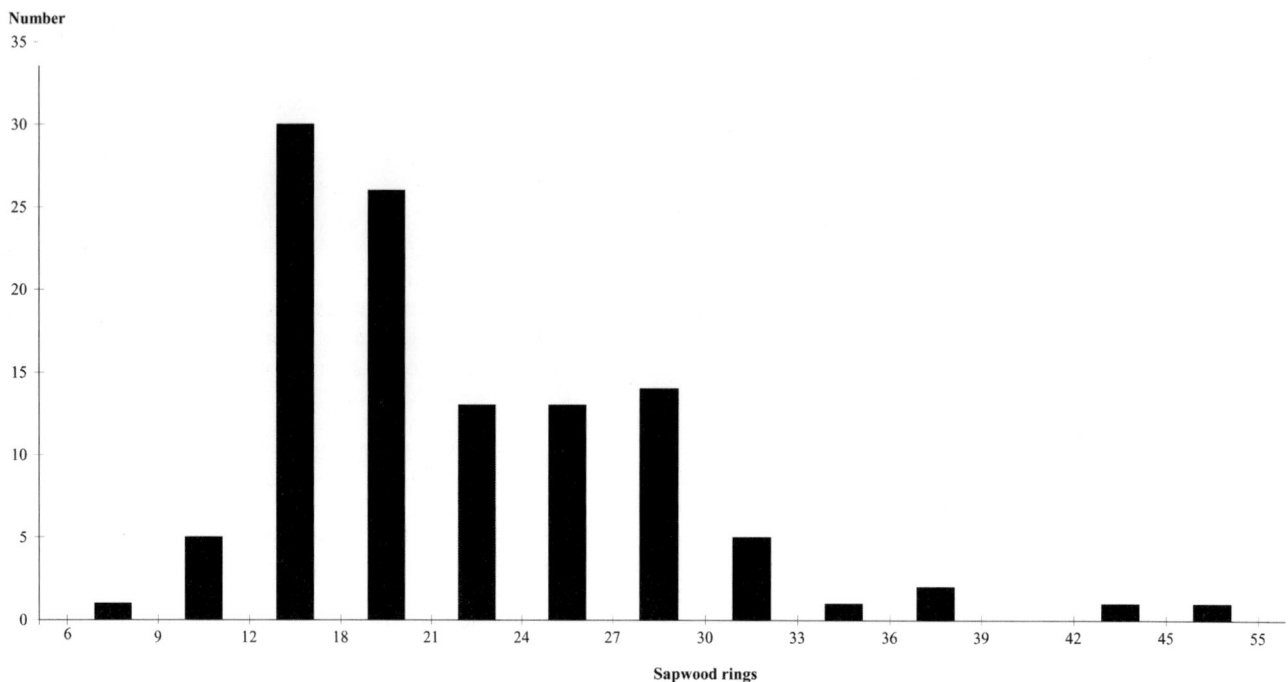

Fig. A1.2. Distribution of sapwood rings in complete samples from the project.

width by the width of the last heartwood rings of an individual sample.[10] Our samples show a very large range of mean ring widths (see below), and the width of sapwood is equally variable, from about 2cm to 9cm (Fig. A1.1); it has only a weak positive correlation with the mean ring width. Thus, this width is of little use in estimating the correction for incomplete sapwood.

At the start of the project, the then accepted standard Southern England sapwood estimate was used, with a range of 15 to 50 rings for approximately 95% confidence limits.[11] During the course of the project, data from the substantial number of sampled timbers with complete sapwood provided an improved estimate for the survey (Fig. A1.2). From this distribution, the 95% probability bounds for individual samples were estimated to be 10 to 43 years, with a modal value of 19 years from the mean heartwood-sapwood boundary. Since then, extensive analysis has provided very similar figures: 9–41 rings for southern England (Warwickshire southwards) and 12–45 rings for the north of the country.[12]

A refinement in the estimation of the likely numbers of sapwood rings has been developed more recently, and has been applied to the calculation of most of the felling-date ranges used here (date ranges in italics in Table 2.2 and the text).[13] Instead of using a simple empirical estimate for a particular geographical location, one model was found to be suitable for the whole of England and Wales. With the methodology of Millard,[14] a Bayesian statistical model is used to produce individual sapwood estimates for samples with the variables: number of heartwood rings present, the mean ring width of those heartwood rings, the heartwood/sapwood boundary date, and the number of surviving sapwood rings (if any).[15] The addition of surviving sapwood to the equation narrows the felling-date range for each sample, although the outer end of the range increases by a few years, most noticeably on those samples with higher sapwood counts. Ring width, rejected as the primary determinant of the number of sapwood rings, is found to have a significant though not dominant correlation with the sapwood estimate.

A particularly significant effect is seen in the application of the COMBINE function of OxCal to a group of samples coming from a single building phase (assumed to be independently drawn from an overall population of trees felled at the same date). The combination of two samples can reduce the felling-date range from about 30 to about 20 years, and if more samples can be included, this 20-year range can be reduced even further. From a statistical viewpoint, this reduced range corresponds to the standard deviation of the *mean*, rather than the standard deviation of each individual measurement. As an example, for LWH-A, six out of eight cores were dated, with heartwood/sapwood boundaries falling between 1534 and 1541 and the latest surviving ring on one sample being that for 1557. The standard sapwood estimate gives a felling-date range of 1558–73, but the OxCal estimate has a much smaller range, 1558–62.

Radiocarbon dating [16]

An alternative approach has been used in the project to date a few buildings for which all the samples are too short to date, or where they failed to match any dated sequences. This is the technique of *radiocarbon dating*. Like tree-ring dating, this technique is also applied to timber samples and, indeed, the cores taken for dendrochronology provide good source material for it.

The essence of radiocarbon dating is the measurement of the amount of ^{14}C, the radioactive isotope of carbon, in the sample. The isotope is created in the atmosphere by the reaction of cosmic rays s with nitrogen and it is then taken up by plant material, such as wood, through photosynthesis. Once incorporated into wood, it becomes fixed and ceases to exchange with the atmospheric radiocarbon. It then undergoes radioactive decay with a half life (the period in which half the atoms have decayed) of about 5,700 years.

In the original radiocarbon dating procedure, the ratio of radioactive to stable carbon was determined by counting its disintegrations in a given time, and comparing this to the original atmospheric ratio.

Three important changes have been made to this procedure, which have greatly improved its effectiveness for dating historic wood. The first involves the measurement of the proportion of radiocarbon. This is now obtained directly by Accelerator Mass Spectrometry (AMS), which gives the $^{14}C/^{12}C$ ratio directly, rather than it being calculated from the radioactive decay rate. This is a much faster procedure, and one that needs much smaller samples, thus allowing it to be applied easily to samples taken from tree-ring cores. AMS also provides the ratio of the stable carbon isotopes, $^{13}C/^{12}C$, which allows the ^{14}C ratio to be corrected for any isotopic fractionation during its uptake.

The second change is the application of *calibration* to the

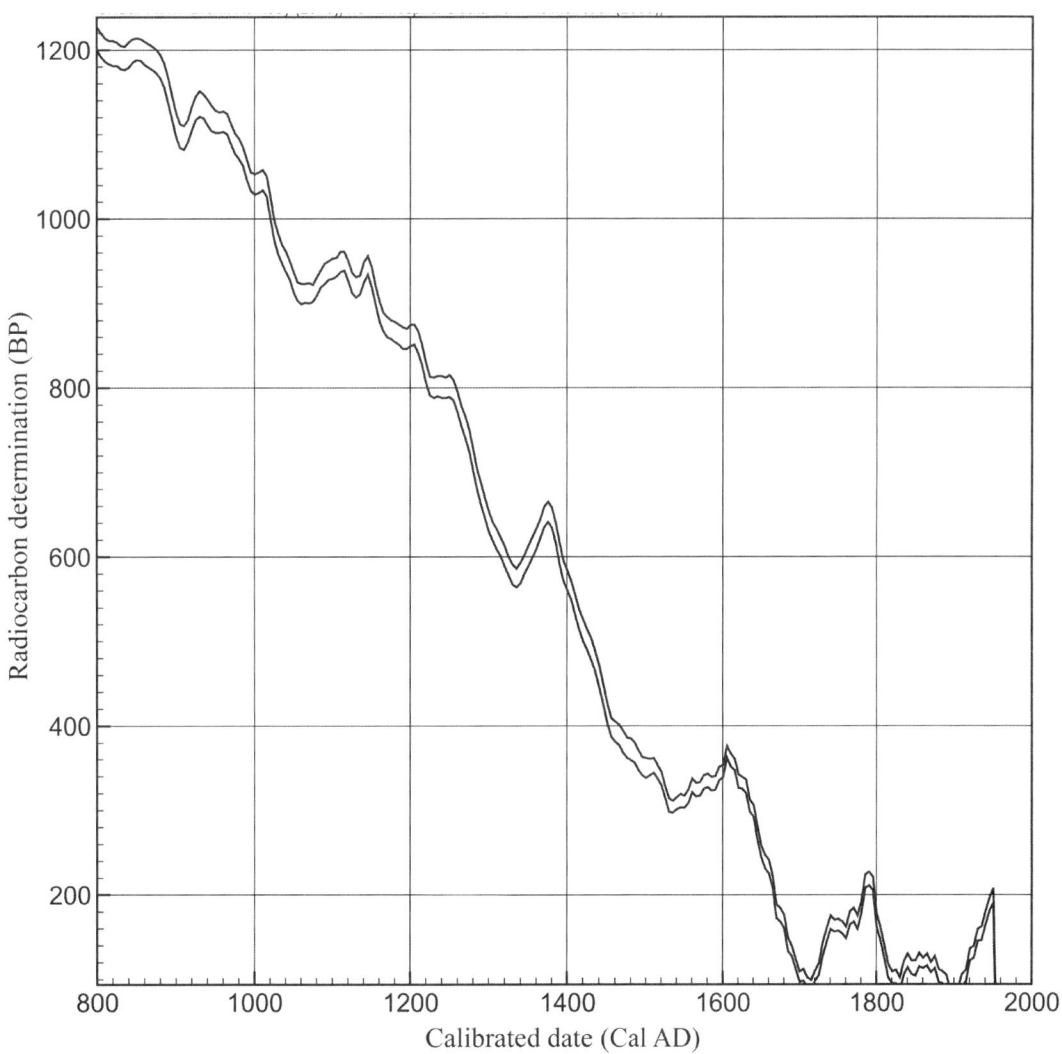

Fig. A1.3. Radiocarbon calibration curve for the period AD 800–2000. (from P. J. Reimer *et al* (2009) *Radiocarbon*, 51(4), 1111–1150).

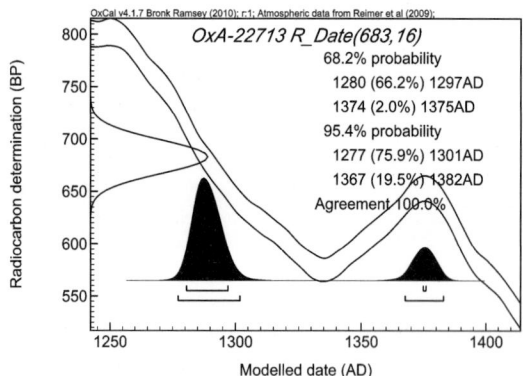

Fig. A1.4. Calibration of the radiocarbon date for the first five rings of sample LON-G21.

results. It was realised early in the use of radiocarbon dating, that the dates obtained for samples of known historic date seemed to be too early. Not only has this been confirmed in later work, but it has been found that the concentration of atmospheric radiocarbon has undergone both short- and long-term variations. This difficulty has been overcome by the extensive dating of material of known age, principally tree-ring dated wood samples, to construct calibration curves. Figure A1.3 gives the most up-to-date curve for the period AD 800–2000, and shows its remarkable departure from the expected simple straight line.

In effect, by using this curve to convert the radiocarbon measurement into the calibrated age, the original radiocarbon procedure has been reversed. Rather than determining the

age from the $^{14}C/^{12}C$ ratio, this information is used to obtain the age by comparison with a series of dated samples for which the ratio is known. The procedure is illustrated in Fig. A1.4, the calibration of the radiocarbon date obtained for the collar purlin of LON-G (see Chapter 8.5). The raw date is 683±16 years BP (left axis). The calibration curve is the diagonal band across the diagram, and the bottom axis shows how the raw date corresponds to *cal AD* dates at either 68.2% or 95.4% probability (approximately 1σ and 2σ ranges). Because this radiocarbon measurement falls on a reflex part of the calibration curve, two possible dates are produced in the 95.4% probability range: 1277–1301 (75.9%) and 1366–1384 (19.5%) (adding to 95.4%). Since the date was obtained from the first five rings of a 25 ring sample that was complete to the bark edge (in fact retaining some bark), these dates have to be increased by 22.5 years, to give *felling-date ranges* of *cal AD 1299–1324* (75.9%) or *1390–1405* (19.5%). Typological arguments indicate that the earlier date range is correct.

The third improvement in radiocarbon dating is specific to multi-ring timber samples, such as tree-ring cores. This is the technique of *wiggle-matching*. Here, at least two and sometimes many dates are determined using different sets of rings from the sample. Thus, not only are the individual dates known, but also the precise calendar relationship between them. The calibration program works out the calibrated date ranges for each determination and also the best fit within these ranges that allows each date to be spaced precisely the correct number of years from all the others.[17]

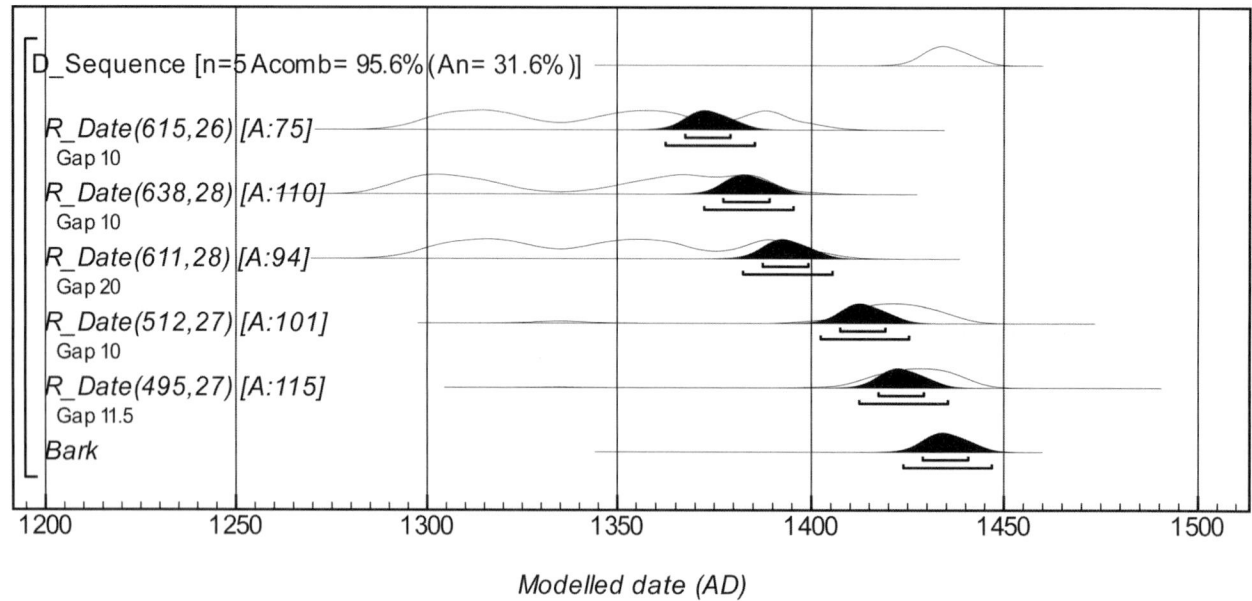

Fig. A1.5. Wiggle-matching of the radiocarbon dates for NWH-A1.

This is illustrated in Figure A1.5, the wiggle-matched dating of NWH-A. Five dates were obtained, each for five tree-rings, spaced at about ten-year intervals along a 67-ring core (complete to the bark edge). The thin lines in the figure shows the calibration of each of these dates, and it can be seen that the top three each covers a wide range, between about 1300 and 1400. Indeed, the radiocarbon dates do not even fall in the known chronological order, because of the ambiguities in the calibration at this period. However, when all the dates are combined, they fit together to give a closely defined *felling-date range* of *Cal AD 1423–1446* (95% probability). The dark profiles on each calibration curve show how the joint probability fits well with the calibration for each date.

For four of the radiocarbon dates used here (HAR-D; STE-E; WOA-A; WOR-A, but not NWH-A or LON-G), a modified version of this procedure has been used. Here, two dates were taken, one from each end of the core, and the combined calibrated dates calculated. Apart from STE-E, the resulting dates have satisfactorily small errors, and it was not necessary to measure any more samples. STE-E still has a bimodal date range (1330–1376 (60.7%); 1382–1421 (34.7%)), but the short length of the core (only 38 rings), and the section of the calibration curve on which it lies means that dating an intermediate sample would be unlikely to improve the precision.

Combined radiocarbon and tree-ring dating

For one radiocarbon-dated sample (STE-E), possible tree-ring dating matches lying within the radiocarbon date range have been examined. Although the sampled core sequence is too short for conclusive tree-ring dating when taken on its own, it does give relatively high *t*-values and a good visual match with a number of local sequences at a final year of 1350. No other years within the radiocarbon date range show significant matches, although a final year of 1446 gives matches at somewhat lower values. The radiocarbon and tree-ring results in combination are considered to determine the felling date satisfactorily. At present, it is not possible to calculate the statistical probability of this match, but qualitatively it is judged to be highly probable.[18] The calibrated radiocarbon felling date range is *cal AD 1330–76 (61%); 1382–1421 (35%)*, and the highest *t*-values are 5.88 with sequence KLYNN_SG; 5.63 with LOW-A; 5.59 with THTASQ02, dating the site sequence *cws13* to 1313–1350. The highest match with final year 1446 is 5.01 with CHILVRTN.

Characteristics of Project Timber

For the project as a whole, only 339 of 966 individual samples were found to be datable (35%), even after the rejection of houses with only wide-ringed timbers.[19] This proportion is lower than in other major studies,[20] and in the general experience of the laboratories concerned. A number of factors can be suggested for this difficulty, ultimately all stemming from the relatively low status of the buildings studied. This affects the nature of the timber and its conversion before use, and has the implication that the carpenters were being more economical than was usual with higher status buildings. The timber may often have been obtained from hedgerows and similar sources where the trees had encountered more human intervention than for timber from more consistently managed woodlands. The frequent use of boxed-heart conversion (p. 79) also causes problems, since each timber has only half the number of annual rings that might be expected from its size. However, the economy in the use of the timber also means that the waney edge is more often preserved than in buildings using higher quality timber and more sophisticated carpentry. As a result, the proportion of precise felling dates to felling-date ranges is relatively high.

Sequence Length and Ring Width

Several specific characteristics of the timber growth rings can be identified which correlate strongly with our ability to date the buildings.[21] The most obvious sample parameter is the number of rings, which can be compared for 332 dated and 374 undated samples from the total of 966 samples (Fig. A1.6); a further 181 samples had fewer than 40 rings, while 79 samples were discarded, 35 because they were not oak and 44 because they were clearly too short to be useful. As expected, the number of rings plays a major part in determining whether a sample can be dated. Almost half of the undated samples have less than 50 rings (167), with only 55 of these samples in this range datable. By contrast, almost half the samples with 50–80 rings were dated, and above this the likelihood of a date increases rapidly.

Long undated samples

A handful of long samples were undated, 17 in all with more than 100 rings. These derive from eleven buildings of which four are undated. It does not seem that any one reason underlies the difficulties with these samples. All have moderately or very narrow rings, including two samples (ANS-A) with such narrow rings that accurate measurement of ring width was extremely difficult. For some of them the ring widths appear to be very even, showing little year-to-year variation. Others have periodic groups of narrow rings, suggesting that they come from trees that had been pollarded or stripped of branches and leaves for fodder at regular intervals; the fluctuating growth under these conditions generally conceals the climatic signal.

Ring widths

The mean ring width is available for 676 samples, 318

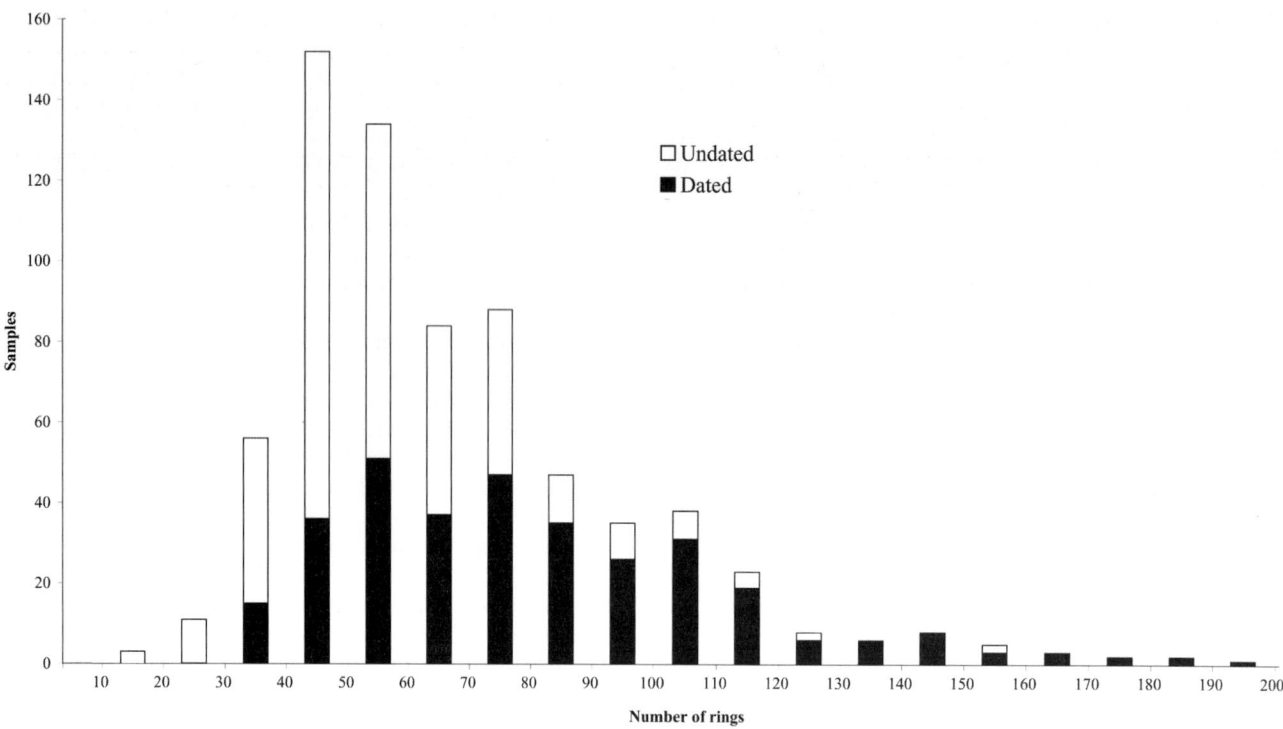

Fig. A1.6. Numbers of rings in dated and undated samples.

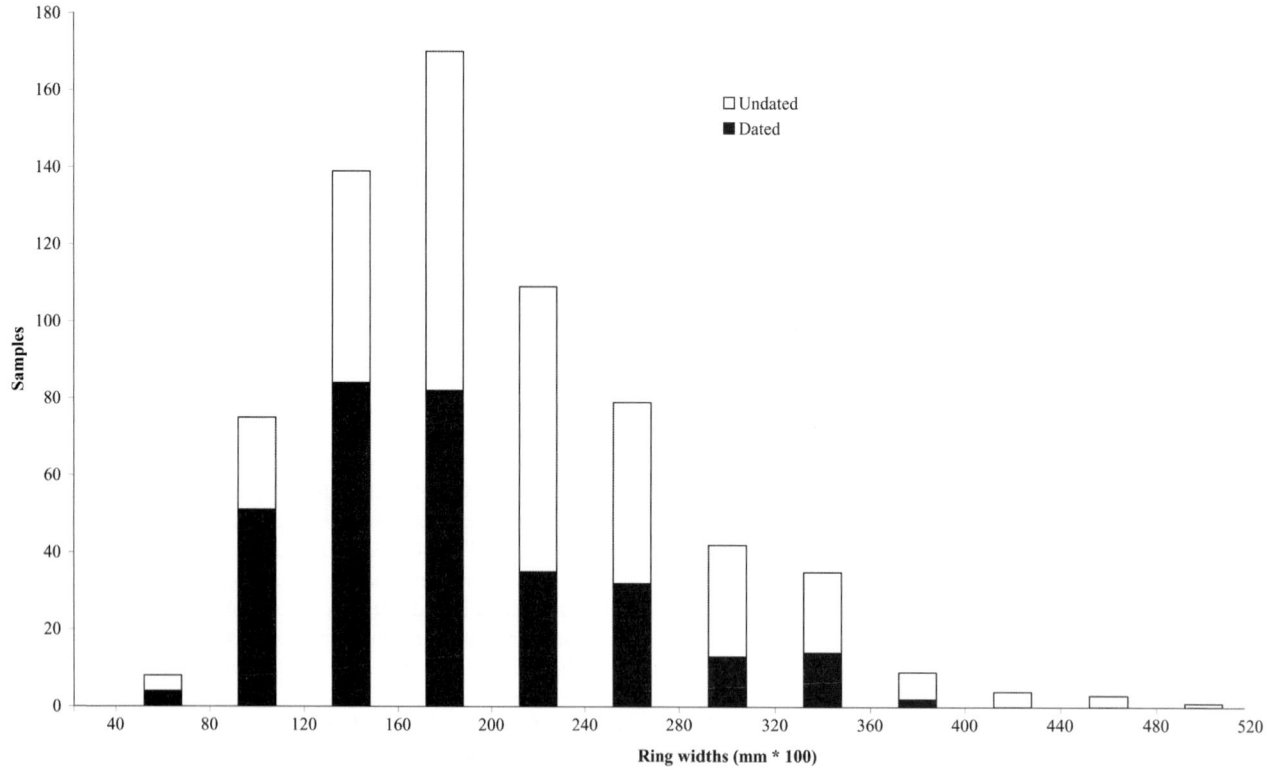

Fig. A1.7. Distribution of ring widths in dated and undated samples.

dated and 358 undated, after the exclusion of undated samples which were too short for measurement to be useful. The widths cover a considerable range (Fig. A1.7), but the differentiation between the dated and undated samples is less marked than might have been expected. The dated samples are on average somewhat narrower, with a mean width of 1.89 mm, compared to 2.15 mm for those undated. It is also interesting that some notably wide-ringed samples proved to be datable, the maximum widths being 3.71 mm (dated) and 4.83 mm (undated). The proportion of dated samples drops off markedly for the wider ring widths, but these statistics suggest that the automatic rejection of relatively wide-ringed samples can exclude some potentially datable samples.

Appendix 2

Location and Dimension Tables

Table A2.1. Lists of buildings and codes.

(a) Buildings surveyed and those studied from documentary evidence (codes in italics), arranged by county and address. For a listing arranged in code order, see Table 2.2 (p. 15).

Code	County	Address	Grid ref
BOT-A	BU	Botolph Claydon, Rosamond Cottage	SP 7320 2451
SKI-A	BU	Hambledon, Old Crown House & Isabel Cottage, Skirmett	SU 7754 9020
HUG-A	BU	Hughenden, Grange Farm, Widmer End	SU 8821 9595
IVI-A	BU	Ivinghoe, Pendyce House, 12–14 Station Road	SP 9447 1623
LON-A	BU	Long Crendon, Abel's Cottage, 43 High Street	SP 6966 0894
LON-B	BU	Long Crendon, Woodpeckers, 25 High Street	SP 6964 0886
LON-C	BU	Long Crendon, Church Green Cottage, 102–104 High Street	SP 6979 0901
LON-D	BU	Long Crendon, 96-98 High Street (96)	SP 6975 0903
LON-E	BU	Long Crendon, Cordwainers, 2 Bicester Road	SP 6942 0862
LON-F	BU	Long Crendon, Dragon Fm, 121 Bicester Road	SP 6864 0916
LON-G	BU	Long Crendon, Sycamore Farm, 9 Bicester Road	SP 6931 0870
LON-H	BU	Long Crendon, Old Bakehouse, 61 Bicester Road	SP 6897 0897
LON-I	BU	Long Crendon, Warwick Farm, 31 Bicester Road	SP 6919 0884
LON-J	BU	Long Crendon, Wapping, 66 High Street	SP 6976 0890
LON-K	BU	Long Crendon, 96-98 High Street (98)	SP 6975 0904
LON-L	BU	Long Crendon, 82 High Street	SP 6968 0895
LON-M	BU	Long Crendon, Lower End House, 72 Bicester Road,	SP 6870 0924
LON-N	BU	Long Crendon, Harfield Cottage, 7 Bicester Road	SP 6934 0866
LON-O	BU	Long Crendon, Manor House, Frogmore Lane	SP 6932 0849
LON-P	BU	Long Crendon, 'Manor Garage' (at Manor House)	SP 6934 0853
LON-Q	BU	Long Crendon, 2 The Square	SP 6939 0858
LON-R	BU	Long Crendon, 27–29 High Street	SP 6965 0888
LON-S	BU	Long Crendon, Eight Bells, 51 High Street	SP 6967 0897
LON-T	BU	Long Crendon, 58–60 High Street	SP 6966 0886
LON-U	BU	Long Crendon, Northend Farm (Bicester Road)	SP 6866 0923
NWL-A	BU	Newton Longville, Jasmine Cottage, 52 Westbrook End	SP 8471 3135
NWL-B	BU	Newton Longville, Ivy Lodge, 46 Westbrook End	SP 8436 3125
NWL-C	BU	Newton Longville, Paradise Cottage, Paradise Lane	SP 8481 3149
NWL-D	BU	Newton Longville, Beverley Cottage, 34 Westbrook End	SP 8436 3135
STC-A	BU	Steeple Claydon, Willow Vale Fm, West End	SP 6946 2686

Code	County	Address	Grid ref
STC-B	BU	Steeple Claydon, Rhenold's Close, 28 North End	SP 6992 2738
STC-C	BU	Steeple Claydon, Well Cottage, 40–44 Queen Catherine Road	SP 7013 2692
STW-A	BU	Stewkley, 28 High Street North	SP 8511 2631
STK-A	BU	Stokenchurch, Kensham Farm	SU 7903 9276
WEE-A	BU	Weedon, Eastgate House, East End	SP 8187 1801
WEN-A	BU	Wendover, 6–8 Pound Street	SP 8672 0776
FOS-A	GL	Frampton-on-Severn, Old House (Advowson Farm)	SO 7470 0751
FOS-B	GL	Frampton-on-Severn, Wildgoose Cottage	SO 7458 0722
ANS-A	LE	Anstey, Green Farm, Bradgate Road	SK 5448 0862
BIL-A	LE	Billesdon, The Gables, 6 Church Street	SK 7189 0275
CAD-A	LE	Cadeby, Church Cottage	SK 4251 0237
CAS-A	LE	Castle Donington, 1 Apiary Gate	SK 4463 2731
CAS-B	LE	Castle Donington, 31 Bondgate	SK 4455 2741
COS-A	LE	Cosby, 9 The Nook	SP 5470 9457
COS-B	LE	Cosby, Coates Barn, Main Street	SP 5478 9484
DIS-A	LE	Diseworth, Plough Inn, 33 Hall Gate	SK 4526 2456
HAL-A	LE	Hallaton, 29 High Street	SP 7889 9665
HAL-B	LE	Hallaton, 34, 36 Churchgate	SP 7863 9663
HBY-C	LE	Harby, Home Farm	SK 744 312
HOB-A	LE	Hoby, Roof Tree Cottage	SK 6686 1716
LWH-A	LE	Long Whatton , 4 Main Street (The Boot)	SK 4758 2363
NEW-A	LE	Newtown Linford, Vine Cottage, 9 Main Street	SK 5201 0989
NEW-B	LE	Newtown Linford, Rose Cottage, 11–13 Main Street	SK 5200 0991
ROT-A	LE	Rothley, Old House, 89 Town Green Street	SK 5813 1233
ROT-B	LE	Rothley, April Cottage, 12 Church Street	SK 5856 1265
ROT-C	LE	Rothley, 13 Fowke Street	SK 5851 1274
ROT-D	LE	Rothley, 91 Town Green Street	SK 5811 1232
SYS-A	LE	Syston, 72 High Street	SK 624 1182
WOE-A	LE	Woodhouse, Golden Cottage, 280 Forest Road	SK 5410 1550
WOE-B	LE	Woodhouse, Old Post Office, 244 Forest Road	SK 5401 1537
BAT-A	NT	Bathley, The Hollies	SK 7763 5913
CLI-B	NT	Clifton, TIL House, 56 Village Road	SK 5446 3500
NOS-C	NT	Normanton-on-Soar, Old Post Office	SK 5184 2303
AST-A	OX	Aston Tirrold, The Cottage, Aston Street	SU 5565 8578
DID-A	OX	Didcot, 26 Manor Road	SU 5206 9034
DID-B	OX	East Hagbourne, Kingsholm	SU 5286 8831
EAH-A	OX	East Hendred, Old Forge, Church Sreett	SU 4587 8858
EAH-B	OX	East Hendred, Inglenook/Penny Green, Catte Street	SU 4591 8885
EAH-C	OX	East Hendred, Godfrey's Farm, 2 St Marys Road	SU 4604 8852
FRI-A	OX	Fringford, Fringford Mill	SP 6132 2873
HAR-A	OX	Harwell, Dell Cottage, Church Lane	SU 4920 8906
HAR-B	OX	Harwell, Church Farm, Church Lane	SU 4921 8907
HAR-C	OX	Harwell, Abbey Timbers, Broadway Hill	SU 4907 8877
HAR-D	OX	Harwell, Pomander House, Townsend	SU 4938 8957
HAR-E	OX	Harwell, Tibberton Cottage, Wellshead Lane	SU 4917 8887
HAR-F	OX	Harwell, Holywell Cottage, Wellshead Lane	SU 4919 8890
LOW-A	OX	Long Wittenham, Terret Close, High Street	SU 5457 9376
LOW-B	OX	Long Wittenham, Cruck Cottage (Cruckfield)	SU 5449 9370
LOW-C	OX	Long Wittenham, 33 High Street	SU 5480 9389
MDM-A	OX	Mapledurham, Mill Farm	SU 6764 7777
MDM-B	OX	Mapledurham, Pithouse, Trench Green	SU 6872 7741

Code	County	Address	Grid ref
MDM-C	OX	Mapledurham, Three Chimneys, Jackson's Lane	SU 6938 7642
MOU-A	OX	Moulsford, Pye Corner	SU 5912 8371
RAD-A	OX	Radley, Thatched Cott, 46–8 Lower Radley	SU 5346 9898
RAD-B	OX	Radley, Bakers Close, 104 Lower Radley	SU 5328 9874
BIF-A	OX	Shiplake, Barn Grounds, Binfield Heath	SU 7395 7933
STE-A	OX	Steventon, Folly Ho, 53 The Causeway	SU 4692 9183
STE-B	OX	Steventon, Tudor House, 67 The Causeway	SU 4676 9174
STE-C	OX	Steventon, 83 The Causeway	SU 4669 9167
STE-D	OX	Steventon, 71 The Causeway	SU 4674 9173
STE-E	OX	Steventon, 39 The Causeway	SU 4699 9186
STE-F	OX	Steventon, Priory Cottages, 127 The Causeway & The Priory, 123–5 The Causeway	SU 4656 9150
STE-G	OX	Steventon, 99 The Causeway [Botleys]	SU 4662 9159
STE-H	OX	Steventon, 87 The Causeway	SU 4668 9166
STE-I	OX	Steventon, 79 & 81 The Causeway	SU 4673 9172
STE-J	OX	Steventon, 35–7 The Causeway	SU 4701 9187
STE-K	OX	Steventon, 12 Milton Lane	SU 4727 9202
STE-L	OX	Steventon, Home Fm, 14–16 Milton Lane	SU 4729 9203
STE-M	OX	Steventon, Green Fm (I), 1 Milton Lane	SU 4736 9207
STE-N	OX	Steventon, Old Farm, 5 Kennel Lane	SU 4748 9204
SUC-A	OX	Sutton Courtenay, Manor Cottage	SU 5035 9416
BRN-H	RU	Braunston, Quaintree House	SK 8328 0676
ALC-A	WA	Alcester, 19 Henley St	SP 0908 5758
ASH-A	WA	Ashow, Trinity Cottage	SP 3107 7037
BIN-A	WA	Binton, Kineton Cottage	SP 1445 5408
BIT-A	WA	Bishops Tachbrook, The Leopard	SP 3148 6150
CUB-A	WA	Cubbington, Old Manor House	SP 3440 6824
WAL-A	WA	Haselor, Cruck Cottage, Walcote	SP 1255 5811
LEW-A	WA	Leek Wootton, Old Forge Cottage	SP 2896 6900
HIW-A	WA	Leek Wootton, Old Thatched Cottage, Hill Wootton	SP 3027 6885
LNG-M	WA	Long Marston, Hopkins, Wyre Lane	SP 1554 4865
LOX-A	WA	Loxley, Loxley Farm	SP 2560 5305
NWH-A	WA	Nether Whitacre, Church End Farm	SP 2334 9308
NEB-A	WA	Newton-and-Biggin, Stag & Pheasant	SP 5309 7816
OXH-A	WA	Oxhill, Old Post Office	SP 3153 4591
POL-A	WA	Polesworth, 64 High Street	SK 2646 0256
ROW-A	WA	Rowington, Holywell Farm	SP 1979 6643
SOU-A	WA	Southam, 26 Warwick Road	SP 4147 6155
STO-A	WA	Stoneleigh, 10 Vicarage Road	SP 3289 7261
STO-B	WA	Stoneleigh, Skep Cottage, 3 Birmingham Road	SP 3293 7281
STO-C	WA	Stoneleigh, High Beams, 8–9 Vicarage Road	SP 3286 7258
STO-D	WA	Stoneleigh, 23–5 Birmingham Road	SP 3296 7276
STO-E	WA	Stoneleigh, Motslow Cottages	SP 3290 7243
STO-F	WA	Stoneleigh, Phoenix Cott, 1 Birmingham Road	SP 3295 7280
STO-G	WA	Stoneleigh, Pypes Mill	SP 3280 7388
STO-H	WA	Stoneleigh, 2 Church Lane	SP 3310 7265
STO-I	WA	Stoneleigh, Bridge Cottage	SP 3328 7282
STO-J	WA	Stoneleigh, Croom Cottage, Birmingham Road	SP 3285 7288
STR-A	WA	Stratford-upon-Avon, Anne Hathaway's Cottage, Shottery	SP 1845 5475
SOF-A	WA	Stretton-on-Fosse, Manor Farm	SP 2223 3826
SUF-A	WA	Stretton-under-Fosse, Old Forge	SP 4502 8131

Code	County	Address	Grid ref
WEL-A	WA	Wellesbourne, 2 School Road	SP 2795 5541
WOA-A	WA	Weston-on-Avon, Low Thatch	SP 1573 5194
WOR-A	WA	Water Orton, The Chestnuts, Church Lane	SP 1765 9139
COU-A	WM	Coundon, Alveston Cottage	SP 3131 8171
ERD-A	WM	Erdington, Lad in the Lane, Bromford Lane	SP 1127 9078
SUT-A	WM	Sutton Coldfield, Smithy, 78 Birmingham Road	SP 1180 9532
WOS-A	WM	Walsgrave-on-Sowe, Cruck House, 14–16 Hinckley Road	SP 3798 8099

(b) Non-project buildings with assigned codes and references. Tree-ring dates are from *Vernacular Architecture* (*VA*). If no source reference is given, information has been taken from the *Vernacular Architecture* date report. For a listing arranged in code order, see Table 2.2 (p. 15).

Code	Cou	Location and source reference	Grid ref	Date ref
X-HAM	BU	Hambledon, Burrow Farm, chamber block	SU 797 856	*VA* 26, 63
X-BEA	BU	New Beaconsfield, Baylins Farm	SU 928 927	*VA* 33, 82
X-STM	BU	Stoke Mandeville, Marsh Lane, Old Moat Farmhouse	SP 827 104	*VA* 39, 133
X-FRI	LE	Frisby-on-the-Wreake, 7 Main Street	SK 695 177	*VA* 39, 123
X-LOU	LE	Loughborough, Warners Lane/Churchgate	SK 536 197	*VA* 15, 66
X-MED	LE	Medbourne, Manor House	SP 803 930	*VA* 33, 110
X-MEL	LE	Melton Mowbray, 5 King Street	SK 750 196	*VA* 39, 108
X-NEV	LE	Nevill Holt, Nevill Holt Hall, great hall	SP 816 936	*VA* 39, 108
X-QUE	LE	Queniborough, 86–8 Main Street	SK 650 121	*VA* 19, 46
X-CHA	OX	Chalgrove, Chalgrove Manor,	SU 630 968	*VA* 39, 109
X-CR2	OX	Crowmarsh Gifford, 17–19 The Street	SU 616 892	*VA* 20, 46
X-CR1	OX	Crowmarsh Gifford, Queens Head	SU 616 892	*VA* 20, 46
X-EAH	OX	East Hendred, Wisteria House & The Stores [Currie (1992)]	SU 460 888	*VA* 30,101
X-HA1	OX	Harwell, Lime Tree House, High Street [Currie (1992)]	SU 492 888	*VA* 12, 39
X-HA2	OX	Harwell, Middle Farm [Currie (1992)]	SU 492 893	*VA* 23, 48
X-MD4	OX	Mapledurham, Whittles Farm	SU 671 784	*VA* 24, 54
X-MIL	OX	Milton, 42–42A High Street [Currie (1992)]	SU 485 923	
X-WAN	OX	Wantage, 57 Grove Street	SU 922 989	*VA* 37,127
X-WHA	OX	West Hagbourne, York Farm [Currie (1992)]	SU 512 878	*VA* 24, 55
X-OAK	RU	Oakham, Flores House	SK 860 088	*VA* 41, 92
X-BUR	WA	Burmington, Burmington Manor	SP 263 379	*VA* 24, 49
X-CLI	WA	Clifford Chambers, Old Rectory	SP 198 521	*VA* 35, 101
X-HIA	WA	Henley-in-Arden, Heritage Centre, 150 High St	SP 150 658	*VA* 33, 87
X-MAX	WA	Maxstoke, Castle [Alcock, Faulkner & Jones (1978)]	SP225 891	
X-SAW	WA	Sawbridge, Red Roofs Farmhouse	SP 504 655	*VA* 26, 49
X-TAN	WA	Tanworth-in-Arden, Old Bell Cottages	SP 114 706	*VA* 31, 98
X-TEM	WA	Temple Balsall, Old Hall [Alcock (1982)]	SP 207 759	*VA* 24, 49
X-UFT	WA	Ufton, 1–2 Ufton Fields [Alcock & Miles (2012)]	SP 3776 6180	*VA* 43
X-WIL	WA	Wilmcote, Glebe Farm	SP 163 581	*VA* 31, 97
X-KNO	WM	Knowle, Cuttle Pool Farm, Cuttle Pool Lane	SP 200 753	*VA* 24, 41

Table A2.2: Rejected sites

County	Address	Grid ref	Comment
BU	Botolph Claydon, 5 Orchard Way	SP 732 246	All trusses plastered internally
BU	Chalfont-St-Peter, Hill Farm	TQ 005 911	Wide-ringed; timbers at Chiltern Museum
BU	Chesham, 78/80 Church St	SP 957 014	Wide-ringed; unclear if oak or elm
BU	Coleshill, Forge House (Fleur-de-lis)	SU 950 950	Four timbers only of phase 1
BU	Long Crendon, 29 High Street	SP 696 087	All timbers elm [*LON-R* in documentary reports]
BU	Long Crendon, 7 Bicester Road	SP 693 087	Much altered. Crucks, all elm or wide-ringed oak [*LON-N* in documentary reports]
BU	Wingrave, Church Farm	SP 870 190	Elm; well-shaped arch-braced cruck
GL	Frampton-on-Severn, Greycroft	SO 746 075	Elm
GL	Frampton-on-Severn, Ye Olde Cruck House	SO 746 075	Elm and very wide rings
LE	Billesdon, 36 Church St	SK 720 026	Elm
LE	Diseworth, 54 Hall Gate	SK 450 240	Few rings
LE	Diseworth, Lillys Cottage	SK 453 245	Few rings
LE	Great Bowden, 21 Manor Road	SP 740 880	Few rings
LE	Great Dalby, Fern Cottage	SP 740 140	Elm
LE	Hoton, 11 Wymeswold Road	SK 575 227	Few rings
LE	Narborough, 34 Coventry Road	SP 542 976	Few remaining timbers
LE	Newton Linford, 59 Main St	SK 510 100	Few rings and few timbers
LE	Swithland, 124 Main St, Loughborough	SK 549 131	Elm
LE	Syston, 1 High St	SK 630 110	Few rings
OX	East Hendred, Dunelm, Horn Lane	SU 460 880	Wide-ringed timbers (recorded as medieval, but not cruck-built, Currie, 1992)
OX	East Hendred, Hickmans Cottages	SU 457 888	All timbers wide-ringed or elm
OX	East Hendred, The Cottage, Horn Lane	SU 458 884	Elm
OX	East Hendred, 2 Newbury Road	SU 459 884	Most timbers wide-ringed or elm
OX	Grove, Ivy Cottage	SU 401 901	Elm
OX	Harwell, Adnams Farm	SU 492 893	Elm: jointed-cruck truss; one oak brace
OX	Harwell, Lockton Farm, Church La	SU 493 891	Elm
OX	Harwell, Seymour Cottage	SU 494 893	Wide-ringed timbers
OX	Long Wittenham, 19 The Cross	SU 546 937	Timbers not oak, possibly chestnut
OX	Long Wittenham, 33 High Street	SU 548 938	Very wide-ringed oak timbers
OX	Long Wittenham, Barley Mow	SU 548 953	Very wide rings
OX	North Moreton, Old Manor Cottage	SU 561 896	Wide-ringed, though good quality timbers
OX	Stanton Harcourt, Smithy Cottage	SP 413 058	2 crucks, both elm
OX	Thame, Langstead Cott, 22 High St	SP 705 060	4 cruck trusses, all wide-ringed
WA	Long Lawford, 86–92 Main St, Old House	SP 474 762	Elm
WA	Monks Kirby, Kingsley Cottage	SP 465 834	Poor quality timbers, wide-ringed, possibly elm
WA	Polesworth, 34 High St	SK 264 065	Wide-ringed, though very massive (largest collar seen)
WA	Sawbridge, Old Farm	SP 503 659	One truss, mostly elm
WA	Snitterfield, Fernside	SP 214 598	Wide-ringed, possibly elm; well-shaped arch-braced cruck

Table A2.3. Plan and truss details and dimensions

P/LT indicates a passage or an inferred lean-to bay. Section (a) includes cruck houses where all or part survives of every bay (Y in the *Complete* column), or where the dimensions of one bay have been inferred (Y?). Less complete cruck houses are listed in section (b) and box-framed houses in section (c). In the column for upper floor area, 0 indicates that the house appears to have had no upper floors; a blank indicates the absence of evidence for upper flooring; all the wings were floored, apart from the service wing of DID-A. Dimensions are external. Heights are measured from the floor to the top of the ridge, and for the walls to the top of the wall plate; a blank indicates that the measurement is unknown and a * that it is approximate. For some wing trusses, the heights have not been recorded. A-br = Arch-braced open truss.

(a) Complete or nearly complete cruck houses

Code	Cou	Type	Complete	Bays	In-line bays Hall	Cham	Serv	P/LT	Truss Width	Ht	Wall ht	A-br	Room lengths Hall	Cham	Serv	P/LT	Wing length	GF Hall	Cham	Serv	P/LT	Wing	Total gf area	Upper main	Upper wing
ANS-A	LE	Cruck	Y?	4?	2	1?	1		18.4	20.4	10.5		32.3	16.07	16.2			595	296	298	0	0	1188	0	
ASH-A	WA	Box-fr & cruck	Y	4	1	1	2		15.4	20.3	11.7		16.7	17.2	31.6			256	264	485	0	0	1005		
BIT-A	WA	Cruck	Y	4	2	1	1		19.5	20.6	10.2	*	23.8	13.8	14.1			462	268	274	0	0	1005		
BOT-A	BU	Cruck	Y?	2	1	1?			19.1	20.6	10.1		14.1	14.1				269	269	0	0	0	537	0	
CAS-B	LE	Cruck	Y	2	1	1			16.5	19.7	9.9		20.3	17.8				336	298	0	0	0	634		
COS-B	LE	Cruck	Y?	2	1	1			15.0	16.7	8.0		16.0	15				240	225	0	0	0	466	0	
COU-A	WM	Cruck	Y?	2?	1	1			17.2	19.2	10.5		13.0	13				223	223	0	0	0	446	0	
DID-A	OX	Cruck (hall)	Y	2	2				15.4	17.1	6.8	*	23.5					358	0	0	0		592	0	
		(wing)		1					13.2	14.9	6.4						17.3					234			
DID-B	OX	Cruck	Y?	5?	1	1	3		16.2	21.8*	12.5		10.3	12.4	38.5			167	201	625	0	0	994	230	
EAH-B	OX	Cruck	Y	3	2	1			17.5	20.5	9.2		34.3	17.1				601	300	0	0	0	900	0	
EAH-C	OX	Cruck	Y	4	2	1	1		18.6	24.0	12.2	*	26.2	13.4	13.6			486	249	252	0	0	988	249	
ERD-A	WM	Cruck & cross wing	Y	3	2		1		18.3	21.8		*	27.2		14.8			498	0	271	0	350	1118		350
				2					15.3	25.2	15.3						23.0								
FOS-A	GL	Cruck	Y	5	2	1	2	P	20.0	21.9	10.3	*	29.1	13.4	21.4	5.1		583	269	429	102	0	1383	269	
FOS-B	GL	Cruck	Y?	2.5?	2		LT?		17.8	22.1	10.6		29.5			7.5		524	0	0	133	0	658		
HAL-A	LE	Cruck	Y?	3?	1	1	1		17.2	20.8			12.4	11.3	11.8			213	194	202	0	0	609	194	
HAL-B	LE	Cruck	Y?	3?	1	1	1		18.7	19.5			17.4	15.4	17.4	3.3		325	287	325	62	0	998	287	
HAR-A	OX	Cruck	Y?	3	2	1			17.5	21.0	10.0		26.6	13.3				465	233	0	0	0	698		
HAR-B	OX	Cruck	Y?	4?	2	1	1		19.5	21.9	10.2		23.4	12	12.0			457	235	235	0	0	927	235	
HAR-C	OX	Cruck & cross wing	Y	3	2		1		20.4	23.4	11.0	*	25.5		11.0			521	0	225	0	332	1077		332
				2					12.9	21.9	13.5						25.5								
HBY-C	LE	Cruck	Y?	3?	1?	1	1		17.8	19.2	9.4		15.0	15	15.0			267	267	267	0	0	801		
HIW-A	WA	Cruck	Y?	3	1	2?	1		19.4	22.7	12.2		16.1	19.5	15.0			312	378	291	0	0	981	378	
HOB-A	LE	Cruck	Y	3	1	1	1		18.0	16.4	7.0		15.5	12.7	16.3			279	228	293	0	0	800	228	
HUG-A	BU	Cruck	Y?	3.5?	1	1	1	LT?	19.9	22.0	12.3		14.5	14.5	14.5	8.0		289	289	289	159	0	1025	289	
LON-A	BU	Cruck	Y?	2.5?	1	1		LT?	18.8	19.3*	8.3		15.0	15		8.0		282	282	0	151	0	715		
LON-B	BU	Cruck	Y?	3?	1	1	1		15.3	19.7	8.6		15.0	15	15.0			230	230	230	0	0	689		

Code	Cou	Type	Complete	Bays	In-line bays Hall	In-line bays Cham	In-line bays Serv	In-line bays P/LT	Truss Width	Truss Ht	Truss Wall ht	A-br	Room lengths Hall	Room lengths Cham	Room lengths Serv	Room lengths P/LT	Wing length	GF Hall	GF Cham	GF Serv	GF P/LT	GF Wing	Total g/f area	Upper floor main	Upper floor wing
LON-C	BU	Cruck	Y	3	1	1	1		18.8	22.5*	10.5		16.3	15.5	13.3			306	291	250	0	0	848		
LON-I	BU	Cruck	Y	3	2	1			19.7	22.6	11.3		20.9	14.5	14.8			411	285	291	0	0	988	285	
LON-J	BU	Cruck	Y	2	1	1			16.5	20.9	10.5		15	13.3				248	220	0	0	0	468	468	
LOW-A	OX	Cruck	Y	4	2	1	1		16.4	18.0	7.2	*	26.0	13.9	9.6			426	228	158	0	0	812		
LOW-B	OX	Cruck	Y?	3	2	1?			17.5	18.5	7.6	*	21.3	10				372	175	0	0	0	547		
LOX-A	WA	Cruck	Y?	4?	1	1	2		18.3	21.0	10.7		16.5	16.5	29.4			303	303	539	0	0	1144	0	
LWH-A	LE	Cruck	Y?	3?	1?	1			16.5	18.0	10.1		16.2	16.2	16.2			267	267	267	0	0	800	0	
MDM-A	OX	Cruck	Y	3.5	2	2	1	LT	19.8	17.1	6.7	*	37.4	18.6		8.0		741	368	0	158	0	1268	0	
MDM-B	OX	Cruck	Y	3.5?	2	1	1	LT?	17.2	19.4	8.2		30.6	11.9		4.8		526	205	0	82	0	813	0	
MDM-C	OX	Cruck	Y	3	2	1	1		18.6	19.3	8.3	*	29.3	11.4				546	212	0	0	0	758	0	
MOU-A	OX	Cruck	Y?	3?	1	1	1?		19.5	25.6	13.2		15.3	11.1	15.0			298	216	293	0	0	807	690	
NEB-A	WA	Cruck	Y?	3?	2?	1?			17.9	20.0	10.7		34.6	17.5				620	313	0	0	0	933	0	
NEW-B	LE	Cruck	Y	3	1	1	1		17.0	17.9	7.9		16.1	15.4	13.6			274	262	232	0	0	768		
NOS-C	NT	Cruck	Y?	3?	1	1	1		18.8	24.2	13.0		18.8	18.7	18.8			354	352	354	0	0	1060	352	
NWL-A	BU	Cruck	Y	3	2	1			17.4	22.7*	10.8		30.5	13.8				532	241	0	0	0	773	241	
NWL-B	BU	Cruck	Y	3	2	1			17.1	20.6	9.5		26.0	13.4				445	229	0	0	0	675	0	
NWL-C	BU	Cruck	Y	2	1	1			15.6	16.8*	7.3		15.5	14.2				242	222	0	0	0	464		
NWL-D	BU	Cruck	Y?	3?	2	1?	2		17.2	20.4	8.9	*	31.7	14.6				546	251	0	0	0	797		
OXH-A	WA	Cruck	Y	4	2	2			17.4	23.2	9.5	*	22.7	13.6	12.3	7.6		461	319	311	154	0	1245		
POL-A	WA	Cruck	Y?	2?	1	1			16.1	19.7	10.5		18.4	19.3				296	310	0	0	0	607	0	
RAD-A	OX	Cruck	Y	2	1	1			15.9	17.5	7.9		18.0	10.5				286	167	0	0	0	453	0	
RAD-B	OX	Cruck	Y	3	2	1			16.5	17.6	6.6		28.8	15.4				476	254	0	0	0	730		
ROT-A	LE	Cruck	Y	3	1	2			18.6	23.0	12.5		16.0	16.1	15.7			297	300	292	0	0	888		
ROT-B	LE	Cruck	Y?	3?	1	1	1?		21.0	22.4	8.8		16.5	13.5	16.0			347	284	336	0	0	966	284	
ROT-D	LE	Cruck	Y	3	1	2			17.6	18.9	8.8		17.2	16.4	18.0			303	288	317	0	0	908	288	
SKI-A	BU	Cruck	Y	4	2	2			17.8	18.7	9.1		27.0	24				480	427	0	0	0	907	427	
SOU-A	WA	Cruck & cross wing	Y?	3?	2	2	1?		19.2	19.6	9.6	*	30.2		14.0		19.0	578	0	268	0	281	1128	0	281
SOU-A (cross wing)				2					14.8																
STC-B	BU	Cruck	Y	2	2	2			18.1	18.8	6.6		16.0	11.3				494	0	0	0	0	494	0	
STC-C	BU	Cruck	Y?	3?	2?	1	1		21.1	21.5	8.8		30.0	14.7				633	310	0	0	0	943	0	
STE-A	OX	Cruck	Y?	3?	2	1?			19.8	18.8	8.3		14.7	14.7	14.7			291	291	291	0	0	873		
STE-B	OX	Cruck & cross wing	Y?	3?	2	1		LT?	21.6	27.6	14.8	*	27.8		12.0		37.5	602	0	260	0	758	1619	0	758
STE-B (cross wing)				2.5?					20.4		15.8														
STE-C	OX	Cruck	Y	3	2?	1			18.5	20.2	14.7	*	30.8	14.7				570	272	0	0	0	842	272	
STE-E	OX	Cruck & cross wing	Y	1.5	1.5				16.5	18.8	7.9	*	13.9			5.5	33.0	239	0	0	95	498	832	0	498
STE-E (cross wing)				3					15.1		13.7														

Main table — complete cruck houses:

Code	Cou	Type	Complete	Bays	In-line bays Hall	Cham	Serv	P/LT	Truss Width	Ht	Wall ht	A-br	Room Hall	Cham	Serv	P/LT	Wing length	GF Hall	Cham	Serv	P/LT	Wing	Total g/f area	UF main	UF wing
STO-B	WA	Cruck	Y?	2	1	1			16.7	17.9	6.8		13.1	15.3				219	256	0	0	0	475	0	
STO-C	WA	Cruck	Y	3	1	2			18.5	17.6	9.6		18.8	17.3	21.3			348	320	394	0	0	1062	320	
STO-D	WA	Cruck	Y	3	1	2			19.2	20.6	10.0		17.9	17.9	18.1			344	344	348	0	0	1036	344	
STO-F	WA	Cruck	Y	3	1	1	1		18.3	20.5	12.5		16.5	17.5	17.0			301	320	311	0	0	932	320	
STR-A	WA	Cruck	Y?	4?	2	1?	1		17.1	19.7	9.3	*	26.7	13.4	15.1			457	229	258	0	0	944		
STW-A	BU	Cruck	Y	3	2	1			20.0	21.3	7.5		32.0	13.9				639	278	0	0	0	917		
SUC-A	OX	Cruck & cross wing	Y?	2 / 3	2				22.2 / 15.3	18.9	7.5 / 12.4	*	27.4				35.6	608	0	0	0	548	1157	0	548
WAL-A	WA	Cruck	Y?	4?	2	1			21.5	20.3	8.9	*	32.1	15.0	18.0			689	322	386	0	0	1396		
WEE-A	BU	Cruck	Y	4	2	1	1		17.2	18.0		*	19.9	9.8	12.3			343	168	211	0	0	722		
WEL-A	WA	Cruck	Y?	3	1	1	1		17.3	17.5	8.4		17.5	17.4	17.4			303	301	301	0	0	906		
WEN-A	BU	Cruck	Y	4	2	1	1		20.3	21.2			31.9	15.9	10.1			648	323	205	0	0	1176	323	
WOE-A	LE	Cruck & cross wing	Y?	2.5? / 2	2			P	21.9 / 16.2	20.4	8.6	*	31.8			6.4	21.2	696	0	0	140	343	1179	0	343
WOE-B	LE	Cruck	Y?	3?	2	1			19.3	21.6	11.1		32.8	16.4				633	316	0	0	0	949	316	
WOR-A	WA	Cruck & cross wing	Y?	3 / 2	2		1		17.8 / 17.2	19.8		*	29.7		13.0		23.4	529	0	232	0	402	1163	0	402
WOS-A	WM	Cruck	Y?	3	1	2?			18.0	21.0	9.5	*	17.3	17.7	9.7			311	319	175	0	0	805	0	

(b) Incomplete cruck houses

Code	Cou	Type	Complete	Bays	In-line bays Hall	Cham	Serv	P/LT	Truss Width	Ht	Wall ht	A-br	Room Hall	Cham	Serv	P/LT	Areas Hall	Cham	Serv	Total area	Upper floor area
ALC-A	WA	Cruck	N	1+					20.4	20.4		*					0	0	0	0	0
BIF-A	OX	Cruck	N																		
BIL-A	LE	Cruck	N	2+	2				18.9	21.9	9.3		15.5				292	0	0	292	
BIN-A	WA	Cruck	N	3?	1	1	1?		18.5	19.5	9.8		15.1	11.48	11.5		279	212	212	704	
CAD-A	LE	Cruck	N	2+	2?				15.1	20.8	12.1		31.5				474	0	0	474	
CAS-A	LE	Cruck	N	2+	2				16.8	18.8	8.9						0	0	0	0	
COS-A	LE	Cruck	N	2+					19.1	19.7	9.7						0	0	0	0	
DIS-A	LE	Cruck	N	3?	1?	2?			17.9	18.7	9.8			11.4			0	205	0	205	
EAH-A	OX	Cruck	N	2+	1+				16.3								0	0	0	0	
FRI-A	OX	Cruck	N	2+					17.0								0	0	0	0	
HAR-D	OX	Cruck & cross wing	N	2+ / ?	2				18.3	21.0	8.2	*	24.0				439	0	0	439	

Code	Cou	Type	Complete	Bays	In-line bays				Truss dimensions				Room lengths: main range				Areas (sq ft)			Total area	Upper floor area
					Hall	Cham	Serv	P/LT	Width	Ht	Wall ht	A-br	Hall	Cham	Serv	P/LT	Hall	Cham	Serv		
HAR-E	OX	Cruck & cross wing?	N	2+ ?	2				22.1	23.8*		*	28.0				618	0	0	618	
HAR-F	OX	Cruck	N	3+	2?	2?			18.6	22.8*	9.7		15.6	15.58	11.6	0.0	290	290	217	796	
LEW-A	WA	Cruck	N	1+					18.1	18.7	10.5						0	0	0	0	
LON-D	BU	Cruck	N	2+	2				18.1	20.4*			29.2				528	0	0	528	
LON-E	BU	Cruck	N	2+	2				18.4	22.8	11.5		39.0				719	0	0	719	
LON-F	BU	Cruck	N	2+	2				19.2	23.2	10.4		27.2				523	0	0	523	523
LON-H	BU	Cruck	N	2+					20.6	20.7							0	0	0	0	
LON-K	BU	Cruck	N	2+	1+	1			18.7	23.4	13.2						0	0	0	0	
LON-L	BU	Cruck	N	2+					16.5	16.9							0	0	0	0	
LOW-C	OX	Cruck	N	2+	2				15.5	16.0*							0	0	0	0	
NEW-A	LE	Cruck	N	3?	1?	2			15.8	17.0	8.2						0	0	0	0	
ROT-C	LE	Cruck	N	3+					18.6	20.3	11.3						0	0	0	0	
ROW-A	WA	Cruck	N	3+	2	1+			18.1	20.4	9.5	*					0	0	0	0	
SOF-A	WA	Cruck	N	2	2	1+			20.7	23.2	10.6	*	22.0	11.1			455	230	0	685	
STC-A	BU	Cruck	N	3+	2?	1			18.0	22.3	10.6		20.6	16.01			371	288	0	659	288
SUF-A	WA	Cruck	N	2+	1+	1			18.5	21.0	11.0		17.7	19.7			327	364	0	692	364
SUT-A	WM	Cruck	N	3?	2	1?			22.0	21.8	10.1	*	32.8				722	0	0	722	
SYS-A	LE	Cruck	N	2+					19.2	20.8	11.1						0	0	0	0	
WOA-A	WA	Cruck	N	2+					15.4	15.7	7.0						0	0	0	0	

(c) Box-framed houses (with the one detached chamber block)

Code	Cou	Type	Complete	Bays	In-line bays				Truss			A-br	Wing length	Room lengths: main range				Areas (sq ft)					Total area	Upper floor area
					Hall	Cham	Serv	P/LT	Width	Ht	Wall ht			Hall	Chamber	Serv	P/LT	Hall	Cham	Serv	P/LT	Wing		
AST-A	OX	Chamber block	N	2		2			13.6	20.9	10.5		24.0					0	0	0		326		326
STE-D	OX	Box-frame	Y	4	1	2	1		18.4	24.3	13.0			15.5	29.6	14.7		285	544	270	0		1098	814
STO-E	WA	Box-frame	Y	4	2	1	1		21.5	23.4	10.5			20.5	11.1	9.5		442	240	205	0		887	0
STO-G	WA	Box-frame	Y	2	1	1			17.7	21.6	12.2			18.2	16.6			316	289	0	0		605	289

Notes

Notes to chapter 1

1   Exemplified, for example, in Hanawalt, B. A. (1986) *The ties that bound: Peasant families in medieval England*, Oxford University Press, 33, and expressed particularly in Andrews, D. D. and Milne, G. (eds) (1979) *Wharram, a study of settlement on the Yorkshire Wolds; vol. 1 domestic settlement, 1: areas 10 and 6*, Soc. Medieval Archaeol.

2   See, for example, Dyer, C. (1986) 'English peasant buildings in the later Middle Ages', *Medieval Archaeol*, **30**, 19–45; Dyer, C. (1989), *Standards of living in the later Middle Ages: Social change in England, c. 1200–1520*, Cambridge University Press, 160f.

3   Johnson, M. (2010) *English houses 1300–1800*, Longman, 77.

4   As discussed in Pearson, S. (1994), *The Medieval houses of Kent: an historical analysis*, London: RCHME.

5   See the fuller consideration of *peasant* in chapter 6.

6   E.g. Barley, M. W. (1961) *The English farmhouse and cottage*, Routledge.

7   Pearson, *Medieval houses of Kent*. The Wealden houses are themselves not uniform in character, ranging from the opulent to the relatively modest.

8   Wrathmell, S. (1984) 'The vernacular threshold of northern peasant houses', *Vernacular Architecture* **15**, 29–33; Wrathmell, S. (1989) *Wharram. Domestic settlement 2: Medieval peasant farmsteads*. York University Archaeological Publications 8.

9   Gardner, M., in preparation.

10 Mercer, E. (1975) *English vernacular architecture*, HMSO.

11 After 1575, we can use these dates to plot regional trends and developments with reasonable precision. (Machin, R. (1977) 'The Great Rebuilding: a reassessment', *Past and Present*, 77, 33–56).

12 Barley, *English farmhouse*, 61.

13 Johnson, *English houses*, 77.

14 E. g. Davis, E. M. (1982) 'Weepers [*recte* Weavers]: a small late medieval aisled hall in Cambridgeshire', *Medieval Archaeol* **26**, 158–161.

15 Alcock, N. W. (1998) 'Smoke bay or open hall? Cuttle Pool Farm, Knowle, Warwickshire', *Vernacular Architecture*, **29**, 82–84.

16 For the most recent views on this problem, see Hill, N. & Alcock, N. (2007), 'The origin of crucks: New ideas revisited *and* A rejoinder, *Vernacular Architecture*, **38**, 8–14.

17 Alcock, N. W. & Hall, Sir R. de Z. (1981) 'Documentary evidence for crucks', in Alcock, N. W. (1981) *Cruck Construction An Introduction and Catalogue*, CBA Research Report, 42.

18 Hill (2005), N. 'On the origin of crucks: an innocent notion', *Vernacular Architecture* **36**, 1–14; Alcock, N. W. (2006), 'The origin of crucks: innocence or naïveté? A response', *Vernacular Architecture* **37**, 50–53;. Hill and Alcock, 'New ideas'. One qualification to the translation of *furca* as *cruck* is that the subtle distinction now made between crucks and base crucks might not have been be obvious to those who wrote the documents. Thus, references to *furcae* in buildings of relatively high status might well refer to base crucks.

19 Prior to the start of this work, just two Midlands crucks had been dated, Kinetoncote, Binton, Warwickshire and Tibberton, Harwell, Oxfordshire. Both are included in this study, and the latter has been re-examined in detail (codes BIN-A and HAR-E).

20 Since publication in hard copy in 1973 and 1981 (Alcock, N. W. *A catalogue of cruck buildings* and *Cruck construction: An introduction and catalogue*), many further examples have been identified and the list is now accessible on-line (http://archaeologydataservice.ac.uk/archives/view/vag_cruck/).

21 Alcock, *Cruck construction*, 77. Recent research on Cumbrian crucks has confirmed both these suggestions (Jennings, N. (2003) *Clay dabbins: Vernacular buildings of the Solway Plain*, Cumberland and Westmorland Antiquarian and Archaeological Society, extra series, XXX).

22 The cruck houses of Radnorshire have been the subject of a detailed and very informative study: Suggett, R. (2005) *Houses and history in the March of Wales: Radnorshire 1400–1800*. Royal Commission on the Ancient and Historical Monuments of Wales. This has demonstrated a chronological succession in the surviving buildings with those of gentry status being the earliest to survive, succeeded by house of lesser status.

23 Alcock, *Cruck construction*, 58.

24 See particularly Currie, C. R. J. (1992) 'Larger medieval houses in the Vale of the White Horse', *Oxoniensia*, 57, 81–244

25 In the lists of buildings and dimensions, the West Midlands houses are separated from those in Warwickshire, but in the tabulations and discussion, they are treated together.

26 Rutland (then in Leicestershire) was excluded, apart from one base cruck house, since its houses are almost entirely

stone-walled, corresponding more to the traditions found in Northamptonshire than to the timber-framed houses of Leicestershire.

27 Recent research in Hampshire has identified a few very early cruck buildings, comparable to some of those in Oxfordshire; see Roberts, E. (2003) *Hampshire houses, 1250–1700*, Hampshire County Council.

28 Survey work by Marsh, W. (1989) *The cruck houses of Frampton-on-Severn: Their interpretation and restoration*, Dissertation, Diploma in Architectural Conservation, University of Bristol. From the original eight houses recorded, two were demolished in the 1960s and two had undergone extensive alterations. Of the remaining four, two proved unsuitable because they were built almost entirely of elm, and only one of those surveyed could be dated.

29 See Tables 2.2c and A2.1b. For details of these houses, the original publications need to be consulted.

30 Happily, this house has since passed into other hands, and we have been able to add it to the project.

31 Alcock, N. W. and Barley, M. W. (1972) 'Medieval roofs with base-crucks and short principals', *Antiquaries J.*, **52**, 132–168.

32 It was already suspected that later base crucks were of rather lower status (Pearson, *Medieval houses of Kent*), but this has proved also to be true of some of the earlier houses.

Notes to Chapter 2

1 The figures in Table 2.1 have been updated to 2010, to include crucks discovered since the start of the project. In 1981, the numbers of cruck buildings known were: Buckinghamshire: 94; Leicestershire: 130; Oxfordshire: 141; Warwickshire: 67 and West Midlands (formerly Warwickshire: 21 (Alcock, *Cruck construction*)

2 Although the technique should always give a result, the date ranges obtained are not always unique, as discussed in Appendix 1. Radiocarbon dating has only recently been applied to any extent to standing buildings, partly because it is substantially more expensive than tree-ring dating. Indeed, the six dates reported here represent more than half the precise dates known to have been obtained by 2011 for English buildings (see the annual lists of radiocarbon dates published in *Vernacular Architecture* from 2009 onwards).

3 When no other information is available, single samples from Warwickshire southwards are given 95% probability ranges of 9–41 sapwood rings; further north, the corresponding range is 11–45 rings. For statistical analysis and mapping, felling date ranges have been assigned central dates, corresponding to the modal (most likely) value of each distribution, respectively 17 and 21 rings. These sapwood ranges and modal values are taken from Miles, D. (1997) 'The interpretation, presentation and use of tree-ring dates', *Vernacular Architecture*, **28**, 40–56.

4 Rackham, O. (1993) 'Medieval timber economy as illustrated by the Cressing Temple Barn', in Andrews, D. D. (ed) (1993) *Cressing Temple: A Templar and Hospitaller manor in Essex*, Chelmsford.

5 These figures include the houses to which radiocarbon dating was applied. For two other houses, radiocarbon dates were obtained

for subsidiary phases. One house (STO-G) firmly dated from documentary evidence is also counted.

6 For mapping, undated base-cruck houses have been taken from the on-line list in the *Vernacular Architecture Cruck Database* (http://archaeologydataservice.ac.uk/archives/view/vag_cruck/, accessed on 1 July 2011) and undated aisled halls from the list in Sandall, K. (1986) 'Aisled halls in England and Wales', *Vernacular Architecture*, **17**, 21–35.

7 For the first two, see *Vernacular Architecture*, **39**, 123 and **35**, 101. For Sawbridge, see Alcock, N. W. and Woodfield, C. T. P. (1996) 'Social pretensions in architecture and ancestry: Hall House, Sawbridge, Warwickshire and the Andrewe family', *Antiquaries. J.* **76**, 51–72.

8 See Alcock. N. W. (2010) 'The distribution and dating of Wealden houses', *Vernacular Architecture*, **41**, 37–44.

9 See the mapping and discussion in Alcock, N. W. (2002). 'The distribution and dating of crucks and base crucks', *Vernacular Architecture*, **33**, 67–70.

10 Alcock & Barley, 'Base-cruck roofs'. Re-examination suggests that Quintree House, Braunston (BRN-H) is more likely to have short principals than base crucks, although the feet of the blades are concealed; however, it is included here with the base-cruck houses. Other Leicestershire houses with short principal roofs have not been mapped.

11 X-WHA and X-HA2.

12 Pearson, *Medieval houses of Kent*; Tonkin, J. W. (1970) 'Social standing and base-crucks in Herefordshire', *Vernacular Architecture*, **1**, 7–11. Typology suggests that the undated Buckinghamshire base cruck, STK-A, may be later in the fourteenth century than any of the dated houses.

13 Sandall, 'Aisled halls'. See also Walker, J. (1999) 'Late-twelfth and early-thirteenth-century aisled buildings: a comparison', *Vernacular Architecture*, **30**, 21–53.

Notes to Chapter 3

1 As well as these houses, some evidence suggests that HUG-A, MDM-B and STE-B had lean-tos at their service ends.

2 At Cupernham Cottage, Romsey, Hants (*inf.* D. Miles) and Husborne Crawley, Beds (Alcock, N. W. and Woodward, P. J. (1976) 'Cruck-frame buildings in Bedfordshire', *Bedfordshire Archaeological J.* **11**, 57–68).

3 LON-F, where only the hall survives. The other fully floored house, LON-J, has only two original bays.

4 STE-C is an apparent exception, with a floored bay and a date of 1365/6, but here the floor can be associated with the fifteenth century reconstruction of the house.

5 The date and nature of the floors at HOB-A and WEL-A is uncertain.

6 As does the undated but probably early/mid-sixteenth century LON-J (Fig. 3.2).

7 However, the crosswing at York Farm, West Hagbourne (X-WHA, 1284/5) (fully described in Currie, 'Larger medieval houses') is attached to the base-cruck hall.

8 E.g. Beresford, G. (1987) *Goltho: The development of an early medieval manor, c.850–1150*, London.

9 The wing at HAR-C could not be dated, but is considered likely to be contemporary with the hall range.

10 The structural form of the DID-A hall the suggests that it is at least 50 years earlier than the wing.

11 Dimensions have been taken as external, since these are generally better established than the internal measurements. Dimensions are tabulated in Appendix 2, Table A2.3.

12 Missing lean-to bays are assumed to have been half the size of ordinary bays.

13 LOW-B is undated, but the form of its crucks suggests an early to mid-fourteenth century date; it has exceptionally short bays.

14 The dominance of two-bay halls becomes more apparent if the incomplete houses (Table A3.2b) are included.

15 BIT-A, DID-A (?), EAH-B, HAR-D, NEW-B, NWL-D, STW-A.

16 Alcock, N. W. and Moran, M. (1984) 'Low open-truss beams (Mantle-beams): Problems of function and distribution', *Vernacular Architecture*, 15, 47–55.

17 Alcock, N. W. (1993) *People at home: Living in a Warwickshire village, 1500–1800*, Chichester, Phillimore, 23f.

18 In such houses as EAH-C, MDM-B and OXH-A.

19 Gardiner, M. (2008). 'Buttery and pantry and their antecedents: idea and architecture in the English medieval house', in Kowaleski, M. and Goldberg, P. J. P. (eds) *Medieval Domesticity*, Cambridge.

20 HAR-F is an Oxfordshire example.

21 See Martin, D. and Martin, B. (2001) 'Detached kitchens or adjoining houses? – a response', *Vernacular Architecture*, 32, 20–33, and papers there referred to.

22 Alcock, *People at home* 50.

23 Alcock, *People at home* 108.

24 Cf. Alcock, N. W. and Currie, C. R. J. (1989) 'Upstairs or downstairs?', *Vernacular Architecture*, 20, 21–23.

25 At Aston Tirrold, the floor was replaced in the fifteenth century at a higher level, thus reversing the relative status of the two floors.

26 Pearson, S., Barnwell, P. S. and Adams , A. T. (1994) *A Gazetteer of medieval houses in Kent*, London, HMSO 101; Currie, 'Larger medieval houses', 162.

27 Alcock & Barley, 'Base-cruck roofs'; Pearson, *Medieval houses of Kent*.

28 Of these houses, eight were examined as part of the project, and three are described in Currie, 'Larger medieval houses'. The final one, LON-O, was included in the project as part of the documentary case study on Long Crendon, and it has neither been dated nor fully recorded. However, it is a very significant example of an aisled-hall to base-cruck conversion, and is therefore included among the houses discussed.

29 The evidence for this end bay (Currie, personal communication) is that the north side of the original timbers in truss I showed no weathering; the tiebeam is grooved for infill. It is also possible that this was a gabled end, adjacent to a chamber block.

Notes to chapter 4

1 Elsewhere in England, a dozen other thirteenth-century cruck houses have been identified; for a list, see Hill, 'Origin of crucks' and Hill and Alcock, 'New ideas'. Two or three crucks are probably or certainly earlier than Lower Radley. The most notable example, as it is a complete structure, is the Royal George, Cottingham, Northamptonshire, dated to 1262 (Hill, N. and Miles, D. (2001) 'The Royal George, Cottingham, Northamptonshire: an early cruck building', *Vernacular Architecture*, 32, 62–7). The cruck house at Upton Magna, Shropshire (1269) (*VA* 26, 70) comprises only two pairs of cruck blades in a house reconstructed in 1425/6, and at Butleigh, Somerset (1263/4) (*VA* 28, 172) only a reused blade survives. For the distribution of these houses, see Fig. 7.1.

2 It is not entirely certain that the surviving upper collar is original, rather than being inserted as a replacement for the lower collar. It was originally recorded as having doubled windbraces and purlins, but close structural examination indicates that the second pair of windbraces and the lower purlins are secondary.

3 This truss has previously been described as a base cruck (Currie, 'Larger medieval houses', 158). However, its only base-cruck feature is the presence of separate upper principals which are also found in other cruck trusses (apex type F2; see p. 84).

4 One of the trusses at 83 The Causeway is dated to 1315–47 and may derive from a separate phase or have been reused from a different house.

5 Lapped arch-braces, though without the joggled halvings are also used at 14–16 Hinckley Road, Walsgrave-on-Sowe (WOS-A, Fig. U), and in a cruck barn at New Shipton, Sutton Coldfield, dated to 1424d (*VA* 27, 96).

6 At HAR-B, the lost central truss seems to have had principals terminating at collar level, apparently without any upper principals supporting the ridge; it was perhaps similar to truss T2 at SKI-A (Fig. H).

7 Although no sapwood remained on the dated samples, with wide-ringed timbers used throughout, it is unlikely that more than a moderate number of rings were lost during conversion. A date in the first part of the fifteenth century is very likely.

8 The undated house, 28 High Street, Stewkley (STW-A, Fig. R), noted previously, contains a number of features suggesting a relatively early date. The only other house with an undated arch-braced truss is 26 Manor Road, Didcot (DID-A, Fig. S), which may be of the earlier fifteenth century; its later crosswing, also cruck-built, is dated to *1517–28*.

9 One dated Warwickshire crown-post truss is in the wing at 150 High Street, Henley-in-Arden (X-HIA, 1345).

10 Precisely how the hall and wing plates were linked is now unclear and, indeed, the truss and presumably the plates have splayed significantly.

11 This type of replacement was first identified at Lime Tree House (Currie, C. R. J. and Fletcher, J. M. (1979) 'The Bishop of Winchester's medieval manor house at Harwell, Berkshire and its relevance in the evolution of timber-framed aisled halls', *Archaeol. J.* 136, 173–192). It also happened at Bramleys, Shudy Camps, Cambridgeshire (E. M. Davis, personal communication). In addition, Handsacre Hall, Staffordshire (demolished) contained timbers from an aisled hall of c. 1175, though its reconstruction as a base-cruck hall in c. 1306 seems to have involved the complete rebuilding

of the earlier house (*VA* **21**.38); the house has not been published in detail.

12 The earliest non-domestic base cruck is the Tithe Barn, Siddington, Gloucestershire of 1245–7 (*VA* **23**, 44). For West Bromwich, see *VA* **41**, 101.

13 The aisles are only intact at Lime Tree House (X-HA1) and Long Crendon Manor (LON-O). At Sycamore Farm the loss of most of both aisles permits only an approximate estimate of the width.

14 All the posts at Lime Tree House, Harwell have been replaced, and this figure presumes that the arcade plates were kept at the same height in the reconstruction. For the same reason, we do not know whether the passing braces reached to the outer walls (as shown on earlier reconstructions), or stopped at the arcade posts.

15 Alcock & Barley, 'Base-cruck roofs'

16 Alcock & Barley, 'Base-cruck roofs'; Tonkin, 'Herefordshire base crucks'.

Notes to Chapter 5

1 Rackham, O. (1972) 'Grundle House: on the quantities of timber in certain East Anglian buildings in relation to local supplies', *Vernacular Architecture*, **3**, 3–8.

2 The only identified use of halving earlier than about 1340 is at the Royal George, Cottingham, Northants of 1262 (Hill & Miles, 'Royal George, Cottingham') where one of the cruck trusses has its blades sawn from a single tree, making them noticeably narrower than the square-section blades of the other truss.

3 Even these substantial blades are not as wide as some examples from Shropshire and the Welsh Marches

4 As well as BIN-A, HAR-F (fifteenth century, T3, not drawn) has the rear cruck blade extended.

5 The same treatment was apparently used in the open truss (T3) at FOS-A (1496/7, not drawn), but the lower parts of both blades were replaced later and the original form is uncertain.

6 Tree dimensions are calculated at breast height.

7 In the house as it exists, only those at the north end of the house appear to have survived intact.

8 Rackham, 'Grundle House'.

9 Rackham, 'Grundle House', but without a detailed breakdown for the Cambridgeshire house; Kirk, J. C. (2004) 'Butts Cottage, Kirdford: the conversion of trees to timber in the rural Sussex Weald', *Vernacular Architecture*, **35**, 12–20.

10 One other example is known to the writer, albeit in a very high quality building, the Round Tower at Windsor Castle, dated to 1354/5.

11 McCann, J. (1978) 'Purpose of rafter holes', *Vernacular Architecture*, **9**, 26–31.

12 Harris, R. (1995) 'Level marks and the sequence of framing', *Mortice and Tenon*, **2** (July), 2–4; Thompson, J. (1996) 'Sussex historic framing', *Mortice and Tenon*, **4** (July), 2–3.

13 Similar bracing has been found at Hickman's Cottages, East Hendred, Oxfordshire (Currie, C. R. J. (1992) 'Larger medieval houses in the Vale of the White Horse', *Oxoniensia*, **57**, 119–20 and personal communication). It has also been

suggested at Upton Magna, Shropshire (Moran, M. (2003) *Vernacular buildings of Shropshire*, Almley, Herefs: Logaston Press, 46–7), but see the CD-report for NWH-A, for a possible reinterpretation.

14 Moran, *Vernacular buildings of Shropshire*, 46–7. An apparently earth-fast cruck has also been reported from Great Fencote, Yorkshire (Harrison, B. and Hutton, B. (1984) *Vernacular Houses in North Yorkshire and Cleveland*, Edinburgh, 175).

15 The crucks at LOX-A pass the sillbeam, resting on padstones whose tops are at floor level. These could well have been inserted below the feet of originally earth-fast crucks.

16 The 'base-cruck' blades at BRN-H are also set into stone walls, but have been cut off at the wall head and the interpretation now preferred is that these were originally short principal trusses, at most extending a short distance down the walls.

17 Smith, J. T. (1981) 'The problems of cruck construction and the evidence of distribution maps', in Alcock, *Cruck Construction*, 5–24.

18 This is also seen at the Royal George, Cottingham, of 1262 (Hill & Miles, 'Royal George, Cottingham').

19 Alcock, *Cruck construction*, 10; 14. Of the 490 cruck houses in the project counties with known apex types, only two others have type B apexes and three have H apexes.

20 Since the measured surveys concentrated on internal trusses, few detailed drawings have been made of end cruck trusses.

21 The only exception is in a very unusual house in the far north of the county, dated typologically to the fourteenth century, Priory Farm, Balscott (Wood-Jones, R. B. (1963) *Traditional Domestic Architecture in the Banbury Region*, Manchester University Press, 42–5). Truncated crucks are also relatively common in Hampshire, to the south of the project counties.

22 It is an interesting illustration of local carpentry styles that the three cruck houses in Steeple Claydon, Buckinghamshire, all of the mid-fifteenth century, have half-hipped (apex V) end trusses with C and F1 apexes internally, rather than the more standard W-apexes (STC-A, STC-B, STC-C, 1448, *1431–6*, 1444/5; Figs. G, F, H).

23 Hewett, *English historic carpentry*, 289 and *passim*.

24 The two pegs between the plate and the arcade post (Fig. 5.5a) are not parallel, but since this is not a halved joint, the pegging does not function to prevent the timbers separating.

25 Hill & Miles, 'Royal George, Cottingham'. The pegging is described in the text but not shown on the section drawing.

26 The second-phase collar of the open truss at IVI-A (*1288-1323*) is also pegged in this way.

27 Joggled joints are also used at a house at Upton Fields, Warwickshire (1407d, *Vernacular Architecture*, **43**, 19), and at New Shipton barn, Sutton Coldfield, Warwickshire (1424d, *VA* **27**, 95).

28 This terminology corresponds to the recommended terminology; *side-halving* is alternatively named *edge-halving*.

29 One part of the ridge was no less than 25 feet long. Unfortunately this roof was destroyed by fire in 2011.

30 At AST-A, the wall plates were examined during renovation work and showed no pegholes.

31 Part of a secondary smoke hood still survives, in the same place as the former louvre, and the present chimney stack has been built within this smoke hood.

32 Interestingly, ANS-A has a small raised roof over the possible louvre position, but with no smoke blackening on its timbers.

33 Thorp, J. (2011) 'Roof carpentry in Devon from 1250–1700' in Walker, J. (ed.) *The English medieval roof: Crownpost to kingpost*, Essex Historic Buildings Group; Alcock, N. W. and Laithwaite, M. (1973) 'Medieval houses in Devon and their modernization', *Medieval Archaeol.* **17**, 100–125.

34 The other side of the louvre has been lost through the insertion of the stack.

35 At EAH-C (1418/20), the wall framing suggests that an original low floor has been replaced. At STE-C (1365/6), the floor is probably associated with the fifteenth century reconstruction of the house, rather than the dated cruck trusses. At HOB-A (1440/1) and WEL-A (1430), the dates of the floors are uncertain. Documentary references (Chapter 6) indicate the existence of some upper floors in the fourteenth century.

36 Some of the braces survive in the cross-wing, some being straight and some curved.

37 Similar infill has survived at 150 High Street, Henley-in-Arden (X-HIA), also of the mid-fifteenth century.

38 A doorway in a similar position (with an ogee head) has been noted at St Owen's Well House, Much Wenlock, Shropshire (1415d) (Moran, *Vernacular buildings of Shropshire*, 282–3).

39 Currie, C. R. J. (1990b) 'Archaic roofs in Hereford and Worcester', *Vernacular Architecture*, **21**, 18–32 (p. 31), has noted the early use of cogged tiebeam joints and suggested that these were the norm before about 1200.

40 Hewett, C. (1980) *English historic carpentry*, Chichester: Phillimore, 91.

41 Long Crendon Manor (LON-O) may use similar joints, but it has not been fully recorded, and its details are not known.

42 Chenevix Trench, J. (1992) 'Another thirteenth-century house for Buckinghamshire?', *Records of Buckinghamshire*, **34**, 14–29

43 These are a regional trait, also being found at West Bromwich Manor House, though the latter's rather earlier date is reflected in the up-braces being halved across the tiebeams rather than springing from the crown post (Jones, S. R. (1975–6) 'West Bromwich (Staffs). Manor-House', *Trans. South Staffordshire Archaeol Hist Soc.* 17, 1–63).

44 Technically, the 'crown posts' are crown struts, since they do not support a plate.

45 CLI-B (1319/20) had an almost identical strap on its tiebeam, although this was removed in the 1990s.

Notes to Chapter 6

1 Addy, S. O. (1898) *The evolution of the English house*, London, xviii; Smith, J. T. (1970) 'The evolution of the English peasant house to the seventeenth century: the evidence of the buildings', *J. British Archaeol. Assoc.* 3rd ser., **33**, 122–47;

Grenville, J. (1997) *Medieval housing*, Leicester, 121–56; Hurst, J. G. (1965) 'The medieval peasant house', in Small, A. (ed.), *The fourth Viking Congress, York, 1961* (Aberdeen, 1965), 190–6; Field, R. K. (1965) 'Worcestershire peasant buildings, household goods and farming equipment in the later middle ages', *Medieval Archaeology*, **9**, 105–45.

2 Hilton, R. H. (1975) *The English peasantry in the later middle ages*, Oxford, 3–19.

3 Hurst, J. G. (1971) 'A review of archaeological research (to 1968)', in Beresford, M. and Hurst, J. G. (eds.), *Deserted medieval villages: studies*, London, 76–144, especially 107–12.

4 Miller, E. and Hatcher, J. (1978) *Medieval England. Rural society and economic change 1086–1348*, London, 158–9.

5 Dyer, C. (2008) 'Building in earth in late-medieval England', *Vernacular Architecture*, **39**, 69.

6 Farmer, D. L. (1991), 'Marketing the produce of the countryside', in Miller, E. (ed.), *The agrarian history of England and Wales*, 3, *1348–1500*, Cambridge, 413.

7 West Yorkshire Archive Service, Leeds Archive Office, MX/M10/3/11, 13.

8 Holden, E. W. (1963) 'Excavations at the deserted medieval village of Hangleton, part 1', *Sussex Archaeological Collections*, **101**, 54–181; Burton Dassett interim reports, *Medieval Archaeol.* **32** (1988), 282–3; **33** (1989), 215–17.

9 Dyer, 'Building in earth', 69.

10 Nottingham University Library, Mi6/170/77; Dyer, 'Building in earth', 69; Poos, L. (1991), *A rural society after the Black Death Essex, 1350–1525*, Cambridge, 78.

11 This is based on Fenwick, C. (ed.) (1991–2005), *The Poll Taxes of 1377, 1379 and 1381*, British Academy, Records of Social and Economic History, New Series, 27, 29 and 37, Oxford, from a sample of villages from Derbyshire, Essex, Leicestershire, Staffordshire and Wiltshire.

12 Dyer, 'English peasant buildings', 19–45 especially 30; Homans, G. C. (1941), *English villagers of the thirteenth century*, Cambridge, Mass., 140–1.

13 Roberts, B. K. and Wrathmell, S. (2002) *Region and place. A study of English rural settlement*, London, especially 5, 26.

14 Westminster Abbey Muniments (WAM), 8362.

15 DeWindt, E. B. (ed.) (1976), *The Liber Gersumarum of Ramsey Abbey*, Toronto.

16 Gloucestershire Archives, D621/M1, M2.

17 TNA, SC2/175/77, 78.

18 Page, P. (2005) *Barentin's manor: excavations of a moated manor in Harding's field, Chalgrove, Oxfordshire, 1976–9*, Oxford Archaeology.

19 John Danby of Allertonshire (Yorkshire) in 1444 had malt and salt meat in his chamber: Durham University Library, Special Collections, Durham Dean and Chapter, Allerton Wills and Inventories, Loc. 8/12; in 1482 Thomas Kirkeby of Clifton (Yorkshire) kept a scythe with bed linen and cushions, probably in a chamber: Borthwick Institute for Historical Research, Dean and Chapter Wills, Kirkeby.

20 Wrathmell, *Wharram*, 31–2.

21 Hurford, M., Jones, M. and Tyers, C. (2010), 'Tree-ring dating and the historical and social context of timber-frame buildings, Norwell, Nottinghamshire', *Trans. Thoroton Soc.* **114**, 37.

22 Birrell, J. R. (1962) 'The forest economy of the Honour of Tutbury in the fourteenth and fifteenth centuries', *University of Birmingham Historical Journal*, **8**, 114–34.

23 Briggs, C. (2009) *Credit and village society in fourteenth-century England*, Oxford.

24 Steane, J. M. and Bryant, G. F. (1975) 'Excavations at the deserted settlement at Lyveden', *Northampton Museum and Art Gallery J.* **12**, 4–56.

25 Riddy, F. (2008) '"Burgeis" domesticity in late-medieval England', in Kowaleski, M. and Goldberg, P. J. P. (eds.), *Medieval domesticity. Home, housing and household in medieval England*, Cambridge, 14–36.

26 Poos, *Rural society*, 183–206 ; Hilton, *English peasantry*, 30–6.

27 Razi, Z. (1993) 'The myth of the immutable English family', *Past and Present*, **140**, 3–44, especially 8–9.

28 Hilton, R. H. and Rahtz, P. A. (1966) 'Upton, Gloucestershire, 1959–1964', *Trans. Bristol and Gloucestershire Archaeol. Soc.*, **85**, 70–146, building 26 (p. 85).

29 Smith, R. M. (1982) 'Rooms, relatives and residential arrangements: some evidence in manor court rolls, 1250–1500', *Medieval Village Research Group Annual Report*, **30**, 34–5; Alcock, N. W. (2003) 'The medieval peasant at home: England: 1250–1550', in Beattie, C., Maslakovic, A. and Jones, S. R. (eds.), *The medieval household in Christian Europe, c. 850–c. 1550*, Turnhout, Belgium: Brepols, 449–68.

30 Watts, G. (2002) 'Medieval tenant housing on the Titchfield estates', *Hampshire Studies*, **57**, 53–8.

31 Durham University Library, Special Collections, Durham Dean and Chapter, Allertonshire wills and inventories, Loc. 8/3, 8/12, 8/17, 8/19 (inventories 1444–99).

32 Razi, Z. (1981) 'Family, land and the village community in later medieval England', *Past and Present*, **93**, 3–36; *idem*, (1993) 'The myth of the immutable English family', *ibid*, **140**, 3–44; Whittle, J. (2000) *The development of agrarian capitalism. Land and labour in Norfolk, 1440–1580*, Oxford, 85–100; Mullan, J. and Britnell, R. (2010) *Land and family. Trends and local variations in the peasant land market on the Winchester bishopric estate, 1263–1415*, Hatfield, 118–31.

33 Mate, M. (1998) *Daughters, wives and widows after the Black Death. Women in Sussex, 1350–1535*, Woodbridge, 50–5.

34 Smith. R. M. (1986) 'Women's property rights under customary law: some developments in the thirteenth and fourteenth centuries', *Trans. Royal Historical Soc.*, 5th series, **26**, 165–94; idem, 'Coping with uncertainty: women's tenure of customary land in England, 1370–1430', in Kermode, J. (ed.) (1991), *Enterprise and individuals in fifteenth-century England*, Gloucester, 43–67.

35 Taylor, C. C. (1982) 'Medieval market grants and village morphology', *Landscape History*, **4**, 21–8.

36 McIntosh, M. K. (1998) *Controlling misbehavior in England, 1370–1600*, Cambridge, 65–7, 119–22; Schofield, P. (1998) 'Peasants and the manor court: gossip and litigation in a Suffolk village at the close of the thirteenth century', *Past and Present*, **159**, 3–42.

37 Maull, A. and others (2001) 'Excavations of the deserted medieval village of Coton at Coton Park, Rugby, Warwickshire', Northamptonshire Archaeology, unpublished report.

38 Evans, D. H., Jarrett, M. G. and Wrathmell, S. (1988) 'The deserted village of West Whelpington, Northumberland: third report, part 2', *Archaeologia Aeliana*, 5th series, **16**, 139–92; Beresford, G. (2009) *Caldecote: the development and desertion of a Hertfordshire village*, Society for Medieval Archaeology Monograph, **28**, 101, 102, 119.

39 Johnson, *English Houses*, 61.

40 Alcock, *People at Home*, 31–4. For cottages in Essex, see Poos, *Rural society*, 74–5.

41 Dyer, 'Peasant buildings', 19–45, especially 24.

42 Sheail, J. (1998) *The regional distribution of wealth in England as indicated in the 1524/5 lay subsidy returns*, List and index Society, Special series 28, 49.

43 Borthwick Institute for Archives, D & C Wills. 1464 Jakson.

44 Suffolk Record Office (Ipswich branch), HA6/51/4/4. 8; here tenants were told in the period 1433–52 to 'raise the sign of the heriot' which was sometimes called the 'cople', similar to the word used for pairs of crucks in western England.

45 Palmer, N. and Dyer, C. (1988) 'An inscribed stone from Burton Dassett', *Medieval Archaeology*, 32, 216–19.

46 Johnson, *English houses*, 157.

47 Hoskins, W. G. (1953) 'The rebuilding of rural England, 1570–1640', *Past and Present*, 4, 44–59.

48 For Buckinghamshire, see Table 2.3; for Shropshire, Moran, *Vernacular buildings of Shropshire*; for Kent, Pearson, *Medieval Houses of Kent*, 148ff.

49 SCLA, DR10/2587.

50 Currie, C. R. J. (1988) 'Time and chance: modelling the attrition of old houses', *Vernacular Architecture*, **19**, 1–9; Currie, C. R. J. (1990) 'Time and chance: reply to comments', *Vernacular Architecture*, **21**, 5–9; Mercer, E. (1990) 'Time and chance: a timely reminder', *Vernacular Architecture*, **21**, 1–3; Smith, P. (1990) 'Time and chance: a reply', *Vernacular Architecture*, **21**, 4–5.

51 Hatcher, J. (1996) 'The great slump of the mid-fifteenth century', in Britnell, R. and Hatcher, J. (eds.), *Progress and problems in medieval England*, Cambridge, 237–72; Bois, G. (2000) *La grande dépression médiéval: XIVe–XVe siècles. Le précedent d'une crise systémique*, Paris; Hare, J. (2011) *A prospering society. Wiltshire in the late middle ages*, Hatfield.

52 Carus-Wilson, E. M. (1959–60) 'Evidences of industrial growth on some fifteenth century manors', *Economic Hist. Rev.* 2nd ser. **12**, 190–205, especially 196.

53 Suffolk Record Office, Ipswich branch, J421/2, f. 3; Bury St Edmunds branch, IC500/2/11, f. 42.

54 Dyer, C. (2005) *An age of transition. Economy and society in England in the later middle ages*, Oxford, 114–25.

55 SCLA, DR5/2357–2360.

56 British Library, Add. Ms. 28208, f. 28r; Carus-Wilson, 'Industrial growth', 197–205; Johnson, M. (1993) 'Rethinking the Great Rebuilding', *Oxford J. Archaeol.* **12**, 117–25.

57 Dyer, C. (1992) 'The hidden trade of the middle ages: evidence from the west midlands of England', *J. Historical Geography*, **18**, 141–57; both places are now in the West Midlands.

58 Dyer, C. (1991) *Hanbury. Settlement and society in a woodland landscape*, Dept of English Local Hist, Univ of Leicester, Occasional Papers, 4th ser, 55–6; Platt, C. (1967) *The monastic grange in medieval England*, London, 106–7.

59 Dyer, 'Hidden trade', 149; Nottingham Univ. Lib., MiM 134/1, 5; *VCH Warwickshire*, IV, 233–5.

60 TNA, E 164/22, f. 155v-156r; *VCH Warwickshire*, III, 112.

61 Lincolnshire Archives, 2 Anc 2/10/1; TNA, SC6/1039/18.

62 Berkeley Castle muniments, select rolls 63.

63 TNA, SC2/207/59, /60.

64 SCLA, DR 18/30/24/17; TNA, SC2/207/79.

65 Litherland, S. and others (2008) 'The archaeology of the Severn Trent southern area rationalisation scheme, Warwickshire', *Trans. Birmingham and Warwickshire Archaeol. Soc.* **112**, 77–124; Palmer, S. C. (forthcoming) 'Medieval sites excavated on the Transco pipeline in 1999', *Trans. Birmingham and Warwickshire Archaeol. Soc.*

66 Blackwell, Worcester Cathedral Library, E series; Hampton Lucy, Worcestershire Record Office, ref. 009:1, BA 2636/164.

67 SCLA, DR75/1–6; ER2/436.

68 TNA, PROB2/452.

69 Palmer, 'Transco pipeline'.

70 Noy, D. (ed.) (2011) *Winslow court books*, Buckinghamshire Record Society, **35–6**. I am most grateful to Dr Noy for making this text available prior to publication.

71 Noy, *Winslow*, 5.

72 Noy, *Winslow*, 402. Brasiar had received three holdings from one John Burnham in 1367, and the requirement probably related to one of these; he disposed of numbers of small parcels of land from the holdings over the next few days. The text reads: *de novo construet unam novam domum in tenemento predicto cum ii paribus de Seules et ii cuttes.*

73 Although *cut* is not recorded in *OED* in any building-related meaning, the phrase 'a stable called a cutting' is found in Somerset in 1608 (TNA, LR2/202, ff. 199–253), and this is best interpreted as a lean-to building. See also p. 129.

74 Noy, *Winslow*, 339.

75 Noy, *Winslow*, 478.

76 Noy, *Winslow*, 484–5.

77 Noy, *Winslow*, 696, 708.

78 Huntington, STG Evidences, Box 23/22; Box 24/10; Box 27/21.

79 This section was originally drafted by John Chenevix Trench who sadly died before the completion of this book. Extensive revision of all the tenement histories has been undertaken in collaboration with Eric Sewell, who has also identified three previously unknown cruck houses. Transcriptions and notes made by the late Christopher Hohler and Joyce Donald and research by Bridget Jones have been of particular use.

80 The total includes Long Crendon Manor (LON-O) and the former monastic tithe barn at Notley Abbey (not further discussed), both built using base crucks, and one house with tiebeams that appear to be reused cruck blades, where the pattern of pegging gives sufficiently strong evidence to accept it as a cruck (see *LON-R*); two other houses, Fennels and Old Vicarage Cottage, have tiebeams that might be reused cruck blades, but only one side of each tiebeam can be seen and the evidence is inconclusive.

81 The major sources documenting the Long Crendon houses are listed in the bibliography. Here and in the documentary histories (see reports, LON-A to LON-U), individual

82 references are not included when the precise reference can be inferred directly from the text, for example the court roll for a specified year.

82 This was initially a cottage industry, until the establishment of a factory in the 1840s. See Donald, J. (1971) 'The Crendon needlemakers', *Records of Buckinghamshire* 19 (1), 8–16.

83 Hearth Tax return (see below); Census abstracts (British Parliamentary Papers), 1801–31.

84 *VCH Buckinghamshire*, IV, 39.

85 In 1563, William Dormer sold his third to John Peers, a London fishmonger, but it was bought back by John Dormer in 1584.

86 Trice Martin, C. (1877) *Catalogue of the archives in the muniment rooms of All Souls' College, Oxford*, 28, Crendon 22, 29. The manor was granted by Isabel Barton's feoffees to Henry VI on 1 April 1442 and regranted by him to the college on 17th May. Two years earlier (Crendon 22), Isabel Barton had sold land in Crendon to the college, to endow masses and obits.

87 *VCH Buckinghamshire*, IV, 41, identifies the Bohun third as that passing to All Souls College, but Christopher Hohler has demonstrated from college deeds that this is incorrect.

88 See Gloucestershire RO, D1447/1/169/2 & 3. The Cannons were a prominent Long Crendon family (see LON-L and LON-O).

89 Even when only one lord is named in a court roll, jurors were sworn for all three lords, e.g. in 1573 (CBS, D/BASM/23/73).

90 In early documents and some secondary sources it is named *Nutley*, but the standard later spelling is used here.

91 Pantin, W. A. (1941) 'Notley Abbey', *Oxoniensia*, 6, 22–43.

92 Dugdale, W. (1817–30) *Monasticon Anglicanum*, new edition, Vol. 6, 277–9.

93 The Abbey's cartulary was destroyed in the nineteenth century, but some notes from it were made in the seventeenth century, Gilbert Jenkins, J. (1954) 'The lost cartulary of Nutley Abbey', *Huntington Library Quarterly*, 17 (4), 379–396. The acquisition by 1390 of one half-virgate, is recorded in CBS, D/BASM 23/9.

94 *VCH Buckinghamshire*, IV, 41; TNA, C54/385 (9 Henry VIII, no. 22); part of this estate belonged to the Warmodeston family in the early fourteenth century.

95 Huntington, STG Box 5/17 (deed, 1219 x 1234); CBS, D/BASM/23/9; Huntington, STG 7/20 (in a deed bundle relating to the Pepir family); Rousham, T6.

96 Huntington, STG 5/10 & 18 (pre-1220); *VCH Buckinghamshire*, IV, 43. Courts were held for the chantry's tenants in the fifteenth century.

97 Morris, J. (ed.) (1978) *Domesday Book, Buckinghamshire*, Chichester, 14,5.

98 Bodl, Ms Top Oxon b. 185–191. As descriptive terms, *yardland* and the earlier *virgate* were used equivalently in the court rolls. The number of customary acres in each yardland is confirmed from the 1824 Abstract of Claims prior to enclosure (CBS, D78/Box1/11); for example, Henry Emerton's holding of two yardlands from All Souls College, is equated to 60 acres.

99 From the 1831 and 1851 census abstracts (http://www.

visionofbritain.org.uk) *VCH Buckinghamshire*, IV, 36 gives 3,348 acres, as in the 1891 census. Whether the difference is the result of boundary adjustments or improved measurement is not clear.

100 This figure needs to be somewhat reduced to take account of the meadows (c. 230 ac) and the small area of commons, which were not considered to be part of the arable yardlands, but were also re-allocated during enclosure.

101 Originally, each arable yardland appears to have been associated with a 'yardland' of lot meadow (each of four acres), but in the course of the seventeenth and eighteenth centuries, the arable and meadow were frequently sold separately.

102 Apart from the Notley Abbey enclosures.

103 CBS, Hohler Transcripts, Rousham, 'Crendon Box', Rental of 1563; CBS, D78/Box1; SGC, CC120131/3. The Dormer demesne was sold as a block in 1611 (Rousham, T109, 20 April 1611, sale of 'the Farm Lands' to Richard Madge and Thomas Chilton); at enclosure, the Duke of Buckingham held a half yardland and 35 customary acres, but these derived from a purchased freeholding rather than being part of the demesne land (CBS, D78/Box1/11; IR/90/Q).

104 CBS, D78/Box1/11; D52/1/32, 33. They may also correspond to the former lands of the Chantry of Thame. Since they were tithe-free, they had undoubtedly been either Abbey or Chantry property at the Dissolution. It is noticeable, that these eight yardlands were only equated to 122 customary acres, rather than the 240 which would be expected, and the corresponding allotment at enclosure was only 60 acres. TNA, E 315/406/1.

105 Huntington, ST 408, 265; CBS, IR/90/Q. All the village woodland was in demesne, most of it (92 ac) in Tittershall Wood, 5½ miles away in Wotton Underwood parish.

106 Rousham, 'Crendon Box', Rental of 1563; CBS, D 78/ Box 1; Windsor, 120. 131/3; ASC, C 24/4; Windsor, XV. 15. 76; Windsor, XV. 15. 88; ASC, C 27/65.

107 For All Souls College: ASC, 53. C21. vii. 52 (1587); For Dormer: Rousham, Crendon box 2 (1549 court of survey); for St George's, Windsor, XV. 15. 52(4) (c. 1560, list of tenants, 14 yardlands); XV. 15. 47 (1562, a rather confused account of rents received, apparently for the Windsor third); XV. 15. 104 (1720 survey). The Dormer survey also includes purchased properties and it is difficult to be sure of the precise number of yardlands in the original manor copyholds.

108 TNA, DL43/1/8 (1336); DL 43/14/3 (1390); these are the only identified medieval surveys or extents for any of the main Long Crendon manors. In 1336, although each of the virgates was held by a different tenant, two of them had a second messuage. The second survey states that 13 tenants each paid 14s for a virgate, but the total given (£9 9s) corresponds to the same 13½ virgates.

109 Bodl, Ms top. gen. e. 64 (undated but c. 1635, from the names given); Ms top. oxon. c. 381/e. 299 (1728); the latter includes four further cottages leased with the demesne yardlands. In 1635, four of the yardland holdings were held by the same tenant, but they had been split up by 1728. The Notley cottage holdings are considerably larger than those recorded for the other manors.

110 E.g. CBS, D/BASM/23/208; CBS, D/BASM/23/193; CBS, D/BASM/23/230, 1815.

111 See, e.g. CBS, CR 134/1, and numerous admissions in CBS, D/BASM/23/134-231. By the nineteenth century, they had often been inherited by absentee descendants of the earlier owners.

112 Rousham, Crendon box 2 (1549 court of survey); ASC, 53. C21. vii. 52 (1587).

113 Rousham, T26 & T23. The second deed includes another property, 2½ yardlands called Digby's, about whose early history little is known. In 1554, Dormer also sold to Bethom a 1½ and two 1-yardland holdings, two cottages and three closes.

114 Bodl, Ms. dd. Bertie. c. 16. At conventional copyhold rate, this would correspond to ten yardlands, but we have no details of its breakdown between rents from land and from houses. In the c. 1635 Notley rental (Bodl, Ms top. gen. e. 64), Sperlings is perhaps represented by a two-yardland holding called 'Guyes'.

115 The 1522 Certificate of Musters assesses 23 people on land rather than on goods, and these may perhaps be identified as the freeholders (Chibnall, A. C. (ed.) (1973) *The certificate of musters for Buckinghamshire in 1522*, London, 141).

116 Rousham, T36 (1554, 3 ½ yardlands; 2 cottages), T37–8 (1555–6, 3 yardlands), T111 (1614, 2 yardlands), T117–122 (1704–8, 5 yardlands; 1 cottage).

117 See LON-S.

118 See LON-F; the cottage sold in 1708 can also tentatively be identified (see LON-B). Tompson's Farm, 64 High Street, was enfranchised in 1614 to John Tompson (Rousham, T111) and remained in this family until it was sold in 1820 to John Hollier (CBS, AR 42/51, P134/2, schedule in deed of 1835).

119 One other Windsor holding, held by the Duke of Buckingham, was enfranchised in 1827 as part of the enclosure process (CBS, IR/90/Q).

120 Bodl, Ms Ch. Bucks 881.

121 *VCH Buckinghamshire*, IV, 42; Rousham, Crendon loose papers, summary of title to Lovedens.

122 Bradbrooke, W. (1932) 'Notes on the Braybrooke Family of Brightwalton', *Berkshire Archaeol. J.* **36** (2), 164–173.

123 CBS, D-X595/1; AR 42/51, P134/1/1–2, /7, /11, /14–15; D-HO/333; two feet of fine from 1657–8 list 12 and 13 recipients respectively for various properties (TNA, CP25/2/537/1657TRIN, /1658/59HIL; PROB 11/333 (1670, will of John Randolph); CBS, DAWf: 51/22 (1682, will of William Cannon).

124 Calculation based on the Land Tax return, CBS, Q/RPL/1/2. It assumes that the acreage and the tax assessment were directly proportional.

125 This has been greatly aided by the card index prepared by Joyce Donald.

126 This disappearance has not previously been suggested. However, not only is most of the village missing from the maps, but the contents list of the seventeenth century map portfolio includes a fifth numbered but now blank page after the four existing Long Crendon maps.

127 CBS, Q/RPL/1/1–53. These changes, which probably reflect the subdivision and combination of individual properties, make the correlation of entries between assessments more difficult.

128 See, for example, the Eight Bells (*LON-S*).

129 This is of Wealden (recessed hall) form, and its timbers have a felling date range of 1483–7 (*Vernacular Architecture*, **29**, 112).

130 Neither the base-cruck barn at Notley Abbey Farm , which served the Abbey demesne, nor a demolished cruck barn at Sycamore Farm are discussed further, as they were agricultural buildings rather than houses. However, the 'barn' at Manor Garage (*LON-P*) is included, as it appears to be domestic in origin.

131 Only one copyhold (*LON-P*) was affected by an ambiguity, with the tenant in 1725 holding two properties, which cannot be distinguished in the earlier court rolls.

132 The copyhold admissions at this period often omit the name of the previous owner, making it very difficult to link them to earlier entries.

133 Dyer, *Standards of living*, 146–150.

134 CBS, D/BASM/23/228–230.

135 SGC, 120. 349, f. 85.

136 CBS, D/BASM/23/227;D/BASM/23/230/73.

137 CBS, D/BASM/23/228/214. What happened to the holding thereafter is unclear, though the steward probably later agreed a smaller fine.

138 CBS, D/BASM/23A, *passim*; Notley manor surveys.

139 CBS, D/BASM/23/197, 208; /228/83/; 228/143/; 228/157; /228/214. Most of these represented the residual rent associated with the house of a former messuage and yardland.

140 TNA, DL/43/1/8.

141 CBS, D/BASM/23/81. Some of these may have been the cottages in roadside enclosures visible on the 1827 map (Fig. 6.3c–d), and some paid quit rents jointly to the three lords, indicating relatively recent creation on enclosures from the manorial waste.

142 *Ibid.* /80.

143 *Ibid.* /82, 86, 87.

144 *Ibid.* /92. k.

145 ASC, 67/hh-aa.

146 CBS, D/BASM/23/102.

147 CBS, DX 727/1, relating to the later 43 Bicester Road.

148 ASC, c 6, 23/48.

149 CBS, D/BASM/23/232, pp. 33–4.

150 *Ibid.* 114–5; 150–1.

151 SGC. CC 120130.

152 CBS, D/BASM/23/164; /228.

153 SGC. CC 120130.

154 CBS, D/BASM/23/227–232 (Court Books), *passim*.

155 Priest, St. J. (1813) *A general survey of the agriculture of Buckinghamshire*, London, 383.

156 CBS, IR/95/Q.

157 This return is probably for 1662, judging from the absence of the exempt names (TNA, E179/80/354); the exemption certificates for 1670, 1671 and 1672 give 23, 14 and 29 names respectively (TNA, E179/80/362/34–6).

158 The better-preserved returns for Warwickshire show that, outside towns, very few of the exempt had two hearths; those with more than this number could not be certified, even if they met the legal requirements.

159 Arkell, T. (2003) 'Identifying regional variations from the hearth tax', *Local Historian*, **33**, 148–74.

160 Bodl. MS Ch. Bucks, 800. He held the farm which later became 3 The Square (*William Thompson* in 1827, opposite P on Fig. 6.3c).

161 Bodl. MS Ch. Bucks, 799.

162 LA, Burnham, 1599/1601, INV 95/117; Howlett, 1604, INV 99/52.

163 LA, Thomas Rawlins, 1607, LCC Admons 1607/207.

164 LA, Hewett, 1618, INV 122/114.

165 Thomas Howlett, CBS, DAWf: 59/11.

166 1560, Thomas Myxbury (CBS, DAWf 5:327); 1575, Margery Coker (DAWf8:18); 1591, Edward Niccols (DAWf 11/303).

167 1633, Roland Burnham (CBS, DAWe: 29 133); 1633, John Greening (DAWe: 29 148A); 1638, Bridget Ridge (CBS, DAWe: 31/316. Coffers were most often identified as standing at the bed foot.

168 Integral dairies are found in Buckinghamshire houses of several layouts, so these examples did not necessarily share the same plan (Chenevix Trench, J. (1983) 'The houses of Coleshill', *Records of Buckinghamshire*, **25**, 61–109, p. 74).

169 Bodl. MS DD Bertie, c 16/5, 11 Hen VII; CBS, D/BASM/23/68; *Ibid.* /71.

170 SGS, CC 120130, entry 9.

171 CBS, DAWe: 43/30.

172 CBS, DAWe: 85/140

173 CBS, D/BASM/23/92. k.

174 CBS, D/BASM/23/30. d.

175 CBS, D. BASM/23/64. a.

176 In seventeenth-century Wiltshire the term seems to have connoted a lean-to (Harvey, B. K. (1992) 'An early seventeenth-century survey of four Wiltshire manors', *Vernacular Architecture*, **23**, 30).

177 CBS, D/BASM/23/30. l;/31. g; /31. b; /31. h; ASC, 22/65; CBS, D/BASM/23/237, /32d (with 5 Hen VII), /32. c; ASC, 22/65/ 12 Hen. VII; D/BASM/23/32. d; /34; /37; /57; Bodl, Ms. dd. Bertie c. 16, 5, 10, 18, 21, 26, 27, 29, Hen VIII.

178 CBS, D/BASM/23/57; *ibid.* /78. This relates to what became Randolph's farm at Lower End, held by John Randolle from the Dormer manor (*Shadk. Godwin* on Fig. 6.3a); no early house survives there.

179 *Ibid.* /50.

180 *Ibid.* /31. b.

181 Bodl. DD Bertie c. 16/5 *passim*.

182 *Ibid.* 26 Hen VIII. It seems that the wardens of the chantry were particularly anxious to make sure that their tenants' houses were well maintained. Their tenant body in Thame cannot have numbered more than 29 or 30, but the 14 courts whose rolls have survived for the reign of Henry VIII record 51 such presentments.

183 *Ibid.* 12 Hen VIII.

184 *Ibid.* 5 Hen VIII; 12 Hen VIII. In the first entry, John Edmundes permitted a cottage to be ruinous through defects [in] the wall plate, groundsill, timbers and thatch.

185 CBS, D/BASM/23/239.

186 CBS, D/BASM/23/62. *Johannes Rygge assumpsit super se ad edificandum sufficienter domum habitacionis duorum spaciorum et dimidii.* These closes were among the properties sold by Michael Dormer in 1554 to Nicholas Bethin, when Wardenwyk is described as lying between a close called Jacke

of Tames (east) and Rogers Lane (west) (Rousham, T36). It can be followed in a deed bundle (CBS D-X34/1–12) to 1736, when it was sold to William Butcher, wheelwright. The plot is identifiable as that owned by John Butcher in 1827 (Fig. 6.3d, north of LON-J). The name Jacotame is found in the 1949 Register of Electors applied to 82 High Street (L on Fig. 6.3d), although it is not known whether this was the traditional name of this cottage or had been coined on antiquarian grounds.

187 This introductory section is based largely on Currie, C. R. J. (1992) 'Larger medieval houses in the Vale of the White Horse', *Oxoniensia*, **57**, 81–244, esp. 82–6. For soils, Jarvis, M. G. (1973) *Soils of the Wantage and Abingdon district*, Memoirs of Soil Survey of Great Britain; for farming regions, Cottis, J. (1985) 'Agrarian change in the Vale of White Horse 1660–1760', Univ of Reading Ph. D thesis, 1–8.

188 For building materials cf Currie, C. R. J. (1976) 'Smaller domestic architecture in North Berkshire, c. 1300 – c. 1650', Oxford, D. Phil thesis, 7–9.

189 WAM, 7263, 22 Apr. 1421. The term for the building (*domus*) probably but not certainly means a house. The tenement was part of Farthing, held of Steventon manor but with a house in in East Hendred. Cf. Currie, 'Smaller domestic architecture', 146.

190 The evidence is discussed in a national context in Rackham, O. (1986) *History of the countryside*, London, Dent, 172–6: 'as far as our documents can tell us, west Berkshire was the seat of its [the open-field's] development.' Cf. also Gelling, M. (1976) *Place-names of Berkshire, Part 3, 1: The old English charter boundaries of Berkshire*, Cambridge, English Place-Name Society, vol 51.

191 Glasscock, R. E. (1975) *The Lay Subsidy of 1334*, London, British Academy, xxviii and map 1. The other areas listed mostly had more drastic post-medieval agrarian reorganization, which may help to account for the disappearance of peasant houses.

192 Titow, J. Z. (1972) *Winchester yields: A study in medieval agricultural productivity*, Cambridge, Cambridge University Press, appendices passim, figures for Harwell and Brightwell; Farmer, D. L. (1977) 'Grain yields on the Winchester manors in the later Middle Ages', *Econ. Hist Rev* 2S **30**, 555–66 describes those manors as 'less successful' (p 556), but they remained at the top of the table for barley and at or near the top for wheat (p 559).

193 Cottis, 'Agrarian Change', 427–9.

194 Currie, 'Smaller domestic architecture', chap 8.

195 Cottis, 'Agrarian Change', 307.

196 Glasscock, *Lay Subsidy*, map 1.

197 For carriage in the medieval period, see e.g. Hall, H. R. (ed) (1903) *Pipe Roll of Bishopric of Winchester, 1208–1209*, London: P. S. King, 15; Holt, N. R. (ed) (1964) *Pipe Roll of Bishopric of Winchester, 1210–1211*, Manchester: Manchester University Press, 60–2; BL Egerton Ms 2418; Hampshire Record Office (Hants RO), Eccl 2/159355; ibid, Eccl 2/159385; TNA, SC 11/83; SC 2/154/44, rot 7; WAM 7301.

198 Currie, 'Smaller domestic architecture', 64–6, 100–5. The decline of the local kersey-finishing industry may have been due to competition from Newbury, which, like other south Berkshire towns, apparently paid aulnage only on broadcloths in 1394 and 1395 (TNA, E 101/343/24), but was a big kersey-making centre in the fifteenth century (Yates, M. (2007) *Town and countryside in western Berkshire c 1327–c 1600*, Woodbridge: Boydell, 83–4). For Lollards, see Plumb, D. (1995) 'The social and economic status of the later Lollards', in Spufford, M. (ed) (1995) *The world of rural dissenters 1520–1725,* Cambridge, 104–126, especially 108, 113–16; McSheffrey, S. (1995) *Gender and heresy: Women and men in Lollard communities 1420–1530*, Philadelphia, 153–60; the lists omit a Steventon copyholder, John Lyford, burnt for heresy (*combustus propter eresim*) at Abingdon on 17 July 1491 (WAM 7411, rot 11).

199 Dyer, 'Peasant buildings', 31 summarizes evidence from accounts of 1430s at Coleshill in the far west of the region.

200 Currie, 'Smaller domestic architecture', 145–6.

201 See STE-H.

202 This material is examined in more detail in Currie, 'Smaller domestic architecture', 146–50; 287–91.

203 Currie, 'Smaller domestic architecture', 114–15; Currie, 'Larger medieval houses', 100–242; Faith, R. J. (1984) 'Berkshire', in Harvey, P. D. A. (ed). (1984) *The peasant land market in medieval England*, Oxford: Clarendon Press, 108–9.

204 Currie, 'Smaller domestic architecture', 106.

205 This and the following paragraphs are based unless otherwise stated on Currie, 'Smaller domestic architecture', 39–42.

206 Currie, 'Larger medieval houses', 175–181.

207 Cottis, 'Agrarian change', 79.

208 Currie, 'Larger medieval houses', 167–71; Currie, 'Smaller domestic architecture', 30, 66–7.

209 Currie, 'Smaller domestic architecture', 73–80.

210 Eg Currie, 'Smaller domestic architecture', 61–2, 68, 73–80; Fletcher, J. M. (1965–6) 'Three medieval farmhouses in Harwell,' *Berks Archaeol Jnl* 52, 55; Currie, 'Larger medieval houses', 125–7, 143–8; Anon (1890–1915) *A descriptive catalogue of ancient deeds in the Public Record Office*, London: HMSO, vi, C7350; cf. Raban, S. (1982) *Mortmain legislation and the English church 1279–1500*, Cambridge: Cambridge University Press, 177–80.

211 This and the and next paragraph are based unless otherwise stated on Currie, 'Smaller domestic architecture', chap 4; Faith, 'Berkshire', 106–77.

212 Hallam, H. E. (ed) (1988) *Agrarian history of England and Wales*, II, 1042–1350, Cambridge University Press, chap 6.

213 Currie, C. R. J. (1987) 'Harwell houses to 1700: an interim gazetteer', in Ashdown, J. and Munby, J. (eds), *Vernacular Architecture Group spring conference, 1987*, 2.

214 In western Berkshire (possibly including the Downs) the mode was 30 acres: Yates, *Town and countryside*, 26.

215 Dyer, C. (1980) *Lords and peasants in a changing society The estates of the Bishopric of Worcester, 680–1540*, Cambridge: Cambridge University Press, 108.

216 E.g. on Arches manor, East Hendred, p. 135.

217 E.g. on Arches manor in the fourteenth century and most dramatically at Steventon in the fifteenth: below.

218 On all the West Berkshire manors studied by Yates frag-

mentation was very rare until at least 1600: Yates, *Town and countryside*, 176.

219 See above, note 209.

220 Cottis, 'Agrarian change', 83–5; Yates, *Town and countryside*, 142.

221 For inflation of fines on copyholds for lives, Yates, *Town and countryside*, 144–5.

222 Currie, 'Larger medieval houses', 152–4.

223 *VCH Berkshire*, III, 485–6, wrongly stating however that Robert Hopkins (d 1838) bought it from the bishop; Hants RO, Eccl 1/155053, Eccl 1/155065.

224 *VCH Berkshire*, III, 486–7; Fletcher, 'Three medieval farmhouses', 63–4.

225 Currie, 'Larger medieval houses', 143–6; *Manorial Documents Register* for Berkshire (on-line).

226 Stenton, D. M. (ed.) (1930) *Great roll of the pipe for the sixth year of the reign of King Richard I, Michaelmas 1194*, Pipe Roll Soc NS **5**, 94; Fletcher, 'Three medieval farmhouses', 47, however stating wrongly that all except the demesne was freehold; Magdalen College, Oxford, Harwell deeds, TS catalogue 1–4, 12.

227 TNA, C133/96, no 25 and E 152/8, rot 4 (both damaged).

228 TNA, SC6/1095/3; Midgley, L. M. (ed) (1942) *Ministers' accounts of the Earldom of Cornwall 1296–1297*, Vol 1, Camden Soc, 3S, **66**, 140.

229 Currie, 'Larger medieval houses', 143–6, 15.

230 Currie, 'Smaller domestic architecture', 73–80.

231 TNA, E 318/41/2229, rot 6.

232 Fussell, G. E. (ed) (1936) *Robert Loder's farm accounts*, Camden 3S, **53**, 37.

233 Englefield, Holloway, Harwell was held on a 600-year lease from the purchasers of Prince's manor, granted on 20 Feb. 1559/60 (deeds in possession of the owners in 1986).

234 Currie, 'Larger medieval houses', 143–6, 152–4; BL Egerton Ms 2418, ff 57–v.

235 BL Egerton Ms 2418, ff 57–8.

236 Hants RO, Eccl 2/159293.

237 Currie, 'Smaller domestic architecture', 110–1, 120–1.

238 Levett, A. E. (1916) *The Black Death on the estates of the See of Winchester*, Oxford: Clarendon Press, Oxford Studies in Social and Legal History, vol 5, 48–9, 76; Currie, 'Smaller domestic architecture', 111–2.

239 Currie, 'Smaller domestic architecture', 121–4.

240 Hants RO, Eccl 2/155878–155920.

241 Hants RO, Eccl 1/121/9, 121/11, 124/7, 125/1–8, 126/1–7, 127/1; Eccl 1/158141, 158142.

242 Thomas Milis: see Currie, 'Smaller domestic architecture', 50–3, 73–80, 120.

243 Pomander House, Townsend (HAR-D); Seymour House, Jennings Lane; Church Farm (HAR-B); The Dell (HAR-A); and Lockton's Farm Outhouse (non-domestic, but perhaps not so originally), all in Church Street; Tibberton Cottage (HAR-E) and Holywell Cottage (HAR-F), Wellshead Lane, and Abbey Timbers, Broadway Hill (HAR-C). The cruck range at Seymour House is a cross-wing now attached to a large post-medieval hall.

244 The Dell, Church Farm and Abbey Timbers (HAR-A, HAR-B, HAR-E).

245 Adnam's Farmhouse, High Street, is the best example, but

fragments of early structures at Pollards, Townsend, and Burr Cottage, Burr Street, (not mapped) may also be medieval (Currie, 'Larger medieval houses', 162).

246 Currie, 'Larger medieval houses', 155–62.

247 Harwell Inclosure Award, John Keat/Keats sen.

248 It is close to the leasehold Englefield Cottage (see note 47).

249 *VCH Berkshire*, IV, 300.

250 *VCH Berkshire*, IV, 294, 297; Berkshire RO, T/M 15 A and B.

251 *VCH Berkshire*, IV, 294, 296–7.

252 *VCH Berkshire*, IV, 299.

253 *VCH Berkshire*, IV, 297–8; National Register of Archives, Eyston (East Hendred) MSS., vol i, court rolls, recognition of John Eyston 12 Oct 1453.

254 Manley, E. R. (1969) *A descriptive account of East Hendred*, East Hendred: The author, 25, 43, 48.

255 The evidence cited in *VCH Berkshire*, IV, 300 does not accord with New College, Oxford, Mss 10346–10375. See also Manley, *East Hendred*, 79.

256 For King's manor in 1607, TNA, LR2/209, ff 57–78.

257 Currie, 'Smaller domestic architecture', 114.

258 Currie, 'Smaller domestic architecture', 61–6.

259 Currie, 'Smaller domestic architecture', 113–14.

260 Currie, 'Smaller domestic architecture', 64–6; *VCH Berkshire*, IV, 294.

261 Information dated 1802 is from Berkshire RO, D/P66/26A-B, which does not number old inclosures but abbreviates the names of their owners.

262 Compare the survival of early houses at Stoneleigh, Warwickshire (below), similarly attributed to conservative estate management.

263 Currie, 'Smaller domestic architecture', fig 17 and plate 39; Currie, 'Larger medieval houses', 119–20. It was rejected for inclusion in the project as its elm timbers could not be dated.

264 TNA, LR 3/1/3, rot 18d (4 Dec. 38 Eliz, described as 'another little close') and rot 19 (12 Oct. 38 Eliz, 'a small pightle on which a cottage is newly built'). The earlier copies mentioned in Currie, 'Larger medieval houses', 119 are almost certainly irrelevant.

265 Berks RO, DP66/26A and B (John Allin).

266 The Stores is a substantial medieval house containing a hall and two jettied cross-wings, dated to 1472/3 (*Vernacular Architecture*, **30** (1999), 101; Currie, 'Larger medieval houses', 118–19). The possibly medieval parts of Meadow Cottages are fragmentary.

267 The Cottage, Horn Lane: the row was owned by 'Robey', either John Robey junior or John Robey senior, respectively a small and a substantial farmer: Berks RO DP66/26A and B.

268 Inglenook-Penny Green, Cat Street (EAH-B).

269 Wythe Cottage, Church Street, and Featherbed Cottage, Newbury Road.

270 Church Street Cottages.

271 Windyridge-Dunelm, Horn Lane, held by William Harris.

272 Briar Cottages, Cat Street.

273 References given only by year are to the corresponding court roll, WAM 7261 ff.

274 For details of descent, Currie, 'Smaller domestic architecture', 21–8.

275 Currie, 'Smaller domestic architecture', 30, 66–8, 226; WAM, 7358–9, 8034. For the 1400 rents, WAM, 7448. The area of Farthing (Currie, 'Smaller domestic architecture', 25) was several times that of the part of it managed or leased directly (e.g. WAM. 7412, rot 34) and thus it probably included freeholder undertenants.

276 For ancient demesne, WAM 7301; for heritable holdings, WAM 7261–7264, 7409–7419. In 1393 and 1398 the court granted some holdings to the tenant 'et suis', apparently making them non-heritable (7261, rott 20, 24), but this seems later to have been ignored.

277 WAM 7301 (1281), TNA, E 106/2/6, rot 4, 8 (1294); E 106/8/5, no 20d (rubbed and partly illegible) (1324). The figures for 1281 are more likely to be accurate than the summary extent figures for 1294 and 1324: for example, 32 half-yardlanders paid 'cherset' in 1401 (WAM 7449). The demesne acreages in those extents are also discrepant, and that for 1294 is almost certainly much exaggerated: Currie, 'Smaller domestic architecture', 29.

278 Currie, 'Smaller domestic architecture', 86–9, 99–105; WAM 7262, rot 19; 7264, rot 5. After 1400, one or two house-and-yardland holdings were split into moieties: e.g. WAM 7662, rot 39. Recent work suggests that involvement in the cloth trade at Steventon was very intermittent and probably marginal from the 1430s until the mid-sixteenth century: e.g. WAM 7410, rott 7, 18; 7412, rot 2; BRO D/A/1/51, inventory of Ellis Cox, 1556.

279 For conditions of tenure, see Currie, 'Smaller domestic architecture', 89–110.

280 WAM 7412, rott 11d, 19, 26d.

281 Four such exchanges in 1428–32, eight in 1438 (besides 19 exchanges of arable), and six in 1439–41: WAM 7264, rott 11–17d, 29d–30, 32–end.

282 Dyer, *Standards of living*, 267–8; WAM 7264, rott 30 (m 2d) -32.

283 WAM 7264, rott 34–35; cf Harvey, B. (1977) *Westminster Abbey and its estates in the Middle Ages* Oxford, 300.

284 WAM 7409 (1441–60).

285 Currie, 'Smaller domestic architecture', 89–110.

286 WAM 7264, rott 26, 29d.

287 WAM 7409, rot 13d sqq.

288 WAM 7409, rot 5d sqq; cf Yates, *Town and countryside*, 198–9.

289 WAM 7412, rott 29d–31d.

290 WAM 7412, rot 21 sqq; cf Yates, *Town and countryside*, 193–4.

291 See STE-F. The ex-Dormer, ex-Yate, and ex-Doo estates were sold in lots between 1558 and 1572: WAM 7418, rott 1–15.

292 WAM 7414, rot 1; 7416, rot 3; 7418.

293 WAM 7415, inner loose pages, f 1d (1548); 7417, 5th sewn sheet (1557); 7418, rot 11(1568).

294 WAM 7418, rott 29–31.

295 WAM, lease book 7, f 93.

296 Currie, 'Smaller domestic architecture', 226–9.

297 Soil Survey of England and Wales sheet 253 (1972–3).

298 TNA, C 241/126/124.

299 Currie, 'Smaller domestic architecture', 22–3.

300 TNA, C 241/155/111.

301 Above, this chapter; Currie, 'Smaller domestic architecture', 100–105.

302 WAM 7261–7264, 7409. After eleven payers in 1430 and nine in 1432, six are recorded in 1446 and five in 1447.

303 WAM 7264, rot 19; rot 33.

304 WAM 7409, rott 3, 13, 16, 18, 20; TM 31 and 40 on Fig. 6.10. Tanners may have also worked further west.

305 WAM 7412, rott 11, 15. See also rot 9 and 7410, rot 9, 7411, rot 5.

306 WAM 7411, rot 7. From 1509 to 1538 tithingmen were elected for each tithing, but they no longer made separate presentments; from 1542 two tithingmen were elected without distinction of ends, and the ends seem to have been ignored thereafter: WAM 7412, *passim*. The division between the ends was probably Highway Lane, although this cannot be conclusively demonstrated.

307 The causeway runs from south-west to north-east; in this section it will be treated as aligned west to east. In the court rolls, it is usually treated as aligned south to north.

308 Tudor House, STE-B, Chapter 8.10.

309 Currie, 'Smaller domestic architecture', 11.

310 Currie, 'Smaller domestic architecture', 11.

311 South of Cat Street, closes TM 77, 77a were called Tun Furlong, indicating that they had been medieval arable, and Pugsden (TM 102–7, 111, Fig. 6. 10) was being inclosed in the late sixteenth century (WAM 7418, rott 16, 28–29d; 7419, rot 10d; WAM 7424, ff 19–26).

312 Currie, 'Smaller domestic architecture', 11.

313 Although c. 1380–1420 there were a few cottages *eo nomine*, sometimes freehold (e.g. WAM 7261, rott 6, 12 (m1); 7262, rott 8, 21), the nine cottagers listed in 1324 (footnote 277, above) probably held *burdewes* or *bordella*, smallholdings with irregular rents and normally no field land; up to 12 of these can be identified later (WAM 7261–7264). In the early fifteenth century a row of three lay in Cat Street (WAM 7263, rot 11d; 7409, rot 24d).

314 WAM 7262, rot 19; 7264, rott 9, 12, 28d, 29d, 33d, 35d; 7409, rott 4, 19d, 30d.

315 Notably Wyresdales, a burdewe, which lay between Green Farm I (STE-M, TM 137) and the brook (WAM 7410, rott 19d, 25d; 7411, rott 17, 21d; 7412, rott 16–17d, 22; 7418, rot 10; 7524, ff 19–26). The hedge line in this part had been straightened before 1839.

316 E.g. WAM 7409, rot 17, 24; 7410, rott 10, 2; 7411, rot 28.

317 WAM 7418, rot 13d; 7524, loose sheets, list of fines.

318 WAM 7419, rott 2d, 13d-14.

319 WAM 7410, rot 22d.

320 WAM 7411, rott 12–13.

321 See STE-G and STE-H.

322 Berks RO, D/A/1/1, 83; D/A/1/114; D/A/1/2, 26.

323 Robert Lyford, Berks RO, D/A/1/201; Thomas Smalbone.

324 Berks RO, D/A/1/51.

325 The 1839 map is Oxford RO, P238/M/1 (key: Berks RO, D/ETY/04, only recognised in 2011); 1842 tithe map and apportionment: Berks RO, D/D1/119/1A-B. An altered tithe map and apportionment were made in 1884, following the enclosure of the open fields (D/D1/119/2). The c. 1835

map of ownership along the line of the railway (with key) is Parliamentary Archives, HL/PO/PB/3/Plan 106.

326 Currie, 'Smaller domestic architecture'. For no 87, a copy of court roll in possession of the owners (in 1972) and copies for nos 77–81 [STE-I] the Causeway, in possession of the Godfrey family, Steventon (in 1986), had allowed their status to be identified.

327 These volumes are WAM CC 292094–292099.

328 These rolls are all in WAM, listed individually in their indexes to manorial documents, apart from two for 1539–42 (TNA, LR 3/1/4; LR 11/57/825). From the mid 1540s they are intermittently supplemented by paper minutes.

329 In the first seventeenth-century gap, minutes survive for a 1604 court, estreats for two in 1609 and 1610, and a list of fines of 1614. If any courts were held in the second gap, when the manor was in the hands of parliamentary controllers and grantees, their work was not recognized by the restored Westminster administration, and many transactions that might have been recorded then are among the 50 admissions in the roll for 1661.

330 The formula defining that feast clearly varied. The Westminster Abbey court officials (monk-wardens and their clerks, or sometimes lay stewards) seem usually to have treated Hock Tuesday as the *third* Tuesday after Easter, whereas the royal officials who drew up the rolls in 1539–41 calculated it correctly as the second Tuesday after Easter. Confusingly, in Henry VIII's reign (accession on 22 April, in the Easter period) there could be two, one, or no Hock Tuesdays in a regnal year.

331 On WAM 7411, rot 5, the courts dated to Tuesday after All Saints 3 Henry VII and Hock Tuesday of year 4 (1487/9) can be shown to belong to the corresponding years of Henry VIII (1511–12) (cf WAM 7412 rot 5).

332 Tracing the holdings from 1664 onwards in the newly-discovered court books and identifying them on the 1842 Tithe Map has been undertaken by Nat Alcock and Heather Horner, with the assistance of Christopher Currie. The latter has tabulated over 2,000 pre-1664 court roll entries, extending his work of the 1970s, and he and Nat Alcock have compiled the ownership sequences for each of the 80 holdings that included houses.

333 These lists are: WAM 57045, the numbered list of admissions; WAM 57046, the 1800 index and WAM CC 292100, the 1890 index. In WAM 57046, each holding is numbered from 1 to 100, and these numbers were re-used in the second index, although with numerous added letters, a, b, etc. for divided holdings. These numbers are included in the individual Steventon reports.

334 Between about 1490 and 1550, cross references to previous court entries show that the tenants' copies were being used to compile the admissions. Even in the middle decades of the fifteenth century, when the rolls seem to be complete, a few entries that should exist cannot be found, indicating that entries must have been accidentally omitted when the engrossed rolls were compiled from the court minutes.

335 Part of 109–119 Causeway, east of the Vicarage.

336 Botleys (STE-G) and 83–5 The Causeway (STE-C). The Chancery suit concerned Botleys (*inter alia*).

337 See Baylis, A. L. H. (1995) *The story of Steventon*, Parchment (Oxford) Ltd, 105, 205. The vicarage comprises a fourteenth-century cross-wing associated with a sixteenth-century hall and a later second cross wing. Tree-ring dating has not been undertaken on it.

338 The Old Vicarage also obviously enjoyed continuity at that period.

339 Stone: STE-K; box-framed: STE-F (mostly), STE-G, STE-H, STE-I, STE-J, and STE-M (which has lost its hall). The box-framed STE-D was built as a subsidiary house for STE-B and descended with it.

340 Currie (1976), 37–8. Doo was never sole lessee of either.

341 WAM 7367.

342 The apparent bunching of firmly dated houses in the thirteenth to fourteenth and the sixteenth century may result more from difficulties in dating fifteenth-century timber than from an absence of fifteenth-century houses. In several undated houses, secondary phases of the early to mid sixteenth century suggest primary construction before 1500.

343 Alcock, *People at home*.

344 A map of Rothley in 1821 exists, but it lacks the necessary key to owners and occupiers that would make it useful in providing the background to the cruck buildings there.

345 Darlington, R. R. (1968) *The Cartulary of Worcester Cathedral Priory (Register I)*, Pipe Roll Society, NS **38**, 319 & 386.

346 Hale, W. H. (ed) (1865) *Registrum Prioratus Wigorn*, Camden Soc, old ser, **91**, 65. See also Alcock, *Cruck Construction*, 33.

347 Bodl, Ms. Trinity 84, p. 65 (Warwickshire County Record Office, microfilm MI-272); this is a miscellaneous 15th century collection of Maxstoke Priory records, including transcripts of earlier documents, here an abstract of a court roll.

348 *VCH Warwickshire*, VIII (1969), 101 (Stoke general history), citing TNA, SC 2/207/18 (f. 6v), Cheylesmore court roll. A written agreement should have been made but it had not been produced or properly sealed, leading to the plea in the manor court. The relevant section of the text reads *'quod idem Williemus edificare in predicto messuagio unum dom[um] continent' iiijor furcis et ij staunsone sumptis in (?) quod Willelmi propriis'* (apparently meaning *at William's own expense*). The *staunsone* can be identified as stanchions, presumably posts.

349 Alcock, *Cruck Construction*, 33, citing Coventry Archives, BA/B/16/352/13; Alcock, N. W. and Blair, J. (1986) 'Crucks: new documentary evidence', *Vernacular Architecture*, **17**, 36–8, 37, citing Coventry Archives, BA/B/16/227/1; Coventry Archives, PA 468/5/3/5/1, deed for a property later acquired by the Drapers' Company.

350 As described in Jones, S. R. and Smith, J. T. (1960–1) 'The Wealden houses of Warwickshire and their significance', *Trans Proc Birmingham Archaeol Soc*, **79**, 24–35.

351 Merton College MCR 6424, m. 3; mentioned in Howell, C. (1983) *Land, family and inheritance in transition : Kibworth Harcourt 1280–1700*, Cambridge: Cambridge University Press, 56.

352 Alcock, *Cruck Construction*, 32, citing Hamilton Thompson, A. (1933) *A calendar of charters and other documents belonging to the Hospital of William Wyggeston at Leicester*, Leicester: Edgar Backus, no. 986.

353 BL Add. Roll 41651; in the following court it was described as ruined (*periorat*).

354 SCLA DR10/2450 and 2472 (references kindly provided by Professor C. Dyer).

355 Alcock (1981) 32, citing SCLA DR 18/30/26/35. The length and descender of the important word missing before *house* match the word *oxe* in the following presentment.

356 Hilton, R. H. (ed.) (1960) *The Stoneleigh Leger Book*, Dugdale Soc. **24**, Oxford: Oxford University Press, 7 provides an outline for the early history of Stoneleigh and its members, which finds support in the pattern of parish boundaries.

357 Hilton, *Leger Book*, xii–xvi; 114–6.

358 *VCH Warwickshire*, VI, 1951.

359 The equivalence of statute acres and open-field yardlands was calculated explicitly by John Goodwin, 'practitioner in the mathematic', in the 1597 survey, matching the 24 yardlands in Stoneleigh village with the 670 acres in its open fields, giving 28 acres on average. Similarly, in Ashow, each yardland comprised 46 acres.

360 As well as these 27 cottages, Stoneleigh village included three without common rights, which had perhaps been created relatively recently.

361 1597 survey and maps: SCLA, DR 18/30/24/279; DR 671/2–3; rentals: SCLA, DR 18/30/24/various; TNA, SC 12/16/43 (c. 1559); /44 (1490); SCLA, DR 10/1523–6 (1488 – c. 1500).

362 Fragmentary only for 1500 and 1501, complete for 1497.

363 The earliest rental of all, for Easter 1466 (SCLA, DR 18/30/24/11) is damaged at its head, with the loss of most of the Stoneleigh village entries, but that for Michaelmas 1468 (/12) is complete.

364 Examined in detail in Alcock, *People at home*. The inventories are held by Lichfield Record Office (copies at SCLA, DR 836/2).

365 One of the two largest houses, that of Thomas Dadley, was the converted gatehouse of Stoneleigh Abbey itself, while Jane Wynter lived at Milburne in a former Abbey grange. Thomas Roweley's house, 11–12 Coventry Road, Stoneleigh, had probably been built within the preceding twenty years.

366 CCC, Diseworth As

367 CCC, Diseworth, A-K. Nichols, J. (c. 1800) *History & Antiquities of the county of Leicester*, III, 745f. *VCH Leicestershire*, II (1954), 3–5, n. 26 states that the parish of Diseworth only included part of the village, but this is a misinterpretation of Nichols, *Leicester*, 745, which states that the manor of Diseworth lay in three parishes, Diseworth itself, Breedon and Lockington. It appears that the portion in Diseworth itself was later regarded as an independent manor.

368 CCC, Diseworth A, 30–58.

369 *Letters and Papers Henry VIII*, **19**, p. 278; CCC, Diseworth Q.

370 CCC, Diseworth, Ag, Agg(1).

371 CCC, Diseworth Ac gives the number of yardlands, adding that each was reputed to contain 18 acres, but dividing the acreage allotted in 1795 by 72 gives a figure of 24 acres.

372 A survey dateable to about 1766 lists 52½ College yardlands (CCC, Diseworth Ac), but a letter of 1767 notes that 7 yardlands had been sold as freeholds (Brompton, S. D. and Hening, P. N. (2000) *Diseworth: The Story of a Village*,

Diseworth: Diseworth Publications, 45) and indeed, the 1698 terrier (CCC, Diseworth Ab) appears to include about 60 yardlands.

373 CCC, Diseworth, Z; TNA, C 12/266/3.

374 CCC, Diseworth, Ad 2, 5. The freeholdings are identified in the 1522 rental and can mostly be recognised in the earlier one.

375 CCC, Diseworth, Ad 3. The names and rents correspond to those given in the conveyance to the college (CCC, Diseworth P; Q), but the latter does not distinguish between free and copyholders.

376 CCC, Diseworth, A3; TNA, SC 2/183/65, /64.

377 CCC, Diseworth, A35. None of the College's free tenants in 1522 owed 4s rent, but James Jerram held a messuage, barn and one virgate for 3s and a pound of cumin; no priory tenant owed 5d chief rent.

378 CCC, Diseworth, Ab; a terrier dated 1658[/9]also survives, but is incomplete, covering only some 40 yardlands, rather than the 60 described in 1698.

379 Leics RO, DE 1107, Cheslyn family of Langley Priory.

380 DIS-A was held by William Orguile in 1695 with ½ yardland, which it had lost by 1795; F had 1 yardland at both dates; D was a 3½ yardland holding that can probably be identified with the 7 hearth house of John Marshall. It may well have been the messuage, close and dovecote with three virgates of land, held by Richard Honye in 1497–8.

381 Alcock and Barley, 'Base-cruck roofs'.

382 Currie, 'Larger medieval houses', 214–240; Alcock, N. W., Faulkner, P. A. and Jones, S. R. (1978) 'Maxstoke Castle', *Archaeol. J.* **135**, 195–233.

383 Currie, 'Larger medieval houses'. It is convenient, though perhaps anachronistic to use the term 'copyhold' for thirteenth century customary tenure; copies of court rolls were undoubtedly being produced by about 1300 (P. D. A. Harvey (1999) *Manorial records*, British Records Association, Archives and the User series, 5, 43).

384 Currie, 'Larger medieval houses', 153–4. The evidence suggests that this had been a customary holding, enfranchised in 1256.

385 This hall and another wing were apparently built in 1316 at a total cost of 27 marks (£18) (Magdalen College, Oxford, Harwell deeds, 72b; Currie, 'Larger Medieval Houses', 147–8).

386 TNA, SC6/HENVIII/109, m 14; Berkshire RO, D/Ebt M 4.

387 E.g. in Herefordshire (Tonkin, 'Herefordshire base crucks') and Kent/Sussex (Pearson, *Medieval houses of Kent*, 76f).

Notes to Chapter 7

1 See also Currie, 'Larger medieval houses'; Alcock, *People at home*, 25–35.

2 The anomalously late example at Weston-on-Avon (WOA-A) is ignored here, since on the most plausible analysis it was not domestic.

3 This was particularly surprising, since the house was originally visited because it had been noted as containing crucks – indeed, correctly so, though they proved to be in an extension rather than part of the primary structure.

4   This contrasts, for example, to the small aisled halls found in Essex (D. F. Stenning, D. D. Andrews, I. Tyers (2003) 'Small aisled halls in Essex', *Vernacular Architecture*, **34**, 1–19.

5   For a summary of thirteenth century crucks, see Hill and Alcock, 'New ideas' and references cited there.

6   See Alcock, *Cruck Construction*, 33, and Alcock and Blair, 'New documentary evidence'. Further *furca* references from the accounts of St Swithin's Priory, Winchester have been kindly provided by B. Harrison: Winchester Cathedral Library, Dean and Chapter Archives: Houghton, Hampshire (1266/7, D & C box 1); Patney, Wiltshire (1270/1, box 59); Michelmersh, Hampshire (1279/80, box 1); Silkstead, Hampshire (1281/2 & 1298/9, box 2); Overton Priors, Atteley, Wiltshire (1291/2, box 2). For a 1284 reference at Sutton Maddock, Shropshire, see Moran, *Vernacular buildings of Shropshire*, 57.

7   Gardiner, M. forthcoming.

8   Currie, 'Time and chance'.

9   These thresholds are similar though not identical to Brunskill's 'Vernacular Threshold' (Brunskill, R. W. (1970) *Illustrated handbook of vernacular architecture*, London: Faber and Faber) which was considered to apply uniformly to Great, Large or Small Houses.

10 See the examples cited in Gardiner, M. (2000) 'Vernacular buildings and the development of the later medieval domestic plan in England', *Medieval Archaeol.* **44**, 159–179; Beresford, *Caldecote*; Wrathmell, S. 'Peasant houses, farmsteads and villages in north-east England', in Aston, M., Austin, D. and Dyer, C. (eds) *The rural settlements of medieval England*, Oxford: Blackwell, 247–67.

11 Cousins, R. (2000) *Lincolnshire buildings in the mud and stud tradition*, Heritage Lincolnshire. One of the present authors (NWA) observed the earth-fast posts and studs of these buildings in houses being demolished in the 1960s.

12 Even the lowest of our houses, DID-A, is 15 feet high. Similar arguments about the difficulty of inserting upper floors in small houses are put forward in relation to houses in Kent (Pearson, *Medieval houses of Kent*, 60ff).

13 At Bromsgrove, Worcs, just outside the project region. Field, 'Worcestershire peasant buildings', 127.

14 Alcock, *People at home*, 35; Coventry Archives, BA/D/11/22/5.

15 Alcock and Woodfield, 'Social pretensions'.

16 Alcock, *People at home,* 26; Alcock, 'Smoke bay'.

17 See Beresford, *Goltho*; Gardiner, 'Domestic plan'.

18 Williams, M. A. (1986) 'The little "big house": The use and meaning of the single-pen dwelling', *Perspectives in Vernacular Architecture*, II, 130–6; *idem* (1991) *Homeplace: The social use and meaning of the folk dwelling in Southwestern North Carolina*, Athens: University of Georgia Press, 38ff.

19 Wiliam. E. (2010) *The Welsh Cottage*, Aberystwyth: Royal Commission on the Ancient and Historical Monuments of Wales, 221.

20 Neither his will nor inventory gives his status, but his inventory value of £55 is in the middle of the range for husbandmen.

21 Alcock, *People at home*, 55.

22 In the seventeenth century, the chamber-end cruck was replaced by a box-framed truss and the house was slightly shortened. The replacement of part of the original floor means that the original stair position is not known, and in the figure, this is placed in the same position as the stair in STO-G.

23 In the Stoneleigh inventories, fire fittings in the halls are rarely mentioned, even when sooted roofs confirm the presence of hearths in both hall and kitchen bays (evidence not available at 2 Church Lane). See Alcock, *People at home*, 49.

24 In 1522, Robert's father had two servants.

25 This room undoubtedly had an open hearth, since the present chimney was only inserted in the late sixteenth or early seventeenth century. What the pot chain hung from is unclear (as in several similar inventories for open-hearth kitchens). Here, a pole is suggested, stretched between the wallplates.

26 Alcock, *People at home*, 50. Peter Brears has noted the absence of tables from early kitchen inventories, and suggested that tables were present, but fixed rather than moveable. Although this is certainly possible in individual cases, it seems unlikely that such tables would have been universally present and never mentioned (Brears, P. (2008) *Cooking and dining in medieval England*, Totnes, Prospect, 205).

27 The inventories generally relate to possessions that have fallen into the lord's hands, either through lack of heirs or through forfeiture from a felon. See Dyer, *Standards of Living*, 170.

28 Alcock, 'Medieval peasant', from which the examples cited are taken; Hanawalt, *Ties that bound*. Inquests for the fifteenth century do survive, but they are buried within the vast body of King's Bench records.

Notes to Appendix I

1   Miles, D. (1997) 'The interpretation, presentation and use of tree-ring dates', *Vernacular Architecture*, **28**, 40–56.

2   Tyers, C. 2008. 'Bayesian interpretation of tree-ring dates in practice', *Vernacular Architecture*, **39**, 91–106.

3   See, for example MDM-A (Chapter 8.6). However, it can reasonably be considered that if an elm sequence matches an oak sequence with a high *t*-value, then the dating is correct.

4   Baillie, M. G. L. and Pilcher, J. R. (1973). 'A simple cross-dating program for tree-ring research', *Tree-ring Bulletin*, **33**, 7–14; Laxton, R. R. and Litton, C. D. (1988) *An East Midlands master tree-ring chronology*, Department of Classics and Archaeology, University of Nottingham.

5   See Pearson, *Medieval houses of Kent*.

6   Laxton and Litton, *East Midlands master chronology*.

7   In the early part of the project, a few tentative tree-ring dates from internal reports were released, some of which were not confirmed by further work. Only those dates included in the present list (Table 2.2) are now considered valid.

8   A master sequence is one formed by the combination of many individual site sequences, a process that enhances the climatic signal contrasted to local influences.

9   This implies that the two master chronologies should themselves match together with a displacement of 114 years, but this only applies to sections of the chronologies of the same length as that being matched.

10   Hoffsumer, P. (1995) *Les charpentes de toitures en Wallonie*, Namur, 38.

11   Hughes, M. K., Milsom, S. J. and Leggett, P. A. (1981) 'Sapwood estimates in the interpretation of tree-ring dates', *J Archaeol Sci.* **8**, 381–390.

12   Miles, 'Interpretation'.

13   Miles, D. (2006) 'Refinements in the interpretation of tree-ring dates for oak building timbers in England and Wales', *Vernacular Architecture*, **37**, 84–96. Calculation of the sapwood estimate is incorporated as a function into the OxCal computer program (Bronk Ramsey, C. (1995) 'Radiocarbon calibration and stratigraphy: the OxCal program', *Radiocarbon*, **37**, 425–30; Miles and Bronk Ramsey, *in preparation*).

14   Millard, A. (2002) 'A Bayesian approach to sapwood estimates and felling dates in dendrochronology', *Archaeometry*, **44** (1), 137–143.

15   Or those known to have been lost in sampling.

16   This section is based on Bronk Ramsey, C. (2008) 'Radiocarbon dating: revolutions in understanding', *Archaeometry*, **50** (2), 249–275.

17   Bronk Ramsey, C, van der Plicht, J. and Weninger, B. (2001), 'Wiggle matching' radiocarbon dates, *Radiocarbon*, **43**(2A), 38 1–9. The term *wiggle-matching* does not as obviously describe the procedure in this form, as it did originally, when the dates were plotted in the form of a calibration curve and then matched to the master curve.

18   Studies are under way to evaluate the probabilities that this and similar tree-ring matches are correct or erroneous, which would allow the combined probability to be calculated (C. M. Tyers, in progress).

19   The statistics given here relate to buildings sampled during the main fieldwork phase, excluding buildings later included in the project.

20   E.g. Pearson, *Medieval houses of Kent*.

21   These results relate principally to individual samples although for dating these were combined into sequences whenever possible.

Bibliography

Abbreviations

Musters, 1522 — Chibnall, A. C. (ed) (1973) *The certificate of musters for Buckinghamshire in 1522*, Buckinghamshire Record Society, **17**,

Subsidy Roll, 1524 — Chibnall, A.C. & Vere Woodman, A. (eds.) (1950) *Subsidy roll for the county of Buckingham, anno 1524*, Buckinghamshire Record Society, **8**

Posse Comitatus, 1798 — Beckett, Ian Frederick William (ed) (1985) *The Buckinghamshire Posse Comitatus 1798*, Buckinghamshire Record Society, **22**

VA — *Vernacular Architecture*.

VCH — *Victoria County History*, cited by county and volume.

VCH Berkshire — *Victoria History of the County of Berkshire*; Harwell in Vol. III (1923); East Hendred and Steventon in vol. IV (1924)

VCH Buckinghamshire — *Victoria History of the County of Buckingham*; Long Crendon in vol. IV (1927)

VCH Warwickshire — *Victoria History of the County of Warwick*; Stoneleigh in vol. VI (1951)

VCH Leicestershire — *Victoria History of the County of Leicester*; vol. 2 (1954) [Langley Priory in *Religious Houses*] (no coverage of Diseworth parish)

Record repositories

ASC — All Souls College, Oxford
BAH — Birmingham Archives and Heritage
Berks RO — Berkshire Record Office, Reading
BL — British Library
Bodl — Bodleian Library, Oxford
CBS — Centre for Buckinghamshire Studies, Aylesbury
CCC — Christ's College, Cambridge
CofE — Church of England Record Centre
Hants RO — Hampshire Record Office, Winchester
Huntington — H.E. Huntington Library, San Marino, California, ST Stowe archive; STG Grenville Evidences.
Leics RO — Record Office for Leicestershire, Leicester and Rutland
LA — Lincolnshire Archives, Lincoln
Lich — Lichfield Record Office
Rousham — Rousham (Cottrell-Dormer) archive (summary list in National Register of Archives report 996); T-numbers refer to Long Crendon deeds.
SCLA — Shakespeare Centre Library and Archive, Stratford-upon-Avon
SGC — St George's Chapel, Windsor, archives
TNA — The National Archives
WAM — Westminster Abbey Muniments
WCRO — Warwickshire County Record Office

Unpublished sources for documentary histories

Buckinghamshire

The major sources used to document the Long Crendon houses are listed below, and are not individually referenced, when the precise reference can be inferred directly from the text, for example the court roll for a specified year. Unless otherwise indicated, baptism, marriage and burial records are taken from the corresponding Long Crendon parish registers.

Long Crendon manorial records

Location	Reference(s)	Description
CBS	D/BASM/23/1–227 (rolls, 1343–1813); /228–235 (vols, 1782–1939))	Long Crendon manor, court rolls, main series. 1343–1939 (with gaps). For the post-medieval period, these have mainly been indexed on cards.
CBS	D/BASM/23a	Notley manor, court rolls, 1720–1826 (many gaps)
Bodl	Ms. Top. gen.c.43–44; Ms. Dd. Bertie.b1	Notley manor, court rolls, 1630–1700 (many gaps) (including some rolls for the main series)
Bodl	Ms. Dd. Bertie.c.27/5; Top. Gen.e.64: p. 116; Top. Oxon.c.381/e.299; Top. Oxon c.381	Notley manor, rentals/surveys, c. 1595; c. 1635; 1728; 1761
SGC	XVII 15.42–3; 44–52	Court rolls: 1521–22; 1558–67

Other sources

Location	Reference(s)	Description
CBS	PR134/1	Long Crendon parish registers
CBS	DVD/1/24	1910 Finance Act Valuation Book for Long Crendon
CBS	IR/95/Q	Enclosure Award and Maps, 1827. See Fig. 6.3 (a–d) for reproductions of portions of the 'Old Enclosures' map relating to the village itself.
CBS	D78/Box1/11	1824: Abstract of Claims prior to Enclosure
CBS	Census	Census returns (microfilms), 1841–1901
CBS	Q/RPL/1/3–53	Land Tax assessments, 1782–1832 (missing some years)
TNA	IR 58/2151–2155	Field Books for 1910 Finance Act Valuations
TNA	(a) E 179/80/354 (b) E 179/80/362/34–6	(a) Hearth Tax return (year missing; probably 1662, as no exempt names included); (b) exemption certificates, 1670–72

Leicestershire

CCC, Diseworth, A-Z; Aa-Ax; Additional, 1–14, deeds.

Map and survey

Date	Reference
1795	CCC, Diseworth, Ag, Agg(1)

Manorial Records

Location	Reference(s)	Description
CCC	Diseworth, Ae	Court rolls, Henry VII – Henry VIII
CCC	Diseworth Ac	Survey, 1766
CCC	Diseworth, Ad 2, 5	Rentals, 1494/5 and 1522
CCC	Diseworth, Ab	Terriers, 1659 and 1695
TNA	SC 2/183/65, /64	Court rolls, Henry VII

Oxfordshire

Steventon manorial records

Location	Reference(s)	Description
WAM	7261ff	Court rolls: 1382ff (few gaps except in 17th century)
WAM	CC 292094–99	Court books: 1664–1925, (continuous)
WAM	56046; CC 292100	Indexes: c. 1800; c. 1890
WAM	7358–9; 8034	Surveys: 1548; 1562–4
WAM	7354; 7355; 7347; 7360; 56665	Rentals: 1590; 1599; 1645–6: (dated from internal evidence); 1686; 1696
Berks RO	D/P119; Film 23	Parish registers; bishop's transcripts; transcript published on CD by Oxfordshire Family History Society

Steventon maps

Date	Source
1839	Oxford RO, P238/M/1; key: Berks RO, D/ETY/04
1842	Tithe map and apportionment: Berks RO, D/D1/119/1A-B
1884	Altered tithe map and apportionment: Berks RO, D/D1/119/2
1835	Railway plan and key: Parliamentary Archives, HL/PO/PB/3/Plan 106

Probate records

At Berks RO, TNA & Wiltshire & Swindon History Centre

Warwickshire

Stoneleigh manorial records:

Location	Reference(s)	Description
SCLA	DR 18/30/24/279	1597 survey and maps
SCLA	DR 671/2–3	Rentals
SCLA	DR 18/30/24/various	Manorial documents, 1497–1600
TNA	SC 12/16/43; /44	Rentals, c. 1559; 1490
SCLA	DR 10/1523–6	Rentals, 1488 – c. 1500

Probate records

For Stoneleigh, at Lichfield Record Office.

Published sources

Anon (1890–1915) *A descriptive catalogue of ancient deeds in the Public Record Office*, London: HMSO.

Addy, S. O. (1898) *The evolution of the English house*, London.

Alcock, N. W. (1965) 'The medieval cottages of Bishop's Clyst, Devon', *Medieval Archaeol.* **9**, 146–153.

Alcock, N. W. (1973) *A catalogue of cruck buildings*, Chichester: Phillimore.

Alcock, N. W. (1981) *Cruck construction: an introduction and catalogue*, CBA. Research Report, **42**.

Alcock, N. W. (1982) 'The hall of the Knights Templar at Temple Balsall, West Midlands', *Medieval Archaeol.* **26**, 155–158.

Alcock, N. W. (1987) 'Kinetoncote, Binton, Warwickshire (SP145541)', *Vernacular Architecture,* **18**, 51.

Alcock, N. W. (1993) *People at home: Living in a Warwickshire village, 1500–1800*, Chichester: Phillimore.

Alcock, N. W. (1998) 'Smoke bay or open hall? Cuttle Pool Farm, Knowle, Warwickshire', *Vernacular Architecture,* **29**, 82–84.

Alcock, N. W. (2002) 'The distribution and dating of crucks and base crucks', *Vernacular Architecture,* **33**, 67–70.

Alcock, N. W. (2006) 'The origin of crucks: Innocence or naiveté? A response', *Vernacular Architecture,* **37**, 50–53.

Alcock, N. W. (2008) 'The Chestnuts Water Orton', unpublished report (copy at WCRO).

Alcock, N. W. (2010) 'The distribution and dating of Wealden houses', *Vernacular Architecture,* **41**, 37–44.

Alcock, N. W. and Barley, M. W. (1972) 'Medieval roofs with base-crucks and short principals', *Antiquaries J.,* **52**, 132–168.

Alcock, N. W., Barley, M. W., Dixon, P. W. and Meeson. R. A. (1996) *Recording timber-framed buildings: an illustrated glossary* (CBA Practical Handbooks in Archaeology 5), 2nd edition.

Alcock, N. W. and Blair, J. (1986) 'Crucks: new documentary evidence', *Vernacular Architecture,* **17**, 36–8.

Alcock, N. W., Braithwaite, J. G. and Jeffs, M. W. (1971–1973) 'Timber-framed buildings in Warwickshire: Stoneleigh village', *Trans Birmingham Archaeol. Soc.* **85**, 178–202.

Alcock, N. W. and Currie, C. R. J. (1989) 'Upstairs or downstairs?', *Vernacular Architecture,* **20**, 21–23.

Alcock, N. W., Faulkner, P. A. and Jones, S. R. (1978) 'Maxstoke Castle', *Archaeol .J.* **135**, 195–233.

Alcock, N. W. and Hall, Sir R. de Z. (1981) 'Documentary evidence for crucks', in N. W. Alcock, (1981) *Cruck Construction An Introduction and Catalogue*, CBA Research Report, **42**.

Alcock, N.W. and Laithwaite, Michael (1973) 'Medieval houses in Devon and their modernization', *Medieval Archaeol.* **17**, 100–125.

Alcock, Nat and Meeson, Bob (2009) 'Radiocarbon dating of a reused cruck blade from Warwickshire and its implications for the typology of cruck construction', *Vernacular Architecture*, **40**, 96-102.

Alcock, N. W. and Miles, Dan (2012) 'An early fifteenth-century Warwickshire cruck house using joggled halvings', *Vernacular Architecture*, **43**, in press.

Alcock, N. W. and Moran, M. (1984) 'Low open-truss beams (mantle-beams): Problems of function and distribution', *Vernacular Architecture,* **15**, 47–55.

Alcock, N. W. and Woodfield, C. T. P. (1996) 'Social pretensions in architecture and ancestry: Hall House, Sawbridge, Warwickshire and the Andrewe Family', *Antiquaries J.* **76**, 51–72.

Alcock, N. W. and Woodward, P. J. (1976) 'Cruck-frame buildings in Bedfordshire', *Bedfordshire Archaeological J.* **11**, 57–68.

Andrews, D. D. and Milne, G. (1979) *Wharram, a study of settlement on the Yorkshire Wolds; vol.1 Domestic settlement, 1 : areas 10 and 6*, Soc. Medieval Archaeol.

Arkell, T. (2003) 'Identifying regional variations from the hearth tax', *Local Historian,* **33**, 148–74.

Arkell, Tom and Alcock. Nat (2010) *Warwickshire hearth tax: Michaelmas 1670 with Coventry Lady Day 1666*, Dugdale Soc. 43.

Bailey, M. (1989) '*A marginal economy? East Anglian Breckland in the later Middle Ages*, Cambridge.

Baillie, M. G. L.and. Pilcher, J. R. (1973) 'A simple cross-dating program for tree-ring research', *Tree-ring Bulletin,* **33**, 7–14.

Barley, M. W. (1961) *The English farmhouse and cottage*, London: Routledge.

Barley, Maurice (1986) *Houses and history*, London: Faber and Faber.

Baylis, A. L. H. (1995) *The story of Steventon*, Oxford: Parchment.

Beresford, Guy (1987) *Goltho: The development of an early medieval manor, c.850–1150*, London.

Beresford, G. (2009) *Caldecote: the development and desertion of a Hertfordshire village*, Society for Medieval Archaeology Monograph, **28**.

Birrell, J. R. (1962) 'The forest economy of the Honour of Tutbury in the fourteenth and fifteenth centuries', *Univ of Birmingham Historical J.***8**, 114–34.

Birrell, J. R. (1979) 'Medieval agriculture', in *VCH Staffordshire*, 6, 1–57.

Bois, G. (2000) *La grande dépression médiéval: XIVe-XVe siècles. Le précédent d'une crise systémique*, Paris.

Bradbrooke, W. (1932) 'Notes on the Braybrooke Family of Brightwalton', *Berkshire Archaeol. J.* 36 (2), 164–73.

Brears, Peter (2008) *Cooking and dining in medieval England*. Totnes: Prospect.

Briggs, C. (2009) *Credit and village society in fourteenth-century England*, Oxford.

Brompton, S. D. and Hening, P. N. (2000) *Diseworth: The story of a village,* Diseworth: Diseworth Publications.

Bronk. Ramsey, C., van der Plicht, J., and Weninger, B. (2001) 'Wiggle matching' radiocarbon dates, *Radiocarbon*, **43**(2A), 381–9.

Bronk. Ramsey, C. (1995) 'Radiocarbon calibration and stratigraphy: the OxCal program', *Radiocarbon*, 37, 425–30.

Brunskill, R. W. (1970) *Illustrated handbook of vernacular architecture*, London: Faber and Faber.

Carus-Wilson, E. M. (1959–60) Evidences of industrial growth on some fifteenth century manors', *Economic Hist. Rev.* 2nd ser. **12**, 190–205.

Chenevix Trench, J. (1983) 'The houses of Coleshill', *Records of Buckinghamshire*, 25, 61–109.

Hallam, H. E. (ed) (1988) *Agrarian History of England and Wales*, II, 1042–1350, Cambridge University Press.

Chenevix Trench, John (1989) 'Willow Vale Farm House, Steeple Claydon', *Records of Buckinghamshire*, **31**, 13–26.

Chenevix Trench, John (1992) 'Another thirteenth-century house for Buckinghamshire?', *Records of Buckinghamshire*, **34**, 14–29.

Chibnall, A. C. (ed) (1973) *The Certificate of Musters for Buckinghamshire in 1522* (London).

Cottis, J. (1985) 'Agrarian change in the Vale of White Horse 1660–1760', Univ of Reading Ph.D thesis.

Currie, C. R. J. (1976) 'Smaller domestic architecture in North Berkshire, c. 1300 – c. 1650', Unpublished D. Phil thesis, Oxford.

Currie, C. R. J. (1987) 'Harwell houses to 1700: an interim gazetteer', in John Ashdown and Julian Munby (eds), *Vernacular Architecture Group Spring Conference, 1987*.

Currie, C. R. J. (1988a) 'Time and chance: Modelling the attrition of old houses', *Vernacular Architecture*, 19, 1–9.

Currie, C. R. J. (1988b) 'Open plank end trusses in the Oxford Region', *Vernacular Architecture*, 19, 32–33.

Currie, C. R. J. (1990a) 'Time and Chance: Reply to Comments', *Vernacular Architecture*, 21, 5–9.

Currie, C. R. J. (1990b) 'Archaic roofs in Hereford and Worcester', *Vernacular Architecture*, 21, 18–32.

Currie, C. R. J. (1992) 'Larger medieval houses in the Vale of the White Horse', *Oxoniensia*, 57, 81–244.

Currie, C. R. J. (2009) 'Another giant 'peasant' house? The site identification of Priory Cottages, Steventon, Oxfordshire', *Oxoniensia*, 74 (2010 for 2009), 185–9.

Currie, C. R. J. and Fletcher, J. M. (1972) 'Two early cruck houses in north Berkshire identified by radiocarbon, *Medieval Archaeol* 16, 136–42.

Currie, C. R. J. and Fletcher, J. M. (1979) 'The Bishop of Winchester's medieval manor house at Harwell, Berkshire and its relevance in the evolution of timber-framed aisled halls', *Archaeol. J.* **136**, 173–192.

Darlington, R. R. (1968) *The Cartulary of Worcester Cathedral Priory (Register I)*, Pipe Roll Society, NS **38**.

Davis, E. M. (1982) 'Weepers [*recte* Weavers]: a small late medieval aisled hall in Cambridgeshire', *Medieval Archaeol* **26**, 158–161.

DeWindt, E.B. (ed) (1976) *The Liber Gersumarum of Ramsey Abbey*, Toronto.

Donald, J. (1971) 'The Crendon needlemakers', *Records of Buckinghamshire*, **19** (1), 8–16.

Dugdale, Sir William (1817–30) *Monasticon Anglicanum*, new edition.

Dyer, C. (1980) *Lords and peasants in a changing society: The estates of the Bishopric of Worcester, 680–1540*, Cambridge: Cambridge University Press.

Dyer, C. (1986) 'English peasant buildings in the later Middle Ages', *Medieval Archaeol*, 30, 19–45.

Dyer, C. (1989) *Standards of living in the later Middle Ages: Social change in England, c 1200–1520*, Cambridge: Cambridge University Press.

Dyer, C. (1991) *Hanbury Settlement and Society in a Woodland Landscape,* Dept of English Local Hist, Univ of Leicester, Occasional Papers, 4th ser.

Dyer, C. (1992b) 'The Hidden Trade of the Middle Ages: Evidence from the West Midlands of England', *Jnl Hist Geog*, XVIII, 141–57.

Dyer, C. (2005) *An age of transition? Economy and society in England in the later middle ages*, Oxford: Clarendon Press.

Dyer, C. (2008) 'Building in earth in late-medieval England', *Vernacular Architecture*, **39**, 63–70.

Evans, D. H., Jarrett, M. G. and Wrathmell, S. (1988) 'The deserted village of West Whelpington, Northumberland: third report, part 2', *Archaeologia Aeliana*, 5th series, 16, 139–92.

Evans, E.B. (1957) 'Seventeenth-century painted overmantels', *Country Life*, **122** (Nov 1957), 1138–9.

Faith, R. J. (1984) 'Berkshire', in P. D. A. Harvey (ed). (1984) *The peasant land market in medieval England*, Oxford: Clarendon Press.

Farmer, D. L. (1977) 'Grain yields on the Winchester manors in the Later Middle Ages', *Econ.Hist Rev* 2S **30**, 555–66.

Farmer, D. L. (1991) 'Marketing the produce of the countryside', in Miller (1991), 324–430.

Feltbower, I. J. and P. V. (1984) 'A First Survey of Sycamore Farm House, Long Crendon', unpublished report.

Fenwick, C. (ed) (1998–2005) *The Poll Taxes of 1377, 1379 and 1381*, British Academy, Records of Social and Economic History, New Series, 27, 29 and 37, Oxford.

Field, R. K. (1965) 'Worcestershire peasant buildings, household goods and farming equipment in the later Middle Ages, *Medieval Archaeol.*, 9, 105–145.

Fletcher, J. M. (1961/2) 'Cruck cottage in Church Lane, Harwell', *Oxoniensia*, **26/27**, 207-214.

Fletcher, J. M. (1965–6) 'Three medieval farmhouses in Harwell,' *Berks Archaeol Jnl* **52**, 55.

Fletcher, J. M. (1968) 'Crucks in the West Berkshire and Oxford Region', *Oxoniensia*, **33**, 85-86.

Fox, H.S.A. (1991) 'Occupation of the land. Devon and Cornwall', in Miller (1991), 152–74.

Fussell, G. E. (ed) (1936) *Robert Loder's Farm Accounts*, Camden 3S, **53**.

Galitzine, Prince Yuri (1980) 'The Quaintree Hall House, Braunston, Rutland', *Rutland Record,* **1**, 25–31.

Gardiner, Mark (2008) 'Buttery and pantry and their antecedents: idea and architecture in the English medieval house', in Maryanne Kowaleski and P. J. P. Goldberg (eds).

Gelling, Margaret (1976) *Place-names of Berkshire, Part 3, 1: The old English charter boundaries of Berkshire*, Cambridge, English Place-Name Society, vol 51.

Grenville. J. (1997) *Medieval housing*, Leicester.

Glasscock, R. E. (1975) *The Lay Subsidy of 1334*, London, British Academy.

Hale, W. H. (ed) (1865) *Registrum Prioratus Wigorn*, Camden Soc, old ser, **91.**

Hall, H. R. (ed) (1903) *Pipe Roll of Bishopric of Winchester, 1208–1209*, London: P S King.

Hall, Linda (2005) *Period house fixtures & fittings: 1300–1900*, Newbury: Countryside Books.

Hall, L. and Alcock, N. W. (1994) *Fixtures and fittings in dated houses: 1567–1763*, Council for British Archaeology, York.

Hanawalt, Barbara A. (1986) *The ties that bound: peasant families in medieval England*, Oxford, Oxford University Press.

Hare, J. (2011) *A prospering society. Wiltshire in the late middle ages*, Hatfield: University of Hertfordshire Press.

Harris, R. (1995) 'Level marks and the sequence of framing', *Mortice and Tenon*, **2** (July), 2–4.

Harrison, B. and Hutton, B. (1984) *Vernacular Houses in North Yorkshire and Cleveland*, Edinburgh.

Harvey, B. (1977) *Westminster Abbey and its estates in the Middle Ages* Oxford.

Harvey, B. K. (1992) 'An early seventeeth-century survey of four Wiltshire manors', *Vernacular Architecture*, **23**, 30.

Hatcher, J. (1996) 'The great slump of the mid-fifteenth century', in R. Britnell and J. Hatcher (eds.) (1996) *Progress and problems in medieval England*, Cambridge, 237–72.

Hewett, Cecil (1980) *English historic carpentry*, Chichester, Phillimore.

Hill, Nick (2005) 'On the origin of crucks: an innocent notion', *Vernacular Architecture,* **36**, 1–14.

Hill, Nick and Alcock, Nat (2007) 'New ideas revisited' *and* 'The Origins of Crucks', *Vernacular Architecture*, **38**, 8–14.

Hill, Nick and Miles, Dan (2001) 'The Royal George, Cottingham, Northamptonshire: an early cruck building', *Vernacular Architecture*, **32**, 62–7.

Hilton, R. H. (1975) *The English Peasantry in the Later Middle Ages*, Oxford.

Hilton, R. H. (ed) (1960) *The Stoneleigh Leger book*, Dugdale Soc. 24, Oxford: Oxford University Press.

Hilton, R. H. and Rahtz, P. A. (1966) 'Upton, Gloucestershire, 1959–1964', *Trans. Bristol and Gloucestershire Archaeol. Soc.*, **85**, 70–146.

Holden, E. W. (1963) 'Excavations at the deserted medieval village of Hangleton, part 1', *Sussex Archaeol. Colls,* **101**, 54–181.

Hoffsumer, Patrick (1995) *Les charpentes de toitures en Wallonie*, Namur.

Holt, N. R. (ed) (1964) *Pipe Roll of Bishopric of Winchester, 1210–1211*, Manchester: Manchester University Press.

Homans, G. C. (1941) *English Villagers of the Thirteenth Century*, Cambridge, Mass.

Hoskins, W.G. (1953) 'The rebuilding of rural England, 1570–1640', *Past and Present*, **4**, 44–59.

Howell, Cicely (1983) *Land, family and inheritance in transition: Kibworth Harcourt 1280–1700*, Cambridge: Cambridge University Press.

Hughes, M. K., Milsom, S. J. and Leggett, P. A. (1981) 'Sapwood estimates in the interpretation of tree-ring dates', *J Archaeol Sci.* **8**, 381–390.

Hurford, M., Jones, M. and C. Tyers (2010) 'Tree-ring dating and the historical and social context of timber-frame buildings, Norwell, Nottinghamshire', *Trans. Thoroton Soc.* **114**, 31–62.

Hurst, J.G. (1965) 'The medieval peasant house', in A. Small (ed), *The fourth Viking Congress, York, 1961*, Aberdeen.

Hurst, J.G. (1971) 'A review of archaeological research (to 1968)', in M. Beresford and J.G. Hurst (eds.), *Deserted medieval villages: studies*, London.

Hutton, Barbara (1982) *Derby Buildings Record Reports* **23** (Feb 1982).

Jarvis, M. G. (1973) *Soils of the Wantage and Abingdon District*, Memoirs of Soil Survey of Great Britain.

Jenkins, J. Gilbert (1954) 'The Lost Cartulary of Nutley Abbey', *Huntington Library Quarterly*, **17** (4).

Jennings, Nina (2003) *Clay dabbins: Vernacular buildings of the Solway Plain*, Cumberland and Westmorland Antiquarian and Archaeological Society, extra series, **XXX**.

Johnson, Ian and Fenley, Pauline (1974) 'Grange Farm, Widmer End', *Records of Buckinghamshire* **XIX**, 449–456.

Johnson, M. (1993) 'Rethinking the Great Rebuilding', *Oxford J Archaeol*, **12**, 117–25.

Johnson, Matthew (2010) *English Houses 1300–1800. Vernacular architecture, social life*, Longman.

Jones, S. R. (1975–6) 'West Bromwich (Staffs). Manor-House', *Trans. South Staffordshire Archaeol Hist Soc.* **17**, 1–63.

Jones, S. R. and Smith, J. T. (1960–1) 'The Wealden houses of Warwickshire and their significance', *Trans Proc Birmingham Archaeol Soc,* **79**, 24–35.

Kirk, J. C. (2004) 'Butts Cottage, Kirdford: the conversion of trees to timber in the rural Sussex Weald', *Vernacular Architecture*, **35**, 12–20.

Laxton, R. R. and Litton, C. D. (1988) *An East Midlands master tree-ring chronology*, Department of Classics and Archaeology, University of Nottingham.

Le Patourel, H. E. J. (1991) 'Rural Building in England and Wales England', in Miller (1991), 820–90.

Leadam, I. S. (1897) *The Domesday of Inclosures, 1517–1518*, Royal Historical Society.

Litherland, S. and others (2008) 'The archaeology of the Severn Trent southern area rationalisation scheme, Warwickshire', *Trans. Birmingham and Warwickshire Archaeol. Soc.* **112**, 77–124.

Levett, A. E. (1916) *The Black Death on the estates of the See of*

Winchester, Oxford: Clarendon Press, *Oxford Studies in Social and Legal History*, vol 5.

Lloyd, Nathaniel (1925) *History of English brickwork*, London, H G Montgomery.

Machin, R. (1977) 'The Great Rebuilding: a reassessment', *Past and Present*, 77, 33–56.

Manley, E. R. (1969) *A descriptive account of East Hendred*, East Hendred:, The author.

Marsh, Warren (1989) *The cruck houses of Frampton-on-Severn: Their interpretation and restoration*, Dissertation, Diploma in Architectural Conservation, University of Bristol.

Martin, David and Martin, Barbara (2001) 'Detached kitchens or adjoining houses? – a response', *Vernacular Architecture*, 32, 20–33.

Mate, M. (1998) *Daughters, wives and widows after the Black Death. Women in Sussex, 1350–1535*, Woodbridge.

Maull, A. and others (2001) 'Excavations of the deserted medieval village of Coton at Coton Park, Rugby, Warwickshire', Northamptonshire Archaeology, unpublished report.

McCann, John (1978) 'Purpose of rafter holes', *Vernacular Architecture*, 9, 26–31.

McIntosh, M. K. (1998) *Controlling misbehavior in England, 1370–1600*, Cambridge.

McSheffrey, S. (1995) *Gender and Heresy: Women and Men in Lollard Communties 1420–1530*, Philadelphia.

Mercer, E. (1990) 'Time and chance: a timely reminder', *Vernacular Architecture*, 21, 1–3.

Mercer, Eric (1975) *English vernacular architecture*, HMSO.

Midgley, L. M. (ed) (1942) *Ministers' accounts of the Earldom of Cornwall 1296–1297*, Vol 1, Camden Soc, 3S, 66.

Miles, D. (1997) 'The Interpretation, Presentation and Use of Tree-ring Dates' *Vernacular Architecture,* 28, 40–56.

Miles, Dan (2006) 'Refinements in the interpretation of tree-ring dates for oak building timbers in England and Wales', *Vernacular Architecture*, 37, 84–96.

Millard, A. (2002) 'A Bayesian approach to sapwood estimates and felling dates in dendrochronology', *Archaeometry*, 44 (1), 137–143.

Miller, E. (ed) (1991) *Agrarian History of England and Wales*, III, 1348–1500, Cambridge.

Miller, E. and Hatcher, J. (1978) *Medieval England. Rural society and economic change 1086–1348*, London.

Moir, Andy (2009) 'Dendrochronological analysis of oak timbers from 71 The Causeway, Steventon, Oxfordshire, England', Unpublished report, Tree-ring Services, ABCA10/09.

Molyneux, N. A. D. (1977) 'The Smithy, 70 Birmingham Road, Sutton Coldfield', Unpublished report (Birmingham City Museum files).

Moran, Madge (2003) *Vernacular buildings of Shropshire*, Almley, Herefs: Logaston Press.

Morris, J. (ed) (1978) *Domesday Book, Buckinghamshire,* Chichester.

Mullan, J. and Britnell, R. (2010) *Land and family. Trends and local variations in the peasant land market on the Winchester bishopric estate, 1263–1415*, Hatfield.

Oxfordshire Buildings Record (2010) '71 The Causeway, Steventon', Unpublished report, OBR.87.

Nichols, John (c. 1800) *History & Antiquities of the county of Leicester.*

Page, P. (2005) *Barentin's manor: excavations of a moated manor in Harding's field, Chalgrove, Oxfordshire, 1976–9*, Oxford Archaeology.

Palmer, N. and Dyer, C. (1988) 'An inscribed stone from Burton Dassett', *Medieval Archaeology*, 32, 216–19.

Palmer, S. C. (forthcoming) 'Medieval sites excavated on the Transco pipeline in 1999', *Trans. Birmingham and Warwickshire Archaeol. Soc.*

Noy, David (ed) (2011) *Winslow Court Books*, Buckinghamshire Record Society, vols. 35–6 (2 vols).

Pantin, W.A. (1941) 'Notley Abbey', *Oxoniensia*, 6, 22–43.

Pearson, S, Barnwell, P. S., and Adams, A. T. (1994) *A Gazetteer of medieval houses in Kent*, London, HMSO.

Pearson, Sarah. (1994) *The Medieval houses of Kent: an historical analysis*, London: RCHME.

Platt, C. (1967) *The Monastic Grange in Medieval England*, London.

Plumb, D. (1995) 'The Social and Economic Status of the Later Lollards', in Spufford, *Rural dissenters*, 104–126.

Poos, L. (1991) *A Rural Society after the Black Death Essex, 1350–1525*, Cambridge.

Portman, Derek (1958) 'Cruck Houses in Long Wittenham', *Berkshire Archaeol. J.* 56, 35–45.

Priest, St. J. (1813) *A General Survey of the Agriculture of Buckinghamshire*, London.

Raban, S. (1982) *Mortmain Legislation and the English Church 1279–1500*, Cambridge: Cambridge University Press.

Rackham, O. (1986) *History of the Countryside*, London, Dent.

Rackham, Oliver (1972) 'Grundle House: on the quantities of timber in certain East Anglian buildings in relation to local supplies', *Vernacular Architecture*, 3, 3–8.

Rackham, Oliver (1993) 'Medieval timber economy as illustrated by the Cressing Temple Barn', in D. D. Andrews (ed) (1993) *Cressing Temple: A Templar and Hospitaller manor in Essex*, Chelmsford.

Razi, Z. (1981) 'Family, Land and the Village Community in Later Medieval England', *Past and Present*, 93, 3–36.

Razi, Z. (1993) 'The myth of the immutable English family', *Past and Present*, 140, 3–44.

Reimer, P. J., Baillie, M. G. L., Bard, E., Bayliss, A., Beck, J. W., Blackwell, P. G., Bronk Ramsey, C., Buck, C. E., Burr, G. S., Edwards, R. L., Friedrich, M., Grootes, P. M., Guilderson, T. P., Hajdas, I., Heaton, T. J., Hogg, A. G., Hughen, K. A., Kaiser, K. F., Kromer, B., McCormac, F. G., Manning, S. W., Reimer, R. W., Richards, D. A., Southon, J. R., Talamo, S., Turney, C. S. M., van der Plicht, J., and Weyhenmeyer, C. E. (2009) 'IntCal09 and Marine09 radiocarbon age calibration curves, 0–50,000 years cal BP.' *Radiocarbon*, 51(4), 1111–1150.

Riddy, F. (2008) '"Burgeis" domesticity in late-medieval England', in M. Kowaleski and P. J. P. Goldberg (eds.), *Medieval domesticity. Home, housing and household in medieval England*, Cambridge, 14–36.

Richmond, A. D. W. (1993) 'The Cottage, Aston Street, Aston Tirrold, Oxfordshire Archaeological Investigations 1991–1992' English Heritage Assessment Report, unpublished.

Roberts, B. K. and Wrathmell, S. (2002) *Region and place. A study of English rural settlement*, London.

Rigold, S. E. (1958) 'The timber-framed buildings of Steventon

(Berks) and their regional significance', *Newbury and District Field Club Trans*, **10**(4), 4–16.

Roberts, Edward (2003) *Hampshire Houses, 1250–1700*, Hampshire County Council.

Rylands, W. Harry (ed) (1907–8) *The Four Visitations of Berkshire*, Harleian Society, vols. 56–7.

Sandall, Kathleen. (1986) 'Aisled halls in England and Wales', *Vernacular Architecture* 17, 21–35.

Schofield, P. (1998) 'Peasants and the manor court: gossip and litigation in a Suffolk village at the close of the thirteenth century', *Past and Present,* **159**, 3–42.

Sheail, J (1998) *The regional distribution of wealth in England as indicated in the 1524/5 lay subsidy returns*, List and index Society, Special series 28.

Smith, J. T. (1981) 'The problems of cruck construction and the evidence of distribution maps', in Alcock, *Cruck Construction*, 5–24.

Smith, J. T (1970) 'The evolution of the English peasant house to the seventeenth century: the evidence of the buildings, *J. British Archaeol. Assoc.*, 3rd ser., **33**, 122–47.

Smith, P. (1990) 'Time and Chance: a Reply', *Vernacular Architecture*, **21**, 4–5.

Smith, R. M. (1982) 'Rooms, Relatives and Residential Arrangements: Some Evidence in Manor Court Rolls, 1250–1500', *Medieval Village Research Group Annual Report*, **30**, 34–5.

Smith, R. M. (1986) 'Coping with uncertainty: women's tenure of customary land in England, 1370–1430', in J. Kermode (ed) (1991), *Enterprise and individuals in fifteenth-century England*, Gloucester, 43–67.

Smith, R. M. (1986) 'Women's property rights under customary law: some developments in the thirteenth and fourteenth centuries', *Trans. Royal Historical Soc.*, 5th series, **26**, 165–94.

Spufford, M. (ed) (1995) *The World of Rural Dissenters 1520–1725,* Cambridge.

Steane, J.M. and Bryant, G. F. (1975) 'Excavations at the deserted settlement at Lyveden', *Northampton Museum and Art Gallery J.* **12**, 4–56.

Steane, J. M. (1985) 'East Hendred The Old Forge', *South Midlands Archaeol*, 15, 75–6.

Stenning, D. F., Andrews, D. D., Tyers, I. (2003) 'Small aisled halls in Essex', *Vernacular Architecture*, **34**, 1–19.

Stenton, D. M. (ed) (1930) *Great roll of the pipe for the sixth year of the reign of King Richard I, Michaelmas 1194*, Pipe Roll Soc NS v.

Suggett, Richard (2005) *Houses and History in the March of Wales: Radnorshire 1400–1800*, Royal Commission on the Ancient and Historical Monuments of Wales.

Taylor, C.C. (1982) 'Medieval market grants and village morphology', *Landscape History,* **4**, 21–8.

Thompson, A. Hamilton (1933) *A calendar of charters and other documents belonging to the Hospital of William Wyggeston at Leicester*, Leicester: Edgar Backus.

Thompson, J. (1996) 'Sussex historic framing', *Mortice and Tenon*, 4 (July), 2–3.

Thorp, John (2011) 'Roof carpentry in Devon from 1250–1700' in John Walker (ed) *The English medieval roof: Crownpost to kingpost*, Essex Historic Buildings Group.

Titow, J. Z. (1972) *Winchester Yields: a Study in Medieval Agricultural Productivity*, Cambridge, Cambridge University Press.

Tonkin, J. W. (1970) 'Social Standing and base-crucks in Herefordshire', *Vernacular Architecture*, **1**, 7–11.

Trice Martin, C. (1877) *Catalogue of the Archives in the Muniment Rooms of All Souls' College, Oxford.*

Tyers, Cathy (2008) 'Bayesian Interpretation of Tree-Ring Dates in Practice', *Vernacular Architecture*, **39**, 91–106.

Walker, John (1999) 'Late-twelfth and early-thirteenth-century aisled buildings: a comparison', *Vernacular Architecture*, **30**, 21–53.

Watts, G. (2002) 'Medieval tenant housing on the Titchfield estates', *Hampshire Studies*, **57**, 53–8.

Webster, V. R. (1954) 'Cruck-framed buildings of Leicestershire', *Leicestershire Archaeol Hist Soc Trans*, **30**, 26–58.

Whittle, J. (2000) *The development of agrarian capitalism. Land and labour in Norfolk, 1440–1580*, Oxford.

Wiliam, Eurwyn (2010) *The Welsh Cottage*, Aberystwyth: Royal Commission on the Ancient and Historical Monuments of Wales.

Williams, Michael Ann (1986) 'The little "big house": The use and meaning of the single-pen dwelling', *Perspectives in Vernacular Architecture*, II, 130–6.

Williams, Michael Ann (1991) *Homeplace: The social use and meaning of the folk dwelling in Southwestern North Carolina*, Athens: University of Georgia Press.

Woodall, Joy (1974) *From Hroca to Anne*, privately printed [Copy in Warwickshire RO].

Wood-Jones, R. B. (1963) *Traditional Domestic Architecture in the Banbury Region*, Manchester University Press.

Wrathmell, Stuart (1984) 'The vernacular threshold of northern peasant houses', *Vernacular Architecture* 15, 29–33.

Wrathmell, Stuart (1989) *Wharram: Domestic settlement 2: Medieval peasant farmsteads*, York: York University Archaeological Publications 8.

Wrathmell, Stuart (1989) 'Peasant houses, farmsteads and villages in north-east England', in M. Aston, D. Austin and C. Dyer (eds) *The rural settlements of medieval England*, Oxford: Basil Blackwell Ltd, 247–67.

Yates, Margaret (2007) *Town and countryside in Western Berkshire c.1327–c.1600*, Woodbridge: Boydell.

Indexes

INDEX OF SUBJECTS

INDEX OF PEOPLE

Site code entries refer to the corresponding pdf files

INDEX OF PLACES

Site code entries refer to the corresponding pdf files

INDEX OF RECORDED BUILDINGS

Site code entries refer to the corresponding pdf files. Bold type identifies the building reports included in Chapter 8